SUSTAINABLE CITIES
IN AMERICAN DEMOCRACY

ENVIRONMENT AND SOCIETY
KIMBERLY K. SMITH, EDITOR

Sustainable Cities in American Democracy

From Postwar Urbanism to
a Civic Green New Deal

❧

Carmen Sirianni

 UNIVERSITY PRESS OF KANSAS

Published by the University Press of Kansas (Lawrence, Kansas 66045), which was organized by the Kansas Board of Regents and is operated and funded by Emporia State
University, Fort Hays State University, Kansas State University, Pittsburg State University, the University of Kansas, and Wichita State University.

Library of Congress Cataloging-in-Publication Data available at

Names: Sirianni, Carmen, author.
Title: Sustainable cities in American democracy : from postwar urbanism to a civic
green new deal / Carmen Sirianni.
Description: Lawrence : University Press of Kansas, 2020. | Series: Environment and
society | Includes bibliographical references and index.
Identifiers: LCCN 2020008297
   ISBN 9780700629978 (cloth)
   ISBN 9780700629985 (paperback)
   ISBN 9780700629992 (epub)
Subjects: LCSH: Urbanization—United States—History. | Urbanization—
Environmental aspects—United States. | Sustainable urban development—United
States. | City planning—Environmental aspects—United States. | City planning—
United States—Citizen participation. | Urban policy—United States—Citizen
participation. | Urban ecology (Sociology)—United States. | Community development,
Urban—Environmental aspects—United States. | Citizens' associations—United States.
Classification: LCC HT123 .S564 2020 | DDC 307.760973—dc23
LC record available at https://lccn.loc.gov/2020008297.

British Library Cataloguing-in-Publication Data is available.

Printed in the United States of America

10 9 8 7 6 5 4 3 2 1

The paper used in this publication is recycled and contains 30 percent postconsumer
waste. It is acid free and meets the minimum requirements of the American National
Standard for Permanence of Paper for Printed Library Materials Z39.48-1992.

For David, forever

Contents

Preface

This book is written with acute awareness of a dual crisis. One is a climate crisis of global dimensions, the other is a crisis of democracy, particularly intense in the United States right now, but also of global scope. *Sustainable Cities in American Democracy* focuses on one piece of this larger pair of crises; namely, to understand how the institutional field of sustainable cities, imperfect yet indispensable in response to environmental degradation and climate change, has emerged and developed over the past decades in the United States and how civic and democratic action has shaped these developments.

The point, for sure, is not merely to understand the world but to change it, to provide a more robust foundation for democratic action to further transform cities in ways that might make them far more sustainable, resilient, and just. Under any circumstances, this would pose an enormous challenge given distributions of power and delineations of complexity. With an unfolding climate crisis that will bring concatenating disruptions to communities and ecosystems for decades to come—even if we can reduce greenhouse gas emissions drastically, as we must—the challenge will be daunting indeed. It will be especially challenging in the face of exacerbated inequalities coming from various directions and aggravated attacks on core democratic norms of free and fair elections, truth-based public discourse, and even rule of law. We live in difficult times and will have to address these challenges from many different angles. Building sustainable and resilient cities represents one such central challenge.

To this end, I examine various kinds of civic associations and grassroots action over the long arc from the end of World War II to the present, especially as they began to explicitly link conservation to the future of our democracy and then begin to develop sustainable cities as a democratic project. These associations include classic multitiered organizations with local, state, and national offices, which were especially important in urban clean water and clean air organizing in the 1950s and 1960s and in helping to constitute the larger civic field to campaign for federal laws. They include professionalized national associations with mass membership but no chapter affiliates, such as the Natural Resources Defense Council, which was largely focused on command-and-control regulation but has since lent critical support to urban alternatives. They include many kinds of local associations, such as bicycle and watershed associations that might be only loosely affiliated through national networks. Some groups challenge city government agencies quite contentiously, while others seek collaboration; many do both at some phase of their development. Some urban groups are fiercely focused on environmental justice, while others fail to frame issues this way until challenged to do so.

In short, the array of civic organizations that has come to play an important role in shaping sustainable cities as a democratic venture is quite variegated. My account utilizes a range of analytic approaches—institutional fields, policy design, urban governance, social movements, democratic theory, public administration, and planning—to understand how diverse civic and professional associations have come to constitute an ecology of organizations that are nonetheless viewed as part of a systemic and coherent project. The institutional field of sustainable cities has emerged with some core democratic norms and civic practices, yet with many tensions and trade-offs that field actors must craft and revise strategically in the face of new opportunities and persistent shortfalls.

In the final chapter, as well as in the postscript on the civics of a Green New Deal, I sketch how we might further build sustainable and resilient cities on much more robust foundations for the decades ahead, while also addressing democratic deficits in our polarized political culture. As we build upon the work of several generations of community activists, we can further leverage the passions and skills of today's youth climate activists for a lifetime of civic and institutional leadership in the many venues where their inspired work and practical wisdom will be critical.

As this book goes to press in early April 2020, we are also in the midst of a coronavirus pandemic that strains our democratic institutions further, yet also reveals the profound civic heroism of so many medical professionals, first responders, and collaborative teams of every skill level and walk of life. May we all learn from them as we work to make our communities more sustainable, our institutions more robust, our planet more inhabitable, and our democracy more resilient for the climate challenges ahead.

Acknowledgments

Many individuals and institutions helped to incubate this book, and some provided direct feedback. The Ash Center for Democratic Governance and Innovation at the John F. Kennedy School of Government at Harvard University provided an institutional home where I was affiliate faculty for formal research exchanges and lively dinners over the past decade. I am especially grateful to Archon Fung, Jenny Mansbridge, Marshall Ganz, Alex Keyssar, Quinton Mayne, Miles Rapoport, and Tim Glynn-Burke, as well as Meira Levinson of the Graduate School of Education. I also wish to thank Christina Marchand for the opportunity to work with the screening committee of the Innovations in American Government Awards on several occasions. Archon also helped with several of the other projects I later mention, and so special thanks to him.

In 2008, I had the opportunity to coordinate twenty scholars and practitioners in the collaborative governance work group of the Obama 2008 urban policy committee, which led me to frame some of the specific themes in this book just as I was finishing another. Special thanks to Bob Weisbourd and Rachel Godsil, who chaired the larger committee, and to Harry Boyte, who coauthored with me several policy papers on civic engagement for the candidate. To several others on the work group, I owe special thanks: Lisa Bingham, Kirk Emerson, Matt Leighninger, Joe Goldman, Beth Noveck, Jim Diers, Jason Corburn, Marshall Ganz, Hahrie Han, John McKnight, Jody Kretzman, Mike Huggins, Lew Friedland, Xav Briggs, Dan Kemmis, and former Seattle mayor Norm Rice, who provided indispensable insight and a welcome venue at the Evans School of Public Policy and Governance, University of Washington. Tina Nabatchi helped with this group and organized several meetings through the Maxwell School of Citizenship and Public Affairs at Syracuse University, in collaboration with the White House Office of Science and Technology Policy, and cofacilitated a workshop in Washington, DC, with me on the use of new technologies in local democratic governance. Thanks also to the participants in this hack-a-thon.

Several people welcomed me onto the US Environmental Protection Agency's team of the Community Action for a Renewed Environment program as its academic advisor, and I benefitted from many conversations with Hank Topper, Rob Brenner, Charles Lee, Jay Benforado, Larry Weinstock, Marva King, and others. Marva embraced us all with her spirit and made the work happen, and she later shared her important dissertation research on EPA community-based programs with me. Together, our team collaborated with one hundred community grantee teams at the national trainings as well as staff from all ten regional offices—an inspired network to which I am deeply and forever indebted. My thanks also for feedback from the participants at my Inaugural Lecture to the Behavioral and Social Sciences Working Group, the Centers for Disease Control and Prevention, and the National Center for Environmental Health, jointly sponsored by EPA Region 4 deputy administrator Stan Meiburg, with Roger Bernier of the CDC. Thanks especially to Dr. Stephanie Bailey, then-chief of health practice at the CDC and formerly of the National Association of County and City Health Officials, for her probing contributions, along with Marilyn Metzler and Bobby Millstein.

The EPA's Innovation Action Council, comprised of deputy administrators from headquarters and regional offices across the country, provided especially probing feedback to my presentation on community-based approaches early in the Obama administration. The EPA also provided me with funding as a coprincipal investigator (with Hank Topper) for Partnering with Communities, which convened representatives of five White House offices, four federal agencies, and innovators among elected local officials, city managers, and environmental justice organizations. It convened at the Brookings Institution, with additional support from the Ash Center. Thanks to Darrell West of Brookings for this opportunity, to Bob Perciasepe of EPA and Peggy Shepard of West Harlem Environmental Action who framed the discussion, to Rob Brenner and Jay Benforado of EPA, Donele Wilkins of Detroiters for Environmental Justice, to Derek Okubo who facilitated the meeting, and to all the other participants. And, to Beth Noveck, deputy chief of the Office of Science and Technology Policy and the director of the White House Open Government Initiative, for our previous joint forum at Brookings on collaborative governance.

Funded by the National Science Foundation, the National Socio-

Environmental Synthesis Center (SESYNC) at the University of Maryland in Annapolis provided support for two workshops on nonstate actors in environmental governance, which Dana Fisher, Kenneth "Andy" Andrews, and I convened. Thanks to Dana and Andy for being such wonderful colleagues in this, and to Margaret Palmer, center director, and Jonathan Kramer for making the center such an exciting place for deep intellectual exchange with practical purpose. Among our participants, Kent Portney and Jeff Berry deserve special thanks for bringing key questions on sustainable cities to the discussions, as did David Hess, Bogdan Vasi, Jennifer Hadden, Suzanne Staggenborg, and Ed Weber on related issues. SESYNC also provided funds for another workshop on civic ecology, where I engaged at length with my research partner, Dennis Chestnut, the executive director of Groundwork Anacostia River DC, an environmental justice and river-restoration initiative. Thanks to Dennis, and to project directors Marianne Krasny and Keith Tidball of Cornell University for this opportunity. Thanks as well to other participants.

I owe special thanks to the Bertelsmann Stiftung in Berlin for the opportunity to discuss Hampton's youth council and participatory planning design, among other innovative urban models, with leaders of the major parties in the Bundestag and other public officials and with other Reinhard Mohn Prize city nominees from around the world. The Asia-Pacific Programme for Senior National Security Officers, Rajaratnam School of International Studies, Nanyang Technological University in Singapore, presented me with a forum to present some of the democratic lessons I learned from Seattle's sustainable city work to civilian and military officials from Asia and Europe with responsibility for responding to climate and other disasters. The Friedrich Ebert Stiftung sponsored my presentation on the potential for university-community partnerships in urban sustainability at Fudan University in Shanghai.

Valerie Lemmie, former city manager of Cincinnati and now board chair of the National Civic League, provided me with much early insight into urban management and its democratic possibilities at several Kettering Foundation meetings, and she introduced me to the National Academy of Public Administration where I have had the opportunity as an elected fellow to draw upon the experience of many colleagues. My former colleagues on the advisory board of the *Journal of the American Planning Association* helped to sharpen my thinking, as did Rachel Weber and Randall Crane, editors of the *Oxford Handbook on Urban Planning*. Aseem

Prakash offered valuable comments on an early paper that I presented on sustainable cities at the School of Public and Environmental Affairs, Indiana University, and he and Nives Dolšak welcomed my initial sketch of a civic Green New Deal for a *Public Administration Review* symposium. Bruce Jennings and his colleagues at the Hastings Center welcomed a related presentation. Elizabeth Kraft, former director of water resources for the League of Women Voters Education Fund, provided insight into a model of leadership that I decided to investigate going back further into the 1950s and 1960s; the league's work in those years proved critical to my understanding of the field.

Thanks also to Miles Rapoport and Heather McGee for sponsoring a forum on collaborative governance with Martha McCoy and Carolyn Lukensmeyer at Demos. Peter Levine and Karol Soltan welcomed me for several seminars at the Jonathan M. Tisch College for Civic Life at Tufts University, especially at their Summer Institute of Civic Studies and Frontiers of Democracy conferences. Thanks to others at Tisch College, especially Kei Kawashima-Ginsberg, Abby Kiesa, Nancy Thomas, and dean Alan Solomont for their continued hospitality. Special thanks to Peter Levine for helping to launch a project at Tisch on the civics of a Green New Deal as I was finishing this manuscript.

At Brandeis University, I benefitted enormously from close collaboration with my research assistants and PhD students, namely Rachel Madsen, over a period of five years, and with Jennifer Girouard, who coauthored an article in the *Oxford Handbook of Urban Planning* that became part of chapter 3; she also coedited a related book on varieties of civic innovation with me. Diana Marginean (Schor) provided research assistance and coauthorship on a project that was critical to my understanding of the role of multiracial youth organizing in urban planning. Stephanie Sofer coauthored an article on the broader field of environmental organizations. Ann Ward has also worked with me in developing the civics of a Green New Deal.

My Brandeis sociology colleague and dear friend for many years, Karen Hansen, gave me feedback and encouragement at every stage and Andrew Bundy took care of us both over dinner on many occasions. Laura Miller provided feedback on the manuscript at a critical stage. Cheri Hansen, our senior administrator in sociology, provided more everyday support and genuine friendship than any faculty member could possibly expect. Thanks also to Lauren Jordahl for support with research grants and travel. And a special shout out to Judy Hanley, our now-retired administrator, whose generous spirit and wonderful but not-always-so-gentle humor I miss on a daily basis. The Theodore and Jane Norman Fund at Brandeis provided essential research support throughout this project. While periodically moonlighting in the junior tutorial on civic engagement and community empowerment in Harvard's Committee on Degrees in Social Studies, I had the good fortune to supervise, among others, the senior honors thesis of Iris Zippora Ahronowitz, who introduced me to two formative groups in urban agriculture and food justice: Nuestras Raices and the Food Project.

Strange as it may seem, I also wish to thank Louis Brandeis, namesake of our university. With other progressive leaders, he helped to found the National Municipal League in the late nineteenth century, which later changed its name to the National Civic League, as it pursued more innovative community-based practices. NCL leaders and staff have been partners and friends for years and have welcomed me on various projects several times, including the All-America City Awards selection committee, which provided insight into dozens of city efforts at civic engagement and sustainability. Special thanks to Gloria Rubio-Cortes, Chris Gates, Derek Okubo, Mike McGrath, and the late John Parr.

Caroline Lee, Michael McQuarrie, and Edward Walker welcomed me to comment on papers at their conference on democratizing inequalities at New York University, from which I learned a great deal and sharpened my own perspective.

Several scholars gave me detailed feedback on all or parts of the manuscript, and I wish to thank Doug McAdam, Clarence Stone, Kent Portney, Lew Friedland, Albert Dzur, Quinton Mayne, Harry Boyte, Peter Levine, and Joel Greifinger. Mike McCall shared an extensive bibliography on participatory geographic information systems.

Thanks to the staff at the University Press of Kansas, especially to David Congdon, series editor Kimberly Smith, Colin Tripp, Michael Kehoe, Karl Janssen, Jenn Bennett-Genthner, and the two anonymous reviewers.

To my dear friend, Lew Friedland, not only for very critical feedback but for the summer Barolo and Barbaresco conversations—and for our shared Italian and Chinese cooking. To my wife Andrea Walsh: my deepest gratitude for critical reading and feedback, and especially for all the ways in which she has helped me focus on the important things. And for sustaining hope in trying times. Finally, to our dear son, David, for his love and deep spirit. Here's to more of his delightful lightness of being!

Acronyms

AASHTO	American Association of State Highway Transportation Organizations
ABCD	assets-based community development
ABW	Alliance for Biking and Walking
ACEEE	American Council for an Energy-Efficient Economy
ACGA	American Community Gardening Association
AFL-CIO	American Federation of Labor-Congress of Industrial Organizations
AIA	American Institute of Architects
APA	Administrative Procedure Act
APA	American Planning Association
ASLA	American Society for Landscape Architecture
ASTM	American Society for Testing and Materials (now ASTM International)
ASU	Arizona State University
BART	Bay Area Rapid Transit (San Francisco Bay Area, California)
BCF	Baltimore Community Foundation
BMP	best management practice
BTA	Bicycle Transportation Alliance (Portland, Oregon), now the Street Trust
C2K	Chesapeake 2000
CAA	Clean Air Act
CANDO	Chicago Association of Neighborhood Development Organizations
CBEP	community-based environmental protection (EPA framework)
CBF	Chesapeake Bay Foundation
CCMP	comprehensive conservation and management plan (NEP)
CCP	Cities for Climate Protection (ICLEI)

CDBG	Community Development Block Grant program
CDC	community development corporation
CEQ	Council on Environmental Quality (executive office of the president)
CEQA	California Environmental Quality Act
CFDI	community development financial institutions
CFP	Community Food Projects Competitive Grants Program (USDA)
CFSC	Community Food Security Coalition
CIAM	Congrès Internationaux d'Architecture Moderne
civic GND	civic Green New Deal
CMAQ	Congestion Mitigation and Air Quality Improvement program
CNT	Center for Neighborhood Technology
CNU	Congress for the New Urbanism
CPD	Chicago Police Department
CSA	community-supported agriculture
CSO	combined sewer overflow
CSU	Community Services Unlimited (south Los Angeles, California)
CWA	Clean Water Act (Federal Water Pollution Control Act Amendments, 1972)
CWC	Catskill Watershed Corporation (New York State)
DCs	district coalitions (Portland, Oregon)
DEP	Department of Environmental Protection (New York City)
DVC	Downtown Voices Coalition (Phoenix, Arizona)
EDF	Environmental Defense Fund
EETAP	Environmental Education and Training Partnership
EGA	Environmental Grantmakers Association
EIS	environmental impact statement
EJ	environmental justice
EPA	US Environmental Protection Agency
FAD	filtration avoidance determination (EPA)
FHWA	Federal Highway Administration
FOE	Friends of the Earth
FPAC	Food Policy Advisory Council (Philadelphia, Pennsylvania)
FPC	Food Policy Council
FSA	food system assessment

FWCA	Fish and Wildlife Coordination Act
FWPCA	Federal Water Pollution Control Act
GAO	US General Accountability Office
GASP	Group Against Smog and Pollution (Pittsburgh and Alleghany County, Pennsylvania)
GCA	Garden Club(s) of America
GFWC	General Federation of Women's Clubs
GGNRA	Golden Gate National Recreation Area
GHG	greenhouse gas
GIS	geographical information system
GMA	Growth Management Act (Oregon)
GND	Green New Deal
GPP	Global Philanthropy Partnership
HEW	US Department of Health, Education, and Welfare
HFFI	Healthy Food Financing Initiative (US Department of Agriculture, Department of Health and Human Services, and the Department of the Treasury)
HHS	US Department of Health and Human Services (after reorganization of HEW)
HOPE VI	Housing Opportunities for People Everywhere (sixth iteration)
HRFA	Hudson River Fishermen's Association
HUD	US Department of Housing and Urban Development
ICLEI USA	ICLEI Local Governments for Sustainability USA (originally International Council for Local Environmental Initiatives)
ICMA	International City/County Management Association
ILG	Institute for Local Government (California)
ILWA	Izaak Walton League of America
IPCC	Intergovernmental Panel on Climate Change (United Nations)
ISTEA	Intermodal Surface Transportation Efficiency Act
LAB	League of American Bicyclists
LEBC	Lake Erie Basin Committee
LEED	Leadership in Environment and Energy Design
LEED-ND	Leadership in Environment and Energy Design-Neighborhood Development
LISC	Local Initiatives Support Corporation

LWV	League of Women Voters
LWVEF	League of Women Voters Education Fund
MALT	Marin Agricultural Land Trust
MIT	Massachusetts Institute of Technology
MOA	Memorandum of Agreement (New York City and several upstate counties, for water filtration)
MPO	metropolitan planning organization
NAAEE	North American Association for Environmental Education
NACTO	National Association of City Transportation Officials
NACWA	National Association of Clean Water Agencies
NAHB	National Association of Home Builders
NAPA	National Academy of Public Administration
NAR	National Association of Realtors
NCI	National Charrette Institute
NCL	National Civic League
NDS	natural drainage system
NEA	National Education Association
NEJAC	National Environmental Justice Advisory Council (EPA-based)
NEP	National Estuary Program (also used for specific estuary programs within this)
NEPA	National Environmental Policy Act
NFSN	National Farm to School Network
NGA	Neighborhood Gardens Association (Philadelphia)
NLC	National League of Cities
NLUPA	National Land Use Policy Act
NOAA	National Oceanic and Atmospheric Administration
NOSB	National Organic Standards Board
NPA	National Parks Association (National Parks Conservation Association)
NPDES	National Pollutant Discharge Elimination System
NPS	National Park Service
NRC	National Research Council
NRCS	Natural Resources Conservation Service (before 1994 Soil Conservation Service)
NRDC	Natural Resources Defense Council
NSAC	National Sustainable Agriculture Coalition
NTI	Neighborhood Transformation Initiative (Philadelphia)

NWF	National Wildlife Federation
NYC	New York City
OAA	Older Americans Act
OEO	US Office of Economic Opportunity
ONA	Office of Neighborhood Associations (Portland, Oregon)
ONI	Office of Neighborhood Involvement (Portland, Oregon)
OSEC	Office of Sustainable Ecosystems and Communities (EPA)
OWOW	Office of Wetlands, Oceans, and Watersheds (EPA)
PHS	Pennsylvania Horticultural Society
PHS	Public Health Service (within HEW, then HHS)
PIRG	(US) Public Interest Research Group
RAE	Restore America's Estuaries
RCW	Rivers Council of Washington
RIC	Rooted in Community
R/UDAT	Regional/Urban Design Assistance Team (AIA)
RWC	Rivers Council of Washington
SCLDF	Sierra Club Legal Defense Fund
SCS	Soil Conservation Service (since 1994 Natural Resources Conservation Service)
SEEC	State Energy Efficiency Collaborative (California)
SEPA	state environmental policy act
SFBC	San Francisco Bicycle Coalition
SFDPH	San Francisco Department of Public Health
SGA	Smart Growth America
SIP	state implementation plan (for the Clean Air Act)
SNAP	Supplemental Nutrition Assistance Program (food stamps)
SPU	Seattle Public Utilities
SPUR	San Francisco Planning and Urban Renewal Association
STB	Save the Bay (Narragansett Bay, Rhode Island)
STPP	Surface Transportation Policy Project (now Partnership)
TFN	The Funders Network for Smart Growth and Livable Communities
TIF	tax increment finance
TNC	The Nature Conservancy
TPL	Trust for Public Land
TVA	Tennessee Valley Authority
UAW	United Auto Workers

UEPI	Urban Environmental Policy Institute (Occidental College, Los Angeles)
ULI	Urban Land Institute
UNFCCC	United Nations Framework Convention on Climate Change
USDA	US Department of Agriculture
USDN	Urban Sustainability Directors Network
USDOT	US Department of Transportation
USGBC	US Green Building Council
VSN	Volunteer Stewardship Network (Chicago, Illinois)
WAC	Watershed Agricultural Council (New York State counties north of New York City)
WHO	World Health Organization
YMCA	Young Men's Christian Association
YWCA	Young Women's Christian Association

CHAPTER ONE

The Sustainable City: Civic Action and Democratic Institutionalism

The concept of the "sustainable city" has emerged over the past several decades as one of the key goals of both environmentalism and urbanism in an era of climate change. It has a distinct trajectory in the United States, which is the topic of this book, but it has many links to similar initiatives in other countries as well as transnational networks and institutions. Because the city is so central to economic development and greenhouse gas emissions, and because an ever-growing majority of the world's population now lives in cities, the question of how to make cities more sustainable and resilient in the face of climate crisis has become ever more urgent. Sustainable and resilient cities are by no means the whole of a robust response to the climate crisis, which has many market, technological, public-investment, and regulatory dimensions, and requires extensive and sustained social movement mobilization. But they are a central component.

In this book, I examine the long-arc trajectory of sustainable cities in the United States to better understand several questions. First, how has civic action shaped the emergence of an urban environmentalism that has now come to be explicitly framed as sustainable cities? Civic action, of course, has been key to conservation movements going back more than a century, as well as to environmental movements in the decades following World War II that led to major legal and administrative frameworks of our era. Civic action has helped shape core legal norms empowering democratic publics with rights to information and voice, and has continued to generate power to enable environmental justice norms and more inclusive grassroots engagement. Analyzing the processes by which civic action has emerged, the repertoires and tool kits it has utilized, and the strategic challenges it has faced at many points along the way is essential to enhancing our capacities as democratic citizens in a self-governing republic, however imperfect and compromised that ideal has often been and however much under threat it is again today.

Second, since urban civic action occurs within and across many kinds of institutional systems—water, land use, housing, transportation, energy, food, commercial real estate—how have civic actors learned to engage institutional actors of various types? To be sure, they have challenged them, protested various planning practices and architectural projects, and have often disrupted and delayed the designs of powerful growth coalitions. But they have also faced choices about how—and how much—to participate in redesign when institutional actors invite them to the table, as has often occurred, if reluctantly. The logic of civic action for urban sustainability is thus fundamentally about managing the dynamic tensions between conflict and collaboration within a larger field of institutional actors that includes elected officials, public agencies, market actors, professional groups, foundations, universities, and cultural organizations. Cities cannot become more sustainable unless they provide greater strategic coherence among such institutional systems, and they cannot become more democratic unless they provide ways for civic actors to engage productively with other institutional field actors and help *modify institutional logics and action repertoires toward sustainability and resilience.*

Civic action, if it is to be sustained and systemic, thus requires a larger framework of what I call *democratic institutionalism*; namely, a complex ecology of forms of civic action that can become progressively aligned with various institutional logics—bureaucratic, professional, market, nonprofit, governance—providing a broad range of public and private goods in cities, but that can be modified to secure greater democracy, sustainability, and justice. Democratic institutionalism is not a romantic or utopian ideal of "real" or "radical" democracy—terms often invoked when arguing for alternative urban futures—but a pragmatic one rooted in how real-world people live diverse lives of commitment in complex communities and institutions of many types. It is an ideal consistent with our best traditions of American democratic pragmatism and provides everyday civic actors with a rich array of options for contributing to the democratic work of our republic.

I use the term *sustainable cities* broadly to include other nomenclature such a *resilient cities, healthy cities,* and *just cities*—terminology that has emerged as part of a long-term process of framing and structuring this field. There exists no single terse and compelling definition that encompasses all dimensions. Each has different emphases, and I explain these in context of their emergence and usage. But the active process of contesting, aligning, and blending frames is essential to what it means to build a field, enhance its legitimacy, and expand the array of actors that might become invested in urban sustainability. Not all field actors ever fully share a common frame as a unified way of interpreting the world around them, and contest entails power and recognition at multiple levels of movements and institutions. Yet the sustainable-cities frame has proven remarkably resonant and integrative across many issues and among networks of field actors operating at various scales and according to diverse institutional logics. Thus, local bicycle movements, national green building, and smart growth associations see themselves operating within a larger sustainable-cities field, as do many grassroots activists in land-use battles with the planners they challenge. Environmental justice activists contest deep racial and spatial inequalities, yet many utilize "sustainability" if appropriately informed by "justice," as in "just sustainabilities" and "just food," and many fight to ensure that bicycle planning is equitable, that green building addresses retrofits in poorer neighborhoods, and that green jobs and training are available for inner-city youth.

The field of sustainable cities tentatively emerged through conflict over the patterns of land use and urban renewal in the decades following World War II, as well as through local civic action for clean water and clean air. Over time, the field developed a distinct identity and then broadened to include a fuller range of professional, political, bureaucratic, market, nonprofit, and civic actors working at various policy scales. Despite considerable progress over the decades, sustainable city strategies have not resolved persistent patterns of power and inequality within urbanism or environmentalism, nor have they adequately neutralized resistance from opponents, such as climate change deniers or property rights movements to restrict land-use regulation. Nor, indeed, have they yet generated sufficient support among broad publics that will face the daunting challenges of resilience and adaptation in the coming decades. Any framing of sustainable cities is thus replete with conceptual tensions, strategic shortfalls, potential trade-offs, and pragmatic choices. We are not at the beginning of a strategic trajectory, nor are we anywhere near the end. We are in a very messy middle, with important signposts generated by field actors of many sorts, but much is uncertain and obscure.

My focus on democratic engagement is driven by empirical dynamics over a seventy-year period (1946–2016). I choose to include the initial decades after World War II because the civic and policy battles over clean water, clean air, and land use, as well as the participatory cultural and legal norms that emerged, prepared the groundwork for thinking and acting more systematically on urban sustainability. The environmental field settlement, based upon new federal laws and command-and-control regulation of discrete pollutants in the early 1970s, has been critically important then and now. But it has proved incomplete, and participatory place-based strategies around built urban environments, ecosystem functions, and community disparities emerged as central complements to regulation among an array of grassroots civic associations. The term *sustainable communities* was used by the mid-1980s, and soon many more social actors entered the field and contributed to framing issues, generating civic and professional practices and tool kits, and fashioning new networks and associations. At various levels of the federal system, public policy and administration also began to contribute to framing and enabling such action.

For instance, the American Planning Association and the American Institute of Architects, two long-standing professional associations, began to respond to local civic action and lend support to field building. Then, with the assistance of the Natural Resources Defense Council and other national environmental groups, they helped to found the US Green Building Council and other networks promoting smart growth, new urbanism, and community engagement. Still other civic associations began to flourish, such as bicycle and pedestrian associations demanding a seat at the table of urban governance, and a new professional association formed that was quite responsive to such democratic urban actors; namely, the National Association of City Transportation Officials. Soon, civic challenges within cities, such as Portland, Oregon; San Francisco, California; and Chicago, Illinois, yielded governance coalitions with an increasingly coherent set of sustainability strategies across the nested fields of energy, land use, watersheds, transportation, and food. City offices of sustainability were established, and learning accelerated through new and established networks of city practitioners—ICLEI USA and the Urban Sustainability Directors Network, as well as the National League of Cities and the International City/County Management Association. National and community foundations also began to invest more strategically in the field, as did the US Environmental Protection Agency (EPA) through various community-based approaches and nonregulatory offices. Climate, sustainability, and resilience planning have diffused more widely and now provide a foundation for still more robust strategies.

My focus on democratic engagement is also motivated by normative and political concerns. With the serious social disruption and institutional crises portended by climate change and the need for creative and socially just responses to resilient adaptation—and, of course, to mitigation—we will need to become more inventive than ever about how we engage civic and institutional actors in configuring urban commonwealths and producing public goods such as clean and sustainable water supplies, flood protection, and resilient shorelines. We will need to engage them in developing just distributions of costs and benefits, cognitive and emotive framings that inspire and sustain democratic hope and engagement amidst signals of futility, and a politics of democratic legitimacy that can hold the worst forms of polarizing populism based upon racial, ethnic, and other forms of scapegoating in check. We cannot achieve greater sustainability without better democracy, certainly not at the urban level, nor arguably on a broader scale. And we cannot achieve better democracy without engaging everyday citizens and civic associations, as well as the many other kinds of actors whose authority, expertise, and resources are critical to sustainability and resilience.

A democratic institutionalist approach seeks to understand how diverse field actors have attempted to align their logics and tool kits over time, and how they might do so on an increasingly more effective and democratic basis in the difficult decades ahead. We do not need to be radical and utopian, but we do need to be normatively rooted and politically imaginative, with the everyday civic grit to move our institutional systems decisively forward through shared public work.

Thinking Institutionally about Urban Sustainability

Sociologists and political scientists have, over the past several decades, reinvigorated institutional analysis across a broad range of research fields. In this chapter, I will introduce several analytic concepts briefly and sprinkle them relatively lightly through the chapters that follow, while occasionally going more deeply into academic debates in the endnotes. My purpose is to provide analytic coherence to the core narratives that constitute the emergence and development of sustainable cities in the United States and enrich the democratic imagination of how we might move forward. The three main clusters of analytic concepts are institutional fields and logics, democratic policy design and feedback, and urban regimes and governance.

Institutional Fields and Logics

The concept of institutional fields has a long pedigree that goes back to the borrowing of metaphors from electromagnetism and fluid mechanics in the physical sciences, as well as gestalt theory in psychology and some early urban theory. But it begins to assume sociological specificity in the 1980s, especially with the work of Paul DiMaggio, Walter Powell, Richard Scott, and John Meyer, among others. The translation from French of the work of Pierre Bourdieu, begun earlier, was generative in linking field with forms of power and capital, including economic, social, cultural, and political capital. The core insight of field theory is that the study of social action needs to be fundamentally relational and mapped within and across institutional domains and diverse types of organizations. Field theory, of course, is far more complex, nuanced, and contested than such a simple sentence conveys, but for the purposes of this analytic introduction, I would elaborate in a few initial ways that draw upon the formulation of "strategic action fields" by Neil Fligstein and Doug McAdam in *A Theory of Fields*, as well as related institutional concepts.[1]

First, it is important to think in terms of strategic action fields because the complex web of actors within distinct fields, as well as across various proximate, nested, and distant fields, make strategic choices in relation to one another, even if they only formalize strategic planning much later in their development, as was the case with the Sierra Club in the broader environmental field. Fields need to be defined flexibly by various indicators of actor types, repertoires, relationships, and cultural markers, as well as by policy boundaries and implementation challenges. Choices within the strategic action fields that constitute the environmental field tend to be driven by normative and cultural considerations of what is right and good for ecological sustainability, species protection, affected human populations, and built environments; by rational calculations of perceived political opportunity, tool availability, risk, cost, and effectiveness; by already embedded or anticipated relationships with other actors. Organizational actors seek to secure legitimacy across fields through multiple sources and criteria, including pragmatic, cultural-cognitive, administrative-legal, moral, and democratic processes of validation that are continually unfolding and often inconsistent. Key actors in field structuration include civic and professional associations, cultural and educational institutions, media, foundations and think tanks, political allies and movement opponents, and market actors and public agencies. The latter typically constitute highly diversified offices within bureaucracies and networks across agencies at various levels of the federal system.[2]

Field actors possess various kinds and degrees of political, cultural, social, and economic power, which lead to episodes and patterns of contestation as well as efforts to broker new relationships and share power on a more distributed and democratic basis—or, of course, to try to consolidate power among narrower bands of privileged actors. Many of these actors are also part of other institutional fields with their own dynamic and shifting cross pressures, emergent policy opportunities, and complex games open to those who are simultaneously insiders and outsiders. The sustainable cities field is narrower than the environmental field but is intertwined with various urban fields (housing, transportation, metropolitan policy) that tend to be less central to environmentalism broadly. The "architecture of field overlap" is thus critical, especially given the distinctive opportunities for environmental issues to draw in other actors who may have previously been distant, unavailable, irrelevant, or unassailable.[3]

Second, what Fligstein and McAdam broadly call "social skills" exercised by movement and institutional entrepreneurs are critical to understanding how fields form, establish boundaries, and reorganize over time. Such social skills help define a field by providing reasons to cooperate, helping actors understand the interests, constraints, and institutional logics that shape the strategic options of other actors while negotiating plausible ways forward. Skilled actors also help provide meaning, identity, and normative grounding. What is "wilderness," "environmental justice," or "sustainable cities," and why should we care? Why and how should we act? And who is the relevant "we"? Social skills are notably important in the environmental field since issues that arise on distinct tracks often reveal opportunities for linkage to other issues, providing opportunities to amplify, extend, align, and bridge "social movement frames," eliciting cooperation from new organizational actors and ordinary citizens and enhancing the democratic legitimacy of the field.[4]

The aligning and bridging opportunities in the field of sustainable cities, most notable over decades-long processes, are partly due to the integrative requisites of urban governance within spatial and jurisdictional borders, as well as across civic and professional boundaries. City officials are pressed to make things work as though they are "of a piece," or to "perform coherence" in the efforts they make, even when achieving and documenting such coherence is enormously difficult. But aligning and bridging also reflect cognitive affinities that emerge within recurrent normative questions of "the good community," which elicit figurative and relational cross-knitting among various framing tropes, such as the livable community, the healthy community, the bikable and walkable community, and the environmentally just community. Skilled field actors enhance legitimacy through such integrative and elaborative work.

Urban civic action on clean water and clean air emerged—or reemerged—immediately after World War II and was quickly tied to new federal laws and norms of public information and participation. The field of sustainable cities then began to take a more distinctive shape with the grassroots highway revolts of the 1960s and 1970s. Actors leveraged participatory and land-use planning components of federal policy designs such as the Model Cities Program and began to incorporate open space, community development, neighborhood planning, healthy community, and watershed ecosystems into a sustainable communities and sustainable cities frame by the mid-1980s. The environmental justice frame began to contest goals and parameters in the 1990s, and then was largely, though often incompletely and uncomfortably, incorporated as part of just sustainabilities. Movement, professional, and market actors built upon the more expansive frame of sustainable cities as they developed the fields of green building, sustainable transportation, and urban agriculture.[5]

Third, if we are to understand the possibilities of democratic action within all the settings where actors can make a genuine difference to protect the environment, generate sustainable practices, and engender resilience in the face of climate and other risks, then we require some conception of "institutional logics" within which they exercise agency. An institutional logic, according to Patricia Thornton, William Ocasio, and Michael Lounsbury, is "the socially constructed, historical patterns of cultural symbols and material practices, including assumptions, values, and beliefs, by which individuals and organizations provide meaning to their daily activity, organize time and space, and reproduce their lives and experiences." While actors are situated in multiple institutional locations, each type of institution tends to have a distinct set of organizing principles, practices, and symbols. Some logics can be grouped under broad categories, such as family, religion, market, bureaucratic, professional, and community logics, yet there are always further specifications that can be made, as well as hybrid forms and re-combinations.[6]

The bureaucratic logics of the EPA, for example, have been primarily determined by command-and-control regulatory statutes and tools since the initial field settlement of the 1970s. However, in response to the perceived shortfalls of command-and-control for place-based strategies, various EPA offices have also come to supply resources and tools for community-based knowledge production, problem solving, and networking among civic associations oriented to sustainability in urban ecosystems and built environments, thus partially modifying bureaucratic logics and aligning them with civic and community logics.

Market logics can be specified by market sector, type of firm, corporate culture, dominant strategy, metrics of performance, regulatory regime, regional cluster, and global network. Strategic action for corporate sustainability, which haltingly emerged as a response to command and control, must now grapple with the distinct logics within market sectors, business organizations, supply chains, and investment institutions, all of which confront democratic challenges from environmental organizations, shareholder resolutions, public pension funds, community stakeholders, and new forms of information transparency. Organizations such as the Environmental Defense Fund and Ceres facilitate strategic leadership development in this part of the larger field of sustainability, although they face daunting challenges given powerful logics of global capital.[7]

Further specifications of logics can be made for various types of civic associations, professions, and educational and cultural institutions. Within the multiple and competing logics in any specific institution or field, some tend to be dominant and others subordinate. But friction typically occurs, given the complexity and layering of units and fields, unequal forms of power, and normative challenges that are made in the name of core mission, new identities, and social justice. Democratic sustainability, as I conceive it in this book, is fundamentally about the complex work of sufficiently aligning institutional logics to serve public purposes, produce public goods, and empower appropriate configurations of democratic publics within local polities, but also within all the relevant institutions where the work of sustainability must occur if we are to become reasonably effective. Democratic institutionalism is not simply about *enhancing democratic voice*, as central as this is, but also about *configuring it* to ensure communication and alignment across logics.[8]

For example, in the green building field that I examine as an important field within sustainable cities, we can see many of these components at work. The initial steps to found the field were taken by architects from private firms in the late 1980s and early 1990s, who were motivated by normative environmental commitments in their own ranks and by profit opportunities in new market niches. They were aided by brokers with the appropriate social skills in several professional associations (the American Institute of Architects and the American Planning Association) and environmental organizations (the National Audubon Society, the Rocky Mountain Institute, and the Natural Resources Defense Council [NRDC]), the latter category with overriding normative values, though flexible on the mix of market and regulatory logics. As a result, a new multi-stakeholder association was established in 1993, the US Green Building Council (USGBC), which came to define itself as a core actor in the field of what it now officially refers to as "sustainable cities and communities."

In developing and diffusing the Leadership in Environment and Energy Design (LEED) rating system, which could be utilized by many sectors of the building industry with its distinctive structure of decentralized firms and temporary organizations of multiple professions and trades, USGBC also drew upon the legitimacy and technical competence of a committee within an established standard-setting organization (the American Society for Testing and Materials). USGBC then developed its own practices for training and certifying over two hundred thousand LEED-accredited professionals and further diffused practices through associations in specific building sectors, such as the Council of Educational Facilities Planners International and the American Association of School Administrators. Champions in some school districts developed democratic governance models for projects that included multiple professions (such as architects and engineers), blue-collar maintenance trades (such as janitors), and pink-collar staff (such as kitchen workers), as well as parent, teacher, student, school board, city council, and other community stakeholders in collaborative design. Bond-voting publics then approved capital investments for green school buildings district wide.

In partnership with NRDC and several smart growth organizations and regional environmental associations, USGBC then developed LEED for Neighborhood Development as a technical tool with applications to whole neighborhoods and a citizen's guide that enabled translation and use by local community groups. They were aided in this by a nonregulatory "sustainable communities" office within the EPA and a for-profit consulting firm. Another cluster of professional groups developed a complementary guide for public officials so that all relevant actors could speak a common language that was nonetheless appropriate to their distinct institutional logics. Tensions among logics of profit, professionalism, and civic and environmental norms have been managed through vigorous USGBC board discussions, by some board resignations—voice and exit, in Albert Hirschman's formulation—and by diversifying the types of groups whose leaders and practitioners are recruited to serve on the board. In view of the urgent need to reduce carbon emissions much faster than has been achieved to date, the green-building field continues to face internal challenges to various logics, metrics, and tools, as well as external challenges from social movements and local governments for more effective regulatory strategies. Its recent LEED for Cities and Communities initiative develops tools that can be utilized for entire cities.[9]

In short, skilled civic and professional actors, as well as other institutional players, have engaged in complex and strategic institutional work over several decades, mobilizing various publics, aligning diverse logics, and developing appropriate tool kits. Understanding how they have been able to do this will help us build the sustainable cities field further.

As this example indicates, two broad types of associations are especially important to sustainable city field dynamics; namely, civic associations and professional associations.

Civic Associations
Civic associations, to be sure, are quite diverse in form. They range from the classic multitiered associations—with national offices and state and local chapters—that Theda Skocpol and her colleagues have analyzed across major periods of US history to professionalized advocacy organizations with members but without chapters (such as NRDC). They also include a broad array of local associations, such as watershed associations, land trusts, open space coalitions, bicycle associations, and environmental and health justice groups. In the early decades after World War II, the League of Women Voters (LWV), organized as a multitiered association that included clean water, clean air, and natural resource programs, was especially effective in civic action, including in many cities. Its multitiered structure,

as well as its "city housekeeping" frame, carved out a distinctive niche in the emerging field while collaborating with other multitiered conservation associations (the National Audubon Society, the National Wildlife Federation, the Izaak Walton League of America), other multitiered women's associations (the General Federation of Women's Clubs), and a wide assortment of local civic groups whom LWV often coached and convened. From the 1970s onward, no other multitiered association played quite this role in further developing the sustainable cities field—and LWV never defined its programs as exclusively urban within the larger fields of water and air pollution—though the Sierra Club and Audubon did make important contributions.[10]

Since then, much of the civic-capacity building has occurred through local associations, sometimes loosely affiliated through networks such as the Association for Biking and Walking and the River Network. To be sure, other associational forms are important to the field, including ones specifically designated with city names, such as Sustainable Seattle, and federal agencies have played important roles in enabling local civic action, as I discuss further. Social movement and institutional roles within the field of sustainable cities are varied, distributed, relational, and dynamic. In some places, a "conservation culture" congeals enough that an agile coalition of groups can, depending on the issues, "rally, react, plan, inform, persuade, compromise, cajole, threaten, lobby, or litigate." Kent Portney and Jeffrey Berry have argued that higher levels of participation across many forms of civic and political activity, as well as greater organizational density of civic and nonprofit groups within a given city, have been important factors in the relative development of sustainable city strategies. Their analyses find partial or strong support in many other studies, though the impact of civic engagement and capacity may be mediated by local political institutions, such as mayor-council and city manager-council forms of government, or multilevel governance, especially states.[11]

Professional Associations

Professional associations must also figure prominently in any analysis of "democracy and association" in environmental fields. Sociologists of professions have typically focused on strategies of closure and credentialing to protect monopolies of competence and to shelter markets for services, or to become increasingly subject to market logics at the expense of social trusteeship.[12] Such practices have often stifled or marginalized local civic knowledge and have legitimated authority upwards in bureaucratic hierarchies. This tendency has been very powerful within environmental fields, since scientific, medical, technical, legal, administrative, planning, and policy expertise have, quite appropriately, been central components of effective solutions.

Nonetheless, professional expertise has been challenged on many fronts by local community groups and civic associations, with claims that experts tend to ignore local knowledge and narrative, utilize inappropriate models of risk, and too-readily exclude alternative designs. These kinds of critiques have prompted democratic theorists and social scientists to recognize alternative norms and practices for collaboration among citizens and professionals who can coproduce and democratize expertise to add public value and enhance legitimacy, as well as to coconstruct "stories of sustainability" to ground democratic agency in shared ecological spaces and "good communities." The terms that theorists use vary but capture the dynamism of such practice across a variety of fields: "civic professionalism" and "democratic professionalism," as well as "street science" and "citizen science."[13]

One key aim of these formulations, as well as the practices that inform them, is to help transform professional identities, thus potentially complementing those social movement and field theories that focus primarily on the identity formation of subordinate groups. At the level of any given city, such as in historian Allison Isenberg's fine-grained study of postwar San Francisco, the extraordinarily complex relations among professionals from land-use, architectural design, and allied-arts fields working among competing civic and environmental visions, market logics, and public power challenge all actors to become more reflexive about negotiating relationships and defining what is democratic, just, and sustainable in their practices.[14]

Professional associations typically protect boundaries, yet over the course of the environmental era, practitioners and academics have also found ways to leverage their associational resources—formal sections, best-practice guides and standards, special programs and trainings, volunteer networks—to enable citizens to engage on a more equal footing with experts from a wide variety of disciplines. Thus, the American Institute of Architects (AIA) and its local chapters, responding to the urban revolts of the 1960s and 1970s, developed volunteer "design assistance teams" from their own ranks and from related professions to enable community groups to participate more knowledgeably in reviewing, modifying, and codesigning construction and transportation projects and, more recently, disaster-recovery and climate-resilience strategies. AIA maintains this program to this day, fifty years after its founding, and it has helped redefine the professional identity of the "citizen architect," now an association goal. The American Planning Association (APA) has also generated a range of tools to enable local community and multistakeholder participation in land-use and sustainability planning, which it now considers a central pillar of the normative and legally binding comprehensive plan. Professional associations in other fields have likewise been important, such as associations of city and county managers, city transportation engineers, and public health professionals. When the Coalition to Restore Urban Waters developed participatory and environmental justice themes to further expand the watershed frame and tool kit in the 1990s, its leading institutional entrepreneur enlisted professional networks cultivated in the National Association of State Wetland Managers and the National Association of State Floodplain Managers. Graduate professional programs in some of these fields have responded by including courses and internships where students learn participatory practice and work in teams with communities.

None of these efforts have been sufficient across professional associations and schools, and none have begun to systematically transform professional identities and practices on the scale that will be necessary, especially in the face of climate disruption. However, to the extent that urban sustainability, resilience, and adaptation will inevitably require the mobilization of knowledge and innovation across many professions and occupations, as well as securing both democratic and professional legitimacy among diverse communities and stakeholders, these models of democratic professionalism hold much strategic promise for field building. In the postscript, I consider ways in which a Green New Deal, or other robust policy design for place-based resilience, might leverage innovative professional practices for broad civic and public purposes.

Democratic Policy Design and Participatory Feedback

A growing body of policy analysis over the past several decades has examined how policy helps to form or construct citizens, sometimes as part of its original design but often as a cumulative and largely unintended consequence. Thus, the citizen of a self-governing democratic republic is partly an artifact of policy design, rather than a primordial actor with fully formed or exogenously generated virtues, preferences, and capacities. Through both resource and cognitive effects, policies form citizens who, in turn, shape further policy opportunities through voting, advocacy, and institutional field building, as well as through hands-on coproduction and public work. Democratic policy design and feedback are the second, key analytic cluster for theorizing sustainable cities as an emergent field, but it is important to distinguish urban and environmental forms from those operative in other social policy areas.[15]

Two of the major social policies that have revealed strong participatory policy feedback over the decades—Social Security and the GI Bill—are both individual benefit programs. Established in 1935, Social Security's programmatic development gradually generated increased resources (money and time), relative stakes (as a percentage of retirement income), and cognitive effects (contributor deservingness and dignity) to enable the building of an institutional field of advocacy and service organizations, as well as increased levels of political participation. The latter extended to seniors with lower incomes, thereby significantly narrowing the class-based participation gap. By the 1960s, the demographic participation and institutional field effects were substantial enough to protect the program from later onslaughts and to help establish related programs, such as Medicare in 1965.[16]

The GI Bill, providing veterans with educational and other benefits after World War II, had powerful civic feedback effects as well, though primarily for men. Administration of the program was perceived as fair and relatively easy to access—the major exception being the South with its segregated educational and training institutions—and the majority perceived educational and training opportunities as providing them with life-transforming experiences. The policy signal they received was that they were deserving and dignified citizens. Since GI Bill users had not been promised such benefits as part of a quid pro quo before enlisting in the military, they also felt a deep sense of gratitude, which elicited powerful normative commitments to give back to their communities by becoming engaged in a range of civic and political organizations. The interpretive effect was one of reciprocity. Those veterans who utilized the GI Bill joined approximately 50 percent more civic organizations, such as parent-teacher associations, neighborhood and homeowner organizations, and fraternal and other translocal groups, than did veterans who did not utilize the bill's benefits. They were also about 30 percent more likely to join political organizations, contact public officials, donate money to campaigns, serve on local boards and councils, and protest. The percentage included those black veterans who became part of the civil rights movement.[17]

Some policy and administrative designs that target the poor, such as Aid to Families with Dependent Children and its successor Temporary Aid for Needy Families, send negative signals that discourage participation and suppress civic dignity, while others, such as Head Start and public housing, tend to send more positive signals, although these vary considerably across states, local political cultures, and implementation strategies.[18] However, the participatory policy feedback literature has focused much less on policy design elements that *intentionally encourage* citizen participation, especially at the city and neighborhood level, than on "large identity-making federal social programs in which the individual is a client" who typically receives cash benefits or their near equivalent, such as the GI Bill's payment of education costs.[19]

"Policy design for democracy," in the touchstone formulations of Helen Ingram, Anne Larason Schneider, Steven Rathgeb Smith, and others, focuses on those design components that intentionally aim to engage ordinary citizens and enable public managers to broker, translate, and synthesize multiple ways of knowing and relational work among participants and stakeholders to solve public problems.[20] In environmental and urban fields, two general approaches that design for democracy are particularly important, although there are overlaps and interactive effects as well as considerable variation depending on legislative statute, type of public agency and public good, and the mobilization of civic and movement actors in shaping policy and administrative design. The first has been the development of legal norms and statutory requirements that provide access to information, public hearings, considered alternatives, judicial review, legal standing, and citizen suits. The second has been an array of programs, sometimes but not always explicit in statute, that provide a mix of resources and tools that enable local civic groups, associational networks, and deliberative multistakeholder partnerships to build organizational and institutional capacity for problem-solving. While somewhat inexact given the mix of components, the first can be called a "rights-based" and the second a "tools-based" environmental policy design for democracy.

Rights-based policy design became important immediately after the war. In 1946, the Fish and Wildlife Coordination Act (FWCA) required that federal agencies prepare "biological surveys" before new dams and other water projects could be launched, which encouraged citizens to become engaged in generating local knowledge, challenging proposals, and building relationships with sympathetic agency and academic scientists who had professional knowledge of fish, wildlife, and the emerging discipline of ecology. Congressional sponsors of FWCA were not only previously networked with the Izaak Walton League of America (IWLA), but also spoke at the 1947 IWLA national convention explicitly linking the future of democracy in the United States to such conservation activism. The Administrative Procedure Act (APA), also passed in 1946 with some of the same congressional sponsors, codified norms of citizen participation in public hearings as a check on growing agency discretion of New Deal state building, and it provided a right to judicial challenge and review, which conservationist Supreme Court justice William O. Douglas interpreted more expansively as he gained the upper hand over Justice Felix Frankfurter's deferent approach to agency discretion.

Reflecting isomorphic institutional tendencies, but in the interests of democratic change rather than reproductive conformity, states introduced their own "little APAs" and diffused them horizontally through the National Conference of Commissioners on Uniform State Laws, thereby generating further cognitive and motivational bases for citizen engagement at state and local levels. Public hearings, while providing the essential right to voice, also furnished incentives and occasions for diverse civic and conservation groups to build ties, foster strategic collaboration, and fashion common frames. Still-stronger rights and norms for public participation were added at different points along the way, especially through the National Environmental Policy Act (NEPA) of 1970 and its required environmental impact statements, spurring the development of isomorphic state environmental policy acts (SEPAs) as well as specific statutory language in national and state laws. The grassroots antitoxics campaign for the Emergency Planning and Community Right to Know Act in the mid-1980s helped to generate the basis for an environmental justice (EJ) movement that became institutionalized by the early 1990s. The movement linked the newly required Toxics Release Inventory (TRI) data from chemical and other firms, as well as other public data, from geographically and demographically distributed risks of local garbage dumps and incinerators to local knowledge and increased grassroots protest. Required data could be leveraged by urban and environmental groups to influence stock market ratings, media coverage, and legal reasoning.[21]

The second tools-based approach to policy design for democracy draws from scholarship across academic and professional disciplines. Ann Swidler provides a core rationale for cultural tool kits in sociological thinking, and this can be extended to the narratives of "best cases" of problem-solving one finds in many tool kits for place-based environmental work. Indeed, "best cases," while sounding a tad technocratic, are often forms of joint storytelling that have arisen from local knowledge and rich experimentation later raised to the level of a recipe from which others can learn to cook, even as they scribble their own substitute ingredients in the margins. Lester Salamon, along with Thomas Dietz and Paul Stern, develop elaborate rationales and examples of tools for environmental policy and problem-solving more generally. The emerging field of urban informatics establishes a foundation for what Daniel O'Brien terms an "urban commons" that is participatory, collaborative, coproductive, and profoundly place-based, especially in its core civic motivational structure built around territoriality and custodianship. Pragmatist democratic theory provides an essential normative foundation for usable tools. The concept of "repertoires" in social movement theory orients much empirical research. Unlike the latter, however, tools in this tradition of theorizing tend to be linked closely to pragmatic problem-solving rather than protest. The two often interact within fields of differently situated and asymmetrically empowered actors or over sequences of strategic choices. Field actors draw upon multiple and different types of tools sequentially over the course of longer trajectories of civic and movement action.[22]

To be sure, the full panoply of concepts within social movement theory is relevant to understand the environmental movement within various institutional fields (urban, wilderness, energy, health, and the like). But the pragmatic dimension is most relevant when examining policy design that is explicitly intended to enhance civic engagement, since nonpartisan public agencies in progressively reformed bureaucracies over the longer arc of American political development are normatively proscribed from directly promoting conflict and contestation.

Tools provided by public policy for urban and environmental problem solving among civic associations and other stakeholder groups take a range of forms and are, to be sure, located within larger policy toolboxes with which they are aligned in various ways. Four general categories of civically oriented tools are particularly important and typically depend upon each other: financial resources; data, mapping, and planning tools; network facilitation; and governance templates.

The first set of tools, *financial resources*, helps associations build capacity to recruit, inform, engage, and train citizens and other community residents, as well as hire staff, so that they can make credible arguments in public forums, do effective public work and coproduction that has impact, and level the playing field between lay citizens and professionals from state, market, and bureaucratic institutions. Thus, as the EPA was helping develop the watershed field in the 1990s and 2000s, it provided grants to build the capacities of local watershed associations and councils, usually requiring a match from other sources (foundations, local donors, and state and local agencies). It also provided grants to enable training networks and institutes (the River Network, the Center for Watershed Protection, and ICMA) to provide a range of other tools (volunteer water-quality monitoring, and online data-storage systems). The National Oceanic and Atmospheric Administration (NOAA) likewise provided matching grants for the National Estuary Program (NEP) though civic intermediaries, such as Restore America's Estuaries, to enable regional groups to do effective ecosystem restoration, including in major coastal cities. Even when public agencies do not provide grants directly to civic associations, but instead distribute funding to local infrastructure projects such as bicycle and pedestrian paths, such policy design motivates action and engages bicycling and pedestrian associations and AARP chapters to take advantage of opportunities to secure further funding and broader legitimacy for sustainable cities that are bikable and walkable, that provide "safe routes to school" for children, and provide "age-friendly streets" for seniors. The Intermodal Surface Transportation Efficiency Act (ISTEA) of 1991 and its successor laws, which also contained rights-based participatory components, spurred both grassroots engagement and collaboration with professional associations.

The second set are *data, mapping, and planning tools* that enable ordinary citizens and civic groups to do complex work. Thus, a city agency and a state university extension program might provide assistance in utilizing geographic information systems (GIS), so critical to place-based planning, ecosystem restoration, and environmental justice, and to meld local and professional knowledge into workable designs for what planning theorist Jason Corburn calls "street science." Other scholars analyze creative combinations of multiple "ways of knowing, including technical, experiential, and artistic."[23] To return to our earlier example, EPA watershed staff developed online planning tools for civic groups but then agreed to coproduce later iterations in conjunction with watershed movement actors when the latter directly confronted them at a headquarters meeting in Washington, DC, and then at the annual River Rally. The aim was to make the data and planning tools more user friendly for local activists. Such policy design for democracy is often not included in statutes but emerges from interactions among agency staff and civic groups. It then might become part of the formal design, as in neighborhood and sustainability planning in Seattle, Washington, where a city office distributed literal toolboxes of materials to institutions in all the relevant neighborhood sites. The coproduction of tools has become increasingly normative through an iterative process that recognizes the reflective practice across networks of actors in many kinds of institutions and at many levels of professional and everyday skills. Civic and professional actors learn how to appreciate what each can contribute to a good tool kit and how their own preferred tools might have drawbacks.

A third set of tools are those of *network facilitation*. To be sure, the main drivers of network formation in the environmental field are civic activists themselves. But public agencies can facilitate networking by helping to fund, convene, and/or legitimate conferences and smaller meetings among grassroots groups, national associations, and other civic intermediaries in emerging movements, as well as among relevant regulatory agencies and professional and trade associations. Such meetings serve as "field-configuring events" among actors who recognize democratic relationships as central to what it means to build a field, even if they do not agree on every aspect of what democratic power and practice might mean in that field. In enhancing network formation among watershed and volunteer monitoring groups, the EPA's Office of Water has, since the late 1980s, cosponsored, sometimes helped fund, and almost always sent mid- and high-level staff to learn, explain, inspire, and build further relationships through multiple types of conferences in the field. The EPA's Office of Environmental Justice and other related offices not only have developed grant programs for local groups (our first category of tools-based policy design) but also have helped facilitate regular convenings of movement leaders and other stakeholders through the National Environmental Justice Advisory Council (NEJAC), first established on a broad interagency basis through executive order of President Bill Clinton (1993–2001) and through other conferences covering a range of issues, such as brownfield redevelopment in inner-city neighborhoods. Authorized by statute, the EPA's Office of

Environmental Education has funded a training partnership that brings together the North American Association for Environmental Education and other national groups, state environmental education networks and teachers associations, and university centers. In all these policy fields, networks have become considerably more robust due to policy and administrative design, though it also takes dissent at such meetings to further reconfigure relationships, redesign tools, and signal the need for more capacity-building resources.[24]

The fourth category among tools-based policy design is the *governance template*. This can be required by statute, formalized as part of grant requirements, or remain part of normative expectations, reinforced by what other actors in the field consider ethical in terms of democracy and social justice and/or effective in terms of results. In Seattle's neighborhood planning policy, which included a significant number of sustainability projects within the 1994 comprehensive plan (Toward a Sustainable Seattle), a template for all participating neighborhoods was codesigned with neighborhood activists, after the latter had protested the otherwise-acceptable planning rubric based upon Jane Jacobs' urban village concept. This new template incorporated deliberative and inclusive visioning, stakeholder analysis and multi-stakeholder collaboration, formal review and feedback by city council and relevant public agencies, and staff training for relational trust building with neighborhood groups. The latter was largely derived from the field of faith-based or institution-based community organizing by an especially skilled actor: the founding director of the department of neighborhoods, who had been trained as an activist in this tradition. Subsequent climate action and sustainability planning in the city has built upon these foundations.[25]

The National Estuary Program, passed by Congress as part of the 1987 Clean Water Act, provided a "management conference" template for all NEPs, each with its own budget, that included collaborative management among multiple stakeholders (community and environmental groups, businesses, universities, scientists, public agencies, and other nonprofits). NEP teams, in turn, developed a range of other types of tools, such as local matching grants for restoration projects, public outreach tools, and an especially comprehensive water-quality monitoring guide for volunteer groups. This guide was coproduced through a national networking process facilitated by the Ocean Conservancy (with public funding), working with hundreds of local monitoring groups and several professional groups.

The National Research Council also assembled a panel of economists to produce a tool for valuing ecosystem services. This tool was essential for convincing those institutions operating according to market logics for business vitality, as well as coastal-city taxation logics for public revenue, to estimate and appreciate the added economic value of protecting and restoring aquatic ecosystems. The NEP policy design and governance template thus enabled field actors to generate additional tools—funding, data, and networking—with the purpose of aligning them appropriately within complex institutional logics to elicit further civic action, public support for investing in restoration, and effective and legitimate local governance strategies.

Participatory policy-design and feedback research pose major questions for how we think about democratic governance and political equality across many areas of policy, not just environmental, and not simply for sustainable cities. Several sets of questions are of special concern for sustainable cities. First, if participatory policy effects tend to be strongest for social welfare programs with mass publics, individualized benefits, and stable identity-based groups—especially seniors, who remain permanently interested constituencies once they qualify—how can environmental policies without such obvious design counterparts, and often more directly linked to place (neighborhood, city, watershed, region), be better crafted and legitimated to enhance capacities for effective and sustained civic action? This is an issue not only across many environmental policy fields. It is also a concern for other policies designed to enhance collaboration among civic actors and other stakeholders seeking pragmatic and just solutions to complex problems, such as urban schooling and policing.[26]

Second, this issue is especially significant in view of systemic tendencies to underinvest in civic skills and capacities *relative to the increasing costs of doing democracy well* in a society with so many complex problems, diverse publics, and highly resourced professional and market actors. It is further compounded by the *relative organizational and administrative advantages* of cash benefits, client services, narrow advocacy, and now social media mobilization and other forms of microtargeting and geotargeting. We must think more deeply about how we might better "invest in democracy" through an array of policy designs with substantial resources and tools that enable communities and institutions to engage their members in democratic processes of sustainability, resilience, and adaptation.[27]

Third, the question of perverse participation effects must be addressed.

Some policy designs might exacerbate disparities in who participates and further deepen civic and political inequality. For instance, a citywide system of neighborhood associations and planning, which might have been key to empowered sustainability strategies in the 1980s and 1990s, may prove increasingly problematic, especially when considering a generation of accumulated single-family homeowner equity among core (and typically white baby boomer) participants relative to a more diverse population of newcomers in the local housing market whose infill housing preferences also make credible claims for sustainability. Of special concern for sustainable cities is that there are already deep patterns of environmental injustice, gentrification dynamics, and spatial inequalities, which might be exacerbated by some forms of policy-induced engagement. Climate adaptation policy options, such as coastal city retreat and resettlement in the face of sea-level rise, may tend to impose asymmetric costs. Other policy designs might demobilize local movements over time, skew participation to some associations over others, and send conflicting messages to local citizens. Or they may elicit participation that is not especially deliberative in terms of workable solutions within realistic budgets, as Superfund (passed in 1980) tended to do before it was reformed in various ways.[28]

As Steven Rathgeb Smith and Helen Ingram argue, "There are no certain strategies for choosing tools that promote democracy."[29] No set of policy design features can guarantee that all relevant questions of democratic, sustainable, and just cities will be addressed fully, or that diverse institutional logics—or even diverse civic logics—will become aligned appropriately. This must remain the essential pragmatic institutional work of skilled field actors engaged in policy learning.

Urban Governance
The institutionalist concept of "urban regime," and its subsequent modifications by Clarence Stone and others, is essential to thinking about the emergence and development of sustainable cities as a field. It has helped shift urban power analysis away from classical pluralism, which sees local government distributing benefits based largely upon shifting popular voting majorities with autonomously formed preferences. Instead, urban regime analysis focuses on relational work across civic, business, professional, union, bureaucratic, and nonprofit organizations that enables the social production of "power to" get things done and "produce" public and private goods, rather than merely distribute them. This approach thus in-

corporates the insight from sociology and political science that employs a "power generating model." In urban regime and subsequent governance analysis, our third analytic cluster, relationships and trust matter not just for single policy decisions, such as a downtown development project or a bond issue, but to facilitate future cooperation, to interpret opportunity costs and acceptable trade-offs, and to establish feasible and credible trajectories forward, thereby enabling regular inclusion into emergent—and more and less stable—coalitions rather than exclusion, which entails costs beyond any specific issue.[30]

While such relationships are typically forged through tough negotiation and public battles, they have the potential to reorient actor preferences and the meaning and mix of public goods, transforming the mesh of governing coalitions in conjunction with the formal authority of mayors, city councils, city managers, and local public agencies. The "new institutionalism" in urban politics builds upon some of the core insights of regime theory by emphasizing that power tends to be widely dispersed and problems highly complex. Governance thus requires marshaling and blending fragmented resources from public, nonprofit, and private market actors and from multiple institutional layers. Coalitional logics may shift from one issue to the next, even from one ballot initiative to the next—and even the next in three consecutive years, as happened with the decision on how and whether to rebuild the Central Freeway in San Francisco in the late 1990s.[31]

Theorists from various traditions have prompted the rediscovery of the generative power of cities. Some urban legal scholars, such as Richard Schragger, and metropolitan governance and fiscal scholars, such as Bruce Katz and Jeremy Nowak, argue compellingly that cities have considerably greater leeway in fashioning more equitable policies, such as minimum-wage laws and labor-friendly community benefit agreements, than the "city limits" literature of a generation ago would lead us to believe. To be sure, powerful trends exacerbate a "new urban crisis" of inequality in some of the most innovative cities. But cities can often leverage place-dependent value, agglomeration logics, and participatory subcultures to challenge economic inequality and to tie urban livability to sustainability. Cities *can* govern, even in an era of mobile, global capital, despite some constitutional limits by state and federal governments and national electoral disadvantages inscribed by economic and political geography. We certainly need new urban policies at the national level. But cities *can* govern much more sustainably, equitably, and democratically if we enable them.[32]

The sustainable city falls at the higher end of the original typology of regimes that Stone and others have analyzed. Stone's "maintenance regime," on the lower rung, tends to reproduce stagnation and fails to respond creatively to new environmental and economic challenges. Moving upward, the "development regime" relies mainly upon elite coordination and conflict management among insiders, facilitated by an abundance of selective incentives (union construction jobs, contractor fees) and other benefits (tax revenues, local spending by tourists) that tend to tie popular constituencies to dominant "growth machine" actors. These include real-estate developers, banks, downtown businesses and hotels, and politicians dependent on campaign finance contributions and public credit for visible achievements. Development logics have defined much of the post–World War II era of cities grappling with the decline of manufacturing and the difficult shift toward postindustrial futures. The sustainable city as an ideal type tends to combine features of Stone's next rungs upward, the "middle class progressive regime" and "lower class opportunity regime," which incorporate, respectively, environmental amenities and class equities. The sustainable city faces far greater challenges of coordination and governance, especially when it attempts to incorporate more robust forms of racial and social justice.[33]

Because strategies for enabling cities to become more sustainable and resilient have sometimes been driven by disasters—a pattern that will almost certainly become increasingly prevalent for civic and policy learning in future decades—democratic actors will have to manage and contain what Kevin Gotham and Miriam Greenberg call "crisis-driven urbanization." This response tends to favor rapid recovery on the terms of growth coalitions dominated by powerful business and financial actors, typically at the expense of vulnerable neighborhoods. Yet, as they argue in their analyses of post-Katrina New Orleans and post-9/11 New York City, such disasters have also generated opportunities for grassroots groups and movements to "dream big" through citywide visioning and other civic processes. Strengthening the sustainable cities field aims to enhance the institutional supports that might make such processes more fruitful.[34]

The sustainable and just city requires mobilizing attentive publics for whom the usual selective incentives are not adequate while also nurturing the capacity of some mix of civic associations to find appropriate ways of translating indispensable contestation into fruitful collaboration. Only then can the production and coproduction of public goods, such as open space, restored watersheds, food justice, affordable housing, energy efficiency, and transportation equity, be achieved without sacrificing those forms of economic growth and business dynamism upon which thriving cities depend—indeed, for which ordinary voters, unions, and minority advocates for expanded economic opportunity will hold elected officials democratically accountable.

At the higher end, sustainable and resilient cities require that the institutional logics of various powerful actors—real estate firms, banks, utilities, planning and transportation agencies, construction unions, disaster management and insurance agencies—align sufficiently and appropriately to the various logics of civic actors that bring new norms and practices into arenas of contestation and collaboration, market regulation and innovation. This has been made more challenging by some recent trends toward "financialization" in urban governance, with real-estate field dynamics among core professional actors that generate perverse effects, including environmental ones. Yet innovative forms of local public finance based upon better processes of valuing public assets, such as land, and leveraging them for public good and sustainability have emerged in the United States and Europe, and we will need to build further upon these. Some goals of the democratic, sustainable, and just city are, no doubt, in tension, and fully compelling theoretical and policy resolutions are not (yet) on the horizon.[35]

Thinking Systemically about Sustainable Urban Democracy

By developing an analysis that draws upon institutional fields and logics, policy design and feedback, and urban governance approaches, I am aligning the study of sustainable cities with the normative and analytic concerns of a "systemic approach to deliberative democracy." This approach has been articulated jointly by political theorists Jane Mansbridge, James Bohman, Simone Chambers, Thomas Christiano, Archon Fung, John Parkinson, Dennis Thompson, and Mark Warren. It proceeds from the assumption that there is no best possible, single deliberative forum. It accommodates multiple ecologies and styles of democratic action and deliberation, and recognizes tensions and tradeoffs, complementarity and displacement, conflict and collaboration operating dynamically at multiple scales and

forms of complexity across levels and types of expertise and local knowledge. Field actors have available a range of recipes and institutional design
choices to construct, realign, and redesign minipublics.[36]

In its efforts to become a more robust institutional field, sustainable
cities can—*indeed must*—accommodate militant grassroots protest on
one end and structured dialogue among diverse stakeholders on the other,
with many forms of relational and coproductive work in between and all
around. In view of the multiple options for and obstacles to various types
of civic action, skilled field actors work to optimize opportunities, recognize limits, and configure and sequence forms, sometimes more successfully than others, to be sure. To achieve appropriate mixes and sequences
often takes a decade or more in many of the cases we shall encounter
and never remains happily stable or uncontested. Theories of public work,
ethical democracy, democratic professionalism, street science, and empowered participation, among others, can further enrich a systemic approach
that locates gaps, identifies power imbalances, and seeks strategic opportunities for democratic action and just sustainability in a very broad range
of institutional settings.[37]

Some analytic approaches to cities are skeptical that various forms of
civic action, collaborative governance, and multistakeholder networks can
generate essential democratic conditions for urban sustainability or help
alter the dynamics of markets and hierarchies, especially within global
capital flows and highly unequal power structures. To some extent, these
differences are reflected in the larger debate in environmental sociology
between the more pessimistic "treadmill of production" versus the more
optimistic "ecological modernization" theories, especially in the context of
climate change.[38] Or they are part of broader radical critiques that purport
to demonstrate that "the dominant environmental strategies are also forms
of denial demonstrably doomed to fail," because they refuse to recognize
the root problem of capitalism and the "necessity for ecological and social
revolution" propelled by a "new [global] environmental proletariat" with
"nothing left to lose." Radical urban theorists place special emphasis upon
periodic rebellions, such as the Paris Commune of 1871, the Petrograd So-
viet of 1917, or Occupy Wall Street in Zuccotti Park in 2015, that might
coalesce into contemporary urban revolution and secure "real democracy."
For some, participation short of urban rebellion is itself tyrannical.[39]

Sociological critics of "the new public participation," such as Caroline
Lee, Michael McQuarrie, and Edward Walker, also offer broad skepticism.

These forms of civic innovation have occurred during an era of dramatically rising inequality and in an institutional context that is far from genuine democratic deliberation. Not only have such innovations legitimated inequality and corporate power when they have been specifically designed by corporate consultants fighting popular resistance, say to a giant box store, but they also perform the very same functions even when, indeed *especially* when, they include multiple stakeholders, greater equality of voice, and have facilitators skilled in deliberative practice in settings not tied to the corporate world. While these critics argue that this is the result of many factors, depending on the community context and policy field, the reason such innovations "democratize inequalities" is because they are initiated by elites and are facilitated by nonprofit and other professional consultants who have formed an "industry" to ply their trade. Their participatory designs, which have "metastasized" like the malignant growth of cancer, almost invariably channel, deflect, and co-opt mass resistance, thereby domesticating social movement forms that *would otherwise emerge* to insist on more general policies in the interest of the broad public good and "true democratization." Instead of nurturing grander forms of social solidarity, the new forms of public participation settle for focusing on public problem solving where citizens and communities may disagree—city planning choices, program budgets, safer neighborhoods, community development.

Some interests are simply irreconcilable, the critics argue, so better to focus on these, with all the repertoires of contentious social movements. Innovation in public participation obscures questions of justice across the wide array of arenas and helps civil society migrate to the state and other elite institutions: "*The end result of all these little steps to empowerment is, unfortunately, not a long journey to social justice but a tightening spiral of resignation and retreat from public life*" (emphasis in original).[40]

While these critical analyses have selective merit and should challenge actors in the sustainable cities field to remain acutely attuned to issues of power and justice as they innovate further, in their starkest form, such critics simply wish away the messy challenges of institutional and field transformation at the urban level in the hopes that they will be rescued by sweeping logics of social solidarity or more contentious forms of organizing. Admittedly, none of the cities, networks, or practices that I examine as part of the broad sustainable cities field could be confidently classified as "strong path-dependent historical institutionalization," and indeed probably no US city yet falls into this category while some in Europe perhaps do. Nor have federal policy designs of the last several decades enabled cities to become sustainable and resilient, although selective ones have helped build some parts of the field, at least up until the 2016 presidential election, and some offer valuable templates for future policy design.[41]

The core question here, however, is not whether or not civic and sustainable city innovations and field building have been sufficient or have stemmed the tide of inequality coming from varied directions—some of the more important ones have little to do with urban dynamics as such. Rather, it is whether or not such innovations have helped lay indispensable foundations for further institutional reform and serve a broader project of democratic hope, efficacy, and justice amidst climate crisis, tempered sufficiently by institutional and political realism so as to be credibly attainable. As Susan Fainstein argues in *The Just City*, the key task is to make the best case we can within the limits of what is feasible in the context of contemporary democratic and capitalist urbanism, albeit with vigorous reforms in regulation, representation, social welfare, redistributive taxation, and, of course, continued independent organizing of many sorts.[42]

The larger questions raised by critics of civic innovation for sustainable cities cannot be settled by theoretical fiat. Since there is little counterfactual evidence—historical, comparative, or contemporary American—that local or global movements of contestation, with postmarket aspirations or encompassing solidarities based upon irreconcilable interests, are capable of institutionalizing and legitimating workable democratic polities at the urban level, the analysis of field building and "alternative pathways" to sustainable cities remains a worthy, indeed essential pursuit of pragmatic and democratic experimentation. Critics have demonstrated, neither conceptually nor empirically, any systemic zero-sum trade-offs between publicly or professionally supported and enabled participation and social movement mobilization. They have certainly not demonstrated that the former has *caused*—in contrast to having *coincided with*—the relative deficits of solidaristic movements in recent decades or that such movements and "true democracy" would flourish *if only* we could find a way to tamp down the new public participation and thus prevent it from channeling, co-opting, and deflecting mass resistance. Structured forms of public participation and social movement mobilization are both needed. Both can use much refinement. Skilled field actors can often generate alignment and synergy across fields that have come to depend on some forms of professionalization of practice, given the complexity of publics, problems, and policies.[43]

Small-scale green enterprises, community trusts, and other forms of cooperative economics can also play an important role in sustainable city strategies. However, these are highly unlikely to displace the core challenges of democratic engagement within and alignment among major institutional systems, which is the focus of my analysis.[44]

Institutionalist theories are perhaps inherently skeptical of analytic approaches that posit radical alternatives and unspecified forms of "true democracy" that would sweep away many of the fine-grained challenges and embedded relationships of building and transforming complex fields, organizational cultures, professional practices, and urban polities on a more democratic basis. *These alone cannot suffice* for robust political, economic, or climate strategies of broader scope. The latter might arguably include, for instance, ways of linking resilient urban infrastructure investment and planning, as well as equitable housing and jobs policies, to a Green New Deal, but one where policy design for public participation is neither an afterthought nor a nemesis. I pursue this topic in the postscript.[45]

Democratic institutionalism and field building elicit a politics of democratic hope and efficacy, even in a period of urgency defined by climate crises and increasing threats to liberal democracy. Indeed, *especially* in such a period we cannot risk experimenting with institutionally unmoored strategies, nebulously encompassing solidarities, unspecified forms of true democracy, or unspecifiable fantasies of postmarket economies, and there is little evidence that mass or local democratic publics would choose to do so.[46]

Note on Methods

This study draws upon a variety of methods. I ground the historical arc of this narrative in secondary works on urban and environmental history, both academic disciplines that have flourished in the past few decades, and I supplement these with biographies and autobiographies, oral histories, and selective organizational archives, framing documents, and action guides. For more recent data on civic and professional associations and other institutional actors, I have reviewed a broad array of annual reports, strategic planning and framing documents, audited financial statements, and board and staff membership affiliations, biographical profiles, and skill mixes (degrees, certificates, prior employment). I have also examined best-practice tool kits, since these provide insight into both tools utilized (drawn from experience) and tools prescribed for civic and government actors. Hence, they are part of strategic interventions to shape and improve the field, even when they are often presented in a less than fully balanced manner. Documents such as annual reports, tool kits, and staff biographies are generally available through a Google search; almost all that I have cited are still available, with the exception of earlier annual reports or strategic plans that organizations choose to remove once they become dated or have been revised or staff bios of those who have since left an organization. I have retained in my files all PDFs and/or hard copies of such data.

I have participated in or reviewed online webinars on current best practice, typically presented by several practitioners from related organizations in a specific field, such as public engagement in transportation planning and watershed restoration. Rating and accreditation guides provide insight into metrics for measuring results and securing technical and professional legitimacy across a field. I have taken field notes at various public meetings and conferences, and I further examine other conference proceedings and participant lists to help understand how civic and professional associations develop relevant sections, enlist actors within and across organizational boundaries, debate strategic orientations, identify barriers, and measure progress.

Many other kinds of sources provide a window into field debates and available models: newsletters, podcasts, blogs, and documentaries produced by civic associations; board and work group meeting minutes and conference call logs; foundation and public agency reports on funded projects and organizations; media coverage; and books by leading practitioners. Career guides provide insight into the emerging shape of opportunities for paid employment within fields and typically provide an inventory of key organizations. I have also utilized general association directories, including those published by leading organizations within specific fields, such as watershed organizations, green building councils, bicycle associations, land trusts, and professional associations.

To understand policy dynamics and design, I have examined city sustainability and climate action plans, climate and smart growth state plans and policies, and federal policies, programs, and evaluations in selected fields, including reports by the National Academy of Public Administration, the National Research Council, and similar groups. I also draw upon secondary scholarship in relevant fields, such as sociology, political science, policy analysis, law, planning, public administration, nonprofit organizations, and urban studies. I restrict repeated references on core analytic concepts from these various academic disciplines except where these are especially important to the context.

I have drawn upon interviews conducted from 2015 to 2019 with association leaders and staff with strategic or programmatic responsibilities, and current or former government officials at various levels of the federal system. Whenever relevant, I have also explored their career trajectories across multiple organizations and over various periods of organizational development. Interviews ranged from forty minutes to two hours.

Plan of the Book

In this chapter, I have presented some broad analytic themes that guide what follows and have posed some normative questions of democratic theory in relation to urban sustainability in the United States. I have also provided selective examples, drawn from more elaborate analyses in later chapters. The core chapters 2 through 7 have a historical arc and are presented largely in narrative form, with analytic concepts interwoven relatively lightly. Chapter 2 covers World War II to the general environmental "field settlement" in the early 1970s. Chapters 3 through 5 are more subfield specific (urban land conflicts; biking, walking, and farming; urban rivers and watersheds). Each has a trajectory beginning *after* the general field settlement, with dynamics specific to each institutional and policy subfield. Chapter 6 (on governance pathways in five cities) briefly goes back into the 1950s to establish each city's initial urban growth machine and governance choices but then also proceeds from the general field settlement to the present. Chapter 7 (on framing and intermediaries) is more conceptual but also largely follows this post-1970s arc. Chapter 8 (on democratic resilience) reviews core analytic themes and presents key field-building and democratic challenges in an age of climate crisis. The postscript explores briefly how some of the core lessons of civic capacity-building and policy design for democracy might be incorporated into a potential Green New Deal. I call this a civic GND, for short.

Chapter 2 provides an account of the development of the environmental field from the end of World War II to the 1970s, and particularly how openings to urban environmental issues emerged. Activism for clean water began immediately after the war, primarily by mobilizing resources from multitiered conservation associations. Critical for catalyzing institutional field building, however, was the League of Women Voters (LWV), which developed the most important strategic organizational niche strategy based upon its experience and knowledge of complex intergovernmental relationships, its women's municipal housekeeping traditions, its previous coalitional work, and its normative commitment to citizens' taxing themselves for public goods. The federal water policy field emerged tentatively, but with various policy designs that further incentivized local knowledge and participation and collaboration among conservation groups, academic scientists, and administrative staff. Local civic action also helped spur urban professional associations, such as the American Municipal Association and the US Conference of Mayors, to become increasingly engaged.

Federal "enforcement conferences" were convened in fifty-one venues between 1957 and 1971, with multiple "sessions," "workshops," and "progress meetings." They represented a policy design compromise in 1956 to stave off actual command-and-control enforcement that seemed unworkable politically and administratively at that point. However, they had the unintentional effect of promoting civic action and field building. To some degree this was built into the logic of the compromise—civic actors can attend and deliberate but should not expect federal authorities to mandate and enforce—but the extent and forms of participatory feedback were quite unexpected when the compromise was first negotiated. These conferences shaped the civic contours of the field in profound ways for more than a decade before the Clean Water Act was passed in 1972. The field of air pollution policy emerged somewhat in parallel with water pollution, though with weaker policy feedbacks. Nonetheless, local urban coalitions, often in conjunction with LWV chapters, played an important role in field building.

In both water and air policy fields, the major federal laws of the early 1970s took the predominant form of command and control, further reinforced by the emergence of a highly professionalized environmental lobby supported by the Ford Foundation's strategy to build the environmental field and the broader public interest law field. Chapter 2 concludes with a discussion of the mix of strategic calculations that undergird the newly settled environmental field, some of which would later help in building the sustainable cities field, especially as command and control could not adequately address issues of urban space, ecosystem, and environmental justice.

Chapter 3 examines the intense conflicts over urban land use that emerged in the 1960s and 1970s and the civic associations that drove them, as well as federal policy designs that responded to them and sometimes further enabled them. It then analyzes the response by some of the established professional associations in the field and the formation of new professional associations in various fields over the following decades as the framing of sustainable cities became more common. Four civic forms or programmatic venues were especially important in the urban land conflicts that initially emerged: Model Cities (a federal program that included various types of civic and other actors), neighborhood associations (in some cases formally recognized by city authorities), community development corporations (which received federal and foundation support and developed as a distinct field of its own), and open space coalitions (including land trusts and greenbelt alliances). This civic action, as well as policy feedback effects of various federal laws—especially NEPA and the establishment of a citizens' advisory within the White House Council on Environmental Quality—prompted a systematic attempt to rethink land use regulation. However, the National Land Use Policy Act failed in Congress in 1975 due to shifting political opportunities in the White House and Congress and divisions among national environmental and urban associations.

Nonetheless, in the following years, the field of land use law and regulation, as well as other forms of local administrative law, continued to expand on many fronts as civic pressure (and countermovements) persisted. Professional associations, such as the American Institute of Architects and the American Planning Association, provided associational resources that enabled citizen participation in urban planning and design and, in the 1990s, lent assistance to the formation of new groups such as the US Green Building Council, Smart Growth America, and the Congress for the New Urbanism. In the ensuing years, AARP also became allied through its livable and age-friendly community strategy.

Chapter 4 analyzes bicycling and walking movements and institutional actors, as well as urban agriculture and its distinct trajectory proceeding largely out of the organic food movement of the 1960s. The bicycle movement, in dormancy for most of the first half of the twentieth century, re-emerged in the early 1970s, but its growth was stifled by divisions among elite club and utilitarian cyclists, exacerbated by legal action within the movement. As the movement began to re-emerge once again in the 1990s, local associations in San Francisco and other major cities made strategic choices to build membership and establish legitimacy on a broader democratic basis, to negotiate spatial scarcities and transportation asymmetries among competing interests, and to find ways to work within urban governance coalitions. Contentious and identity-forming civic action in the streets transformed into collaborative action, though never completely and never without distinct cultural strategies. New dynamics among national associations, as well as the participatory requirements and funding streams of the ISTEA policy design (1991) and its successor statutes, enabled further growth of local bicycle and pedestrian associations as part of "complete streets," "safe routes to school," and "healthy community" coalitions, in conjunction with groups focused on opportunities for seniors and families. Participatory and field-building policy feedbacks were considerable.

Within urban agriculture, I focus on several civic and institutional forms, especially community garden systems, food policy councils, and food justice strategies. These have manifest themselves in different cities, including Philadelphia, New York City, Seattle, and Los Angeles while some of the federal programs have helped support local innovation more broadly. National associations and networks have leveraged local innovation but have often fragmented in ways that reflect the enormous complexity of the broader field of food advocacy, sustainability, and justice. Opportunities to secure greater strategic collaboration have suboptimized, both within the extended deliberative processes of the National Organic Standards Board and within and among the major associations, with different strategic and issue emphases and racial tensions. A comparison of food policy design with ISTEA in transportation provides insight into why this might be so.

Chapter 5 examines further shifts in the field of water policy after the Clean Water Act (CWA) of 1972, especially the emergence of the watershed and estuary movements. Urban watersheds have been an important, but by no means exclusive, part of this field since many cities lie along or at the juncture of rivers, and because major coastal cities lie within estuary watersheds that extend thousands or even tens of thousands of square miles inland across hundreds and thousands of rivers and streams into other urban, suburban, and rural areas. In an era of climate change, coastal cities are especially vulnerable. As many arid western cities become even hotter and drier, further challenges have emerged to manage water resources equitably and effectively, including protecting aquifers, renegotiating claims to riverine supplies, reducing consumption, and managing growth. CWA contained one section that required integrative and participatory planning across entire basins, including nonpoint as well as point-source pollution, but it was largely sidelined in the 1970s due to the timetables, tools, staff capacities, political priorities, and public preferences manifest in the overall command-and-control policy design. This began to shift in the 1980s with greater scientific understanding of watersheds as integrated ecosystems, the further development of conservation biology as a field, and with additional policy designs, such as the Chesapeake Bay Program and the National Estuary Program, the latter part of the 1987 revisions of CWA.

Civic action began to manifest itself in the formation of watershed associations and councils, friends of the river and stream groups, citizen monitoring of water quality, trashed urban stream networks, and the development of a distinct watershed frame among civic and professional actors at many levels. Several national civic associations, such as the River Network and Restore America's Estuaries, have played particularly important roles in building the field, along with local, state, and regional groups, as well as groups focused primarily upon advocacy within the command-and-control framework, such as American Rivers and Clean Water Action. In turn, the EPA complemented this field building with tools, financial resources, and support for further civic networking through its Office of Wetlands, Oceans, and Watersheds, established in 1991, as well as through various other incentives for states. Other community-based strategies across the agency reinforced such work through the Clinton, Bush, and Obama administrations. The chapter concludes with two innovative cases that have had impact across the field; namely, natural drainage systems in Seattle and the New York City model of collaborating with upstate watersheds to preserve natural filtration while also providing resources for local watershed communities for sustainable farming, forestry, and other community development strategies.

Chapter 6 provides a further window into local field building processes by examining several cities over a long trajectory—World War II to the present—to understand alternative pathways to sustainability within complex urban governance systems. The chapter first analyzes the processes of change in three cities—Portland, San Francisco, and Chicago—that tend to be ranked by many scholars and practitioners as having made significant progress toward sustainability on multiple fronts and that have also tended to play leadership roles within regional, national, and international networks. These cities differ in various ways, but all have had significant episodes of grassroots contention over economic and spatial development strategies, as well as multistakeholder collaboration, over many decades. I then add two other cases—Baltimore and Phoenix—where sustainability strategies face more serious obstacles but that cast further light on the range of pathways potentially available. Such case studies, to be sure, have their limits, especially for understanding some of the smaller and medium-sized cities hit hard by deindustrialization and that are taking tentative steps to revitalize themselves, often with some mix of sustainability strategies. While there is much to learn from the trajectories of cities in this chapter, a fuller understanding can only come from further comparative case study research.

Chapter 7 examines two key processes that operate across various fields and cities, namely *framing* "sustainable cities" as an integrative set of cognitive components among the various watershed, biking, green building, urban farming and forestry, and other fields, and *enabling* integrative practices among various agencies and organizations at the city level and among cities. Framing has become an important concept in social movement theory, as well as in policy and communication studies, and I thus examine how emergent framing processes in the sustainable cities field have become enriched by aligning and bridging selectively with the frames of "healthy cities," "assets-based community development," and "environmental justice." This fecund cross-fertilization has helped fashion sustainable cities as an emergent urban "master frame." Unlike many social movement frames that build primarily upon us-versus-them identity tropes, the sustainable cities frame seeks to locate opportunities for collaborative action among various kinds of civic and professional associations, multiple stakeholders in arenas of contention, and public agencies at all levels of the federal system. Integrative framing and practice at the city level are increasingly facilitated by *city institutions*, such as a sustainability or resilience office; *city processes*, such as community visioning and planning; and *city tool kits*, such as geographical information systems and other digital platforms that permit visualization of multiple forms of data, interactive dynamics, and comparative scenarios. The federal government, and especially the US Environmental Protection Agency over several Democratic and Republican administrations, has helped facilitate and complement the framing work of movements and among other agencies. I return to some of the emotive elements of framing in the final chapter's discussion of urban resilience work as a way of constructively managing emotions of fear, denial, and despair, as well as democratic faith and hope.

In the second part of chapter 7, I discuss how various intermediary organizations that have adopted urban sustainability framing have attempted to enable pragmatic and integrative work at the city level, especially among those directly responsible for sustainability and resilience agendas across agencies, plans, and practices. I focus on two major intermediaries: ICLEI USA, which is part of the global ICLEI network within the United Nation's institutional framework, and the Urban Sustainability Directors Network (USDN), which was established to add more robust peer learning among staff directly tasked with driving and integrating sustainability work. I also examine their relation to urban generalists and multi-issue professional and advocacy associations of long standing, such as the National League of Cities (NLC), the International City/County Management Association, and the US Conference of Mayors. While these are not leaders in technical or civic innovation, they have very broad reach and can generate legitimacy for sustainable city work among association members who may face skepticism and even opposition among other actors in their home cities.

Chapter 8 revisits several themes in the analytic narratives of the previous chapters, with a view to further field building for urban democratic resilience in the face of more disruptive climate change in the years ahead. In line with my general framework of sustainable cities as a strategic action field, I focus on three sets of strategies that will require heightened attention. The first is a *civic politics of risk and resilience* capable of tapping local sources of political trust, civic virtue, and bonding social capital while further developing bridging and linking social capital for more just and more robust action across cities and regions. The second is an *institutional politics of democratic professionalism* that can further engage professionals as civic partners across the broad range of institutions that will need to be mobilized for effective and fair resilience and adaptation. Many professional associations are poised to take further action toward linking citizens and experts in a politics of democratic resilience, and the time is ripe for a national strategic initiative among leading associations and foundations. The third strategy is a *cultural politics of hope* that can grapple with the complex mix and sequence of emotions that climate change raises. Movements help shape and manage emotions, as do institutions. Yet, in an era of climate crisis, they are vulnerable to pulls and tugs toward a sense of futility and despair. While there are many cultural traditions across the political spectrum that can help nourish hope in the difficult and uncertain work ahead, the field building and institutional practice of sustainable cities, however incremental and incomplete, provides a major resource for democratic faith and hope.

In the postscript, I explore a potential policy design of a civic Green New Deal (or similarly ambitious program of alternative nomenclature) that seeks to enhance civic capacity building and participatory policy feedback. Should an ambitious Green New Deal (GND) become possible, it could be designed in such a way as to enhance the potential of a civic politics of risk and resilience, an institutional politics of democratic professionalism, and a cultural politics of hope. A robust civic framing could increase political chances of enactment, reduce conflict over implementation, and diminish popular resistance in communities wary of technocratic and statist overreach. Whatever the appropriate mix of market mechanisms, regulatory tools, technological innovations, and public investments that we might choose for an ambitious Green New Deal, we will nonetheless need a broad set of strategies for engaging local communities and youth, civic and professional associations, workers and employers, educational and cultural institutions, and multistakeholder partnerships in ways that are effective for mitigation and resilience while generating widespread trust and democratic legitimacy. A strategic approach to a policy design of investment in civic capacity can help inoculate us from policy backlash and a politics of rage and chaos, futility and despair.

I explore briefly how federal grants and other tools can enable community partnerships, democratic professional initiatives, worker and employer collaboration, and other multistakeholder models to generate effective work on climate across many fields. I also suggest some ways that strategic coordination and metagovernance can be enhanced within and across federal agencies to enable appropriate designs and limit perverse consequences. These include civic GND mission statements and strategic frameworks for all relevant federal agencies, interagency working groups, citizen advisory committees, and a dedicated White House office.

Contentious climate movements must challenge power and open up political opportunities, but a civic design for a Green New Deal will be essential to building trust and collaboration across many types of communities and institutions to build sustainable, resilient, and just cities and to enable the transformative work that will be needed. Movement contention and civic policy design are not inherently zero-sum but open to synergies of many kinds. *Sustainable Cities in American Democracy* seeks to enhance these analytically to interpret the world, as well as practically to change it.

CHAPTER TWO

Urban Water and Air in the Early Postwar Decades: Movement and Settlement

In this chapter, I examine the development of the environmental field from the end of World War II to the beginning of the 1970s, when "field settlement" occurred. The focus remains on those aspects of the field that provide openings for action at the urban level and thus does not take up issues such as wilderness, which constitutes an important part of the larger field and to which urban activists are certainly connected. I begin with an overview of those institutional field dynamics that fueled postwar suburbanization, and then I turn to the emergence of clean water as an issue that catalyzed action across urban, suburban, and rural communities.

Existing multitiered conservation associations, including civic associations such as the League of Women Voters (LVW), began to frame clean water as an issue immediately as the war ended, and their democratic engagement in this emerging field was buttressed by two 1946 federal laws: the Fish and Wildlife Coordination Act and the Administrative Procedure Act. Both had isomorphic effects at the state level. However, the route to strong federal action was circuitous because of limited federal administrative capacities and deference to states, which enjoyed cooperative relationships with local industries that resisted federal controls. Participatory policy feedback was gradually strengthened with further legislation and federal enforcement conferences as well as a political opportunity structure that provided new openings with the 1958 midterm elections and then the presidential elections of 1960 and 1964. Unlikely environmentalists assumed new roles in Congress that linked federal finance, administrative systems, and meaningful lifeworlds, buttressed by a more robust public sphere around water.

The LWV exercised especially noteworthy social skills to mobilize publics locally and regionally while providing trustworthy knowledge based upon complex relationships with a broad array of field actors in industry, academia, and at all levels of government. LWV chapters brought institutional logics to public light, systematically mapped opportunities for action, and creatively aligned a broad array of civic and professional actors in various river basin, coastal, and Great Lakes cities and communities. Professional associations, such as the American Municipal Association and the US Conference of Mayors, which had members who were in the most direct line of pressure from local publics and were held directly accountable for problem-solving and governance, also became persistent voices for clean water action at all federal levels. Clean air manifests similar civic and policy dynamics, though with weaker participatory policy feedback through federal enforcement conferences. Nonetheless, cities like Pittsburgh, Pennsylvania, provide evidence of the important field-building role played by LWV, as well as the skillfully blended civic repertoire that could be deployed in diverse institutional settings.

The passage of the Clean Air and Clean Water Acts in the early 1970s was buttressed by the National Environmental Policy Act, signed by Richard Nixon on New Year's Day of 1970; it was viewed as the Magna Carta of environmentalism. Initially, its self-executing environmental impact statement (EIS) policy design—which helped generate enormous data for civic use and thus reduced knowledge asymmetries across the field—was viewed in competition with the explicit command-and-control designs of the other statutes. Earth Day followed in the spring and generated further public support and institutional resources to build the field further. The US Environmental Protection Agency (EPA) was pieced together from various other federal agencies by executive order of the president, with approval from Congress, and began operations in December.

Despite creative grassroots energy, command and control established the core policy design features of the 1970s as the environmental decade and defined the parameters of field settlement. This was the result of many factors, including the relative availability of tools and metrics, industry resistance, deep distrust between the two major political parties controlling different branches of government from 1969 to 1977, and the emergence of environmental law as a field. Older multitiered conservation associations, as well as newer national environmental organizations, made rational strategic choices to professionalize and become effective players in this emerging field settlement. Conflicts over urban land had begun to emerge, but without coherent links among the major urban and environmental organizations or compelling models of place-based ecological and urban dynamics. With settling, however, this soon began to change.

The Suburban Industrial Complex

Various socioeconomic trends in the immediate postwar period set the stage for the broadening of the earlier conservation movement and the emergence of environmentalism as a full-blown institutional and policy field. One of the most important developments was the consolidation of what historian Adam Rome terms the "suburban industrial complex." This included a home-building industry operating with bulldozing equipment that could level vast tracts of land, construct hundreds or even thousands of units at a time utilizing mass-production techniques, and bypass, at least initially, the spatial and fiscal challenges of municipal sewer construction through the installation of individual septic tanks. Such construction could ignore the physical contours and ecological functions of wetlands, steep slopes, and floodplains. Large-scale builders, responsible for only 5 percent of the housing market in 1938, claimed 24 percent in 1949 and 64 percent by 1959. The federal government provided loan guarantees for builders and mortgage insurance for buyers, including for utilities built into new homes, thus further cementing support from manufacturers and power companies, along with coal companies, the railroads that shipped coal, and the miners who extracted it. Suburban sprawl provided endless speculative opportunities for real-estate firms whose brokers professionalized, and federal highway dollars subsidized automobile travel for work and play. Businesses within the suburban industrial complex were represented by powerful trade associations, such as the National Association of Home Builders and the National Association of Realtors; construction unions provided additional intermediaries capable of further structuring sectors and exerting influence across various subfields.[1]

This larger institutional field was buttressed by a timber regime in the national forests that functioned as a classic iron triangle of private timber interests (whose own lands had become depleted during the war), a US Forest Service primarily driven by board feet metrics, and congressional representatives from timber states who dominated appropriations committees. The latter acted with foremost attention to local logging jobs and the designated 25 percent of timber sale tax receipts that went directly to supporting local school and road construction. As a result, timber production increased from 3.5 to 9.3 billion board feet per year during the 1950s alone.[2]

To be sure, these suburban institutional field dynamics were energized by pent-up consumer demand for housing after years of depression, stagnant urban home construction, cities crowded with war workers, the rapid demobilization of some fourteen million men and women, and the mass migration of blacks into northern cities. Suburban development expressed itself as a civic ideal melding freedom, beauty, and order, albeit tinged by deep shades of racial inequality.[3] To a large extent, these field dynamics were powered by the civic hopes and dreams of individuals and families, as well as democratic choices expressed through various institutional forms at all levels of the federal system, though with their own democratic deficits. Homeless vets at a public hearing could certainly capture the democratic imagination.[4]

A hydropower institutional field, symbolized by some of the great dams of the New Deal–era—the Grand Coulee, Bonneville, and Boulder—was also poised to expand enormously after the war. Industry and population were projected to grow further and require vast new sources of relatively cheap electricity. Even in the historically arid West, agriculture and ranching could thrive if enough dams and channels could be constructed to irrigate fields and grasslands and provide electricity; water law evolved to accommodate and incentivize these developments through the "prior appropriation" doctrine. Spectacular cities such as Las Vegas, Nevada; Los Angeles, California; and Phoenix, Arizona, could grow in the desert. The US Department of the Interior's Bureau of Reclamation, operating in the West, and the US Army Corps of Engineers represented politically powerful bureaucracies with proven technical and institutional capacities with clear stakes in such a vision, even if they often competed with each other and with private power companies.[5]

Other sociodemographic changes set the stage for postwar environmentalism. Birth rates, incomes, and family assets increased substantially, and average family labor-market time decreased. Popular demand for outdoor recreation soared, including for urban and suburban parks serving families and neighbors and venues for hunting, fishing, and hiking. In the quarter century after the National Park Service (NPS) was established in 1916, visitation grew from a few hundred thousand to over twenty-one million, only to see a decline during the war. But by 1955, visitation was over fifty-five million, with an ambitious new Mission 66, marking the upcoming fiftieth anniversary, in place to guide still further growth. Some sought wilderness experiences without roads, but many also drove miles to see wilderness from their car windshields, perhaps only then to seek deeper meaning by leaving their cars behind. With rising education and greater economic security, more people sought environmental amenities, including open space, aesthetic vistas, clean air, and clean water.[6]

While postwar suburban, timber, and hydropower institutional dynamics included democratic components, civic associations set about to modify or reverse such dynamics in multiple arenas and across emergent environmental fields such as wilderness, clean water, and clean air. The wilderness movement, of course, was primarily focused on nonurban land, although the increasing growth of cities in the West allowed local activists to mobilize civic action through the famous battles leading up to the Wilderness Act of 1964, and then later through its participatory feedback effects (see chapter 1). Clean water and clean air emerged as prime concerns within cities, but typically had many cross-boundary dimensions as well.

Clean Water

The pollution of waterways had been a long-standing issue in US history. Industrial wastes had increased many times over with the growth of industry during the war. Industrial output over the previous half century had risen some 700 percent, containing a dizzying number of new chemicals in the postwar period, most of which had not been rigorously tested for human health or ecological impact. Organic wastes from concentrated population growth in cities and suburbs, as well as the introduction of phosphates for dishwashing, fertilizers and pesticides for gardens and farms, led to the regular appearance of algae blooms and cultural eutrophication, thus depleting oxygen from the water and leading to massive fish kills. These were increasingly noticed by commercial fishermen, recreational anglers, and nearby homeowners, and were often among the first signs of hazard to be reported by civic associations and sportsmen's groups. Popular public beaches were closed at the height of the summer due to bacterial levels, as were shellfish beds, with economic costs to fishing and tourism industries.[7]

In the mid-1960s, Lake Erie was declared dead, and in 1969, estimated fish kills rose to forty-one million, more than the amount in the previous three years combined. In January and February 1969, an oil-rig blowout off Santa Barbara befouled miles of Southern California beaches and killed thousands of marine mammals and sea birds. Only a few months later, the oil wastes on the Cuyahoga River in Cleveland caught fire, as they had done on other occasions over the years and on other "burning rivers" of the Great Lakes region.[8]

In addition to pollution, drought conditions plagued many states, especially in the Northeast and Midwest in the late 1940s mid-1950s, and most severely from 1963 to 1967, leading to mandatory curbs on water usage in cities such as New York. At the leading edge of suburbanization, Long Islanders saw their "groundwater commons" of aquifers threatened by DDT-spraying county health officials, and by "taking" and "dumping" from polluting industry, as well as by their own neighbors, who by the tens of thousands saw their septic tanks fail and "poured household wastes into the same porous ground from which their drinking water came." Many conservationists and ecologists on the island began to build the bridge to public health and thus to a new environmentalism.[9]

Civic and Professional Action and the Dynamics of Policy Design

Citizen action on water pollution emerged immediately and persistently after World War II, although it took several phases of movement building and lawmaking to produce the landmark Clean Water Act of 1972. Key to developments was the combination of two factors: civic action by multitiered associations and participatory policy feedback through jurisdictionally distributed federal enforcement conferences that, despite the name, did little enforcing. The federated/federal alignment of these two institutional features was especially fertile.[10]

Early action occurred primarily through conservation groups such as the Izaak Walton League of America (IWLA), the National Wildlife Federation (NWF), and the National Audubon Society. The League of Women Voters (LWV) provided distinctive new capacities to the field, especially after its 1956 convention voted to make water resources a national program. Each one of these was structured as a multitiered civic association, with a national office, state chapters, and local affiliates. Perhaps most initially important was IWLA. As soon as the war ended, executive director Kenneth A. Reid identified water quality as a strategic goal. While focused primarily on water pollution and the loss of marshland that were of chief concern to its core constituency of fishermen and hunters, its magazine,

Outdoor America, was open to a broad range of views, and by 1946, it aspired to spearhead a national alliance of all conservation groups for which there was much talk at other national conventions and in conservation journals. Indeed, in his keynote address to the Audubon Society's national conference in November 1945, Ira N. "Gabe" Gabrielson, wildlife biologist and director of the US Fish and Wildlife Service, urged increased civic activism and much greater cooperation between birders and their sometime adversaries among hunters and sportsmen. Without concerted civic action and informed public scrutiny, Gabrielson feared that wildlife would suffer grievously due to all the federal water construction projects currently in the planning stages. Reid then initiated letter writing campaigns to Congress through state chapters. William Voigt Jr., head of IWLA's western office in Denver, began a national speaking tour urging land and water law reform and federal water pollution regulation to a broad array of civic groups beyond the typical conservation constituencies.[11]

There was considerable messiness in testing new approaches and managing institutional turf in specific states and communities. Because IWLA became part of the conservation establishment in states like Wisconsin, where it remained closely tied to the Conservation Department and rural small-town and northern county legislators in an institutional iron triangle, it had considerable difficulty transitioning its red-shirt sportsmen membership to broader problems of urban water pollution and more administratively coherent state regulation. By the late 1960s, however, it had managed to check the powerful business lobby in the new superagency, the Department of Natural Resources, which then became a model for many other states.[12]

Two important federal laws enhanced opportunities for citizen participation as early as 1946, as noted in the previous chapter. The Fish and Wildlife Coordination Act (FWCA) was spearheaded by Willis A. Robertson (D-VA), a conservative member of the House elected to the Senate in November. He established the requirement that federal agencies prepare "biological surveys" before new dams and other water projects could be launched. Such surveys were rudimentary compared to later environmental impact statements (EIS), for which they set precedent; indeed, Henry "Scoop" Jackson, whose 1969 NEPA bill would establish federal EIS requirements, was an enthusiastic member of Robertson's committee. Biological surveys motivated citizens to generate further local knowledge and find continuing opportunities to collaborate with sympathetic agency and academic scientists who possessed professional knowledge of fish, wildlife, and ecology—the latter now emerging more broadly as a legitimate disciplinary approach, particularly in terms of watershed ecosystems. Indeed, the act required Congress to spend money to fund the work of civic and scientific critics of dams and other construction projects as a form of investing in democracy. As a former chair of Virginia's first Game and Inland Fisheries Commission in the 1920s, Robertson enjoyed close relationships with IWLA leaders before and during the war, as well as with NWF; they regularly exchanged views on the importance of building a broad movement in the face of an impending conservation crisis, with water pollution as the most pressing problem. At IWLA's 1947 national convention, he told the delegates that "the work of the Izaak Walton League, and of all the conservationists engaged in a similar program, is now definitely linked to the preservation of our democracy." This policy design thus emerged partly from embedded movement work over decades and elicited further civic knowledge and action going forward.[13]

The second 1946 law, the Administrative Procedure Act (APA), was passed only a few days prior to FWCA, with support from some of the same key members of Congress. While it had no specified environmental goal, APA's constraints on the New Deal state's vast expansion of agency discretion would be layered into virtually all environmental conflicts, laws, and rulemaking in subsequent years. The APA required public hearings for federal projects, with some significant restrictions but under expansive norms for broad public participation across a wide range of issues that galvanized civic action, associational capacity building, media coverage, and the democratization of relevant knowledge. The APA also introduced a very expansive right of judicial review, further catalyzing civic challenge by a broad array of interests and eroding agency discretion and secrecy, especially once Supreme Court Justice William O. Douglas, an outspoken conservationist, began gaining the upper hand over Justice Felix Frankfurter's deferent interpretations of agency discretion. Reflecting isomorphic tendencies, albeit agentic and change-inducing ones within the legal field, states enacted "little APAs" partly by adopting principles in the federal APA, but especially by borrowing horizontally from model state APA laws through the National Conference of Commissioners on Uniform State Laws. This generated further cognitive and motivational bases for citizen engagement at state and local levels. Indeed localist administrative law, often submerged and neglected in legal scholarship, provides a fruitful blurriness and porousness between governmental action and public participation. These two federal laws, in short, generated participatory policy feedback that encouraged civic engagement across a broad array of environmental issues and arenas.[14]

Lawmaking specifically on water began to manifest an unmistakable trajectory toward nationalization, though it faced various obstacles within federalism and provided opportunities for what Paul Milazzo calls "unlikely environmentalists" to become effective entrepreneurs within the decentralized congressional committee system. The 1948 Federal Water Pollution Control Act (FWPCA), a temporary law extended in 1953 and then amended in 1956, established the federal government's constitutional authority to regulate water pollution on interstate waters, buttressed by Article I's Interstate Commerce Clause in the US Constitution. However, policy entrepreneurs in Congress, who had gained much greater influence due to the restructuring of the committee system, traded potential federal policing authority for a developmental program that distributed federal construction dollars to states and communities to help build new wastewater treatment facilities—a well-worn path for building New Deal liberalism. This choice was shaped by two major factors. First was the absence of a robust enough national movement or public-interest lobby to counterbalance business lobbyists and state officials who jealously guarded their regulatory prerogatives and their cooperative relations with local industries. Second, the relatively weak federal bureaucracy—in the form of the Division of Water Supply and Pollution Control within the Public Health Service (PHS) at the Department of Health, Education, and Welfare (HEW) created only in 1953—was hesitant to frame water pollution as a health issue.[15]

Clean water was thus linked to water supply and was an essential ingredient in future economic development. This distributive and developmental policy design could generate sufficient support from groups such as the American Municipal Association (now the National League of Cities) and the US Conference of Mayors, whose thousands of members were most immediately pressed by ordinary local citizens as well as organized civic associations about adequate water supply during years of drought in the late 1940s and mid-1950s, especially in the Northeast and Midwest. Quite persistent questions of water quality also began coming from suburbs. The Senate Select Committee on National Water Resources, which began meeting in early 1959 and held public hearings in twenty-four cities around the country—many if not all monitored by the LWV and multi-tiered conservation groups—was dominated by western senators who cared little about water pollution. But this committee also surprisingly gave water pollution pride of place due to new technical models, arguing that the country was not running out of water but of clean water. This helped make water pollution a key component of the much broader field of natural resources, though the Senate committee still recoiled from stricter enforcement.

Some twenty thousand copies of the final report, released in late January 1961, were requested by civic groups, elected officials, and the press. This was far greater than similar reports of this kind—perhaps akin to the downloading from a PDF link in an influential newspaper op-ed or tweet today—and it helped frame President John F. Kennedy's "Message on Natural Resources" to Congress a month after his inauguration, in which he declared that the "pollution of our country's rivers and streams has . . . reached alarming proportions." In addition, investing federal dollars in constructing 6,685 new treatment plants projected during the debate on the 1956 amendments appealed to organized labor, a very powerful constituency in Congress, and had precedent in both the 1930s New Deal public works projects and the 1946 Hill-Burton hospital construction grants. While the Eisenhower administration (1953–1961) recognized the constitutional authority of federal regulation of water pollution, in 1960, it vetoed a further extension of the 1956 amendments, including the proposal to make matching grants permanent, primarily for budgetary reasons. Kennedy immediately proposed to reverse this.[16]

The political opportunity structure was shifting considerably. Democrats had made large gains in the Senate in the 1958 midterm elections, from forty-nine to sixty-four seats, and soon, but predictably, courts would mandate congressional redistricting to reflect postwar population shifts from rural to urban and suburban areas, much more favorable to environmental issues such as water.[17] Dwight Eisenhower, as a concession accompanying his veto, agreed to call a National Conference on Water Pollution. This was the first conference of its kind and was convened under the auspices of the Public Health Service, which was now willing to act more energetically to stem its increasing bureaucratic marginalization, attributable to its deferent service orientation to state and local governments; the decline of waterborne diseases in the postwar period due to its own successful sanitary engineering work also prompted action. After six months of planning, the conference met in December 1960, following the election of Kennedy but before his inauguration. Despite the conference's overwhelmingly male and technical orientation, Katie Osbirn, president of the General Federation of Women's Clubs, and Suvia Whittemore, director of the League of Women Voters and chair of its Water Resources Committee, served on the steering committee, along with officers from IWLA, NWF, and the Wildlife Management Institute, directed by Gabrielson, a key civic partner after he had left the US Fish and Wildlife Service. They were joined by leaders of the US Conference of Mayors, the American Municipal Association, and the AFL-CIO, all core constituencies favoring federal matching construction grants.[18]

Osbirn and Whittemore made plenary presentations to the conference. Whittmore offered an example of a broad civic and multistakeholder strategy along Missouri River communities to support such grants, based on organizing work with over five hundred organizations. While the formal eighty or so core participants at the conference were carefully selected from those primarily with technical backgrounds (engineers, economists, sanitarians, scientists, industrial plant managers), the template of shared national civic leadership on water pollution policy had now been established for the field. This field-configuring conference was open to some twelve hundred participants in all, many of whom were activists from LWV, ILWA, and other associations whose previous engagement provided the cultural and organizational rationales for such a template.[19]

Carving Out a Strategic Niche: The League of Women Voters

In helping catalyze vigorous citizen action around water, LWV leveraged its structural advantages as a multitiered association to develop a distinct and indispensable niche among other civic groups in this field. Its national office and state chapters distilled lessons on water action from local leagues during the late 1940s and early 1950s; its national convention in 1956 voted to make water a national program after being pressed insistently by several hundred local leagues, including many cities and twenty state boards. This decision came on the heels of several national conventions that had put water resources on the program but specifically in the wake of severe drought and flooding in different parts of the country and debate and passage of the 1956 FWPCA amendments. Like the General Federation of Women's Clubs, with whom it often collaborated on citizen advisory groups and advocacy coalitions, the league employed a "housekeeping" frame. In fact, Osbirn's opening sentence to the 1960 national water pollution conference was: "Water pollution has been termed our national housekeeping problem." *Good Housekeeping* published an article earlier that year that singled out the work of the league and utilized the housekeeping frame explicitly. The league's profoundly relational view of urban coproductive and strategic institutional action was deeply rooted in women activists' civic, professional, and narrative resources and practical tool kits going back to the Progressive Era, including a frame of "city housekeeping."[20]

Yet the league clearly made a strategic choice based upon its scan of the field of conservation organizations, many of whom it recognized as "doing valuable work" but who were not as nearly well-equipped as the league to understand the intricate complexity of intergovernmental relationships within and across all levels of the federal system and across the broadest geographical range of cities and communities. The "water resource field," Jane Freeman argued in her presentation to the 1956 LWV national convention, offers an especially good case of intergovernmental relationships: "[Our members believe that there is] no field today where our unique contribution of background and techniques can be employed more fruitfully, for our own satisfaction and the public good." Clearly, the league had begun to develop and test its own practical theorization of institutional fields.[21]

League practice contained a variety of components: generating and/or translating usable knowledge from scientific, administrative, management, and civic sources; leveraging its multitier structure to facilitate interorganizational relationships and action; and campaigning on an ethic of civic responsibility to help finance water pollution remedies, such as wastewater treatment plants.

First was a serious commitment to objective research on the threats to water resources and quality in the distinct river basins, watersheds, and communities in which leagues were engaged. LWV chapters gathered scientific, policy, and administrative reports from wherever they could, discussed them in study groups, and held face-to-face meetings with university scientists, agency staff, company engineers, and elected officials to refine their own knowledge, build relationships, and identify barriers. In effect, leagues cultivated their understanding of the institutional logics that might be at work among the various actors in the field; and league leadership represented the most refined and extensive application of "social skills" to better (re)align these logics of any civic or movement organization in the field of clean water in the postwar decades.[22] Leagues also put together press kits for other civic groups and newspaper editors, translating technical reports for everyday civic communication on a scale that was unmatched. While in some campaigns for clean water (such as Lake Erie) the footprints they left in news coverage are quite clear and direct, local and state leagues and the national office were involved in passing on reports, press kits, and other materials to local and national editors, such as *Good Housekeeping*, *House & Garden*, *American Home*, and *Better Homes and Gardens*, which began to cover septic tank failure and groundwater contamination in the 1950s. Leagues served as a vital link between public health and urban planning professionals who were on the forefront of calls for more effective regulation, on the one hand, and the lay public, on the other.[23]

Leagues mastered the intricacies of local, state, and federal regulations; identified conflicting requirements; and even estimated agency staff capacities and needs, utilizing knowledge that insiders shared with them. Because of its careful research, as well as its willingness to entertain multiple perspectives and options, the league was viewed as a trustworthy broker and was invited to present at innumerable local, state, and federal conferences. They also served on steering committees and in other leadership roles, such as at the First National Conference on Water Pollution in 1960. Whittemore also served as chair of the panel on citizen action at the 1965 White House Conference on Natural Beauty, a gathering of eight hundred that included the leadership of virtually all major conservation groups, in addition to leaders from education, science, law, media, architecture, business, philanthropy, youth groups, and government at all federal levels. Many league activists were later named to state and local planning commissions and one to the Federal Water Pollution Control Administration Advisory Board when it was created. To be sure, the league did not simply wait to be invited but typically put itself forward quite insistently, justifying its claims in terms of broad representativeness and its unexcelled level of civic expertise on water issues in every region of the country.[24]

While league research was measured and nonpartisan, local committees shared documents with those who would argue more stridently, thus expanding the civic ecological mix. In *Death of the Sweet Waters*, a widely read account that pulls few punches, the author acknowledges his use of their abundant research files, credits them as doing the "best country-wide job" in educating the public, and dedicates his book to the "League of Women Voters of the United States." Unsurprisingly, his wife was a league activist.[25]

In some cases, such as the Delaware and Columbia River Basins, local leagues did extensive basin surveys, prompted in part by the national office's "Know Your River Basin" strategy, launched in 1958. In its own best-practices handbook, titled *The Big Water Fight: Trials and Triumphs in Citizen Action on Problems of Supply, Pollution, Floods, and Planning across the U.S.A.*, the league's nonprofit education fund provides an extensive case study of the Sudbury, Assabet, and Concord River Basins in Massachusetts, in which fourteen local leagues crisscrossing thirty-six towns and cities had collaborated. The survey, funded by a public-spirited local brewer, classifies each town in terms of population (and projected growth), highway routes, water sources, municipal sewage systems, industrial waste disposal, zoning, planning, and regulatory mechanisms. It provides background information on precipitation, hydrology, soil, and climate as well as multiple types of water usage and an array of competing interests that citizens will need to address. In line with the league's niche strategy, the basin survey covers a very broad range of state and federal agencies and programs that have purview over specific problems in the basin.

However, it also includes an inventory of relevant civic organizations—town by town—that can or already do contribute to water governance. These include granges, LWV chapters, land trusts, garden clubs, 4-H clubs, development commissions, and the relatively new conservation commissions, which had spread to all but six of the towns in the initial survey (1963) and all but four at the time of further update. The basin survey served, in effect, as a strategic map and template for public action across an entire field, bounded by place but not institutionally limited to it.[26]

Second, because the league understood that water was a cross-boundary issue potentially spanning many jurisdictions, it utilized its multitier structure to facilitate interorganizational work of various sorts. In larger basins, it formalized this through interleague committees, where well-worn league processes for democratic responsibility and accountability (local, state, national) could be employed, although local leagues sometimes circumvented the slower and more polite official procedures. Interleague committees then helped educate and coach leaders in an array of nonleague groups and coalitions. In the battle to save Lake Erie, which captured the nation's attention in the mid-1960s, some thirty-one local leagues across four states (Ohio, Michigan, Pennsylvania, and New York) established the Lake Erie Basin Committee (LEBC), whose initial research report served as the basis for an explosion of press coverage and calls for civic action. The Save Lake Erie Now Campaign enlisted newspapers, television, and radio across these and several other states, as well as nationally. The series in the *Cleveland Press*, edited by Betty Klaric, which ran from 1964 to 1972, was among the most successful media campaigns in environmental history up to that point. Klaric enjoyed continual access to the LEBC and local leagues, often highlighted their work in her coverage, and, as the first woman president of the area's newspaper guild, helped bring a concerted focus to water pollution and related issues in the region.[27]

Due to the work of the LEBC and other interleague basin committees around the country, the Public Health Service chose the league to spearhead a national effort to develop leadership for water action among a wide array of civic organizations. Called Schools for Citizens, this program began with three-day seminars on land and water use in several regions around the country in 1965, with more planned for the following year. The seminars were cosponsored by PHS, which also provided funding. Participants were then encouraged and coached to organize one-day seminars in their local areas. The March 1965 Lake Erie Land and Water Use Seminar for Community Leaders included presentations by nationally recognized scholars. One such scholar was Lynton Caldwell of Indiana University who would go on to help draft the National Environmental Policy Act (NEPA) of 1970, which included important requirements for public participation and environmental impact statements. This three-day meeting was followed by one-day seminars in cities and towns around the lake, some cosponsored by groups like the Camp Fire Girls and the General Federation of Women's Clubs, while others were cosponsored by United Auto Workers (UAW) locals, with appearances by top leaders such as Walter Reuther. Leagues organized "go-see tours" by bus and boat for the leaders of other civic organizations and candidates for municipal office so that they could see and smell sewage waste, fish kills, and algae blooms, thus further moving the field toward a model of "street science," melding lay and professional knowledge.[28]

The water pollution group at HEW during the 1960s was most impressed by the work of the league across basins, as Rebecca Hanmer, a staffer who later become a senior executive in the EPA's Office of Water, recalls. So was the Conservation Foundation, which hired Sydney Howe as its president in 1965 to help create stronger ties with grassroots activists, including LWV. In cities across the country, the league began to play a similar role in leading workshops and helping form other organizations on clean air; it then continued work on clean ground water at an impressively high level of quality, often with public funding, for several more decades. Its tool kits were especially clear, compelling, and usable. As I discuss more in this chapter and further in chapter 5, however, the command-and-control design of the Clean Water Act, as well as the relative administrative disadvantages of its section 208 on participatory basin planning in the 1970s, largely squandered the opportunities for the kind of civic action for which the league had been notable, at least until new framing opportunities for watershed planning and restoration emerged in the 1980s.[29]

A third component of league practice was its consistent effort to get citizens to understand the need for paying increased taxes and water rates or supporting bond issues that could be used to finance local wastewater treatment plants. While the league understood the need for greater enforcement of regulations and for business investments to reduce industrial waste as an externality, it recognized that citizens themselves must assume responsibility for clean water. When they did not, the league was willing to invoke a much stronger rhetoric of civic shame and obligation, as was enforced in a league flyer that challenged local citizens in no uncertain terms: "You are Guilty . . . You are Guilty of Pollution." Typically prompted by LWV chapters and similar organizations, cities and counties led the way in 1957 to 1961, in effect laying the civic foundation for what would become more robust local-state-federal matching mechanisms. Where states had introduced some cost sharing, local officials had an incentive to invest. But the initial formulas of the 1956 FWPCA limited the federal cost share to 30 percent of a project's total cost or $250,000, whichever was smaller. This represented a significant burden for local communities, especially for larger cities requiring expensive treatment facilities and suburbs that had not yet made initial investments in sewer systems. Local and state officials thus often depended upon the league to educate local voters and generate support for bond referenda, whether or not there were federal or even state matches.[30]

When Governor Nelson Rockefeller of New York State put a $1 billion bond issue on the ballot in November 1965 to finance his Pure Waters program—most of which was for municipal treatment facilities—his proposed federal-state-local match formula was 30–30–40. This was still a large investment from localities, with the 30 percent federal match prefinanced by the state as a way to move projects forward and pressure Washington to alter its formula, increase overall funding, and lift the caps further (then at $600,000 per project). Rockefeller mobilized state bureaucracies, such as the public health department, for public education on clean water, and he developed a partnership with the State Charities Aid Association, which in turn led to the formation of the Citizens' Committee for Clean Water. Comprised of thirty-two groups, this coalition developed a campaign of mass mailings, television commercials, speeches, editorials, and a "Get out the vote" effort. The league was a core partner and strategist. Indeed, the committee's report on the overwhelming four-to-one victory in favor of the largest bond issue in the history of the state, including large majorities in the less-certain upstate counties, singled out the "periodic county-by-county checks with the field virtually everywhere in New York State—and where a lack was noted, an eleventh-hour effort was made to stimulate a drive by a unit of at least one of the Committee's member organizations, more often than not the League of Women Voters."[31]

The Federal Enforcement Conference as Participatory Policy Feedback

The federal enforcement conference, included in the 1956 FWPCA, proved to be a policy design that increasingly encouraged public participation and press coverage, partly in recognition of emergent norms but largely as an unintended consequence of legislative compromise that avoided stricter enforcement mechanisms. Neither political coalitions nor federal and state administrative capacities were credibly available for strict enforcement, even in the most advanced of states.[32] However, the surgeon general, as head of PHS, could convene such a conference at the request of a state that perceived itself unduly burdened by water pollution from another state, such as along a shared river or when studies showed that the health and welfare of citizens in one state were endangered by pollution from another. The conference was informal in the sense that no testimony was offered under oath and no recommendations had the force of law. If, after six months, the secretary of HEW decided that insufficient progress had been made, he or she could establish a hearing board that would then convene a formal public hearing, resulting in further recommendations to be followed, if necessary, by the secretary filing a suit in federal court against recalcitrant polluters. From January 1957 to February 1971, the

HEW secretary and then the secretary of the interior (following a bureaucratic reorganization of water pollution programs in 1966) convened a total of fifty-one enforcement conferences. In only three cases, however, was a formal public hearing scheduled, and in only one case did the HEW secretary file an actual suit.[33]

This policy design, however, catalyzed significant public participation. In addition to representatives from industry and city, state, and interstate agencies, the enforcement conferences were open to the public and the press; any interested party could offer testimony. The intent was to spur genuine dialogue on problem areas, health risks, available technologies, and projected costs to specific businesses and municipalities, with the goal of achieving pragmatic consensus among reasonable people motivated by community spirit. This point was argued by Murray Stein, chief of the enforcement branch from 1956 to 1970, as a matter of public philosophy and proven effectiveness. In many cases, it seems remedial action occurred but not on a scale or at a pace to satisfy conservation groups, local and regional press, or citizens from homeowner associations, unions, or as independent civic entrepreneurs who attended. For instance, David Blaushild, a local Chevrolet dealer from Cleveland, Ohio, funded his own massive publicity campaign and delivered several hundred thousand petitions to the Lake Erie enforcement conference.[34]

Due to press coverage and group mobilization, and especially on occasions when a noxious oil slick, suffocating algae bloom, or massive fish kill had recently come to the public's attention, large numbers attended. Because the conferences sought some reasonable degree of public consensus, many held multiple sessions, workshops, and progress meetings extending over several years. The Lake Erie conference held five sessions from August 1965 to June 1970; the Colorado River conference held six sessions between January 1960 and July 1967. The first session of the Lake Michigan conference, whose convening was politically contested, dragged on for a full nine days during January, February, and March 1968, followed by several other sessions and workshops in subsequent years. The Environmental Protection Agency (EPA), which became operational in December 1970, persisted with enforcement conferences during its initial years through its regional offices, even as it rapidly expanded enforcement staff.[35]

Networking among citizen groups and across professional and institutional boundaries was extensive. Local public hearings or city council meetings pressed for additional sessions and debated conference issues before and after sessions. This established a dynamic that made the en-forcement conference a virtually ongoing affair in some places. It was cov-ered widely in the press and in conservation publications, with vernacular translations of complex technical issues, and with meetings sometimes rotated among various cities in a river system or Great Lake basin. Public talk—and "side talk"[36]—of this sort was highly educative and motivating, yet it could be labeled a mere talkathon that frustrated those who wanted to see results. Indeed, the conferences became occasions for organizing and coalition building, crafting community resolutions, presenting petitions, articulating criticisms, monitoring progress, and demanding enforceable standards. They also became occasions for electoral competition in races for city council, mayor, and even governor. Governors, indeed, typically attended the conferences to make substantial presentations. Secretary of the Interior Stewart Udall, a strong conservationist who served for eight years under both Kennedy and Lyndon B. Johnson, oversaw the new water pollution administration established in 1966; he utilized the enforcement conferences, especially through personal appearances in the Great Lakes region, as an occasion for public education on strengthening regulation.[37]

In short, though they did little formal enforcing and added to the per-ceived delay that the 1956 revisions were intended to reduce, these fed-eral enforcement conferences provided significant policy feedback and systemic deliberation, both within and around the actual conferences. They organized what was perhaps the most robust and distributed public sphere for clean water action of the 1960s, incorporating lay and profes-sional knowledge, legitimating iterative and accountable review, providing incentives to communicate across associational boundaries, and opening a broad window of publicity into the institutional logics of corporate and government actors.

Muskie's Policy Moves: Publics, Institutions, Lifeworlds

Edmund S. Muskie, first elected in 1958 after a term as Maine's gover-nor, became chair of the Senate's subcommittee on air and water pollution within the powerful Public Works Committee in early 1963. He would then chair Public Works and become the key figure in the passage of the Clean Water Act of 1972, but only after further policy reframing and leg-islative compromise that resulted in the Water Quality Act of 1965, the Clean Water Restoration Act of 1966, and competing approaches con-

tained in the National Environmental Policy Act of 1970.[38] Wedded largely
to a developmental discourse—one that increasingly incorporated ecological concepts—he was committed to educating the public and listening to
their daily life experience and local knowledge during the hearings he held
in eight cities over the next few years. In addition to the hearings, speeches,
and media appearances, however, he did something quite extraordinary.
With $200,000 of his committee's budget—approximately $1.6 million
in today's dollars—he arranged for the production of a film called *Troubled Waters*, the first-ever documentary film by the Senate. Narrated by
Hollywood star Henry Fonda, edited by a professional journalist, shot by
the camera crew from PHS's Communicable Disease Center, and with
transportation provided by an air force plane, the film resonated deeply
with the public by embedding water into everyday life, work, and ritual
activities. Its opening images included an infant's baptism, a child's bath-
ing, a surgeon's scrubbing, a mother's cooking, a fisherman's trout catch,
and a woman's watering of her garden. It then positioned these activities
alongside images that captured both aesthetic assault ("rivers of blood"
from slaughterhouse waste) and health risks (an adult leading kids out of a
stream with a "No Swimming" sign). Pollution was both real and ritual, as
with the "autopsy of a doll" floating in Lake Michigan rubbage. The film
was intended for widespread viewing in schools and by civic and community groups, such as LWV chapters and garden clubs, and was built upon
the cultural narratives already employed in civic settings.

The film's cognitive framing was not contentious, despite some images
of clear frustration. At times, its emotive framing bordered on passive resignation, as when an older man with his fishing rod tells an inquiring boy
that the stream would no longer yield a catch due to thermal pollution
from a plant upstream. He comes nonetheless because "I like to sit and
think." The frame's diagnosis is that "all these uses of water," including by
industrial plants that produce so many of the goods that we enjoy, are "legitimate," but not when they spoil use by others. "A man competes against
himself for the precious water," on his job, at home, in his recreation. But
there are some "who don't think we should have to fight with each other
over who has the right to pollute the water." Indeed, "there is a river, the
psalmist sang years ago, the waters of which shall make glad the city."[39]

What the Sierra Club's film *Wilderness River Trail* provided as an educative resource for civic associations in the battle over Echo Park in the early
1950s, the Senate's *Troubled Waters* did for the campaign for clean water in

the mid-1960s. When elected lawmakers, administrative officials, and civic organizations learn how to collaborate over a long campaign and make a significant investment in civic democracy, the boundaries between the logics of system and lifeworld, in the terminology of Jürgen Habermas, are more permeable than theorists might sometimes imagine.[40]

Public opinion on water pollution began to shift decisively by the end of 1965 and then especially after the dramatic oil-rig blowout off Santa Barbara, California, beaches in January 1969, followed by the oil fire on the Cuyahoga River, Ohio, in June. That month, the League of Women Voters spearheaded the Citizens Crusade for Clean Water. This coalition was initially composed of thirty-one leading civic associations and conservation groups. They included the NWF, Audubon, the Sierra Club, the Wilderness Society, Trout Unlimited, the Wildlife Society, and IWLA, which then became coordinator. Also involved were municipal, county, and state government associations (the National League of Cities, the National Association of Counties, the National Association of Soil and Water Conservation Districts, the US Conference of City Health Officers, the US Conference of Mayors, and the Association of State and Interstate Water Pollution Control Administrators); labor unions (AFL-CIO, UAW, and the United Steelworkers of America); and professional groups (the American Institute of Architects, the American Institute of Planners, the Society of American Foresters, the American Fisheries Society, and the American Association of University Women). These were the key leaders in the field of organizations favoring more robust water action, minus the many smaller unaffiliated groups. Of the latter, many were supportive, but only the South Jersey Shellfisherman's Association made the original list. Muskie asked that the full list of organizations in the Citizens Crusade be read into the *Congressional Record* on July 7. Even some industry groups joined, since the immediate purpose was to pressure Muskie and Congress to spend the full amount already allocated for matching sewage treatment grants, a huge backlog of which had begun to build up due to LWV and similar local campaigns and strategic moves on prefinancing matches by public officials, such as Governor Rockefeller in New York.[41]

The final passage of the 1972 Clean Water Act Amendments (CWA) was determined by a variety of other factors. First, new environmental lobby groups had come onto the scene, including the Environmental Defense Fund (EDF) in 1967, the Natural Resources Defense Council (NRDC) in 1970, and Environmental Action, which was created to organize Earth

Day in 1970. Ralph Nader's public interest movement also took a keen interest in clean water. Second, Nixon realized the potential threat from Muskie in the upcoming 1972 election and initially tried to outbid him for middle-class environmental support while appointing some excellent staff to head the EPA and the White House Council on Environmental Quality (CEQ). The latter had been established by the National Environmental Policy Act (NEPA), with Nixon taking photo credits at its signing on New Year's Day 1970 next to Senator Henry "Scoop" Jackson (D-WA), the bill's main sponsor and one of Muskie's legislative and potential 1972 Democratic presidential primary rivals.[42]

The political opportunity provided by competing elites that motivated bidding up was complemented by a third factor; namely, an administrative move by the US Army Corps of Engineers several years earlier to revitalize the Rivers and Harbors Act (commonly known as the Refuse Act) of 1899, which requires permits for dredging and other modifications of waterways. It also enables citizen whistleblowers to collect up to half the fine in any settlement for violation. Originally a navigation act to free waterways from obstruction, the law—technically a criminal statute—began to receive a much broader interpretation as an environmental statute by the Supreme Court beginning in 1960 in *United States v. Republic Steel*, with Justice Douglas in the lead, and then again in 1966 in *United States v. Standard Oil Company*. By the late 1960s, federal courts were ruling that almost any substance deposited in waterways, however inadvertently, was refuse. The corps' action was also prompted by a congressional oversight report by the House chair on the subcommittee on the Great Lakes. The corps then issued a handy tool kit enabling citizen informers to bring suit and collect their share of the fines, which led to a flood of citizen calls to the regional offices of the Department of Justice, since nearly all industrial plants in the nation with outflow pipes were operating without permits.[43]

To be sure, citizen groups were already pressing for enforcement of the act, and the Hudson River Fishermen's Association distributed ten thousand "Bag-A-Polluter" postcards up and down the river valley to make reporting to its own office extraordinarily simple. The practice was endorsed by the US attorney for the Southern District of New York, Whitney North Seymour Jr., who had both civic and professional ties to local activists. The Nixon administration began to prosecute dozens of cases in late 1969 and early 1970, and CEQ issued stronger requirements for public hearings and access to permit information.[44]

The Clean Water Act of 1972 was passed overwhelmingly when Congress overrode a veto by the president, who objected to its fiscal implications. But with robust civic action in communities, new organizations for environmental lobbying and litigation, dramatically shifting public opinion, participatory policy feedback through the enforcement conferences and Refuse Act, other legal and administrative handles, and the creative use of public hearings and film embedded in everyday life and ritual by a leading member of the Senate, it is hardly surprising that the Conservation Foundation, with a grant from the EPA to help train citizens, prefaced its water quality handbook with the statement that the CWA "contains one of the strongest requirements for participatory democracy in the whole federal statute book."[45]

Clean Air

The Clean Air Act (CAA), passed in 1970 and revised several times since, has a policy trajectory similar to the Clean Water Act (CWA). In response to rising public pressure during World War II, though largely put on hold under the patriotic rationale of war production, lawmakers and administrative officials felt compelled to organize a series of national air pollution symposia and technical conferences beginning in 1949. Officials were responding to public concern over illnesses and deaths during the infamous smog emergency in Donora, Pennsylvania, in 1948 and to the repeated smog alerts and protests in Los Angeles beginning several years before this and then continuing, though episodically, during the 1950s and 1960s. In addition, serious concerns were raised in many other areas of the country by farmers whose crops were harmed, homeowners for corrosion to their houses and potential loss of equity, the real estate industry that feared decline in purchases, hotel owners who saw individuals and groups cancel reservations, and urban growth coalitions that saw threats to business more generally. The first National Air Pollution Conference was convened by HEW in 1958, but the air pollution control act of 1959 reflected the agency's reticence to lead without further research and its deference to polluting industry, as well as to local and state officials who jealously guarded their authority.[46]

Both Congress and the White House became more receptive to federal regulation after the election of Kennedy in 1960, and especially once the US Conference of Mayors, the American Municipal Association, and the National Association of Counties helped to draft the Clean Air Act of

1963. While this act required public hearings and included token enforcement powers, if requests were made by governors, it did not seem to utilize the enforcement conference mechanism, which became so important to the clean water campaign. To be sure, the press in some cities, such as Los Angeles and Pittsburgh, did become quite energetic in developing staff, providing coverage, and consistently editorializing the need to address air pollution. But even in 1966, after two previous conferences, the Third National Conference on Air Pollution had only a small handful of civic activists presenting. Esther Peterson—assistant secretary of labor, special assistant to the president for consumer affairs, and recent director of the Women's Bureau—gave general recognition to citizen organizing and made the case for citizen rights to safety and information. Only one representative of the General Federation of Women's Clubs, along with one from the National Audubon Society, were on the steering committee. None of the other women's and conservation groups asked questions of the technical experts, at least that were recorded in the 667 pages of proceedings. However, Carolyn Pearce, president of GFWC, did frame her contribution in terms of "self-government" in the opening sentence to her presentation "Volunteer Organization Activities and Air Pollution Control," and referred to various public conferences that GFWC was organizing in different parts of the country.[47]

Public concerns over air pollution continued to increase and were reinforced by isomorphic institutional dynamics from the field of water pollution expressed through civic groups mobilized on *both* water and air. In addition, congressional committees, especially Muskie's, had joint responsibility for *both* issues. Nonetheless, the six conservationist and health groups that testified on air pollution before Muskie's committee in 1967 were uncoordinated and ineffectual, in comparison to three years later.[48]

Local Action: Pittsburgh and Alleghany County

In Pittsburgh, the League of Women Voters and dozens of women's clubs had been organizing over the hazards of smoke since the early 1940s and, along with other civic, business, and union stakeholders, had achieved significant progress by 1960. This was partly an unintended consequence of cleaner natural gas for homeowners, and diesel-electric for railroad locomotives, becoming more available as an alternative to coal. Historian James Longhurst provides the most in-depth city and county case study of how civic activists came to shape clean air policy and the required state implementation plans (SIPs) once the CAA had finally become law in 1970. In the "Smoky City" of Pittsburgh, which is part of Alleghany County in Pennsylvania, home to steel mills and other heavily polluting industries, several women from LWV, along with several others, organized GASP (Group Against Smog and Pollution), which soon grew to hundreds and then perhaps as many as four thousand in the early 1970s. Their action was enabled by public hearing requirements as well as by the specific clause liberalizing citizen standing in the Air Quality Act passed by Congress in 1967, for which Senator Muskie had held public hearings in cities across the country.[49]

The core of women leaders was complemented by male GASP members, some connected by marriage and other family ties with shared concern for their children's health as well as by memberships in conservation groups. GASP men were drawn primarily from technical and academic backgrounds, and they reached out to a wide range of professionals in virtually all relevant institutional settings, such as scientific, technical, medical, and legal disciplines in local and regional academic institutions as well as in government and industry research institutes.

Local female activists understood themselves in terms of the "participatory democracy" of other 1960s movements and in discourses that highlighted the role of citizens and mothers. The quite contentious citizens who appeared before the Alleghany Board of Public Health in September 1969, and then compelled it to extend its hearings for three days, were coached months before by LWV, working together with the Federation of American Scientists and the Western Pennsylvania Conservancy. Such coaching became a common practice in large cities across Pennsylvania and other cities, from Gary, Indiana, to Missoula, Montana.[50] Due to its work in Pittsburgh, GASP was singled out by the EPA as a model for mobilizing local participation for the required SIPs. Headed by William Ruckelshaus, who would later become quite renowned for his citizen-driven and community-based approach, the new EPA provided grants for the national LWV to conduct trainings during its 1972 Leadership Summer for Citizen Action in fifteen states and produce films such as *Don't Hold Your Breath (Fight for It)*. Some league members were later recruited into EPA regional offices to help the agency with its public participation programs.[51]

Before the Clean Air Act was passed, GASP began with an imaginative and humorous public-education campaign involving characters such as "Dirtie Gertie, the Poor Polluted Birdie," with Bake-Offs and sales through the Girl Scouts, the YWCA, home economics classes in schools, church and synagogue kitchens, garden clubs, and other women's groups. Large downtown department stores as well as small shops were also enlisted to sell cookies and the thousands of copies of its message-laden cookbooks. It also publicized the campaign through Dirtie Gertie window displays. Kids barged into city council meetings with posters saying "I Belong Here," a claim to a "right to the city" that became a model for clean air organizing in other cities.[52] As in its clean water campaigns, the league provided research and contacts to intergovernmental functions as well as links to many other kinds of civic and professional associations, including many experts willing to testify formally when needed. GASP, as a separate organization, could be more impolite when met with stonewalling by agencies charged with developing the SIPs, and it forcefully represented citizens on the air pollution control advisory committee as well as on the county variance board. The latter could negotiate settlements, permit extra time to come into compliance, and encourage flexible solutions while monitoring progress—all of which were necessary given the enormous technical, bureaucratic, legal, and political complexity of air pollution regulation as it unfolded during the decade of the 1970s.[53]

Because of GASP organizing, the public hearings of the variance board had to be held in large auditoriums, and members of the public watched as their representatives cross-examined industry lawyers and municipal officials, offered surprise counter evidence, and presented slide shows of smoke fumes from specific facilities. Nonetheless, they were deeply committed to a pragmatic approach that could achieve results in this incredibly intricate field, shaped by perhaps the most complex of any federal environmental law ever written. In short, league and GASP women had developed an appropriately flexible mix of civic styles and social skills: diligent research, playful activities, maternal rhetoric, expertise and professionalism, forceful argument and performative rhetoric in formal settings, and pragmatism that was attentive to the multiple institutional logics at work. The latter included public health bureaucracies, school systems, housing authorities, and businesses of multiple types and sizes, each of which manifest a different mix of opportunities, constraints, and timelines for effective remediation. Actors within each type of institution were provided with opportunities to demonstrate that they were "honorably engaged." Grassroots action thus layered civic honor within the cultural construct of institutional logics, to be verified relationally and in public.[54]

This mixed repertoire, appropriately deployed in differentiated institutional settings with multiple logics, was enabled by the civic and professional ties that GASP and LWV had developed over the years, including ties with leading researchers and technical innovators in the region and by the EPA's role in funding and legitimating civic action within the legal and administrative framework established by Congress and the president.

National Environmental Policy Act

During the last days of December 1969, a Democratic Congress passed the National Environmental Policy Act (NEPA) with a broad bipartisan consensus. It was immediately referred to in the press as the Magna Carta of American environmentalism. At a White House ceremony on New Year's Day, the Republican president, who initially had his own preferred approach, signed the bill to great fanfare in a live television broadcast, signaling it as his first official act of the new decade. Earth Day would follow in a few months, as would the creation of the Environmental Protection Agency later in the year. The passage of landmark legislation on clean air and clean water, among other areas of environmental policy, soon followed, marking the 1970s as "the environmental decade." NEPA remains a cornerstone of this policy field, though its impacts have been debated and contested to this day and is now under assault by the Trump administration.

The idea for NEPA began largely with the work of Lynton Caldwell, a professor of political science and public administration at Indiana University who wrote an article in 1963 in *Public Administration Review*, the most prestigious journal in its field and published by the American Society for Public Administration. Caldwell made the case for integrating public policy and public administration across the various disciplines and agencies that had responsibility for the environment. Indeed, he is usually credited with coining the term *environmental policy* in this article. Caldwell had decided several years earlier to shift the focus of his distinguished but typically narrow academic career by beginning to study ecology across social science and natural science disciplines. He was deeply influenced by the writings of famed ecologist Aldo Leopold (whom he had met in 1946), helped found the Indiana chapter of The Nature Conservancy (TNC) in the late 1950s, and was involved in the struggles to preserve the Indiana Dunes National Park from further industrial development.

The receptiveness he perceived in the Kennedy and then Johnson administrations, and in the public's response to Rachel Carson's *Silent Spring* in 1962, convinced him to move forward on the policy front as well as through quite influential efforts to transform academic training across the country, thus building a critical component for further development of the environmental field across research, teaching, practice, and policy. He received early and repeated support from the Conservation Foundation (founded in 1948), which even agreed to pay his salary as he was asked to serve as a special consultant for the powerful Senate Interior and Insular Affairs Committee, headed by Henry "Scoop" Jackson. This relationship was initially brokered by the foundation's president, Samuel Ordway Jr., and then by his successor, Russell Train. Train became a key advisor and catalyst in the Nixon administration, and then became undersecretary of the Department of the Interior, the first head of the newly proposed Council on Environmental Quality (CEQ), and the second administrator of EPA. Caldwell wrote several other papers and influential reports that shifted agencies such as HEW in the late 1960s and framed the distinctive approach of NEPA.[55]

Several components were key to NEPA. First, it was intended to be self-executing, primarily through the requirement for environmental impact statements (EIS), in a way that environmental planning and regulation were not. The EIS policy design, despite its initial barriers and wide variation in subsequent implementation, requires a systematic, interdisciplinary, and ecological approach to the assessment of environmental impacts and adverse effects. It also requires the consideration of alternatives in balancing different values (ecological, economic, technical), thus enabling—even jolting—federal bureaucracies and cross-agency networks in their fields to reason more deliberatively and engage relevant publics in such deliberation.[56]

Several environmental groups (the Sierra Club, NWF, LWV) sent their leaders to testify on behalf of this requirement, but even Michael McCloskey of the Sierra Club, the lead witness, confessed to not having seen the importance of the EIS requirement. Nor did anyone seem to be aware of how much public and private business information would be generated and disclosed to citizens, thereby becoming difficult to ignore, all at a relatively limited cost to local citizen groups or larger environmental organizations and thus reducing information asymmetries in the field quite significantly. This represents a major policy feedback effect that enhanced civic learning, motivated further search for local knowledge, provided the basis for action in various venues, and helped in "making bureaucracies think." It also epitomizes systemic deliberation among differentiated field actors.[57]

NEPA generated demand for environmental planners with training in hydrology, biology, geology, and botany, thereby shaping university programs and professional career paths in ways that would over time enhance capacities for collaborative land and watershed management and sustainable city approaches. Some environmental groups, to be sure, were skeptical of NEPA, and press coverage was virtually nonexistent after the initial New Year's Day telecast. Many preferred Muskie's emerging approach, which stressed specific legislative standard setting and policing mechanisms, though Muskie and Jackson were eventually able to work through their intense disagreements over administrative mechanisms and congressional turf to see NEPA and other legislation as complementary. Representative John Dingell's bill in the House was generally consistent with Jackson's approach, and Senator Gaylord Nelson weighed in on the importance of public participation so the conference committee, meeting in December, could offer NEPA as its holiday gift to the nation.[58]

The self-executing EIS requirements—which served as a template for nations around the world—were specified in the famous Title I, section 102(C), and were later extended with more specific guidance through CEQ and executive orders. While NEPA had limited scope in city-level planning, except where projects received federal funds or fell under federal laws, many isomorphic state versions of NEPA—or SEPAs, and later TEPAs for tribal areas—institutionalized environmental impact assessment for state projects, and some of these extended EIS to local government actions as a cascading effect, thus encouraging more open and participative planning procedures across diverse policy fields that became relevant to building the sustainable cities field and eventually addressing climate change explicitly in some cases.[59]

As a second key feature, NEPA established CEQ as an office within the White House to issue annual reports on the state of the environment and to advise the president on overall policy. Its model was the Council of Economic Advisors, established by the Employment Act of 1946. Nixon's preferred Environmental Quality Council—drawn from the heads of various federal agencies, making it potentially slow, turf driven, and distracted by other policy concerns—quickly proved an embarrassment for a president trying to establish strong credibility in this field, and even his own key advisors, especially Train, worked behind the scenes in favor of Jackson's bill. Third, while NEPA did include a broad mission statement protecting ecosystems and promoting human health and welfare, the preferred clause of both Jackson and Caldwell that "each person has a fundamental and inalienable right to a healthful environment" was excised in favor of a weaker statement ("should enjoy"), which did not raise constitutional concerns that might prompt endless litigation. Subsequent attempts to include strong rights language have repeatedly failed.[60]

Institutional Dynamics in the Emergent Environmental Field

On April 22, 1970, a massive but quite decentralized teach-in took place in some fifteen hundred colleges and universities and in ten thousand schools and a multitude of other community settings, such as churches, temples, parks, libraries, YMCAs, businesses, hotels, and government buildings. As Adam Rome notes, Earth Day was somewhat of a misnomer, since events occurred over the course of an entire week, with numerous other events in the months preceding. At the University of Michigan in March, fourteen thousand people joined the tip-off event in the basketball arena on the first day of four, which included one hundred and twenty-five different activities, including a congressional subcommittee hearing. Some fifty thousand participated across Ann Arbor. Earth Day events around the country built upon the work of many who had become active within and through the federal conferences on water quality and natural beauty, civic and conservation associations, women's clubs and LWV chapters, and scientific and professional associations that had called for greater public debate on the environment, population growth, and nuclear fallout. Accounts of Earth Day discussions and debates signaled spillover from other participatory movements of the 1960s—student, antiwar, counterculture, women's liberation, civil rights, and black power movements—yet organizational competition revealed worry about displacement of energies into environmental causes.[61]

Earth Day enriched the institutional field of US environmentalism in many direct and indirect ways. Grassroots activism increased significantly and fueled the growth of some of the established associations, such as the Sierra Club and Audubon, as well as new organizations on the national, state, and local levels. Cofounded by David Brower in 1969 after he had been forced to resign as Sierra Club executive director, Friends of the Earth ratcheted up its political and legislative work, as did a subsidiary group called the League of Conservation Voters. Environmental Action arose directly out of the extensive organizing network of Earth Day, led by Dennis Hayes. To signal worthy endorsements or important targets for defeat, all three groups developed rating systems and/or voter handbooks, and these yielded success already in the 1970 and 1972 congressional elections. They also quickly boosted the number of lobbyists working in Washington. Earth Day catalyzed the development of permanent environment and ecology beats among leading newspapers. It also encouraged the publication of mass-market paperbacks and environmental handbooks, thereby strengthening the environmental public sphere.[62]

Having been comprised of events in a broad array of schools and universities, Earth Day gave a huge boost to environmental education. The National Association for Environmental Education (now the North American Association for Environmental Education, NAAEE) grew from a group of US community college educators in 1971 and has become the premier association in the field, bringing together many state associations of environmental educators, programs of youth associations (YMCA, 4-H) and national multitiered associations (Audubon, NWF). It has also brought together national curricular projects originally housed in state natural resource and fish and wildlife agencies. The Environmental Education Act of 1970, passed by Congress several months after Earth Day (though repealed under the Reagan administration in 1981), provided funding for various initiatives; its later iteration in 1990 exhibited institutional resilience at all levels and enabled NAAEE to spearhead the Environmental Education and Training Partnership (EETAP) with the leading organizations in the field. Significant funding from EPA's Office of Environmental Education, as well as from the National Science Foundation, was critical to further building the training capacities of state associations and NAAEE itself, and hence the professional legitimacy of the field, including its field of research. EETAP facilitated the development of standards and guidelines for excellence in schools and less formal settings. The 1990 act also established the National Environmental Education and Training Foundation to bring further resources to the field, and the Council of State Governments collaborated to develop a model act for state legislatures. These educational programs deeply shaped individual and collective identities critical for movement building and likely tempered the sectarian identity dilemma in the environmental movement.[63]

Command and Control as Field Settlement

Nonetheless, despite the enormous creativity of civic and conservation associations and other forms of grassroots action during tumultuous times, including the creation of important countercultural organizations, the environmental field in the 1970s "settled," to borrow the term of Neil Fligstein, Doug McAdam, and others.[64] This settlement privileged command and control by federal regulatory actors and was authorized by specific congressional statutes over distinct media of pollution. It was also enabled by enhanced technical tools, frequently resisted by industry and other regulated actors, enforced through the courts if necessary, and monitored by a set of environmental organizations with growing memberships and public legitimacy. The latter increasingly professionalized to enable them to act effectively within this complex set of relational field dynamics. To understand in broad outline how this happened provides insight not only into the parameters of democratic action over these first decades of US environmentalism, but it also indicates some of the challenges that emerged in the years following for urban and other place-based approaches.

First, industry foot dragging or outright resistance in the two decades leading up to the 1970s, often reinforced by cultural and technical deference among state agencies with underdeveloped administrative capacities, set civic and conservation groups and congressional entrepreneurs on the path of heightened federal action. Depending upon the specific policy field and its distributed authority design under federalism, regulatory tool kits included requiring "best available technologies," or even "technology forcing" requirements, setting permit standards, mandating ambitious deadlines, establishing uniform standards on specific types of pollution, closing waste dumps, and banning some substances entirely. Such tools were often highly imperfect, even speculative, given the state of technology, environmental health science, and the uncertain causal chains in complex ecological systems. However, under the divided rule of a Republican president, whose environmental motives were primarily strategic, and a deeply distrustful Democratic congress, statutes left less room for administrative discretion than they otherwise might have—and even less when the Clean Air Act and the Clean Water Act were further amended in 1977. Something akin to multipurpose or multiuse resource management, as in the Forest Service or the US Army Corps of Engineers, did not appear administratively feasible or legally manageable for reducing discrete pollutants. The EPA provided funding and technical assistance to build state administrative capacities and to improve professional standards as well as for water pollution treatment infrastructure—an area where distributive benefits could offset some of the regulatory conflict. Through its ten regional offices, the EPA also provided significant decentralization and flexibility to enable more collaborative relationships with state and local actors.[65]

The relatively low-hanging fruit of point-source pollution enhanced the capacity for legitimation of command and control, even in the face of rising economic, political, and ideological criticism on grounds of cost-effective performance and the proper reach and role of federal power. Such criticism increased steadily over the decade of the 1970s, and eventually helped lead to the election of Ronald Regan in 1980 and his attempted unsettling of the field. Where regulations were difficult to implement, deadlines virtually impossible to meet, or results hard to measure, enforcement efforts provided plenty of room to enact organizational myth and ritual, as did legislation itself.[66] Nonetheless, despite missed deadlines, court litigation, and institutional challenges all around—especially given the added financial and transaction costs of such a fragmented system—command and control eventually set in motion organizational changes within industry in terms of building environmental staff capacity, compliance offices, and technological innovation, and then more strategic managerial approaches to sustainability, at least selectively. The latter have proceeded largely on a separate track from sustainable cities and, though quite incomplete, provide an important foundation for climate action today.[67]

Second, existing federal agencies could be retooled and the major new one, the EPA, could be pieced together with a presidential reorganization plan, enacted through executive order, from more than a dozen units in three federal departments (HEW, USDA, and the Department of the Interior) and several independent agencies, already operating under media-specific statutes. More tools were soon added with the Clean Air Act and Clean Water Act, and laws on toxics, pesticides, and solid wastes. For Nixon, this EPA design was a second-best choice; his first was a larger, more integrative agency. But it avoided a potential clash with Congress and the traditional constituencies of the Forest Service and the US Army Corp of Engineers, and indeed the claims of other departments (the Department of the Interior, the Department of Commerce, HUD, USDOT, HEW, and the US Army Corps) to become the foremost environmental agency. This bureaucratic reorganization strategy left the EPA as a kind of "holding company," and, according to Richard Andrews, more fragmented than it might otherwise have been under its own overall "organic act." It deprived the administrator greater authority to set program and budgetary priorities, both within the agency and across congressional subcommittees, or to integrate management across these bureaucratic silos, a condition that has largely persisted and become embedded in agency subcultures. For a variety of reasons, subsequent attempts to grant EPA formal cabinet status have failed, though the administrator has typically been granted cabinet rank.[68]

Despite having thematized public participation as a way to enable citizens to decide the "kind of life [they] want and the risks they will accept to achieve it," as William Ruckelshaus put it in a law journal article early in his term, the EPA's first administrator chose an aggressive standard-setting and enforcement strategy to ensure the agency's timely legitimacy among environmental organizations and congressional Democrats. It quickly demonstrated to the broader public that the agency was not subservient to the White House or to the business community. Targeting a limited number of big-business polluters also played to the popular narrative of corporate villainy, though big cities also took their share of blame. Ruckelshaus made competent management and recruitment a high priority against all attempts at politicizing top appointments by either Congress or the president, but his own legitimacy internally depended on accommodating staff inherited from other agencies. When Ruckelshaus left in April 1973 to head the FBI during the Watergate scandal, the EPA's second administrator, Russell Train, maintained much of this approach through the presidency of Gerald Ford (1974–1977).[69]

Though likely the best available to the EPA under two Republican presidents and relentlessly intensive and adversarial oversight by Congress, these initial field-positioning and relational strategies seriously constricted the agency in "fostering public debate and public understanding." As Marc Landy and his colleagues have argued, these are arguably an "agency's highest calling" and vital to fostering the "capacity of citizens for successful self-government" amidst constrained resources, imperfect tools, and competing policy priorities. As a result, agency support for public participation programs, including staff capacity to enable these, was half-hearted and erratic. President Jimmy Carter (1977–1981), a Democrat, increased support for such programs, as did Senator Edward Kennedy, who later admitted that the forms available at the time were neither deliberative nor collaborative enough to gain much traction. By then, the much more evident costs of environmental regulation—especially in a period of significant economic slowdown, inflation, and "panic at the pump"—increasing scrutiny by the Office of Management and Budget, and the still-uncertain future of the agency led EPA leaders to fashion public health as its core mission in the mind of the public. They especially targeted cancer in the age of "the Chemical Revolution." This occurred before Love Canal, though it was reinforced by it and quickly brought sizable budget increases, anticipating the new emphasis on toxic substances in contrast to conventional pollutants, not to mention the broad and balancing ecological mission of NEPA or place-based strategies in cities.[70]

As a result, some of the community and relational capacities developed by associations such as the League of Women Voters and other local groups on clean water and clean air in urban settings were not leveraged optimally into the ensuing decades, even as others began to appear.

Emergent Logics among Civic Associations

A further factor in field settlement was that the emergent logic of environmental organizations, both the older conservation organizations and the newer ones created in the late 1960s and 1970s, was designed to build and deploy organizational resources to make effective use of the opportunities provided by monitoring implementation, ensuring adequate EIS documentation, litigating through the courts, legitimating further regulation on scientific and technical grounds, and, of course, by congressional lobbying through decentralized committee structures under Democratic control. The latter proliferated further due to the new laws that could provide the hooks upon which to hang future litigation. During the 1970s, at least eleven standing committees in the House and nine in the Senate, as well as one hundred or so subcommittees, exercised some jurisdictional oversight over the EPA.[71]

Environmental law congealed as a field of its own shortly after a conference at Airlie House in Warrenton, Virginia, in September 1969, sponsored by the Conservation Foundation; leading law professors, litigators, advocates, and congressional staff from the Muskie and Jackson committees participated. Specific field-building components—the *Environmental Law Reporter*, the Environmental Law Institute, the *Environmental Law Review*, law school conferences, new curricula, and law school clinics—soon followed. The Ford Foundation developed a broader strategy to build the field of public-interest law and nonprofit law firms; provide economic, institutional, and regulatory justification; and develop the Council for Public Interest Law to act as an association across the broader field. Two program officers at Ford, Gordon Harrison and Sanford Jaffe, along with several other foundation officers, took the lead, with Harrison and Ned Ames focusing on environmental law. Professor Joseph Sax of the University of Michigan Law School, a prominent actor in building the field, published his book, *Defending the Environment: A Strategy for Citizen Action*, which coupled civic action tightly to court action. The book had an introduction by Senator George McGovern, the soon-to-be nominee of the Democratic Party for president, reiterating the argument that "access to the courts of the United States is *the most effective* means for citizens to participate directly in environmental decisions and may be *the only way* to assure that democratic processes are brought to bear on environmental problems."[72]

With the substantial increase of staff attracted by shared environmental values to the EPA and other federal environmental departments and offices, as well as the direct staffing of important positions from professionalized environmental groups—both representing normative structuration processes at work—a distinct relational field-building dynamic emerged: agency staff consulted with professional staff in the major advocacy organizations, many of whom also shared social networks through friends, spouses, former law and graduate-school classmates, and previous activism. These agency staff could report back to their colleagues on the probability of court action. Such authoritative anticipation would produce feedback effects in agency deliberations and policy recommendations.

The steep organizational costs of maintaining and further building local grassroots capacities in the multitiered associations, where they already existed; developing networks from the diffuse array of newer participatory organizations; sustaining the more radical national ones; or blending emergent participatory forms with the new environmental law organizations made the strategic choice to professionalize across much of the associational field quite rational.[73] While models of revenue generation in such groups can be quite complex, it does seem that real revenues among environmental groups remained relatively flat during the late 1970s. Organizations such as the Environmental Defense Fund and the Natural Resources Defense Council could legitimate themselves as voices for the environmental movement by enlisting increasing numbers of members through direct mail; with visible action on prominent disputes (often allied with local and regional groups); through scientific, technical, and legal competence; and by demonstrated results in blocking some projects or helping to pass further legislation. To be sure, some of the conundrums of policy design for democracy, such as the perverse liability design for Superfund that heightened conflict in urban communities while delaying remediation, were also the result of lobbying by major environmental organizations, which developed a stake in persistent, contentious mobilization at the grassroots to get sites named to the National Priorities List. The Superfund program itself became a "full-employment program for lawyers" on all sides, partly due to the interpretive effects of Love Canal.[74]

The lineaments of these civic and institutional developments were quite complex and do not lend themselves to easy narratives of grassroots wisdom or professional myopia. For all the shortcomings within the dynamics of this field settlement—especially for urban ecosystem, built environment, and environmental justice, as we shall see—a radical strategic alternative never generated significant political or organizational credibility.

Conclusion

In the early decades after World War II, conservation associations immediately began to take up issues of clean water, and while they were not initially focused on urban issues per se, local chapters of multitiered associations, such as the Izaak Walton League of America, began to form coalitions with other groups that pressed for action in cities around the Great Lakes and along major river systems, such as the Missouri and Colorado. Other multitiered associations, such as the National Wildlife Federation and the National Audubon Society, joined in identifying citizen action on clean water as key to democracy in the decades ahead. The League of Women Voters, with its legacy frame of city housekeeping from Progressive-Era women's organizing, developed an important organizational niche among them that built key components of the field through civic research on community impact, institutional logics, and basin frameworks for further action—and, in some places, on clean air as well. Together, these associations, as well as numerous unaffiliated groups whom they brought into coalition and often coached, established the template of shared civic leadership in developing a national policy agenda through federal enforcement conferences and other field-configuring events, as well as though laws and norms that increasingly recognized rights to information and voice among ordinary citizens. Formal policymaking, while responding to enhanced national political opportunities and technical models from the late 1950s onward, and responding to organizations such as the American Municipal Association and the US Conference of Mayors whose members were typically in the most direct line of local pressure, also built upon lifeworld resonances from civic organizing and even Senate filmmaking.

The emerging environmental field, much broader than early conservation or the urban clean water and clean air struggles of these years, settled around command-and-control regulation by the early 1970s. This was inscribed in federal statutes, such as the Clean Water Act and the Clean Air Act, soon followed by other laws. It was enforced by new bureaucracies, such as the EPA, and stronger enforcement and technical tools all around, buttressed by increasingly professionalized environmental groups with the capacity for researching, lobbying, monitoring, mobilizing, and contesting in court. Despite much creative local organizing, this field settlement was quite rational and strategic for the newer organizations that could develop membership without chapters, such as the Environmental Defense Fund and the National Resources Defense Council, as well as for many of the older multitiered conservation organizations. It could deliver some very important results quickly and hence solidify public support, achieve much symbolically even when tools were imperfect or had unintended consequences, and could provide much-needed balance to corporate power resisting the environmental movement and a very wide swath of public opinion.

Field settlement, to be sure, is always relative and "a work in progress." Only after the election of Reagan in 1980, who ominously though ultimately unsuccessfully unsettled the field, would the Kendall Foundation convene the leaders of nine—soon the "Group of Ten"—of the foremost national organizations to further "rationalize the field" by bringing increased comity (amidst funding competition), division of labor, and strategic collaboration. Several other environmental funders also participated in this effort. By the mid-1970s, and then especially during the early Reagan presidency, corporate and conservative actors emerged to oppose both the civic and regulative dimensions of this settlement, with some degree of success.[75]

However, they were not able to prevent various other forms of democratic participation and place-based ecological and urban models from emerging. One of the most important was the field of sustainable cities, which encompasses many forms and frames of community and grassroots action, as well as professional, market, network, and bureaucratic logics of institutional development.

CHAPTER THREE

Urban Land Conflicts and Professional Shifts

This chapter examines the land-use conflicts that emerged in and around cities beginning in the 1960s. These conflicts elicited action from a variety of forms of civic association at the local level and attempts at the federal level to pass a national land-use law that would enable more creative responses by building further institutional capacities in states. These conflicts also prompted responses by leading professional associations in the field of land use, such as architects and planners, and responses in overlapping fields, resulting in the emergence of other associations for new urbanism, smart growth, and green building.

I begin by examining the civic associations and policy designs that proved most consequential in prompting a sustained federal review of land-use planning in the early 1970s; namely, Model Cities, neighborhood associations, community development corporations (CDCs), and open-space councils and alliances. Two of them—Model Cities and CDCs—had federal policy supports. At the local level, there were often organizational crossties and interactive dynamics among these and several other organizational types, such as multitier environmental organizations, ethnic associations, and community action agencies. The federal land-use task force, which was established in the early 1970s to review recent developments and perhaps build this field, helped frame the debate on a national land-use law. Despite early signs that this would pass, the bill generated significant opposition and lost the president's support before failing in Congress in 1975. The various urban and environmental groups that might have collaborated more effectively on the proposed legislation did not display sufficient mutual interest or strategic coherence at this point. Nonetheless, land-use laws of various sorts proceeded to be enacted at various levels of the federal system, thereby building local land-use law as an institutional field and enhancing opportunities for civic challenge and innovative participation.

In response to local civic engagement and conflict, participatory norms and practices found increasing resonance among some established professional associations, such as the American Institute of Architects and the American Planning Association, as well as other professional associations specifically focused on urban governance, such as the National League of Cities (NLC) and the International City/County Management Association (ICMA). By the mid-1980s, a sustainable cities frame began to emerge; it further reprised such participatory norms and linked them directly to the design of the built environment and urban ecosystem functions. New associations emerged in the 1990s to build the field more systematically, such as the Congress for the New Urbanism, Smart Growth America, and the US Green Building Council, with many ties to each other, to environmental organizations, and to networks of federal, state, and local staff in relevant agencies (environment, housing, transportation, planning). These associations then helped draw AARP and its chapters into the field of the built environment, which, in turn, served as conveners of civic coalitions.

Civic Openings and Policy Options

The open space movement began in the late 1950s, primarily as pushback from architects and planners to bulldozing for suburban development, although they were supported by various civic groups. They soon became more expansive in framing open space to include urban environments likewise being bulldozed and reshaped by the building of the interstate highway system. While there were stipulations on the acquisition of open space in the Housing Act of 1961, the largely voluntary campaign led by journalist William H. Whyte was outpaced by urban and suburban development, the appropriation of large tracts for interstate highway construction, and resistance by new suburbanites to taxing on top of their local sewer and school costs. In August 1972, after a decade of commissions and the drafting of several national land-use bills in Congress, the Task Force on Land Use and Urban Growth was created by the Citizens Advisory Committee on Environmental Quality. It was established by presidential executive order in conjunction with—and as policy feedback of—the passage of NEPA in 1970 and the creation of the White House Council on

Environmental Quality (CEQ), from which the task force borrowed its executive director.[1]

CEQ had also commissioned a study of innovative laws in several states by two prominent land-use lawyers, provocatively titled *The Quiet Revolution in Land Use Control*, to be followed by an influential study on the "takings" issue, also commissioned by CEQ. The chair of the nongovernmental task force was environmental philanthropist Laurance S. Rockefeller; funding was provided by the Rockefeller Brothers Fund. Perhaps as significant, however, was that the deputy chair was Paul N. Ylvisaker, who was instrumental in shaping the Ford Foundation's urban programs in the early 1960s, and President Lyndon B. Johnson's Model Cities Program, both of which aimed to accommodate or even mobilize participation by urban residents, including poor communities, in renewal and development projects. At least three other members of the task force brought overlapping perspectives: Vernon Jordan was the executive director of the National Urban League, which focused on civil rights and equity for inner city communities and whose previous executive director, Whitney M. Young Jr., had served on the original Model Cities task force; Virginia Nugent was chair of the League of Women Voters' national land use committee, which could leverage LWV's extensive experience in urban water and air; and James W. Rouse was CEO of the Rouse Company, a developer of planned communities and an emerging funder in the community-development field—though only after an early career favoring expressway construction through the central cities. Task force executive director William K. Reilly later went on to head the Conservation Foundation and then the EPA (under President George H. W. Bush, 1989–1993) and held an urban planning degree from Columbia University. While engaging professionals, the report recognized that "a generation of experts has produced fewer important changes in the growth process than five or so years of sustained citizen action."[2]

Urban civic action during the 1960s and early 1970s manifested itself through at least four major forms that directly, indirectly, and often jointly began to feed into the emerging open space movement and participatory urban planning practices; namely, Model Cities, neighborhood associations, community development corporations, and open space coalitions. Each of these generated new institutional linkages to various public agencies, to other community and environmental groups, and to other public and private actors that helped build the field of urban sustainability.[3]

Model Cities

First, the Model Cities Program (1966–1974), announced by President Johnson for the newly created Department of Housing and Urban Development (HUD), aimed at revitalizing urban areas through comprehensive and participatory planning. Model Cities represented an important, albeit flawed, policy design for democracy to the extent that it provided funding, technical assistance, and cognitive signals that incentivized local action by community groups to engage in claims making, problem solving, program innovation, and collaboration with various other civic and neighborhood associations and civil rights groups as well as with public and private agencies that were often also targets of protest. Model Cities was intended to reign into authoritative city structures the "maximum feasible participation" of the Community Action Program within the president's Office of Economic Opportunity (OEO), begun two years earlier. This participation mandate was prompted by the irrepressible claims of the civil rights movement for voice in urban development and by the pluralist and Jeffersonian framing opportunities available to Johnson; namely, to provide a seat at the table with other interests and institutions, but to serve the purpose of democratic community.[4]

Nonetheless, a requirement for "widespread citizen participation" remained in Model Cities, testifying to a normative shift in the urban field backed by legislatively granted rights for community groups to appeal exclusion from the process. City officials yielded to well-organized local pressure and accommodated or even encouraged engagement through pre-existing community action agencies, which spawned independent civic associations, local service nonprofits, and urban leadership development on a broad scale, including among women and minorities. Federal grants were targeted to areas specified in city applications, covering at most ten percent of population, but contiguous neighborhoods often organized in emulative and isomorphic fashion to gain a voice in other city planning and renewal efforts; city staff often worked sequentially or simultaneously across programmatic and neighborhood boundaries. While HUD remained ambivalent about participation—more so once Richard Nixon was elected in 1968—local administrators improvised in response to citizens' insistent demands for "partnership" and their own common-sense understanding of heuristics that could legitimate programs in citizens' eyes.[5]

Local administrators also improvised to develop means of conflict resolution among the many contending claims of community groups. HUD's chief advisor on citizen participation, Sherry Arnstein, strongly criticized programs where engagement remained ritualistic and manipulative, and she got approval for advisory guidelines and best practices for the one hundred and fifty Model Cities funded, as well as a technical assistance fund to build citizen capacities. At times, the agency held up applications until the citizen-participation design was clarified or strengthened. Municipal agencies confronted well-organized, even militant community leadership in many cities. Model Cities, though highly underfunded relative to the number of municipalities included and unable to coordinate effectively across local or federal government agencies, reached beyond social service agencies to a broad range of municipal services. For the first time, it established extensive participation in land-use planning, such as housing demolition and construction, transportation routes, and freeway construction. Evident in some cities by the 1950s, what came to be called the "freeway revolt" against the bulldozing of urban neighborhoods, especially those of blacks, Latinos, and ethnic whites, also generated many new organizations capable of local and legal action. Some were tightly networked in cities like Baltimore, Maryland, as well as more loosely through the Highway Action Coalition, a national antifreeway network.[6]

The Johnson administration's new US Department of Transportation (USDOT), established in 1966, became responsive at the highest levels. It reined in the Bureau of Public Roads and its state highway allies, and publicly valorized the revolts in a national tour. It supported laws for greater public participation and multiple hearings that could slow down projects, and in some cases, directly brokered agreements favoring communities in the twenty-five or so cities it closely monitored as stalemated. Nixon's new secretary at USDOT, renowned highway supporter and former governor of Massachusetts John Volpe, soon also became responsive to the freeway revolts, as well as to the new constraints of NEPA, and either actively supported or acquiesced in local decisions to not build controversial highways. He even created a new assistant secretary position to help respond to the revolts.[7]

In urban and regional transportation, the extent of public pressure for new modes of participation can also be gleaned from the large array of practice guides and handbooks published or commissioned by public agencies at every level of the federal system, including civil rights organizations and university centers, and by analyses in a broad array of scholarly journals across professional disciplines. While Model Cities encouraged the participation of the poor, ensuring some confrontation with existing agencies, it required conflict resolution as a condition for continued support. Indeed, quite a few of the Model City agencies and programs persisted beyond 1974 with funding from the new Community Development Block Grant (CDBG) program, which also contained requirements for participation. Much of what would emerge under the rubric of collaborative urban and environmental planning and problem solving grew from this milieu.[8]

Neighborhood Associations

Second, neighborhood associations also experienced considerable growth from the late 1960s onward. In many cases, this was a direct or indirect spinoff of Community Action and Model Cities; in other cases, this resulted from Alinsky-style community organizing and, in some cases, it was both. In some cities, neighborhood groups and various coalitions among local stakeholders were given new vigor and shape, as was the case in the Mission District in San Francisco, where local organizations developed strategic responses to changing institutional configurations from the Progressive Era through New Deal federal highway, public works, and housing programs to participatory designs of Community Action and Model Cities. Neighborhood associations are typically open to all residents living within geographical boundaries defined by historical identities and/or city service districts, though boundaries and identities might be shifting and contested internally, pragmatically, and discursively as prescribed by local social scientists, planners, and other service providers, as in the classic case of Chicago sociology. Neighborhood associations tend to meet on a regular basis. During this period, many cities came to recognize them officially through city council resolution or other mechanisms, with administrative linkages to planning or community development agencies.[9]

However, only a few cities institutionalized them on a citywide basis as relatively robust local policy designs for democracy. Such citywide systems provided strong requirements for the inclusion of residents from all neighborhoods on a nonpartisan basis, with clear lines of communication to city agencies. As independent civic groups, neighborhood associations could raise money and incorporate as nonprofits, but they also received core funding from the city to hire local staff or bring in consultants. This helped them build capacity to engage in land-use decision-making and neighborhood planning—their most important areas of focus and efficacy.

Analyzed by Jeffrey M. Berry, Kent E. Portney, and Ken Thomson in *The Rebirth of Urban Democracy* (1993), citywide systems of neighborhood representation, as developed in Portland and St. Paul, proved quite robust in terms of their capacity to work with a broad range of other types of civic groups, including Audubon, the Sierra Club, LWV chapters, and open space councils and coalitions. This book was especially important because it systematically analyzed one organizational archetype within larger multi-organizational fields, opening channels over time to citizen and professional concerns with developing more sustainable cities as this field was about to experience major growth in the 1990s. It tested important theories of participatory democracy in relation to structural design.[10]

While we lack a rigorous quantitative analysis of the "organizational ecology" of such groups in this period, much evidence points to complementary dynamics. Those cities that later borrowed institutional design features from these citywide systems and added still others have also enabled collaboration across an array of civic associations in neighborhood planning (community councils, open space and watershed groups, senior and youth groups, ethnic associations) and city agencies. In Seattle, Washington, for example, the intense conflict of earlier periods, though not completely gone, generally resulted in multisided learning among activists, city councilors, mayors, planners, and other public administrators. Some of these cities, in fact, have been in the forefront of sustainability and climate action planning in recent years.[11]

Community Development Corporations

Third, the neighborhood, civil rights, and tenants' rights movements of the 1960s and 1970s spurred the growth of local community development corporations (CDCs). These were initially supported by an OEO program and then by critical field-building investments of the Ford Foundation and various other foundation, banking, and corporate partners. Community development soon included a wide range of intermediaries, seen by many as key to its emergence as a robust field, operating through loosely structured networks and enabled through various policy tools. These have included the Community Development Block Grant program (1974), the Community Reinvestment Act (1977), the Low-Income Housing Tax Credit (1986), and the Community Development Financial Institutions (CDFI) Fund (1994). The most general-purpose capacity builder in the field, the Local Initiatives Support Corporation (LISC), was established in 1979. It developed local offices in some thirty cities, typically on the basis of pre-existing CDC networks and citywide associations, with strong relational and/or programmatic ties to city agencies (housing, community development, neighborhoods, parks), and then increasingly to green building, smart growth, community agriculture, and similar associations and partnerships.[12]

Other foundations and regional networks, as well as some twelve-hundred CDFIs (community development loan funds, banks, and credit unions), provide a range of financial, technical, and other capacity building assistance. Banks, corporations, church dioceses, and local universities have been drawn into local community development systems, further enhancing their institutional embeddedness. Living Cities—originally the National Community Development Initiative established in 1991—brought in additional funders, some of whom had programmatic interests and cognitive frames beyond housing and physical infrastructure, which helped the field operate across multiple urban practices, including environmental. These and other intermediaries (Enterprise Foundation, NeighborWorks, Center for Community Change, Development Training Institute) helped to catalyze further growth to approximately two thousand CDCs by 1990, three thousand six hundred by 1998, and some four thousand six hundred or more by 2005. However, CDCs remain concentrated in large and medium-sized cities, and the mortgage and foreclosure crisis weakened the field in the late 2000s.[13]

While there has always been tension between professionalization and grassroots participation in the field, and division of labor between community organizing and community development networks, no credible radical option for fundamentally reconfiguring this institutional field has ever emerged in any US city despite periodic calls to do so. Diversification of activities beyond housing has also been evident. These include practices that engage residents in assets-based and coproduction activities utilizing neighborhood residents' local knowledge, skills, and networks in urban and neighborhood market revitalization, community health and participatory planning, brownfield redevelopment, sustainable communities, and environmental justice.[14]

Open Space Councils and Alliances

Fourth, by the time that the Task Force on Land Use and Urban Growth met in 1972 to 1973, open space councils and land trusts, planning and conservation leagues, greenbelt alliances, and foothill committees had begun to emerge, and some national, state, and local chapters of conservation associations began to focus on open space, especially the National Audubon Society. The Save the Dunes Council, founded in 1952 as an offshoot of Chicago progressivism, waged a prolonged albeit successful battle that brought successive parcels into the National Park Service (and Indiana state parks) amidst the otherwise heavily industrialized southern shores of Lake Michigan, where steel mills had consumed the dunes for much of the previous century. The Austin Environmental Council, a coalition of two dozen groups, was formed in the Texas capital in the late 1960s upon the foundations of several open space and greenbelt groups, as well as the local Sierra Club chapter. These and other open space groups, intertwined with creek groups that crisscrossed the city due to its distinct topography, came to define the development of Austin as an environmental city to this day. County conservation leagues and seashore protection groups were active in open space, land-trust, and park designation efforts across the San Francisco Bay Area, sometimes in collaboration with the Sierra Club, Audubon, and TNC chapters. In the mid-1960s in Phoenix, Arizona, the Teen Committee to Save Camelback Mountain, with chapters at twenty-six schools and a petition 322 feet and 6 inches in length, mobilized high school students through dances and concerts to stop encroaching development; an expanded Mountains Preserve emerged over the next decade with further civic action, city funding, and federal support.[15]

Around the country, professionals in several federal agencies, such as the US Geological Survey and the Soil Conservation Service, also played important roles in research, convening, and public education. They wrote newspaper articles, engaged in TV appearances, and hosted public talks with civic groups, municipal officials, and builders. Guidebooks, such as *Open Land for Urban America*, were produced as collaborative efforts of leaders from all levels of Audubon, several federal agencies (especially the US Forest Service), state conservation departments in New York and Wisconsin, nonprofit organizations, such as the Open Space Institute and the Urban Land Institute, and several private development corporations, such as the Rouse Company. The Open Lands Project in Chicago issued *Open Land in Urban Illinois: Roles of the Citizen Advocate*, which detailed the practices of local land activists, especially women, organized into groups such as the Wilson Bog Committee, the Thornton Creek Preservation Association, and the Peacock Prairie Preservation Project. They confronted and negotiated directly with developers and planning agencies. They routinely made their public case before other conservation groups, church groups, women's clubs, and garden clubs, which brought media attention—quite in parallel with LWV clean water and clean air actions of the period, discussed in chapter 2.[16]

National Land Use Policy Act

Nonetheless, the National Land Use Policy Act (NLUPA)—supported by a wide array of citizen activists, prominent legal and planning associations, federal and state officials, and progressive developers—failed to pass in 1975. Initially introduced on January 1, 1970, by Senate interior committee chair Henry "Scoop" Jackson on the very day that his NEPA legislation was signed by the president and revised to bring the Nixon administration on board (especially through CEQ), the act was designed to build institutional capacity at the state level through various federal incentives and sanctions. States, in turn, would build capacity and bring greater coherence to local land-use planning, where jurisdictional fragmentation and economic competition typically undercut solutions to cross-boundary problems such as regional traffic congestion and ecological degradation. Even rudimentary zoning was absent in the great number of cities, towns, and counties across the country in 1970. The peculiar complexity of land-use issues, which entailed potential triggering of popular opposition and a realistic assessment of congressional support, ruled out action-forcing policy designs such as the Clean Air Act (1970) and the Clean Water Act (1972).[17]

However, the Nixon administration withdrew its support in 1974 due to increasing opposition from organized interests and grassroots public opinion and the changed political circumstances of Watergate that led the endangered president to seek more conservative support in Congress. The National Association of Home Builders (NAHB) and the National Association of Realtors (NAR) mobilized, especially after the housing slump that accompanied the 1973 recession, since they perceived any such increase in planning or regulation as delaying projects and adding costs. But grassroots opposition to NLUPA, often spurred by NAHB and NAR, also came from small farmers and urban and suburban homeowners who feared losing existing or potential investments for retirement savings or for new home purchases if planning came to impose restrictions on building. The threat to private property rights, articulated in the public debate on "takings," had broad resonance. This was not just another command-and-control policy design framed as us versus them, where the power of big corporations or irresponsible public agencies should be restricted and many technical solutions could be imposed.[18]

The land use bill also faltered, as Margaret Weir argues, because a coalition of urban and environmental interests could not be placed on a secure foundation. The US Conference of Mayors and the National League of Cities offered qualified support but were far more interested in community development block grants (CDBGs; introduced in 1974 as part of Nixon's New Federalism), other unrestricted block grants, and revenue sharing. At the federal administrative level, HUD competed with the Department of the Interior to become the lead agency, but HUD also had close institutional ties to development interests. For most African American urban activists, NLUPA represented, at best, a remote form of good government and, at worst, a distraction from the primacy of economic and job growth—hence urban growth machines, except where land-use conflicts were highly localized and lent themselves to claims of "community control." Some environmental organizations could mobilize direct action to stop the construction of a new highway extension or power plant, but they had little organizational capacity for or cultural affinity to the kind of deliberative planning that would require a balancing of interests. Building state capacity to guide local land-use policy, or to bring the various types of civic groups discussed above into workable coalitions, did not play to the organizational strengths of the big nationals, such as the Environmental Defense Fund and the Natural Resources Defense Council, at least in these early years of the field settlement discussed in chapter 2. However, after the act's demise, NRDC published a handbook on citizens' legal rights in land-use cases and later became quite involved in smart growth, new urbanist, and green building movements, as we shall see.[19]

The Sierra Club represented a partial exception in this early period, and during the next decade, it published a framing document on sustainable communities by Sim Van der Ryn and Peter Calthorpe that would shape emerging movements. Indeed, the volume grew from a cross-disciplinary solar cities design workshop of three dozen participants—architects, planners, ecologists, biologists, community organizers, food-systems specialists, transportation engineers, entrepreneurs, and others—who met for a week together in 1980 at the Westerbeke Ranch near Sonoma, California. It was sponsored by the Solar Energy Research Institute. The explicit goal:

to develop a "vision" of sustainable communities based partly on pragmatic learning from distinct prototype communities in different parts of the country. William H. Whyte's *The Social Life of Small Urban Spaces* appeared in 1980, following upon several decades of his writing and campaigns against sprawl and for open space. Others began writing in this vein as well. The first widely utilized tool kit of "building blocks" for US and Canadian cities, Mark Roseland's *Toward Sustainable Communities* was published in 1992, with a preface by the secretary general of ICLEI-Local Governments for Sustainability (see chapter 7). It was then significantly revised in 1998, in 2005, and in 2012 to respond more fully to emerging debates on civic action, social capital, and the core value of democracy— thereby *"mobilizing citizens and their governments"* (emphasis in original). This tool kit is based upon considerably more integrative framing than the volume by Van der Ryn and Calthorpe, and subsequent editions display the considerable plasticity of this emerging frame.[20]

Although the dominant liberal interpretation by Frank Popper of the failure of NLUPA at the time saw it as a blow to much-needed centralized regulation, the institutional and legal legacy was more complicated. Popper revised his own view several years later in analyzing an array of centralized state land-use laws, as well as land-use provisions of federal laws on water, air, coastal zone management, mine reclamation, and flood disaster protection. It revealed a much more pragmatic and unobtrusive extension of regulation. The "quiet revolution in land use control" had, by 1975, "achieved at least 20 new environmentally-oriented state land use laws, mostly in the northeast, the upper Midwest, and the far West." A second generation of such laws, both comprehensive and single-purpose, was already underway by the mid-1980s.[21]

In addition, under continued pressure from civic and environmental groups, local governments gained a wide array of legal authority to regulate land use and other environmental problems, expanding the field of local environmental law quite significantly as part of the larger environmental law field. While NEPA had limited scope in city-level planning, except where projects received federal funds or fell under federal laws, at least twenty-two isomorphic state versions of NEPA—or SEPAs—institutionalized environmental impact assessment for state projects. Some of these extended EIS to local government actions, thus encouraging more open and participative planning procedures. Apart from NEPA and SEPAs, local administrative law has also evolved to provide many handles for public participation, and, since the 1970s, a loose overlay of legal and political tools for "legal neighborhoods" that could be further realigned and refined to address sustainability has evolved rather dramatically.[22]

Established and Emergent Professional Associations

Civic engagement and public participation also came to be promoted by several established professional associations. As Royston Greenwood, Roy Suddaby, and C. R. Hinings argue, such associations can play an important role in "theorizing" change across fields by managing debate within a profession, legitimating new approaches, reframing professional identities, and representing themselves differently to other field actors. In our cases, they can also enable an array of new associations in smart growth, new urbanism, green building, cycling, and walking.[23]

Professional associations, as I argued in chapter 1, can play an important role in developing the field of sustainable cities and aligning appropriately with grassroots and democratic movements that challenge growth-machine dynamics, thereby manifesting core norms and practices of "democratic professionalism" or "civic professionalism."[24] This almost never happens smoothly but is the result of strong challenges within and outside professional associations, as occurred in the land-use conflicts of the 1960s and 1970s. However imperfect and incomplete such alignments have been so far, they are clearly significant in providing new tools, cognitive resources, and associational linkages that have helped to build the field. Several long-established associations among planners and architects have been especially important not only in their respective areas of competence but in nurturing several associations in green building, new urbanism, and smart growth. This has increased crossties in board memberships and collaborative projects, convergence in framing, borrowing of tools, and staff mobility across sectors of the field. Here I examine several established and newer associations while indexing a broader array that have also lent themselves to the work of building sustainable cities.

In the 1960s, community design centers—some affiliated with universities and utilizing students as interns—were established to offer low-cost services to grassroots groups, especially in poor neighborhoods. These centers affiliated in 1977 as the Association for Community Design, which maintains a strong participatory and social justice approach in its annual conferences and local practices. Urban Design Associates, which was cofounded by exiled South African antiapartheid activist David Lewis in a Pittsburgh neighborhood in 1964, viewed the emergent "urban design as a language of democracy, a way of linking the individual and the family to the city—house, porch and street, neighborhood, city." The first sentence of its fiftieth anniversary report announces its practice as "urban design and architecture based on democracy in action." It has developed over five decades as a design firm that works with public agencies and housing authorities, nonprofits and CDCs, and larger private development corporations. It maintains its commitment to participatory principles and charrette practices, which are increasingly fine-grained and well aligned with recent advances in visualization tools. Other consulting firms, including the Urban Land Institute (ULI) and various professional schools, have endorsed public involvement through multi-stakeholder design processes.[25]

While a diverse set of community visioning and participatory planning methods have emerged over the past several decades, sustainable city and new urbanist approaches often utilize the charrette, an intensive collaborative design and planning workshop that occurs over multiple, consecutive days. The term comes from the practice of solving architectural design problems *en charrette*, as students placed their designs for jury critique in a circulating cart (*charrette*) at the École des Beaux-Arts in nineteenth-century Paris. It was revived in a new form after World War II and then adapted to the post-1960s participatory movements and mandates by including local neighborhood groups, other stakeholders, and multidisciplinary design teams of professionals, sometimes within a Model Cities planning process.

American Institute of Architects
The American Institute of Architects (AIA), founded in 1857 and currently with some eighty thousand members in three hundred state and local chapters, has developed an important model with its Regional/Urban Design Assistance Teams (R/UDATs). The R/UDAT project, begun in 1967 with input from David Lewis, fully recognized that citizens were in open revolt in many cities over urban renewal and redevelopment practices, often tied to racial segregation, and that this revolt was part of a broad array of participatory, civil rights, neighborhood, and other movements. Indeed, during this period, AIA invited Whitney M. Young Jr., president of the Urban League, to address its national convention, at which he chastised that "you are most distinguished by your thunderous silence and your

complete irrelevance." This deliberately self-inflicted shaming by association leaders led to a prestigious AIA award that now bears his name. The R/UDAT stance was profoundly normative—"making urban democracy work"—rooted in an explicit Jeffersonian ethos, indicated by Thomas Jefferson's famous argument: "I know of no safe depository of the ultimate powers of society but the people themselves: and if we think them not enlightened enough to exercise their control with a wholesome discretion, the remedy is not to take it from them, but to inform their discretion."[26]

In the R/UDAT model, cities and towns initiate contact with AIA, which assembles a national pool of volunteers from its own state and local chapters and from professionals in other disciplines (planning, sociology, economics, political science, engineering), partly nurtured by crosslinks among their associations. AIA thus leveraged its multitier professional structure horizontally among other professions, as well as across geographical, jurisdictional, and civic association boundaries, to reduce the problem of capture by local authorities and enhance the degree of openness in urban regime and governance dynamics. To reduce costs to cities, maximize public good over private gain, and ensure that the public does not perceive them as hired guns for developers or city officials, team members receive no compensation other than travel expenses; they are also barred from accepting commissions from work resulting from their recommendations. As Joel Mills, senior director of the Center for Community Design at AIA, notes, recruiting volunteers has been surprisingly easy (aside from scheduling). Although team members "work like crazy and get no pay," they prize having the opportunity where "they don't have a client and can thus practice more purely. . . . And they are always learning from the interdisciplinary design." Of course, they can also put such prestigious service on their resumes, thus signaling and certifying high-level practice and trustworthiness. Mayors, city planning agencies, developers, and even grassroots advocacy groups and nonprofits that may have initiated contact with AIA are not viewed as clients. The team announces its normative stance at the beginning of the charrette as it commits to "serving the public interest," which tends to win over initial skeptics. Teams are politically astute and aware of the propensity among various actors to want to control process and outcome, if they can, and thus teams are ready to "navigate" troubled waters of power, inequality, and conflict.[27]

After receiving a request—now formalized as an application form that itself prompts serious reflection on goals, barriers, prior failures, local partners, and diverse stakeholders—the national AIA office puts out a call for volunteers to work as a team, which then prepares research for several months in advance, including one-on-one and group interviews and oral histories. Letters of support from neighborhood groups, civic associations, and educational institutions, as well as elected officials, public agencies, businesses, and the local (or state) AIA chapter, are prerequisites for the acceptance of an application. AIA provides up to $15,000 toward the cost of the process and requires a match of $5,000 from the community (for a service whose estimated average value is over $180,000). The team then visits the city or town over four intensive days of multistakeholder design charrettes. These are typically accompanied by two open town meetings of several hundred citizens, with participation by elected city officials, planning and design staff, and private developers.

The charrettes have a dual governance structure: public meetings are the responsibility of a citizens' steering committee while design workshops and reports are the joint responsibility of this committee and the visiting team. Central to the R/UDAT approach is utilizing citizens as resources —"local 'authorities' on almost every subject"—and providing a forum of open democratic exchange that could reveal the "treasure troves of local inputs and perceptions" while also providing the opportunity for citizens to learn from experts across disciplines. The latter ideally includes developers explaining how they put together financing for projects. The architects' drawings "were not hardline and prescriptive designs imposed 'from above,' but were tentative, exploratory, sensitive and uncertain, as though searching to uncover meanings." By the fourth day, the joint group produces a book, typically sixty to one hundred pages, for release at a news conference and further discussion at a second town meeting, with a presentation of key recommendations and drawings. The recommendations then proceed through established channels in each city, with strong normative force of the participatory process and further team visits, if needed, to help move the process along.[28]

By the mid-1980s, when a formal review was conducted by ten of the architects and planners who had served on multiple teams, some 572 volunteers from twenty-three professions had served as team members, many on repeat assignments, along with three hundred and sixty students from sixty-five schools of architecture; by its fiftieth anniversary, over one thousand professionals from forty disciplines had served. Such multidisciplinary design teams were later recommended in 1996 by President Bill Clinton's

Council on Sustainable Development, though without attribution. Today, community project reports and a formal guide are available on the AIA website as is normative recognition in the AIA's handbook of professional practice. Cities that have been in the forefront of sustainable design, such as Portland, Oregon, and Austin have often utilized a R/UDAT process for an important phase of their development. Many of the three hundred or so AIA state and local chapters provide volunteers for projects outside their immediate area. An increasing number of universities are providing courses or internships that supplement R/UDAT work. Team members testify to R/UDAT's impact on transforming their professional identities, which has helped spur AIA's conception of the "citizen architect" and its leadership institute's focus on professional leadership, civic engagement, and public policy, rooted in values of equity, human rights, sustainability, and economic opportunity. The AIA Resilience Network focuses on hazard mitigation, disaster assistance, and climate adaptation and resilience.[29]

Inclusive citizen participation remains a core value of R/UDAT and, drawing upon its lessons, local AIA chapters provide direct input into city sustainability and climate-planning efforts without charrette processes, often through their participation on steering committees and task teams (typically credited in the city's published planning documents). Thus, AIA as a professional association utilizes its chapter structure; its local capacity to coach, convene, and collaborate; and its centrally recruited volunteer teams in ways that cross-fertilize each other and leverage member and association capacities and networks. R/UDAT staff regularly meet in Washington, DC, with organizations such as the Urban Land Institute (ULI), the Mayors' Institute on City Design, and the EPA's Smart Growth office. They also meet at each other's conferences, thereby cultivating a learning network. Local projects often attract the support of foundations, as well as city departments, planning commissions, and federal agencies. AIA's Center for Communities by Design has also incorporated green building and healthy city frames. R/UDAT has further developed sustainability and resilience teams that work in collaboration with the Urban Sustainability Directors Network and the New England Municipal Sustainability Network.[30]

According to the center's longtime staff member and director Erin Simmons, the requests for assistance increasingly come from citizen groups and nonprofits, and not primarily from city staff. The team follows the vocabulary preferred by the community, avoiding terms such as *climate change* and *climate mitigation* if they appear too "nasty," even though the planning may nonetheless include these and related issues. In 2011, the Center for Communities by Design was named Organization of the Year by the International Association for Public Participation (IAP2), the most widely respected practitioner network of its kind. In the case of the Rockaways R/UDAT that was conducted in 2013 after Hurricane Sandy severely hit this South Queens neighborhood, team recommendations placed special emphasis on bringing greater coherence and collaboration to a civic sector that was at once impressive in activity yet cacophonous in voice—partly due to existing inequalities and neighborhood balkanization. Drawing upon experience from other cities, the team saw its role as helping the community design and build appropriate civic capacity for the long run, especially in situations where disaster and climate change may generate significant divisions on future rebuilding or prompt retreat from the shore.[31]

The American Institute of Architects, of course, works in other ways to enhance professional training and practice to enable sustainability and mitigate climate change, especially through its AIA+2030 Online and Professional Series Certificate Programs. Architecture 2030 is a separate nonprofit think tank, created in 2002 by Edward Mazria, which has focused on the radical reduction of greenhouse gas emissions from the built environment by the year 2030. Its goal is zero emissions by the middle of the century. It has spurred the development of 2030 Districts in nineteen cities, with 388 million square feet of commercial building space and some 960 member organizations. It licenses the online professional training series to AIA chapters and other organizations—some 30 percent of members have taken the series as of 2018—although AIA has its own educational portal for high-performance building. In 2006, AIA committed to the 2030 challenge, as have other green building, new urbanist, and smart growth organizations, and 40 percent of all architecture firms.

American Planning Association
Planning associations have also provided important norms and tools. Some of what have become core concepts in sustainable urban design have drawn from a longer history of utopian visions and systematic rethinking in the profession, such as the City Beautiful movement, while others have broken new ground that linked urban form and ecological function. Ian McHarg's *Design with Nature* (1969) proved especially generative in this

regard and helped to train many landscape architecture and planning students from his program at the University of Pennsylvania. His methods, which progressively permitted quantifying and visually displaying ecological values of hydrology, soils, vegetation, and other natural resources for land use suitability, became the basis for geographical information systems (GIS) and contributed significantly to environmental impact statements (EIS). Anne Whiston Spirn, Forster Ndubisi, Frederick Steiner, Douglas Farr, and others have broadened and deepened this approach to urban ecological design, landscape architecture, community ecology, and planning.[32]

The 1960s and 1970s witnessed considerable activism in the planning profession, manifest in the development of new organizations in major cities; the emergence of city-enacted, if organizationally conflicted, community planning systems; and new norms favoring participatory democracy. *The Death and Life of Great American Cities* by Jane Jacobs (1961), which emphasized vibrant street life in neighborhoods, influenced a generation of planners, as well as some mayors, such as Neil Goldschmidt in Portland, Oregon (see chapter 6), who were willing to innovate in participatory neighborhood governance. Some planners brought participatory norms directly from prior engagement in Students for a Democratic Society and a successor group called Movement for a Democratic Society. Others worked in the context of various federal programs, beginning with the Housing Act of 1949, which mandated city planning as a condition for funding, thereby establishing planners' leverage as gatekeepers to federal funding and increasing their influence within political power structures. In some cases, as with Community Action and Model Cities, participation was mandated by program design or was elicited by NEPA and SEPAs.[33]

In 1959, sociologist and urban planner Herbert Gans raised important criticisms of the discipline in the leading planning journal, and his collected essays are explicitly informed by the norm of "democracy in all spheres of life." His classic 1962 book, *The Urban Villagers*, established an important framework for empirical analysis of the impact of planning on class and ethnic subcultures. Other social scientists, practitioners, and planning academics developed concepts of "advocacy planning" and "equity planning." Under challenge in various cities against top-down and racially biased practices, the major professional societies such as the American Society of Planning Officials and the American Institute of Planners—which merged into the American Planning Association (APA) in 1978—began to lend support to communities. The Council of Planning Librarians published a substantial bibliography entitled "Citizen Participation in Planning," whose author would become, in subsequent years, an important voice in collaborative urban and environmental governance. Nonetheless, while citizen engagement in planning became increasingly normative, ecological functions, such as watersheds and natural hazards, remained poorly integrated into local planning practice in the 1970s. As we shall see with watershed planning in chapter 5, only in the 1980s when ecological models began to reveal affinity for multi-stakeholder policy designs were synergies taken to a new level of institutional development.[34]

Professional school curricula manifest genuine, if uneven, "learning from turbulence," as the number of planning programs and enrolled students expanded significantly and new students raised questions of equity and authority in their training and in their subsequent practice. Widely assigned textbooks began to progressively incorporate new norms. Articles in the *Journal of the American Institute of Planners*, the *Journal of the American Planning Association*, and other planning and related professional journals also reflected this shift, as did many subsequent planning guides on various aspects of urban sustainability such as urban river restoration. Engaging the public actively and through methods that progressively went beyond standard public hearing formats toward community visioning, multistakeholder collaboration, and design charrettes gradually became normative in the planning field.[35]

Some planning theorists, such as Judith Innes, provided well-elaborated justifications closely linked to theoretical debates in communicative ethics, deliberative democracy, and network governance. John Forester further enriched the understanding of planning practice by initially informing deliberative theory with Paolo Freire's "pedagogy of the oppressed" and John Gaventa's "power analysis," and then with the use of narrative to uncover the complexity of planners acting with stakeholders in pluralistic and conflictual settings and across multiple institutional logics, where generating trust is critical. As he recounted vividly his own teaching of several generations of planning students at Cornell University, he would take off his shoe in class and tell students that "your job is to figure out what it's like to be in the other's shoes. . . . This is what it's like to be an actor in the field."[36]

More direct attention to substantive issues of sustainability in urban planning emerged in the 1990s, thus interweaving democratic process and ecological content. The APA progressively generated further policy guidance, metrics, and best-practice standards, and then, in 2010, it convened a series of task forces beginning to learn from recent models and new pilots to systematically produce sustainability standards for the comprehensive (or general) plan. Enjoying legal authority in most urban jurisdictions, the comprehensive plan became the profession's archetype over the previous half century since 1964, when T. J. Kent first published *The Urban General Plan*. The point of departure in 2010 was that "planning for sustainability is the defining challenge of the 21st century." These new standards included (among others) "authentic participation," "livable built environment," "harmony with nature," "healthy community," and "interwoven equity" in housing, services, and environmental justice. Philip Berke, director of the Institute of Sustainable Communities at Texas A&M University and who joined the APA team with David Godschalk, recounted how the participatory sustainability model was becoming further embedded in recent years in APA practices, awards, standards, and staff support. He argues, however, that there is still much further to go on equity and environmental justice in the planning profession. The next big challenge, he says, will be for universities to produce a new generation of scientists—including hydrologists, civil engineers, and planners—who can produce information for use by ordinary people in their communities, including youth in inner cities, to enable "citizen science" through the full range of apps and data uploaded into the cloud.[37]

In 2011, Community Planning Assistance Teams, largely modeled on AIA's R/UDAT but without the resources to subsidize team travel, were relaunched after a leadership change at the American Institute of Certified Planners, a commission within the APA. Beginning in 1995, they built upon several experiments and have been coordinated by Ryan Scherzinger, whose activist identity was formed through antiracist community organizing in Louisville, Kentucky. Some state chapters (most ambitiously in California) have also developed models for community assistance. The APA has established a Sustainable Communities Division, which had over one thousand members by 2016. The major career guide for the planning field rests upon the core notion of enabling others through participation and consensus building to enhance sustainable cities, healthy communities, new urbanism, and climate planning. In the APA's comprehensive text *Planning and Urban Design Standards*, the second major chapter—following only the introductory synopsis of types of plans and preceding twenty-one other chapters—is now titled "Participation"; such norms and practices were once add-ons of secondary or tertiary importance.[38]

Strategic choices for building the knowledge base for participatory practice in the planning field have been generally wise and appropriate. As sociologist Lily Hoffman has argued, those radical planners whose engagement tended to undermine their own expert claims to knowledge led to their marginalization, even as the American Institute of Planners was quick to learn from the challenges of the late 1960s. To be sure, relatively robust community-planning models persisted in some seventy neighborhoods across New York City, with support from the Center for Community Planning at Hunter College. While some in the post-1960s decades were influenced by the radically participatory writings of social ecologist Murray Bookchin, who nurtured broad vision and identity formation, those who remained in planning tempered these with more complex multistakeholder processes, institutional designs, and data tools. Planning scholars and practitioners have adapted geographical information systems (GIS), visualization, and other information-rich tools to better enable lay publics in community settings to understand complex choices and alternative scenarios, thus further enhancing pragmatic democratic opportunities in the field. Urban informatics now makes possible a conception of the "urban commons" that is participatory, collaborative, and coproductive.[39]

Among the newer associations, established with some help from the more established ones, are the Congress for the New Urbanism (CNU), Smart Growth America, and the United States Green Building Council. AARP has also become active in place-based work and has increasingly collaborated with some of these organizations.

Congress for the New Urbanism

In 1993, six architects convened the CNU, which has held congresses every year since. The six included Peter Calthorpe, Andrés Duany, Elizabeth Moule, Elizabeth Plater-Zyberk, Stephanos Polyzoides, and Daniel Solomon. After his coauthored book on sustainable communities was published by the Sierra Club in 1986, Calthorpe had published another book, this time with the prestigious Princeton Architectural Press that helped further develop the frame of sustainable cities and new urbanism. The term *congress* was borrowed from the Congrès Internationaux d'Architecture Moderne (CIAM, 1928–1959), which was emulated for its capacity to transform the field and for its principles of open membership around agreement with a charter. However, CIAM's "functional city" design and planning model deteriorated into "zoned urban sprawl." Not all accept this delineation of the related fields of architectural design and city planning, or which factors (design, political, bureaucratic) might be most responsible for the decline of historical neighborhoods and the rise of sprawl. New urbanism has thus had to vigorously defend itself against prominent academic critics and alternative conceptions of "landscape urbanism."[40]

To be sure, as new urbanist planning theorist Emily Talen argues, there have been serious tensions among the main planning cultures of the past century in the United States, as well as failures within each, including those that have placed significant emphasis on community, ecology, self-governance, and regionalism. The core challenge, in her view, is to knit together valuable components of these planning traditions in pragmatic and pluralistic ways that are sensitive to context and place, and to work within realistic political and economic structures while also being alert to diversity and equity in a far more robust melding of vision and incremental strategy.[41]

In 1996, the Charter of the New Urbanism was fashioned at CNU's fourth congress and signed by 266 attendees. Its frame reprises themes in the emerging smart growth movement, as well as some of the broader community building, healthy communities, and other movements of the preceding years (see chapter 7). Its opening sentence conveys its broad reach and integrative intentions: "The Congress for the New Urbanism views disinvestment in central cities, increasing separation by race and income, environmental deterioration, loss of agricultural lands and wilderness, and the erosion of society's built heritage as one interrelated community building challenge." Central to its vision is the "restoration of existing urban centers and towns within coherent metropolitan regions." While design alone is hardly enough for such a big challenge, the design of dense, mixed-use, diverse (age, income, race), and walkable neighborhoods, with additional public transit and bicycle alternatives to the automobile, can encourage citizens to "take responsibility" for their blocks, local parks, community gardens, and watersheds. "We are committed to reestablishing the relationship between the art of building and the making of community, through citizen-based participatory planning and design." They are also committed to reinforcing the "culture of democracy" through civic buildings and public gathering places.[42]

At the annual congresses, these normative commitments to participatory design remain strong, including among many of the design firms making presentations. The National Charrette Institute, initially led by Bill Lennertz from the firm of Duany Plater-Zyberk, has refined charrette practice enormously over a thirty-year period among many of the key players in the CNU orbit; it is now housed at Michigan State University's School of Planning, Design, and Construction and is well embedded within Michigan Extension, the Michigan Municipal League, and many city planning processes. According to Andrés Duany, "Bill Lennertz effectively played the St. Paul role in spreading the charrette as a gospel of local democracy." NCI has refined charrette practice enormously, especially for large complex design and planning challenges, and it has developed tools, training, and certification in a way that builds capacity across the field and in conjunction with other professional associations, design firms, public agencies, and schools of architecture and planning. At its conferences, CNU combines participatory design with increasing attention to "just sustainabilities." This follows a strong commitment to "the just city," articulated in CNU's strategic plan and drawn from normative planning theorists such as Susan Fainstein. CNU's board chair, Michaele Pride, brings a long commitment to public engagement, social justice, and institutional collaboration, forged early on by her response to the civil unrest in Los Angeles, California, in the wake of the Rodney King police beating verdict in 1992; she helped found the Design Professionals Coalition to provide assistance in rebuilding.[43]

The second edition of the essays accompanying the charter in 2013 refines the frame after more than a decade of further experience—and criticism—in architectural design and urban and metropolitan planning, as well as through a conversation with still more expansive concerns of sustainability, ecology, and climate change. Recently, CNU has turned attention to problems of the suburbanization of poverty, housing affordability, healthy communities, and the threats and opportunities of self-driving vehicles. It has likewise begun to thematize especially-difficult issues of real estate and resilient communities in the face of climate change, coastal retreat, and receptor city accommodation. However, as executive director Lynn Richards puts it, its expansive framing remains in tension with its continued search to more precisely define its "specific niche and added-value . . . in a field that has become so crowded and filled with issues so broad."[44]

CNU is a nonprofit with twenty-eight thousand dues-paying members and nineteen state, regional, and local chapters that formed since 2004, largely through a "branding agreement" with the national office. It has had a budget of approximately $1.8 million over the past several years and a national staff of seven. After fashioning its charter, CNU has continued to cohere innovative architects and planners in local, state, and regional coalitions, and to refine practice while in dialogue with other leading smart growth and green building associations and firms that have completed thousands of projects across the United States and internationally. Its yearly congresses attract professional, nonprofit, and civic associations across the new urbanist and smart growth fields (Center for Neighborhood Technology, AARP Livable Communities, National Association of City Transportation Officials, Project for Public Spaces, and NRDC), along with many design, engineering, transportation planning, and real estate firms; public officials; and consultants in collaborative process, disaster response, and resilience. After some initial difficulty, new urbanism has also won adherents within schools of architecture, such as the University of Michigan's Taubman College and the University of Miami's School of Architecture, both of which have had favorable deans—Doug Kelbaugh and Elizabeth Plater-Zyberk—with long tenure. They have trained many students in new urbanism and collaborative charrette practice, as have an increasing number of schools of architecture.[45]

CNU recruited its current executive director Richards from the EPA's Office of Sustainable Communities. Along with HUD and USDOT, this office has provided support for new urbanist and smart growth policies and projects. Beginning in the early 1990s, HUD gave a huge boost to new urbanism with its HOPE VI public housing design, which was extended in Barack Obama's Choice Neighborhoods, with the intention of deconcentrating the poor out of large housing projects and enabling civic relationships in mixed-income communities. However, policy design and results have been contested.[46] CNU's executive director at the time of the initial publication of its charter in book form, Shelley Poticha, went on to lead the Partnership for Sustainable Communities under President Obama, and then established HUD's Office of Sustainable Housing and Communities; the three agencies provided several hundred million dollars in regional planning grants and other assistance over its first five years, leveraged in many cases through state programs and local partnerships. Senior staff, some of whom had worked together for years as part of various advocacy coalitions, held listening sessions around the country and incorporated the views of environmental organizations and those representing low-income neighborhoods who were fearful of new urbanism and smart growth that reinforced residential segregation. Building partly upon ISTEA's transportation planning mandates (see chapter 4), requirements for community engagement and multistakeholder visioning were strengthened as a result. As Karen Chapple argues, "The deep experience of many cities with sustainability planning" by the time of the Obama initiatives, as well as grant guidance by foundations with decades of experience in community development and social equity, enabled increasingly robust regional work, albeit with persistent obstacles due to limited funding and persistent bureaucratic silos.[47]

Cultivated by EPA's Community-Based Environmental Protection (CBEP) framing and strategy in its ten regions (see chapter 7), as well as through coalitions such as the Surface Transportation Policy Project (STPP), these networks of federal staff provided an indispensable anchor for building the associational field of new urbanism, as we shall also see with smart growth and urban watersheds.

Smart Growth America
Smart Growth America (SGA) was founded in 2000 as a coalition of organizations that provides leadership training, tool development, technical assistance, and policy advocacy. At the national level, key coalition partners include the APA, CNU, and NRDC, along with the Trust for Public Land (TPL, a major land trust organization) and the San Francisco Bay Area Greenbelt Alliance. But also involved is a widening circle of groups with emphasis on social justice and community development, such as Policy Link and the Local Initiatives Support Corporation (LISC). At the state and regional levels, SGA affiliates include 1000 Friends of Oregon, created in January 1975 to defend the state's land-use management act of 1973 (see chapter 6). It established "citizen involvement" as the first of nineteen planning goals to incorporate into local comprehensive plans. Other state groups imitate its "friends" nomenclature and structure (a core of regular small donors) in Florida, Iowa, Maryland, Wisconsin, and Pennsylvania (the latter with its "10,000 Friends"). New Jersey Future, which was founded in 1987, helped nurture smart growth policies under Governor Christine Todd Whitman (1994–2001), who then brought such commitments to her job as first EPA administrator under President George W. Bush, further energizing staff in the EPA's smart growth office—the latter rebranded and reorganized over a period of several decades with the sustainable communities office. At the local and regional level, smart growth

and new urbanism have represented overlapping approaches around which a sustainable communities discourse emerged.

SGA affiliates also include a range of other smart growth and transportation alliances, coalitions, and partnerships. This includes the Chesapeake Bay Foundation, a watershed advocacy and restoration group active across several states and Washington, DC, with a prominent role in the development of the watershed movement (see chapter 5) and a force behind Maryland's smart growth movement. Some states have multiple affiliates, though fully half have none. SGA's budget was close to $2 million in 2007, a modest amount relative to the range of projects it undertakes. These include the SGA Leadership Institute and the Governors' Institute on Community Design, both headed by Parris N. Glendenning, the former governor of Maryland (1995–2003) who led smart growth efforts in his state through two terms in office. He significantly shaped the broader movement in its early years, though the state was hardly alone or even the most consistently effective.[48]

The governor's team began to use the phrase "smart growth" during the spring and summer of 1996, at the very same point the EPA established the Smart Growth Network under the initiative of Harriet Tregoning and Geoffrey Anderson. Some groundwork had been prepared by President Clinton's Council on Sustainable Development, a federal advisory committee created by executive order in 1993 that included sustainable communities. The council included equity, stewardship, and a strong emphasis on civic engagement among its core goals. The latter was partly the product of the Reinventing Citizenship initiative among civic groups, academic centers, and Clinton's Domestic Policy Council. The Smart Growth Network was a partnership of government, civic, professional, and business organizations, and grew to include a range of affiliates (AIA, APA, ICMA, LISC, NRDC, CNT, CNU, ULI, and the American Society of Landscape Architects [ASLA]); various national land-trust associations; and several federal agencies, among others. Tregoning would become one of the founders of SGA in 2000, thus further leveraging federal support to build the associational field; under Obama, she served as director of HUD's Office of Sustainable Housing and Communities. Anderson, head of the smart growth office at the EPA, became the second executive director of SGA in 2008 and served for the next decade.[49]

SGA also initially hosted and now staffs the National Complete Streets Coalition, formed in 2005 to spread the complete streets movement. Based on earlier studies of livable streets, the complete streets frame focuses on safe, multimodal forms of transportation, with cycling, walking, and public transport options (in addition to autos and delivery trucks) that accommodate everyone, including seniors, people with disabilities, and children, especially going to and from school. As recounted by Barbara McCann, a key leader in the movement during its first decade who then went on to become director of policy development, strategic planning, and performance at USDOT under Obama, framing was a very deliberate exercise among smart growth leaders. It was inspired by academic framing studies and by the challenge of escaping an overly technical terminology that the bicycle movement was then utilizing in Congress. They selected "complete streets" because it had an inclusive simplicity that could appeal to many street users, potential national coalition partners, and prospective adopters at the local level. It could also highlight safety, which had broad public appeal and deep professional resonance among otherwise skeptical transportation engineers.

The coalition assembled a broad array of national civic associations in biking and walking (see chapter 4) as well as professional associations, such as the American Public Health Association, the Institute of Transportation Engineers, and the American Society of Landscape Architects (ASLA). From early on, AARP has been a donor and has served on the steering committee. A core group of major design and transportation firms has enlarged in recent years, even though some have dropped off the steering committee, which now accommodates participation in strategic direction without requesting visible support for specific advocacy campaigns that might be politically divisive among the constituencies with whom they work. For the National Association of Realtors (NAR), this has been an amenable structural feature as well. At its tenth anniversary in 2015, the coalition could report that one thousand communities had passed complete streets ordinances. The California Complete Streets Act of 2008—cosponsored by SGA, the California Bicycle Coalition, AARP, other professional associations (planners, landscape architects, transportation engineers), and civic groups (biking, walking, disability)—mandates the use of complete streets principles in the revision of city and county general plans. Several other states have followed suit.[50]

Executive director Emiko Atherton, whose identity as a civic and professional actor was forged in the fecund mix of neighborhood and transportation planning in Seattle and King County during the 1990s and early 2000s, is a staunch proponent of social and racial equity in smart growth. She sees her role as managing the strategic balance among interests and perspectives for the sake of building a robust field across many types of organizations operating with diverse institutional logics. Because transforming narrow professional practices and turf-laden agency cultures through champions on the inside has been a central goal, the complete streets movement has devoted research and workshops to the finer details of implementation through multidisciplinary and multiagency teams within city government as well as through multistakeholder processes involving the public, such as charrettes, and ongoing relationship building and information sharing among advocates, traffic engineers, and other staff. Indeed, changing the professional culture of construction engineers and the institutional logics of their work is recognized as a key, indeed inescapable, challenge.[51]

The National Association of City Transportation Officials (NACTO) has also become a partner in the complete streets coalition. NACTO emerged in 1995 as a coalition of city transportation departments to challenge the design standards of the dominant and predominantly rural highway builders of the American Association of State Highway and Transportation Officials (AASHTO), which represents state DOTs. As the number of member cities and transportation agencies has grown, and with it core staff (from three to twenty-three between 2012 to 2018), so has NACTO's commitment to engaging community-based organizations and bicycle associations in local planning and codevelopment of national guidelines on participation for cities across the country. It has published community-engagement guides that recommend hiring staff ("on-the-ground engagement teams") who can build relationships with lower-income, minority, and disabled communities traditionally marginalized by planning, and reducing financial barriers to using bike-sharing through various discounted public-benefit and service-program sign-ups. In 2013, the USDOT recognized NACTO's standards as legitimate options for bicycle and pedestrian "facility design flexibility." NACTO guides on urban street design, bikeways, transit design, and urban street stormwater are among the most attractive and user-friendly ones available. Because design manuals are among the most important tools at the local level, NACTO's guides provide legitimacy and usable templates, and in the case of smaller jurisdictions with limited staff and resources, they can sometimes serve as the official manual.[52]

AASHTO, in response, took nearly two more decades after NACTO was established to incorporate multimodal approaches into its strategic planning, although it published pedestrian and bicycle guides in the interim. In Atherton's estimate, for the complete streets movement, it remains to be seen whether or not AASHTO's recent revisions to the "Green Book"—viewed as an ironic term within the movement—will have significant traction among those three dozen or so laggard state DOTs. AASHTO's shift has been partly prompted by smart growth leadership coming from Maryland and other states, but it is clearly due to the threat posed by NACTO and other multimodal organizations. As its recent strategic plan notes of threats, "Other organizations with a more multi-modal focus may chip away at AASHTO's ability to represent all state DOTs." In 2017, AASHTO restructured its organization and added a Council on Active Transportation with a focus on biking, walking and other active modes within a multimodal network. While they have taken some time to play out, these competitive field dynamics promise much greater attention to sustainable transportation and community engagement, which NACTO has leveraged strategically as democratic legitimation.[53]

SGA also provides key staff support for other alliances and coalitions that fit specific policy niches or advocacy campaigns, including LOCUS, which is a network of real estate developers and investors who advocate for sustainable and walkable development. In 2006, the Growth Management Leadership Alliance, which had provided significant direction to the smart growth movement for nearly two decades, merged with SGA. Don Chen, SGA's founding executive director (2000–2008), had close ties to other strategic actors in the field, including NRDC, before his time at SGA; he subsequently moved to the Ford Foundation, where he directed its program in Just Cities and Regions, further incorporating social justice goals, policy designs, and local practices into the movement.[54]

AARP and Livable Communities

AARP and the National Association of Area Agencies on Aging are also partners in the National Complete Streets Coalition. In the context of active aging under conditions of extended lifespans and improved senior health and mobility of recent decades, unintended, long-arc policy feedback persists from the Social Security Act of 1935 and the Older Americans Act (OAA) of 1965. As noted in chapter 1, the Social Security Act has enhanced cognitive, motivational, time/income, and organizational capacities for civic engagement over many decades, and the 622 Area Agencies on Aging (AAAs, established in 1973 under OAA reauthorization) have provided an institutional basis to begin leveraging work on livable communities. While their institutional logic is primarily to coordinate, provide, and advocate for home and community-based services, 70 percent of AAAs now have Livable Communities projects, which are promoted by the National Association of Area Agencies on Aging—though the AAAs are not typically robust partners in local consortia.[55]

Established in 1958 and originally the American Association of Retired Persons, AARP has developed its own Livable Communities program, with tool kits, grants, annual conferences, and a national network of more than two hundred member communities committed to "age-friendly" planning and design. As part of an association with thirty-eight million members, Livable Communities is backed by AARP's robust capacity for advocacy at national, state, and local levels. It is also enabled by its propensity to collaborate with major professional associations such as the American Planning Association and the National League of Cities, both of which have chapter structures. AARP educates its members about a wide array of innovative models and partnerships across the field through its series of publications, called *Where We Live: Communities for All Ages*, and provides an ecumenical vocabulary and organizational map for situating and catalyzing such work.

While primarily a national advocacy and service organization, AARP has developed state chapters in all fifty states and local chapters in many cities, thus lending it some of the advantages of classic multitiered associations. Active and inclusive civic participation is a core goal for "age-friendly" planning for all age groups, and not simply for seniors, thus adding the design of built environments to participatory policy feedback dynamics—though, to be sure, these are still much weaker than its core incentives based on individualized benefits. This frame is one AARP has borrowed from the World Health Organization's Age-Friendly Cities and Communities Program, launched in 2006 as an extension of WHO's healthy community approach; AARP's Network of Age-Friendly Communities is an affiliate. Since so much of the funding for walkability and access, as well as de facto bike paths (via curb cuts), has come through requirements of the Americans with Disabilities Act (1990), with the far more stringent requirements and enforcement mechanisms of a civil rights act, the convergence of these various smart growth and complete streets movements has been further enhanced.[56]

As the director of AARP's Livable Communities program Danielle Arigoni notes, city chapters function as "neutral conveners and facilitators" when they develop "local consortia." These might include neighborhood associations, disabled veterans' groups, local realtors, bicycle associations, universities, and many other organizations assembled in different configurations, depending on the specific community. Public health advocates and agencies, concerned with the epidemic of obesity and diabetes, have been major supporters of complete streets policies at the local, state, and federal levels. Some state AARP directors are more supportive of local Livable Communities work than others, depending partly on their own policy emphasis. A state director focused on fraud scams against seniors (in the AARP Fraud Watch Network) might not assign as much importance to Livable Communities as another state director with a background as a mayor or as a business leader working through the local chamber of commerce. Leaders and volunteers in Livable Communities are fundamentally "relational" in their approach since they bring together various kinds of associations and seek collaboration with local DOTs and other agencies. Local campaigns can produce great success, yet they can sometimes be risky for the organization. As Arigoni noted, in 2016, AARP went "in whole hog" for Measure M in Los Angeles County to fund major public transit improvements, as well as pedestrian and bike connections and local street improvements (in addition to highways). It proved a resounding success with 71.5 percent of the vote. But other campaigns might fail. Indeed, they might even lead to some backlash against AARP, which depends on broad nonpartisan support from seniors across the country. It can become vulnerable to member dissent and threatened exit to competing organizations during contentious policy battles, as happened during the Clinton health reform.[57]

Within the organization, there is also some risk, since most offices and staff at headquarters have a focus on "selling [AARP] products," not engaging communities in place-based design. Arigoni, to be sure, was recruited because of her place-based background—first as a planner and then as senior staff at the EPA's Office of Smart Growth, and then at HUD, where she helped lead various initiatives on sustainable communities, affordable housing, and climate preparedness and resilience. After Hurricane Katrina in 2005, and especially after Hurricane Sandy in 2012, funding at HUD for disaster-resilience planning, primarily through the Community Development Block Grant Disaster Recovery Program, increased substantially. Arigoni also worked across agencies in the Urban Waters Federal Partnership, the tri-agency Partnership for Sustainable Communities (EPA, HUD, and USDOT) and in Obama's White House Council on Climate Preparedness and Resilience. AARP has thus been able to enrich its place-based work due to its capacity for network learning among an array of smart growth and sustainable city actors in long-established professional associations and newer associations, as well as through federal staff in offices that have developed policy designs to foster community-based work through funding, coproducing tools, and convening some of these very same networks and their local partners. The EPA model for this—which for aging and smart growth stresses continued engagement in communities, service on nonprofit boards and commissions, intergenerational interaction, and the design of retirement communities as part of neighborhood planning, as in the Northgate neighborhood in Seattle—thus has broader relevance, as we shall see in chapters 5 and 7.[58]

US Green Building Council

The US Green Building Council (USGBC) has been another key intermediary in the sustainable cities field, focused specifically on developing a system of voluntary standards for buildings and certification for professionals, known as Leadership in Environment and Energy Design (LEED). USGBC was founded as an unusual multisector and multistakeholder nonprofit in April 1993 by David Gottfried, Mike Italiano, and Rick Fedrizzi, with some sixty private firms from the dozen or so sectors within the building industry. Also included were several environmental organizations: NRDC, Audubon, and the Rocky Mountain Institute, the latter founded in 1982 with an emphasis on market-based and soft-energy paths. Lending assistance were also several professional associations that had already developed a commitment to the environment and to participatory planning. Among the latter was AIA, which hosted the founding meeting of USGBC and designated its recent student organization president Lynn Simon a key staff person and then board member. AIA had held the brainstorming luncheon session on sustainability at its annual 1992 conference in Boston, which helped profoundly transform the professional identity of young real estate developer Gottfried. His core autobiographical and field metaphor was transition from "greed to green."[59]

Italiano, who had some building experience through his work as a Superfund lawyer, drew upon the American Society for Testing and Materials (now ASTM International), founded in 1898. ASTM was central to the development of industrial engineering standards and steel and concrete quality testing throughout the twentieth century and was thus quite typical of a broad range of standard-setting organizations. However, in response to the movements and regulations from the 1960s onward, it also engaged in developing consumer products safety, occupational health and safety, and environmental standards. Indeed, ASTM's official history refers to new partnerships with such advocacy groups, open to their formal participation with ASTM financial support (if needed), which paralleled normative debates for financing public participation at the federal level. ASTM also heralds its own consensus-building method, dating back to its 1908 prescription for technical committees, as the "genius" of the organization.[60]

Along with Italiano, Gottfried began attending AIA's committee on the environment, and then became chair of ASTM's green building subcommittee, thus further leveraging professional association expertise, networks, legitimacy, and normative commitments. The two men also sought to leverage networks and social learning on energy efficiency and industrial ecology. Such learning was a response to federal regulations in various fields as well as to sustainability practices and organizational cultures that had begun to develop within several industry sectors, other professional associations, within several offices at EPA and the US Department of Energy, and among corporate environmental managers. One thousand such managers were members of the ASTM environmental assessment and risk management committee. Normative commitments among those who served on these various committees did not preclude periodic USGBC board disputes to adjudicate and adjust the balance between market metrics, technical requirements, and core values. Affiliated environmental groups (NRDC, EDF, Audubon) and their membership networks also reinforced environmental norms. David Brower, first executive director of the Sierra Club and founder of several other environmental organizations, became a personal mentor to Gottfried in the later years of his life. These groups quickly signaled commitment to their memberships, to other environmental organizations, and to the emergent green building and sustainable cities fields by commissioning their own green building projects, if they had not already done so. Such normative expectations soon spread to other nonprofits, often driven by donor networks.[61]

USGBC lists as the first of its strategic goals to "catalyze and lead the building sector's active participation in the movement to achieve sustainable cities and communities." It has continued to build its capacity by affiliating some twelve thousand member companies and certifying over two hundred thousand LEED-APs (accredited professionals), along with developing some seventy-six regional chapters (as of 2015). The latter are engaged in working across professional boundaries and working with civic groups and public agencies at the local and state level, where most networking, education, public forums, and increased advocacy for mandatory standards occurs. Its board, which contains members from many building-industry sectors, has become increasingly more inclusive of those from the fields of public health, education, urban planning, and environmental justice. To signal fair treatment of all building projects and thus ensure further legitimacy across the field, a separately incorporated nonprofit was established in 2008, the Green Building Certification Institute, which manages registration and certification through LEED-Online. USGBC's 2012 to 2014 annual budgets of $64 to $76 million were drawn overwhelmingly from its building registration (intent) and certification (final product) fees, professional accreditation, workshop, and other education fees, and from its annual Greenbuild International Conference and Expo attended by some twenty-five thousand professionals and nine hundred exhibiting companies. Member dues accounted for approximately 15 percent of the total.[62]

LEED rating is based upon a system of prerequisites and credits grouped under core categories such as water efficiency and energy and atmosphere. These expanded from an initial five categories (in the first formal 2000 version) to twelve in version 3, so that credits can be earned for awareness and education (in homes) and neighborhood design, both of which directly reward a civic feature (individual/family education and neighborhood/community engagement). Buildings can earn status as Certified, Silver, Gold, or Platinum on a 110-point scale, with an increasing number of specific LEED products tailored to different market segments. USGBC considers its LEED rating system "voluntary, consensus-based, and market driven." While this characterization draws upon the ASTM legacy noted previously, it has accommodated the highly decentralized structure of the building industry in which temporary organizations of owners (private, public, nonprofit), as well as architects, consultants, engineers, and contractors among various trades, form to design and complete particular projects, then reconfigure themselves for other projects, with particular attention to value-added and reputational heuristics. Key field actors have worked toward "appropriate fit" among various institutional logics.[63]

This structurally constrained strategic choice for field building by USGBC was reinforced by its environmental organization networks open to market-based solutions, though never exclusively so and never precluding pressures within the organization and its chapters to press for green building mandates at the local, state, and federal levels. Even though USGBC has moved further toward advocacy for green building policies and codes at all levels of the federal system, it nonetheless maintains its consensus-based identity, indeed refining it quite meticulously through organizational governance processes that seek to enhance the "quality and integrity of the LEED brand"—hence, legitimacy within the industry more broadly. Any substantive revision in the prerequisites and credits can only occur through "a process based on principles of transparency, openness, and inclusiveness." Proposals are vetted through a public comment form or Pilot Credit Library process, with specified periods for review, further comment, refinement by a balanced multistakeholder consensus body (if needed), and a democratic membership vote based proportionally upon individual votes within each USGBC member organization. An appeals process (on procedural grounds) is also available. Any member of the public who creates a free site-user account can also review and comment on the draft.[64]

Consensus-based multistakeholder processes can also emerge at the building site or the school district, or it can spill over into other nonprofit sustainability projects not directly related to building. School building comprises a very large market in the construction industry. In the Poudre School District of Fort Collins, Colorado, the fourth largest city in the state with some twenty-seven thousand students in more than fifty buildings in the late 1990s, initial attempts to institutionalize green building and get bond approval from voters (required for capital projects) had limited success until the operations department facilitated a process of "inclusive visioning" in 1999. This permitted skeptical voices, including those of self-declared climate skeptics, to have a seat at the table in fashioning a vision of "high performance buildings." This vision encompassed a range of goals for fiscally responsible energy savings and improved learning and working environments while enabling a systematic process of "relationship building" (led by district operations staff). This generated trust, respect, and mutual accountability across professional categories (architects, engineers, teachers), blue- and pink-collar trades and staff (plumbers, custodians, HVAC, kitchen), as well as across potential political divisions among school board members and the broader public, including parents of school-age children. The collaborative process reduced the risk to administrators when making bold choices. In this "flat-team" approach, "everybody's job is important" and staff are "empowered" to contribute knowledge and help drive change, as Michele Meyer and her colleagues, including Bill Franzen, district operations supervisor at the time, argued.[65]

Over the next six years, the district generated wide external recognition and legitimacy with awards from USGBC, the American Association of School Administrators, the Council of Educational Facilities Planners International, the American Council of Engineering Companies of Colorado, and the EPA, among others. As this recognition secured additional local legitimacy among voters and elected officials, the district could proceed to develop a more ambitious "sustainability management system" (SMS) in 2006, with an explicit goal of stewardship and an ethic of sustainability in all its practices within new and older buildings as well as in transportation (bus, bike, walk) to and from school. Cultivating student awareness of energy use and water conservation became an explicit goal of design, operations, and curriculum, although there are some clear differences among schools, from which policy learning has proceeded systematically.

Student learning on sustainability has led to still other partnerships—for instance, with the Colorado Alliance for Environmental Education, a professional nonprofit association and an affiliate of the North American Environmental Education Association (NAAEE). The district's cable TV station airs shows on sustainability, including one in which students analyze climate data in the context of school building energy use. The expanded district team, still comprising multiple professions and trades, has also come to include city and state government agencies and state university centers on climate and sustainability—with the intent to partner with still more community groups in citywide sustainability leadership. The SMS process was initially facilitated by the Brendle Group, a for-profit consulting firm in Fort Collins with experience in green building and staff networks to APA sustainability committees, ICLEI USA, and the Colorado Clean Energy Cluster, a nonprofit economic development organization.[66]

The visioning process introduced in the Poudre School District reveals the significant potential for synergies among professional collaboration; workplace democracy across blue-, pink-, and white-collar lines; direct democracy in bond approval; and partnerships among various public agencies, nonprofit associations, and for-profit firms. These operated within the standard model of representative democracy in council, mayoral, and school board elections. Skilled field actors in the local arena combined and leveraged this mix of democratic institutional, relational, and deliberative practices in ways that were distinctively creative—indeed intentionally "systemic," as in the normative-analytic approach of political theorist Jane Mansbridge and her colleagues.[67]

The USGBC took LEED a step further with the formal release of LEED for Neighborhood Development (LEED-ND) in 2010, refined further in later iterations and in a recent LEED for Cities and Communities initiative. LEED-ND uses rating systems in an integrative fashion for entire neighborhoods and across a variety of sectors (housing and business building design and location, transportation, open space, ecological functions, green infrastructure, community gardens, food access), thus serving as a broad approach to neighborhood sustainability and environmentally sound land development. Among its core goals are the community's own "sense making" of meaningful places; hence, citizen engagement in the planning and everyday maintenance process, as well as walkability and bikability, diverse housing types, and multiple levels of affordability—the latter serving equity and social justice. Civic spaces (community centers, libraries, schools, places of worship, and civic buildings) are central and earn key credits in the overall rating.[68]

With Raimi+Associates, a for-profit consulting firm with staff experience in new urbanism, healthy communities, and comprehensive and participatory planning, NRDC developed *A Citizen's Guide to LEED for Neighborhood Development*. It did so in collaboration with the Congress for the New Urbanism and USGBC, and an array of other national, regional, and local groups (Smart Growth America, Greenbelt Alliance, 1000 Friends of Minnesota, Defenders of Wildlife, Cumberland Region Tomorrow), lending it broad legitimacy in the smart growth movement. Matthew Raimi had also worked on piloting LEED-ND and Building Blocks for Sustainable Communities with EPA's technical assistance team. The citizen's guide translates rigorous and complex standards that can claim professional legitimacy and impartial weighting, into everyday language for use by local neighborhood and community groups to enable them to better decide whether to oppose or support a development project over a typically three-stage process (conditional approval, precertified, and final certification at completion). It also provides tools for developing "long-term working relationships with developers and other stakeholders," should they so choose. LEED-ND can likewise serve as a tool for formalized neighborhood planning, where standards of accountability, inclusivity, and relational work across stakeholder boundaries are strong, as in Seattle, which was the first city (in 2000) to develop LEED standards as a policy for public construction by one of the leaders of the green building movement, Lucia Athens. The city has since developed one of the fifteen high-performance downtown districts in the country, in conjunction with AIA, Architecture 2030 (a separate nonprofit founded in 2006), and other partners.[69]

Indeed, having the LEED-ND tool for citizen groups incentivizes cities to be more systemic in their neighborhood planning and design criteria; it promises to enhance and diffuse civic knowledge and lower transaction costs for planning agencies, private firms, and citizen groups themselves, who can utilize the detailed checklist provided in the guide—its "'crib sheet' for every LEED-ND credit and prerequisite"—while also sparking "the creativity and expertise of citizens and advocates." Here the guide is clearly recognizing that community groups—whose number and density tend to correlate with the spread of green building practices among cities—prize local knowledge and autonomous input, even if the tool provides them with technical expertise that has been refined through practical experience and collaborative work across professional boundaries. Citizens can also use the criteria to audit comprehensive plans and zoning codes. Soon after LEED-ND was first published, HUD lent it further legitimacy by including its location criteria in various grant applications, including its Sustainable Communities Regional Planning Grants.[70]

In addition to coproducing a similar guide for local officials—which serves as a map of organizations across the field, with relevant resources, authority, and partnering opportunities—USGBC collaborated in 2012 with ICLEI USA, the Urban Sustainability Directors Network, the National League of Cities, and the Center for American Progress to develop a complementary consensus-based rating system: the STAR Community Index. This includes a considerably broader range of goals, objectives, and measures (community health, quality jobs and living wages, emergency prevention and response). These core partners were joined on the steering committee by many innovators from cities and counties, several federal agencies, and other professional associations, most notably APA and ICMA. Among the various paths that communities take, this guide recognizes the first as "democratic commitment to local sustainability" and includes measures of civic engagement, partnerships, and collaboration. Building upon this STAR Community Index, USGBC has also begun training and certifying whole cities—such as San Jose, California, and Hoboken, New Jersey—in using its Arc SKORU performance platform to enable LEED for Cities and Communities to integrate green building, watershed strategies, healthy community plans, and resilience and climate action plans into comprehensive planning. It also includes values and metrics for affordable housing and environmental justice. Integrative framing of sustainable cities, as I discuss further in chapter 7, enables and is enabled by such platforms.[71]

Nonetheless, some within the green building movement argue that certifications by USGBC have slowed considerably since its big growth period in 2005 to 2009. Jerry Yudelson, who has considerable experience writing and consulting in the field, presents the most sustained and critical diagnosis from within the movement also shared by some others. In his view, USGBC and LEED, despite enormous successes in shaping the field, have hit a wall due to several factors. First, the inclusion of environmental groups on the board, while critical for early legitimacy, has left a legacy of idealism that tends to trump market realism, especially in those sectors where smaller and non-elite builders cannot afford the delays, cumbersome procedures, and high costs of certification relative to the value they receive. Second, the tendency to add ever-more categories to LEED, while desirable in many ways, tends to distract from the most pressing needs to lower overall carbon emissions far more quickly than green building has been able to do. Category inflation makes the process too rigid and bureaucratic, driven by the new army of certifiers, and fails to respond adequately to customer experience. Third, there are various exit options, including registering but not completing LEED certification, not registering at all but still designing to LEED specifications, or utilizing competing certification systems now offered by other professional or industry associations.

Solutions to these challenges, according to Yudelson, lie in paring down the number of categories to focus on carbon emissions, water usage, and waste. Critical will be to utilize the full panoply of internet-enabled cloud, mobile devices, apps, transparency, and big data tools to streamline the process and make it less costly. This would attract market actors, building portfolio managers, home owners, and the other sectors (education, health care) that, despite some notable innovations, experience significant barriers. Here, Yudelson's argument parallels more general ones, such as those of Beth Noveck about the need to wed such information technologies to broader engagement in creating public value.[72]

In his comparative study of thirty-five voluntary programs for green building and low carbon cities in six countries, including the USGBC and several other US initiatives, Jeroen van der Heijden also sees significant weaknesses in producing sufficient impact yet also a pathway forward. The core structural feature of the building field is "a very, very long tail without a head"; that is, hundreds of millions of small voluntary improvements that are possible in hundreds of millions of commercial and residential buildings with many millions of property owners and builders (the tail) but for whom there exists no highly concentrated group of high emitters (the head) whose behavioral change can shift the rest. The field thus generates "leadership delusion," with strong incentives to present a narrative of more successful performance than demonstrably exists. If we factor into this analysis those real-estate field dynamics driven by financialization, which can generate speculative boom, construction debris, and suboptimal energy usage overall, the picture becomes even murkier. Nonetheless, according to van der Heijden, these voluntary green building programs and diffusion networks serve as a kind of research-and-development mechanism, with significant capacity for legitimating mandatory programs among field leaders, or hybrid ones that combine and sequence voluntary and mandatory approaches to achieve greater impact at a much quicker pace. A "rolling rule regime" might transform leading practice into baseline mandatory standards after a fixed period, say five to ten years, while still incentivizing early adopters in the market. New York City's recent Climate Mobilization Act prescribes benchmarks and fines to guide massive building retrofits and the scaling up of the retrofit industry.[73]

Conclusion

During the initial postwar settlement in the broader environmental field in the 1970s, the field of sustainable cities began to craft a distinct identity. As argued in chapter 2 and in this chapter, it was in some ways already on civic and professional association agendas in prior decades, focusing on issues such as clean water, clean air, and open space, all of which had place-based parameters of one sort or another. The intense land-use and other urban conflicts of the 1960s and 1970s, which were manifest in a variety of sometimes-competing but often complementary associational forms—Model Cities, neighborhood associations, community development corporations, and open space councils—and some participatory policy feedback loops further reinforced these dynamics, as did normative shifts and practical tool kits. Policy feedback through the Task Force on Land Use and Urban Growth, a product of the Citizens Advisory Committee on Environmental Quality that was established through NEPA and CEQ with White House support, registered the civic and professional groundswell for greater democratic and institutional capacities. While the National Land Use Policy Act ultimately failed due to changed political calculations, real estate industry and grassroots property rights opposition, and still incoherent coalitions among urban and environmental actors in the field, efforts to enhance citizen engagement continued and were further reinforced by shifts in regulatory and legal fields in many cities and states, as well as through some federal land-use programs. By the early 1980s, "sustainable cities" was being fashioned as a distinct frame, substantially different though skillfully aligned with the command-and-control tools of the environmental field settlement, as would happen in other arenas where spatial dynamics and ecosystem functions would further come to the fore.

Civic organizing became gradually more effective at least partly because it met with receptiveness within some established professional associations, such as the American Institute of Architects and the American Planning Association, and because these helped enhance further capacity building through distinctively branded new associations, such as the Congress for the New Urbanism, Smart Growth America, and the US Green Building Council. Several of the multitiered civic and environmental associations (Sierra Club, Audubon), as well as nonchapter-based professionalized environmental groups (NRDC, Rocky Mountain Institute), also served as important field actors in building institutional relationships; developing tool kits for citizens and public officials; and enhancing normative purpose in a field with diverse civic, professional, market, and bureaucratic logics. Skilled strategic actors among these various associations, public agencies, and private firms have become increasingly persistent in attempting to align their various logics. Each of these organizations has grappled in creative, if incomplete, ways with developing crossties among each other and with many other associations and institutions that have come to define the field as well as through emergent conflicts and framing challenges that manifest themselves in terms of environmental justice, healthy cities, food justice, restored rivers, and eventually disaster resilience and climate action planning, as we shall see in the following chapters.

CHAPTER FOUR

Biking, Walking, and Farming in Cities

This chapter examines several important components of the larger field of sustainable cities. The first two—biking and walking—are directly related, since claims for greater and safer road space for bicycles led to coalitions with less visible groups concerned with walking safely in urban neighborhoods. The major federal policy design that emerged in the early 1990s tied the two sets of issues together, with substantial policy feedback. Urban farming proceeds largely on a separate track, with more difficult spatial trade-offs and fewer positive feedback effects, though all three have come to use the framing of sustainable cities in one way or another.

The bicycle movement, which began relatively early yet went through long periods of quiescence and ineffectiveness, became a key player in both local politics and at the national level in the 1990s. In this section, I first examine dynamics at the local level, especially in the shift from militant Critical Mass protests to more institutionalized forms of democratic negotiation, as city governments provided openings for civic collaboration and bicycle associations made strategic choices to broaden their movement, expand their membership bases, and form coalitions with pedestrian and other groups to work on street design and cultural norms, including "rights to the city" by nonautomotive actors. At the national level, the legacy of an organization wedded to the elite of high-performance club cyclists resulted in cultural and legal strategies that hampered the broadening of the movement. However, as local associations had begun to find ways to work within the norms of urban democratic governance, as federal policy design provided new participatory incentives and mandates, and as new national organizations emerged as competitors, the shape of national biking and pedestrian advocacy shifted significantly to grow the field. The Intermodal Surface Transportation Efficiency Act (ISTEA; pronounced "ice tea") of 1991, and its successor acts, provided funding, required state pedestrian and bicycle coordinators, and mandated public participation at all key points in transportation planning. Significant participatory policy feedback became part of field dynamics thereafter.

Urban agriculture emerged in its most recent phase from the social movements of the 1960s and 1970s, and especially those movements broadly focused on organic food and sustainable agriculture. While food movements of recent years are quite variegated in organizational form and frame, and display clear tensions between movement and institution, here I focus on three overlapping innovations: citywide community gardening systems, food justice strategies, and food policy councils. I also examine some of the federal policies that have supported community-based approaches and compare these to ISTEA. For various reasons, policy design in urban agriculture has had considerably less participatory feedback and field building effects than has ISTEA in urban transportation.

The Bicycle Movement

In recent decades, the bicycle movement has been important at virtually all levels of civic action for livable and sustainable communities. Its roots go back to the late nineteenth century, when the League of American Wheelmen was founded, and especially to American Youth Hostels in subsequent decades. But the movement had become largely dormant as the automobile gained supremacy in market production, federal highway policy, consumer culture, traffic engineering practice, and legal liability standards. Local bicycle clubs and coalitions, however, began to spring up in major cities from the early 1970s onward due to technological changes (ten-speed gear shifts), baby boomers coming into early adulthood, and the participatory civic and political culture change that prompted expanded claims for bicycle rights in sharing the roads. The countercultural "small is beautiful" ethos of E. F. Schumacher and other theorists such as Jane Jacobs and Ivan Illich, who stressed slower movement on streets that could nurture civic relationships, also played an important role, as did local bike shops, small collectives, and community cycling centers with face-to-face norms of mutual aid, appropriate technology, and democratic participation. The oil shocks of 1973 and 1979 provided further economic and national security rationales as well as some federal spending in the highway act of 1973, though states could also use this funding option for roads. Framing contests within the movement, however, deferred political opportunities for two more decades, as we shall see.[1]

Exceptional Early Adopter: Davis, California

Beginning in the 1960s, Davis provided an early model because of its unusual circumstances. As a university town whose agricultural annex (to UC Berkeley) had recently been converted into a full-fledged University of California campus, physical expansion proved opportune for a bike-loving chancellor to ask its architects to plan for bike paths winding through the sprawling campus. Faculty and graduate students, some of whom had recently spent time in the Netherlands, one of the global leaders in bicycle travel, experimented with street design in collaboration with the city's public works director. New students were urged to bring their bikes to school and, within a few years, a bicycle coalition, bolstered by environmentalists in the community, had gotten the city council to expand bicycle paths to city streets, though with a good deal of slippage as the city itself changed in the following decades. Other cities had considerably more difficulty than this, sometimes facing more contentious politics and at other times experiencing extended interludes. In most cases, they developed action repertoires and frames that expanded public support and forged more effective political coalitions, and they learned to work collaboratively with city agencies to transform professional practices and metrics.[2]

Strategic Choices in Building Local Fields: From Confrontation to Collaboration in San Francisco and Other Cities

San Francisco provides a case in point. In 1971, neighborhood and environmental activists, along with bicycle enthusiasts, organized the San Francisco Bicycle Coalition (SFBC). They succeeded in quickly getting bicycles into the transportation master plan, and getting bike access to the Golden Gate Bridge and the Bay Area Rapid Transit (BART) system by 1975. But, as in most cities, utilitarian cycling (to work, shop, school) lagged after the bike boom of the early 1970s, though some progress was made within public agencies. Then, SFBC sponsored an event in September 1992, initially called Commute Clot but soon renamed Critical Mass, in which riders militantly "clogged" the avenues and "corked" the traffic from cross streets to assert their claims to space and their "right to the city." Critical Mass rides were soon scheduled for the last Friday of every month and grew from several dozen to several hundred and, on some occasions, even more. The first event was partly inspired by the radical tactics of Earth First!, which was actively spiking trees in Northern California protests against redwood logging and by protests against the Gulf War, in which some four hundred bicyclists disrupted traffic to the Bay Bridge for two hours. While Critical Mass retained a protest edge with a quasi-anarchist leadership ethos and sometimes clashed with the police as it spread to other cities, it evolved largely into "bicycle's defiant celebration," providing cultural resources and identity formation within a quite diverse and imaginative movement, while also providing some "radical flank effects" that helped publicize cycling's claims to space. Chris Carlsson could sustain the radicalism of Critical Mass in San Francisco from his paid organizational position as newspaper editor of the International Longshore and Warehouse Union, a union strategically though quite unusually privileged in the global chain of trade to be able to maintain its own longstanding militant practices and principled solidarities.[3]

Bicycle activists in San Francisco, however, soon concluded that they had to address how to generate broad democratic legitimacy and accountability for urban governance among multiple constituencies vying over relative spatial scarcities, physical risks, and transportation asymmetries deeply embedded in culture and systems that manifested in the sunk costs in vehicle ownership, insurance policy, garage space, and home location. Like many local bicycle associations over the years, they had to reconstruct the street as commons or a common-pool resource. SFBC thus increasingly distanced itself from Critical Mass as part of its strategic choice to build the local field further. Several factors were most prominent in this choice.[4]

First, Mayor Willie Brown (1996–2004), after a sharp and escalating confrontation with a Critical Mass ride in 1997, opened the doors of democratic opportunity by asking SFBC for a list of priority bike projects, by sponsoring public hearings citywide, and by directing agency staff to work collaboratively with SFBC. Second, SFBC responded to the opportunity to expand its public support and grow its membership by incorporating broader themes of public health, safe cycling for families and children, and other components of complete streets and healthy community frames. Indeed, cyclists in leadership were growing older and having families, thus lessening the relative civic allure of confrontation in the streets by young and fit (and mostly male) cyclists with drivers and police. SFBC's expanded frame came to stress rights *and* responsibilities, and therefore it focused a great deal of attention on educating adult bikers and children as well as car, taxi, and bus drivers on safe practices and proper etiquette—now included in "a rules of the road" safety video on the city website—while not relaxing focus on police injustices in bicycle and pedestrian cases.

Rights to the city were negotiated and reframed and not simply valorized as the radical claims of the excluded. These shifts were also intended to defuse some of the backlash—fueled by talk radio—that had begun to build in outer neighborhoods and nearby suburbs as well as among drivers more generally who resented the loss of car lanes and lane width in favor of bike lanes. The Coalition of San Francisco Neighborhoods (on the west side) became part of this opposition, thus pitting one civic form for livable neighborhoods against another, with the result of an injunction against further bike space for almost five years. Third, because metrics favoring rapid automobility were woven into the "levels of service" standards that had become widespread in the United States over previous decades, SFBC began to research alternate multimodal metrics to adjust the meaning of service to biking, walking, and buses on shared and safe streets.[5]

These strategic choices have enabled SFBC to grow its dues-paying membership to over ten thousand, with a full-time staff of sixteen and a budget of $2.4 million. It also strengthened its advocacy capacities. Bicycle ridership in San Francisco has increased significantly across the city since 2007, most notably on those streets that have completed projects. Public support has grown, and with it funding from the city for projects and infrastructure. SFBC has also expanded its donor base significantly, mostly in the form of small and medium-sized contributions from individuals and small businesses. It has modest support from some of the larger firms whose workforce transportation preferences and financial interests are well aligned with bicycle mobility and new urbanism. It has hired community organizers, some bilingual, to garner support with neighborhoods, ethnic groups, local merchants, families, and schools for bond issues and providing design input for specific bicycle lane and trail projects. Staff and volunteers have also done extensive one-on-one relational work with staff at the municipal transportation agency, as well as with the planning, health, and environmental departments, to build trust and to ensure effective knowledge sharing and smooth implementation.[6]

SFBC draws ecumenically from several Alinskyite organizing traditions, as well as from the US Public Interest Research Groups (PIRGs), and is forming a leadership academy for its members to balance SFBC staff expertise—indispensable for highly technical transportation planning and implementation—with further grassroots capacity. Combining the two is indeed seen by its leadership as a "big existential question." Over the previous two decades, SFBC has also become well-linked to civic associations such as the Alliance for Biking and Walking, the League of American Bicyclists, the Bay Area Open Space Council, the San Francisco League of Conservation Voters, the Sierra Club, and SPUR, a good government and regional-planning group central to San Francisco governing coalitions for more than a half century (see chapter 6). In 2018, with staff support from the National Association of City Transportation Officials (NACTO), six major California cities joined San Francisco in a statewide California City Transportation Initiative.[7]

Brian Wiedenmeier, a decade-long SFBC member who became executive director in 2016, brings state PIRG experience as a young organizer and a master's degree in public administration. The latter stressed concepts such as civil society and network governance that have remained critical to his thinking. Today, this is not an uncommon occurrence among staff within local civic associations and public agencies, including his own staff and some of their partners, testifying to how academic training in certain fields shapes framing and strategizing. Wiedenmeier works collaboratively with major business associations to pass such measures as the recent $150 million bike and pedestrian bridge projects. Yet he is a critic of those high-tech firms that proffer a dystopian vision of autonomous vehicles that fails to understand that "civic space is key" and that "mobility plays a central role in democracy."[8]

In the past several years, SFBC has also incorporated transportation justice into its framing, advocacy, and problem-solving practices. SFBC began to work with racial justice groups, especially for black bikers most at risk of being cited for minor violations by the police that might then escalate into violent confrontation. In one major public dispute over the lack of bicycle, pedestrian, and child safety beneath the tangle of freeway arteries known as "the Hairball," where many of the homeless camp due to the city's housing crisis, SFBC chose to work with homeless advocates to establish a navigation center as a temporary shelter and service center rather than simply demand safety from the authorities, as they would have done in earlier years. This choice risked diluting mission and focus in the eyes of SFBC's internal critics yet was pursued as normatively just, as well as strategically wise, to further expand support for bicycle issues in the city. However, redesigning the Hairball will take many years and considerable resources. Bicycle strategies that reach into poor and minority communities cannot on their own address deep spatial, housing, and wage inequalities that constrain bikable and walkable cities from becoming more "just cities" with "just sustainabilities."[9]

While bicycle movements in other major cities have many distinct qualities, they also came together through national coalitions and networks, they shared lessons, and made strategic choices informed by local opportunities and through network learning. A critical moment was the formation of the Alliance for Biking and Walking in 1997, the result of a conference among some of the more robust local alliances, with the SFBC playing an important role. While local trajectories and bike-friendly climatic conditions vary, the developmental civic and political logics displayed in San Francisco have had strong parallels in other cities.

In Portland, Oregon, oppositional and performative cultural and identity practices—from Critical Mass and the Belligerantes to the Sprokettes and Pedal Palooza—have been essential to movement building, as has the threat of lawsuits against police arrests for blocking traffic. Yet the early development of city land-use and sustainability planning from the 1970s onward (see chapter 6), support at the state level for a minimum 1 percent of transportation funds to be spent on biking and pedestrian improvements, and many important links to elected city councilors ("commissioners") and department administrators, whose leaders were often cyclists themselves, yielded early results in building bike infrastructure, writing a bike master plan, and eliciting relatively high levels of ridership, especially after 1993. Funding from ISTEA during the 1990s elicited further participation, as well as collaborative multistakeholder practices at the local level, including with businesses and the police department, on appropriate norms and practices for motorists, cyclists, and pedestrians alike.[10]

The Bicycle Transportation Alliance (BTA), initially founded in 1990 as the Portland Area Bicycle Coalition, has been central in building the local field. Over time, it developed a broader frame to include healthy communities, walking and transit advocacy, neighborhood greenways, and gender equity through Women Bike. It then changed its name to The Street Trust to reflect this more inclusive frame—"Trust" signaling both assets and relationships. Staff and board affiliations and formal partners have expanded over time to include Oregon Walks, Northwest Trails Alliance, Kaiser Permanente, the Sierra Club, Audubon, and the American Heart Association, among others, in the successful advocacy campaign for a $1.3 billion, ten-year state investment (with $125 million for Safe Routes to School).[11]

The Street Trust's strategy has come to include more vigorous efforts at bicycle equity, especially in East Portland where the critique of the movement as predominantly white and gentrifying, resulting in erasure of black culture distinct to the area, most strongly emerged. As executive director Jillian Detweiler recounts, Portland was unusually fortunate in the 1990s to have secured bike safety as part of the curriculum of all fifth graders in the public schools, but when budgets were cut back, the Street Trust focused on bringing the Safe Routes to School curriculum to all twenty-two low-income Title 1 schools. Equity has become increasingly prominent due to internal self-reflection on core values, in conjunction with a major funder (Meyer Memorial Trust), though some members remain skeptical, especially when equity coalitional logics have led to prioritizing an affordable housing bond while delaying a transportation bond campaign for several years.[12]

While Transportation Alternatives (Trans Alt) was founded in New York City in 1973, it only developed staff capacity in the early 1990s and expanded rather steadily thereafter to a staff of thirty-three (full and part time), with ten thousand dues-paying members in 2016 and a core of organizers and activists in every borough. There had been a few failed attempts to build selective bikeways on major Manhattan streets and one great success with the Westside (or Hudson River) Greenway, later extended to several other edges of Manhattan. The bike group's history is marked by similar culturally formative events and confrontations by Critical Mass with the police, as in San Francisco and Portland, and an expansive frame that began to include walking, public transit, and public spaces. It also exercised successful pressure at the department of transportation around the number of bike fatalities, although Trans Alt supporters had to stage a "die in" of mournful prostration in Washington Square Park in July 2019 to protest their recent rise again. Neighborhoods in the outer boroughs have often been divided at public meetings since the lack of parking space had, over the years, led to the widely accepted practice of double parking, thus competing for new bike-lane space. The increasing presence of Amazon delivery and Uber and Lyft vehicles pulled over to the side has only added to spatial competition.[13]

Bike advocacy efforts, however, yielded limited results until Mayor Michael Bloomberg (2002–2013) appointed Janette Sadik-Khan as transportation commissioner in 2007. Bloomberg was a strong mayor with a clear commitment to combat climate change, and his deputy mayor for economic development was already at work on a sustainability plan for the city (PlaNYC). Sadik-Kahn served for six and one-half years. She hired well-known advocates from Trans Alt, the Project for Public Spaces, and consultants trusted by the cycling community. She also drew upon experience from cities such as Copenhagen. As Inbar Kishoni, deputy director for public engagement at the city's DOT, explained in a compelling and humorous online training webinar organized by NACTO, "street ambassadors" in her office have developed a panoply of ways to meet and talk to residents where they typically congregate—at libraries, shopping centers, churches, and senior centers. They utilize one-on-ones, fun-filled design tools for kids and adults on the street, and online tools and public forums to envision street alternatives and address the concerns of multiple constituencies, from local businesses concerned with curb loading spaces and times to local groups such as the Harlem Bike Network.[14]

National Bicycle Advocacy

Bicycle advocacy at the national level has evolved considerably over the years based upon local strategic choices and affiliations, competitive organizational dynamics among key national associations, and public policy design. The League of American Wheelmen, dormant or regionally based for many decades, was revived in 1964, hired staff in 1973, and changed its name to the gender-neutral League of American Bicyclists (LAB) in 1994. It promoted John Forester's *Effective Cycling* and John Allen's *Bicycling Street Smarts*, two widely used guides. But the league remained primarily committed to the elite of high-performance club cyclists, who viewed the newcomers as evidence of the "toy bike syndrome," the title of Forester's influential article in the October 1973 issue of *Bike World* that signaled diminutive discounting in the core framing dispute within the movement over several decades.

The league's club structure, whose logic was to enable local clubs to learn about each other's upcoming rides, generated persistent problems of organizational maintenance and advocacy capacity. Under the influence of Forester, the league opposed separate bike lanes, partly because it feared— perhaps realistically—that relatively underdeveloped bicycle associations in the 1970s lacked the political capacity to prevent such dedicated lanes from providing the rationale for excluding cyclists from other roads. Forester himself, disturbed by the "new cycling populism," litigated a case under the Consumer Product Safety Commission that weakened the domestic bicycle industry and its trade association (which provided much-needed if never-adequate resources for the movement), eroding government support for expanded cycling and demoralizing the broader movement.[15]

However, the league was increasingly drawn into the mainstream mix as local groups—such as the San Francisco Bicycle Association, the Bicycle Transportation Alliance of Portland, the Chicagoland Bicycle Federation, the Washington Area Bicycle Alliance, and the Cascade Bicycle Club—broadened their base and forged links to pedestrian and other livable streets and healthy community groups. City bicycle planning coordinators became complete streets and livable neighborhood coordinators during the 1990s. The league also began to shift as other national organizations entered the field, especially when new funding became available under ISTEA in 1991. The selection of Andy Clarke as LAB's executive director in 2004, who was previously director of the Association of Bicycle and Pedestrian Professionals, provided a clear break with the Foresterites, and he went on to serve for twelve years. In this case, the transfer of professional experience, as well as his previous networks through the Rails to Trails Conservancy and the Surface Transportation Policy Project, seems to have directly spurred civic associational growth.

Clarke provided, in his words, a "2.0 version" of a more mature and broad-based organization, and then helped it transition to a "3.0 version" that focuses on the bigger picture beyond bikes. The league helped in the formation of Safe Routes to School, for which it developed a curriculum, and the National Complete Streets Coalition. Its 2015 to 2018 strategic plan articulates a "shift of paradigm" that incorporates health, environment, economic and community development, inequality, diverse communities, and multistakeholder partnerships—all under the rubric of adding value for the mutual benefit of all sectors of society. National summits have sessions on building partnerships with health agencies and organizations. LAB received funding from the Robert Wood Johnson Foundation to facilitate change within the organization and across the field, and for nearly a decade, they enjoyed what Clarke calls "remarkably hands off" support from a "dream funder" called Bikes Belong (now PeopleForBikes), an industry trade group and foundation. Since the movement at national and local levels had to respond to vigorous critiques of racial inequality in street design and relative investments in different neighborhoods, the league's reframing has been accompanied by recruiting staff and board members from social justice activists and critics.[16]

The league has grown to perhaps twenty-five thousand dues-paying individual and family members, seven hundred and fifty bicycle clubs, seven thousand affiliated nonbike organizations, and several dozen larger bicycle and law firms. It has provided training for several thousand bicycle instructors around the nation. Training, of course, is a technical and aesthetic resource—it helps one ride competently and look the part—but also a civic one that enables responsible etiquette during competitive encounters over space. Critical to organizational growth was the insurance program that the league offered to clubs and advocacy groups (e.g., for their riders and licensed bike instructors) as well as its refusal to build a branded and exclusive chapter structure, which, according to Clarke, would not have been consistent with the cultural ethos or information needs of local groups unless it had been accomplished much earlier. LAB lobbies Congress, especially with its mass lobby during its annual National Bicycle Summit. In 2010, some 730 cyclists descended on four hundred congressional offices.[17]

The transformation of LAB was partly the product of earlier field-configuring events. The Bicycle Federation of America (Bike Fed) was founded in 1977 after the Bike-Ed '77 conference, convened jointly by the USDOT and the Consumer Product Safety Commission, as a way to leverage the organizational resources of the one-time Bikecentennial, an official series of bike tours recognized and funded by the 1976 bicentennial commission over a period of thirty months. The Bike Fed became the counterpoint to LAB during the latter's most elitist phase. It was built largely under the leadership of two directors who would leave their posts at the National Highway Traffic Safety Administration (Katie Moran) and US-DOT (Bill Wilkinson) during the bike-unfriendly Reagan years, though not before channeling some grant money to help build the organization. The Bike Fed convened local activists and professionals across the field of traffic safety and planning, broadened its focus to health (in collaboration with the Robert Wood Johnson Foundation), and sponsored the biennial ProBike conference beginning in 1980. The Bike Fed eventually changed its name to the National Center for Bicycling and Walking. However, in the mid-1990s, the bicycle movement still lacked a national organization with a sizable individual and associational membership committed to everyday, utilitarian cycling in separate bike lanes. It could not take full advantage of the new opportunities posed by broadening of the sustainable cities field and federal funding nor could it respond effectively to emerging threats to bike programs in ISTEA as it approached reauthorization in 1997.[18]

Under the initiative of the Bike Fed, some two dozen leaders of local and state bicycle alliances met at the Thunderhead Ranch in Wyoming in 1996 to form the Thunderhead Alliance, soon renamed the Alliance for Bicycling and Walking (ABW), as a counterweight to LAB, becoming perhaps the main impetus for the latter's own transformation. Indeed, the two organizations have had a joint program, called Advocacy Advance, to develop training and tools for more effective local work. ABW has developed an organizational membership base composed of local and state bicycle alliances, pedestrian groups (Oregon Walks, Los Angeles Walks), joint organizations (BikeWalk Alameda, Minnesota Safe Routes to Schools), open space coalitions (Seattle Neighborhood Greenways), and others. Its board has included leaders of some of the more robust local alliances; in 2015, SFBC's longtime executive director (Leah Shahum) and subsequent one (Noah Budnick) both served. ABW has several sponsor organizations, including PeopleForBikes (originally Bikes Belong), which is largely an industry group with a nonprofit foundation arm run by former Chicagoland Bicycle Federation director and ABW founding chair Randy Neufeld. It is explicitly committed to the bicycle movement. TREK, a major manufacturer, is also a sponsor, as is Kaiser Permanente, signaling links to health. Other partner organizations include AARP, the National Complete Streets Coalition, and the Safe Routes to School National Partnership.[19]

Intermodal Surface Transportation Efficiency Act (ISTEA): Biking and Walking

The Bike Fed, in conjunction with organizations such as the Rails to Trails Conservancy (RTC), founded in 1986 to broker the conversion of abandoned railroad tracks through the land-trust model, played a central role in convening the Surface Transportation Policy Project (STPP). David Burwell, a Cape Cod lawyer who helped found RTC, served as STPP president for more than a decade. This coalition initially included AIA and APA (architecture and planning professionals), EDF and NWF (two mainstream national environmental groups), the Center for Neighborhood Technology (CNT, a major Chicago-based innovator for local solutions), Friends of the Earth (a more radical national and international group), and other organizations and coalitions. It was hosted by the National Trust for Historic Preservation and funded by Pew, Surdna, Joyce, and a few other foundations whose numbers expanded quite considerably over the next decade. The Sierra Club, NRDC, SGA, and several grassroots community-organizing and environmental-justice networks also later joined, further diversifying the mix and lending the coalition greater clout. With help from an AIA staffer on STPP who formerly worked with New York senator Daniel Patrick Moynihan, chair of the Senate Environment and Public Works subcommittee on transportation, and who reminded him of his early article criticizing the chaotic and destructive spread of highways through cities, STPP successfully crafted ISTEA, which supplanted the original interstate highway bills passed from 1956 onward.[20]

ISTEA linked transportation to environmental values more strongly than several previous transportation acts, placed much greater emphasis on intermodal approaches, and created two new programs: Transportation Enhancements and Congestion Mitigation and Air Quality Improvement (CMAQ). These increased funding for walking, biking, and related cultural and aesthetic enhancements, in addition to money for rails-to-trails projects. While the bulk of the allocated $24 billion in funding (1991–1997) still went to roads, spending on these other programs was set at 10 percent and delivered some $677 million to bicycle and pedestrian facilities in its first four years. This was an unprecedented amount but fell short of authorization due to the sluggish and uneven obligation of funds by state agencies and other administrative challenges at the local level. In this participatory-feedback design, the amount spent, as well as the larger amount authorized, spurred further mobilization by cycle advocates, the bike industry, and community groups; by local officials and some non-profits sponsoring enhancements; and by professional associations such as the National League of Cities, the National Association of Counties, and the US Conference of Mayors. In 1994 and 1996, the Federal Highway Administration (FHWA) sponsored conferences with hundreds of stakeholders to assess and showcase achievements and to continue to work out administrative kinks. STPP had a grassroots coordinator (Laura Olsen) on staff, who helped affiliate some eight hundred groups by 1996.[21]

Local engagement was enabled by the ecology of local groups in any given city. In Chicago, the Center for Neighborhood Technology and the Neighborhood Capital Budget Group formed a coalition that hired an architect to help the transit authority plan six inner-city station sites on a rapid-transit line, and in Portland, Oregon, neighborhood associations worked with the city council to develop a community action plan to calm neighborhood traffic (see chapter 6). Obligation rates increased steadily due to these various efforts. Together, these groups resisted attempts by highway interests to eliminate the programs in subsequent iterations of ISTEA, beginning with the Transportation Equity Act for the 21st Century of 1998 (TEA-21), followed by SAFETEA-LU in 2005, MAP-21 in 2012, and FAST Act in 2015. By 2004, states and counties had implemented more than ten thousand bicycle- and pedestrian-related projects representing $3.7 billion in federal expenditures in addition to state matching grants, generating still further incentives to organize in national coalitions and participate locally.[22]

In addition, ISTEA required states to name a pedestrian and bicycle coordinator to facilitate nonmotorized alternatives, thus providing institutional leverage within state DOTs. Most had been appointed after and as a response to ISTEA, and the FHWA convened them at a national conference in 1993, with forty-five states sending delegates. ISTEA also mandated public participation at all key decision points in transportation planning and explicitly included diverse and traditionally underserved stakeholders. This was hardly a new idea, since many of the battles of the late 1960s and early 1970s were around transportation projects, and the federal highway act of 1968 required public hearings. Indeed, the USDOT had published its own two-volume compendium on effective participation practices coauthored by Sherry Arnstein, Model Cities' chief advisor on public participation and whose own analysis of moving up "the ladder of citizen participation" is renowned and widely reprinted in scholarly and activist circles alike. In addition, a good number of states established bicycle-advisory groups to expand citizen participation. From 1979 to 1992, the USDOT filed more environmental impact statements (EIS) than any other federal agency, and in 1991, it was a defendant in more NEPA claims than any other federal agency. Drafters of ISTEA resisted attempts to use the new mechanisms to preempt NEPA, testifying to the cumulative impact of public participation norms, laws, and practices, albeit with significant backsliding under Reagan in the 1980s.[23]

Indeed, the Reagan administration engaged in a pointed attack on those federal staff that had created the Interagency Council on Citizen Participation to voluntarily share models and lessons across federal departments. However, much of the networked learning among federal staff and others in the burgeoning field soon shifted to a successor organization, the International Association of Public Participation Practitioners (IAP3, now the International Association for Public Participation, IAP2). This move represented a nimble strategic response among practitioners in this overlapping professional field.[24]

In a virtuous cycle of participatory feedback, ISTEA was implemented in the 1990s amidst burgeoning bicycle associations, environmental-justice groups, and healthy community coalitions as well as professional associations, new urbanist coalitions, and national environmental groups that were far more knowledgeable and attentive to the role of transportation for sustainable cities and regions. Under ISTEA, state DOTs and the Metropolitan Planning Organizations (MPOs) specifically designated to implement the law had to allow public review and comments, including of a plan to involve the public. It also had to demonstrate explicit consideration and response to public input—in short, they adopted rights-based participatory and deliberative design requirements. They had to consider all reasonable alternative transportation investments in a corridor prior to selecting a project, which spurred collaborative decision-making before a plan was put forth and then likely rejected. CMAQ dollars have funded collaborative planning among civic associations and local public agencies, with social media complementing traditional meetings in some recent initiatives. Working with STPP, the Federal Transit Administration funded the Community Empowerment Project to pilot public highway education and civic capacity building in five communities, including those with low-income and minority youth. MPOs reported that public involvement, despite having many challenges, was the biggest change ISTEA made in their transportation planning and professional training processes. Greater public involvement produced better decisions responsive to the public's needs and generated broader and stronger public support.[25]

A "Citizen's Guide" to ISTEA funding and participation requirements was quickly developed and widely circulated by the Campaign for New Transportation Priorities. The "ISTEA Planners Workbook," edited by a team from APA and AIA, identified the requirements of ISTEA and related laws (Clean Air Act Amendments, NEPA and similar state laws, and the Americans with Disabilities Act, passed in 1990) to further clarify and strengthen the role of the public in transportation planning. It recommended innovative methods in community visioning and collaborative planning and specifically named those utilized by the Program for Community Problem Solving, a nonprofit partnership led by William Potapchuk with national associations such as the National League of Cities (NLC), the International City/County Management Association (ICMA), and the National Civic League. Public engagement practices and guidelines recommended by FHWA in 2015 have continued to be refined and enriched considerably over several decades. Guidelines include transportation fairs, games, computer simulations, and social media. Special attention has been devoted to engagement by minority, low-income, disabled, and EJ groups that might be structurally disadvantaged or may have what this federal bureaucracy has come to recognize as diverse "communication and learning styles"—not your great grandfather's bureaucracy of Max Weber, to be sure, nor your mother's street-level bureaucracy of Michael Lipsky.[26]

The American Association of State Highway Transportation Officials (AASHTO)—and many of the state DOTs it represented—pushed to narrow the types of groups involved and to make public involvement optional for the states while environmental and smart growth groups have worked to strengthen and broaden it. However, as part of the dynamic of policy feedback among this complex array of organizational types in the emerging institutional field, the National Association of City Transportation Officials (NACTO) was founded in 1995 during the first ISTEA funding cycle as a counterweight to AASHTO, which it has ever more effectively become (see chapter 3). Nonetheless, as Margaret Weir and her colleagues show, the "striking success" of ISTEA in engaging and empowering bicycle advocates, environmentalists, and emerging policy networks in overall metropolitan planning was more evident in implementation where major cities could also generate vertical power with top-down and bottom-up initiatives. This was more evident in Chicago, with Mayor Richard M. Daley able to work with a well-organized business sector and community organizing groups, than in Los Angeles, where network collaboration remained more diffuse. In the latter case, the policy feedback cycle was considerably less virtuous and more vulnerable.[27]

Urban Agriculture

Urban agriculture has emerged as part of much larger fields of sustainable agriculture and organic food movements, especially after the participatory communes and co-ops of the 1960s. While today there are various institutional forms that extend beyond city limits, such as the alternative regional food district in the San Francisco Bay Area, farmers markets, and community-supported agriculture (CSA), here I focus on urban systems of community gardens, food justice, and food policy councils. Federal policies have helped spur innovation, yet policy designs have had considerably less participatory feedback and field-building effects than ISTEA has had in the field of transportation.[28]

Community Gardens

Community gardens have a long history in the United States, associated especially with wartime mobilization through "victory gardens," though the more recent phase since the 1960s and 1970s has been closely linked to grassroots activism for neighborhood revitalization, organic food for healthy eating, and environmental and ecological values. One core model is the "urban garden program" directly supported by city agencies in partnership with neighborhood and sometimes citywide or statewide civic groups (Denver Urban Gardens and the Pennsylvania Horticultural Society), as well as by some networks and institutes within university extension programs. Hybrid organizational forms are quite varied, though community gardeners almost always seek government as a partner and to formalize support in city plans and budgets. The American Community Gardening Association, a binational group in the United States and Canada founded in 1979, lists New York; Newark, New Jersey; Philadelphia, Pennsylvania; Minneapolis, Minnesota; and Boston, Massachusetts, among those cities with the most community gardens. Its survey of members counts 88 percent as urban gardens, mostly for food growing, and 61 percent are located on government-controlled land. Gardeners, who are typically chosen from long waiting lists or other formal application processes, plant, till, and harvest the produce; do some design, construction, and art work (often as part of a required number of hours on common tasks); and pay annual fees based upon plot size, often subsidized for low-income members. They cannot typically sell their produce but can donate part or all of it. Some gardens, as in Seattle, set aside part of the land specifically for this purpose.[29]

Seattle, a northwest port city with a moderate climate, a long growing season, and a population of 668,000 in 2016, has one of the most institutionally robust systems of this type, although like many others it emerged amidst often difficult land-use conflicts among local groups and development interests. Several factors stand out in field building for Seattle's community gardens. First, the city has a rich history of civic, countercultural, and urban ecological engagement, much of it place-based and linked to

Model Cities and neighborhood associations known locally as community councils. In 1974, a Northwest Conference on Alternative Agriculture was organized in Ellensburg in the central part of the state and drew upon a loose network of ecotopian, bioregionalist, and food co-op activists from Seattle and elsewhere. As Seattle's population has become increasingly diverse, with immigrants and refugees from Southeast Asia and East Africa adding to Latino, African American, and East Asian groups, ethnic and other associations achieved official recognition in the neighborhood system—although this system was reorganized in 2016 partly in response to perceived inequalities of voice.

Second, innovation by the city occurred early, with the donation of an old truck farm in 1971 by the Picardo family (initially managed by a nonprofit), quickly followed by the addition of eight more community gardens on city owned land within a few years, and then more by the end of the decade. This formalized the P-Patch program, in honor of the Picardos, but with the "P" culturally inscribed in the mantra of "passionate people producing peas in public."[30]

Third, while the P-Patch program grew slowly during the tight city budgets of the early 1980s, it was complemented by other forms of institutionalization, especially the establishment of a department of neighborhoods in the late 1980s, whose neighborhood-matching fund for various civically driven improvement projects helped finance further gardens; and the neighborhood planning program of the 1990s, which was the result of vigorous and often-contentious civic initiative to modify in a more collaborative participatory policy design the otherwise notable 1994 comprehensive plan called Toward a Sustainable Seattle. The department of neighborhoods incorporated P-Patch into its structure in 1997. Neighborhood planning across thirty-eight diverse neighborhoods generated sufficient democratic legitimacy through a variety of methods: inclusive multistakeholder visioning and continuous relational work, public accountability through city council and agency review, shared tool kits and expertise among neighborhood planning groups and relevant city agencies. As a result of such increased legitimacy, the $198.2 million Pro Parks Levy was passed in 2000, which included further funding for community gardens.[31]

Finally, as Jeffrey Hou, Julie Johnson, and Laura Lawson argue in their richly detailed and photographed study of the system, Seattle's community gardens have benefitted by an emergent and expansive web of other supportive institutions. These have included Washington State University King County Extension, with its master gardener and food education programs; the design-build studio at the University of Washington, whose students and faculty have assisted the civic gardeners who perform the bulk of physical labor; and the Seattle Housing Authority, with its Cultivating Communities and Cultivating Youth gardens for low-income residents. The P-Patch Trust raises additional funds to support low-income community gardens and gardener fees, and Lettuce Link assists low-income gardening families and children and distributes extra produce from various gardens to food banks and women's shelters across the city. The Seattle Tilth Association offers workshops and operates a children's garden. Additional land is provided by Seattle Public Utilities, Seattle City Light, and the Department of Parks and Recreation.[32]

As is the case with many local environmental capacity-building projects around the country, including the YMCA of the USA's Earth Service Corps established at the Greater Seattle YMCA in 1989, AmeriCorps VISTA volunteers have been involved in community gardening. Headquartered in Seattle, Starbucks and various architecture, design, engineering, and green building firms have also contributed funding, labor, and expertise. The Race and Social Justice Initiative, initially introduced within the department of neighborhoods, added an explicit racial equity tool kit to community garden planning, which has significantly expanded food-security gardens in low-income and immigrant communities.

The local field of community gardening has become institutionally thick, with many complementary relationships and functions across public agencies, nonprofits, universities, and civic and ethnic associations, including those of low-income, minority, and refugee status. King County, within which Seattle is located, also has a high rate of direct marketing from farms to urbanites, partly due to the nature of the land and its suitability to vegetable farming in contrast to ranching or wheat farming east of the Cascades.

The individual gardens help provide healthy food, nutrition education, farming skills, cross-cultural produce, and recipe exchanges. They also serve as venues for recreation and leisure; public art; public space for birthdays, weddings, anniversaries, and holiday celebrations; and locations for informal civic deliberation and relationship building for garden governance and other civic projects. Civic and institutional thickening strategies are thus complemented by culturally embedding and enriching ones. Guided by a city transportation map to the gardens, they also attract visitors across the city and tourists nationally and globally. Highly skilled social actors have left a model that, while still burdened by high housing prices, gentrification pressures, and spatial segmentation nonetheless represents profound civic initiative, variegated institutional collaboration, and social justice values. One such actor is Jim Diers, the founding director of the department of neighborhoods who helped broker many of the civic, public staff, and elected leadership relationships for the larger field-building enterprise.

Philadelphia also has a history of urban gardening among its older African American migrants from the South and its various ethnic groups from Europe, Asia, and Latin America. But over recent decades, the strategic choices of urban gardeners have proceeded from very different conditions than those in Seattle. A politically reformed city by the 1950s but with highly segregated neighborhoods and institutions in the throes of urban renewal and black resistance, Philly had become deindustrialized with the loss of one-quarter of its population from 1950 to 2000. This resulted in a land legacy of somewhere between forty thousand and sixty thousand vacant lots and building structures (houses, housing projects, docks, warehouses, factories, derelict railroads, canals, and landfills). But by the 1990s, with strong economic growth under Mayor Ed Rendell, it was nonetheless well positioned to implement Center City redevelopment strategies to attract new businesses, cultural institutions, college-educated workers, and empty nesters. Amidst the gentrification that accompanied new growth in finance, real estate, information, hospitals, and higher education, urban gardening re-emerged as a local food and community self-determination strategy among African Americans in distressed neighborhoods. It also became a culturally hip, ecological, and (sometimes) socially just identity-building strategy among young educated whites, many from liberal arts colleges and universities in the surrounding region. This combination has produced some profound tensions within the local movement, though they have been relatively well managed among the interlocking associational networks and city institutions that have emerged to support urban agriculture.[33]

Key among the associations has been the Pennsylvania Horticultural Society (PHS), which, in the early 1960s, began to leverage its more than century-old legacy to bridge gaps between mostly female suburban gardening clubs and inner-city neighborhoods. PHS built upon organizing styles of the Neighborhood Gardens Association (NGA, 1953–1977), which in turn drew upon community development practices and partnerships among settlement houses, community centers, and other local institutions. PHS then consolidated various gardening and tree growing projects under Philadelphia Green in the 1970s. When it turned to the increasing problem of vacant land in the 1990s, it utilized the assets-based community development (ABCD) frame to view vacant lots as potential assets and connect ABCD to comprehensive community-development strategies and urban land trusts promoted especially by the Trust for Public Land, a key nonprofit in the broader land-trust movement. With $100,000 from its own PHS fundraising, and another $250,000 from the city's office of housing and community development, Philadelphia Green hired eight staff to work directly with community groups, providing training, technical assistance, gardening tools, and other resources. Partnerships were developed with CDCs and LISC, with funding from the local Pew Charitable Trusts and William Penn Foundation, and with further institutional support from Penn State University Extension and the Greening Studio at the University of Pennsylvania.[34]

With its $21 million budget, PHS maintains its Green City Teachers and Tree Tenders programs. The recent development of its Urban Forest Cloud for online data collection and management system is also linked to watershed restoration. In 2017, it also invested $500,000 in its LandCare Re-Entry Initiative for previously incarcerated persons, thereby creating forty jobs and five Community LandCare organizations. Groups with more litigious and contentious repertoires, such as the Garden Justice Land Initiative and Soil Generation, pressed for greater racial and income inclusiveness. They achieved this partly through representation and leadership in the Food Policy Advisory Council (FPAC), a version of the food policy councils discussed further.[35]

Political opportunities became more favorable but also much more complex, with the election of mayor John Street in 2000 and then Michael Nutter in 2008, both African Americans who served two terms. Street launched the promising Neighborhood Transformation Initiative (NTI), which included urban gardening as part of neighborhood revitalization and a broader strategy for structural demolition and land acquisition. However, he did not implement this conundrum-laden policy in a way that generated sufficient trust and democratic legitimacy in neighborhoods with unhappy memories of urban renewal and through processes that were also administratively manageable, given the huge inventory of properties. Tensions often played out between local gardening groups, who wanted longer and more permanent leases than the typical one-year lease—if there was a lease at all—and city council and city agencies that preferred to keep land options open for projects that might generate more revenue for city services and further private economic development. While urban gardening supported some job training and development, it never credibly promised comparable development strategies for the city overall.[36]

Nonetheless, community mobilization managed to gain increasingly greater recognition and institutional support for urban agriculture. The Philadelphia Water Department, an institutional leader in green infrastructure (see chapter 5), lent its support to urban gardening. Mayor Nutter's wife (Lisa Nutter) had been part of the group that helped produce the foundational study *Old Cities/Green Cities: Communities Transform Unmanaged Land*, led by J. Blaine Bonham Jr., longtime executive director of PHS and Philly Green. Nutter lent further support with a Greenworks vision; the creation of the FPAC in 2011; development of the *Green City, Clean Waters Plan*; and favorable revisions in the zoning code and comprehensive plan. The Philadelphia Land Bank, promoted by PHS since 2000 and established by legislation in late 2013, has developed an ambitious strategic plan to streamline the acquisition, leasing, and sale of vacant land. This includes community gardens and open space, in collaboration with the Neighborhood Garden Trust (successor to NGA). It also facilitates some of the original goals of NTI. As a policy design, the Land Bank is intended to enhance public accountability, community representation, and transparency (including web access), and partly builds upon prior neighborhood and district planning.[37]

But the continued contest over urban land is manifest in the existence of a least two coalitions: (1) the Philadelphia Land Bank Alliance, a multistakeholder group that includes urban agriculture advocates, affordable housing, community development groups, and real estate and building interests; and (2) the Campaign to Take Back Vacant Land, which includes faith-based, labor, neighborhood association, and other community organizing groups that favor more permanent urban agriculture, community land trusts, healthy communities, and affordable housing.[38]

Just Food
The frame of food justice combines many of the components of the broad critique of the industrial food system as well as a specific critique of the

racial and class inequities of this system *and* of many alternative food models. It also selectively appropriates some of the components of these movements in the interests of environmental and social justice values and expanded coalitions. The latter include immigrant and workers' rights but also outreach to community development and transportation equity. The food justice movement's prognostic framing of institutional and policy alternatives still has many tensions and unresolved questions, to be sure, not the least of which is the mix of movement and institutional components and the degree to which food justice is radically transformative or can and should be accommodated within more democratized political, civic, consumer, and corporate cultures.[39]

Activists and agencies within New York City have attempted to address food justice for various reasons. Central among these is the fact that three million people—in a total population of eight and one-half million—live in neighborhoods with few or no grocery stores and supermarkets. The Hunts Point terminal in the South Bronx serves as the hub of supply for fresh fruits and vegetables, with some fifteen thousand truck trips each day, though it is less accessible to the smaller bodegas that cannot afford the vehicles and travel time. As a result, people in these neighborhoods pay more for less and are more likely to suffer from diet-related illnesses, such as diabetes and heart disease, or choose to spend their food dollars (and gas miles) in suburbs. In response to and sometimes in partnership with civic associations, food justice activists and land trusts coordinated through the Trust for Public Land, city government has developed a range of policies. Initially, during the 1970s crisis that witnessed widespread arson and housing abandonment, the city formalized a community garden program called Operation Green Thumb and, in 1995, brought it within the New York City Department of Parks and Recreation as Green Thumb, which now has some six hundred gardens under its jurisdiction. Land tenure, however, has often remained uncertain, given real estate development and affordable housing pressures and sometimes unfavorable administrations, especially under Mayor Rudolph Giuliani (1994–2001). He was checked only by grassroots protest and a state court order, which led to a community gardens settlement with more favorable rules for review and protection early in the administration of Mayor Michael Bloomberg.[40]

Recently, greater attention has been given to the food justice potential of community gardens, as in the city-block Red Hook Community Farm run by Added Value, a youth nonprofit in Brooklyn, and the New Farms

Development Project for immigrants, in partnership with Cornell Extension. New York Botanical Gardens provides assistance to many projects in the Bronx. In contrast to Seattle, the large majority of community gardens in New York are in neighborhoods that are overwhelmingly African American and/or Hispanic, and low-income, though these areas also have a lower density of other forms of open space and are under strong gentrifying pressures, sometimes accompanied by ethnic and new immigrant conflict. In addition, the New York City Housing Authority, with some 345 public housing developments, now also supports community gardening in terms of land-use policy and training for adults, youth, and children. The city has brought on board other agencies, such as the New York City Department of Buildings, DCAS Real Estate Services, the Department of Sanitation, and the School Construction Authority, to move various other components of community and school gardens forward, although it has lagged behind some other cities in including food and agriculture in formal city plans.[41]

Activists have recently become more energetic in bringing food justice issues to community gardens, CSAs, and farmers markets. They have also mobilized around immigrant struggles for cultural heritage and self-determination and female, youth, and LGBT empowerment. They have linked these to other environmental justice issues, such as polluted land sites, street traffic, and highway construction. Organized in 2010, Black Urban Growers (BUGS) organized to provide a citywide voice, and soon spread to other cities as well. The range of other food justice groups includes Just Food and Green Guerillas, who typically work with associations and coalitions in historically low-income and minority neighborhoods (Harlem, Bedford-Stuyvesant, East New York). They also work on other projects housed within community development corporations, educational, health, and other nonprofits, although there are persistent racial disparities in power and resources among local groups.[42]

Nonetheless, as Lindsay Campbell shows, urban agriculture has been institutionally underdeveloped relative to other urban sustainability strategies in New York, such as urban forestry. The latter became an important component of PlanNYC, Mayor Bloomberg's formal sustainability plan in 2007, with strong administrative support from the Department of Parks and Recreation and a robust collaboration with the New York Restoration Partnership. The private fundraising capacity of the partnership complemented significant capital investments from the city. The Million-

TreesNYC campaign had several notable advantages. These included relatively simple *metrics*—number of trees and ten-minute walk to parks for all—to motivate volunteer planting and stewardships across the city and to provide public accountability and political credit; *land* readily available in the sprawling park system and in public right-of-ways in front of homes and local businesses, where administrative mandates for planting could be enforced; and *framing* that was consistent with a competitive city seeking to attract and retain skilled employees and enhance real estate values while also targeting social justice goals by giving priority to neighborhoods with less tree cover and greater vulnerability to health impacts of urban heat islands, poor air quality, and lack of appealing venues for exercise.

Urban agriculture, by contrast, was not even mentioned in the initial PlaNYC, and when it was put into the revision of 2011, which included broader public engagement, there were no new capital investments available due to budget cutbacks in the wake of the financial crisis and recession. Land for urban agriculture is relatively scarce in such a built-out city, and opportunity costs are far more pronounced since parcels of land could be credibly developed for commercial and residential uses that include affordable housing, which could generate strong public support. No city agency comparable to the Department of Parks and Recreation existed to drive change, and civic and movement groups had relatively loose coalitions. In addition, framing was more problematic since the ability to produce food within city limits was constricted and thus displaced credible discourse to regional, upstate-downstate solutions or other nutritional health and hunger strategies.[43]

South Los Angeles, a sixteen-square-mile district with twenty-eight distinct neighborhoods and a population of some nine hundred thousand in a city of more than four million, has developed a food justice movement as part of, in the words of Neelam Sharma, "building a sustainable community." Sharma is executive director of Community Services Unlimited (CSU), a local nonprofit. Known previously as South Central LA, the area suffered from many of the historical inequities of black ghettoes, including redlining, white flight, and the famous riots in Watts in 1965 and those occurring after the failure to convict police officers responsible for the filmed beating of Rodney King in 1992, which led to one thousand physical structures destroyed overall. South LA is now home to many Latinos, in addition to African Americans. Rooted in the Black Panthers organizing around food in the 1960s, CSU has generated a variety of "just food" projects, including a Village Market Place and a mini-urban farm (Expo) that provides a venue for Garden Gateway workshops and youth education. The latter provides gardening skills and nurtures "critical consciousness" for a community-led agenda for health and sustainability within systems dominated by the industrial food system.[44]

Organized by CSU, Earth Day South LA provides a distinct event that includes food justice and other service groups while also utilizing the repertoire of the fairs and festivals that one typically finds at farmers markets. Enabling residents and especially youth to tell their stories as an essential part of building identities and cultures to support its work, CSU utilizes many local, face-to-face, and digital forms of communication. At the same time, CSU's strategic field building includes funding and other support relationships with federal, state, and municipal programs; funding with large private foundations and universities; and links to key community development and community economic development intermediaries. Indeed, it established itself as a fundable organization in 2004 only after it demonstrated its capacity to execute an ambitious "community food assessment." This mobilized local knowledge and professional expertise through a multimethod and participatory research process that geographically mapped the deficits in food access in the area and paired this with ABCD mapping of the neighborhood's assets. While yielding innovation and funding staff, CSU's local field-building strategy is contested by those in the community who see it as a threat to a genuinely radical and transformative enterprise. But the political-opportunity structure that informs CSU's strategic choices also includes various other programs for neighborhood empowerment and community gardening that are provided by the city and county of Los Angeles—that includes county public housing and the City Department of Neighborhood Empowerment, representing neighborhood councils. Along with CSU, these and many other groups and institutional actors are represented on the county's Los Angeles Food Policy Council.[45]

Food Policy Councils
Initially conceived in a landscape architecture class in 1977 at the University of Tennessee, food policy councils (FPCs) were first institutionalized in Knoxville in October 1981 by resolution of the city council. Their diffusion was slow despite official support from the US Conference of Mayors in the mid-1980s. But they have spread considerably since then to some 282 in

2015, sometimes under related nomenclature. These numbers are inexact and they include state and county FPCs as well as those either authorized by city government or formed within cities by multistakeholder coalitions, sometimes with foundation funding and/or extension staff support but often with some material and institutional support from the city. The latter provides legitimacy, but at times there are tensions with voice in the sense of the practical freedom of expression and the range of actors at the table. While some FPCs arise and then disappear within a few years, the overall number has shown a notable incline since the mid-2000s. Many of the early ones were motivated by rising food prices and Regan administration cuts in nutrition programs, but broader issues of sustainable agriculture, just food, and citizen engagement within local and regional contexts have driven the latest wave. In addition, since the late 1990s, planning at the urban and regional level for healthy food and more equitable access has become part of the repertoire of the American Planning Association and a good number of academic planning programs.[46]

FPCs take on a range of four sets of tasks. Not all do the full panoply, though additional ones tend to emerge with greater organizational capacity and credible accomplishments. First among these tasks is serving as a deliberative forum for food issues among the diverse array of organizations. These might include food security and antihunger activists, family farmers, local restaurant and retail businesses, food workers, and farm worker unions, as well as environmentalists, planners, nutritionists, and other public health workers. Community gardens, CSAs, and farmers markets might also send representatives. Many see the forums as ways to build a broader food movement from many disparate ones and take a food systems perspective. Dissemination of practical tool kits, public-involvement guides, food-system assessments, and newsletters to their respective organizational memberships, other networks, and broader publics can lend them further "democratic anchorage," as can the use of other online tools by civic associations. Outside speakers from local organizations and universities, as well as national networks, often take up one hour of a typically two-hour meeting; many fill in gaps of knowledge or present new perspectives and linkages among issues.[47]

Second, FPCs aim to coordinate among various sectors—minimally production, distribution, and consumption—while ideally including processing and food-waste recovery. They link advocacy, market, and nonprofit groups as well as government agencies and institutions such as schools and farm-to-school projects. Third, FPCs evaluate and advocate for policy. Most begin with some research that maps and assesses local and regional food access and security—the standard template has become the Food System Assessment—and then proceed toward policy proposals, including rerouting bus lines to provide greater access to healthy food, establishing urban agriculture guidelines and inclusion into comprehensive planning, securing land for community gardens and urban agriculture through zoning, and supporting mandatory menu labeling. The Austin-Travis County Food Policy Board, originally established by city ordinance in Austin, Texas, in 2008, provides official policy advice. FPC policy advocacy may also include support for federal legislation, such as the 2009 Childhood Nutrition Reauthorization Act.

Finally, FPCs often engage in some implementation, such as the establishment and expansion of farmers markets and creating the infrastructure for them to handle food stamps, farm-to-school programs, institutional food-purchasing programs, and affordable housing for farmworkers (though the latter is more likely to be addressed by state or county FPCs). Effective FPCs often generate spin-off organizations and projects for implementation or engage partners in coproduction.

At the city and county levels, most FPCs are the result of grassroots action and operate with limited paid staffing, whereas state FPCs are more likely to be integrated into a state agency and have dedicated staff. State councils, of course, can set policy that enables or requires action at the local level. Members tend to be appointed by public officials (especially at the state level) and/or self-select, though sometimes through a formal application process that attempts to balance a broad range of actors. Housed at Food First, an important national and international food research and action organization established in the 1970s, the Oakland, California, FPC has an elaborate selection process for its two-dozen-member council and it has multiple sources of funding (city, county, foundations, Kaiser Permanente), as well as an ambitious agenda across many policy issues. It grounds its mission explicitly in food justice, grassroots action, and community development. Yet it also includes representation among food, health, and other sustainability professionals, businesses, and labor, and interacts frequently with elected officials and city staff.[48]

In addition to urban gardeners, businesses, nonprofits, and conservation groups, the Denver Sustainable Food Policy Council includes members from several city departments as well as the Colorado State University

Extension. The Indy Food Council in Indianapolis, Indiana, includes representatives from city and county agencies, nonprofits, and large institutions such as the Purdue Cooperative Extension and LISC. It also organizes outreach events in neighborhoods and provides small grants to spur community engagement. However selected, the aim is generally to involve those who have interest, skills, diversity, network relationships, and some authority to move issues forward. Partner and allied organizations also range widely, from federal agencies to faith-based groups; food banks and school districts; Leagues of Women Voters and local grocers' associations; local chefs; and national, state, and local environmental organizations.[49]

In Seattle, however, the P-Patch program and relatively robust interdepartmental cultures and team practices were nurtured by the neighborhood planning process; the 2012 Food Action Plan was thus developed by a broad interdepartmental team, coordinated by the Office of Sustainability and Environment. It was authorized in 2008 and later approved directly by the city council, with community listening sessions to inform the process. Its related Fresh Bucks program, initially instituted by a private funder and then largely financed out of the city's general fund, provided $200,000 to match food stamp purchases at farmers markets. The Seattle King County FPC that had been active at an earlier phase was no longer present in the development of the later action plan, nor has there been much presence of food issues on other citizen advisory boards and commissions.[50]

While FPCs have a good deal of potential to link grassroots action to urban policy, they also have a variety of limitations. They can be narrow in terms of focus (antihunger, sustainable agriculture) and tend to neglect the broader range of issues that make up local and regional food systems. In some cases, spin-off projects consume much time and preempt efforts to keep a more general FPC functioning. FPCs also display the usual tensions of achieving greater racial and class diversity as well as managing multistakeholder processes. Even the well-funded FPC in Los Angeles in the mid-1990s displayed tensions between movement and institutional politics as well as among various movement advocates with specific issue niches, which led to its demise within three years. However, it was re-established as a forty-person independent multistakeholder initiative by Mayor Antonio Villaraigosa in 2011, and it receives support from several foundations, Kaiser Permanente, one city and one county agency, the Urban and Environmental Policy Institute (UEPI) at Occidental College, and the United States Department of Agriculture (USDA).[51]

Political pressure from big agricultural interests tends to display itself at the state level, but should FPCs diffuse further and become more institutionalized at the local level, one can expect much greater political opposition, especially if they tackle big issues where corporate profits are directly at stake such as school, university, and other institutional purchasers. Some cities experience more obstacles from state governments than others due to urban/rural divisions and partisan splits mapped over these. Virtually all FPCs, especially at the local level, face significant capacity-building and resource challenges. Even cities like Seattle or counties like Marin in California disposed to take up food system challenges may face organizational competition shaped by existing agency cultures and networks, alternative forums for participatory input, and the pace of emerging political opportunities that might encourage mayors, city councilors, or county supervisors to streamline the food policy process, or to at least avoid redundancy.[52]

Federal Policies and National Networks

Federal food policy is complex and contested, with lines of division that cut in many directions among industry sectors, among nonprofit advocacy and public interest organizations, and among highly contested frames within the organic food sector. The key policy battles have been fought around the Farm Bill, periodically up for reauthorization every six years, and within the National Organic Standards Board and its public forums held outside of Washington, DC, headquarters at the USDA. Here I explore a few policies that have provided some support for urban- and community-based agriculture and then draw comparisons between federal food policy and ISTEA in the field of transportation.[53]

Several federal initiatives have attempted to advance community-based and healthy food. The Community Food Projects (CFP) Competitive Grants Program, established by the 1996 Farm Bill that has been extended several times since then, has provided funding for matching grants to nonprofits that seek to develop comprehensive responses to local food, farm, and nutrition issues, especially for low-income communities. Projects that provide innovative linkages between two or more sectors of the food system, as well as between nonprofit and for-profit actors, and that emphasize ABCD strengths are favored. While relatively small at $16 million over the first six-year course of funding, the CFP grants raised the visibility of such innovations as part of more systemic responses, and have since generated perhaps $100 million for hundreds of nonprofit groups. Funded groups, such as Nuestras Raices and The Food Project, became leaders in the field. Funding expanded modestly under George W. Bush and Barack Obama. In 2016, projects could be funded from $10,000 to $400,000 and from one to four years. The 2016 grant cycle was authorized at $8,640,000, roughly in line with many other community-based grant programs in environmental areas and with similar process goals of building capacity for multistakeholder and civic collaboration.[54]

In 2010, the Healthy Food Financing Initiative (HFFI) was created as a partnership among three federal agencies (the USDA, HHS, and the Treasury Department) to address the problem of food deserts in both urban and rural areas. The 2014 Farm Bill authorized $125 million for HFFI grants and technical assistance through the USDA, while HHS utilized its community economic development office to provide $44.5 million (as of 2015) through community development corporations (CDCs), which are part of a well-developed institutional field seeking to further diversify (see chapter 3). The treasury likewise built upon this infrastructure by providing an additional $22 million through its Community Development Financial Institutions Fund and by providing tax credits through CDCs. Community Services Unlimited, the food justice group in south Los Angeles previously discussed, received two grants under HFFI to help expand its Village Marketplace. The East Los Angeles Community Union also received a grant to revitalize a vacant building for retail space, in partnership with wholesale distributor Titan Foods and with the UC extension providing community education on healthy foods. In Minneapolis and St. Paul, Minnesota, the Latino Economic Development Center utilized funding for its Immigrant Enterprise Healthy Foods Fund to support the development of new full-scale retail grocery stores and commercial kitchens, and the East Bay Asian Local Development Corporation built a full-service grocery store within walking distance of four low-income census tracts in Oakland. The Greater Jamaica Development Corporation has implemented the Healthy Corner Store Initiative in locations near Special Supplemental Nutrition Program for Women, Infants, and Children (WIC) in three of the most diverse neighborhoods in Queens, New York (Jamaica, Corona, and Flushing). These and other kinds of projects have begun to address food desert problems in cities from Miami, Florida, to Cleveland, Ohio; Boston to Pittsburgh, Pennsylvania; Nashville, Tennessee, to Portland, Oregon.[55]

These federal programs provide important templates for further field building, as do several others, such as farm-to-school programs.[56] However, compared to ISTEA (1991) and its successor laws in transportation, which generated significant participatory feedback and field building for biking and walking, federal farm policies seem to have had a much more modest impact for urban agriculture. Several interacting factors help account for this. First, ISTEA was crafted and then further refined by a relatively coherent coalition within the Surface Transportation Policy Project (STPP) that included well-established professional associations (AIA, APA, NLC), large mainstream environmental groups (NRDC, EDF, NWF, Sierra Club), and major foundations (Pew, Surdna, Joyce). Second, its policy design included several billion dollars in authorized spending over several cycles for its two programs most relevant to biking and walking, which would further motivate civic organizing at the city level. The policy design also specified participatory requirements for transportation planning, and the Federal Highway Administration convened field actors to share learning. Policy design and learning were informed by several prior decades of highway revolts and NEPA suits—with significant political leverage to block or delay major projects—as well as by practitioner testing and broad diffusion of appropriate forms of public participation to help move alternatives forward.

Third, the ISTEA design fostered coalitional logics at the local level among biking, pedestrian, and trail groups, eventually drawing in AARP chapters as well. It also helped to trigger the formation of the National Association of City Transportation Officials (NACTO) in 1995, a key professional association, as well as the Alliance for Biking and Walking (ABW) in 1996. The latter was responsive to strategic opportunities emerging at the local level (as in San Francisco and other cities) for collaboration with elected officials and transportation professionals, as well as to their strategic choices to broaden democratic legitimacy in the negotiation of spatial scarcities and transportation asymmetries. In response to competitive organizational dynamics locally and nationally, the transformation of the League of American Bicyclists (LAB) represented still another virtuous feedback loop after several decades of elite cycling politics.

In contrast, urban agriculture has not benefitted from similar dynamics, although several of the small-grant food programs have had capacity-building effects, and a mimetic version of STPP emerged with the Kellogg-funded Farm and Food Policy Project (FFPP) for the three-year period leading up to the Farm Bill of 2008. Why? First, in the 1990s, urban agriculture lacked a coherent coalition of prestigious professional and advocacy groups to shape policy design for urban or metropolitan approaches within the organic food field, and networks within the latter were themselves highly fragmented. The organic movement that re-emerged in the 1960s generated a large consumer base that was concerned about purity and health, as well as social distinction; a producer base worried about fraudulent claims by nonorganic farmers and distributors and the entry of big firms at all levels carving out a large part of the burgeoning market during the 1980s, especially once national standards seemed proximate. To secure sufficient trust and legitimacy across the field, organic farmers and their state and regional associations had, by the late 1980s, moved from loose philosophy to specified standards. Food scares, especially the widely publicized one in 1989 about alar on apples, a cultural symbol with wide resonance, sparked federal action and a field settlement that tended over time to marginalize the transformational vision of decentralized agriculture based on participatory governance.[57]

The resulting Organic Foods Production Act of 1990 established a national certification process to be worked out through a specified multistakeholder representation schema among a wide array of groups on the National Organic Standards Board (NOSB), a democratic design reflecting movement mobilization that had unusual statutory power and some unexpected participatory feedback effects. This process required much negotiation over identity within the advocacy coalition that heavily relied upon powerful national consumer and environmental groups to get the act passed, and who also possessed relative advantages within administrative rulemaking. Consumer groups were primarily concerned with health, testing, and labeling; environmental groups were primarily concerned with pesticides, biodiversity, water quality, and supply. Under a hostile Gingrich Congress elected in 1994, each group worried that its own policy preferences might be at risk by inclusionary overreach in the separate campaign for a Community Food Security Empowerment Act. Organic farmers were the weakest voice on NOSB, although they did manage to open the process through public meetings convened across the country, which has left a democratic institutional legacy in the field.

But urban farming and food justice groups did not have a single seat on the fifteen-member board. Opposition to one set of industry proposals in the 1997 proposed rule—the big three of irradiation, sewage sludge, and genetically modified organisms—did nurture movement solidarity within

NOSB, which was expressed quite intensively during the public comment period. But solidarity did not persist. Sponsored by the Kellogg Foundation (Integrated Farm and Food Systems Network) and the National Campaign for Sustainable Agriculture, various network initiatives for sustainable agriculture in the 1990s had significant difficulty negotiating identity beyond mere conflict avoidance, leading to suboptimal strategic thinking across the broader field. This was argued in an MIT doctoral dissertation by Kathleen Merrigan who was lead staff member on NOSB and later deputy secretary of agriculture under Obama. Self-induced vulnerabilities have lingered. Actors within these networks did not generate sufficient skills to reciprocally appreciate and, hence, better align diverse institutional logics.[58]

Second, neither the Organic Foods Production Act nor other farm bills authorized spending for urban and other community-based initiatives on a scale approaching ISTEA in the 1990s and 2000s, nor did they specify participatory requirements for local food planning. The field had not experienced the intense urban conflicts that occurred in transportation and land use over several decades, where mobilized neighborhoods could impose enormously costly delays. Sustainable urban agriculture did not benefit from a similar legacy of participatory design theorizing and practice, nor from the many intermediaries that had emerged to facilitate deliberative and collaborative planning, nor indeed from network learning coordinated through the relevant federal agency. As Brian Obach has argued, participatory design remained largely rooted for several decades in prefigurative models of co-ops and collectives. These were self-limiting in institutional support that might be otherwise available. Food policy councils, largely free of prefigurative utopianism, have since gained considerable momentum, and urban farming has been included in a growing number of comprehensive city plans. FPCs are now positioned to benefit from the broader legacy of participatory institutional design.[59]

Third, the various organic food and general farm bills have not encouraged coalitional dynamics at the local level in ways similar to ISTEA, nor through various feedback loops among national associations, such as the Association for Biking and Walking, the League of American Bicyclists, and AARP. At the local level, food groups often have quite disparate policy goals (urban farm production, food security distribution, and identity and cultural politics). Land use for farm plots might be credibly counterposed to other highly visible and worthy goals, such as affordable housing or offices, warehouses, and factories that produce more jobs and greater tax revenues for other city services. Each of these might generate greater advocacy and electoral support, even among poor and minority groups, than urban food and farming. The negotiation of spatial scarcity frequently generates what appear to attentive publics as significant opportunity costs or zero-sum options more frequently than, for instance, allocating space for bicycle lanes alongside already existing streets or for trails on abandoned rail tracks.

While there are important networks and intermediaries across the broader and overlapping fields of sustainable agriculture, food justice, and urban agriculture, few seem to have cohered further from food policy design. Formed in 1979, the American Community Gardening Association has remained quite small in staff and budget, though it holds an annual conference. It does not seem to provide much that city-based coalitions or formal municipal offices, typically within departments of parks and recreation or at public housing authorities, offer in terms of technical assistance, although several staff from such organizations serve on its board. Its grant funding and regranting to local groups remain minimal. The Farmers Market Coalition provides education, training, networking, and advocacy. Part of its framing is to enhance the "public space" and "town square," in addition to helping build the capacity of markets, but it remains relatively limited in its urban strategies. The National Sustainable Agriculture Coalition (NSAC) was formed in 2009 as the result of a merger of two organizations: the Sustainable Agriculture Coalition that had emerged from the farm crisis of the 1980s, and the National Campaign for Sustainable Agriculture, a network established in 1994 with some one hundred and fifty affiliated organizations but growing to perhaps three thousand by the end of the decade. NSAC's focus, however, is primarily rural. The National Farm to School Network, now a project of the Tides Center, emerged in 2007 as an initiative of the Community Food Security Coalition and UEPI. Its cofounder and executive director, Anupama Joshi, coauthored the book *Food Justice*.[60]

Founded in 1994, the Community Food Security Coalition (CFSC) articulated a frame in which "community food security is a condition in which all community residents obtain a safe, culturally acceptable, nutritionally adequate diet through a sustainable food system that maximizes community self-reliance and social justice." CFSC was founded after a meeting of Robert Gottlieb of UEPI, Mark Winne of the Hartford Food

System, and Andy Fisher of Seeds of Change, followed by a larger conference in Chicago. It then led the broad coalition of food and environmental groups that lobbied successfully for the inclusion of the Community Food Projects Competitive Grant Program that was authorized in 1996 and then reauthorized in 2002 and thereafter. However, its more ambitious attempt to include a Community Food Security Empowerment Act as part of the 1996 Farm Bill, which faced the first Gingrich Congress, never had a chance of passing and revealed some profound tensions within the coalition in the face of very real risks to other preferred programs, such as those that were priorities to antihunger groups that remain skeptical of community-based solutions.[61]

CFSC conferences grew steadily in size, and it published an influential set of guidebooks, research reports, and newsletters widely read across the food security and food justice movement. Nonetheless, CFSC was unable to sustain itself through its second decade. Due largely to tensions over relative racial representation, the Growing Food and Justice Initiative emerged in 2008 as a spin-off network led by Will Allen and Erika Allen, who had organized the Growing Power food projects in Milwaukee, Wisconsin, and Chicago. The National Farm to School Network, cultivated within CFSC, sought its own funding and organizational niche. CFSN was incorporated into UEPI, a prominent action research center under the direction of Gottlieb, but was later disbanded.[62]

The youth food justice movement, while representing a key dimension of organizing at the local level in many cities, has not been able to sustain itself robustly in broader networks. Rooted in Community (RIC) is a "loosely identified collective" of one hundred or so affiliated groups without a board of trustees or a strategic plan since its founding in 1999, although it is under the fiscal sponsorship of the Earth Island Institute.[63] Weakness is partly due to the general challenges of maintaining community youth-development networks beyond the city level or without institutional supports—made relatively more difficult when the target group is narrowed to high school-aged youth, as occurred with RIC. But the problem also stems from the fact that this wing of the food movement is often the most prone to imagined radical alternatives not tempered by longer term work to build institutional relationships and achieve pragmatic goals.[64]

In response to these kinds of problems, Mark Winne—longtime urban food activist, writer, and cofounder of CFSC—recently issued a poignant challenge in his book *Stand Together or Starve Alone: Unity and Chaos in the U.S. Food Movement.* His subject is the much broader field, which contains many vibrant movements—local food, antihunger, environmental sustainability, farmworker organizing—but also a decided propensity to work in separate silos, if not often at cross purposes. Movement sectors, according to Winne, generate self-righteous ideological rationales for segmentation rather than complex institutional strategies for collaboration. Urban agriculture has itself been the target of criticism, and its advocates "have brought on some of this opprobrium themselves with exaggerated claims of economically feasible food-production methods as well as unsupported claims of creating many new jobs." Nonetheless, he argues, urban farming and gardening have contributed in a variety of ways to life in the built environment and an expansive framing of "community food security," which includes building social capital and local engagement, can serve the larger movement. This argument gains further traction if we recognize how complex governance dynamics in cities, which require ongoing tests of local democratic legitimacy and engender recurring opportunities for movement-institutional partnership, have tended to contain fragmentation.[65]

Conclusion

Biking and walking, as well as urban agriculture, have helped constitute and further enrich the sustainable cities field over a period of decades despite various lags, detours, and obstacles along the way. The bicycle movement was spurred yet also impeded in the wake of technological, cultural, and generational changes manifesting in the late 1960s and early 1970s. Early innovators, such as Davis, California, proved the exception to the rule, until bicycle associations in various other cities were able to make more complex strategic choices to transition from identity-forming contestation over rights to the city to broader forms of alliance with other civic and professional associations, collaboration with elected officials and city agencies responsible for urban governance, and negotiation with other stakeholders vying over spatial scarcities and transportation asymmetries deeply embedded in culture and systems. Operative "rights to the city" were relationally reconstructed through a rich repertoire of civic and institutional practices.

Bicycle associations thereby grew their memberships and expanded the kinds of frames they drew upon, such as healthy cities, while also managing the distinctive cultural legacy of Critical Mass through an array of other types of public celebrations of biking that included families, women, and children—all in the interest of reconstructing the street as commons. Today, even NACTO, the leading professional association, promotes such celebratory cultural practices in major cities throughout the country. Managing strategic choice and culture has nonetheless sometimes required legal and political hardball in the face of police practices and the recurrence of bicycle injuries and deaths.

Strategic choices and organizational shifts at the local level prompted a major shift in national advocacy, especially with the creation of the Alliance for Biking and Walking, which in turn had feedback effects upon the strategic direction of the League of American Bicyclists. Many of these shifts were further enabled by the policy design of ISTEA, whose main advocacy coalition (STPP) enlisted major professional associations, environmental groups, and foundations. The participatory policy feedback effects spurred further mobilization at the grassroots, incentivized by available funding and empowered by requirements for public participation, layered further into NEPA and other requirements and by state pedestrian and bicycle coordinators to provide appropriate institutional handles for collaboration.

Urban agriculture developed from the organic food movement and democratic co-ops of the 1960s and 1970s. It has since manifest itself through a variety of organizational forms, including community gardens and food policy councils and various strategies for urban food justice. As an institutional field—with linkages to rural and metropolitan networks, state and national policy development, and national and global market dynamics—urban agriculture has been enabled especially by formal city agencies (parks, housing, neighborhoods, community development) and by collaboration across networks of local and regional growers, university extension agents, institutional purchasers (schools, hospitals), CDCs, and land trusts. Responding to various producer, consumer, environmental, and large market-actor concerns, federal policy helped rationalize the field with the Organic Food Production Act of 1990, which provided opportunities for multiple stakeholders in the field to establish standards through the National Organic Standards Board during the following decade.

These opportunities were not optimized due to significant and still-lingering divisions among movement actors and allies and policy designs that did not adequately incentivize civic mobilization and collaboration. Some policies during the Bush and Obama administrations helped build community capacity further, but scale was limited by the politics of farm bills, even when policy design was promising. Those posing more radical solutions over several decades never generated sufficient organizational capacity, network collaboration, or democratic legitimacy to alter the general direction of building the field.

CHAPTER FIVE

Urban Rivers and Watersheds

The Clean Water Act (CWA) of 1972, as we have seen in chapter 2, was passed into law after several decades of civic organizing and participatory policy feedback, which enabled creative policy entrepreneurship by Senator Edmund Muskie to leverage resonant lifeworlds in which ordinary citizens in cities across the country experienced threats to water. However, because CWA was largely command and control by design, the one section that might have enabled public participation on a watershed level was severely constrained.

This chapter examines these initial constraints in the 1970s and then turns to some of the policy innovations that provided opportunities to develop and refine a watershed frame and help build a watershed field beginning in the 1980s. First, the chapter analyzes why section 208 of CWA, intended to engage citizens and other stakeholders in basin-wide planning, did not live up to its promise, even as it promoted some learning and capacity building. Two federal policy designs emerged soon thereafter that were considerably more successful in engaging stakeholders; helping to motivate grassroots local, regional, and national network formation; and incorporating holistic watershed approaches that went beyond command-and-control tools and templates, thus complementing and supplementing the initial CWA design. The Chesapeake Bay Program in 1983 and the National Estuary Program in 1987 were policy designs that significantly reoriented the field of water protection and restoration at a time when both political and ecological limits of additional command-and-control strategies were becoming evident. Neither program was specific to urban areas or municipal planning, but both encompassed cities of various sizes, including major coastal cities and metropolitan areas.

If Restore America's Estuaries became the major national association addressing urban coastal issues, the River Network became the premier national intermediary in building a broad watershed movement that included hundreds of local watershed associations, councils, and alliances, as well as state associations, some fully independent of and others sanctioned and partially funded by state governments in multistakeholder policy designs—the latter especially in western states. Civic action on rivers and estuaries prompted the formation of a dedicated office at the US Environmental Protection Agency (EPA) and other offices and initiatives across federal and state agencies that built technical, institutional, and still-further civic capacity for watershed work. The EPA's Office of Wetlands, Oceans, and Watersheds provided funding, developed tools, and enabled networks across the field among civic and watershed groups as well as among professional associations, state and local agencies, and various other nonprofit and for-profit institutions.

The challenges of urban floodwater, stormwater, drinking water, and coastal protection have nonetheless continued to grow with further urban and suburban development, persistent contests over the scope and enforcement of CWA and related laws, and in the face of climate change. Environmental groups such as American Rivers and Clean Water Action, founded in the early 1970s, have maintained important roles in the command-and-control segments of the watershed and policy fields. The chapter concludes with case studies from two policy areas that further extend ecological and watershed approaches while by no means remaining separate from the regulatory dynamics of water. Both have been highly regarded models and have been utilized as partial templates to build their fields further. The first is the development of natural drainage systems for stormwater in Seattle, Washington, and the second is New York City's partnership with watershed communities north of the city to protect and further enable natural filtration of the city's water supply.

Watersheds as Civic and Policy Development

Watersheds became an intriguing way of thinking about natural resource governance when John Wesley Powell, famous explorer and second director of the US Geological Survey, presented a report to Congress in 1878, and then made a more public plea in 1890 for hydrologic units to become local "watershed commonwealths." While the proposal never had much credibility amidst the already existing tangle of local government jurisdictions and the evolution of the field of water law ignorant of hydrologic dynamics, the core idea gained some traction over the next decades, partly due to several great floods followed by federal flood control acts, large dam building projects, and the creation of the Tennessee Valley Authority (TVA) in 1933 and the Soil Conservation Service (SCS) in 1935. By 1949, SCS had helped to institutionalize over two thousand soil conservation districts—now called conservation districts, with their own national association of three thousand districts—fashioned around land and water dynamics at the small watershed scale by means of a policy design that empowered local landowners through formal elections. Some policy development occurred over the next two decades, especially with the Water Resources Planning Act of 1965. The passage of the CWA of 1972 generated further opportunities, though the route to a more robust watershed approach proved considerably more circuitous than some of the drafters might have imagined.[1]

Clean Water Act, Section 208

Section 208 of CWA, referred to by the House Committee on Public Works as "the most important aspect of a water pollution control strategy," was envisioned as the main vehicle for integrated water-quality planning for both point and nonpoint pollution for every river basin in the country. It mandated that states and local governments, including regional planning agencies and other designated institutions such as highway departments and conservation districts, develop twenty-year area-wide plans that cover urban stormwater runoff, agricultural runoff, and runoff from construction activity. Planning should include financing as well as ecological and administrative components. Section 208 is the only section of the 1972 act to address nonpoint pollution and required the use of best-management practices (BMPs) to do so. Section 208 also contained a variety of sanctions for states and localities, including the potential withholding of funds for water treatment facility construction. A citizen suit provision enabled challenge in court, and a successful suit (*Natural Resources Defense Council v. Costle* in 1977) ensured that all areas of the country, not just designated critical areas, were subject to planning. The policy design incorporated a requirement for public participation in section 101(e).[2]

Nonetheless, the potential for aligning this new administrative design with further civic capacity building appropriate to the challenges of water-sheds was seriously constrained. First, the overall command-and-control logic of CWA, with its high-priority metrics and deadlines especially oriented to controlling discrete chemical pollutants rather than its core stated goal of ecological restoration, tended to crowd out section 208 planning in terms of EPA staff attention, dedicated funding, and degree of explicit regulatory mandate and program guidance, thus delaying implementation for several years. Congress even failed to appropriate all the authorized funds and thus shifted the burdens to states and localities, which were not generally predisposed to meet new public participation requirements. Hence, they found ways to evade them, especially since the threat of major sanctions, such as the withholding of construction grants provided by section 201 of CWA or imposing temporary moratoria on sewer connections, was not fully credible in view of the power of organized lobbies—including environmental ones—when vying for federal dollars and the potential for political embarrassment should such facilities not become operative in a timely fashion. Thus, while the policy design recognized that construction grants without planning might provide incentives for further development and thereby *increase* nonpoint pollution, it could not by itself generate the political or civic will to act upon this insight, nor could the citizen suit provision be utilized against state and local agencies that dragged their feet or did not implement BMPs.[3]

Second, public participation was required in five other water quality programs administered by the EPA. To be sure, this reflected the relatively strong normative support for public participation in the emerging water quality field and among the act's drafters, but it was also easy for Congress to create broad mandates yet react testily should preferred programmatic goals be delayed. This confronted civic and environmental groups with attention- and resource-rationing dilemmas: choose to focus their participation on higher priority programs, such as the permit program of the National Pollutant Discharge Elimination System (NPDES, section 402 of CWA), or spread their limited organizational attention and resources even more thinly. In line with the emergent CWA norm and legislative history that EPA actively promote public participation, the agency provided a training grant to the Conservation Foundation to conduct one-time workshops in all ten EPA regions, which seemed to enhance knowledge and interest among a range of civic and environmental groups.[4]

However, the most effective civic organization that the EPA might arguably have chosen for long-term civic capacity building in the field would have been the League of Women Voters, given its multitiered national structure extending into all states and numerous communities, its continuity of engagement and extent of cross-cutting networks in basins nurtured over nearly two decades, and its broad legitimacy in terms of epistemic evenhandedness among multiple stakeholders and agencies, including EPA and the US Army Corps of Engineers. In the early 1970s, the corps's famous "fishbowl planning" engaged the Puget Sound LWV in helping to develop almost a dozen alternative plans for public consideration. By then, however, the League of Women Voters was competing for members in the larger ecology of activist organizations with second-wave feminist groups and other environmental organizations.[5]

At the local level, organized constituencies among farmers, home builders, and other industry groups made their presence felt in these water quality planning processes given their open democratic design. And a bias toward further development was buttressed by a powerful demographic trend: new family formation resulting from the coming of age of the baby boomers. Neither EPA staff nor the consultants hired to help facilitate participation had yet developed multistakeholder designs to intentionally balance pluralist voice, equity, accountability, and trust in the interests of pragmatic consensus formation and shared work, which would only later emerge as an important component of watershed field building.

The North Carolina section 208 water quality planning process, which extended over a two and one-half-year period beginning in December 1976, attracted chapters of multitiered environmental groups, such as the Sierra Club, Audubon, and NWF as well as LWV, whose representative became cochair of the policy advisory committee. It also attracted freestanding local and regional groups, such as the Wilmington Clean Water Association and the Clean Water Association of Coastal North Carolina. Yet some of these groups were more interested in new state mandates than in participatory planning that yielded only voluntary strategies, partly because they realistically perceived disproportionate industry influence among state agencies but also because they recognized that broader publics were quite responsive to industry arguments that water quality plans would constrict economic development and home-building activity and would constrain property rights. These arguments paralleled those emerging in the debate on the National Land Use Policy Act (NLUPA), which had been defeated in Congress in 1975 (see chapter 3). At this early stage of post-CWA watershed policy, not only was federal land-use authority relatively weak and in tension with other command-and-control tools but neither smart growth nor watershed movements had yet emerged to reframe the debate.[6]

However, section 208 seems to have triggered learning about policy substance and dialogic process in the state, possibly even more so in terms of long-term leadership development in some civic and professional networks where legal and regulatory challenges were mounted in the early 1980s. Out of eight existing grassroots groups, this occurred through the formation of the North Carolina Coastal Federation, which also campaigned successfully to have the Albermarle and Pamlico Bays designated as part of the National Estuary Program in 1987 and mobilized active citizen involvement in its collaboratively developed conservation plan. Basin planning efforts manifesting similar patterns elsewhere in the 1970s are unclear. Congress, however, eliminated section 208 grants in 1981 when Ronald Reagan came to office, though it did not repeal the section itself.[7]

The Chesapeake Bay and National Estuary Programs

Two other federal policy designs were particularly important to building the watershed field in the 1980s: the Chesapeake Bay Program, established by agreement of several states and the District of Columbia in 1983, with a dedicated office at the EPA, and the National Estuary Program, which was partly modeled on the Chesapeake program but derived statutory authority from the 1987 amendments to the Clean Water Act. It now extends to twenty-eight designated estuaries of national significance, such as Puget Sound and Tampa Bay. Estuaries are especially complex ecosystems because they combine freshwater fed by inland rivers and streams with saltwater maritime environments subject to tides and the regular influx of saline water into semienclosed coastal areas. Their most common names are bay, sound, harbor, inlet, and lagoon. Due to the complex and synergistic interaction among major threats (population growth, coastal development, agricultural runoff, overfishing), and the many types and scales of actors that operate in their ecological systems and institutional fields, they are recognized as especially appropriate for forms of adaptive management and multistakeholder collaboration.[8]

Chesapeake Bay

As the nation's largest estuary—approximately two hundred miles long, north to south from Havre de Grace, Maryland, to Norfolk, Virginia, and varying in width from 3.4 miles to 35 miles—Chesapeake Bay has fifty major freshwater tributaries, such as the Susquehanna and Potomac Rivers, and an overall watershed area of some sixty-four thousand square miles—fifteen times the size of the bay itself, extending to six states and the District of Columbia. Its relative shallowness of twenty-one feet on average makes it especially vulnerable to shifts in temperature and wind as well as nutrient overload from agriculture and metropolitan sprawl, although it also faces major stressors from toxic chemicals and other pollutants. Population doubled in the region between 1950 and 2000, and the average amount of land per person has increased four to five times over the forty-year period since 1970. After an accelerated period of deterioration of the bay in the postwar period, the Chesapeake Bay Foundation (CBF) was established in 1967 as an advocacy and environmental-education organization. It grew into a civic association with extraordinary legitimacy that could compel vigorous debate on the future of the bay in the public sphere of major local and regional media, including its own influential *Bay Journal,* and in the halls of state legislatures and Congress. This public debate, given further force by the devastating floods of Hurricane Agnes in 1972, was buttressed by two major research projects, each lasting seven years. One was coordinated by the US Army Corps of Engineers and released in 1973, and the other was by the EPA and released in 1983. Scientists from many institutions contributed to these and other ongoing research efforts, and the 1977 revisions of CWA authorized the EPA to develop a program for the bay.[9]

The policy design that emerged had several important components. First, the states of Maryland and Virginia established an advisory commission in 1980 that generated the momentum for direct legislative collaboration, resulting in the Chesapeake Bay Agreement in 1983 and facilitated by William Ruckelshaus who had returned to head the EPA after the removal of Reagan's initial administrator. Pennsylvania joined in 1985, and other states (New York, Delaware, and West Virginia) with land and rivers in the watershed have collaborated on various projects. The agreement was formalized at a governors' summit (including the Washington, DC, mayor) attended by many other elected officials, scientists, local and state administrators, and user and civic groups that had become active across the bay, and thus signaled serious purpose for sustained action. A special Chesapeake Bay Commission was established to guide the process and has remained institutionally anchored in the three state legislatures. The agreement was renewed in 1987 and again in 2000, the latter commonly referred to as C2K (Chesapeake 2000), with a more ambitious and specific set of goals under five major categories, including the restoration and protection of living resources, vital habitat, water quality, improved land use, and stewardship and community engagement.[10]

Second, the Chesapeake Bay Agreement was voluntary and granted the EPA no additional regulatory authority, although it did not foreclose further state regulatory action, as with Maryland's Chesapeake Bay Critical Areas Law and mandatory blue-crab harvest limits, or Philadelphia's regulatory strategies to manage stormwater on a watershed basis and through multistakeholder partnerships. Nor did it cede any of its CWA command tools to motivate innovative watershed and green infrastructure approaches. Indeed, CBF has served as a policy advocate and watchdog, monitoring state implementation of the Clean Water Act and various state laws and sometimes going to court. With the new agreement in place, EPA could provide a fuller range of assistance beyond the initial scientific study as part of its Chesapeake Bay Program; its executive council was designed around continued tristate and DC representation.

In addition to scientific, technical, and policy analysis, EPA assistance has taken the form of support for collaborative planning and restoration projects, with technical assistance and small grants for citizen monitoring, environmental education, stream teams, and hands-on restoration projects. Established in 1971, the Alliance for Chesapeake Bay came to largely serve as the nonadvocacy institution coordinating many of these activities and convening the Citizens Advisory Committee for the program, a familiar and often surprisingly effective way for citizens to exercise influence over public bureaucracies, as argued by political scientist Susan Moffitt. A science advisory committee and local government advisory committee are also part of this structure.[11]

The Local Government Advisory Committee provides technical assistance to various jurisdictions and local agencies, thus further building their administrative capabilities as well as their capacities to work with civic and environmental groups. The Delaware River watershed, with some 13,539 square miles with 838 separate municipalities, is only one of six in the Philadelphia, Pennsylvania, region. The city of Philadelphia, the first US city to establish an office of watersheds, utilized the emerging template of stakeholder participation in watershed partnerships and educational outreach that was diffused through the local government advisory and other mechanisms. In this case, the Pennsylvania Horticultural Society (see chapter 4) became a key partner along with specific neighborhood associations as part of a later mayoral strategic neighborhood transformation initiative. A still-further Model Neighborhoods program for Green Street stormwater management engaged residents and nonprofits. The city's Green City, Clean Waters program extends these initiatives in an agreement with the EPA and through collaboration among fifteen city departments (housing, schools, parking, streets, parks, planning, health, commerce, and others). By 2016, it showed significant results by its fifth anniversary, with another twenty years of commitment to invest in green stormwater infrastructure.[12]

The Bay Partner Communities Program has catalyzed many local projects, of which there were approximately one thousand by the mid-1990s. Funding support through these various programs, as well as stewardship and advocacy opportunities emerging at the grassroots level, sometimes with CBF support, have nurtured civic associations of many sorts, including watershed associations, stewards and friends groups on many rivers and streams, and environmental education initiatives through schools and youth groups. While this policy design has many shortcomings given the extent and pace of the threats to bay health and some of the political deficits of voluntary approaches, as well as the enormous estimated costs and projected financing shortfalls of restoration of the C2K strategy, it has incentivized numerous forms of collaborative civic and local government action at a time, especially—though by no means only—at its inception when further federal command-and-control legislation did not appear to be either politically feasible or ecologically adept.[13]

National Estuaries

The National Estuary Program (NEP), authorized by section 320 of the 1987 amendments to CWA, drew upon the Chesapeake Bay policy design, but extended it to many more estuaries. NEP has several core features. First, EPA can accept a petition from governors to designate an estuary of national significance, with renewable federal funding after a three-to-five-year initial grant, if the petitioning state or states agree to establish a multistakeholder management conference for the local NEP. This conference is typically housed in a federal or state agency, university, or non-profit organization that serves as fiscal agent. The designated NEPs, which grew from an initial round of five in 1988 and have sometimes reorganized and developed nomenclature more appropriate to place or practice (e.g., the Puget Sound Partnership), are encouraged to raise further funds from public and private sources and develop a wide range of other institutional relationships not dependent upon EPA, whose funding may decrease over time even while programmatic links and the legitimacy that come with federal program status are enhanced.

Second, the management conference must include several categories of actors: other public agencies (local, state, and federal), businesses, academic institutions, environmental and community groups, and a representative from the EPA regional office. However, an essential aspect of an NEP baseline "institutional analysis," as it is formally called, is to map early a broader range of the organizations in its institutional field that may provide distinct tools (regulatory, voluntary, incentive-based, planning, natural resource, public education, technical assistance), and hence civic, political, economic, and administrative opportunities and obstacles that may present themselves. In effect, the NEP policy design incentivizes core actors to imagine, map, and build, in the terminology of Neil Fligstein and Doug McAdam, a "strategic action field" within each estuary.[14]

Third, the NEPs develop a shared vision for the protection and restoration of the estuary, as well as a comprehensive conservation and management plan (CCMP), to which core stakeholders commit. The CCMP entails the development of a wide-ranging set of adaptive strategies over time but contains no new regulatory authority, although the local NEP and its stakeholder groups and other civic and environmental partners might—and often do—advocate for enhanced regulatory powers through the appropriate state and local authorities, such as the implementation of local land-use and sediment controls. Fourth, NEPs typically have a range of appropriate committees (technical and scientific, policy, and local government) to enhance their capacities as well as a citizens' advisory committee intended to broaden public participation and civic initiative well beyond the groups that may be represented on the management and other committees.[15]

NEP policy design thus has several civic components, though these may be developed in a more and less robust fashion depending on the specific estuary and the mix, mobilization, and receptiveness of various civic groups and institutional partners. The two most important components are the core representational design within the management conference that enables one or more civic, watershed, or estuary groups to help determine vision and strategy, and hold the partnership accountable for implementation and results; and the broader citizens' advisory committee that enables outreach to dozens or even hundreds of other civic associations and institutions such as schools, museums, and nature centers. The latter represents the intention to widen and deepen "democratic anchorage" in the field;[16] namely, the capacity of core civic and environmental groups to reach into their own broad-based memberships and affiliated networks to form public opinion and facilitate democratic deliberation around issues that emerge within the much narrower management conference. In addition, the policy design aimed to enlist members and affiliates to do some of the actual work through coproduction (water quality monitoring; restoration of riparian buffers or oyster beds; and environmental education with statewide associations, local school districts, or national multitiered youth groups). To facilitate coproduction, NEPs provide various types of grants to local groups, sometimes networked through a bay-wide association, to enable staff and training capacity.

Best practice within the emerging network of NEPs, which over time have come to call themselves a *network* rather than just a federal program, is diffused through personal relationships, conferences, reports, websites, and tool kits to which various network partners contribute for broad use. Thus, NEP partners learn from each other how to best translate complex scientific findings from their academic partners to broader publics so that ecological threats and potential restoration benefits can be understood in the vernacular and become coupled to resonant cultural narratives and visuals about special places, iconic species, family, and community memories. I observed this vividly in staff presentations and civic interventions at community meetings when the Puget Sound NEP was being reshaped and renamed a decade ago, which resulted—after a few missteps—in a more collaborative, democratic professional, and decentralized institutional design around "local integrating organizations" with the capacity to develop strategic action agendas and ecosystem recovery plans across distinct areas of the sound.[17]

NEPs also develop and utilize analytic tools for estimating the economic costs and benefits of estuary services (pollution filtration, fishing, tourism).

In this they have been aided by academic economics, sometimes directly by economists and businesses who take part in official committees or special work groups, and by elaborate sets of tools that have been specifically developed by the National Research Council and other researchers. These kinds of tools are especially important for community decision-making when CCMP recommendations may call for a bond issue to fund sewer upgrades or green infrastructure investments. They enable understanding of comparative benefits and costs of investing in improving estuary and ecosystem services—indeed, in understanding the very concept of such services.[18]

In short, NEP multistakeholder policy design, institutional field analysis, and practical tool kits enhance opportunities for aligning ecological, cultural, and civic logics with market, regulatory, and revenue-generating local governance logics.

NEP has also provided the institutional framework to build the capacities of local groups to enhance monitoring of estuary health. The second iteration of *Volunteer Estuary Monitoring*, a 396-page manual, provides a good sense of the meticulous combination of technical knowledge and civic practice represented by the EPA's collaborative work with some of these organizations and their local partners. Developed in partnership with the Ocean Conservancy, this method manual covers all manner of project planning, the organizing of volunteers, safety management, and the testing of the broadest spectrum of nutrients, oxygen, toxins, alkalinity, temperature, salinity, turbidity, bacteria, submerged aquatic vegetation, and other living organisms—each has a chapter.

The process for developing the manual, however, is as significant as the product. With EPA funding, the Ocean Conservancy had been conducting regular trainings for local networks of volunteer groups since 1998 in all twenty-eight NEPs—some six hundred groups in all as of 2005. During development of the manual's second edition, the Ocean Conservancy worked with experts in each technical area of monitoring and shared the draft with all its local group trainees over the previous two-year period. As part of an expansive watershed movement network, prominent volunteer monitoring organizations around the country contributed case studies. The final draft was reviewed by a broad array of leading practitioners from these groups, universities and extension services, local and state agencies, EPA regional and headquarters offices, and the US Fish and Wildlife Service. From local knowledge and organizing methods on one end to laboratory science and rigorous quality assurance technique on the other, this network has produced and refined a form of democratic knowledge indispensable to the stewardship of estuaries throughout the country.[19]

In a comparative study of twenty NEP and ten non-NEP estuary programs based upon a sizable survey of stakeholder participants and interviews, Mark Lubell found that the NEP design enhances communication and trust among stakeholder groups, including those with strongly divergent beliefs about the primacy of environmental values versus property rights. It also enhances beliefs in the importance of scientific knowledge—especially in knowledge generated through the NEP process in conjunction with academic and other scientists—to grapple with problems that are complex, diffuse, and boundary spanning, and thus do not lend themselves well to the simpler application of command-and-control methods to control point-source pollution. Stakeholder inclusiveness tends to moderate deeply held value-based views and generates trust among those with strong value positions at different ends of the belief spectrum. Conservatives with strong property-rights beliefs are less likely to distrust other stakeholder groups, including public officials and environmentalists; strong environmentalists, while still wary of the role of economic interests, are more likely to recognize fairness in the NEP process and see it as yielding better environmental outcomes. Overall, NEPs seem to enhance social capital and trust as well as the belief in institutional performance.[20]

Founded in 1995, the most important national civic association in the estuary field is Restore America's Estuaries (RAE). It is a coalition of regional groups, such as the Chesapeake Bay Foundation, North Carolina Coastal Federation, Save the Bay (San Francisco), Tampa Bay Watch, and Save The Bay (STB) in Narragansett Bay. STB was one of the key civic innovators in this arena extending back two decades prior. It was initially called the Narragansett Bay Homeowners Association and was in coalition with other local groups to stop the building of an oil refinery and twin nuclear power plants; it then broadened its perspective to include civic collaboration and restoration across the bay's watershed and convened similar groups on the national level in the late 1980s (with the help of an EPA grant). The NEP policy design furnished the key organizing incentive for RAE, and the Pew Charitable Trusts played the key convening and funding roles in its founding. In the late 1990s, RAE became especially active in helping pass the Estuary Restoration Act of 2000, which was enacted with strong bipartisan support and authorized $275 million over five years for restoration projects; it then lobbied for the Magnuson-Stevens Fishery Conservation and Management Reauthorization Act of 2006.[21]

These policies have provided significant funding for community-based restoration projects through the National Oceanic and Atmospheric Administration's (NOAA) Restoration Center at its National Marine Fisheries Service—with a further boost from the American Recovery and Reinvestment Act in 2009—as well as through EPA, the US Fish and Wildlife Service, and the Natural Resources Conservation Service at USDA, all of which have sat on the interagency restoration council along with the US Army Corps. While NOAA has had some two dozen partners—including multi-tiered associations such as Ducks Unlimited working across all one hundred and thirty US estuaries—in the period from 2000 to 2005, RAE received $8,717,249 from the Restoration Center, which it distributed to local groups in its network. They, in turn, leveraged $9,136,416 directly and a further $8,404,916 through its member groups and other partners. In collaboration with NOAA and an extensive network of scientists, restoration practitioners, and program managers—and as stipulated in the Estuary Restoration Act of 2000—RAE developed an elaborate national strategy document to restore coastal and estuarine habitat. It also serves as the key sponsor of a biennial conference that enlists participants, now including international ones, from across the estuary and coastal habitat field. It also facilitates other programs for its member organizations. The Digital Coast at NOAA now adds economic, land cover, and satellite tools; it includes a sea level rise viewer and land cover atlas to enable coastal communities to plan more effectively and transparently.[22]

In the face of projected sea level rise due to climate change and the institutional biases toward ineffective and costly forms of coastal hardening strategies, such as those for bulkheads and sea walls, RAE has focused attention on "living shorelines," such as saltmarsh and oyster reefs, and has framed this as a way of protecting estuarine ecosystems and property interests of waterfront landowners subject to water damage. In 2015, it convened the first Living Shorelines Summit along with partners from The Nature Conservancy, which has been quite active on this front. Joining them were the California Coastal Conservancy, California Sea Grant, and various university centers, along with representatives from several federal agencies (the EPA, the NOAA, and the army corps). RAE was then designated through a cooperative agreement with the EPA to establish a Living

Shorelines Academy to further diffuse science, policy, tool kits, databases, and hands-on practices among volunteers. In view of the uncertainties of sea-level rise estimates, RAE's approach is based on a multiscenario approach to planning.[23]

Watershed Associations and Councils

The postwar struggle for clean water legislation, as we have seen in chapter 2, engaged a range of multi-tiered associations, such as the League of Women Voters and the Izaak Walton League of America (ILWA), and elicited new organizing by local and regional groups around specific rivers and lakes, from the Hudson River to Lake Erie, from the Colorado River to the Northwest salmon fisheries. The policy designs of section 208 of CWA in the 1970s, and then more ambitiously of the Chesapeake Bay and National Estuary Programs in the following decade, generated further incentives and resources for civic organizing, so that by the late 1980s and early 1990s, a distinctive watershed movement began to emerge in many parts of the country, including inland areas not directly linked to estuaries. Movement actors, both at the local level and through various state and national associations and intermediaries, worked to build a broad watershed field with its own distinctive cognitive framing, cultural symbols, scientific research, organizational forms, institutional supports, practical tool kits, and action repertoires. EPA further helped nationalize the movement while also recognizing state, regional, and local distinctions and authorities.[24]

The civic impetus at the local level was typically protective: stop some unwanted development or source of pollution to preserve a cherished water body or culturally emblematic fish species, such as "totem salmon" on the Mattole River in Oregon and Northern California. Such struggles, especially for Native American tribes, may have interwoven generations of cultural meaning, placemaking, community feeding, and economic trading. For others, it was direct pollution where people swam and fished or where waterfront property values, children's health, or family memories were suddenly threatened. This protective ethic manifested itself in the formation of groups with nomenclature such as "friends" or "stewards" of a specific stream or lake. Indeed, when the River Network and the Rivers, Trails, and Conservation Assistance Program of the National Park Service surveyed the field of existing groups and institutions in 1998, these were by far the most common names, along with "adopt a stream" and similar nomenclature, which state directories of groups such as Save the Salmon, with far more thorough listings, likewise confirmed.[25]

Volunteer—or "citizen"—water quality monitoring also drew upon this protective ethic, buttressed in part by distrust of the amount, quality, and place-specificity of data being produced by public agencies. Various "lake watch" and "river watch" networks, as well as "student congresses" within the environmental education field, began to emerge, some with support from ILWA and state water offices hungry for low-cost data, enhanced legitimacy, or both. The first national conference of volunteer water monitoring groups convened in 1988 and then biennially throughout the 1990s, until its meetings were merged with those held by professionals in the field. The proceedings were published, and a growing list of some five hundred groups had been generated by 1994. In addition, "riverkeeper" and "baykeeper" boats, modeled on the Hudson Riverkeeper, were equipped with monitoring equipment and could also provide onboard education about illegal dumping practices and the overall health of specific bodies of water. Many watershed groups now have such nimble and well-equipped craft, and the Waterkeeper Alliance was founded in 1999 to diffuse the practice nationally, and then internationally.[26]

Two broad field-building strategies were especially important during these years, and they proved largely complementary and coconstitutive. The first was pursued by the River Network and its various watershed association partners, the second by the Office of Water at the EPA, also with its various institutional partners and networks. Together, they drew in multiple kinds of actors to fashion a more robust watershed frame and an increasingly sophisticated and usable set of tools. The George H. W. Bush administration (1989–1993), and then especially the Clinton administration (1993–2001), provided the initial political opportunity, but field building continued through the administrations of George W. Bush (2001–2009) and Barack Obama (2009–2017).

River Network

Founded in Portland, Oregon, in 1988, the River Network has developed into one of the most important capacity-building intermediaries in the watershed field and the sponsor of the annual River Rally that includes local watershed associations, state associational networks and agency officials, and other national groups (American Rivers, Groundwork USA,

Waterkeeper Alliance). Civic action and civic professionalism have been interwoven into the core of its identity and practice for three decades. It has placed increased emphasis on environmental justice (EJ) as it continues to reinvent its mission at a time of fewer federal resources to support broad training initiatives, yet it maintains a strong emphasis on multistakeholder partnerships as an indispensable part of watershed work. Indeed, as Kyle Dreyfuss-Wells—CEO of the Northeast Ohio Regional Sewer District encompassing Cleveland and sixty-one other communities, past chair of the National Association of Clean Water Agencies (NACWA) Stormwater Management Committee, and Stormwater Professional of the Year—put it in her 2019 address to the River Rally, "It is *way more fun, way more exciting, and way more authentic* for utility directors and staff to partner with communities, and to get on the right side" (emphasis in original).[27]

In the early 1990s, the River Network hired a field organizer to conduct an itinerant field survey of river groups. Peter Lavigne, who had experience with two of the more venerable watershed associations in New England, began to organize and affiliate "watershed associations," "watershed councils," and "watershed alliances" around the country. With a grant from the Henry P. Kendall Foundation of Boston, the River Network then convened the Watershed Innovators Workshop in June 1995 in Cummington, Massachusetts, in collaboration with Trudy Coxe, the decade-long director of Narragansett's Save The Bay, who was then serving as secretary of the Massachusetts Executive Office of Environmental Affairs. Forty innovators attended, mostly from civic associations and public agencies. They had been identified by their peers across the country; their biographies listed prior affiliations to multi-tiered associations and national advocacy groups (Audubon, the Sierra Club, the National Wildlife Federation, Clean Water Action, Nuclear Freeze) and to various other public agencies, with a broad distribution of civic experience and technical background.

The meeting emphasized the need for a more holistic approach to watersheds—rather than simply regulating pollutant by pollutant, permit by permit—as well as civic involvement in the scientific and management process and the value of local knowledge, with special responsibilities of scientists to empower communities, including tribal and EJ communities. It also recognized that the diverse spectrum of watershed groups included independently organized nonprofit "watershed associations," more typical in the East, and "watershed councils," more common in the West and typically constituted, often with state authorization, as multistakeholder groups. This structural distinction within the larger organizational ecology, while not fully determinative of the degree of empowerment of environmental groups or of democratic accountability within multistakeholder designs, nonetheless shaped perceptions of strategic opportunities and traps within the watershed field and among critics in the broader environmental movement.[28]

With further funding from Kendall, the River Network then extended its learning process for several more years through its Four Corners Watershed Innovators Initiative, which convened four further meetings, one in each corner of the United States: Washington State, California, Florida, and Massachusetts. Each meeting was preceded by the circulation of a substantial report of the watershed activities, policies, and organizations in that state, typically written jointly by civic and agency staff. Thus, the Washington report was authored by the director of the nonprofit Rivers Council of Washington, the director of the Yakima River Watershed Council, and a senior policy analyst from the Department of Ecology, which was the chief regulatory agency, with close ties to the Puget Sound NEP, an organization it later absorbed administratively in its third institutional iteration as the Puget Sound Partnership. These background reports were followed by reports of meetings as well as general analyses written by two University of Wisconsin researchers, including one commissioned by the National Academy of Public Administration (NAPA), which had been playing an important analytic role in community and state innovations for both the EPA and Congress during the preceding five years.[29]

The EPA's Office of Wetlands, Oceans, and Watersheds

While the River Network and its partners were exploring watershed practices in leading states and establishing a template for other states with significant isomorphic effects, the EPA was developing its own strategies, which, over the 1990s and then into the 2000s, became increasingly ambitious and linked to these civic initiatives. In 1991, based partly upon its experience with the same watershed associations in New England's Region 1 that informed the River Network strategy, the Office of Water set up a dedicated Office of Wetlands, Oceans, and Watersheds (OWOW). In 1994, staff from other offices joined in developing a framing document known by the site of the key meeting as the Edgewater Consensus. This framing document was included in the EPA's strategic planning, which produced a scan of two hundred other place-based projects and then a more ambitious Community-Based Environmental Protection (CBEP) strategy (see chapter 7). It further enlisted staff across other relevant offices who considered themselves an agency network with cognitive affinities to ecosystem science and shared normative commitments to empowering communities. It included links to similar networks in other agencies and among civic groups. The staff in these EPA networks cohered into the Office of Sustainable Ecosystems and Communities (OSEC), although the EPA's deputy administrator, a champion of this approach, was unable to secure a viable way to sustain separate funding for the office given turf battles amidst flat overall agency budgets. Nonetheless, OSEC moved watershed approaches and other community-based thinking forward significantly by the end of the decade.[30]

A further opportunity presented itself when Congress, just before Republicans took control of the House under Newt Gingrich in 1995, commissioned NAPA—the most prestigious organization in the public administration field and the one with a congressional charter—to further examine alternatives to command and control. The NAPA panel was led by DeWitt John, who had just published his book *Civic Environmentalism* with the Congressional Quarterly Press and was well connected to those in the National Civic League (NCL) who had been energetically pressing for community-building innovations across various policy fields; its community visioning and strategic planning handbook became widely utilized in cities around the country. Indeed, NCL had just convened a major national initiative beginning in 1994 among prominent nonprofit organizations under the board leadership of John Gardner, the former HEW secretary, the founder of both Common Cause and Independent Sector, and a recent author of a widely read book called *On Leadership*. NAPA published a series of reports, including ones examining watersheds, that elaborated on the importance of community-based approaches while not backing away from the core functions of federal regulation. These reports were generally consistent with reports by other prestigious nonprofit, academic, presidential, and multistakeholder projects appearing in the latter part of the 1990s, including from Enterprise for the Environment, Yale University, the Aspen Institute, and the President's Council on Sustainable Development.[31]

Although there were complex twists and turns in watershed and other community-based approaches at the end of the Clinton administration and into the Bush presidency—which preferred the frame of "cooperative conservation"—the EPA helped build the watershed field quite substantially, especially in ways that can be grouped into three categories: funding, tools, and networks. First, drawing upon its experience in the Chesapeake Bay and National Estuary Programs, the EPA provided funding for watershed groups that were organized as independent nonprofits at the local level. It did this through a Watershed Assistance Grant program administered through the River Network, focused on building local organizational capacity and not just completing projects. These grants were part of a strategic Clean Water Action Plan that the EPA developed with seven other federal agencies and the TVA. Thus, the core idea of funding local civic capacity secured broad legitimacy within the federal government and represented a longer arc of strategic alignment between administrative agencies and movement groups, though one that has been continually constrained by budgets and periodically disrupted by politics.[32]

When the subsequent Targeted Watershed Initiative grants shifted greater grant selection authority to states and tribes, the EPA set aside several million dollars to be distributed on a competitive basis to national and regional intermediaries with proven training and field-building capacities, such as the River Network, the Center for Watershed Protection, the Southeast Watershed Forum, and the International City/County Management Association (ICMA). These organizations, in turn, helped build the capacity of states and local governments for such work with their local watershed associations. In this policy design for democracy, the EPA thus utilized national and regional civic intermediaries to help build local and state government capacities for collaboration. State policy designs, motivated by other aspects of EPA guidances and funding incentives, such as CWA section 319 nonpoint source grants, incentivized the formation of statewide watershed associations. A case in point is the Colorado Watershed Assembly, which collaborated in its workgroups with EPA Region 8 and state staff but was governed by its independent member associations. The latter grew from six to forty within two years of the mid-1990s shift in state policy built around watersheds—a very clear policy feedback effect. The assembly, in turn, developed a wide in-state network with *other types of groups* focused on water quality and environmental education, including the League of Women Voters of Colorado Education Fund, and holds the broad annual Colorado Watersheds Conference. During the Obama administration, the Urban Waters Federal Partnership, led by EPA with thirteen other agencies, sponsored the Urban Waters National Training Workshops.[33]

Second, OWOW and other offices at the EPA developed a set of watershed tools that civic groups could utilize in their work of monitoring, planning, and restoration. In many cases, though sometimes only when the agency was pressured by independent groups, these tools were coproduced by a set of partners in a larger network, of which the EPA and other federal agencies were a part. In most cases, network actors treated each other as equal and valued partners, linked through distinct forms of knowledge, practice, and trust generated through collaboration rather than hierarchical authority. As discussed prior, this was clearly the case in the development of Volunteer Estuary Monitoring, with the Ocean Conservancy acting as intermediary between hundreds of local groups and with various professional actors. But it was also inscribed in the regular diffusion of technical and scientific tools, state and local agency policies, and civic practices through the *Volunteer Monitor*, a quarterly online journal, and in the development of other monitoring manuals for specific types of watersheds. The nonprofit Center for Watershed Protection, with support from the EPA, developed a series of manuals for restoring small urban watersheds in which it had been working. Key partners of the River Network redesigned the online Watershed Plan Builder to accommodate local user needs; in this case, they had to pressure Diane Regas, the director of OWOW who had previous and then subsequent experience as a national environmental association leader, to assemble her technical staff to listen to grassroots users and training intermediaries. She did this first at Washington, DC, headquarters and then at the next River Rally—for both practical and symbolic purposes. OWOW's Watershed Academy produced webcasts on a broad range of tools, which were typically presented by two or three partners from relevant networks of federal, state, and local agency professionals, academic centers, and civic groups.[34]

Third, EPA facilitated networking across the field. This is evident already in the way that it provided funding through nonprofit intermediaries to train local, state, and regional association leaders or build upon their networked local knowledge and tool kits. But the EPA also facilitated various conferences as "field-configuring events," either as a direct partner in organizing events or by lending legitimacy and sending staff to participate in various plenary and regular sessions. These meetings ranged from several hundred to several thousand participants, plus teleconferencing to other sites for some meetings, and with one or several major civic associations in the lead. They included the River Network's annual River Rally, regular biennial citizen water quality monitoring conferences, national and regional multistakeholder watershed forums, the "trashed rivers" conferences of the Coalition to Restore Urban Waters, and RAE's national conferences on coastal and estuarine habitat restoration. The range of types of participating organizations varied from one conference to another depending on pre-existing solidarities and homophilies on one end, to emergent opportunities for relationships and trust among actors operating with diverse institutional logics on the other. EPA's field-building and legitimation strategy included assembling a very broad array of civic, conservation, and watershed groups; Indian tribes; professional and business associations; local, state, and federal agencies; and university extension and K–12 environmental education groups.[35]

These two broad field-building strategies—by the River Network and OWOW—have been complemented by others at the state, metropolitan, and local levels and with tool kits enabling creative configurations of deliberative planning, cultural engagement, and hands-on restoration. Anne Taufen analyzes such multiple "ways of knowing" urban watersheds in her study of the restoration of the Los Angeles River. Funding from California's Prop 50 bond of $3 billion for water projects in 2005 incentivized—indeed required through Integrated Regional Water Management plans—collaboration among multiple public agencies as well as the conservancies and watershed groups that had been active for two decades. Project planning tools enabled the deliberative evaluation and ranking of grant projects according to their multiple benefits, including "service to disadvantage communities." Friends of the Los Angeles River and the Los Angeles County Bicycle Coalition produced a guidebook for walks and rides to enable more people to fall in love with the river and thus work actively to protect and restore it. James Rojas, senior transportation planner and founder of the Latino Urban Forum, developed art and design charrettes to engage neighborhoods and children in actively imagining how to restore the river and its public spaces.[36]

American Rivers and Clean Water Action

Other kinds of river advocacy groups, as well as national groups such as the Sierra Club and NRDC, have been important to building urban watershed strategies and building the broader field of water protection and conservation. American Rivers was founded in 1973 as the American Rivers Conservation Council—shortening its name in 1987—largely in response to the Wild and Scenic Rivers Act of 1968. When the National Parks and Conservation Association rejected a direct advocacy role for classifying rivers under the jurisdiction of the National Parks Service, American Rivers was founded to perform this role and to campaign against the construction of new dams on "wild rivers." The organization grew modestly in terms of staff and budget in its first three decades, but into the twenty-first century, it became significantly more strategic in its growth and campaigns. It developed a sizable professional staff of seventy-five and an annual budget of some $12 to $15 million. It campaigned effectively, often with local groups and other national partners, to remove hundreds of dams, a trend that has accelerated with a clearer understanding of their ecological impacts. By 2016, American Rivers had organized staff into four major regional councils (California, Colorado, Montana, and the Northwest), but also led or collaborated on campaigns for dam removal, river restoration, and green infrastructure in other parts of the country, including cities such as Milwaukee, Wisconsin; Pittsburgh, Pennsylvania; and Atlanta, Georgia. Its strategic plan for the years 2014 to 2018 aimed to further strengthen its advocacy role for rivers at national, state, and local levels while also mobilizing volunteers, especially youth, for its annual National River Cleanup.[37]

While generally avoiding the watershed frame unless a local partner such as the Yakima Nation utilizes it, American Rivers often employs similar language—"basins" and "ecosystems" as *ecological content*, and "diverse stakeholders," "common ground," "win-win," "partnering with local governments, water utilities, and community groups," and "mov[ing] from water conflict to a new era of cooperation" as *participatory process*. This language was chosen partly because it "resonated in media stories," thereby opening space within local public spheres. Lisa Hollingsworth-Segedy, director of the river restoration team of twelve, brings a fine-grained relational repertoire to contentious settings where dam removal typically triggers concerns about potential loss of community icons, family memories, and fishing buddies. She coaches her team to do one-on-ones and small group walks on the river banks and taps her training in storytelling and puppetry to facilitate community conversations at local events that include families and children. Architectural drawings and photos from other dam removal projects help communities envision aesthetic, recreational, tourism and other cobenefits. In Pennsylvania, she could progressively draw upon seventy-five dam removal projects with before and after photos and testimony from local citizens who had once been profoundly skeptical, even threatening that "no amount of protest [by environmentalists] will ever remove this dam."[38]

American Rivers has evolved in this manner partly in response to networks of other field actors (the Pisces Foundation, NRDC, local water managers, and high-level staff at the EPA's Office of Water) and partly in response to political opportunities and funding during the Obama administration, which supported its work in river restoration in four states in the Potomac Highlands, part of the Chesapeake Bay watershed and, of course, the city of Washington, DC ($1.8 million from EPA in 2011). Since 2001, it has also received funding for regranting to local groups from NOAA's Community-based Restoration Program ($700,000 in 2012 and similarly in 2013) and from other federal, state, and local agencies; foundations; corporations; multitier civic associations (the Sierra Fund, the National Wildlife Federation, The Nature Conservancy, Trout Unlimited); and nonchapter environmental groups (the Environmental Defense Fund).

Clean Water Action was founded in 1971 as the Fisherman's Clean Water Action Group and, drawing from resources and staff from Ralph Nader's network of public interest organizations, became a watchdog coalition of state and local groups on the implementation of the Clean Water Act (CWA) under the decades-long leadership of David Zwick who coauthored an influential early report. It continues to play an important role in organizing grassroots groups and coalitions through its thirteen state offices, with some eighty-eight staff at national, state, and city offices. Clean Water Action maintains a focus on drinking water and related issues, partly under the rubric of "healthy communities" and increasingly includes a broader menu of tools, such as green infrastructure, smart growth, and conservation outreach and education. It is particularly attuned to contamination from fracking, as well as lead in drinking water, and was a major organizer around the Flint, Michigan, lead-contamination response. Its key campaign is Put Drinking Water First, "from watershed to water tap." While its 501(c)(3) Clean Water Fund steers clear of endorsing candidates for Congress and other offices, Clean Water Action itself is quite engaged in advocacy, electoral work, enforcement suits, permitting battles, and administrative rulemaking, including efforts to implement and protect the EPA's 2015 Clean Water Rule on the inclusion of streams and wetlands in CWA coverage.[39]

Sustainable Urban Water Systems

As the watershed approach emerged largely in response to the limits of command and control of CWA, the field has continued to become more complex in response to further challenges of floodwater, stormwater, drinking water, drought, and coastal protection, especially in an era of climate change. Careful studies of the interactions of all of these, such as at the state level in California or Arizona, reveal enormous complexity for institutional, legal, economic, hydrologic, and ecological systems, as well as for urban and regional governance, which also makes the problem of equity in water especially complex. For instance, for the problem of overpumping of groundwater, the complexity of hydrologic models may outrun the knowledge capacity and civic will of local associations, even as the passing of time with each new subdivision and irrigation well generates new advocates for permissive pumping, thus leading to perverse participatory feedback. Local civic groups, public agencies, and other institutions have continued to be innovative in their responses, further deepening sustainable city frames and tools, though the challenges proceed at a worrisome pace and scale. Here I examine how selective cities have responded to several of these issues and in the process have helped to build the urban watershed field.[40]

Seattle's Natural Drainage System

Most urban stormwater systems were built before World War II and combine stormwater and sewage in "gray infrastructure" that entails enormous costs to upgrade or replace. Stormwater events of increasing frequency, intensity, and duration entail rising incidents of combined sewer overflow (CSO) in which wastewater from homes, businesses, and other institutions is combined with rainwater from impermeable surfaces, such as parking lots, streets, sidewalks, and roofs, and directly flows into local water bodies, thereby bypassing treatment plants. This threatens public health and aquatic species, and violates the Clean Water Act's 1972 NPDES requirements and its later CSO control policy of 1994. Indeed, hundreds of cities have repeatedly been found in violation, which has prompted the search for green infrastructure, such as more permeable pavements, bioswales along roads to retain and filter rainwater, ecological landscape designs, tree plantings, and the preservation of wetlands and open spaces. The EPA sanctioned such strategies in the 2000s.

Many of these practices can complement or supplement still-needed gray infrastructure and can show a return on investment, in terms of costs relative to status-quo scenarios, which is often a critical factor for securing support from taxpaying and bond-voting publics. A good number of technical models and tools have been developed to measure impacts and costs for stormwater management as well as for drinking water and flood water, and these have been widely diffused through organizations such as The Nature Conservancy and the Natural Resources Defense Council. TNC's Urban Water Blueprint was developed in conjunction with C40 Cities, the International Water Association, and the Rockefeller Foundation's 100 Resilient Cities initiative. The EPA's *Protecting Water Resources with Smart Growth* draws upon contributions of a wide network of university scholars, state agencies, watershed associations, Sea Grant and university extension programs, and Smart Growth alliances.[41]

Beginning in the late 1990s, Seattle provided an early model for natural drainage systems (NDS) that captured attention in the field by securing prominent awards, including the Innovations in American Government Award from the Kennedy School of Government at Harvard. It then persisted in its national leadership role, as evidenced by its funding (with the Summit Foundation) and design guidance in the development of the elegantly presented and user-friendly *Urban Street Stormwater Guide*. This was issued as the official guide by the National Association of City Transportation Officials. Its forward was written by the director of the Seattle DOT, who was NACTO vice president, and the general manager/CEO of Seattle Public Utilities (SPU). Each of these agencies had experienced significant culture changes in response to the neighborhood planning processes of the late 1990s—initially a rather contentious add-on to the comprehensive plan Toward a Sustainable Seattle—and to the early implementation phase into the next decade, which established decentralized interdepartmental teams working in collaboration with neighborhood plan stewardship groups. When Denise Andrews, a young policy analyst at SPU, responded to Mayor Paul Schell's (1998–2002) Millennium Challenge to spur innovative projects by assembling an interdisciplinary team that included a civil engineer and a landscape architect, she explicitly aimed to combine citizens' local knowledge of stormwater runoff with professional knowledge.[42]

Various urban creek groups had begun to form earlier; one of the earliest was the Carkeek Watershed Community Action Project in 1979, inspired by a local resident leading a Girl Scout group through a local park, which discovered the degraded creek in 1965, and began to work on restoration over the years following. Mayor Schell also initiated the Urban Creeks Legacy Program in 1999, which placed greater emphasis on urban runoff and spurred NDS. This included the HOPE VI redesign of the High Point public housing project in the Longfellow Creek watershed in the lower-income Delridge neighborhood of West Seattle, owned and managed by the Seattle Housing Authority. It piggy-backed NDS onto the new urbanist and green building features of the design and included sixteen hundred residences in a mix of low-income, affordable, and market-rate units. The Delridge neighborhood plan was facilitated by long-time Filipino-American public housing resident and Delridge activist Ron Angeles in his role as department of neighborhoods staff.

Though applied differently in locations with varied cultural norms, development challenges, and hardened infrastructure obstacles as well as citizen protest and mayoral shifts, NDS has emphasized "strategies of infiltration, flow attenuation, filtration, bioremediation with soils and plants, reduction of impervious surface coverage, and provision of pedestrian amenities." As Andrew Karvonen argues, this was to be accomplished as much as possible with "ecorevelatory design" features that would serve as a civic educational feedback mechanism visibly revealing relationships between human actors and natural processes. In addition, the burgeoning watershed movement manifested itself in the 1993 transformation of the mission of the nonprofit Rivers Council of Washington (RCW) to protecting and restoring all watersheds in the state. RCW's change of mission led it to contact some eight hundred subwatershed citizens' groups in its 62 Watersheds of Washington Campaign; it found that three hundred and seventy of them were engaged in significant watershed work.[43]

The policy design of neighborhood planning in Seattle also encouraged watershed association, land-trust, open space, and other groups besides community councils to join in deliberative and collaborative work and thus increased the chances over time that stormwater runoff would become an issue for attentive local publics. This helped to drive a process where Green Streets are now codified in the city's land use code (complemented by a Complete Streets ordinance) requiring private developments to incorporate green stormwater infrastructure into their design. Other cities working with NACTO have likewise proceeded to institutionalize such designs from which the NACTO tool kit extensively draws. It also foregrounds neighborhood equity for those areas that have historically borne disproportionate water and air pollution burdens and lack of open space. In multiple kinds of feedback loops and relational dynamics, the field-building process for green stormwater infrastructure has thus drawn from grassroots activism, institutionalized neighborhood planning as a policy design for democracy, civic professionalism, bureaucratic culture change at the local level, and extensive organizational and professional networking at the state and national levels. For-profit developers and contractors, albeit sometimes with difficulty, have adjusted to new requirements, and nonprofit and for-profit consulting firms have often played key technical and relational roles in moving projects forward.[44]

Natural Filtration for New York City

New York City (NYC) delivered water to its inhabitants through shallow wells in the seventeenth and eighteenth centuries, and then through hollow logs under the streets followed by cast-iron pipes that drew water from reservoirs constructed in Manhattan, beginning with one on Broadway on the Lower East Side in 1776, the year the Declaration of Independence was signed. As the city grew, such a system proved completely inadequate, and a decision was made to dam the Croton River in Westchester County to create the Old Croton Reservoir in 1842, delivering water through an aqueduct. This was followed by decades of further building of reservoirs and aqueducts in nearby counties and ensuring the ascendance of engineering authority in water policy. During the first half of the twentieth century, and then especially in the 1950s, the Croton and the west-of-Hudson Catskill-Delaware systems were further expanded by condemning wide swaths of land, and by 2008, these three watersheds delivered 10, 50, and 40 percent, respectively, of the 1.8 billion gallons of water consumed daily by residents, workers, and businesses in the city and just north of it.[45]

As historian David Soll analyzes in *Empire of Water*, the politics of bringing water to the city were complicated by power plays among highly asymmetrical regional actors, regulatory constraints, and Supreme Court rulings, among other factors. But by 1990, the watershed approach had been gaining credibility, and the city faced a momentous strategic choice that went beyond what it could achieve by its recent conservation efforts through water metering and toilet replacement. It could choose to spend an estimated $6 to $8 billion dollars to build a new water filtration plant (plus $350 million annually to operate it), which would almost certainly trigger a rate revolt among the city's homeowners, landlords, and businesses and lead to potential displacement of several hundred thousand lower-income people from their homes and rent-controlled units. Or, it could choose to refine a watershed approach in the Croton and Catskill-Delaware watersheds—375 square miles and 1,597 square miles, respectively—in such a way that local communities, farmers, foresters, and other businesses would willingly collaborate to enable the city to retain its largely natural filtration supply (though a plant has been required at Croton, where Putnam County and Westchester County development pressures were greatest).

The drinking water field contained fierce opponents of this latter approach, including leading environmental groups and five of the six scientists on the EPA panel convened to review NYC's eventual application. The EPA's 1989 Surface Water Treatment Rule—under the 1986 amended Safe Drinking Water Act of 1974, further amended in 1996 to protect water supplies at their source—permitted application for a waiver to pursue the second strategy, but the waiver needed to be reviewed and renewed periodically and had many specified conditions; otherwise, the EPA reserved the authority to require a new filtration plant. Other large cities that had natural filtration, such as San Francisco, Seattle, and Portland, Oregon, drew their supplies from federally protected watersheds, so New York's challenge was quite distinct.[46]

Several kinds of institutional actors enabled an innovative and collaborative approach that has achieved national and international prominence over the course of nearly three decades, though not without repeated obstacles, political and legal conflicts, and threats of exit. One was the NYC Department of Environmental Protection (DEP), whose drinking water control division had offered a rationale for such an approach in 1987. Several years later, Albert Appleton, the former conservation chair of the city chapter of the Audubon Society, had been appointed commissioner by Democratic mayor David Dinkins (1990–1993), who himself had been pressured by a coalition of environmental and union groups to campaign on the issue of clean water. The first nonengineer to hold this position, Appleton had deep commitments to ecology but also a lecturing style that put off many in upstate communities. In any case, Dinkins' policy plate was otherwise full and little happened. Appleton was succeeded by Marilyn Gelber, an appointee of Republican mayor Rudolph Giuliani (1994–2001), from the city's planning department. The first female DEP commissioner, Gelber brought considerably greater relational skills to her dealings with watershed communities, took all their phone calls on her personal line, and re-established enough trust to proceed, though she also credited working with a Republican city government and soon thereafter with a Republican governor as facilitating such trust with the skeptical watershed communities. She attended nearly every meeting of the several hundred it took to close the deal but admits that trust was primarily established by "side talk" during lunch hours. This was notably manifest when she first sent a pitcher of beer to the watershed table at Schneller's beer garden in Kingston, New York; they returned the civic gesture. Soon, city, state, and local watershed communities regularly sat at mixed tables, eventually joined by environmentalists when they were invited to attend the formal sessions.[47]

Second, each of these city commissioners built upon foundations established by the state's deputy commissioner of agriculture, Dennis Rapp, who had organized a series of watershed agricultural forums to explore how various agricultural practices were harming the watershed. But he also listened to dairy and other farmers' concerns about the costs of implementing new management practices that were less reliant on capital intensity, pesticides, and fertilizers. He respected their deep sense of not wanting to lose local control and individual autonomy to a system dominated by such a powerful actor as New York City, or indeed to the state. Farmers were even more fearful, however, of new water regulations of minimum footage setback that would make it extremely difficult if not impossible to farm where rivulets and streams meandered through almost all farmland in the area. Rapp was placed on a short leash by skeptical state regulators, but he persisted in brokering agreements, partly because he had experience as a midwestern farmer himself. These democratic forums led to a joint task force, and then to what became known as the Whole Farm Program, which enlisted voluntary participation to introduce best-management practices, tailored farm by farm, and was assisted by local Cornell University Extension agents and soil and conservation district staff.[48]

Third, two new organizations were established to oversee and enable action: the Catskill Watershed Corporation (CWC) and the Watershed Agricultural Council (WAC). CWC was established as an independent corporation in 1997 as part of the New York City Watershed Memorandum of Agreement (MOA). This was signed by federal, state, and city agencies; a coalition of environmental organizations; and watershed municipalities. It enabled the city to receive from the EPA a filtration avoidance determination (FAD), thus saving it billions of dollars, in return for effective and accountable efforts to protect and improve the watersheds.

Activists on the Hudson had fought important battles that helped form the environmental movement in earlier years.[49]

Robert F. Kennedy Jr., a prominent environmental lawyer with NRDC and a leader of the Riverkeeper on the Hudson and of its emergent national and international alliance of waterkeeper organizations, became a key player in the negotiations after his initial exclusion. Like many environmentalists, he first favored a stronger regulatory approach because of his highly detailed knowledge of institutional failures and outmoded regulations in the watershed. Indeed, he was involved in repeated suits against the governor, the New York State Department of Health, and many upstate towns. However, he also took up the offer of a successful real estate agent to do volunteer work for six months; Kennedy then asked her to estimate the cost of buying all the raw land in the Catskill watershed. Her estimate was far lower than the cost of building a new filtration plant. Other options had to be possible, Kennedy thought, and Governor George Pataki agreed to help with negotiations.[50]

In return, the MOA required New York City to fund a wide range of watershed projects. As it was implemented and the FAD was renewed in 2002, 2007 (for ten years), and 2017, fundable projects came to include land acquisition and local economic development and employment initiatives as well as subsequent wastewater treatment upgrades, stormwater retrofits, septic rehabilitation and replacement, flood hazard mitigation, and road and bridge repair. Planning, zoning, and mapping grants are also provided to towns and villages through CWC's Sustainable Communities Program, including some to enable the movement of homes and businesses out of floodplains. Various grants for community development, arts, watershed education in schools, and other business loans and grants have also been available through the organization. Some have even been targeted to professional engineers, designers, and inspectors to bring them up to speed on community engagement and watershed work. Through many venues, watershed communities have been transforming everyday culture and civic professional norms, farming and forestry practices, and planning capacities for the challenges of flooding and general resilience.

While there was initially little watershed identity—in contrast to town identity—among upstate residents, CWC had its origins in the more contentious and litigious Coalition of Watershed Towns that resisted the city's effort and was driven by long memories of home and farm, even graveyard, dislocation as the reservoirs were built through "imperial edicts" of eminent domain. Locals openly suggested to applause at public meetings that the reservoirs be blown up. Even in negotiating sessions, Kennedy recalls the chair of CWC threatening to meet the governor on Route 23 with shotguns, and that they (CWC) would "make the Oklahoma City bombing—which had just occurred about a month before—look like child's play." Indeed, the first page of CWC's 2016 annual report still calls attention to the fact that its successful partnership with the city was built upon the power of vivid memories of displacement and was purchased "at a great price, a price we must never forget." Given historical, cultural, and contemporary policy tensions, the MOA also created a Watershed Protection and Partnership Council to help resolve disputes but to also deal with related issues of reservoir waterfowl management, wastewater management, and stream and riparian protection. CWC itself has an elected board largely from elected local town officials in several of the counties within these watersheds, but also with reserved seats for New York City, New York State, and an environmentalist (appointed by the governor) operating according to super-majority voting rules.[51]

The Watershed Agricultural Council (WAC) was established as a nonprofit in 1993 in the wake of the agricultural forums to oversee the creation and implementation of voluntary individual farm plans, known as Whole Farm Plans. In addition, Gelber credits a CWC member for reaching out to her on her first day in office and repeatedly after that to explore how to build trust with the city, when all her lawyers were immediately suggesting that there was no other option than litigation. The longer history of the relationship of the city to the Catskill area reveals significant collaboration, so perhaps this legacy persisted under the surface of conflict. The farm plans include water quality goals achieved through less capital-intensive agricultural practices, thus saving on costs and improving profit margins. The initial condition negotiated with the city required an at least 85 percent participation rate among farmers, which was exceeded handily. With 94 percent of its funding over the past two decades coming from the city, WAC has since expanded from a staff of three to nearly fifty, with an additional twenty-four contracted through its partner agencies such as local Cornell Cooperative Extensions, county soil and water conservation districts, the USDA Natural Resource Conservation Service, and the US Forest Service.

With the memorandum of agreement, WAC's mission has likewise expanded over time to include private forest management plans, as well as conservation easements on the model established by the land-trust movement in prior decades, with the intent of applying for formal certification by the Land Trust Alliance, a key intermediary in the field. Such easements, now constituting approximately one-third of protected land, entail legal obligations to protect the land in perpetuity, thereby complementing the city's fee-simple purchase of critical watershed lands while limiting the direct reach of city ownership. A "willing seller, willing buyer" provision at fair market rates was key to the MOA, which also included a local community review process and payment of taxes on the land by the city. As of 2016, WAC oversaw more than three hundred and fifty active whole farm plans and had completed over thirteen hundred forest management plans, covering one hundred and twenty thousand acres of forests, in a blend of scientific and local knowledge, as in Jason Corburn's concept of "street science." These various tools aim to protect farming and forestry as viable economic lifestyles while helping maintain natural filtration for the city's water supply. WAC views the development of partnerships as central to its mission and practice, and it includes noncouncil members on many of its thirteen committees. Its 2016 strategic plan explores a much broader New York State Conservation Partnership Program.[52]

While many challenges have remained for implementing the MOA since 1997, other opportunities have been generated by the agreement. One dispute over Croton led mayor Michael Bloomberg to fund an ambitious renaissance of parks throughout the Bronx—including lower-income neighborhoods in the South Bronx—the city borough bordering the watershed just north of the city. The Bronx River, alongside which I once drove to college daily and supervised summer youth work teams who endangered their health by insisting on swimming in it during lunch hour, has also been significantly restored. A dispute on the monitorial tone of watershed signage proved the DEP nimbler than it previously had been in responding to what local watershed residents saw as an issue of civic respect. Dispute resolution allowed much greater local control over recreation and deer hunting on city-owned buffer lands without cumbersome permitting rules signaling distrust.[53]

Nonetheless, development pressures in the Catskill-Delaware watershed have increased significantly, and fracking likewise became a contentious issue before it was banned statewide in 2015. The renewal of the EPA waiver in 2007 without significant input from watershed communities also led to contentious legal action, although CWC and WAC remained resilient institutions in the face of this. Much of this resilience was due to the extensive public participation at local meetings and network support for learning new farm and forestry practices, in addition to the alignment of interests made possible by the cost structures of hard and soft infrastructure and the opportunities for sustainable community development funded by a large city.[54]

But critical was the design, deliberation, and trust building of the negotiations that led to the MOA. By Kennedy's count, some two hundred and seventy meetings took place over two years, almost all of which were attended personally by Gelber, when Kennedy thought that the initially projected eighteen was too many. When issues are complex and dignity is at stake, perhaps democracy sometimes requires too many meetings. Or perhaps, as Justin Freiberg and his colleagues argue, "early stakeholder involvement through participatory planning processes guided by local leadership," a key to success so far, should receive added attention.[55]

Conclusion

The period since the passage of the Clean Water Act in 1972 has been one in which the field of urban watersheds has emerged with increased salience, refined framing, elaborate tools, and enhanced civic and institutional capacities. This has partly been a response to some of the inherent limits of command and control at national and state levels. But it has also proceeded in the face of repeated threats to core regulatory tools that can complement ecological approaches. In our New York City case, an EPA regulator worked productively with the negotiating parties on 157 requirements that the city would have to meet to get the filtration avoidance determination. This represents another instance where skilled field actors sought to better align institutional logics—regulatory, advocacy, community, small farm and forest business, urban finance—to achieve ecological outcomes while mixing and testing a variety of democratic practices within broader systemic deliberation in a field where power asymmetries are pervasive.

While CWA was drafted with ecological goals, citizen engagement at the watershed level remained a poor second cousin in the early years due to relative EPA financial and staff resource commitments and the metrics, tools, and timetables of the regulatory design. Major environmental organizations favored the pre-eminence of command and control, suited to their own technical competencies, organizational capacities, and avenues of influence, such as lobbying, the courts, and regulatory implementation. Elected officials and constituent publics were also heavily invested in seeing measurable results from low-hanging fruit relatively quickly. While there may have been some alternatives for building local civic capacities for watershed work in the early years (such as through the League of Women Voters), much of this would inevitably have hinged upon the coconstitutive development of a watershed frame among academic scientists, policy analysts, agency officials, legal theorists, and grassroots watershed movement networks, followed by much more ambitious civic organizing and greater institutional alignment among public agencies at all levels of the federal system.

In the early 1980s, local and state actors in the Chesapeake Bay, with support from the EPA, crafted the first major policy design for collaborative strategies to protect and restore an estuary. The design did not displace CWA regulations but complemented them with a voluntary framework to enable further action and capacity building by watershed associations and stewardship groups, local governments and other institutions, multistate programs, and technical and financial support by the EPA and eventually other federal agencies such as NOAA. This model became the basis for the more ambitious National Estuary Program as Congress turned to amending CWA in 1987. As the number of NEPs grew to twenty-eight and formed a strategic network for learning, so did many of the smaller one hundred estuaries borrow components in a process that was moderately isomorphic. The Office of Wetlands, Oceans, and Watersheds (OWOW) at the EPA, created in 1991, offered the institutional framework for sharing lessons across estuaries as well as other watersheds and river systems that were in the process of generating their own protective associations, councils, and alliances. These cohered into a watershed movement over the course of the 1990s, parallel to civic and collaborative action on estuaries but in many regions nested within the riverine systems that were also part of estuaries, as well as within the purview of federal land-management agencies that are largely beyond the scope of this study.[56]

National groups, such as Restore America's Estuaries and the River Network, along with foundations such as the Pew Charitable Trusts and the Kendall Foundation, helped build the national civic infrastructure for watershed work, but federal agencies also supplied important funding and other forms of assistance and, in the case of the EPA, encouraged states— key actors within the federal policy design of water pollution control—to utilize a watershed approach, thus further incentivizing watershed associations and networks that could work at the state and community levels. California, for instance, has recently utilized Proposition 1 water bond funding ($1,495,000,000) for a policy design on urban rivers and watershed protection and restoration that includes grants to various conservancies, some with several dozen complementary projects on green streets, stormwater, high school campus infrastructure, and similar projects.

Other offices, programs, and networks within the EPA raised the profile and legitimacy of civic environmentalism and community-based work, as did prominent professional associations, such the National Academy of Public Administration, and other prestigious university, nonprofit, and presidential reports. Through the Estuary Restoration Act of 2000 and the Magnuson-Stevens Conservation and Management Reauthorization Act of 2006, Congress provided further funding to build the estuary field and enable civic associations and intermediaries to enhance capacities and thus provide tools, metrics, and further resources to legitimate federal funding. The EPA managed to pull together funding for local watershed groups as well as several intermediaries that would help develop the technical and organizational capacities for complex watershed work. It also served to develop and in many cases coproduce tools suitable for watershed planning, monitoring, management, and collaboration among stakeholders, including civic associations and community groups. The EPA, in short, became a key strategic actor in forming and nurturing the diverse networks that have come to constitute the watershed movement and the watershed field.

Other organizations that have focused primarily upon advocacy and litigation, such as American Rivers and Clean Water Action, as well as many of the major environmental organizations, such as the NRDC and the Sierra Club, have played vital roles in the larger field of water protection that has enabled local urban watershed strategies. In some cases, such groups have integrated aspects of watershed framing, such as American Rivers. In other cases, they have remained wary of specific agreements, such as NRDC's eventual refusal to sign the NYC Watersheds MOA in 1997 even though the Riverkeeper and the NYC PIRG did. In the latter case, all retained a watchdog role. In some cases, such as the Chesapeake Bay Foundation, watershed work has been driven by advocacy but has nonetheless integrated watershed education and volunteer restoration activities.

As cities continue to innovate on various and often multiple components of watershed protection and restoration, as our Seattle and NYC cases and others demonstrate, the need for strong advocacy above the level of the urban watershed remains vital in the face of threats from new technologies and industry strategies, such as fracking, as well as many attempts at regulatory rollback, which have existed throughout this entire period but which have reached new levels of systematic assault under President Trump's EPA administrators. Watershed and other strategies to enhance the resilience of coastal cities will become relentlessly more important in the years ahead, as will the challenges of democracy that accompany them, as chapters 7 to 8 examine. But first, in chapter 6, we look at the dynamics of several urban regimes or governance systems as they have attempted to build more sustainable cities across a range of issues and reveal multiple pathways for moving forward.

CHAPTER SIX

Governance Pathways to Urban Sustainability

This chapter examines how some cities have developed political trajectories, governance strategies, and local institutional fields that foster urban sustainability while also engaging civic groups and hence leveraging and promoting democratic engagement as a core part of field building. The three primary cases—Portland, Oregon; San Francisco, California; and Chicago, Illinois—are generally ranked at the high end of institutional development and governance capacity, as discussed in chapter 1, though they are hardly without persisting challenges on many fronts. While other cities cannot replicate their trajectories, they can and do learn from many of their promising practices. The two other cases—Baltimore, Maryland, and Phoenix, Arizona—also display progress on sustainability but under considerably more difficult conditions. San Francisco and Chicago (along with Seattle, Washington, and Chattanooga, Tennessee) were among the primary cities visited by President Bill Clinton's Council on Sustainable Development in the 1990s, from which key lessons were drawn for the broader field, including for federal agencies. San Francisco and Chicago have also been among the twenty-three US cities in the global 100 Resilient Cities Network.

To be sure, a fuller analysis of urban governance and just sustainability in these cities would include many other policy areas, such as affordable housing and minimum-wage laws, as well as more systematic analysis of shifting civic, political, and business coalitions. Other cities, especially some of the smaller and medium-sized ones harder hit by deindustrialization, experience much greater difficulties in developing sustainable city strategies. Thus, there is much to learn from the trajectories of cities in this chapter but much that only further comparative research can clarify, including large-N studies.

Portland leveraged its Progressive-Era traditions of civic participation and direct democracy to challenge the dominance of downtown business and growth machine actors by the late 1960s, and then quickly institutionalized a neighborhood system open to various environmental, land-use, and open space groups. A state growth management act in 1973, followed by the election of a mayor responsive to neighborhood associations and local participation in planning, provided the context to institutionalize citizen access to relevant public agencies, develop an energy office and a citizens' energy commission, create a Metro planning authority through ballot initiative—all done in the 1970s—and then develop the country's first climate action plan in 1993 (updated several times since). These were followed by an office and a commission for sustainable development in 2000. If there has been one early adopter that stands out among US cities, it is certainly Portland.

San Francisco, encountering postwar population decline in the face of suburbanization, developed a vigorous growth coalition in the 1950s whose vision of the "Manhattanization" of downtown met with local resistance in these and other neighborhoods. While some projects, especially proposed freeways cutting through the city, were blocked, it took sustained organizing over several decades and through failed ballot initiatives to shift the balance of power among city supervisors and mayors toward planning that was more accountable to neighborhoods. The Bay Area's open space, urban creek, estuary, and greenbelt movements complemented these shifts as did local participation and policy design in the federally designated Golden Gate National Recreation Area. San Francisco's contentious pluralism was also moderated by the emergence of collaborative strategies within various city departments, nonprofits, and neighborhood and civic groups.

Chicago's future also looked bleak after the war due to white flight, suburbanization, massively segregated public housing, and other forms of racial inequity and conflict. Land use in the Loop tangled with railroad yards and aldermanic privilege made it especially difficult to plan coherently. Mayor Richard J. Daley's election in 1955 enabled a growth coalition to cohere but also met significant pushback from neighborhoods, including white ethnic ones. Harold Washington's election as the first black mayor in the 1980s helped to open the governance coalition significantly, but his untimely death shortly into his second term generated uncertainty until

Richard M. Daley was elected in 1989 and proceeded to serve the longest of any mayor in Chicago's history. He built upon some of Washington's legacy of community empowerment and began a halting, but eventually more coherent, shift toward sustainable city practices. His climate action plan of 2008 leveraged many of the grassroots neighborhood, community development, foundation, and ecological restoration networks of previous decades.

Following these three core cases, the chapter examines two others that help to expand our understanding of opportunities and obstacles existing in other cities. Baltimore represents a city that is predominantly black and has not been able to stem population loss in the way that Chicago has. Nor has it been able to effectively link its postindustrial strategy based upon medical and educational institutions to revitalization of proximate neighborhoods in distress. While there exist tensions in sustainability framing among key networks, there also exists opportunity for social learning across them. Phoenix, the fifth most populous city in the country, lies in the arid desert Southwest that is steadily getting hotter and has built upon a strategy of suburban subdivision sprawl and aggressive annexation, massive water allocations and overdrafts from the Colorado River, and coal power drawn from relatively distant Navajo lands. Nonetheless, in the late 1980s, an innovative multistakeholder visioning process lasting eighteen months, combined with council restructuring to better implement changes and provide more equitable representation, has led to some innovation in light rail, water conservation, transit-oriented development, affordable housing, and downtown arts activism with broad purpose. Growth dynamics, while lessened in the wake of the housing crash of 2008, nonetheless remain strong, and the conservative state legislature and anti-immigrant politics constrain more robust movement forward toward just sustainability.

Portland

In the 1970s, Portland, Oregon, began to display some of the components of field building that have led to its becoming widely recognized as one of the leaders in the sustainable cities movement. The city has a long history of populist participation and middle-class radicalism going back to the Progressive Era, and the state was a pioneer in its direct democracy reforms. Women were especially active through women's clubs and LWV chapters through the postwar decades. Nonetheless, it was not until the late 1960s and early 1970s that civic activists and other reformers began to shift the political culture away from uninspired downtown business and professional leadership and toward citizen-driven sustainability, albeit with some cooperation of businesses and the local American Institute of Architects (AIA) chapter. By 2015, Portland had grown to over six hundred thousand residents, approximately three-quarters white and the remainder divided in roughly equal proportions among Asian, Latino, African American, and a very small percentage of Native Americans. Over the previous decades, the city and metro area had experienced major shifts away from steel manufacturing, ship building, and forest products, among several other industries, and toward high technology, but also with corporate headquarters of various major sportswear and other firms. The city itself sits at the juncture of the Columbia and Willamette Rivers and serves as a port city inland from the Pacific Coast.[1]

Several factors have been especially important in building the sustainable cities field in Portland. First, Portland developed a quite-vibrant neighborhood movement partly upon the foundations of the federal Community Action and Model Cities Programs, and then strengthened the infrastructure of neighborhood associations to the point where a citywide system was institutionalized through the Office of Neighborhood Associations (ONA) in 1974. ONA provided contractual funding through officially recognized District Coalitions (DCs), which served as umbrellas and representatives of the dozen or so neighborhood associations that might fall within a given district. While the DCs were accountable to the city for basic fiscal and operational matters, they had considerable autonomy over hiring, firing, and agenda setting. Their focus was largely though not exclusively on land use, open space, environment, housing, parks, traffic, and transportation. The system represented a form of what democratic theorist Archon Fung has called "accountable autonomy." The city council set broad policy priorities and appointed the ONA director, yet initiative resided with the neighborhood associations working within the DCs. These various associations, including some unlikely allies in the environmental groups, collaborated with businesses and planners in the development of a plan to revitalize downtown during the years immediately preceding ONA, with a good deal of focus on pedestrian, public transit, and retail uses. They hence built a stock of social and political trust that would prove useful going forward and could modify growth-machine dynamics.[2]

Tension recurred between the various levels of the formal system (on budgets, service-delivery functions, development issues), even leading to several cases of temporary non-renewal of contracts for some DCs. Much of this reflected growing pains associated with eventually transforming ONA in 1997 into ONI—the Office of Neighborhood Involvement— to become more inclusive of ethnic and immigrant associations, multicultural organizations, youth groups, neighborhood business associations, and other groups that worked across neighborhood boundaries. The city thus recognized that multiple stakeholders, and not just traditional neighborhood associations typically dominated by homeowners, required a seat at the table, and it has continued to invest through ONI in relational leadership and capacity building that valorizes diversity and collaboration. Many other types of urban environmental groups—dozens of "friends" of specific streams, wetlands, and parks—formed either from neighborhood associations or in relationship with them. Watershed groups have had an especially important presence, as has planning to revitalize the Willamette River as a working harbor that is healthy, green, embedded in neighborhoods, and a source of civic partnership and education. Local chapters of multitiered environmental associations, among the densest in the nation in membership, also had many ties to these various local groups. DC staff have received training designed to broker relationships across various community groups, neighborhood business associations, and public agencies, as in many of the best models nationwide.[3]

Second, Oregon passed the first state Growth Management Act (GMA) in 1973 with support from urban as well as rural interests and bipartisan support in the legislature. This act required cities to establish urban growth boundaries through the preferred tool of comprehensive planning and placed emphasis on citizen involvement. The new law established a Land Conservation and Development Commission, with a "citizen involvement advisory committee" deeply influenced by neighborhood association practices in Portland and several other cities; it proceeded to send out one hundred thousand invitations for citizens to participate in land-use planning workshops in thirty-five locations, with some ten thousand who eventually participated over several phases. Even as the National Land Use Policy Act was faltering in Washington, DC, and thus would not provide support for capacity building in the states (see chapter 3), the civic association, 1000 Friends of Oregon, was founded by environmentalists and others, with the backing of Governor Tom McCall (1967–1974), to act as an independent watchdog of the implementation of GMA. It also became an important educator and technical assistance provider, as well as advocate, across the state on land-use issues.[4]

As Portland mayor, Goldschmidt also strengthened citizen advisory boards and created bureau advisory committees, which gave citizens an inside view of the working of public agencies and budgets, opportunities to build relationships with staff, career avenues into formal staff positions, and a role in setting agendas. These lasted some two decades. Goldschmidt also established a citizen's planning commission to counterbalance the development commission, a key reform in modifying urban regime and growth-machine dynamics. As activist-scholar Steven Johnson, who studied these processes meticulously over the long arc of civic development in the city, noted some thirty years later, "Portland's official civic life—indeed, much of the city's bureaucracy—is dominated by yesterday's street activists."[5]

The mayor reconfigured the metropolitan bus system around a downtown transit mall and provided the early impetus that resulted in the city's famous light-rail system in the mid-1980s. In response to the national oil crises of 1973 and 1979, he made energy conservation part of land-use planning, established an energy office and a citizen energy commission, and introduced the first municipal energy policy in the nation before leaving to become President Jimmy Carter's transportation secretary. In addition, in 1978, citizens in the Portland region voted to create Metro, the only elected regional government in the country, to coordinate land-use planning and urban growth boundaries across twenty-four cities and parts of three counties. While not especially vigorous during the deep and prolonged state recession of the 1980s tied largely to the wood products industry, in the following decade Metro began to engage citizens, environmental and civic groups, business interests, and local jurisdictions in developing alternative growth scenarios projected for the next fifty years. These included a system of green spaces approved in a major levy and supported by vigorous organizing among the one hundred groups affiliated with Friends and Advocates of Urban Natural Areas (FAUNA). These also included multimodal transportation options supported by Portland's bicycle coalition and funded by the Intermodal Surface Transportation Efficiency Act (ISTEA) in its initial round of grants (see chapter 4).[6]

The early round of public involvement in strengthening Metro capacities and authority in the 1990s relied upon sending five hundred thousand copies of a tabloid—one for every household—outlining four alternative growth scenarios and trade-offs and coupled these with extensive public hearings and workshops, presentations to local civic and environmental organizations, and cable TV and local news media coverage. Metro planning director John Fregonese, known widely as "Frego," was deeply committed to community involvement and had a video produced of the preferred alternative and vision that had emerged through public deliberation; it was widely advertised and distributed free of charge through the local Blockbuster and other video rental stores, resulting in an estimated fifty thousand views. Metro has since coproduced GIS tools for citizen and professional collaboration in visualizing and evaluating the impacts of land-use options across a complete base map of land parcels, now available with extensive layers of community data on the Regional Land Information System website (RLIS Discovery). These tools have been utilized effectively in planning workshops, larger public meetings, civic association offices, and is now on activists' laptops, tablets, and smart phones. Much of the land-use planning within Portland and Metro incorporates new urbanist design principles and green building practices, and it has been enabled by a decades-long process of nurturing what Ethan Seltzer has appropriately called a "culture of inhabitation."[7]

Third, with broad support from civic and environmental associations, such as 1000 Friends of Oregon and the Bicycle Transportation Alliance, the city began to develop the first climate action plan in the nation. City councilor Mike Lindberg, Goldschmidt's former planning director in charge of implementing the city's energy policy (and a former neighborhood activist), leveraged several other networks to move the city and the broader movement forward. One was in his role as chair of the National League of Cities' energy and environment committee, which became responsive to the Brundtland Commission's 1987 report on sustainable development and the UN's Intergovernmental Panel on Climate Change (IPCC). The second was his leadership in getting Portland to join with thirteen other United States, Canadian, and European cities in ICLEI's Urban CO_2 Reduction Initiative, which began to learn from each other in a network design and further diffused innovations nationally and internationally (see chapter 7). The climate action plan of 1993 was coordinated by Susan Anderson, who eventually went on to head the Bureau of Planning and Sustainability until 2018, providing important leadership continuity. The city adopted a set of Sustainable City Principles in 1994, under three-term mayor Vera Katz (1993–2005), followed by climate plan updates in 2001, 2009, and 2015, each of which has further enriched and integrated the framing, including restored watersheds, urban forests, sustainable businesses, food systems, and green building. The city has built strategic partnerships among professionals, civic groups, and trade associations. Ongoing institutional innovation included the creation in 2000 of the Office of Sustainable Development and the Sustainable Development Commission of Portland and Multnomah County. These systemic efforts enabled the city in its "institutionalization of sustainability as a core business driver" and as "a way of life" across city bureaus.[8]

In addition, some sixty environmental, housing, church, and social justice groups formed the Coalition for a Livable Future, which over its twenty-year history (1994–2015) placed emphasis on urban sustainability projects. Many other civic groups generate and diffuse green practices and participate in third-party certification processes. Citizen engagement has remained important to these and many other initiatives. Open planning workshops were held as the climate plans were being developed, and an Equity Work Group engaged environmental justice (EJ) leaders and communities of color in the 2015 climate plan. Equity was also highlighted as the foremost concern in the Portland Plan, with "partnerships" across civic, nonprofit, market, and public agencies as the main driver of change. A specific "diversity and civic leadership" program was built around five community-based organizations: the Center for Intercultural Organizing, the NAYA Youth and Elders Council, the Latino Network, the Immigrant and Refugee Community Organization, and the Urban League of Portland. In the early 1990s, Portland State University developed an explicit civic mission to "Let Knowledge Serve the City" and an ambitious array of community-based learning initiatives that engage undergraduate, as well as graduate and professional school students and faculty, in sustainability projects of various sorts, including with neighborhood associations and nonprofits, local businesses, and major institutions such as the Portland International Airport.[9]

San Francisco

San Francisco faced the postwar period in moderate decline, with projected losses of population and industry to the suburbs and without a coherent strategy for future development. As a peninsular city of approximately forty-seven square miles with no room for physical growth outward, its racially homogeneous white population (with only 3 percent ethnic Chinese in 1940) was supplemented by wartime black workers from the South who continued to grow as a percentage of residents to some 13.4 percent by

1970. Latinos and Asians also grew. Overall population, however, declined from 775,000 in 1950 to 740,000 in 1960 with still-further losses over the next two decades. The completion of the Bay Bridge and the Golden Gate Bridge during the New Deal ensured suburbanization, and industry found new opportunities (electronics, auto, defense) in Santa Clara Valley to the south and in the East Bay, where the Port of Oakland would soon display relative advantages in shipping and inland distribution routes. The Bay Area Rapid Transit (BART) system, planned by a broad array of business leaders through the Bay Area Council, would link suburban commuters and downtown jobs while omitting station placement in selective minority neighborhoods, such as Hunters Point.[10]

In the face of these challenges and a sclerotic city redevelopment agency—albeit in a consolidated city/county government from its 1932 charter revisions—downtown business leaders and real estate developers formed a growth coalition through the Blyth-Zellerbach Committee, with selective support from nonprofits and a blue-ribbon citizens group of its own creation, the San Francisco Planning and Urban Renewal Association (SPUR), to mobilize support for bond issues and legislative changes. Having helped elect several mayors willing to cooperate, their plans converged, for the most part, on the "Manhattanization" of downtown, especially but not only south of Market because of steep land grades and firmly entrenched users in several other potential areas.[11]

This vision would accommodate large new office towers to house the "Wall Street of the West" as well as many other global firms that could drive development and extend the reach of business across the Pacific Rim, which had been a focus of U.S. military involvement and now presented trade and other opportunities. It would also position the city and its region well relative to Los Angeles. Over time, information workers and other largely white collar jobs could be further drawn to the city and help to transform it on a postindustrial basis. Citizens across the city, including some prominent activists, union leaders, and black workers, were very supportive of the economic and aesthetic transformation of the skyline that ensued, even if some influential voices in architecture and allied professional fields began to generate alternatives for enhanced civic engagement, critical design journalism, and retaining public ownership of renewal land.[12]

Pushback began to cohere over a long arc of resistance to the most untrammeled manifestations of this vision and eventually in the mid-1990s to an official plan for a sustainable city. First, as in so many other cities, neighborhood groups resisted. They resisted both the proposed new freeways, especially during the 1956–1966 period in which activists conducted the first and most far-reaching revolt in the nation, and many of the other land-development projects that promised to disrupt or destroy their neighborhoods, as happened in the African American neighborhoods of the Western Addition and its commercial and cultural center in the Fillmore. While the City of San Francisco did not move to institutionalize the growing number of neighborhood associations, as did Portland, it nonetheless witnessed their increased mobilization, along with multiform coalitions among public interest land-use lawyers, human service, housing, and ethnic nonprofits, and several environmental groups, especially the venerable Bay Area chapter of the Sierra Club. Perhaps the most famous early and prolonged battle, beginning in the mid-1960s, occurred over the proposed development of the Yerba Buena Center, which threatened to displace several thousand retired men, many militant longshore unionists, who made their homes in single-occupancy residential and transient hotels whose ties to place and to each other were deep.[13]

The successful battle over the proposed development of a vast international furniture mart in the north waterfront in the late 1960s and early 1970s mobilized civic professionals across the design field, as well as neighborhood groups, in favor of "urban environmentalism"; land stewardship and alternative uses, such as affordable housing; and in opposition to the discounted sale pricing and "vacationing" of public streets for those who had been secretly buying up private parcels. With broad cultural resonance, the new skyscrapers were regularly anthropomorphized and cartooned as tombstones and monstrous file cabinets. The unsuccessful battle against the Transamerica Pyramid in the same area further enhanced the participatory ethos and the legal tool kits available, including the California Environmental Quality Act (CEQA) of 1970, eventually transforming planning as an integrative urban-environmental practice in the city, though, as planning historian Jasper Rubin argues, often only after a "tangle of argumentation and fractured purposes" resulting from the proliferating civic initiatives across the waterfront for years on end. In the Mission District, especially strong civic networks and political capital going back to the early twentieth century enabled a rapidly diversifying neighborhood to establish favorable terms for citizen engagement through multiple phases of city plans for urban renewal, BART station openings,

Community Action and Model Cities, and to prompt more generalized learning and culture change among city agencies on planning collaboratively and pragmatically with neighborhood, local merchant, faith-based, and Latino groups.[14]

While there was strategic maneuvering on land purchases by the city's redevelopment agency, shifting mayoral and supervisor alignments, repeated efforts to compromise and litigate (including a NEPA suit), as well as HUD action through its regional office, which all played a part in the outcome of Yerba Buena, it was the election of George Moscone as mayor in November 1975 with strong citywide support that led to a much more open planning process for Yerba Buena, though it was one that did not shift the balance of power enough on the planning commission to slow down growth. Moscone's assassination (along with gay supervisor Harvey Milk) in 1978 set this process back, and downtown development continued apace, though the legacy of struggles over land use eventually led to far more participation in neighborhood planning as well as the impetus toward sustainable city strategies within the city's planning and other departments.

Two groups, San Francisco Tomorrow (founded in 1970) and then San Franciscans for Reasonable Growth (founded in 1979 as a more progressive spinoff), led the way in the 1970s and 1980s, brokering relations with a very broad array of neighborhood associations, tenant unions, small business associations, public employee unions, and Democratic political clubs. While the coalitions—with internal tensions—lost most ballot initiatives, they compelled the planning department to set limits on building height in neighborhoods. In addition, the environmental impact review (EIR) requirements of CEQA—modeled on NEPA but partly propelled by the earlier freeway revolts against highway planning—added a requirement to mitigate negative impacts in 1976, which led to public hearings, changed planning practices, and linkage policy arguments for improved mass transit and more affordable housing from fees extracted from new downtown development. These linkage policies, which were the first of a major US city, had many deficits in terms of effectiveness but also on grounds of fair process of implementation, though they were improved and institutionalized in due course. Despite several key losses through citizen ballot initiatives earlier and again in 1979 and 1983, the controlled growth movement gained cumulative strength and amplified support across various social cleavages even under the less favorable progrowth mayor Dianne Fein-stein (1978–1986), who was nonetheless responsive to the movement. EIR requirements, enforced through persistent litigation by famed land-use lawyer and slow-growth activist Sue Hestor and others, became increasingly effective in generating transparency and public discourse, as did the capacity of the movement to produce sophisticated cost-benefit analyses of impacts on city revenues and services to counter those of the growth coalition, dislodging some of its key claims to exclusive expertise. Chinatown organized to produce its own downzoning plan to block high-rise development, preserve affordable housing, and protect the cultural integrity of the neighborhood, as did the Tenderloin.[15]

Eventually, with more consistent support from a new generation of black leaders no longer willing to buy the many false promises of jobs, as well as some temporary ambivalence among downtown businesses facing relatively high vacancy rates, the movement broke through with the passage in 1986 of Proposition M, an "accountable planning initiative"—one that represented a profound transition in power relations and political culture among various activist and stakeholder groups alike. This proposition specified annual caps on office building construction and hence competition among development proposals to respond to civic claims for mitigation and public amenities. The caps could be exceeded only by regularly scheduled citywide ballots and included eight sets of substantive policy priorities, such as neighborhood diversity, affordable housing, and open space and parks, as well as a distinct goal of job training for low-income and minority residents in any proposed growth and development plans.[16]

The complex redevelopment plan for Mission Bay, a massive 315-acre expanse of abandoned and toxic railroad yards and warehouses in the China Basin District just south of downtown, has illustrated the new political culture. Perhaps clumsily sequenced by the city in its negotiations with the developer, public participation among some fifty civic groups in the fourth version of the plan in the 1990s—of at least six over nearly four decades—resulted in an agreement for significant affordable housing, minority and female hiring, open space and wetlands restoration, child care and senior centers, and eight-story limits for 4.8 million square feet of new office space. A temporary downswing in the real estate market, and then the entry of the University of California, San Francisco, to build several new medical school buildings, altered the plan, but civic groups remained engaged and ultimately quite supportive of the resulting project. Considerable racial and gender equity in hiring, training, business contracting, and affordable housing was achieved, in addition to a comprehensive open space system and biking and walking street design. It has served as a model for several other large-scale developments. Innovative and equitable low-carbon transportation, parking, and housing strategies, such as in the Market and Octavia areas, also manifested this legacy of civic activism and collaborative planning.[17]

Second, San Francisco's trajectory toward urban sustainability was shaped by the city's open space, urban creek, food district, estuary, and greenbelt movements during these years, which have functioned as an "exceptionally effective network of organizations," according to geographer Richard Walker. It reaches deep within the city but also extends to many countryside, suburban, and coastal areas across nine counties and into regional sustainable communities planning. Groups such as the Sierra Club Bay Chapter and Save the Redwoods League, of course, go back many decades earlier, as does the California Federation of Women's Clubs' advocacy for city, county, and state parks. Direct action groups organized against several nuclear power plant projects and helped deepen participatory socialization in the 1970s and 1980s. The Save San Francisco Bay Association (now Save the Bay), founded in 1961, drew support from various more-established groups and reached outward to newer local groups across the sixty thousand square miles of the estuary watershed. Wetland and habitat restoration has proceeded under the auspices of the California Coastal Conservancy, with various civic and professional partners. Local conservation leagues, trail committees, and friends of park and stream groups have received support from Audubon, The Nature Conservancy, and the Trust for Public Land to facilitate land purchases and transfers.[18]

The Greenbelt Alliance—renamed and restructured twice since its founding in 1958—has been an especially important player. It combines grassroots activism with science-based policy and multistakeholder collaborative work with civic and environmental associations, land trusts and local farm groups, planning agencies and commissions, as well as with real estate development and green building groups, affordable housing and environmental justice organizations, and elected officials. Its board members and staff have been drawn over the years from a wide array of organizations converging on smart growth, participatory neighborhood planning, and sustainable cities and regions. The Urban Creeks Council, founded in 1982, built upon various day-lighting and stream restoration initiatives already under way and soon became part of a much broader national watershed movement (see chapter 5). Its work has also left a long local legacy, visible more recently in the institutionalization of citizen participation in formal watershed planning to reduce stormwater runoff. Still other organizations across the Bay Area display various degrees of embeddedness based upon place and issue yet surprisingly oriented toward collaborative action, especially on sustainable development, as Christopher Ansell has argued. With strategic leadership of Save the Bay, such networks have served as the foundation for an ambitious sea-level rise initiative, institutionalized through a new San Francisco Bay Restoration Authority, as Bay Area voters in nine counties agreed in 2016 to a parcel tax that will fund $25 million per year for twenty years for shoreline remediation and wetland restoration. The first allocation for eight projects was approved in early 2018.[19]

While the creation of the Golden Gate National Recreation Area (GGNRA) in 1972 was spurred by groups across the Bay Area region under the auspices of People for a Golden Gate National Recreation Area and fell largely under the federal auspices of the National Park Service (NPS) and the Department of Defense (which transferred decommissioned military installations), local groups within San Francisco proper were engaged on a site-by-site basis fighting against other planned developments, such as a federal prison, high-rise apartments, and two likely segregated schools. Urban regime dynamics, however, were far less important than federal bureaucratic politics and congressional policy entrepreneurship, especially by US representative Philip Burton, who became GGNRA's bold and effective champion in Washington. Assembling parcels into a coherent system, and then further modifying and expanding boundaries to more than twice their original size, has taken persistent and creative civic initiative. In addition, managing the park to meet the expectations of so many different communities in a way that generated sufficient democratic legitimacy and pragmatic cooperation has challenged civic leaders and park officials alike. They had to plan collaboratively so that multiple goals (recreation and tourism, ecology and environmental education, community history and culture) could be addressed together, and so that distinctive sites, prior uses, perceived prerogatives, surrounding neighborhoods, and transportation from diverse areas of the city, received their appropriate due. The battles over unleashed dogs and the hiker-mountain biker wars were but two of the many intense conflicts.[20]

Burton had insisted that the 1972 law require a citizens advisory committee that included leading activists and underrepresented minority groups. At first no one knew what such a committee was supposed to do, since the Federal Advisory Committee Act (FACA) had just been passed. Nor did anyone anticipate that it would become such an effective deliberative forum and broker among contending groups. The four hundred initial meetings and workshops convened by park planners—especially Doug Nadeau, who sought to set a national standard for NPS and other agencies—generated a framework for increasingly diverse and inclusive collaborative governance among park managers, landscape architects, and civic and user groups that has paid many dividends in the decades since. Indeed, it helped to establish GGNRA as a model urban park. The advisory was discontinued by Congress in 2002 and, while clearly a loss, its legacy had been thoroughly established by then. Persistent tensions between public use and natural resource protection have been mitigated by engaging the public directly in stewardship and restoration, including through formal partnerships with the San Francisco Unified School District Environmental Science Center, the San Francisco Conservation Corps, the Marine Mammal Center, the Headlands Center for the Arts, and dozens of other centers and institutions housed in GGNRA's 1,231 historic structures.[21]

For instance, Fort Mason served as the venue for a series of meetings in 1986, convened by the bioregionalist Planet Drum Foundation, among groups active in a range of issues of city sustainability in San Francisco. These meetings resulted in significant networking thereafter as well as a 1989 book called *Green City Program for San Francisco Bay Area Cities and Towns* that covered what would become core dimensions of sustainable city strategies. It also positioned Beryl Magilavy, one of the coauthors, to become chair of the new citizens' advisory committee on sustainability planning to the board of supervisors, and then to staff official city efforts on sustainability planning in the mid-1990s. The park was also the venue of a twentieth anniversary Earth Day bike rally in 1990 that directly led to the resuscitation of the San Francisco Bicycle Coalition. In addition to independently formed civic groups, the Golden Gate National Parks Association (now Parks Conservancy) was established in 1981 as a cooperating nonprofit that generated funding for community-oriented design with distinguished architects; stewardship, citizen science, and habitat restoration programs; and green building. It has since been thoroughly integrated into park planning and operations. The Presidio Trust was enabled by congressional legislation to further the work of governance in this area of the park.[22]

Third, several other aspects of San Francisco's political, bureaucratic, and planning cultures have either directly or indirectly enhanced opportunities for sustainable city development. Much of this is now reflected in the collaborative, participatory, and EJ ethos of the San Francisco Department of the Environment's work, and even its reporting icons. To varying degrees, these cultural dimensions reflect the emerging institutional capacities to turn the city's famed contentious pluralism toward inclusive and collaborative work, albeit with persistent independent organizing. The department of public health (SFDPH), drawing upon the healthy cities frame, first introduced its community-based approach to the gay community's struggle against HIV/AIDS in the early 1980s, and Mary Pittman took the lead in the department on this issue. Pittman, who became a leader in the American healthy cities movement, had been a graduate student at the University of California, Berkeley, under Leonard Duhl, a leading theorist of healthy cities worldwide (see chapter 7). Based upon extensive listening among pre-existing gay organizations that highlighted problems such as eviction and loss of jobs, the health department built relations with landlords and employers to align itself with the challenges of "field formation" in the gay identity movement under the distinct threat of HIV/AIDS.[23]

SFDPH has continued to integrate the social determinants of health more generally, including with land use and the built environment, into its practices over the following decades, with explicit normative emphases on democracy, equity, power, and place as relational and narrative. It included a wide array of community groups as actors in shared governance over strategies and the co-production of tool development, such as with community health impact assessment tools. SFDPH's healthy communities work has also drawn other city departments (planning, police, redevelopment, parking and traffic, transportation, recreation, and parks) into local partnerships, and it has developed networks with groups across the spectrum of sustainable cities work. The police department had undergone a profound shift toward liberal and tolerant cosmopolitanism and community cooperation, linked to securing conditions for economic growth, in the two and one-half decades after 1950. This served it well when developing measured responses to contentious politics of various sorts, such as the Critical Mass bicycle rides in the 1990s (see chapter 4), hence further opening strategic options for groups such as the San Francisco Bicycle Coalition to enable collaboration and broaden democratic legitimacy.[24]

In addition, immigrant nonprofits have developed forms of administrative advocacy that enhance collaboration with city agencies, build cross-sectoral and cross-organizational networks, and frame issues to strategically foreground common benefits and linked fates across the entire population. As Els De Graauw argues, they also serve as "strategic sites through which city officials and city agencies can communicate" with a large and growing proportion of (immigrant) city residents. To accommodate rising demands for youth civic engagement, the city institutionalized a youth commission in 1995, composed of seventeen youth between twelve and twenty-three years of age. Though appointed by supervisors and the mayor, they were embedded in a broad range of youth advocacy and organizing groups, nonprofits serving girls and young women, LGBTQ and ethnic groups, schools, and environmental education, health, and service organizations.[25]

Due to these various trajectories of grassroots struggle, mobilization of resources from established multitier environmental associations, the formation of coalitions specifically tailored to control growth, urban regime shifts that opened new political possibilities, and innovation within various city bureaucracies, San Francisco positioned itself on a pathway to more robust and coherent sustainable city work. Indeed, its long arc of civic mobilization on multiple fronts, in conjunction with business and philanthropic networks, has likely helped the Bay Area in its regional economic development relative to Los Angeles. The Transamerica Pyramid, a touchstone of grassroots opposition in the early 1970s, was awarded Leadership in Energy and Environmental Design (LEED) Platinum Status by the US Green Building Council (USGBC) in 2011 after its renovation, and it now stands as a symbol of the city's commitment to sustainability. Nonetheless, the empowerment of some types of civic groups, such as neighborhood associations, in this long trajectory has arguably generated distinct obstacles to aligning sustainable city strategies with affordable housing strategies under conditions of strong job and population growth, especially with the dot.com boom of Silicon Valley beginning in the mid-1990s. However, affordable housing, community development, and public housing institutional fields have continued to become more robust and engaged in recent decades.[26]

Chicago

In the face of postwar suburbanization and the distinctive spatial legacy of railroad yards that carved up major parts of the city's land, and an entrenched system of aldermanic privilege that made it impossible to plan in a way that emulated the famous Plan of Chicago early in the century, the future of the Windy City in the 1950s looked bleak. Office investment and downtown retail were largely stagnant, if not in clear decline, as were property values. Racial divisions deepened with white flight and the rapid southern in-migration of African Americans, many into segregated neighborhoods and then massive public housing projects. Others competed for space in white neighborhoods that themselves had deteriorated over the decades. Overall population began to decline in the 1950s, eventually by over one-fifth as the effects of deindustrialization began to be more severely felt in the 1970s and early 1980s, and did not begin to recover until the 1990s, albeit inconsistently thereafter. The 1955 election of Mayor Richard J. "Dick" Daley, a Cook County Democratic machine boss, provided opportunities for a highly fragmented set of business-led civic organizations to form a growth coalition, organized as the Central Area Committee. It intended to forge a degree of business and developer consensus within the Loop and focused on making it and the surrounding ten-square-mile area a more robust center of finance and retail, as well as of professional white middle-class residence, to anchor the city's economic future.[27]

Daley's newly established department of city planning and its initial 1958 plan for the central area, provided the institutional basis for development that would more productively utilize former railroad land and be less dependent on highways and slum clearance, including in white ethnic areas from which there had been major resistance in the preceding years. As Larry Bennett argues, the plan offered an "unambiguously postindustrial vision," though one realized only decades later under the next mayor Daley. That this strategy would succeed in the face of the many Loop skeptics and other sources of institutional resistance was hardly a foregone conclusion, but within a decade, the foundations had been clearly laid, if never fully institutionalized, in robust planning institutions.[28]

Civic engagement in neighborhood development, city planning, and urban sustainability emerged in various forms and stages over the next several decades. First, neighborhoods and community organizations mobilized to resist parts of this agenda and to gain a seat at the planning table. When Daley was unable to negotiate a reasonable price for purchase of railroad land in the South Loop for a new University of Illinois campus in the early 1960s, for instance, he rammed through the council an urban renewal plan (with federal dollars) to build the campus in a white ethnic neighborhood just outside the central area that would displace some eight thousand Greek and Italian residents and six hundred and thirty businesses—to fierce local protest, a major lawsuit, and much embarrassment to the mayor. While the campus came to serve many from ethnic working class and minority backgrounds, the mayor backed down in the face of neighborhood resistance to the long-planned Central Expressway in the early 1970s. The city experienced its share of urban riots based on widespread racial grievances in the 1960s and, in some places, persistent organizing in public housing and other venues for decades to come. The contentious community organizing of Saul Alinsky had its birthplace in Chicago, though the model would undergo major changes after his 1972 death toward more relational and deeply faith-based—albeit ecumenical—practices, diffused through some two hundred city federations and several major national organizing networks, including in Chicago. Another Alinsky-inspired group, the Citizens Action Program, led a vigorous campaign on clean air.[29]

Various other Alinsky projects became part of the emerging community development field, with a good number of CDCs, several networks that focused on housing rehabilitation and construction jobs, several university centers that provided research support and direct faculty and student engagement, a handful of broader civic and advocacy organizations, and funders such as the Joyce Foundation, the Chicago Community Trust, the Woods Charitable Fund, and the MacArthur Foundation. In 1979, eight CDCs and other nonprofits came together under the umbrella of the Chicago Association of Neighborhood Development Organizations (CANDO), which grew to one hundred and fifty member organizations a decade later, and then to two hundred or so by the mid-1990s. In 1982, many helped establish the Community Workshop on Economic Development. In addition, National People's Action, which was central to passing and monitoring the federal Community Reinvestment Act of 1977, developed its initial template between a local group, representing the Edgewater and Uptown neighborhoods and the Bank of Chicago; it remained engaged through its various network partners across the city and then helped institutionalize a partnership of the two citywide networks, CANDO and the Rehab Network, with the bank. The formation of these civic networks represents but a slice of the complexity of Chicago as a city of neighborhoods, with multiple dimensions of civic efficacy, nonprofit density, and leadership ties across neighborhoods, as analyzed by sociologist Robert

Sampson. But they cohered during this period in ways that would shape strategic options for years to come.[30]

Second, the most vigorous effort to shift the basis of the city's development toward greater neighborhood participation, local economic development, and racial equity occurred during the years of Harold Washington's mayoralty (1983–1987). Daley had died in office in 1976 and was succeeded by two relatively ineffectual mayors. Washington, a black politician from the South Side who had risen steadily through the Daley machine to become a US representative from the First District in 1980, won the Democratic mayoral primary in a three-way race with 36 percent of the vote. This secured him victory in the general election of April 1983, though on a much narrower basis than would have typically been the case in this heavily Democratic city. Washington's disillusion with the machine, however, was evident much earlier, and his campaign brought together white liberal reformers, black civil rights and empowerment organizations, and a broad array of black, white, and Latino neighborhood groups and institutions within the community development field.[31]

Previously, Daley had incorporated black and Latino leadership into the machine, albeit in subordinate positions, but such deference and the machine structure itself were in retreat by then. With social movement fervor and mobilizing, the campaign set out its core goals in *The Washington Papers* in 1983. These were crafted for implementation in the city's official development plan called *Chicago Works Together*, though without much input from neighborhood groups, and then again in *Chicago Works Together II*, where neighborhood and community development groups, as well as labor and business groups threatened with further deindustrialization, had some eighteen months to contribute ideas. Metaphors such as "jobs not square feet" of downtown development informed the overall framing.[32]

After Washington finally rejected the proposed World's Fair—part of the city's 1983 central area plan—because of its projected costs and limited impact on permanent jobs, a network of planners, especially in the department of economic development and the mayor's office, led the way with planned manufacturing districts, downtown linkage proposals, more human service and Community Development Block Grants channeled through community-based organizations, and a reorganized CDBG formula that shifted a greater proportion of federal funds toward black neighborhoods, albeit in a period in which the Reagan administration was making significant cuts overall. The planning department was placed under the leadership of Elizabeth Hollander, who had trusting relationships with downtown business, developer, and architectural communities, and an explicit commitment from the new mayor to respect professional practice. While she worked to maintain these relationships through the ups and downs of conflict over major development projects and her own periodic disagreements with the mayor himself, she leveraged her normative commitments to participatory democracy and social justice from the civil rights movement to appreciate the wisdom of engaging communities much more directly in development projects.[33]

A policy design to formalize neighborhood planning boards, which had considerable support in the neighborhoods, seemed too much at risk of capture by aldermanic institutional power, as had happened with the department of neighborhoods under the immediately preceding mayor Jane Byrne. Therefore, Hollander and a subcabinet of staff with related responsibilities in various departments developed the practice of holding what they called "community forums" and making neighborhood-specific data much more accessible, which proved a major undertaking in a city that understood the informal uses of information as power and thus kept it highly secret when it collected it at all. Two of this "affirmative neighborhood information" group members—Jody Kretzmann and John McKnight— soon went on to elaborate the "assets-based community development" frame and tool kit (see chapter 7). But they understood that just prying out data through Freedom of Information Act methods might assist advocacy and protest (e.g., against slumlords) without effectively serving broader neighborhood development.

Hollander's group also utilized the mayor's presence at community forums to directly engage the questions and suggestions of ordinary residents, which he did with great verve for hours on end, typically with key professional staff on hand to add expertise to these democratic conversations. Washington came early, often to a reception before the forums, and stayed as late as local people wanted or until almost everyone else had drifted back to their homes for the evening. With grace and humor, he engaged more skeptical, even hostile, neighborhoods, some in white ethnic districts on the southwest side openly resisting his agenda on the council. He then planned bus tours for them, with aldermen and press in tow, to demonstrate how new neighborhood investments through a general obligation bond could improve their streets, sewers, and sidewalks as well. These engagement practices helped create enough public pressure to finally break the logjam on the council to approve the bond, and then led to formalizing neighborhood planning through multistakeholder processes that included homeowners, renters, local businesses, institutions, and aldermen. While the initial amounts of funding were relatively modest, larger projects and more comprehensive approaches also emerged, including a Neighborhood Land Use Task Force that broadened its approach to industrial area community organizations and the industrial real estate community.[34]

The obstacles facing the Washington administration were daunting. First, the aldermanic system resisted fiercely in what was widely described as the "Council Wars," in which Edward "Fast Eddie" Vrdolyak and Ed Burke led a majority group of twenty-nine of the fifty aldermen to ferociously oppose Washington's proposals. Thus, for instance, when the neighborhood forums began to prove popular, the council slashed the budget of the department of neighborhoods, which was coordinating outreach. This resistance was only broken with a federal redistricting ruling and a special election in early 1986 that shifted power on the council. Second, this relatively small window of political opportunity was cut short still further by Washington's death from a heart attack in November 1987, just six months after his re-election. Developing institutional capacity—staffing, training, funding, information, and especially organizational culture change—as well as civic capacity appropriate to and aligned with the emerging challenges of fair and effective engagement in complex land use issues were thus further hampered. To many, Washington appeared administratively ineffective. To others, following a widely read post-mortem series by John McCarron, urban affairs writer for the *Chicago Tribune*, many community groups pursued an unrealistic ideal of inner-city industrial renewal not only out of misplaced idealism but because of narrow organizational self-interest that would sacrifice downtown growth and undermine more effective employment strategies for those they claimed to serve.[35]

Washington was followed by two interim mayors, one for only eight days until the council agreed upon Eugene Sawyer, a long-serving black alderman from the South Side. Richard M. "Rich" Daley, eldest son of the former mayor, was elected for a regular (albeit initially two-year) term in 1989, and then proceeded to serve for the longest of any Chicago mayor in history until he voluntarily stepped down in 2011. Rich Daley's political evolution was long and complex, breaking further from the machine legacy of his father in important ways, yet he was often impatient and imperious in using concentrated power to further transform Chicago into a world-class city, tourist mecca, and "city of spectacle," in close alignment with the business community. In doing so, he utilized complex instruments of financialization across a range of powerful real-estate institutional field actors to fuel a speculative bubble while imposing "collateral environmental damage" from energy waste and construction debris dumped especially in low-income communities of color. His strategies also exacerbated certain spatial agglomeration logics already apparent in central area plans of decades prior: finance, retail, and corporate headquarters clustered in and around the Loop; increased housing nearby for the professional middle classes whose work, play, biking, artistic, and shopping preferences drew them in; and further insulation from spatial spillover from relatively nearby high-crime areas and large public housing projects slated to be demolished through HOPE VI redesigns and the broader Chicago Plan for Transformation.[36]

Nonetheless, in Eleanora Pasotti's felicitous formulation, Daley incorporated parts of Washington's legacy, as "patronage logics" were progressively replaced by "brand logics" in which multicultural values and metaphors of public space played a key part in political trust, partnership, and opinion formation. He retained or appointed new liberal advisors, including Valerie Jarrett as commissioner of planning and development, who became an important bridge with neighborhoods as well as a major player in corporate and foundation circles, into which she brought Michelle and Barack Obama. Daley cultivated support from a gay and lesbian community whose effective politicization over the decades had been enabled by local black civil rights leaders and by Mayor Washington. In some important ways, Daley was quite responsive to community empowerment and planned industrial corridors, both by sector and by district—some twenty-six corridors by 2013 representing 16 percent of all land within city limits.[37]

But long-term strategic calculations were shaped by splits within business leadership favoring real estate over industry in the city's economic development planning; for instance, in lakefront condos on the southeast side over steel reinvestment, already evident under Washington and manifested in deep worker and community pessimism. Political calculations shifted to strengthened aldermen working through the resource and status rewards of tax increment finance (TIF) districts, which have considerable flexibility but low transparency—leading to more recent calls for general reform. Yet even here, participatory budgeting has emerged in nine wards over the past decade, initiated by alderman Joe Moore of the Forty-Ninth Ward, to provide further civic voice to the distribution of aldermanic "menu money," with a network of civic, parks, transportation, youth, and religious groups, as well as foundations and university centers, serving as resources to neighborhood groups.[38]

Daley also pursued multiracial inclusion at the elite level and opened the doors to civic groups that had begun to work more vigorously on sustainability than had been evident in even the best of the Washington-era community planning. Perhaps the clearest example of Rich Daley's willingness to innovate at the intersection of neighborhoods and bureaucracies was community policing, which he crafted in conjunction with neighborhood activists in the citywide Chicago Alliance for Neighborhood Safety, founded in 1981 and whose agenda had been supported by major foundations and endorsed by the city's key newspapers, with some experiments under Washington. Once he recognized the strategic political opportunity presented by community policing in a city with growing black and Hispanic voters and a declining white population through the 1980s, Daley invested considerable city, state, and federal resources—with a very robust independent evaluation unit at Northwestern University—to ensure broad outreach to all neighborhoods, significant training for both police officers and neighborhood leaders, and administrative coordination across all city agencies whose activities could contribute to neighborhood safety.

The policy design included local beat meetings and district advisories that enabled significant civic participation, democratic deliberation, and joint problem-solving among residents and beat officers. It also incentivized engagement by specific kinds of nonprofits within and across neighborhoods whose agendas and styles were well aligned with issues of family safety, child development, neighborhood cleanup, and local business revitalization. Recent crises, partly the result of disinvestment in training for both officers and civilian organizing staff, have prompted a renewed call for community engagement and community policing as a "core philosophy infused throughout the CPD."[39]

Nonetheless, on neighborhood revitalization, the Daley administration was constrained by the system of aldermanic prerogative, where individual aldermen still exercise a good deal of formal and informal power over land use, zoning, permits, and funding (CDBG, TIF, and regular discretionary funding), while other aldermen defer in return for similar treatment. Zoning reform in 2004, which was preceded by open community meetings and distribution of an educational CD-ROM designed for public understanding (followed by accessible Internet features), added transparency and enabled new urbanist sidewalk and open space features. But aldermanic dynamics prevailed under Chicago's Empowerment Zone federal grant in the 1990s, despite considerable community participation in the initial planning process. Comprehensive strategies, especially any that might cross jurisdictional boundaries, are at a structural disadvantage compared to the usual funding competition and logrolling. Comprehensive strategies for community development that mobilize many kinds of assets, including the social capital of neighborhood residents, the resources of local institutions (universities, hospitals), and market actors, have largely drifted to public-private partnership configurations, some with quite robust neighborhood planning. This is especially the case with the New Communities Program, supported by local foundations (MacArthur and others) and intermediaries (Chicago LISC), with lead nonprofit agencies in sixteen designated community areas of seventy-seven official ones in the city that are selected on the basis of demonstrated capacity. Part of the problem of the Chicago Association of Neighborhood Development Organizations (CANDO), which disbanded in 2002, had been the highly uneven capacity of its member organizations.[40]

A third component in Chicago's pathway toward a sustainable city can be seen in Daley's early commitment to various green design projects. That he would commit to these was not a foregone conclusion. One incident captures some of the early flavor of his shift. As Suzanne Malec-McKenna tells it, she and Gerald Adelmann went to talk to the mayor in 1993. Adelman was executive director of Openlands, founded in 1963 to protect open space, forest preserves, and water resources in the Chicago area, and she was then on staff. Shortly after they walked into the room, the mayor simply announced that "we are privatizing the Bureau of Forestry. That's all there is to it!" They argued with him vigorously for forty-five minutes of what was scheduled as a twenty-minute meeting; she recalls leaving in tears. To her surprise, Daley called her back and offered her a job as assistant commissioner for the environment, initially over natural resources, and then later as commissioner in her seventeen-year tenure at the department. He appreciated her forthright honesty as well as her patience in educating this son of the white ethnic working-class neighborhood of Bridgeport. "No," she told him, "prairies were not just a pile of bird poop!"

He loved trees and "became the biggest nature advocate government has ever seen by the time he left office."[41]

Daley supported tree plantings along sixty-three miles of street medians, the restoration of dozens of school parks, a green roof on city hall, and the establishment of the Chicago Center for Green Technology, which was housed in a LEED Platinum building that offered classes and other resources. As a mayor clearly committed to economic development, he justified greening quite explicitly in terms of its cobenefits for corporate-headquarter and young-professional recruitment. Some of his early greening was accelerated as the Democratic National Convention approached in 1996, which would provide the opportunity to leave behind lingering national memories, associated with his father, of the police violence against antiwar protesters at the 1968 convention. He also reformed the parks department, a bastion of patronage, and had two hundred thousand trees planted during his first decade, with an ambitious open space plan going forward to be coordinated with community policing initiatives for safe spaces in all neighborhood greening projects. He authorized major grants to fund Greencorps Chicago, training low-income youth for greening jobs as they helped complete over eleven hundred projects with schools and block clubs across the city.[42]

Working closely with the Chicagoland Bicycle Federation—which renamed itself Active Transportation Alliance in 2008 when it officially incorporated pedestrian and transit advocacy into its mission—Daley established the Mayor's Advisory Bicycle Council, which issued the Bike 2000 Plan in 1992, later ambitiously updated as the Bike 2015 Plan. Mayor Rahm Emanuel's Streets for Cycling Plan 2020 further built upon multi-stakeholder community workshops and an online survey to help design a 645-mile system, triple the previous length, which includes neighborhood routes with attention to equitable and low-stress access with three key elements: protected bike lanes, neighborhood greenways, and urban trails. The city also worked for more than a decade with a local friends group and the Trust for Public Land, which convened extensive neighborhood visioning and design charrettes, to convert the old Bloomingdale Line through four ethnically and economically diverse neighborhoods on the northwest side into The 606, a festive yet functional bike trail, walkway, and park. Federal transportation dollars from ISTEA and successor laws funded this and other projects.[43]

The Chicago Brownfields Initiative, launched in 1993 in response to the unintended consequences of the federal Superfund's cost and liability design that delayed cleanup, proceeded to help remediate dozens of contaminated sites on some thirteen thousand acres as of 2006 that had been the source of blight, crime, and health hazards, especially in communities of color. With multistakeholder participation that frequently, though not consistently or by municipal code, included a neighborhood association, faith group, and/or community development corporation, the initiative also spurred redevelopment in the form of affordable, subsidized, and market-rate housing; factories and jobs; parks and open space; community and job-training centers; family and Head Start centers; and tax revenues from those projects that revived market activity directly and indirectly—though not without some tendencies toward gentrification, especially in the larger housing developments. Indeed, the EPA and its Region 5 office in Chicago showcased the city in helping to build a municipal brownfields movement nationwide, which was also a central actor in the EPA's Community Action for a Renewed Environment and collaborative EJ grants programs.[44]

Daley's trips to European cities provided other models for him and his staff, and his greening efforts also served as a complement to some of his grand architectural and public space projects, such as Millennium Park. These greening projects helped him respond to some of the criticisms of the city's institutional vulnerability to heat waves, as occurred in 1995, but with less vulnerability to another heat wave in 1999, likely due to better institutional responses. Indeed, a 1999 settlement agreement with ComEd, the local power company that had failed to meet state energy conservation goals, generated substantial funding of several million dollars annually for the city's Environmental Action Agenda for the next twelve years or so. The core rationales for urban sustainability, meant to serve as guidelines for the city council and the Chicago Plan Commission in reviewing development projects, were elaborated in *Adding Green to Urban Design: A City for Us and Future Generations*, which received input from a range of civic and professional groups, including those representing green building, bicycles, architecture, river restoration, neighborhood associations, community development, open space, parks, real estate, and local chambers of commerce.[45]

Several of Chicago's environmental and nonprofit organizations became especially important in leveraging civic relationships during these years and moving the city's climate planning forward. The Center for Neighborhood Technology (CNT), founded by Scott Bernstein in 1978, published the *Neighborhood Works* magazine for two decades, which helped diffuse innovative tool kits and pragmatic "neighborhood technologies" across a broad range of Chicago community development groups and local business networks struggling to come into compliance with environmental regulations (dry cleaning, electroplating, metal finishing). It also helped develop sustainable manufacturing practices and energy efficient buildings in low-income neighborhoods. The EPA's Design for Environment program funded CNT to help catalyze a national voluntary network for multistakeholder small manufacturing projects such as these, which included business owners, shop-floor workers, unions, neighborhoods, and professional designers. CNT offered one-stop energy conservation services to some one hundred and fifty community-based nonprofits and provided research within EJ coalitions, as in the case of battles around siting of waste incinerators and recycling alternatives.[46]

While CNT grew its staff and consulting practice to spur innovation in cities across the country, it has remained deeply embedded in the community-development field in Chicago, as recounted by Julia Parzen, long-time CNT board member and later chair as well as a key practitioner in this field. CNT thus enjoyed substantial local civic legitimacy in addition to its growing technical expertise and professional legitimacy. It was part of various coalitions during Harold Washington's mayoralty, and Chicago community organizer Barack Obama had served on its board. Bernstein cofounded and later chaired the Surface Transportation Policy Project, which helped design ISTEA, and served as one of the most central brokers (along with the Chicago Bicycle Federation) of its metropolitan network for implementation, as Margaret Weir and her colleagues have shown. He also served on the President's Council for Sustainable Development in the 1990s, cochairing its task force on metropolitan sustainable communities. CNT has continued to broaden its partnerships and board interlocks with other smart growth, green building, and transportation equity organizations. It thus positioned itself to work as one of the core partners in the Chicago Climate Task Force, and was responsible for developing the greenhouse gas emissions report and several other research papers funded by various foundation partners. CNT had at least one representative at every climate plan meeting, including all task force meetings, research advisory committees, sector groups, and organizational summits.[47]

Chicago Wilderness, another nonprofit partner helping to move the city forward on climate planning, grew from the Volunteer Stewardship

Network (VSN) created by Steve Packard in the late 1970s to restore prairie wildflowers and ecosystems in the urban forest preserves within the city of Chicago proper, Cook County, and eventually other surrounding counties of what historian William Cronon characterized as "nature's metropolis." Aided by the Sierra Club, Audubon, and several other groups that agreed to publish the schedules of VSN workdays, the group grew to some five thousand volunteers from neighborhood associations, garden clubs, Girl Scout and Boy Scout troops, and unaffiliated citizens interested in hands-on work and drawn to becoming "citizen scientists" of restoring prairies as they once existed before large European settlement. From a new position within the Illinois Conservancy, Packard spread the model to other state branches of The Nature Conservancy (TNC), though not without tension with some of its professional managers wary of amateurs. Eventually the project moved to Audubon, where it became Chicago Wilderness, and was then incorporated as an independent nonprofit in 1996.[48]

Much of the city's open space plan, as well as specific district plans, built upon the work of stewards over previous years, which they had done in collaboration with city and county forest staff, among the core governance partners. In the late 1990s, Chicago Wilderness became embroiled in intense political controversy, and was even subject to formal moratoria on its work for several years, as some neighborhood groups questioned its methods (controlled burns, deer removal) as well as its democratic legitimacy to speak for communities or, indeed, to speak for nature in the sense of controlling public and private meanings—aesthetic, recreational, symbolic, and wildlife.[49]

In response, Chicago Wilderness has further structured itself as a broad partnership of many kinds of associations and institutions. It informed itself first through a democratically sophisticated social science and humanities debate facilitated by the US Forest Service's North Central Research Station in the late 1990s to respond deliberatively and relationally to such local contentiousness. Some of this work was directly brokered by Malec-McKenna, a founding board member and a public official at the time. Then Chicago Wilderness began to further enrich its repertoire by stressing active discovery and storytelling in the construction of personal and civic identities in relation to nature. Positioning itself strategically within local governance dynamics defined by neighborhood resistance, electoral calculations, and bureaucratic accommodation (city, county, and federal), Chicago Wilderness thus came to deploy—alongside its original civic claims based upon volunteer work and restoration science—deliberative, relational, and narrative practices in complex sequences and combinations.[50]

Chicago Wilderness assembles in a biennial congress—some seven hundred participants in 2014. It is now comprised of several hundred member organizations, ranging from homeowner and park associations, advocacy coalitions, land trusts, friends groups, and local chapters of several multi-tiered environmental associations (the Sierra Club, Audubon, the Izaak Walton League, the National Parks Conservation Association, and TNC). It also includes corporate groups, cultural and educational organizations (the Field Museum, the Shedd Aquarium, the Lincoln Park Zoo, and university programs), and CNT, as well as city, county, state, and federal forest, park, and other land use and natural resource agencies, many of which have provided resources in the form of staff, space, volunteers, information, and grants. Its leadership focus on climate change has been land conservation (hence carbon sequestration), groundwater, green infrastructure, and biodiversity, which it links to its environmental education commitment to Leave No Child Inside. While some affiliations are relatively loose and not backed by consistent dues contributions and strategic commitments, Chicago Wilderness draws upon many sources of legitimacy and combines them in ways that are quite synergistic: through volunteer work, citizen science, associational networks, institutional prestige, professional knowledge, business contribution, and cultural status.[51]

The Chicago Climate Action Plan began as a nonprofit initiative in 2006, but with agreement of the mayor it was reconceived as an official city planning process. The lead person within government was Sadhu Aufochs Johnston whom Daley had moved from head of the department of environment into the mayor's office as his chief environmental officer while he also personally challenged his entire cabinet at an off-site retreat to "green every department or find other jobs." The key catalyst in the civic and philanthropic community, however, was Adele Simmons, who, as founder of the Global Philanthropy Partnership (GPP), served as cochair of the task force with Johnston. As head of the MacArthur Foundation for a decade (1989–1999), Simmons brought global stature and relationships, including with the Clinton Foundation, which provided the initial funding for the task force facilitator, Julia Parzen, who had also done earlier work in the community development finance field. With GPP's home offices in Chicago, Simmons also brought extensive relationships to the community-based groups that MacArthur had funded over the years—which included low-income and minority groups focused on environmental justice and brownfields—as well as to foundation heads and program officers in the local philanthropic community, several of whom (Joyce, Chicago Community Trust, and others) joined the effort. Simmons and others also enlisted experience from cities such as Seattle, as well as from other urban sustainability networks (ICLEI USA, US Conference of Mayors). Joyce Coffee, one of the core group of champions who had worked together over the years, was tasked to coordinate teaching across some forty city agencies.[52]

A persistent issue from the early 1990s, environmental justice concerns emerged more strongly in the election of 2011 and into the mayoralty of Rahm Emanuel due to grassroots protest, such as the successful campaign to close coal-fired power plants in Little Village and Pilsen, two predominantly Latino neighborhoods, and for participatory neighborhood and multistakeholder planning in their reuse. Other relatively effective grassroots efforts for bicycle equity, as well as collaborative projects with LISC and the Chicago New Communities Program, raised related issues. Sustainability strategies also took on an added metropolitan focus. With their networks beyond the city limits, CNT and Chicago Wilderness helped identify practitioners at the metropolitan level, as did several multitiered or multiunit organizations (the National League of Cities, the American Planning Association, the US Green Building Council, the US Conference of Mayors, and the Sierra Club's Cool Cities). They worked to surface, classify, and compare sustainable city practices and planning techniques, meld key standards, and fashion the template of the Greenest Region Compact of Chicagoland's Metropolitan Mayors Caucus. The review of plans also revealed that civic engagement and citizen commissions were normative, even though it did not attempt to analyze relative effectiveness. The compact was endorsed by ninety-five of the two hundred and seventy-five cities, towns, and villages in the region and was originally initiated by Mayor Daley and signed as a simple pledge in 2007, following on the opportunity provided by the US Mayors Climate Protection Agreement in 2005.[53]

However, these various initiatives, including participatory neighborhood planning have all occurred as core functions of city planning—in contrast to deal making, specialized federal grants, and the proliferation of more than one hundred and fifty TIF districts—have eroded in recent years. While there have been significant reconfiguration and improvements in services in some poor neighborhoods, the cost has been the displacement of many.[54]

Each of these three cases, though highly compressed, provides a window onto pathways to sustainable cities that have been developed within the opportunities and constraints of specific urban governance systems. They also reveal the interdependence of emergent local strategies with those of other actors operating across fields, including civic and professional associations and state and federal agencies. The following two cases of Baltimore and Phoenix add further distinctiveness and complexity to this pragmatic understanding of alternative pathways and to the opportunities and constraints that field actors will need to further map in the coming years.[55]

Baltimore

While Baltimore has been a core city in Chesapeake Bay protection and restoration efforts going back to the middle of the 1980s—hence, part of the watershed field—only in 2009 did the city council pass a sustainability plan. The city's real takeoff began in 2004 when the city council created a green building task force and engaged the regional chapter of USGBC; the report recommended the creation of a sustainability office as well as the broadening of policy scope beyond green building. As Mayor Martin O'Malley became governor of Maryland in 2007, city council president Sheila Dixon succeeded him and established the Office of Sustainability within the planning department, with a twenty-one-member Commission on Sustainability, which linked government efforts to broader civic, business, labor, and environmental networks engaged across a spectrum of policy issues, from energy and construction to job training and public health.

Public engagement, including youth civic engagement, is the first core value discussed in the plan. Participation was designed into the planning process, including the recruiting of some twenty-six "sustainability ambassadors" to link city agencies and neighborhood meetings. The plan itself listed an array of potential implementation and funding partnerships, signaled by a visually attractive set of strategy icons. While distinct from some earlier civic efforts through neighborhood associations and faith-based community organizing in Baltimore, as well as a federally funded Empowerment Zone, sustainability planning had an important civic and institutional legacy to build upon, but also a deep legacy of neighbor-hood segregation. Cheryl Casciani, who has deep roots in neighborhood revitalization and community development, that includes her position as the director of neighborhood sustainability at the Baltimore Commu-nity Foundation (BCF) and a board member of the Funders' Network for Smart Growth and Livable Communities (TFN), has served as chair of the sustainability commission for a decade. She has been a facilitator of dialogue and a bridge across various policy network framings. She was also able to help bring funding to the table after the 2008 recession. Thus, the city's food policy director was initially hired as a consultant to BCF. Casciani remains profoundly committed to civic engagement, including in those neighborhoods that are preoccupied with "rats and trash" rather than "trees and grass." She is clearly one of those skilled social actors who has helped build the local field of sustainable cities in a democratic manner, with important links to national networks.[56]

Sustainability in Baltimore has three main sets of framings or perspec-tives, according to Eric Zeemering's Q-sort methodology that assigns rela-tive weight (salience) to various responses to questions about the meaning of sustainability and then links these to specific local policy networks. He does this in ways demonstrating openness to the agendas of organizations with alternative saliences, hence productively contesting framings and po-tential social learning. The first definitional framing is *environmental sus-tainability*, which places emphasis on watersheds in the Chesapeake Bay, storm water management, GHG emission reduction, tree planting, urban forests, and local habitat. Blue Water Baltimore emerged in 2010 as a local coalition of four watershed associations and the Baltimore Harbor Wa-terkeeper. It utilizes volunteer river cleanup, monitoring, and restoration methods; environmental education partnerships with public schools; ad-vocacy and legal strategies; and native plants sold through the Herring Run Nursery (which brought in more than 10 percent of its nearly $3 million in revenues in 2015). The board and staff of Blue Water Baltimore include some who have served at the highest levels of strategic work on the Chesapeake Bay for decades in nonprofit, state government, and federal agency roles.[57]

In addition, Tree Baltimore works through the city's forestry division within the Baltimore Department of Recreation and Parks, as well as with state and federal agencies, and maps tree cover in the interest of reducing the heat island effect. The Parks and People Foundation works with neighborhood and environmental groups across the city. Bike Maryland and the Farm Alliance of Baltimore City also collaborate with such groups; the latter receives support from the University of Maryland Extension. Baltimore City Public Schools is a key institutional player, partly because of state standards for environmental literacy and state funding for sustainability initiatives in school buildings, but also because of a Green Schools Network that can maneuver nimbly around bureaucracy. Network links among organizations operating within the environmental sustainability frame are the densest among the three.

The second framing of *sustainability as urban rebuilding* places emphasis on revitalizing neighborhoods, reducing crime, attracting local businesses and jobs, expanding opportunities through transit-oriented development, and rehabilitating vacant and abandoned properties (estimated at thirty thousand in the 2009 sustainability plan). This framing receives support from prominent economic development organizations, such as the Greater Baltimore Committee (established in 1955) but also the Downtown Partnership, which focuses on the urban core. It also receives support from many of the CDCs that constitute the community development field in struggling inner-city communities, including the intermediary Central Baltimore Partnership. The third framing is *sustainability as civic health and justice*, which emphasizes public engagement and institutional partnerships (especially with nonprofits), the rights and interests of disadvantaged communities, job training, and neighborhood revitalization. Here, we also find CDCs and other local nonprofits, health and food justice alliances, healthy baby initiatives, and Civic Works, which has enrolled some two hundred and fifty AmeriCorps volunteers each year. Environmental justice and civic environmentalism provide key bridges to the first two frames, though network linkages are the least dense among the three.[58]

Some policies manifest greater potential for coalition and strategic action than others, such as rehabilitating vacant and abandoned properties in a majority-black city that has lost significant population over the decades, while others, such as improved storm water management, not only show less potential but also generate framing opposition more broadly, such as a modest water fee being labeled a "rain tax." While the subsequent mayor, Stephanie Rawlings-Blake (2010–2016), de-emphasized sustainability and then resigned in the aftermath of protests around the death of a black man (Freddie Gray) in police custody, it is not yet clear whether or not her successors have the strategic leverage to make urban revitalization and police reform part of a larger sustainable city agenda. Previous efforts have been notable, if uneven, especially when Mayor Kurt Schmoke could draw upon a variety of federal grants during the Clinton years, such as community policing, HOPE VI housing, and Empowerment Zones. But the shift from manufacturing to postindustrial development strategies built around medical and educational institutions with geographical proximity to distressed neighborhoods has yet to elicit sustained leadership from city government, thus leaving such strategies overly dependent upon quasi-public corporations, such as East Baltimore Development, Inc., with limited commitment to community engagement and public transparency.[59]

Phoenix

"A horizontal hymn to unsustainable development" is how sociologist Andrew Ross opens his book *Bird on Fire: Lessons from the World's Least Sustainable City*, a subtitle that has continued to spur public debate and has prompted concerted action. Phoenix, a desert city of approximately 1.6 million people, is part of the fastest growing US metropolis over the past half century. Now with over four million people, its six-lane arterial roads and canal networks spread out to connect single-family tract housing across the metro area. In the 1950s alone, the city's area increased tenfold through annexation and its population grew fourfold. Phoenix has very little rainfall; it ranks the highest of cities with days over ninety-nine degrees Fahrenheit and its average nighttime temperatures, due partly to urban heat-island effects, have risen eleven degrees over this period. Its model of development has been based on cheap land sustained by even cheaper water largely allocated by historical pacts on diversions from the Colorado River (in addition to the local Salt and Verde Rivers) as well as the doctrine of prior appropriation that holds that "first in time is first in right." The state's groundwater act of 1980, designed to stem overdraft from rivers and aquifers in the face of pressure from President Carter to restrict water pork unless coupled with conservation, has steadily weakened over time, and an extended drought beginning in 2002 has further exacerbated problems.[60]

The city attracted people from various parts of the country, but notably many midwestern white retirees in search of affordable and air-conditioned homes, often with private swimming pools and membership-only golf courses in racially segregated subdivisions. Cultural narratives, such as consuming "the desert oasis lifestyle," have informed political, economic, and planning choices. Younger workers were recruited to aerospace industries and then to electronics factories and call centers, many of which later moved offshore. Those employed in such industries at low-wage and nonunionized jobs, especially Latinos and African Americans, were compelled by deed restrictions—later by zoning codes, and then covenants, conditions, and restrictions (CC&Rs)—as well as affordability, to settle in south Phoenix where industrial facilities with more than their share of environmental hazards were concentrated, even while the "power lines" of electricity generation from coal extended far out of the metropolitan area into Navajo lands. Other Phoenicians settled in white working-class suburbs such as Maryville, whose industrial zone also became the site of toxic pollution and protest by the late 1980s. Many were also attracted by subprime loans before the housing bust of 2008; by this time, Phoenix trailed all other major cities in per-capita income.[61]

While it is the epicenter of Goldwater conservatism with strong libertarian ideologies and antitax sentiments, Phoenix nonetheless suppressed from its consciousness how much of its growth was based on the flow of federal dollars for the aerospace industry, road and highway infrastructure, water reclamation projects, and home mortgage guarantees and tax credits. Its main industry has been land speculation and home construction, with concomitant boom and bust cycles especially exaggerated in Phoenix. While now a majority Democratic city, its form of government had become council/manager during the municipal reform movement of the early and mid-twentieth century and was heavily influenced by real estate interests. It was also constrained by a conservative state legislature, lax enforcement of groundwater regulations, and a tax law that prohibited more than 10 percent of city budgets to come from property taxes.[62]

Some scholars of Phoenix and the larger Valley of the Sun contest the "least sustainable city" designation, though they certainly recognize that there are many challenges going forward. Portney's influential set of national rankings, based upon various indicators of sustainable and smart growth *activities*, places Phoenix in a tie for seventh place among the fifty-five largest US cities.[63] Grady Gammage Jr., a local scholar and influential voice within the city, recognizes that arid western cities built around the automobile and single-family homes, "need to change and evolve dramatically." Nonetheless, he makes an extended case that Phoenix is considerably more sustainable than typically thought and has a viable trajectory forward. While Phoenix, like much of the Southwest, has faced serious drought in recent years, Arizona's limits on groundwater pumping since

1980 have protected the aquifers of central Arizona relatively well, argues Gammage; its shift away from agricultural uses of land to subdivisions has decreased overall water use. Homeowners have further reduced per-capita water consumption—high by national urban standards—and new construction of homes with swimming pools is plummeting to as low as 10 percent. Solar energy has advanced considerably, including recent shifts on Navajo land, and has much greater potential if political and institutional obstacles can be overcome. The light rail system, finished in 2008 and coincident with the flow of students from Arizona State University's Tempe campus—which decided to become an institutional model of sustainability—to its newer downtown Phoenix campus, has been relatively effective in riders per mile compared to peer cities; its success led to the ballot approval of a $30 billion transportation plan in 2015, which included further light rail extensions, bike lanes, and bus improvements.

Light rail has, in turn, spurred greater housing density and transit-oriented development, although overall housing density in Phoenix has not been especially low. In 2009, Mayor Phil Gordon (2004–2012) announced the intention to make the city the greenest in the nation, and his successor, Greg Stanton (2012–2018), appointed its first sustainability officer to help meet the challenge of the Ross epithet. Some other recent studies of the Colorado River system, while not underestimating the enormous complexity and uncertainty of the challenges, see considerable evidence of strategies for conserving and sharing water, as well as for collaboration and restoration.[64]

Movement toward making Phoenix more sustainable has been driven in part by civic action, though as a newer city with such rapid growth and constant churn, the city has lacked much of the civic infrastructure upon which many older cities have relied. As civic life was beginning to stabilize by the early 1980s, Terry Goddard co-chaired Citizens for District Elections to replace at-large council elections to give more leverage to neighborhoods and civic associations and to spur council diversity; the measure passed in 1982. When elected mayor (1984–1990), Goddard increased participation in neighborhood planning and established the basis for a new neighborhoods department. Inspired by the work of the National Civic League (NCL) on civic engagement and community visioning, and prompted by NCL-affiliate Neal Peirce's widely read 1987 "Peirce Report," Goddard and the city's planning director, Rod Engelen, convened the Phoenix Futures Forum in 1988. The report had been commissioned by the publisher of the city's two major newspapers, the *Arizona Republic* and the *Phoenix Gazette*, and was delivered on the same Sunday to over five hundred thousand homes. Herb Ely drove the work of the policy committee on a virtually daily, full-time basis for fifteen months. As an attorney and counsel with the NAACP, he had drafted Arizona's civil rights act of 1965, and he had defended and often joined black youth in protest events.[65]

Chris Gates, NCL vice president, facilitated the process, which included four major forums spaced several months apart followed by a "civic summit" and various work group meetings and mini-forums throughout. The Futures Forum enabled multistakeholder deliberations at the neighborhood and city levels lasting some eighteen months. The city, along with several private organizations and the mayor—from his personal retirement fund as a sign of his deep commitment—provided funding, and some three thousand five hundred participated in the forums and work groups. Ninety-five people served on a general policy committee and two hundred and fifty people served on nine task forces. A final report and vision statement was issued in January 1990, along with a commitment to an implementation process. Not surprisingly, given previous deliberative planning efforts by an American Institute of Architects R/UDAT team (see chapter 3), growth emerged as the core issue. Environmental, neighborhood, religious, and nonprofit groups met with business, labor, and educational groups, as well as city officials. Mayor Paul Johnson (1990–1994) reorganized the city council subcommittee structure to align more effectively with the Forum's subsequent six action groups, which included: (1) arts, culture, and recreation; (2) basic economic resources; (3) citizenship and governance; (4) environment and resources; (5) neighborhoods and community; and (6) transportation and urban form. New civic, professional, and business leaders emerged in a variety of areas and were drawn into further efforts as "action partners."[66]

In 1993, the city also implemented a Neighborhood Initiative Area program aimed to include many forms of community-based action and innovation, especially in lower-income and blighted areas, each with an interdepartmental team to coordinate efforts across agencies and to help catalyze integrative neighborhood planning that engaged ordinary residents. To be sure, the absence of vast pockets of concentrated poverty made it more feasible for the city to target manageable areas. The combination of professionalized institutionalization and civic engagement has won the city recognition, with awards by some of the most prominent organizations in the governance field, including those from NAPA and ICMA, as well as NCL's All-America City Award. Nonetheless, while the institutional infrastructure survives and extends to even larger areas of revitalization, such as West Phoenix, the rapid appreciation of home prices prior to 2007 followed by the housing bust—especially severe in Phoenix—dispersed or debilitated many of the homeowners key to the process.[67]

Artists have become very active in downtown planning. Their presence became increasingly important as the city began systematic efforts to improve the arts in the mid-1980s, with a 1 percent budget line from city construction projects designated for public art. Many artists lived and/or rented studio space in the poorer parts of downtown vulnerable to development pressures. They organized to oppose a third sports stadium and then brought together a broad coalition whose vision was built around environmental sustainability, affordable housing, and inclusive participation. The Downtown Phoenix Arts Coalition spurred the formation of a larger Downtown Voices Coalition (DVC), whose members also included the Community Housing Partnership, Arizona Chain Reaction, the Phoenix Historic Neighborhoods Coalition, and LISC Phoenix.

DVC's 2004 report, *Downtown Voices: Creating a Sustainable Downtown*, was open to the much broader framing of sustainable cities, which had progressed in many other cities by then. It clearly built upon the legacy of the participatory and multistakeholder process of the Phoenix Futures Forum, which persists in the DVC to the present day and serves as a counterweight to the pressures of the more traditional growth machine. DVC itself, as well as community development groups such as Chicanos Por La Causa, have led several affordable housing initiatives, and LISC has developed a Sustainable Communities Initiative to link housing affordability to energy and transportation issues, the latter of which seems to be leading to considerably greater use of biking, walking, and public transport, especially among millennials. Chicanos Por La Causa also has a representative on the fifteen-member Citizens Transportation Commission that oversees the plan.[68]

The most recent city plan update contains a full array of sustainable city components, from green building to complete streets, open space to healthy neighborhoods. For the first time, such planning had input from representatives of the neighborhood planning groups, which have grown quite steadily over the past three decades; the earlier seventeen-point Green City program had been assembled somewhat hastily with the help of ASU's Global Institute of Sustainability to take advantage of the political opportunity of the American Recovery and Reinvestment Act (ARRA) stimulus funding under Obama. How current initiatives play out will depend on many factors in the civic, political, desert, and environmental justice landscapes of the city itself, the metropolitan area, and at state and national levels. With the steadily increasing growth and geographic dispersal of Latinos across the city's neighborhoods, immigration politics will play a key role. However, the central challenge will remain managing water consumption in extended drought and possibly mega-drought conditions in a way that enhances participatory governance, civic responsibility, and social equity. This seems achievable, but only if the city, other municipalities, and the state can begin to collaborate much more ambitiously in growth management, infrastructure investment, and conservation of groundwater assets.[69]

Conclusion

Cities have generated various pathways to sustainability, though some are more constrained than others by patterns of urban governance over decades. Portland, San Francisco, and Chicago reveal pathways that tend to place them in the higher rankings among U.S. cities. Each has had a robust civic infrastructure that was further developed and aligned with the challenges posed by postwar land use, energy, water, transportation, and economic development while also modifying some growth machine dynamics. Each found ways to combine and/or sequence high degrees of contestation with new forms of collaboration across the field of urban and environmental groups and institutional actors, including government agencies, and through changes in political opportunity opened by electoral competition.

Portland demonstrated advantages due to its particularly strong neighborhood movement in the late 1960s and early 1970s and its capacity to quickly leverage political opportunity at local and state levels to institutionalize neighborhood voice, relational practice, bureaucratic openness, participatory land-use planning, and even energy planning within a decade. These positioned the city to take early advantage of ICLEI's global learning network design in the early 1990s, and then to develop the nation's first climate plan (with multiple iterations since). It further institutionalized sustainable development through a city office and commission and through community-based learning and research at Portland State

University. Portland's sustainability director was also a key practitioner in the development of USDN (see chapter 7). While many cities have struggled to incorporate environmental justice into sustainable city practices and institutional development, Portland's latest climate action plan has been quite intentional in the way it has included five specific community-based organizations representing diverse racial and ethnic populations in its Equity Work Group.

San Francisco did not institutionalize neighborhood associations in the way that Portland did, but civic activists opposed to the Manhattanization of downtown exercised persistent leverage through ballot measures and environmental review suits to control growth and expand participation. A breakthrough in planning practice and governance culture came only in 1986 with the passage of a ballot proposition for accountable planning, and successive mayors became responsive to sustainability concerns. The contentious pluralism of the city was also modified by a range of collaborative strategies in various city departments and across parts of the nonprofit field, including healthy community coalitions, HIV/AIDs organizing, youth development, immigrant organizing, community development, and environmental justice. In addition, the city drew upon an exceptionally rich network of Bay Area groups, including some of the legacy multitiered ones, engaged in open space, parks, watersheds, alternative food, and bicycling, many of which had refined their strategic thinking in response to persistent struggles over effectiveness, equity, and democratic legitimacy.

In Chicago, resistance to the growth coalition assembled by Mayor Richard J. Daley took the form of various community organizing projects inspired by Saul Alinsky, but also cohered into a community development and participatory planning field that provided a critical part of the coalition that supported Mayor Harold Washington, the city's first black mayor, in the mid-1980s. This window of political opportunity did not stay open for long, given white aldermanic resistance and the early death of Washington. Yet, Mayor Richard M. Daley managed to keep some of this legacy alive and found ways to progressively institutionalize it, even as some initiatives blocked by aldermanic logrolling were spun off to public-private partnerships. A robust community-policing design and implementation, beginning in the early 1990s, proved especially noteworthy despite significant slippage that exacerbated racial tensions; calls for strengthening the core design and philosophy are a prominent part of recommendations by the task force, headed by Lori Lightfoot, who was elected mayor in 2019 by an overwhelming majority. A sustainable city agenda also emerged in the early 1990s with tree planting, bicycle planning, and brownfield redevelopment. These efforts positioned the mayor to draw upon a network of organizations and foundations that had been active for several decades on green community and business development, urban forest restoration, environmental justice, and green building. Several of them, with strong ties among their leaders, enabled the mayor to commission and develop the city's first climate action plan, released in 2008.

Baltimore and Phoenix have not been as well positioned as these three cities, yet they have nonetheless managed to bring issues of sustainability to the fore. As part of the Chesapeake Bay watershed and its various institutional strategies, driven by influential civic actors, state legislatures and agencies, and a dedicated program at the EPA, the framing of Baltimore's sustainable city has been primarily environmental, with significant community development actors playing important brokerage roles but achieving much less traction on civic health and social justice. This is especially true in poorer black neighborhoods, including those proximate to the medical and educational institutions that have anchored the city's recent postindustrial economic development. Phoenix, a city of desert sprawl, civic churn, and tenuous water faces significant challenges of sustainability, not the least of which is a state political culture favoring libertarian and conservative approaches to environmental issues as well as intense conflict over immigration. Nonetheless, neighborhood and arts activists have managed to place issues of equity and sustainable growth on the agenda, as have faculty and administration at Arizona State University, recent Phoenix mayors and city plans, and LISC Phoenix, the major community-development institution in the area.

The future of *none* of these cities' sustainability strategies is secure, especially in face of heightening climate crises and recent federal turmoil since the 2016 presidential election that has disrupted public agencies most responsible for various aspects of sustainable, healthy, and just cities. Coronavirus stresses at the local level, as of this writing in early 2020, will likely exacerbate challenges. Nonetheless, we can expect many cities to move forward as they discover further ways in which environmental sustainability, economic vitality, community health, and social justice can complement each other. Various professional intermediaries in the field—from the National League of Cities and the International City/County Management Association to the American Planning Association and the American Institute of Architects, ICLEI and the Urban Sustainability Directors Network to civic and environmental intermediaries such as the Natural Resources Defense Council, Restore America's Estuaries, and some of the legacy multi-tiered associations—all have come to recognize sustainable and resilient cities as core components of US democracy. We turn to some of these in the following chapter.

CHAPTER SEVEN

Framing and Enabling
the Sustainable Cities Field

In the historical narratives of previous chapters, I have examined how civic, professional, government, and other actors at various levels of the federal system have built the fields of new urbanism and smart growth, green building, biking and walking, urban farming, and watersheds. They have done so through conflict and collaboration, sometimes with policy supports, often circuitously, and almost always with an eye on how to accommodate or enhance democratic engagement to help transform communities. In specific cities, local field building has proceeded within the context of governance dynamics that have attempted to reconfigure various forms of power over many decades. Along the way, actors in these various arenas have positioned their work in relation to emerging conceptions of the "sustainable city," not as a lazy and hazy summer umbrella term but as a dynamic and often conflictive blending of components that further indexes power and democracy, equity and justice.

In this chapter, I first examine how the urban sustainability frame has become integrative and enriched by other frames, such as "healthy cities," "assets-based community development," and "environmental justice." While framing could never be complete and comprehensive, especially in the face of complexity and uncertainty in an age of climate crisis, sustainable cities now serves as a master frame within urbanism, especially when appropriately modified or accompanied by the "just city" and the "resilient city."

In the second half of this chapter, I discuss how various intermediary organizations that have adopted urban sustainability framing have attempted to enable pragmatic and integrative work at the city level, especially among those directly responsible for sustainability and resilience agendas across agencies, plans, and practices. I focus on two major ones: ICLEI USA and the Urban Sustainability Directors Network (USDN), but I also examine their relation to urban generalists, such as the National League of Cities (NLC), the International City/County Management Association, and the US Conference of Mayors, which bring very broad reach as well as potential legitimacy for sustainable city work among association members who may face skepticism and even opposition among other actors in their home cities.

Enriching Frames

Sustainable cities framing has drawn from many sources over several decades and continues to be fashioned with creativity and contest over the relative configuration and normative weight of specific components. As Meg Holden argues, sustainability is a "slippery" concept in many ways; it can be vague and encompass various values (ecology, economy, equity) that are in tension and often quite fiercely contested among theoretical approaches. Yet, it has also proved "sticky" in its ability to "organize urban policy, planning, and institutional design in new and useful ways," primarily through the pragmatic engagement of many kinds of actors. Here, I discuss some of the ways that field actors have spliced together various components of a richly variegated yet coherent frame of sustainable cities, as well as those factors that motivate and enable integrative stances.[1]

As social movement theories conceive it, framing is a cognitive process of assigning meaning, akin to bricolage by assembling and splicing together components from various sources, amplifying them to apply to additional problems, and developing bridges among related framing devices. Movement entrepreneurs select and modify frame elements for a perceived strategic fit to political events and opportunities, to enhance resonance with popular beliefs and lifeworlds, and to motivate engagement by potential adherents while also demobilizing opponents and gaining bystander support. Diagnostic components analyze the causes of problems and attribute blame while prognostic components indicate how solutions might be generated. However, action can and often does precede ideation, and local interactionist and discursive processes influence the framing work of movement entrepreneurs. Injustice is often, though not always, a core component of movement frames. Insisted by a second wave of theorizing, frames are not simply cognitive but also contain cultural and emotive components, such as ways of narrating and performing anger and shame, despair, and hope. Movement actors continuously dispute among each other how frames might reconfigure, and a broader range of actors in multiorganizational fields further shape the processes of splicing, combining, and aligning. Hence the attention to framing in policy studies, political communications, urban branding, and organizational culture and strategy.[2]

As we have seen so far, the cognitive core of what has become the sustainable cities frame was initially crafted around participatory civic action to secure clean water and clean air in specific places and to protect neighborhoods from disruptive development driven by downtown business and real estate interests as well as by unresponsive highway and planning bureaucracies, especially toward urban ethnic and racial minorities. Civic actors, such as the League of Women Voters chapters but also Model Cities coalitions, might flexibly calibrate skills and styles, cognitive and emotive features, in ways that were angry yet relational, righteous yet alert to appropriate institutional logics, and demanding of federal regulation yet sensitive to built places, proximate neighbors, and inhabited ecosystems. While still overly enmeshed within actual or imagined command-and-control tool kits and policy designs in the initial decades, such civic actors sought to secure and protect "good communities." In response to the limits of command and control, they began to borrow narrative templates and action repertoires from the emerging field of environmental dispute resolution from the early 1970s onward; these problematized legal conflict and stalemate and the deleterious effects the latter might have on everyday community life. Such repertoires were diffused through the National Association of Environmental Professionals as well as through other professional associations and institutes. By the early 1970s, open space became part of the framing mix, and land-use planning was placed on the agenda by local activists, planning and architecture professionals, and by the White House Council on Environmental Quality (CEQ) and its citizen advisory committee.[3]

Beginning in the 1980s, a specific watershed frame was developed by self-described "shedheads," with cultural resonance to the "Deadheads" that devotedly tailed the famous 1960s Grateful Dead rock group on their concert tours. The watershed frame responded to advances in ecology and conservation biology, to the perceived limits of command-and-control regulation (especially but not only due to Reagan administration constraints), and to the opportunities presented by multistakeholder strategies of protection and restoration. Ecological urban design began to extend some of Ian McHarg's original insights on designing for nature in landscape architecture. By the mid-1980s, due to increasing recognition of affinities among actors in these various fields, the framing of sustainable communities, in the works as early as the meeting at Westerbeke Ranch in 1980, was formally articulated with the publication of the edited volume by Van der Ryn and Calthorpe in 1986 called *Sustainable Communities*, and then with far greater conceptual elasticity and practical tool kits by Mark Roseland's *Toward Sustainable Communities* in 1992. The United Nations Brundtland Commission's report on sustainable development in 1987, which had a chapter on the "urban challenge," generated a specific local government initiative through ICLEI in cities globally.[4]

The framing endeavors that emerged largely on separate tracks for the first several decades had, by the mid-1980s, manifested a far more elastic and fecund cross-fertilization over the next decade and beyond, albeit in a period when other federal policy supports for the urban poor were considerably weakened. New urbanism, green building, and smart growth represented further cognitive contributions in the 1990s, each with distinct emphases within places of neighborhood, city, and metropolitan scope, yet each also recognizing affinities among themselves within a more encompassing frame of sustainable communities. "Complete streets" and "age-friendly communities" added new components in the 2000s. Local projects, such as urban river restoration, began to highlight *cobenefits*—itself an important frame-bridging term—such as flood reduction, ecosystem health, community health through recreation and trails, diverse cultural celebrations, and local economic development. Such cobenefits resonate within and across multiple frames.

Three additional frames also further enriched the general frame of sustainable cities: "healthy cities" and "healthy communities" (typically used interchangeably), "assets-based community development," and "environmental justice." Each has a distinct origin, trajectory, and set of challenges, yet all have come to borrow freely from each other in their key framing documents, cross-references in bibliographies, book endorsements, and best-practice guides. They are woven into the broader discourse on sustainable cities and communities. Best-practice guides sometimes rebrand cases that have arisen within one frame, such as assets-based community development, with another frame, such as smart growth, as in the case with the

Dudley Street Neighborhood Initiative, although such rebranding is often the result of strategic blending that occurs locally.[5]

Healthy Cities

The term *healthy city* was coined in its contemporary version by Leonard Duhl, a professor of planning at the University of California, Berkeley, when speaking at an international conference in Toronto in 1984, which soon led to the Toronto Healthy City Project and the World Health Organization (WHO) Healthy Cities Project, the latter eventually growing to several thousand urban partnerships worldwide. Duhl had been deeply influenced by various forms of participatory and community-based health improvement projects before and during the War on Poverty in the 1960s. His work—first at the National Institute of Mental Health, then at HUD, and finally working with Peter Edelman as an advisor to Senator Robert F. Kennedy—was instrumental in bringing a place-based and integrative conception of health into Model Cities, though this was hardly its focus. Some neighborhood health centers—later renamed community health centers—shared this vision, but their practices narrowed considerably due to various policy compromises and funding streams, especially Medicaid.[6]

Healthy community projects were diffused in the United States through the National Civic League (NCL), with modest funding from the Public Health Service (PHS) at the US Department of Health and Human Services (HHS) in the late 1980s, as NCL was in the process of reinvention (and name change from the National Municipal League) to stress civic action and community building. Drawing upon the experience and networks of John W. Gardner (secretary of HEW in the mid-1960s and board chair of NCL in the mid-1990s), and Dr. Philip Lee (assistant HEW secretary in the mid-1960s and again in the mid-1990s), HHS established a healthy communities office to promote this model. It received added emphasis after the failure of the Clinton health plan in 1994, as recommended in a meeting in the secretary's office with Peter Edelman (then-counselor to the HHS secretary), key agency staff in healthy communities and health reform, and a network of scholars and practitioners.[7]

State-funded networks (California, South Carolina, Massachusetts) and various institutional partners (Health Research and Education Trust of the American Hospital Association) and foundations (Kellogg, Robert Wood Johnson, California Endowment) helped to further develop the frame and build the healthy-communities field. While the movement had difficulty sustaining its key intermediary (the National Coalition for Healthier Cities and Communities), its core tenets that health improvements had to address various environmental determinants of health (housing, street design, urban food, open space) by empowering multiple community and institutional stakeholders to collaborate continued to be diffused through the American Public Health Association, the Interfaith Health Program, the Centers for Disease Control, and schools of public health.[8]

As planning theorist Jason Corburn and others argue, the healthy communities frame includes the community as coproducer of relevant urban expertise and avoids the reductionism associated with single behaviors, diseases, and risk factors. It aims to incorporate the full complexity of social, spatial, economic, and environmental factors that interact to produce population health and illness as well as the systemic inequalities that impede environmental and health justice. Effective democratic urban governance, including multistakeholder partnerships at the neighborhood level, is a key component of the healthy city frame.[9]

Assets-Based Community Development

Fashioned especially by Jody Kretzmann and John McKnight in their work at Northwestern University with Chicago nonprofits in the late 1980s and early 1990s, "assets-based community development" emerged in framing disputes within and across several fields. The first was the community development field, where so much emphasis had come to be placed on the "bricks and mortar" of housing. The second was the Alinskyite community organizing field where, despite the emphasis on associational and institutional relationships and "power with" in several of the major networks, the focus on social justice tended to direct communities toward claims on outside resources. And the third was the human service field, which even in its community-based nonprofit variant that emerged so strongly in the 1960s with federal policy design and funding changes, tended to focus on residents as clients with deficiencies—the "deficits model"—rather than as citizens and coproducers.[10]

In contrast, assets-based community development (ABCD) framing focused on the capacities of individuals and the work of associations, no matter how small, as well as the resources that local institutions and local land could provide to help communities mobilize "from the inside out" while not ignoring larger contexts of power and resources. The 1993 handbook *Building Communities from the Inside Out*, followed by a training video, supplied highly usable tools and numerous examples for mapping the assets of communities. Within the next decade, the ABCD Institute was providing training through its national network of practitioners to hundreds of CDCs, neighborhood associations, local nonprofits, community foundations, and the United Way. Also engaged were university extension services, AmeriCorps programs, healthy community coalitions, associations of public health practitioners, and local, state, and federal agencies for youth development and people with developmental disabilities. Many schools of social work, public administration, and urban and environmental planning incorporated ABCD framing, tool kits, and case studies into curricula. Community grants through public agencies often included ABCD criteria, thus adding a policy feedback component.[11]

Environmental Justice

Environmental justice (EJ) is the most challenging frame to contest and enrich the sustainable cities frame since it foregrounds systemic inequalities that are generated within cities due to decisions made by many kinds of actors on the siting of hazardous waste incinerators, landfills, and other noxious facilities, as well as other forms of spatial clustering of dirty industry, segregated housing, inadequate transportation, open space, food access, and the like. The EJ frame emerged from local community struggles in the early 1980s and scholarly studies that began within a few years, resulting in the formal convening of movement actors in a summit in 1991. This prompted the recognition of the issue of "environmental equity" under George H. W. Bush's EPA administrator William Reilly, the executive director of the Task Force on Land Use and Urban Growth created by the citizen's advisory committee within CEQ in the early 1970s (see chapter 3). Carol Browner, the next EPA administrator under Bill Clinton, adopted the movement's justice framing language. During the previous decade, she had been a lawyer for the National Toxics Campaign, a grassroots initiative where early frame incubation and organizer training occurred. Two EJ movement entrepreneurs served on the president's environmental transition team. Clinton's EJ executive order in 1994 provided greater administrative scope across other agencies—through the Interagency Working Group on Environmental Justice, coordinated by the EPA—and incorporated multistakeholder and movement voices in the newly established National Environmental Justice Advisory Council (NEJAC).[12]

Environmental racism and injustice manifest through inequalities in permitting and regulation, local political power and growth coalitions; and market dynamics on locational choices, agglomeration economies, and land values that have inscribed within them historical legacies of racial segregation. Strategic choices to reduce the potential of local resistance—that is, by putting noxious facilities in neighborhoods where there is likely to be least pushback—also became common. To be sure, the vast literature on environmental justice parses these dynamics in different ways, which adds to the strategic complexity within the EJ movement of linking the diagnostic dimension of framing to the prognostic; namely, what is to be done to reduce or eliminate environmental injustice. To develop the prognostic, field actors are continually testing strategic alternatives, such as direct action, the uses and limits of the law, or the relative weight and efficacy of contentious and collaborative approaches. The latter provide significant opportunities for frame bridging with healthy communities and ABCD and have been sanctioned by several NEJAC reports that draw upon various community-based framing initiatives within EPA and among its partners in the field. Locally, the term *partners* could be fiercely contested, as it was in the years following the Flint water crisis of 2014. The frame of "just sustainabilities," developed by Julian Agyeman and Robert Bullard among others, provides further bridging opportunities, although its tendency to posit radical institutional prescriptions sometimes places it at the edges of the civic and policy spaces where most of the main field actors, including many grassroots groups with contentious origins and periodic battles, have chosen to operate strategically. Nonetheless, enriching the normative debate on the institutional dimensions of the "just city"—especially in terms of equity, democracy, and diversity as well as the tensions among them—remains an essential task for sustainable cities work.[13]

Framing Anchors and Integrators

Several further features of framing sustainable cities are important to highlight, and these distinguish them from framing processes within contentious social movements that gravitate toward "us versus them" identity tropes. The three I discuss here are framing anchors and integrators within cities, federal framing processes, and professional interlocutors.

First, city institutions, processes, and tool kits serve as what I call *framing anchors and integrators. City institutions*, such as a sustainability office, chief resilience officer, or interagency partnership, provide authorization and incentive to identify cognitive and operative complementarities. *City processes*, such as multistakeholder and inclusive visioning, and sustainability and climate planning, provide opportunities for disparate civic, professional, agency, and other field actors to add their preferred perspectives and practices to the overall mix, but they also have to justify themselves as part of a consequential composite that enhances pragmatic credibility and broader democratic legitimacy as a result. *City tool kits*, such as community and sustainability indicator projects, GIS and cloud-based platforms, 311 reporting systems, and LEED for Cities and Communities enable comparison of metrics, visuals, and scenarios and combine in multiple ways, providing ordinary citizens, diverse stakeholders, and authorized officials ways of imagining the complex contours of a sustainable city and potentially generating accountability for how its specific components can be systematically knit together. Each of these three sets of framing anchors and integrators tend to pull disparate pieces together into more firmly grounded and holistic blends and admixtures.

Civic groups, such as bicycle associations, help drive the process or respond in kind by broadening agendas, diversifying boards, and developing more inclusive nomenclature, such as the Street Trust in Portland (see chapter 4). The aligning and bridging opportunities emerge partly due to cognitive affinities but also because the challenges of urban governance within local spatial and jurisdictional boundaries generate normative questions of "the good community" or "the good city," including how to make it work coherently.[14]

At community forums and other public meetings where they are authorized to share stories and articulate values, ordinary citizens tend to make connections among issues, seek partners, suggest cobenefits, and explore what it might take to reduce barriers to action. Contingent rationales often emerge. For instance, complete streets cannot be realized, its framers argue in prognostic and pragmatic fashion, *unless* civic actors such as bicycle associations, AARP chapters, and neighborhood associations can get city transportation engineers to *work with them*, and *unless* civic groups can come to appreciate the technical and safety norms and institutional logics *within which such professionals operate*. The citizen or resident as coproducer—for example, of bike lane design and bicycle safety skills—adds a civic identity that further reinforces such dynamics. While not necessarily displacing other identities, such as a righteous senior or a disabled veteran in a complete streets coalition, the coproducer identity tends to temper us-versus-them identity framing. The greater the apparent need for practical collaboration to realize objectives, the greater the incentive for multiple actors to speak a common language, or to at least become multilingual and capable of code switching.

While there are clear normative overlaps and cognitive affinities among many of the components of these and related frames discussed thus far, organizations in the sustainable cities field become multilingual and amplify their initial framing for strategic reasons as well. Frame bridging enhances the potential for broad democratic legitimacy, strategic alliances, and funding worthiness (from taxes, bonds, foundation, and government grants), as well as for shared board membership, staff recruitment, and institutional recognition.

Second, federal institutions contribute to framing by responding to contentious claims, convening an array of field actors that include those making such claims, and developing "framework" statements. During what was a critical period of cross-fertilization in the latter part of the 1990s, the EPA's deputy administrator Fred Hansen—second in command and operational chief—established a process to fashion the EPA's Framework for Community-Based Environmental Protection, known as the CBEP approach (pronounced "see-bep"). Key coordinators utilized the terms *framing* and *framework* interchangeably, although with greater institutional and policy emphasis for the latter, which had become a commonly utilized template in federal agencies. Various types of associations and organizations contributed potential cases and practices over a five-year period, including NEJAC, which contained leading representatives of the EJ movement, and the Seattle City Council.[15]

The latter was at the height of its neighborhood planning to enhance participatory processes for its own Toward a Sustainable Seattle comprehensive plan. City councilor Richard Conlin, who oversaw the council's process, had been a cofounder in 1991 of the civic group with the identical name Sustainable Seattle, and he was key to developing its frame and sustainable indicators tool kit through extensive community forums. Local discursive creativity in the forums filtered upward through several levels of the federal system (city, King County, other cities in the county, governor's sustainability panel, and the EPA) and then outward to other cities and through media strategies elaborated in the local public sphere. The participatory processes ensured that qualitative and culturally framed metrics—sometimes linked to rich storytelling—were included with quantitative ones. The Seattle indicators, highlighted in the extensive CBEP tool

cities frame has many challenges not the least of which in the coming decades are managing climate movement emotions of anger and fear, even panic and despair, in the face of ever-more worrisome scientific prognoses and political barriers, and linking these to a politics of democratic hope and institutional resilience, to which we return in the concluding chapter.[20]

Enabling Intermediaries

As we have seen, the sustainable cities field, has been enabled by intermediary civic and professional associations, from the Association for Biking and Walking and the River Network to the American Planning Association and the US Green Building Council. Indeed, institutional field building is central to the work that intermediaries do. Here, I consider the emerging relationships among intermediaries of various types and with city actors who utilize their services and inform their practices.

Some intermediaries have directly tutored city actors from a range of cities that vary in many ways, including on comparative indices of planning and institutionalization of relevant policies as well as developmental trajectories and political cultures of larger and smaller cities in a specific region. Intermediaries act in ways that are meant to diffuse best practices, even when some cities are less receptive due to administrative and fiscal capacity, political culture and structure, and ecological and climate challenges. They are key carriers of isomorphic tendencies within fields, including *mimetic* versions that encourage imitation in the face of uncertainty and ambiguity, *normative* ones that derive from professional standards and identities and/or civic norms and identities, and *coercive* ones that, for Paul DiMaggio and Walter Powell, include authoritative standards as well as softer forms of persuasion and invitation by state actors and coordinated funding by philanthropies.[21]

Government actors, as well as nonprofit funders and funder networks are often engaged in systematic learning from local innovators, and then help facilitate further network learning among them in expanding and virtuous circles of the willing. Intermediaries accelerate the shift from early adoption, often determined by exceptionally favorable city characteristics, to broad diffusion based upon what is recognized as legitimate structural form. Transnational networks for urban sustainability have also proliferated in recent decades, varying in regional scope and issue focus, but frequently collaborating formally and informally with each other to learn and lobby, even while guarding distinct brands.[22]

While quantitative studies of large numbers of cities affiliated with any one intermediary in the United States do not provide the kind of data that permit specification of dynamic patterns *among* types of intermediaries, nor do they clarify *multiple simultaneous* or *sequential memberships* among networks competing in the same institutional space, certain patterns are emerging more clearly. First, city offices—whether a specific agency or a general sustainability office—draw upon expertise and best practice from intermediaries with specialized knowledge and tools suitable for each area of policy. Thus, city practitioners draw upon such groups as the US Green Building Council (USGBC) for green building, the River Network and Restore America's Estuaries for watersheds, the League of American Bicyclists, the Association for Biking and Walking, and the National Association of City Transportation Officials (NACTO) for bike and pedestrian alternatives. In the development of a city's sustainability or climate action plan, local chapters or affiliates of such organizations are often active on steering and advisory committees; their participation is often the result of advocacy and relational work over previous years. City practitioners also draw upon state and federal offices charged with promoting specific approaches, often working with or even helping to form new networks that can, in turn, assist local civic associations and public agencies. EPA offices, for instance, have played this role for watershed, environmental justice, and smart growth networks.

Research and/or consulting from academic scholars, university institutes, National Academy of Sciences panels, and private consulting firms provide further specialized depth available to local innovators. Arizona State University's Global Institute of Sustainability, for instance, has developed the Sustainable Cities Network for partners in the Phoenix area, which helps to diffuse practice from USGBC and other intermediaries. Consulting firms such as Raimi+Associates might play key brokerage roles and synthesize expert knowledge for local officials. Nonprofits, such as the American Council for an Energy-Efficient Economy (ACEEE)—established in 1980 and now with a staff of fifty supported by foundations and contracts with utilities, corporations, public agencies, and other nonprofits—might be enlisted by a sustainable cities intermediary to provide its members with basic level training though workshops and online webinars. ACEEE's City Clean Energy Scorecard tool for measurement and policy has been developed with a wide array of organizations across the energy, environment, and urban fields, including many of those discussed here, ensuring a rich mutual exchange of relevant knowledge. Its Energy Efficiency and Equity Working Group, with organizational participants such as WE ACT for Environmental Justice that have been active across the most important movement, federal, and local New York City venues for several decades, has provided ACEEE essential guidance on EJ issues.[23]

Generalist associations serving cities across a broad panoply of issues, such as the National League of Cities (NLC), the International City/County Management Association (ICMA, primarily US focused), and the US Conference of Mayors, likewise rely upon more specialized intermediaries to help them develop and legitimate new sustainability approaches, tool kits, and templates suitable to their members. None of these organizations is in the forefront of ecological, technical, or civic innovation. But they are critical to diffusion, since their broad membership attends conferences, reads best-practice guides and association magazines, becomes engaged in sections, and relies upon the legitimacy of these key professional associations when they initiate programs locally where they are likely to face uncertain results, skeptical colleagues, budget-conscious city councils, wary taxpayers, and (in some cities) organized grassroots ideological and business opponents. In addition, despite multiple institutional logics and tensions in their roles, these intermediaries have made basic commitments to public participation and often stress the indispensability of community engagement for the success of sustainability initiatives. Some have developed or coproduced participation tool kits that are tailored to specific challenges at neighborhood and city levels, such as those of NLC and some of its state affiliates.[24]

Two other important intermediaries—ICLEI USA and the Urban Sustainability Directors Network (USDN)—have added yet-other important components to the diffusion of sustainability practices that many cities, including those on diverse pathways, have utilized. If the USGBC and the River Network are specialists and NLC and ICMA are generalists, ICLEI and USDN are specialized generalists. They work on a broad array of issues yet remain focused on sustainability convergences. None of these categories are rigid and definitive, of course, since even highly specialized organizations rely upon others with yet-more refined and specialized competence, and specialized organizations are often under pressure from other actors in the field to address questions of broader import, such as environmental and climate justice.

ICLEI USA

ICLEI was founded as the International Council for Local Environmental Initiatives at the 1990 UN Inaugural Congress of Local Governments for a Sustainable Future, with Jeb Brugmann serving as its secretary general for the first decade. It then changed its name to ICLEI-Local Governments for Sustainability in 2003. It is a nonprofit membership organization of local governments, as well as national and regional local government associations, with a privileged role representing cities in the United Nations Framework Convention on Climate Change (UNFCCC). It is thus able to consult with cities and associations around the world, utilize global staff at its main office in Bonn, Germany, and participate in Conference of Parties meetings such as Paris in 2015, where it was quite active in leveraging support from global cities. Initially comprised of two hundred local governments from forty-three countries, ICLEI has grown to some fifteen hundred cities, towns, and regions, with a regional office structure.[25]

ICLEI USA was founded in 1995 and now has its main office in Denver. Membership fees in the United States are on a sliding scale, ranging from $600 in 2014 for cities under a population of fifty thousand to $8,000 for cities over 4 million. The ICLEI USA board is drawn from those in city government in elected positions as well as key staff in planning, water management, energy, and transportation. Some board members have played strategic roles in increasingly aligned groups, such as the US Conference of Mayors and the National League of Cities (and its state affiliates); in conservation and environmental groups, such as the Trust for Public Land, the Sierra Club, and Clean Water Action; and from professional groups across virtually the entire spectrum of sustainable city work. ICLEI USA utilizes a movement rhetoric to signal commitment to concerted action by cities as well as broad civic action and linkages to related movements. In addition to staff with various technical and market backgrounds (renewable energy, real estate and construction, information technology), some have recently developed experience in community organizing and environmental justice, especially collaborative approaches that have been drawn from movement actors within the National Environmental Justice Advisory Council (NEJAC) and EPA offices. In cities such as Oakland, California, this was partly a response to EJ movement criticism of ICLEI's earlier public participation advice to the city.

ICLEI has been explicit since it earliest Agenda 21 framing and action guides about its normative commitment to "community-based action," "participatory governance," and to "a participatory sustainable development planning process," which have been norms promoted by United States and European cities and by city partners throughout the developing world. Terms such as *citizen-driven* and *cocreation*, as well as *just, equitable, inclusive*, and *diverse*, permeate presentations from the podium by top ICLEI staff as well as by local practitioners at major meetings, such as its World Congress in Montreal in June 2018, and in its strategic vision documents.[26]

ICLEI USA develops a range of tools (often with partners), enables peer learning through conferences and workshops, provides technical assistance, and advocates for policy at the national level, such as when Barack Obama was first elected. Its core template for member cities consists of five milestones that include conducting a sustainability assessment, establishing goals, developing a local plan, implementing policies and measures, and evaluating progress and reporting results. Its *Sustainability Planning Toolkit*, developed with the mayor's office of planning and sustainability of New York under Michael Bloomberg, presents a nontechnical guide for proceeding through these milestones, including assembling a team, generating buy-in from elected officials, mobilizing research and analysis, engaging stakeholders and the broad public in an inclusive and transparent manner, remaining accountable to the public, and institutionalizing the planning and updating process. It offers case examples and points users to a wide array of other tool kits provided by civic and professional intermediaries and public agencies at all levels of the federal system.[27]

ICLEI USA's *Preparing for Climate Change: A Guidebook for Local, Regional, and State Governments* was developed in 2007 by the Center for Science in the Earth System at the University of Washington, in collaboration with King County, Washington, under its three-term county executive Ron Sims (1997–2009), who was later deputy secretary at HUD under Obama. As Sims noted, with a nod to Yogi Berra, "The Future Ain't What It Used to Be," which became the theme for the county's October 2005 conference, cosponsored with forty organizations from government, nonprofits, and businesses, from which the tool later emerged. In line with ICLEI's Climate Resilient Communities program, launched earlier in 2005, the guide is quite ambitious in specifying climate resilience and adaptation challenges, including how to frame responses to the typical arguments for delay presented by local officials. It remains rooted in a deep commitment to civic engagement and community partnerships throughout. The guide received input from senior staff of various agencies in the city of Seattle, whose interdepartmental teams during the neighborhood planning process in the Toward a Sustainable Seattle comprehensive plan, as well as in the Puget Sound NEP, brought much experience in collaborative civic and professional work. NOAA, which also has had much experience with NEPs and community restoration projects, including those facilitated by Restore America's Estuaries, funded the production of the guidebook.[28]

In 2016, with ecoAmerica, ICLEI USA also produced *Let's Talk Communities and Climate: Communication Guidance for City and Community Leaders*. This guide further enriches what scholars such as Bogdan Vasi found in ICLEI's earlier work; namely, its capacity to help participating cities in "frame alignment," so that innovations would be viewed as compatible with other public values and governance requirements. Foremost among these is cost-consciousness for elected officials and taxpaying publics, and hence the potential cobenefit of the city saving money through energy efficiency, although other cobenefits such as clean air and reputational advantages have also been prominent. In addition, local actors may be motivated to join ICLEI to help "reframe policy agendas and add political weight to particular coalitions within the local arena" and thereby shift urban regime dynamics. While *Let's Talk Communities and Climate* does not ground itself in the emerging literature on culture and emotion in popular climate attitudes and political differences (see chapter 8), it does offer compatible guidance on developing narratives and speech styles that connect with lived experience of scientifically grounded threats across various urban systems that have the potential to motivate morally rooted, community-enhancing, and hope-inducing action by citizens and stakeholders.[29]

From its earliest days, ICLEI has provided software enabling cities to measure GHG emissions and hence their progress in reductions, and even as it has seen other competitors emerge to work with city staff, such as the USDN, it has retained a strong market edge with its software packages. Its latest is Clear Path, which is a cloud-based tool enabling collaboration to develop emissions inventories, forecast multiple trajectories, and visualize alternative planning scenarios, all of which are key to professionally sound and democratically accountable local governance of climate mitigation. ICLEI members have access to the software along with technical assistance in utilizing it effectively. Bloomberg Philanthropies provided funding for ICLEI to train twenty cities to use it to meet the Compact of Mayors commitments. Clear Path is also offered free to any city that signs the Global

Covenant of Mayors for Climate and Energy, which focuses on strategic planning for mitigation and adaptation in a just and inclusive manner.[30]

This software is also an essential part of California's State Energy Efficiency Collaborative (SEEC), which the state has developed with nonprofit partners ICLEI USA, the Institute for Local Government (ILG), and the Local Government Commission, and which is funded by the four largest investor-owned utilities in the state. SEEC is the most ambitious attempt at the local city and county government levels to respond to the landmark state law AB 32, or the Global Warming Solutions Act. It has enlisted over four hundred local and county-level units of government (approximately 80 percent of the total in the state), facilitated by the institutional infrastructure of ILG that was founded in 1955. ILG has strong links to its parent organizations, the three local government associations in the state: the League of California Cities, the California State Association of Counties, and the California Special Districts Association. It has four staff in its sustainable communities program, a greater number than the National League of Cities, and has had what is arguably the most robust program in public engagement and collaborative governance of any state municipal league, directed for many years by Terry Amsler. Additional capacity and civic leadership development occurs through CivicSpark, a governor's AmeriCorps initiative that recruits ninety fellows per year—some enlisted by intermediaries such as ICLEI—demonstrating how other states and cities could utilize AmeriCorps far more ambitiously if Congress increases funding and directs it to urban sustainability challenges. California thus provides a model for how an intermediary such as ICLEI USA can leverage other institutional networks, funding sources, and state policies to facilitate innovation in hundreds of cities, towns, and counties, most of whom are not formal ICLEI members.[31]

ICLEI USA's strategic decision to leverage these kinds of networks in California, and in other states such as Colorado and through the Chicagoland Metropolitan Mayors Caucus, has played to its legacy strength in software tools, and it responds to the fact that, as executive director Angie Fyfe readily admits, "some cities felt that they had outgrown us." Fyfe had come to ICLEI after serving as the director of the Colorado chapter of USGBC and the governor's energy office, preceded by a career in commercial real estate. After significant ICLEI staff reductions during the previous five years, she was quite strategic in repositioning it among intermediaries, emerging state policies, and constricted federal policies near the end of the

Obama administration, upon whose advisory committee for the Energy Efficiency and Conservation Block Grant (EECBG) program of $3.2 billion she had served.[32]

ICLEI's previous growth pattern is instructive. While only a few US cities—such as Portland, Oregon, among the cases in chapter 6—were part of ICLEI's initial Urban CO_2 Reduction Project (1991–1993), over the next seven years, some seventy-nine US cities enlisted by city council resolution or some other formal decision to become part of over four hundred global cities that participated in the Cities for Climate Protection (CCP) campaign, including Portland, San Francisco, and Chicago, but neither Baltimore nor Phoenix. Cities with compatible environmental programs, as well as previous experience in a similar learning network, such as the US Department of Energy-sponsored Clean Cities Coalition or the National Association of Local Government Environmental Professionals (both established in 1993), were considerably more likely to join ICLEI's CCP, as were those with spatial and administrative proximity to early adopters.[33] The 1990s, as we have seen, witnessed the burgeoning of bicycle and pedestrian associations; participatory policy feedback from ISTEA; the emergence of national green building, new urbanist, and smart growth organizations; the strengthening of the local land-use legal field; fecund frame bridging across fields; and the increasing receptivity of national professional associations of city officials, planners, and architects. EPA offered critical support for community-based strategies. The formal decision to join ICLEI entailed a commitment to measure baselines and progress as well as to plan, implement, and monitor some set of strategies that specific cities would decide were culturally appropriate, administratively feasible, and politically justifiable—criteria that were in full recognition of the norms of democratic pragmatism operating at the city level.

Growth in city participation in ICLEI's CCP program continued at roughly the same rate until 2005, when US mayors (led by Greg Nickels of Seattle) signed the Mayor's Climate Protection Agreement, partly in response to the failure of the United States to ratify the Kyoto Protocol as it took effect. In 2006, former vice president Al Gore was featured in the Academy Award–winning documentary *An Inconvenient Truth*, and in 2007, he shared the Nobel Peace Prize with the Intergovernmental Panel on Climate Change. From 2006 to 2010, ICLEI USA experienced a nearly six-fold increase in its CCP participation, with seven hundred local governments overall, five hundred and sixty-five of which were cities and towns. But a steep decline occurred over the next several years.

Several factors seem to have played a role. The rise of the Tea Party movement, which targeted ICLEI and climate action at the local level, likely had an impact on the withdrawal of some cities in Texas, Florida, and Virginia. Tea Partiers were active in other cities as well, but some had much greater capacity to resist them. My observations of the May 2013 town hall that took place before the Seattle City Council ratified the city's first climate action plan perhaps reveal a pattern in cities more support-ive of ICLEI and the Mayor's Climate Protection Agreement. Several Tea Partiers arrived very early and got themselves listed for the first three con-tributions from the public as city council president Sally Clark and cli-mate program director in the office of sustainability Jill Simmons (among others) listened from the platform. When the initial angry crescendo was finished, the hearing shifted gears seamlessly to a very substantive and con-structive exchange between city officials and local citizens, which had been preceded by other forms of public engagement preparing the groundwork for this meeting.[34]

In addition, fiscal stress in some cities after the Great Recession of 2007 to 2008 may have played a role, as did perhaps the difficulty some cities had in proceeding through all five of ICLEI's prescribed steps. But ICLEI had no enforcement mechanisms, and it is likely that many cities who terminated their membership continued on their sustainability pathways, though sometimes narrowing their broader community strategies, or be-gan to utilize membership in other networks, such as USDN and 100 Resilient Cities.

Urban Sustainability Directors Network

With the institutionalization of offices of sustainability in Portland and several dozen other cities in the first decade of the 2000s, a new interme-diary emerged. As Nils Moe, managing director of the Urban Sustainabil-ity Directors Network (USDN) and a founding member from the city of Berkeley, California, noted, "Without ICLEI, none of this would have been possible. . . . But we needed a peer-driven network." Sustainability directors and their staff are responsible for ensuring that the many compo-nents of sustainability from the various nested and overlapping fields and types of field actors are implemented and advanced in a coherent citywide fashion. ICLEI has placed great emphasis on mayors, and ICLEI's World

Congresses, as at the Palais des congrès in Montreal in June 2018, honor mayors' contributions with great ceremony, as mayors and other leaders from each region of the globe ascend to the stage in their distinctive and colorful garb, projected on two huge screens in the auditorium to great applause, conveying an emotionally uplifting message of diverse leadership in the common mission of sustainable and just cities. For the founders of USDN, mayors are important, but what was needed was a much nimbler form of peer networking among core practitioners and beyond GHG emissions reduction.[35]

The initiative to found USDN in 2009 was the product of two individuals who had been central to the development of the first Chicago Climate Action Plan in 2008: Sadhu Aufochs Johnston, the city's sustainability director at the time, and Julia Parzen, the facilitator of the planning process. Steven Nicholas, who, as a senior planner, had been a cofounder of the influential nonprofit Sustainable Seattle and then became the city's sustainability director for eight years (2000–2008), was also a key founder. Together they published *The Guide to Greening Cities* with Island Press, the premier nonacademic environmental publisher. Amanda Eichen, a senior staff person with Nicholas in Seattle, also did significant outreach to other directors around the country and, with funding from the Surdna and Summit Foundations, several dozens of them met in Chicago in 2009 to form the network. The Global Philanthropy Partnership (GPP), the same funder that helped initiate Chicago's planning process, served as initial fiscal sponsor, though other large and medium-size foundations have since provided support. Only recently did USDN seek freestanding nonprofit 501(c)(3) status of its own. Its normative commitment to citizen participation, neighborhood planning, environmental justice, and social equity is robust.[36]

While USDN has a staff of nineteen distributed around the country, it remains committed to horizontal network governance principles that informed its founding but took several years to implement. Indeed, its reflective practice for peer learning and trust building has been quite exceptional—as is evident in its Regional Networks Leadership Academy, facilitated by Julia Parzen and Peter Plastrik in 2013; its continued refinement of peer learning processes; and its members' own call for ever-higher active participation requirements among themselves. To the outsider, these requirements at first appear overly prescriptive, even monitorial, but serve as a form of mutual self-discipline to enable learning. In addition, USDN incorporates sophisticated networking measurements, maps, and models to guide further network development, and it facilitates the adoption of "smart cities" technologies and apps. Its collaboration with the Innovation Network for Communities has been especially important in this regard. As of 2018, USDN facilitated ten regional partner networks among its two hundred or so member cities (including a network in Canada), comprised of core members and their local affiliates who may choose not to join USDN, at least initially. Among these regional partner networks are the New England Municipal Sustainability Network, Green Cities California, the Great Lakes Climate Adaptation Network, and the Southeast Sustainability Directors Network, which administers an innovation fund as large as that of the main network.[37]

During any given year, USDN also hosts some twenty or so user groups on specific topics, such as urban water systems and urban food systems, which encourage sustainability directors to pursue one or several topics in much greater depth than can be achieved in general monthly calls, and which likewise draw upon research and tools provided by external specialized intermediaries such as the American Council for an Energy-Efficient Economy, which USDN enlists in member trainings. As Garrett Fitzgerald, strategic collaborations director, notes, USDN "does a lot of curating" that is sometimes "virtually impossible" since there may exist in the broader field "some 200 documents on green infrastructure alone." The members-only part of the USDN website is designed to further enable focused, safe, and trustworthy exchange of information. Some user groups choose to spin-off from USDN, such as the Green Infrastructure Leadership Exchange, which is focused on stormwater and grew from a USDN grant and conference. In 2014, USDN was part of a global cities effort to develop "deep carbon reduction planning" with the US cities of Portland, San Francisco, Seattle, Boston, Boulder, Minneapolis, New York, and Washington, DC, as founding members of the Carbon Neutral Cities Alliance. USDN continues to provide organizational support in collaboration with the Innovation Network for Communities and the C40 Cities Climate Leadership Group, a global network of megacities.[38]

Membership in the USDN network provides access to funding of various sorts, especially as ARRA funding (beyond membership fees) was terminated. Several philanthropies—Summit, Bloomberg, Kresge, McKnight, JPB, Kendeda, and Surdna, among others—contributed to a regranting fund to members on a competitive basis, determined by a steering committee from cities (and not by staff). This innovation fund grew from a modest $100,000 in its first year, doubling each year thereafter for the next two years, and then settling into the range of $500,000 to $1 million per year. This is still relatively modest but enough to motivate cities to take risks and to form multicity partnerships, such as in Boulder, New York, and Vancouver (British Columbia), to test specific approaches. The Funders' Network for Smart Growth and Livable Communities (TFN) has pooled some $2 million in funding from thirty-five foundations for the Partnership for Places, which puts a premium on city partnerships with community foundations. A smaller but highly popular fund enables teams composed of the sustainability director and staff from other offices to visit another city for a day and one-half to help accelerate its own innovation. In addition to profiling many of these grants and innovations, the "Urban Sustainability Bulletin" provides a wide survey of initiatives and innovations to inform its members.[39]

Philanthropic Foundations

Foundations have played a strategic role in shaping the field of environmental organizations since the Ford Foundation's investments in developing the Environmental Defense Fund and the Natural Resources Defense Council in the late 1960s and early 1970s, and with the Conservation Foundation's critical work even earlier (see chapter 2). Today, there are other major environmental funders, such as the Pew Charitable Trusts, which has played a central strategic role among other foundations, national organizations, and program areas. In addition, the Environmental Grantmakers Association (EGA) was founded in 1987 to provide networking, strategic thinking, and research across the entire field, summarized in its *Tracking the Field* volumes beginning in 2007. Grants from the more than two hundred EGA members increased substantially as EGA consolidated its member base over its first twenty years and grew modestly over the past decade, representing roughly 40 percent of total environmental grant dollars from US foundations.[40]

The Funders' Network for Smart Growth and Livable Communities (TFN), founded in 1999 with thirty members, now includes over one hundred and fifty foundations involved in strategic conversations, framing work, and tool sharing on building and integrating the field across its issue silos, expanding its resources, and further developing its partnerships, including how to address issues of race, equity, inclusion, green jobs, and other concerns of leaders from environmental and social justice fields. The Just Cities and Regions program at the Ford Foundation, initially under the direction of a key leader from the smart growth movement (Don Chen), has combined urban sustainability with social justice in housing, economic development, and planning. Community foundations have demonstrated increasing capacity over several decades to become strategic actors that seek to integrate issues and develop new community leadership capacities, and sustainable city networks have increasingly been working with them.[41]

While the largest environmental organizations receive the bulk of foundation grants, the percentage for the top four (based on the four-firm concentration ratio in industry) declined from 41 percent to 21 percent in the 1989 to 2005 period, and the percentage of the top thirty-one likewise dropped, especially when increased investments in state and local chapters were factored in. Environmental nonprofits have been considerably more reliant on foundation grants, as well as dues and individual gifts, than the nonprofit sector as a whole—46 percent of total income in 2005 compared to 12 percent—which receives a much greater proportion of its funding from public sources due to dedicated streams of public funding for health and social welfare services that are channeled through nonprofits. Government grants and contracts have nonetheless also been important in funding environmental organizations; such funds are typically designated for research, education, ecosystem restoration, land trusts, and similar projects rather than for advocacy activities.[42]

Foundation priorities in funding certain types of environmental organizations over others have often been questioned by activists and academics alike. The major charge is that foundations are more comfortable with grants that go to mainstream organizations with professional leadership and accountability mechanisms than to more innovative, grassroots, contentious, and radical organizations, leading to a conservative bias in who receives money.[43] This funding bias clearly exists, yet the critique is too-often made in a way that is analytically unhelpful and politically misleading. It typically rests on little more than an unquestioned ideological assumption that radical or contentious means better, more effective, and truly transformative without any credible test of organizational sustainability and strategic judgment or any metric of strategic impact, project performance, movement-building outcomes, or reciprocal accountability to institutional partners, donors, or even to grassroots members.

These are all questions that foundations must remain alert to as they negotiate priorities with other actors in the broader environmental or sustainable cities fields. It is no less a democratic challenge than remaining responsive to promising approaches emerging at the grassroots, which the staff, board, and members of EGA and TFN arguably do. There is certainly much room to question foundation priorities on various grounds, not the least of which is building the local community and civic leadership capacities to engage in effective sustainable city, ecosystem, environmental justice, health, and climate action partnerships. Yet, simply presuming that foundations should fund organizations *because* they have more radical protest repertoires or discourses hardly provides a sound normative or strategic guide to building the sustainable cities field or democratizing environmental politics and policy.

Conclusion

Sustainable cities framing has emerged through decades-long civic struggles over the contours of urban and place-based environmental development, splicing together components from different policy arenas and responding to welcome opportunities and strident challenges. In each distinct field, actors have had to do much cognitive as well as practical work to legitimate new approaches, whether this be establishing a credible watershed frame with robust ecological and civic components not generally referenced in command and control, or elaborating a healthy cities frame that is less dependent on discrete disease and risk factors and more attuned to the social organization of space, power, and inequality. Even fields with community-based practices, such as nonprofit housing development and nonprofit social services, have been challenged by assets-based community development and relational organizing to focus more on community strengths rather than deficits—or "power with" rather than "programs for." Hence, framing is almost always reframing as well. Such shifts have helped provide the foundation for still-more integrative framing as the sustainable and resilient city, yet still with ongoing contests over the meaning and metrics of a "just sustainability" and a "just city." Even when it has not always been able to sustain robust local organizations or national networks, the environmental justice movement has had a very substantial impact on framing in virtually every single field within sustainable cities.

In Neil Fligstein and Doug McAdam's formulation, skillful social actors do much of the cognitive splicing and strategic aligning work to build a field. In the sustainable cities field, this is further facilitated by *city institutions*, such as a sustainability office or a chief resilience officer, designed to provide coherence across public agencies and bureaucratic silos. *City processes* that engage citizens, such as the various forms of multistakeholder visioning and participatory planning that have become increasingly recognized as requisite for urban democratic legitimacy, provide further integrative opportunities, as do many of the *city tool kits* that provide GIS and other forms of spatial, digital, and visual data for civic and professional actors alike. These institutions, processes, and tool kits enable further skillful action to align and integrate disparate frames and to fashion sustainable cities as an urban master frame—incomplete and imperfect, to be sure, yet relatively sticky and increasingly embedded in institutional practices and cultural norms.

While social movement and city actors have done much of the framing work, staff in the EPA have contributed to core framing through "community-based environmental protection" and "collaborative environmental justice" conferences, through framework statements, and in the search and dissemination of relevant cases and tool kits from across various fields. Should the political opportunity present itself, any framing of the civics of a Green New Deal (see the postscript) would have to build upon the field-configuring work of the EPA as well as other agencies that have actively engaged civic and other partners, such as NOAA, HUD, USDOT, and USDA. More important than ever, public investments in green infrastructure, broadly conceived, will have to be paired with appropriate investments in civic infrastructure and the cognitive and emotive framing that can inspire and mobilize communities and institutions of many types for the gritty and uncertain pragmatic work ahead.

Intermediaries have been critical in developing the sustainable cities field in a strategic fashion over several decades. Previously existing urban generalists, such as the National League of Cities and the American Planning Association, have placed increasing emphasis on sustainability and have developed strategic relationships with more specialized associations, such as the United States Green Building Council, the National Association of City Transportation Officials, and the American Council for an Energy-Efficient Economy. Generalist urban sustainability networks, such as USDN and ICLEI USA, tutor, curate, and facilitate knowledge exchange for those who are most directly responsible for integrating professional and civic practice at the city level. While we lack in-depth ethnographic studies of the dynamic interaction among city staff, civic associations, and professional intermediaries in any given city, or across cities for comparative analysis, their field-building strategies appear quite skillful and have often been accomplished with modest resources.

The complexity of the challenges they face in helping to shift and align institutional logics across multiple systems, and in ways that generate appropriate forms of professional, cultural, and democratic legitimacy, can hardly be underestimated, however—especially as climate impacts become more severe. Further private investments through foundations, and especially public investments through federal grants in an ambitious Green New Deal, would enable such intermediaries to build further institutional capacity and do so in ways that enhance civic engagement in problem-solving and urban resilience.

CHAPTER EIGHT

Democratic Resilience: Civic Action, Democratic Professionalism, and a Culture of Hope

Sustainable cities have emerged as a complex and dynamic institutional field in the United States over a long arc of development that has been intricately tied to democratic engagement in myriad forms. The latter have included civic action at all levels of the federal system and through classic multitiered associations, highly professionalized advocacy organizations, established and novel professional associations, and local community groups capable of contesting power and coproducing public goods. Norms of democratic participation have been progressively embedded in law and policy, and selective policy designs have had participatory feedback effects. Professional associations have aligned practices, tools, and templates to accommodate and even enable innovative forms of engagement appropriate to complex problem-solving and shared expertise, thereby modifying claims of technocratic authority within urban management systems. Some market sectors have also been responsive.

Certainly, such developments have been *neither sufficient nor secure*. Some cities have progressed further than others in addressing specific problems of natural and built environments and of empowering diverse communities and stakeholders. All confront how to better design participation and collaboration and weave norms of a just city into a more democratic and sustainable city. Over the next decades, the institutional field will undoubtedly confront challenges that are at least as difficult, if not far more so, as they have been over the past several if it is to generate appropriate resilience strategies that are effective, democratic, and just.

Indeed, such norms will be vigorously contested in the face of the what are certain to be considerable disruptions to cherished places, valuable housing and business assets, and community health. Climate change will prompt further field-building strategies while it also generates conundrums for action that are democratically legitimate, socially just, and ecologically sound. No one should underestimate these challenges. No one should conclude from the analytical narrative of institutional field building thus far that the future of sustainable and resilient cities in the United States is assured or that robust democratic norms and practices can be appropriately refined and secured. Much work remains, and we will have to accomplish it in a world facing interlaced climate and democratic crises.

In this concluding chapter, I first recap some of the main contours of field building over the past decades, and then I turn to several key challenges that need to be addressed in the years ahead. While I point beyond the election of 2016, I do not directly address the grave challenges that have been posed specifically by the Trump administration, partly to provide clear time boundaries for empirical analysis and partly due to the lack of availability of key federal staff for interviews, as encountered by other scholars of current environmental politics and policy. Much damage has been done, much repair will be needed, and the specifically political challenges going forward are indeed daunting. Here, I focus on three broad strategies that have direct relevance to urban sustainability in the United States as a democratic project for the longer run: (1) a civic politics of risk and resilience, (2) an institutional politics of democratic professionalism, and (3) a cultural politics of hope. The broader institutional field of sustainable and resilient cities, and of sustainability more generally, has many other challenges, to be sure, and skilled actors will have to knit together strategies as appropriately as possible. Minimally, any list of these would have to include national and state regulatory strategies, global climate agreements and multilevel governance, corporate sustainability strategies, carbon pricing, disaster management and insurance, and grassroots protest and climate justice movements—locally, nationally, and globally.[1]

Were a Green New Deal (GND)—or some other robust set of policy initiatives that invest in place-based sustainability and resilience—to become possible after the presidential elections of 2020 or 2024, it could not conceivably succeed without a sustained civic politics of risk and resilience, an institutional politics of democratic professionalism, and a cultural politics of hope. Whatever the appropriate mix of market mechanisms, regulatory tools, and public investments that we might choose for an ambitious GND, we will nonetheless need a broad set of strategies for engaging local communities, civic and professional associations, workers and employers, educational institutions and multistakeholder partnerships in ways that are effective and that generate widespread political trust and democratic legitimacy. There can be no programmatically and politically sustainable GND without such trust and legitimacy. A GND will thus have to invest not only in resilient energy, transportation, agriculture, and water systems, as well as green jobs across the economy. It will also have to invest substantially in the civic capacities that can make such big plans and projects responsive and accountable to communities and workers and enable productive and collaborative work with professionals, businesses, and many other kinds of institutional actors whose ingenuity and commitment will be required for sustained action over many years. Anything short of this will likely generate far too much policy backlash and leave a GND vulnerable to charges of being statist, elitist, and technocratic. I take up these issues in the postscript on the civic GND.

Sustainable Cities: Building the Field in Its First Decades

In the previous chapters, I stressed several lines of argument to help understand the long arc of civic and institutional development of sustainable cities. First, the field began to take shape in the early decades after World War II, largely due to grassroots civic action against threats to urban water, air, land, and neighborhoods. Some forms of action were leveraged by classic multi-tiered associations, such as the League of Women Voters, the Izaak Walton League, and the National Audubon Society, while others represented relatively novel stand-alone groups to protect specific urban rivers, neighborhoods, and greenbelts. The latter proliferated in numbers, types, and extra-local networks—watershed associations, land trusts, bicycle associations, forest stewards, community gardens, environmental justice—after the initial environmental field settlement of the 1970s proved limited in terms of civic action around place and ecosystem. Some had been nurtured within or alongside neighborhood associations, antihighway coalitions, and Model Cities planning in the 1960s and 1970s, which indicated still-other sources of grassroots urban action. However, the highly professionalized environmental groups, whose strategic choices were key to achieving this critical field settlement, were for the most part organizationally and cognitively unsuited to the novel forms of urban-environmental civic action, although some later proved important in brokering new associational relationships (green building, smart growth, new urbanism) that have lent distinctive identities, frames, and tool kits to sustainable cities and its various nested and overlapping fields.

Professional associations have become essential actors in constituting sustainable cities as a field of democratic action. While by no means dominant among the vast array of urban professionals, the norms and practices of democratic professionalism have become key to several important professional associations such as the American Planning Association (APA), the American Institute of Architects (AIA), and the National Association of City Transportation Officials (NACTO). Each helped fashion ways to accommodate contentious grassroots action over difficult cycles of mutual learning and to develop templates and tool kits for planning, building, and transit that have engaged local publics, civic associations, and other organized stakeholders in collaborative problem-solving and coproduction. Professional schools in these and related fields (public administration, landscape architecture, public health, environmental and water management) have progressively incorporated democratic professional norms and practices into classroom curricula and internships, even as they have deepened and refined core professional knowledge to support sustainable practices. Professional expertise that is highly technical, such as energy efficiency, might be "double brokered" for civic use, such as when the Urban Sustainability Directors Network (USDN) enlists the American Council for an Energy-Efficient Economy (ACEEE) to provide 101-level training for its affiliated sustainability directors who, in turn, collaborate with various civic and other stakeholders at the city and neighborhood levels.

Through sometimes circuitous and often contentious learning processes, civic and professional actors have developed social skills that have proven to be appropriate to field building within and across nested, proximate, and distant fields. Thus, they have developed a variety of frames tailored to specific problem areas—restored watersheds, complete streets, smart growth, just food, green building—but have also worked across boundaries to find ways of bridging and aligning frames as well as incorporating core components of others, such as healthy cities, assets-based community development, and environmental justice. Accompanying such frames, actors have also produced tool kits ranging from simple how-to-get-started guides to elaborate manuals and online planning and data tools covering civic, ecological, technical, institutional, and (sometimes) market dimensions of informed strategic action. Many handbooks are coproduced by a range of field actors who bring not only specific forms of knowledge but also distinct modes of legitimating action. Actors within these fields build relationships among each other through regular forms of networking. They include each other on boards, provide staff mobility across diverse types of organizations, co-produce and disseminate tool kits within each other's networks, and induce each other to embrace new voices and sources of local knowledge and street science.

Of course, they also skirmish to protect some boundaries and brands, compete within shared institutional spaces and markets (for services, funding, affiliates, policy attention), carve out niches, and adjust amidst competition—as with ICLEI and the USDN, Smart Growth America and the Congress for the New Urbanism, the Alliance for Biking and Walking, and the League of American Bicyclists. Many, if not most, have also explicitly adopted sustainable cities as a kind of master frame, though this concept was originally developed to understand social movement affinities across cycles of protest rather than cycles of contention and collaboration to forge a complex institutional field with multiple sources of democratic action and legitimacy.

Field actors have also demonstrated considerable skill in steering among various forms of democratic deliberation in a way that political theorist Jane Mansbridge and her colleagues would recognize as "systemic." This systemic approach is particularly suited to analyzing plural ecologies of democratic action within a multiorganizational field such as sustainable cities with many types of actors and institutional logics: civic, professional, bureaucratic, and market, with many variations within them and combinations among them. It recognizes tensions and trade-offs, and hence the necessity for strategic and normative judgment. It is alert to power and resource imbalances among diversely situated actors, communities, and identities, and it often generates self-corrective mechanisms. My own conception of "democratic institutionalism" builds directly upon this systemic view but with added attention to how skilled actors align institutional logics—deliberatively, relationally, epistemically, pragmatically—across various types of organizations to produce and coproduce multiform public goods that can constitute sustainable and resilient cities, and to enlist still other actors who are willing and able to coproduce.[2]

While still under-theorized in terms of public work and relational repertoires, the systemic approach to deliberative democracy can make room for the multiple ways in which actors seek to secure discursive agreement, trust, and legitimacy as well as a sense of shared work with ongoing reciprocal accountability and mutual learning. Thus, a bicycle association might further diversify its board and staff, prioritize racial equity in citywide bicycle planning and biking skills within schools, participate in broad community forums and at city hall, forge local coalitions with AARP for age-friendly streets, collaborate and build trust with transportation engineers to develop workable street designs, and lobby through state and national networks for multimodal funding with participatory policy feedback that further enhances civic motive and capacity. A planning process for transit-oriented station design may build upon such components and include intensive charrette deliberation over several days.

Deliberative democracy in this systemic approach remains a core norm, but skilled actors test and redesign in ways appropriate to context, responsive to contest, and alert to competing yet potentially complementary forms of knowledge. Skilled field actors borrow and generate relational practices designed to elicit trust amidst the many sources of distrust, including some that will likely persist indefinitely in one form or another. Skilled practitioners also design and redesign to progressively align diverse and often divergent institutional logics to better serve democracy and sustainability, and hence to regenerate hope and commitment even amidst imperfect and incomplete tools and templates. Indeed, the sustainable cities field provides perhaps one of the most robust cases for linking institutional field analysis with deliberative democratic systems, and many of its practitioners have become notably skillful over time.

A second line of argument in this book has been that civic action has helped to generate pathways to sustainable cities by reconfiguring local urban regimes and governance, in some cities much more than others, to be sure. Early urban regime analysis, as well as more recent "new institutionalist" approaches to urban politics and governance, emphasize that power struggles, together with relational strategies, can reorient actor preferences, enlist new actors from nonprofit and for-profit sectors, and change the meaning and mix of public goods. They can also generate new power resources for producing such goods and embed their production in planning and technical systems. Mayors and city councils can respond creatively to pressure from below and opportunity for partnership from alongside. *None of these strategies* are without potential traps and trade-offs, and even skillful actors and networks can misjudge opportunities or delude themselves about impacts.

Three cities analyzed in chapter 6 represent relatively strong path-dependent institutionalization of a sustainable city over several decades while two are considerably weaker. Portland, Oregon, leveraged civic action into a robust system of neighborhood associations in the early 1970s, generated power in mayoral and city council elections, utilized state legislative opportunities to begin land-use and then energy and light-rail planning, and in the 1990s, it began sustainability and climate action planning in a more integrated fashion. The city has become increasingly responsive over time to much greater diversity in the types of civic, environmental, and social justice groups making relevant claims for a just and sustainable city, and its Sustainability at Work program now provides sector-specific tools, with lists and maps of certified green businesses across the city. Civic challenges in San Francisco were not institutionalized in a neighborhood association system but took other forms and went through a more prolonged series of tough-fought ballot initiatives before securing accountable land-use planning and more responsive mayors and city councils. The city also benefited from robust open space, urban creek, estuary, food district, urban park, bicycle association, and other forms of civic action that, despite (or perhaps because of) its famous contentious pluralism, managed to develop many forms of innovative collaboration, often reinforced by actors within key urban bureaucracies.

Chicago also traversed a path of highly contentious struggle and deep ambivalence until black community and other civic and political reformers generated an opportunity to break the stranglehold of white aldermanic power during the mayoralty of Harold Washington in the mid-1980s, whose death early into his second term left much uncertainty but also a legacy that mayor Rich Daley could leverage for his own strategic purposes. A network of groups that were mobilized around community development, environmental justice, brownfield revitalization, bicycle mobility, and urban forest stewardship generated the broader leadership that provided the mayor with new strategic opportunities to fashion a more sustainable city and to forge a climate action plan over the next two decades.

Sustainability strategies in Baltimore have been relatively robust in terms of watersheds, stormwater management, and urban greening because of the legacy of Chesapeake Bay restoration, which had its own program at the Environmental Protection Agency (EPA). But as a majority black city wrestling with deindustrialization and long-term population loss, it has struggled to link these to its local community-development actors and to neighborhood revitalization, including in those areas proximate to its educational and medical institution-based "eds and meds" economic development strategies, where quasi-public corporations show limited commitment to community engagement. Phoenix has been, in many ways, an unlikely case for moving along a trajectory of sustainability due to its development model based on cheap land, sprawling subdivisions, and water diversions from the overextended Colorado and Salt-Gila River systems in a highly arid state with strong libertarian and antitax political traditions and now highly polarized conflict on immigration. But it has nonetheless begun to generate sustainability strategies that engage artistic, community development, black and Latino, and downtown renewal groups, as well as support from Arizona State University.

Highly compressed case studies of urban governance trajectories among several cities over many decades have clear limits, even when supplemented by other cases, such as neighborhood planning, natural drainage, and community gardening in Seattle; natural filtration from upstate communities in New York City; urban agriculture in New York City and Philadelphia; or those studies that provide data on programmatic uptake in a relatively large number of cities.[3] However, such cases should prompt further comparative case-study research on urban governance for sustainability since they provide windows into a form of institutional inquiry that complements the broader analysis of strategic action fields across networks and policies at the national level. Indeed, strategic choices among skilled actors are intricately and reciprocally—if almost never optimally—intertwined at virtually all levels.

For instance, the early developmental trajectory of citizen engagement on land use and city energy innovation within Portland positioned it to contribute to network learning among a broad array of cities through ICLEI in the 1990s and 2000s. The San Francisco mayor's choice to accommodate militant bicycle association demands helped develop a template for collaboration with city agencies and broader democratic legitimation that had direct impact on other groups within the emergent Association for Biking and Walking in the 1990s, which in turn had indirect (and competitive) feedback effects on strategic choices within the more established, yet elitist League of American Bicyclists a decade later. The Chicago mayor's choice to develop a climate action plan in 2008 built upon opportunities generated by an array of community development, racial justice, and urban environmental groups over several decades, and then spun off staff and a funder to form the Urban Sustainability Directors Network, which has developed two hundred city affiliates and a broader network of funders a decade later.

None of these cities, however, has secured sufficient institutional and path-dependent dynamics for the challenges of democratic and just sustainability and resilience in the decades ahead. Much more work remains to be done.

A third line of argument is that policy design has been important in configuring democratic field dynamics and relationships. Policy, of course, is always important, but in some instances, it is especially critical for shaping how ordinary citizens and civic associations engage in shaping the contours of a field. While there has not been—and perhaps could not be, for reasons discussed in chapter 1—the kind of participatory policy feedback design for sustainable cities comparable to that of Social Security or the GI Bill, field actors have utilized both rights-based and tools-based policy and administrative designs to further generate and strengthen forms of engagement appropriate to specific fields emergent within sustainable cities. Civic associations in the field of water leveraged some of the rights-based information requirements of laws passed immediately after World War II and then the federal enforcement conferences prescribed in the 1956 Federal Water Pollution Control Act to mobilize constituencies within dozens of cities and metropolitan regions. They developed relationships among themselves and with potentially sympathetic lawmakers and regulators, generated a much broader public sphere for water deliberation in multi-stakeholder settings and in broadcast and print media, and enriched resonant cultural narratives of water in everyday life. The latter could then be deployed in civic settings through film and in formal public hearings in cities across the country by the key policy entrepreneur in the Senate in his campaign for the Clean Water Act of 1972.

While the specific section of that law devised to institutionalize deliberative basin planning displayed clear limits in the overall policy design, ecologically refined watershed models then helped to generate support for more robust designs that could locate specific roles for citizen science, monitoring, restoration, and collaboration in complex ecosystems. These manifested in the Chesapeake Bay and the National Estuary Programs of the 1980s, and then in further tools-based design components (funding/training, network facilitation, data/planning, multistakeholder management templates) in the 1990s and beyond for other kinds of watersheds, including small urban watersheds and major inland and coastal city ones.

The Intermodal Surface Transportation Efficiency Act (ISTEA) of 1991 and its successor laws provided policy feedback through its funding design that helped incentivize grassroots and joint action among bicycle associations, pedestrian groups, AARP chapters, trails conservancies, and smart growth and new urbanist coalitions as well as among established professional associations, such as the National League of Cities, the American Planning Association, the American Institute of Architects, and the newly created National Association of City Transportation Officials. It also required states to name bicycle and pedestrian coordinators, thus providing civic and professional groups with an institutional handle within state DOTs. In addition to NEPA requirements for environmental impact statements, civic and professional groups could also utilize the specific normative requirements for public participation in transportation planning and reflectively leverage years of conflict for more collaborative approaches. Policy design for urban agriculture, as well as in broader sustainable food fields, did not contain as robust components for participatory and network feedback effects, although local food policy councils are now positioned to institutionalize voice more productively.

In a range of other policy areas, various offices at the Environmental Protection Agency, the National Oceanic and Atmospheric Administration, and the Department of Housing and Urban Development, among others, have instituted matching-grant, training, and technical assistance programs, as well as field-configuring events and networks, to enable community-based innovation. *None* of these policy designs has ever been funded at sufficient levels due to congressional budgetary constraints, competing demands within agencies and among environmental lobbies, or lack of robust statutory support. But they do provide essential policy templates upon which to build, especially for a concerted civic strategy within a Green New Deal or some other ambitious climate mitigation and resilience approach. We need to build bigger and better policy wagons, to be sure, but we do not have to reinvent every wheel.

Missed policy opportunities have also been evident. The most important was probably the failure to pass the National Land Use Policy Act (NLUPA) in 1975, which would have enabled states to help build local capacities among cities, towns, and counties. While partly the result of post-Watergate political recalculations, the failure represented the inability to secure a more robust coalition among national environmental and urban groups due largely to divergent policy preferences and organizational repertoires as well as real estate industry opposition with strong grassroots property-rights mobilization. The field was not yet ready for the kind of policy design that emerged within the CEQ-sponsored deliberations in the early 1970s, yet it was more than ripe for the many initiatives on land use that continued to emerge within the local land-use legal field, within local planning and administrative law practice, and through new state growth management strategies.

Strategic Action for Democratic Resilience: Moving Forward

If building a strategic action field for sustainable cities has been a protracted, arduous, and imperfect process over many decades, the challenges we face in the coming decades will be at least as daunting, if not far more so. First, of course, we face political obstacles at the national level; as of this writing, we have a Republican administration deeply wedded to ideological denial of climate change and materially wedded to fossil industries that fuel denialism as a popular countermovement. Republicans in Congress also lean strongly in this direction, even if there is a change in administration. Cultural and religious differences overlay and infuse such organized denialism and party polarization.[4] While not as evident in many cities that can count on environmental values and progressive political coalitions, such organized resistance restricts federal agencies from implementing programs that can help build civic and other institutional capacities at the local and state levels. Many of the institutional supports for sustainable city networks and programs in federal agencies, as underfinanced as they have always been, have been systematically undermined over the past several years. Some budgets have been zeroed out, many staff have left, others have been reassigned to safer offices, and many have been intimidated from speaking with independent researchers and potential civic partners.

Second, the disruptions of climate change to cities and communities in the United States will be felt on a much greater scale in the coming years, even if we can turn the corner on effective mitigation nationally and through effective global agreements, and even if we can become a net contributor to effective resilience strategies in more vulnerable and explosively growing cities around the world, especially the global south. Many coastal cities in the United States will be compelled to retreat from the shore, at least partially, and some will not likely survive in their present form, leading to loss or displacement of businesses, homes, and other real estate or institutional assets, such as health-care and higher education institutions. This may also occur due to drought, wildfires, and floods in noncoastal regions. Many people will be displaced from homes, neighborhoods, churches, and jobs—some beyond their home cities and counties—and while insurance and buyouts may be designed to respond creatively, such movement will trigger significant disruptions in real estate values and markets, albeit with institutional logics of denial for an extended period to help prop up market values. Displacement will trigger a deep sense of loss of memory and place and disruption to social networks upon which ordinary people rely. Sizable displacement will also generate grounds for conflict among those being relocated and those within receptor communities. These conflicts will be inevitably interlaced with issues of race, income, and immigration status. They will trigger defensive place-strategies rather extensively and provide further fuel for intense right-wing populist resistance.[5]

To leverage sustainable city field building for a more robust politics of democratic resilience in the decades to come, I would highlight several broad and intertwined strategies that are drawn from scholarship but also from the active work already under way by some of the key intermediaries in this book and by the many cities with whom they have been working. These three strategies focus on a civic politics of risk and resilience, an institutional politics of democratic professionalism, and a cultural politics of hope. Resilience, of course, has many dimensions, from hard infrastructure to soft psychology and much in between. Judith Rodin, in *The Resilience Dividend*, informing much global work by the Rockefeller Foundation and its many partners in the 100 Resilient Cities network, provides a baseline definition: "Resilience is the capacity of any entity—an individual, a community, an organization, or a natural system—to prepare for disruptions, to recover from shocks and stresses, and to adapt and grow from a disruptive experience." To adapt means to learn, to revitalize, and to generate resilience dividends from new opportunities, and not just to recover from the storm and rebuild the house as it once stood. The broad strategies I outline here are focused on the civics of resilience, both at the local community and city level, but also through civic partnerships enabled by professional and policy actors at all levels.[6]

Civic Politics of Risk and Resilience

The first broad strategy is to forge a civic politics of risk and resilience that is highly localized yet also establishes robust links across cities and regions.

In his comparative study of three cities that were presented with the choice to accept or reject the building of National Biocontainment Laboratories in the early 2000s, sociologist Thomas Beamish developed the concept of the "civic politics of risk," which he used to clarify political and cultural repertoires, civic virtues, and legacies of trust and distrust between specific communities and trustee institutions (government, universities). These repertoires tended to shape public discourses into distinct clusters and eventual public decisions. His clusters are instructive, though not meant to be comprehensive for discrete risk disputes or broader resilience strategies: *red* in Roxbury (Boston, Massachusetts), with an emphasis on direct action by racially aggrieved groups in the name of social justice; *green* in Davis (California), with stress on shared governance and antimilitarism in a pastoral environment; and *blue* in Galveston (Texas), with a more deferential and conciliatory posture toward trustee institutions yet a strong sense of civic virtue. In none of the cases, including the one (Galveston), whose deep sense of moral responsibility in the name of a common good helped determine a positive decision on the proposed lab, did the technocratic arguments of risk assessors win the day.[7]

If we move from the singular and relatively well-bounded risk dispute to city resilience as a concatenating, interlacing, and periodically lurching series of risk disputes, urban development opportunities, and distributive logics of potential costs and benefits, we can further appreciate Beamish's insight that this kind of work invariably elicits resonant narratives and memories of grievance, even betrayal, yet also of past accomplishment, collaboration, and hope. Developing a trust-building civic politics of risk and resilience over an extended period and across multiple disputes infused with competing certainties and ambiguities is one of the core strategic tasks of local field actors and a sine qua non of democratic urban governance in the face of climate change.

Extending a trust-building civic politics of risk and resilience to states and regions, as well as to federal policy, will also be critical, since socially just sustainability and resilience strategies cannot be accommodated within cities alone, especially when we factor in regions that have disproportionately greater concentrations of potentially stranded fossil fuel assets and stranded workers and communities that will need support for "just transitions." Strategies must be developed within "an uneven landscape of risk and resilience" across neighborhoods, many of which are vulnerable to exacerbated inequalities and among powerful institutional actors, some of whom are well-positioned to profit disproportionately from disaster and can frame the meaning of disaster on their own terms and with racial and other myths and metaphors. Technocratic practices of even the most well-intentioned and competent public and private agencies will never generate sufficient democratic legitimacy in the face of the tough choices that climate adaptation will present. Civic media technologies, however, instead of fueling polarization, can enhance community engagement, democratic problem-solving, and just cities if we design them appropriately.[8]

A civic politics of risk and resilience must include strategies to build upon existing stocks of social capital and to further develop new stocks appropriate to the specific challenges of sustainable and resilient cities. Existing stocks of social capital have proven a critical resource in disaster response and recovery, as Unites States and comparative research has shown. Communities with strong social ties, dense networks of local associations, and robust traditions of mutual reliance tend to generate timely information, local initiative, protective measures toward the most vulnerable, rapid recovery and rebuilding, and political capital to ensure responsiveness from institutions. The strong ties of *bonding social capital* also have a potential dark side, leading in some cases to ethnic, racial, or religious exclusion and violence, and thus must be viewed as a "Janus-faced resource," as Daniel Aldrich argues, which needs to be complemented by *bridging social capital* and *linking social capital*. Bridging forms of social capital connect group members to extra-local networks and reach across boundaries of potential or actual ethnic, racial, and religious cleavage. Linking forms connect group members to institutionalized power and authority.[9]

Policy should enhance the capacities for a local civic politics of risk and resilience, enhance opportunities for further bridging and linking social capital formation, and encourage bonding solidarities while restraining their dark side. For instance, Seattle neighborhood planning within the Sustainable Seattle comprehensive plan included a requirement for stakeholder analysis to ensure diverse representation in deliberations, and all thirty-eight eligible neighborhoods agreed to this as a condition for funding. The neighborhood planning office, with strong norms of social justice reinforced by mayoral and city council support (linking social capital), used the threat of second-round funding denial to encourage collaboration among neighborhoods within planning areas that were differently situated (by income, race, home ownership rates, immigrant status), and in some initially resistant cases there emerged shared board memberships in community councils and civic associations (bridging social capital). Watershed partnerships have in some cases been designed with institutional structures, formal processes, and informal mechanisms to build trust, enhance mutual learning, and engage in joint restoration work across different types of stakeholder groups (bridging social capital) within state-sanctioned policy frameworks and federal agency engagement (linking social capital). Although there is no set formula for how to optimally enhance the various forms of social capital while limiting negative externalities, there are numerous examples in the literature on urban and environmental governance upon which to build.[10]

Institutional Politics of Democratic Professionalism

Second, a broad strategy of strengthening democratic professionalism within and across the many types of institutions that can enable urban resilience is of central importance, and indeed an indispensable complement to a localized civic politics. Democratic professionalism builds upon the strong historical traditions of public trusteeship but complements its claims to expertise and authority with forms of local knowledge generated by everyday citizens, marginalized communities, engaged students, and civic associations. It seeks to accommodate and enable local knowledge and to engage lay actors in coproducing knowledge and mutually adjudicating claims of epistemic truth and practical effectiveness. Democratic professionals work in teams with local civic actors, facilitate deliberation among diverse groups, and engage across narrow disciplinary boundaries with other professionals. They recognize that their own claims to legitimacy and trustworthiness are often vulnerable without broader forms of civic insight, local practice, and deliberative public scrutiny.[11]

A robust politics of democratic professionalism does not require that all professionals practice at some ideal level but that enough of them work in ways appropriate to the problems and communities they encounter and that the institutions in which they work enable the best mix possible of professional norms and civic practices. Not every coastal scientist needs to cofacilitate a public meeting, coauthor a civic guide on green infrastructure, or get her feet wet planting eelgrass, but enough of her colleagues need to work with coastal communities to enable effective, collaborative, and resilient responses to sea-level rise. And many delight in getting their feet wet.

Or keeping their feet dry in other waters. As Kyle Dreyfuss-Wells—Northeast Ohio Regional Sewer District CEO, professional of the year and past chair of the National Association of Clean Water Agencies (NACWA) Stormwater Management Committee—framed her plenary presentation to the 2019 River Rally in Cleveland, "It is *way more fun, way more exciting, and way more authentic* for utility directors and staff to partner with communities, and to get on the right side" (speaker emphasis).[12]

The professional associations we have encountered in previous chapters have laid important foundations, but *none* of these have been able to diffuse tools and templates on a broad enough scale or transform professional identities in ways that sufficiently anchor democratically resilient institutional cultures and logics. That many have come so far is impressive; that so much more is still to be done in the face of urgent climate challenges is imperative.

In virtually every field relevant to urban sustainability and resilience, individual professionals, work teams, professional associations, academic departments, and public agencies are available for a more robust democratic professional strategy. As we have seen, urban and regional planners have often responded nimbly and creatively to civic claims for engagement and partnership over several decades and have promoted democratic sustainability norms and practices over the past decade. City transportation engineers in NACTO have done likewise when pressed by bicycle associations and AARP coalitions. Architects have been in the forefront of new urbanism, and green builders have developed tools for LEED for Neighborhood Development and multidisciplinary work teams across blue-, pink-, and white-collar lines. Stormwater professionals have been working with watershed associations and local environmental justice groups and Groundwork trusts. More than a decade ago, the Association of State Floodplain Managers formalized a climate adaptation approach based upon inclusive partnerships.

Confronted with raging wildfires, local fire departments in the urban West have found that their line personnel are often engaged with neighborhood associations as educators, partners, information sharers, and planners in mitigation strategies, and indeed many are willing to risk their lives but also expect homeowners and communities to become actively engaged in building their own capacities for hazard reduction. A major textbook for professionals in preparedness, hazard mitigation, and climate adaptation is clear that "resilience is everyone's responsibility," and that professionals need to supply the appropriate tools to make "bottom up resilience" and a "whole community approach" possible.[13]

Most everyday citizens, however, especially in vulnerable communities, have no idea that professionals can be trustworthy and productive partners in sustainability and resilience. Most professionals likewise have little sense that ordinary citizens and diverse urban residents can make their own work more effective, democratically legitimate, and worthy of public support—and indeed might help insulate them from the nastier forms of right-wing populist backlash they may face when trying to utilize their best expertise and even formal authority in responding to climate challenges. It is thus perhaps time to launch a strategic initiative across the entire field of sustainable and resilient cities that would do what several of the civic renewal initiatives in the late 1990s did for community building, deliberative problem-solving, and service learning; namely, raise the visibility of work already occurring, link networks across civic and professional association boundaries, help produce new tools and sources of funding, and deepen strategic initiatives in specific professions. Professionals—and their associations and graduate schools—need to become highly visible partners of communities in democratic resilience work.[14]

Cultural Politics of Hope

Third, a cultural politics of hope needs to be further embedded in the pragmatic and strategic work of sustainable and resilient cities. Several decades of scholarship have carved out a vital place for the sociology of emotions in the study of social movements so that rational and strategic action can no longer be neatly separated from emotions such as anger and shame, dignity and despair, apathy and hope. Movements develop cultural tool kits to construct and manage emotions, to integrate emotive elements with cognitive ones in framing processes, and to motivate action in deep and ongoing fashion. Climate denial is not only the result of an organized countermovement or a deficit in information but also reflects a "cultural schism." It can operate in everyday life, even in well-informed and progressive communities, so as not to frighten children at school or to dishearten dinner guests at home—or, indeed, to assuage shame and guilt for one's own personal lifestyle or national energy choices. Climate futility can even be clever and entertaining.[15]

Generating and managing emotions tend to create "strategic dilemmas" for movements, whose "moral batteries" are set by polarity between positive and negative posts, as James Jasper has argued. Stigmatized groups, for instance, can mobilize pride of identity but risk reinforcing negative stereotypes among the broader public. Nurturing strong internal solidarities may come at the expense of support among outsiders. Emotions within movements are never simple. They interact with each other, come in complex configurations and sequences, exercise differential appeal over the life course, and often have racial and gendered manifestations. They are also coconstructed relationally within institutional fields of multiple organizational and cultural logics. Actors thus need to be alert to strategic dilemmas and learn to make and modify strategic choices to generate the most appropriate mix and sequence of emotions.[16]

The sustainable cities field has been grappling with emotions from its earliest days. At their national conventions and in local work, League of Women Voters activists expressed moral shock and anger over urban water pollution yet also developed repertoires of emotionally restrained and respectful dialogue with experts in agencies and industries. Critical Mass bike riders staged performances of aggressive presence in face of threatening motor vehicles and intimidating police yet many have reconfigured joyous militancy into family celebration and gender irony as they have renegotiated space, and still others return to outraged yet nonviolent civil disobedience in the face of continuing fatalities. Environmental justice activists erupt in righteous indignation and sometimes unrestrained anger, at toxic waste sites near children's play areas or at the scourge of asthma and lead poisoning among their own kids. Yet many have also embraced their professional partners, body and soul, when they come to the table to help solve problems, as I have witnessed at trainings and celebrations among EPA community grantee teams. Few of these kinds of emotional movement displays, sequences, and strategies have unfolded seamlessly or without second-guessing, and none of the fields within sustainable cities should be imagined as having achieved the most optimal emotive mix or institutional fit.

However, these movements and the broader field of sustainable cities must learn to navigate one major strategic dilemma especially well in the coming years of climate disruption; namely, managing the emotions of fear, dread, and anger at the negative battery pole and the joy, faith, and hope of urban resilience work at the positive pole.

Sustainable city organizations and networks are already quite conscious of this dilemma. Acutely aware of the dangers of inaction, they stoke the fires of fear of what may happen to cherished places, to beloved children and grandchildren, to home assets hard-earned over decades of work and savings. Climate change, indeed, requires a multifaceted "sociology of loss." No one needs to tell those who work as grassroots leaders or professionals in climate and sustainability how difficult it sometimes becomes to manage their own emotions. Some integrate meditation practices into their strategic conferences. With some surprise, I first witnessed this at the Garrison Institute's Climate, Mind and Behavior Conference in June 2013 in Garrison, New York, where senior Natural Resources Defense Council (NRDC) staff, US Department of Housing and Urban Development (HUD) officials, Harvard scientists, evangelical preachers, and assets-based community-development practitioners from Chicago regularly sat together contemplating in silence between their animated discussions. Pride of accomplishment, even exuberant celebration as well as renewed emotional commitment among city leaders and organized stakeholders, characterized much of San Francisco's Global Climate Action Summit of September 2018. These grassroots activists and national associations, political and business leaders, professionals and investors feel this work deeply and profoundly. At the River Rally in Pittsburgh in May 2014, jointly sponsored by the River Network and the Waterkeeper Alliance, participants danced heartily to the music of a Chicago blues band on the final evening as if to embody the sensuous joy of a dam's demolition or a river's restoration.[17]

Or, as the *Troubled Waters* film produced through a committee in the US Senate in the 1960s put it, "There is a river, the psalmist sang years ago, the waters of which shall make glad the city."[18]

The social movement and institutional work of urban sustainability cannot do without both battery poles charging, discharging, and recharging. But emotions of democratic hope, faith in co-creation and creation care, and pride in everyday resilience work are at risk of being overwhelmed by a deep and recurrent sense of futility and despair. To be sure, despair is driven by uncomfortable facts staring at us starkly and darkly: statistics on warming trends, species extinction, massive wildfires, sea-level rise, and social conflicts already triggered by population displacement around the world. Biblical floods resonate. Cities and civilizations are lost.

Emotions of futility, however, can also be exacerbated by cultural and intellectual tropes that refuse the test of sustained democratic practice. On the cultural right, climate denial can morph into religious end-time prophecy, with all its ecstatic and fanatic joys. End-time prophets among some urban scholars on the left, who preach that "the city is always going to hell," provide little institutional design to instantiate paeans to urban revolt. Climate crisis will likely feed further "chaos incitement" to burn down the whole democratic cosmos, which already has a major foothold in the polity. To counter these, diverse cultural, religious, and intellectual traditions offer many sources of hope and civic motivation. The untidy, imperfect, and incremental work of institutional field building of sustainable cities in the United States is now assuredly one such source—a vital and practical resource for ongoing and indeed *expedited* strategic action suffused with democratic faith.[19]

Postscript: Toward a Civic Green New Deal

Should an ambitious Green New Deal (GND), or some other robust strategy to address place-based issues within a larger climate policy, become politically feasible, it could be designed in such a way as to enhance the potential of a civic politics of risk and resilience, an institutional politics of democratic professionalism, and a cultural politics of hope, as outlined in the previous chapter. Making these a core part of its framing and design would enhance its chances of enactment and implementation, diminish popular resistance in communities wary of technocratic and statist overreach, and generate sufficient trust and mutual respect to help contain cultural and political polarization. Together these would reduce the risks of seesaw governance—up, down, up again, and perhaps down yet again for major federal policy such as a GND or other robust policy design, which is bound to have unanticipated costs and risks. Developing the appropriate mix of market mechanisms, regulatory tools, and public investments in technology and infrastructure for the larger policy design of a GND will require trial and error, to be sure, as will further institutional field building for sustainable and resilient cities and communities of every type. This is the heart of a democratic institutional pragmatism.[1]

Most certainly, grassroots mobilization and protest—often with righteous desperation and dogged disruption by young people who justifiably fear being robbed of a viable and noble future—will be needed to jolt us forward and help us sustain political momentum. Groups such as 350. org, Sunrise, and others have been leading important campaigns. But also essential will be forms of civic collaboration through which everyday citizens and neighborhood residents, workers and employers, professionals and students can accomplish ongoing resilience work together and hold each other democratically accountable for results over an extended period. Hundreds of thousands, and eventually millions, of young activists would welcome community and career pathways to resilience work, some no doubt through expanded AmeriCorps programs that focus on conservation, disaster response, river restoration, and reforestation. Career, community, and national-service pathways for young people can include sophisticated digital planning and engagement tools beyond polarizing social media platforms. Indeed, we would irreparably, unforgivably betray their idealism if we refused them the practical tools they might need for a lifetime of coproductive engagement for sustainable, resilient, democratic, and just communities. *We owe them nothing less.*

The civic contours of a GND—let's call it civic GND for short—could build upon some of the policy designs we have encountered in this book and add many others, yet with much greater strategic coordination by public agencies and far more substantial public funding appropriate to the magnitude, scope, and likely duration of climate challenges. To be sure, it would be essential to strengthen and expand rights-based tools for public participation in all areas where public investment and planning will impact neighborhoods, cities, watersheds, and regions. As clumsy, conflictual, or co-optative as some of the participatory designs resulting from mandates have often been, ordinary citizens and organized stakeholders have frequently proven capable of refining them, adjusting deliberative components and power balances, and responding to normative and practical deficits.

Public participation practices have grown in sophistication over previous decades, as conceded by even some of its more exacting critics who favor social movement mobilization as a binary alternative. They could be refined still further by clearer legal mandates, greater public funding, and more appropriate forms of training in universities, professional schools, neighborhood departments, community design centers, public libraries, schools, and youth development programs. In highly complex institutional arenas and among diverse publics facing extraordinarily knotty challenges of sustainability and resilience, professionally trained facilitators, organizers, and coaches are often indispensable. Thus, a civic GND should strengthen legal mandates and administrative norms for public participation as well as enhance practical tool kits and training capacities to enable refined practice suitable to specific institutional fields, community settings, and problem scenarios. It should help structure markets for the best and most appropriate forms of training, coaching, and facilitation.

This is an appropriate use of federal policy design and funding while also welcoming and encouraging multiple forms of independent organizing. The latter, however, are not a proper use of direct public finding unless carefully delimited to the public problem-solving activities of such groups, as is routinely delineated in many grant programs already. We should seek to enable synergies, wherever appropriate, and not permit ourselves to be disabled by presumed zero-sum or binary alternatives.[2]

Here, I sketch several core components of what could serve as the lineaments of a civic GND for the coming decades. These might be aligned and sequenced in various ways, depending on perceived political opportunities and relative urgency in specific fields. They are intended to further institutionally embed civic forms and practices while providing opportunities to reflect, revisit, and revise. They seek to be deliberatively systemic within and across various institutional fields and policy challenges while remaining open to pragmatic tests of efficacy and normative challenges of equity and justice. Further efforts to refine these should, to be sure, engage scholars from a broad array of disciplines and agency practitioners at all levels of the federal system. They should also engage community groups, professional associations, and civic intermediaries. Some already have the kinds of experience needed for policy design and implementation and others will find incentives to engage creatively. I offer these proposals as an initial foray.

Let me briefly outline several key components of a civic GND as a policy design for democracy. These include: (1) funding for a diverse array of federal grants, based upon a congressionally stipulated percentage of overall GND funding; (2) mission statements and strategy frameworks within and across federal agencies; and (3) strategic coordination through a White House civic GND office, in collaboration with a range of citizen advisory committees.

Federal Funding for a Civic GND

Federal grants could and should serve as key mechanisms to generate appropriate civic skills, capacities, and tool kits aligned with the range of other planning, design, ecological, and digital tool kits that communities and multistakeholder partnerships will need to do effective work. Such grants can take many forms, as evident in previous chapters. They can be provided by federal agencies as competitive project grants directly to local groups, teams, partnerships, and institutions engaged in ecological restoration, multistakeholder planning, disaster response, and other forms of inclusive problem-solving. They can also be provided to states, cities, and other local jurisdictions as block grants and categorical formula grants, accompanied by strong norms of public participation, diversity, inclusiveness, and collaboration. Federal funding and administrative support can prioritize the most vulnerable communities, but grants should be available broadly while incentivizing collaboration across lines of race, income, neighborhood, and region.

In complex institutional fields with many kinds of professional actors, civic GND funding should also enable professional associations and professional schools to advance civic professionalism in training, practice, and mission. Where participatory work practices are essential to effective energy, infrastructure, transportation, and other green resilience projects, grants could be provided to unions, trade associations, and central labor councils to encourage the development of appropriate civic and collaborative skills and organizational capacities.

Congressionally Authorized Funding

Funding for a civic GND needs to be substantial and systemic, not a tiny add-on to explore program innovation or mollify the grassroots with a dozen or so grants per year in each policy area. To be sure, funding should be distributed according to appropriate criteria and on timetables that are manageable and support learning among networks of grantees and agency staff, as happens in many grant programs. Yet funding for place-based grants to community groups and projects tends not to attract the active attention of major national environmental organizations, and indeed sometimes attracts their passive opposition if it seems to threaten their own preferred regulatory tools or internal allocation of agency funds.

One possible way around this funding dilemma would be for Congress to stipulate a minimum percentage funding rule for any GND or similar climate legislation. This could establish a minimum baseline rule of 1 to 5 percent for the civic GND of all relevant federal spending that would impact neighborhoods, cities, regions, coastlines, and other ecosystems. Thus, for every $1 trillion in overall GND investment, the 1 to 5 percent rule would yield $10 to $50 billion for civic GND as an investment in civic infrastructure appropriate to and aligned with the larger federal investments in green infrastructure, broadly conceived. Let's call this the *1-to-5 percent civic GND funding rule.*

Such a rule could and should be justified in terms of a clearly defined mission of civic GND to foster effective, collaborative, and equitable engagement from all sectors of US society. It would then relieve the budgetary process of permanent competitive struggles between the *green infrastructure* and the *civic infrastructure* of a GND. A relatively modest and appropriate, but clearly specified, overall investment percentage would signal a fundamental commitment by Congress and the president to involve ordinary citizens and diverse communities in developing local and regional solutions. It would also hold in check statist overreach and political polarization. A civic GND would be prominently branded as an investment in civic democracy, in addition to its substantive goals of sustainability and resilience. Its policy design would signal how a GND intends to value the civic skills and coproductive work of ordinary citizens and diverse partners. Let us put our money where our civic republican mouths are if we genuinely intend to keep our republic amidst the coming decades of climate crisis. That is the overriding message of the funding design.

Federal Grants to Communities, Cities, and Civic Associations

Federal grants to communities represent a well-worn path that incentivizes and enables cities and/or local community partnerships to craft suitable strategies for sustainability and resilience. Administrative form can vary, with states playing greater and lesser roles, but the core feature is that communities can leverage federal funding to enable associational capacity building and active engagement among local partners. They can also leverage further funding from states, cities, foundations, and institutions—as in matching grants and other matching in-kind and volunteer work contributions.

Watershed grants have been distributed through various programs at the EPA and NOAA directly to local groups, through state programs and civic intermediaries, or with civic intermediaries funded separately to provide capacity building. Such grants have helped to build the field by enabling cities and states to shift to watershed approaches as well as by enabling intermediaries such as the River Network, Restore America's Estuaries, the International City/County Management Association, and the Southeast Watershed Forum to build the capacity of affiliated groups to do watershed planning, citizen monitoring, and ecosystem restoration. Often such grants are accompanied by the coproduction of practical tool kits usable by ordinary citizens, students, and partner institutions. The EPA's Environmental Justice Collaborative Problem-Solving grants, as well as grants from the Community Action for a Renewed Environment (CARE) program, have also funded local partnerships. Other agencies, as well as interagency partnerships, have provided grants for community food security, regional planning, and environmental education.

Again, the design of such grant programs can vary and is open to revision due to federal oversight, city and state authority claims, independent evaluation, and critical feedback from local civic groups and partners. Civic GND grants can be directly attached to larger public investments in green infrastructure; hence, they can be tightly aligned or can travel across program areas to ensure appropriate targeting and proportionality. Substantial increases in funding through a civic GND would enable significant scaling up and would further incentivize local engagement.

In addition, civic GND grants can also be available to faith-based groups. Many faith traditions are developing responses to climate crisis under rubrics of environmental justice, responsible stewardship, and creation care. Groups such as Interfaith Power and Light, Young Evangelicals for Climate Action, the Episcopal Ecological Network, and the Evangelical Environmental Network engage their members in various forms of stewardship. Federal funding to such networks, coordinated through the faith-based office in the White House, could become an important means to engage communities of faith in local work. To be sure, there have been some tricky issues of separation of church and state, but the diverse Advisory Council on Faith-Based and Neighborhood Partnerships appointed by President Barack Obama seems to have navigated these reasonably well.

Federal grants for faith-based organizations working on climate change, community resilience, and ecological stewardship could generate deep and sustained civic motivation to act, provide new sources for a politics of hope, and defuse some of the cultural polarization around climate change.

Grants to Professional Associations and Professional Schools

Professional associations are central actors that can help shift institutional and policy fields toward a more robust democratic or civic professionalism. A civic GND should help them do so. Federal grants could go to professional associations to encourage strategic initiatives focused on the civics of professional practice, such as the development of core principles, best-practice guides, tool kits, awards, sections, internships in communities, consulting teams, and strategic plans to transform their professions to be able to work more effectively, collaboratively, and extensively with communities. Those professional associations that already have such initiatives—the American Institute of Architects, the American Planning Association, the National Association of City Transportation Officials—could be asked to serve on citizen advisory committees within relevant federal agencies to help design such grants. Of course, intermediaries such as ICLEI USA and the Urban Sustainability Directors Network, the National League of Cities and the International City/County Management Association, would be key here as well.

In virtually every field that has relevance grappling with climate change in communities and regions, there exist innovative professionals who have worked collaboratively with diverse communities and stakeholders, and some associations have developed mission statements, engagement strategies, tool kits, and textbooks for refining civic professional practices. This is true not just for architects, urban planners, and city transportation engineers, but also for clean water agencies, hazard mitigation and disaster preparedness professionals, state and tribal wetland and floodplain managers, western wildfire teams, and multidisciplinary associations of adaptation and resilience professionals. Civic GND grants should be designed in such a way to encourage core visioning and baseline strategic planning for professional associations, and they should help those that have already begun doing this to roll out ambitious strategies to their sections, local chapters, and selective partnerships. The latter would incentivize professional associations to collaborate with community groups and civic intermediaries that might receive grants under the previous category of federal grants to cities and communities and vice versa, thus fostering strategic partnerships from multiple directions. A key design principle: provide many grant portals to incentivize action and enlist partners, wherever they might be.

Let's say, for instance, that $50 million—a mere drop in the GND bucket—were made available competitively over the first grant cycle, for an average three-year grant of $1 million. By the end of the third year, some fifty professional associations across the most important fields of climate planning and resilience would have had the opportunity to develop and begin implementing a strategic initiative for blending civic and professional practices in ways most appropriate to the challenges they face.

They would have articulated core principles of practice, developed several new tool kits, implemented innovative pilot projects in a range of their chapters, and engaged in learning that could feed back into citizen advisory committees in relevant federal agencies for iterative policy redesign. At joint annual workshops, grantees could share best cases, celebrate successes, honor champions and emerging young professionals, and reflect on persisting barriers.

Another round of funding could deepen and broaden practice and generate still further incentives for emulation. Community partners could join them at such workshops in signaling the moral and practical power of collaborative democratic action to solve problems. Fifty professional associations in this position could also lend a movement ethos to the diffusion of civic professional practice without loosening their commitments to professional legitimacy and accountable governance. Having visible and broad engagement among civic professionals would further legitimate climate action in the eyes of publics and legislatures across the country.

Competitive grants to professional schools (and *their* associations), as well as college and university programs in relevant disciplinary fields, could also advance civic practices considerably. They would be a most suitable complement to grants for professional associations and could be developed jointly with them, thus again incentivizing initiative from multiple directions. A wide array of programs might be eligible, including for insurance and real estate, sustainability management in industry and retail, computing and engineering, and still others—not just some of those mentioned previously or the usual college majors for community-based learning. The educational priority of such professional programs is, of course, the analytic and technical core of such disciplines. However, civic GND grants would encourage students to learn how their disciplines impact communities, how they might communicate more effectively for broad public purposes, how they can collaborate and coproduce with community partners, and how they might step up for a life of civic leadership as they move through various stages of their professional careers. One can imagine grants to develop core civic GND courses in each relevant discipline and develop community internship programs.

Campus Compact, the American Association of State Colleges and Universities, and similar organizations promoting civic engagement and service learning could be eligible for similar grants. University extension programs, many with practitioner and research networks that have deep commitments to local knowledge and civic participation in sustainability work, could also be funded more substantially. Of course, federal grants to further build the field of environmental education in K–12 schools is essential. With expanded funding for national and community service programs, we can begin to see a range of diverse pathways for youth leadership and civic professional development over a lifetime of commitment to create sustainable and resilient communities. No climate action strategy worth its salt could neglect such initiatives.

Grants to Labor Unions and Trade Associations

Still another type of competitive federal grant could be made available to unions, central labor councils, labor-community coalitions, trade associations, and local chambers of commerce to enable them to further develop and diffuse best-participatory practices in green building, industrial ecology, sustainability management in retail, and other forms of corporate citizenship and employee engagement to ensure collaborative skill development at every level. Some building trades, as well as state and city building trades councils, are beginning such work in collaboration with the US Green Building Council, and many others are available in transportation and energy sectors and elsewhere. Such grants might shift the internal dynamics of unions that remain overly wedded to fossil fuel models, as can various forms of retraining and community development for hard-hit workers who would likely be central to other core programs within a GND.

Likewise, some leading companies are pursuing models of "embedded sustainability," with sustainable business strategies embedded in communities and networks. These models vary, but most emphasize the cocreation of solutions with stakeholders, including community groups, nonprofits, and regulators. They are leveraging local knowledge, self-organizing communities of practice, and engaging employees and even youth task forces.

Federal agencies such as the Labor and Commerce Departments could administer such grants to ensure that an all-hands-on-deck strategy to combat climate change and develop resilience strategies truly means hands and heads, as well as hearts, are broadly available for transforming the way we work and do business in our everyday lives. Priority might be placed on grants that include labor-management cooperation in developing collaborative leadership and participation strategies for their firms and industries. Imagine a grant category for a city's central labor council, chamber of commerce, and community-labor coalition to collaborate in developing best-participatory work practices for a sustainable city. Stir into the pot vocational and community college programs. Then imagine the first five to ten cities that step forward to help us learn how this might be done more broadly and deeply.[3]

The Department of Education, or some more appropriate agency, could also provide grants to school systems that emulate all or parts of the Poudre School District approach in Fort Collins, Colorado, for professional, blue-, and pink-collar staff in collaborative green building design as well as in student, parent, and community participation. These are models that are transferrable, and civic GND grants to other school districts can make them more so.

Workplace democracy, a noble ideal going back more than a century and sometimes embedded in institutional practice in the United States and Europe, will mean little in the coming years if it cannot develop the appropriate mix of participatory, team-building, and technical and information skills to help make our private businesses and public services sustainable. A GND must empower labor not just in rights, wages, and benefits, as important as these are, but also in collaborative decision making and resilience skills, refined in arenas still defined by labor-management contestation on other levels. Workers and unions that can step up to the plate for this kind of civic GND will have still-further strategic leverage and broader public support in making all workplaces more rewarding, democratic, and just.[3]

Prominent CEOs stressing the need for a new capitalism that is more equitable and sustainable can provide leadership on the broad civics that must inform sustainable business strategies. Imagine grants that enable and incentivize collaboration among worker and employer associations to raise such perspectives to new prominence in their industries or across a city or region. Environmental organizations, such as the Environmental Defense Fund and Ceres, would almost certainly step forward to help businesses and investors with creative proposals, as they have been doing on related projects for the past several decades. Perhaps competitive federal grants can make it shameful for business and labor leaders to not at least apply for such civic GND grants. Can they afford to be turned down because they are not perceived as innovative enough to warrant support from the Commerce and Labor Departments for, say, a three-year, $1 million grant to develop a collaborative strategy? Let's do the simple math again and ask what fifty such grants might do in the first three years to spur new initiatives and establish models that can be diffused widely for the next round of $50 million or $100 million, still only a few drops in the bucket of projected overall GND spending. The civic leadership of labor and business are both essential for a GND that empowers everyday people in communities and workplaces of all kinds.

Corporation for National and Community Service

National service programs, especially those institutionalized through AmeriCorps beginning in the early 1990s, can play an important role in a civic GND. Melissa Bass, who has analyzed national service as "public policy for democracy" in its three main periods of expansion (1930s, 1960s, 1990s), argues that the AmeriCorps variant has increasingly embedded itself into state service commissions and civic innovations of recent years. This makes AmeriCorps available for robust partnerships with the types of community-based groups, as well as the civic and professional associations, discussed throughout this book. Again, enlisting partners through multiple grant portals can be reinforced as a core design component. Within the range of civic activities and "teachings" of democracy that have characterized national service programs, AmeriCorps programs have generated ample space for hands-on public work to solve common problems and co-produce public goods. They also build civic leadership through teamwork while also guarding against activities that can be perceived as partisan and hence potentially undermine broad support.[4]

Such programs, funded and partially organized through the Corporation for National and Community Service (CNCS), can play a critical role in sustainability and environmental stewardship, disaster response, and a range of other community-building initiatives. FEMA Corps works directly with the Federal Emergency Management Agency and can further bring to scale its "whole community" approach, first developed by the agency in 2011. The Earth Service Corps of the YMCA works on environmental service, habitat restoration, and leadership projects through school and club projects. The Corps Network, funded partially through CNCS, includes some one hundred and thirty local corps administered by cities, states, and nonprofits. They enlist young adults (ages sixteen to twenty-five) and veterans (up to age thirty-five) in disaster response, river restoration, reforestation, park conservation, wildfire fighting and prevention, and home weatherization, among other activities.

A civic GND could increase funding for such groups, strengthen multi-stakeholder state service commissions that regrant as well as raise additional dollars, and foster partnerships of many kinds. The numbers enrolled in such programs, for a long time stuck at seventy-five thousand per year due to lack of appropriations for the full authorization of two hundred and twenty-five thousand (under the Edward M. Kennedy Serve America Act), could be increased stepwise but quite significantly while avoiding the conundrums and potential backlash of calls for universal service.

Strategic Coordination and Policy Learning

Central to a civic GND that aims to mobilize civic, professional, and institutional assets for the sustained work of resilience and transformation are strategically configured policy and administrative designs that provide the kinds of participatory feedback enabling community problem-solving locally and regionally while constraining potentially perverse effects. Among the latter are exacerbating participatory inequalities, eroding independent organizing, or promoting unjust outcomes. Any systemic attempt to institutionalize an appropriate mix of designs must thus be both vigilant and corrective. Tackling climate change and resilience over the next decades is perhaps the most complex strategic challenge that our system of governance has ever faced. It thus requires strategic coordination, policy reflexivity, and democratic accountability on a scale unmatched. A civic GND cannot be simply an afterthought or an add-on, nor indeed a handout.

A GND promises a bigger state, to be sure, but if it is not simultaneously a better state, a more civically embedded and democratically accountable state, it will almost assuredly collapse of its own weight, with a lot of help from honest skeptics as well as outright opponents. It will likely be replaced by something far worse. Neither progressive state builders nor social movement mobilizers nor urban rebels should assume that we will not have to *design* a civic GND to get appropriate mixes and feedbacks, and to avoid policy backlash. These will not emerge spontaneously and independently, although civic spontaneity and associational independence must remain key components of any overall mix of organizational ecologies and policy designs.[5]

To begin to design policy strategically for a civic GND, I suggest considering several institutional components become appropriately part of congressional authorization of any GND.

Civic Missions and Strategic Frameworks
of Federal Agencies

The first institutional component I propose is that all GND funding that directly impacts communities, regions, and workplaces should require relevant federal agencies to develop civic GND mission statements—the *why* of appropriate civic engagement in any broader policy architecture and institutional field—as well as strategic planning frameworks mapping pathways for the *how* of getting there. Mission statements should include a core discussion of democratic norms and policy messages as well as the dignified and coproductive roles and identities of policy targets as civic agents. Strategic framework documents should include a wide panoply of relevant tools: grants, data and planning tool kits, best cases and shared narratives, governance and participation templates, and networking designs to ensure knowledge sharing, policy learning, and mutual accountability among civic, government, business, and other field actors. The mission and framework statements, of course, can be combined.

The strategic framework documents of federal agencies should consider various recipes and design choices that might be most appropriate for specific clusters of policy problems and response scenarios and yet less so for others, informed by closely aligned ecological and social scientific knowledge as well as with "multiple ways of knowing" and "street science." A policy for urban watershed planning and restoration might elicit civic and deliberative recipes similar to some aspects of bicycle planning but not others; policy design for strategic retreat from the shore might appropriately draw upon a very different mix. Such policy designs should also consider potential unintended and perverse consequences, such as participatory inequalities and environmental injustices, and should develop methods for remaining alert and responding appropriately as needed.

Interagency working groups, as has occurred with the environmental justice interagency group to implement Executive Order 12898, could align agency strategies, and citizen advisory committees could inform policy and help provide metrics of impact and public accountability. These advisory committees would include multistakeholder representatives from relevant associations within each policy field or agency purview, consistent with the Federal Advisory Committee Act (FACA) requirement of balance. Design of mission statements and strategic frameworks should be a shared endeavor among federal agencies and civic and professional associations, rooted in learning from local and state agencies, grassroots community groups, and actors in the broader institutional field.[6]

In his far-reaching analysis of potential components of a GND, Jeremy Rifkin builds upon the experience of "peer assemblies" in several regions of Europe, and he suggests ways that these might be laterally scaled in the United States as complementary forms of governance suitable to the "distributed, open-sourced, and laterally scaled design and engineering principles" of a green post-carbon-energy future. These assemblies would include representatives from labor unions and chambers of commerce, elected officials and civic associations, and economic development agencies and universities, among others. While the participatory design details of these assemblies remain vague, Rifkin has one proposal that is quite consistent with my stress on strategic federal coordination to enable distributed governance of distributed energy and green infrastructure: that Congress provide a three-year grant to each state, conditional upon a match, to "establish and staff an operational center whose sole purpose is to organize and coordinate peer assemblies across their cities and counties for the express purpose of preparing Green New Deal roadmaps," suitable to each city and region.[7]

A White House Office and Citizen Advisory Committee

The second institutional component is a White House office of civic GND, working with appropriate staff at the Office of Management and Budget that would provide overall strategic direction and a national civic GND advisory committee that would advise the White House/OMB group to provide robust civic guidance, learning, and feedback across all GND-related fields. The national advisory committee would build upon the work of the relevant citizen advisory committees, interagency working groups, and perhaps state peer-assembly centers. It would also draw from leading scholars and practitioners of public engagement and policy design from the National Academy of Public Administration, the International City/County Management Association, the American Planning Association, the National League of Cities, the American Society for Public Administration, and similar professional groups as well as leading professional schools, advocacy groups, and major organizations experienced in public participation. Business and trade associations, as well as labor organizations, would also have appropriate representation, all consistent with FACA. As in the National Environmental Justice Advisory Council, prominent EJ groups would also have a voice.

The White House office, along with civic GND federal agency staff and citizen advisory committees, can hold regular workshops and conferences with civic and professional associations to provide relevant input, feedback, and further strategic initiatives across the larger field. Foundation funding would, of course, also be welcome in such endeavors, as would the collaboration of the Funders Network for Smart Growth and Livable Communities, the Environmental Grantmakers Association, and other strategic funder networks.

The overall design of a civic GND must be a shared endeavor, with appropriate evaluation and continual revision along a pathway that will be filled with much uncertainty, significant contention, and enormous disruption by climate-related events. If designed and implemented well, a civic GND can manage these challenges in ways that contain conflict and steer civic energies toward public work that is coproductive, pragmatic, hopeful, and just.

Whether in this or some other variant, mechanisms for strategic coordination of civic policy design and iterative learning will be needed if a very large federal initiative such as a GND, with an extraordinarily ambitious overall goal yet with many differentiated local and institutional actors and fields, is to generate appropriate mixes of civic engagement. It is highly unlikely that one or two big participatory policy feedback designs—as in Social Security or the GI Bill discussed in chapter 1—could be crafted to serve this purpose.

Many other policy design components are available, and many others could be invented along the way, to be sure. But all such designs have unintended and potentially perverse consequences in need of revision and rebalancing that is well attuned to specific institutional logics, field dynamics, and power plays. No systemic ecology of deliberative, relational, and coproductive forms of engagement are without such risks. Strategic field actors thus need to remain highly alert to how these can best be configured and reconfigured to achieve overall policy goals, enhance equity and legitimacy, and revitalize our civic democracy. An ambitious GND intent on saving our communities, our country, and our planet for democratic habitation should attempt no less.

Concluding Thoughts

A civic GND is not all there is to civics in an era of climate change, to be sure. Social movement action remains an essential ingredient for shaking up our politics and waking up our populace. It will bring many people, especially youth, into the arena of vital contestation and help ensure that, even as we begin to make more progress, we do not become lazy and lulled. Movement protest challenges power imbalances at the national level as well as in the many community and institutional venues that do not take unjust distributions of power, resources, and risks seriously enough. Movement mobilization can ensure that we shift the balance of power in Congress and elect a supportive president to be able to enact, fund, and sustain a GND, even if we may still disagree about its size and components, and, indeed, its nomenclature. Climate justice for the most vulnerable communities must remain foremost, both in movement action and in the design of a civic GND. There can be many synergies, though some will also see unwarranted trade-offs.

An important and distinct federal role in a civic GND is warranted for a variety of reasons. First, a GND would be a federal program, and thus the federal government, in collaboration with state and local governments as well as civic and other associations, has a responsibility to try to get the civic mix right given the range of challenges in various community settings and institutional fields in which federal action will play out over the coming decades. If large public investments are to be made by a GND, then some commensurate investments in a civic GND should be made to ensure effective, appropriate, well-aligned, and legitimate civic action. There exists much precedent for such a federal role, many available civic repertoires and tool kits, and persistent interest among a broad array of community groups for federal support.

Second, as important as movement repertoires are in generating grassroots power, they have significant limits for sustaining collaborative public work with democratic accountability. Unhinged from other forms of civic and pragmatic institutional action, climate movement rhetoric sometimes tends toward metaphors of "all-out war" to repair all forms of historic oppression in one interconnected and inseparable bundle of social justice programs and to "change virtually all aspects of society on an extremely tight deadline."[8]

Such overwrought rhetoric may mobilize, but it will not institutionalize, and it may very well erode social and political trust and legitimacy needed to sustain broad-based action over decades. Movements contest but often do not make for reliable governance partners unless they, or some of the actors within them, shift their civic styles. Bicycle movements have contested militantly but have collaborated with city traffic engineers in street design. Environmental justice groups have protested vehemently yet have often joined with professionals and public agencies to restore urban rivers or to anchor healthy community partnerships to reduce childhood asthma. A civic GND should leave as much room as possible for style shifts and blended forms and should promote learning from multiple directions, but its overall goal must be to enhance public problem-solving and democratic governance. Democratic governance, especially for such extended and uncertain challenges as climate change poses, must not only respond to conflict but must also seek to contain it and help direct it to coproducing public value with broad legitimacy. Government rightly invests in civics to promote democratic governance and broad collaboration. It does not rightly invest in protest that promotes conflict, *as important as other resources for movement contestation will assuredly continue to be.*

Third, a civic GND must manage the cultural and emotional facets of climate change over the coming decades of certain disruption and tempting despair. As social movement theorists argue, all movements face strategic dilemmas on emotions. They develop cultural tool kits to construct and manage emotions, to integrate emotive elements with cognitive ones in framing problems and solutions, and to motivate action in deep and ongoing fashion. Movements cultivate anger, elicit shame, and generate hope in various mixes and at diverse junctures of political opportunity, as argued in the previous chapter. Today, our polity is divided on climate change not only due to an organized countermovement of denial or a deficit in information but because of a cultural schism. End-times prophets appear on the right and on the left, and ordinary citizens will hear recurring messages of fatalism and despair, as well as desperate utopianism.

A robust civic GND must anchor democratic faith and hope by enlisting us in deeply meaningful stewardship and the pragmatic work of making our communities and institutions sustainable, resilient, and just. And it can provide pathways, tool kits, and resources to enable our young people to sustain an engaged and robust democracy throughout their lives and those of their own children and grandchildren. Shame on us—civic, movement, political, professional, religious, cultural, educational, business, and labor leaders alike—if we cannot develop the policy and institutional supports to enable their work.

Notes

Chapter 1. The Sustainable City: Civic Action and Democratic Institutionalism

1. Neil Fligstein and Doug McAdam, *A Theory of Fields* (New York: Oxford University Press, 2012); Daniel N. Kluttz and Neil Fligstein, "Varieties of Sociological Field Theory," in *Handbook of Contemporary Sociological Theory*, ed. Seth Abrutyn (New York: Springer, 2016), 185–204; Walter W. Powell and Paul J. DiMaggio, eds., *The New Institutionalism in Organizational Analysis* (Chicago, IL: University of Chicago Press, 1991); W. Richard Scott, *Institutions and Organizations: Ideas, Interests, and Identities*, 4th ed. (Thousand Oaks, CA: SAGE, 2013); Mustafa Emirbayer and Victoria Johnson, "Bourdieu and Organizational Analysis," *Theory and Society* 37 (2008): 1–44; Peter A. Hall and Rosemary C. R. Taylor, "Political Science and the Three New Institutionalisms," *Political Studies* 44 (1996): 952–973; B. Guy Peters, *Institutional Theory in Political Science: The New Institutionalism*, 4th ed. (Northampton, MA: Elgar, 2019).

2. Stephanie Moulton and Jodi R. Sandfort, "The Strategic Action Field Framework for Policy Implementation Research," *Policy Studies Journal* 45 (2017): 144–169; Ann Mische, "Relational Sociology, Culture, and Agency," in *SAGE Handbook of Social Network Analysis*, ed. John Scott and Peter J. Carrington (Thousand Oaks, CA: SAGE, 2010), 80–97; David L. Deephouse, Jonathan Bundy, Leigh Plunkett Tost, and Mark C. Suchman, "Organizational Legitimacy: Six Key Questions," in *The SAGE Handbook of Organizational Institutionalism*, ed. Royston Greenwood, Christine Oliver, Thomas B. Lawrence, and Renate E. Meyer, 2nd ed. (Thousand Oaks, CA: SAGE, 2017), 27–54. On strategic planning in the Sierra Club, see Michael McCloskey, *In the Thick of It: My Life in the Sierra Club* (Washington, DC: Island Press, 2005), 176–179.

3. Elizabeth A. Armstrong and Mary Bernstein, "Culture, Power, and Institutions: A Multi-Institutional Politics Approach to Social Movements," *Sociological Theory* 26 (2008): 74–99; Elisabeth S. Clemens, "The Democratic Dilemma: Aligning Fields of Elite Influence and Political Equality," *Research in the Sociology of Organizations* 43 (2015): 221–242; Hayagreeva Rao, Calvin Morrill, and Mayer N. Zald, "Power Plays: How Social Movements and Collective Action Create New Organizational Forms," *Research in Organizational Behavior* 22 (2000): 237–281;

Rhonda Evans and Tamara Kay, "How Environmentalists 'Greened' Trade Policy: Strategic Action and the Architecture of Field Overlap," *American Sociological Review* 73 (2008): 970–991.

4. Neil Fligstein, "Social Skill and the Theory of Fields," *Sociological Theory* 19 (2001): 105–125; Fligstein and McAdam, *A Theory of Fields*; Paul J. DiMaggio, "Interest and Agency in Institutional Theory," in *Institutional Patterns and Organizations: Culture and Environment*, ed. Lynne G. Zucker (Cambridge, MA: Ballinger, 1988), 3–21; Robert D. Benford and David A. Snow, "Framing Processes and Social Movements: An Overview and Assessment," *Annual Review of Sociology* 26 (2000): 611–639.

5. Julian Agyeman, *Introducing Just Sustainabilities: Policy, Planning, and Practice* (London: Zed Books, 2013); Rebecca L. Henn and Andrew J. Hoffman, eds., *Constructing Green: The Social Structures of Sustainability* (Cambridge, MA: MIT Press, 2013); Jeffrey Tumlin, *Sustainable Transportation Planning: Tools for Creating Vibrant, Healthy, and Resilient Communities* (Hoboken, NJ: Wiley, 2012).

6. Patricia H. Thornton, William Ocasio, and Michael Lounsbury, *The Institutional Logics Perspective: A New Approach to Culture, Structure, and Process* (New York: Oxford University Press, 2012), qtd. on 2; Roger Friedland and Robert R. Alford, "Bringing Society Back In: Symbols, Practices, and Institutional Contradictions," in *The New Institutionalism in Organizational Analysis*, 232–263.

7. Chris Laszlo and Nadya Zhexembayeva, *Embedded Sustainability: The Next Big Competitive Advantage* (Stanford, CA: Stanford University Press, 2011); Rebecca Henderson, Ranjay Gulati, and Michael Tushman, eds., *Leading Sustainable Change: An Organizational Perspective* (New York: Oxford University Press, 2015); Andrew J. Hoffman and Marc J. Ventresca, eds., *Organizations, Policy, and the Natural Environment: Institutional and Strategic Perspectives* (Stanford, CA: Stanford Business Books, 2002); Bronagh Ward, Sakis Kotsantonis, Veena Ramani, and Hannah Saltman, *Systems Rule: How Board Governance Can Drive Sustainability Performance*, Ceres and KKS Advisors, May 2018, https://www.ceres.org/systemsrule; Sarah A. Soule, *Contention and Corporate Social Responsibility* (New York: Cambridge University Press, 2009); Walter W. Powell, Doug White, Kenneth Koput, and Jason Owen-Smith, "Network Dynamics and Field Evolution: The Growth of Interorganizational Collaboration in the Life Sciences," *American Journal of Sociology* 110 (2005): 1132–1205. For an institutionalist approach to corporate social action that could be extended to city sustainability logics and strategies, see Christopher Marquis, Mary Ann Glynn, and Gerald F. Davis, "Community Isomorphism and Corporate Social Action," *Academy of Management Review* 32 (2007): 925–945.

8. My formulation here partly addresses a suggestive point raised by Thornton, Ocasio, and Lounsbury, *Institutional Logics Perspective*, 56 and 67–68, that democracy is a potential feature *within* each institutional order. However, it can also

play a normatively aligning role *across* institutional logics. The two are mutually constitutive.

9. Albert O. Hirschman, *Exit, Voice, and Loyalty: Responses to Decline in Firms, Organizations, and States* (Cambridge, MA: Harvard University Press, 1970).

10. On multitiered civic associations generally, see Theda Skocpol, *Diminished Democracy: From Membership to Management in American Civic Life* (Norman: University of Oklahoma Press, 2003); Theda Skocpol, Marshall Ganz, and Ariane Liazos, "A Nation of Organizers: The Institutional Origins of Civic Voluntarism in the United States," *American Political Science Review* 94 (2000): 527–546; Theda Skocpol, Ariane Liazos, and Marshall Ganz, *What a Mighty Power We Can Be: African American Fraternal Groups and the Struggle for Racial Equality* (Princeton, NJ: Princeton University Press, 2006).

11. For analyses of the diversity of organizational forms and the heterogeneity of challenger roles across the entire environmental field, see Carmen Sirianni and Stephanie Sofer, "Environmental Organizations," in *The State of Nonprofit America*, ed. Lester M. Salamon, 2nd ed. (Washington, DC: Brookings Press, 2012), 294–328; Stephanie Bertels, Andrew J. Hoffman, and Rich DeJordy, "The Varied Work of Challenger Movements: Identifying the Challenger Roles in the U.S. Environmental Movement," *Organization Studies* 35 (2014): 1171–1210; and on conservation culture, see Angela C. Halfacre, *A Delicate Balance: Constructing a Conservation Culture in the South Carolina Low Country* (Columbia: University of South Carolina Press, 2012), qtd. on 3 ("rally, react, plan"). See also Kent E. Portney, *Taking Sustainable Cities Seriously: Economic Development, the Environment, and Quality of Life in American Cities*, 2nd ed. (Cambridge, MA: MIT Press, 2013); Kent E. Portney and Jeffrey M. Berry, "Participation and the Pursuit of Sustainability in U.S. Cities," *Urban Affairs Review* 46 (2010): 119–139; Kent E. Portney and Jeffrey M. Berry, "The Impact of Local Environmental Advocacy Groups on City Sustainability Policies and Programs," *Policy Studies Journal* 44 (2016): 196–214; Kent E. Portney and Zachary Cutler, "The Local Nonprofit Sector and the Pursuit of Sustainability in American Cities: A Preliminary Exploration," *Local Environment* 15 (2010): 323–339; Mark Lubell, Richard Feiock, and Susan Handy, "City Adoption of Environmentally Sustainable Policies in California's Central Valley," *Journal of the American Planning Association* 75 (2009): 293–308; Lenahan O'Connell, "The Impact of Local Supporters on Smart Growth Policy Adoption," *Journal of the American Planning Association* 75 (2009): 281–291; Jungah Bae and Richard Feiock, "Forms of Government and Climate Change Policy in US Cities," *Urban Studies* 50 (2013): 776–788; George C. Homsey and Mildred E. Warner, "Cities and Sustainability: Polycentric Action and Multilevel Governance," *Urban Affairs Review* 51 (2015): 46–73. On various local civic configurations, see Dana R. Fisher, Erika S. Svendsen, and James Connolly, *Urban Environmental Stewardship and Civic Engagement: How Planting Trees Strengthens the Roots of Democracy* (New

York: Routledge, 2015); Kenneth T. Andrews and Bob Edwards, "The Structure of Local Environmentalism," *Mobilization* 10 (2005): 213–234; Elizabeth A. Moore and Tomas M. Koontz, "A Typology of Collaborative Watershed Groups: Citizen-Based, Agency-Based, and Mixed Partnerships," *Society and Natural Resources* 16 (2003): 451–460; Phil Brown, Rachel Morello-Frosch, and Stephen Zavestoski, eds., *Contested Illnesses: Citizens, Science, and Health Social Movements* (Berkeley: University of California Press, 2011).

For related studies of local civic ecologies, civic efficacy, "blended" or "hybrid" civic and movement forms, see Robert J. Sampson, *Great American City: Chicago and the Enduring Neighborhood Effect* (Chicago, IL: University of Chicago Press, 2012); Robert J. Sampson, Doug McAdam, Heather MacIndoe, and Simón Weffer-Elizondo, "Civil Society Reconsidered: The Durable Nature and Community Structure of Collective Civic Action," *American Journal of Sociology* 111 (2005): 673–714; Doug McAdam, Robert J. Sampson, Simón Weffer-Elizondo, and Heather MacIndoe, "'There Will be Fighting in the Streets': The Distorting Lens of Social Movement Theory," *Mobilization* 10 (2005): 1–18.

Some scholars have developed large data sets to analyze the organizational ecology of the US environmental movement, sometimes linked to international groups along a global north/south axis. While these studies have led to valuable insights on patterns of organizational foundings, competition due to increased density, political opportunity, and cultural production (especially of books), they do not tend to be finely grained enough to grasp the challenges of strategic choice, democratic legitimation, and institutional capacity building within strategic action fields or local governance systems. See Jason T. Carmichael, J. Craig Jenkins, and Robert J. Brulle, "Building Environmentalism: The Founding of Environmental Movement Organizations in the United States, 1900–2000," *Sociological Quarterly* 53 (2012): 422–453; Erik W. Johnson and Scott Frickel, "Ecological Threat and the Founding of U.S. National Movement Environmental Organizations, 1962–1998," *Social Problems* 58 (2011): 305–329; Paul McLaughlin and Marwan Khawaja, "The Organizational Dynamics of the U.S. Environmental Movement: Legitimation, Resource Mobilization, and Political Opportunity," *Rural Sociology* 65 (2009): 422–439; Wesley Longhofer and Evan Schofer, "National and Global Origins of Environmental Association," *American Sociological Review* 75 (2010): 505–533.

12. Andrew Abbott, *The System of Professions: An Essay on the Division of Expert Labor* (Chicago, IL: University of Chicago Press, 1988); Eliot Freidson, *Professionalism, the Third Logic: On the Practice of Knowledge* (Chicago, IL: University of Chicago Press 2001); Magali Sarfatti Larson, *The Rise of Professionalism: Monopolies of Competence and Sheltered Markets* (New Brunswick, NJ: Transaction, 1979); Steven Brint, *In an Age of Experts* (Princeton, NJ: Princeton University Press, 1994). See also Mark E. Warren, *Democracy and Association* (Princeton, NJ: Princeton University Press, 2000).

13. Albert W. Dzur, *Democratic Professionalism: Citizen Participation and the Reconstruction of Professional Ethics, Identity, and Practice* (University Park: Pennsylvania State University Press, 2008); William M. Sullivan, *Work and Integrity: The Crisis and Promise of Professionalism in America* (San Francisco: Jossey-Bass, 1995); Jason Corburn, *Street Science: Community Knowledge and Environmental Health Justice* (Cambridge, MA: MIT Press, 2005); Michael Méndez, *Climate Change from the Streets: How Conflict and Collaboration Strengthen the Environmental Justice Movement* (New Haven, CT: Yale University Press, 2020); Barbara Eckstein and James A. Throgmorton, eds., *Story and Sustainability: Planning, Practice, and Possibility for American Cities* (Cambridge, MA: MIT Press, 2003); Caren Cooper, *Citizen Science: How Ordinary People Are Changing the Face of Discovery* (New York: Overlook Press, 2016); Janis L. Dickinson and Rick Bonney, *Citizen Science: Public Participation in Environmental Research* (Ithaca, NY: Comstock Publishing Associates, 2012). See also Frank Fischer, *Democracy and Expertise: Reorienting Policy Inquiry* (New York: Oxford University Press, 2009); Judith E. Innes and David E. Booher, *Planning with Complexity: An Introduction to Collaborative Rationality for Public Policy* (New York: Routledge, 2010); Raul Lejano, Mrill Ingram, and Helen Ingram, *The Power of Narrative in Environmental Networks* (Cambridge, MA: MIT Press, 2013).

14. Elizabeth A. Armstrong, *Forging Gay Identities: Organizing Sexuality in San Francisco, 1950–1994* (Chicago, IL: University of Chicago Press, 2002); Alison Isenberg, *Designing San Francisco: Art, Land, and Urban Renewal in the City by the Bay* (Princeton, NJ: Princeton University Press, 2017).

15. Suzanne Mettler and Joe Soss, "The Consequences of Public Policy for Democratic Citizenship: Bridging Policy Studies and Mass Politics," *Perspectives on Politics* 2 (2004): 55–73; Suzanne Mettler and Mallory SoRelle, "Policy Feedback Theory," in *Theories of the Policy Process*, ed. Christopher M. Weible and Paul A. Sabatier, 4th ed. (New York: Routledge, 2017), 103–134; Andrea Louise Campbell, "Policy Makes Mass Publics," *Annual Review of Political Science* 15 (2012): 333–351; Donald P. Moynihan and Joe Soss, "Policy Feedback and the Politics of Administration," *Public Administration Review* 74 (2014): 320–332. For the broad range of relevant factors, such as time, money, and civic skills, see Sidney Verba, Kay Lehman Schlozman, and Henry E. Brady, *Voice and Equality: Civic Voluntarism in American Politics* (Cambridge, MA: Harvard University Press, 1995).

16. Andrea Louise Campbell, *How Policies Make Citizens: Senior Political Activism and the American Welfare State* (Princeton, NJ: Princeton University Press, 2003).

17. Suzanne Mettler, *Soldiers to Citizens: The G.I. Bill and the Making of the Greatest Generation* (New York: Oxford University Press, 2005); Christopher S. Parker, *Fighting for Democracy: Black Veterans and the Struggle against White Supremacy in the Postwar South* (Princeton, NJ: Princeton University Press, 2009).

See also Kathleen J. Frydl, *The G.I. Bill* (New York: Cambridge University Press, 2009).

18. Joe Soss, "Lessons of Welfare: Policy Design, Political Learning, and Political Action," *American Political Science Review* 93 (1999): 363–380; Joe Soss, Richard C. Fording, and Sanford F. Schram, *Disciplining the Poor: Neoliberal Paternalism and the Persistent Power of Race* (Chicago, IL: University of Chicago Press, 2011); Sara K. Bruch, Myra Marx Ferree, and Joe Soss, "From Policy to Polity: Democracy, Paternalism, and the Incorporation of Disadvantaged Citizens," *American Sociological Review* 75 (2010): 205–226.

19. Elaine B. Sharp, *Does Local Government Matter? How Urban Policies Shape Civic Engagement* (Minneapolis: University of Minnesota Press, 2012), qtd. on 13.

20. Helen Ingram and Steven Rathgeb Smith, eds., *Public Policy for Democracy* (Washington, DC: Brookings Press, 1993); Anne Larason Schneider and Helen Ingram, *Policy Design for Democracy* (Lawrence: University Press of Kansas, 1997); Anne Schneider and Mara Sidney, "What Is Next for Policy Design and Social Construction Theory," *Policy Studies Journal* 37 (2009): 103–119; Martha S. Feldman, Anne M. Khademian, Helen Ingram, and Anne L. Schneider, "Ways of Knowing and Inclusive Management Practices," supplement, *Public Administration Review* 66 (2006): S89–S99; Martha S. Feldman and Anne M. Khademian, "The Role of the Public Manager in Inclusion: Creating Communities of Participation," *Governance: An International Journal of Policy, Administration, and Institutions* 20 (2007): 303–324. These studies link empirical research with normative democratic theory.

21. Archon Fung, Mary Graham, and David Weil, *Full Disclosure: The Perils and Promise of Transparency* (New York: Cambridge University Press, 2007); Shameek Konar and Mark Cohen, "Information as Regulation: The Effect of Community Right to Know Laws on Toxic Emissions," *Journal of Environmental Economics and Management* 32 (1997), 109–124; James Hamilton, "Pollution as News: Media and Stock Market Reactions to the Toxics Release Inventory Data," *Journal of Environmental Economics and Management* 28 (1995), 98–113; Michael Schudson, *The Rise of the Right to Know: Politics and the Culture of Transparency, 1945–1975* (Cambridge, MA: Harvard University Press, 2015). For a foundational statement on institutional isomorphism, see Paul J. DiMaggio and Walter W. Powell, "The Iron Cage Revisited: Institutional Isomorphism and Collective Rationality in Organizational Fields," *American Sociological Review* 48 (1983): 147–160.

For another policy feedback model in the environmental arena during the early decades after World War II, see James Morton Turner, *The Promise of Wilderness: American Environmental Politics since 1964* (Seattle: University of Washington Press, 2012). Turner analyzes how the Wilderness Act, with limited acreage of US Forest Service lands, established a public process for designating tens of millions more acres from other federal land agencies over a ten-year period. This included intermediate timetables and tools (maps, legal descriptions). These helped motivate and enable citizens and associations, such as the Sierra Club and the Wilderness Society, that had been especially active over the previous decade organize effectively around each potential new designation. The act was a policy compromise, to be sure, but had the largely unintended effect of linking opinion formation in the broad public sphere to place-based civic engagement, nationally coordinated trainings, and federal representative democracy for Congressional approval for each proposed area.

22. Ann Swidler, "Culture in Action: Symbols and Strategies," *American Sociological Review* 51 (1986): 273–286; Lester M. Salamon, ed., *The Tools of Government: A Guide to the New Governance* (New York: Oxford University Press, 2002); Thomas Dietz and Paul C. Stern, eds., *New Tools for Environmental Protection: Education, Information, and Voluntary Measures* (Washington, DC: National Academy Press, 2002); Daniel T. O'Brien, *The Urban Commons: How Data and Technology Can Rebuild Our Communities* (Cambridge, MA: Harvard University Press, 2018); Christopher K. Ansell, *Pragmatist Democracy: Evolutionary Learning as Public Philosophy* (New York: Oxford University Press, 2011); Xavier de Souza Briggs, *Democracy as Problem Solving: Civic Capacity in Communities Across the Globe* (Cambridge, MA: MIT Press, 2008); Meg Holden, *Pragmatic Justifications for the Sustainable City: Acting in the Common Place* (New York: Routledge, 2017); Ben Minteer, *The Landscape of Reform: Civic Pragmatism and Environmental Thought in America* (Cambridge, MA: MIT Press, 2006); Michael C. Dorf and Charles F. Sabel, "A Constitution of Democratic Experimentalism," *Columbia Law Review* 98 (1998). For a qualified assessment of democratic pragmatism, see John S. Dryzek, *The Politics of the Earth: Environmental Discourses* (New York: Oxford University Press, 2013), 99–121. For analyses of "repertoires of contention" in social movement theory, see Charles Tilly and Sidney Tarrow, *Contentious Politics*, 2nd ed. (New York: Oxford University Press, 2015).

23. Corburn, *Street Science*; Anne Taufen Wessels, "Ways of Knowing the Los Angeles River Watershed: Getting from Engaged Participation to Inclusive Deliberation," in *Varieties of Civic Innovation: Deliberative, Collaborative, Network, and Narrative Approaches*, ed. Jennifer Girouard and Carmen Sirianni (Nashville, TN: Vanderbilt University Press, 2014), 23–44; Sheila Jasanoff, "A New Climate for Society," *Theory, Culture & Society* 27 (2010): 233–253.

24. For an important general contribution, see Joseph Lampel and Alan D. Meyer, "Field-Configuring Events as Structuring Mechanisms: How Conferences, Ceremonies, and Trade Shows Constitute New Technologies, Industries, and Markets," *Journal of Management Studies* 45 (2008): 1025–1035.

25. Carmen Sirianni, "Neighborhood Planning as Collaborative Democratic Design: The Case of Seattle," *Journal of the American Planning Association* 73 (2007): 373–387.

26. Dennis Shirley, *Community Organizing for Urban School Reform* (Austin: University of Texas Press, 1997); Clarence N. Stone, Jeffrey R. Henig, Bryan D. Jones, and Carol Pierannunzi, *Building Civic Capacity: The Politics of Reforming Urban Schools* (Lawrence: University Press of Kansas, 2001); Archon Fung, *Empowered Participation: Reinventing Urban Democracy* (Princeton, NJ: Princeton University Press); Wesley G. Skogan, *Police and Community in Chicago: A Tale of Three Cities* (New York: Oxford University Press, 2006).

27. On relative underinvestment, see Carmen Sirianni, *Investing in Democracy: Engaging Citizens in Collaborative Governance* (Washington, DC: Brookings Press, 2009), 13–25; Chris Wells, *The Civic Organization and the Digital Citizen: Communicating Engagement in a Networked Age* (New York: Oxford University Press, 2015). On the problem of undersupply in collaborative governance networks, see Mark Schneider, John Scholz, Mark Lubell, Denisa Mindruta, and Matthew Edwardsen, "Building Consensual Institutions: Networks and the National Estuary Program," *American Journal of Political Science* 47 (2003): 143–158.

28. For discussion of some of these problems, see Sharp, *Does Local Government Matter?*; Campbell, *How Policies Make Citizens*, 138–145; Randy Shaw, *Generation Priced Out: Who Gets to Live in the New Urban America* (Berkeley: University of California Press, 2018); Kenneth A. Gould and Tammy L. Lewis, *Green Gentrification: Urban Sustainability and the Struggle for Environmental Justice* (New York: Routledge, 2016); Winifred Curran and Trina Hamilton, eds., *Just Green Enough: Urban Development and Environmental Gentrification* (New York: Routledge, 2017); Orrin H. Pilkey, Linda Pilkey-Jarvis, and Keith C. Pilkey, *Retreat from a Rising Sea: Hard Choices in an Age of Climate Change* (New York: Columbia University Press, 2016); Liz Koslov, "The Case for Retreat," *Public Culture* 28 (2016): 373–401; Mara S. Sidney, *Unfair Housing: How National Policy Shapes Community Action* (Lawrence: University Press of Kansas, 2003); Marc K. Landy, Marc J. Roberts, and Stephen R. Thomas, *The Environmental Protection Agency: Asking the Wrong Questions* (New York: Oxford University Press, 1990). On the relative challenges of participatory innovation to achieve justice and not just legitimacy and efficacy of governance, see Archon Fung, "Putting the Public Back into Governance: The Challenges of Citizen Participation and Its Future," *Public Administration Review* 75 (2015): 513–522.

29. Stephen Rathgeb Smith and Helen Ingram, "Policy Tools and Democracy," in *The Tools of Government*, 565–584, qtd. on 579.

30. Clarence N. Stone, "Urban Regimes and the Capacity to Govern: A Political Economy Approach," *Journal of Urban Affairs* 15 (1993): 1–28; "Reflections on Regime Politics: From Governing Coalition to Urban Political Order," *Urban Affairs Review* 51 (2015): 101–137; *Regime Politics: Governing Atlanta, 1946–1988* (Lawrence: University Press of Kansas, 1989); Marion Orr and Valerie C. Johnson, eds., *Power in the City: Clarence Stone and the Politics of Inequality* (Lawrence: Uni-

versity Press of Kansas, 2008); Stephen L. Elkin, *City and Regime in the American Republic* (Chicago, IL: University of Chicago Press, 1987).

31. Jonathan S. Davies and Jessica Trounstine, "Urban Politics and the New Institutionalism," in *The Oxford Handbook of Urban Politics*, ed. Karen Mossberger, Susan E. Clarke, and Peter John (New York: Oxford University Press, 2012), 51–70; Vivien Lowndes, "Rescuing Aunt Sally: Taking Institutional Theory Seriously in Urban Politics," *Urban Studies* 38 (2001): 1953–1971; Jon Pierre, *The Politics of Urban Governance* (New York: Palgrave Macmillan, 2011); David Kaufmann and Mara Sidney, "Toward an Urban Policy Analysis: Incorporating Participation, Multilevel Governance, and 'Seeing Like a City,'" *PS: Political Science & Politics* 53 (2020): 1–5, along with the accompanying symposium. For a helpful classification of nonprofit organizational roles, see Christof Brandtner and Claire Dunning, "Nonprofits as Urban Infrastructure," in *The Nonprofit Sector: A Research Handbook*, ed. Walter W. Powell and Patricia Bromley, 3rd ed. (Stanford, CA: Stanford University Press, 2020), 271–291.

32. Richard Schragger, *City Power: Urban Governance in a Global Age* (New York: Oxford University Press, 2016); Bruce Katz and Jeremy Nowak, *The New Localism: How Cities Can Thrive in the Age of Populism* (Washington, DC: Brookings Press, 2017); Sara Hughes, *Repowering Cities: Governing Climate Change Mitigation in New York City, Los Angeles, and Toronto* (Ithaca, NY: Cornell University Press, 2019); Gerald E. Frug and David J. Barron, *City Bound: How States Stifle Urban Innovation* (Ithaca, NY: Cornell University Press, 2008); Susan E. Clarke and Gary L. Gaile, *The Work of Cities* (Minneapolis: University of Minnesota Press, 1998); Richard Florida, *The New Urban Crisis: How Our Cities Are Increasing Inequality, Deepening Segregation, and Failing the Middle Class—and What We Can Do About It* (New York: Basic Books, 2017). On the historical and structural roots of urban political disadvantage in Congress and state legislatures, especially manifest in economic and political geography within winner-take-all districts, see Jonathan A. Rodden, *Why Cities Lose: The Deep Roots of the Urban-Rural Political Divide* (New York: Basic Books, 2019). On the nationalization of political behavior, reflected partly in the decline of state and local political engagement, see Daniel J. Hopkins, *The Increasingly United States: How and Why American Political Behavior Nationalized* (Chicago, IL: University of Chicago Press, 2018).

33. Stone, "Urban Regimes and the Capacity to Govern"; Clarence N. Stone, Robert P. Stoker, et al., *Urban Neighborhoods in a New Era: Revitalization Politics in the Post-Industrial City* (Chicago, IL: University of Chicago Press, 2015), especially ch. 9 and table 9.1, for an analysis of structural shifts since the early postwar challenges of redeveloping the urban core. See also Peter Dreier, John Mollenkopf, and Todd Swanstrom, *Place Matters: Metropolitics for the Twenty-First Century*, 3rd ed. (Lawrence: University Press of Kansas, 2014), 192–236; John H. Mollenkopf, "The Post-War Politics of Urban Development," *Politics and Society* 5 (1975): 247–

296; Harvey Molotch, "The City as Growth Machine: Toward a Political Economy of Place," *American Journal of Sociology* 82 (1976): 309–332; John R. Logan
and Harvey Molotch, *Urban Fortunes: The Political Economy of Place*, 20th anniversary ed. (Berkeley: University of California Press, 2007); Peter Hendee Brown,
How Real Estate Developers Think: Design, Profits, and Community (Philadelphia:
University of Pennsylvania Press, 2015). On the multiscalar dimensions of urban
growth machines, see Neil Brenner, *New Urban Spaces: Urban Theory and the Scale
Question* (New York: Oxford University Press, 2019). Urban governance must be
situated within the broader context of the city in US political development over
long periods of time. See especially Richardson Dilworth, ed., *The City in American Political Development* (New York: Routledge, 2009).

34. Kevin Fox Gotham and Miriam Greenberg, *Crisis Cities: Disaster and Redevelopment in New York and New Orleans* (New York: Oxford University Press,
2014); David W. Woods, *Democracy Deferred: Civic Leadership after 9/11* (New
York: Palgrave Macmillan, 2012); Kathleen Tierney, *The Social Roots of Risk: Producing Disasters, Promoting Resilience* (Palo Alto, CA: Stanford Business Books,
2014), 125–159; *Disasters: A Sociological Approach* (Cambridge, UK: Polity, 2019);
Francesca Polletta, "Just Talk: Public Deliberation after 9/11," *Journal of Public Deliberation* 4 (2008), art. 2; Peter F. Burns and Matthew O. Thomas, *Reforming New
Orleans: The Contentious Politics of Change in the Big Easy* (Ithaca, NY: Cornell
University Press, 2015), who examine reform avenues in a patronage city.

35. Rachel Weber, *From Boom to Bubble: How Finance Built the New Chicago*
(Chicago, IL: University of Chicago Press, 2015); Josh Pacewicz, "The City as a
Fiscal Derivative: Financialization, Growth Coalitions, and the Politics of Ear-
marking," *City and Community* 15 (2016): 264–288; Kevin Fox Gotham, "The Secondary Circuit of Capital Reconsidered: Globalization and the U.S. Real Estate
Sector," *American Journal of Sociology* 112 (2006): 231–275. For innovative forms of
local public finance, see Katz and Nowak, *New Localism*; Bruce Katz and Luise
Noring, "The Copenhagen City and Port Redevelopment Corporation: A Model
for Regenerating Cities" (Washington, DC: Brookings Institution, 2017); Dag
Detter and Stefan Fölster, *The Public Wealth of Cities: How to Unlock Hidden Assets
to Boost Growth and Prosperity* (Washington, DC: Brookings Press, 2017).

36. Jane Mansbridge, James Bohman, Simone Chambers, Thomas Christiano,
Archon Fung, John Parkinson, Dennis F. Thompson, and Mark E. Warren, "A
Systemic Approach to Deliberative Democracy," in *Deliberative Systems: Deliberative Democracy at the Large Scale*, ed. John Parkinson and Jane Mansbridge (New
York: Cambridge University Press, 2012), 1–26; Jane Mansbridge, "A Systemic Approach to Civic Action," in *Varieties of Civic Innovation*, 239–246; Archon Fung,
"Recipes for Public Spheres: Eight Institutional Design Choices and Their Consequences," *Journal of Political Philosophy* 11 (2003): 338–367. For a different way
of formulating broad discursive systems, see David Owen and Graham Smith,

"Two Types of Deliberative System" (paper presented at the 2013 American Political Science Association's Annual Meeting & Exhibition, Chicago, IL, August 29–September 1, 2013).

37. For some democratic concepts that might further complement systemic deliberation and enrich democratic institutionalism, see Harry C. Boyte, "Reframing Democracy: Governance, Civic Agency, and Politics," *Public Administration Review* 65 (2005): 536–546; Harry C. Boyte and Nancy N. Kari, *Building America: The Democratic Promise of Public Work* (Philadelphia, PA: Temple University Press, 1996); Fung, *Empowered Participation*, especially on accountable autonomy; Richard L. Wood, *Faith in Action: Religion, Race, and Democratic Organizing in America* (Chicago, IL: University of Chicago Press, 2002), especially on ethical democracy; Dzur, *Democratic Professionalism*; Corburn, *Street Science*. In a similar spirit is James G. March and Johan P. Olsen, *Democratic Governance* (New York: Free Press, 1995), whose "logics of appropriateness" in the construction of publics, forms of knowledge, and responsibilities and accountabilities rely upon a conception of governance through "cobwebs of connections in an ecology of communities" (177).

38. For an analysis of these contrasting approaches, see Robert J. Antonio and Brett Clark, "The Climate Change Divide in Social Theory," in *Climate Change and Society: Sociological Perspectives*, ed. Riley E. Dunlap and Robert J. Brulle (New York: Oxford University Press, 2015), 333–368.

39. John Bellamy Foster, Richard York, and Brett Clark, *The Ecological Rift: Capitalism's War on the Earth* (New York: Monthly Review Press, 2011), qtd. on 423 and 440; David Harvey, *Rebel Cities: From the Right to the City to the Urban Revolution* (London: Verso, 2012); Erik Swyngedouw, *Promises of the Political: Insurgent Cities in a Post-Political Environment* (Cambridge, MA: MIT Press, 2018), who argues that multistakeholder participatory forms within urban governance "succumb . . . to the 'tyranny of participation'" (137), yet, in selective and preferred urban rebellions, democratization is actually "the act of the few who become the material and metaphorical stand-in for the many; they stand for the dictatorship of the democratic—direct and egalitarian" (132). This type of thinking reflects the analytic incapacity of this approach to theorize democracy as broadly based and institutionally complex; the logic of capital reduces and degrades virtually all complex questions of civic and institutional engagement among citizens and diverse stakeholders. For some nuanced gradations on forms of urban democracy within this critical tradition, see Mark Purcell, *Recapturing Democracy: Neoliberalization and the Struggle for Alternative Urban Futures* (New York: Routledge, 2008).

For social movement and institutionalist analyses of the promise *and distinct limits* of such urban rebellions in Europe, see Carmen Sirianni, "Workers' Control in the Era of the First World War: A Comparative Analysis of the European Experience," *Theory and Society* 9 (1980): 29–88; "Councils and Parliaments: The

Problems of Dual Power and Democracy in Comparative Perspective," *Politics and Society* 12 (1983): 83–123. A fuller analysis and critique of the forms of urban action within this important body of work must remain beyond the scope of this study.

40. Caroline W. Lee, *Do-It-Yourself Democracy: The Rise of the Public Engagement Industry* (New York: Oxford University Press, 2015), qtd. on 26. See also Caroline W. Lee, Michael McQuarrie, and Edward T. Walker, "Rising Participation and Declining Democracy," in *Democratizing Inequalities: Dilemmas of the New Public Participation*, ed. Caroline W. Lee, Michael McQuarrie, and Edward T. Walker (New York: New York University Press, 2015), 3–22.

41. Davies and Trounstine, "Urban Politics and the New Institutionalism," qtd. on 61 ("strong path-dependent historical institutionalization"). For some European models, see Timothy Beatley, *Green Cities of Europe: Global Lessons on Green Urbanism*, 3rd ed. (Washington, DC: Island Press, 2012); Mark Luccarelli and Per Gunnar Røe, eds., *Green Oslo: Visions, Planning, and Discourse* (Burlington, VT: Ashgate, 2012); Jens Stissing Jensen, Matthew Cashmore, and Philipp Späth, eds., *The Politics of Urban Sustainability Transitions: Knowledge, Power and Governance* (New York: Routledge, 2019).

42. Susan S. Fainstein, *The Just City* (Ithaca, NY: Cornell University Press, 2010). For an analysis of core tensions and paradoxes of urbanism, see Robert A. Beauregard, *Cities in the Urban Age: A Dissent* (Chicago, IL: University of Chicago Press, 2018). See also Steven A. Moore, *Alternative Routes to the Sustainable City: Austin, Curitiba, and Frankfurt* (Lanham, MD: Lexington Books, 2007). For a potentially complementary approach to habitation as a critical handle for embedding more just and responsive market institutions, see Fred L. Block, *Capitalism: The Future of an Illusion* (Berkeley: University of California Press, 2018).

43. Many of the best models of social movement and independent community organizing likewise build in careful training, often by professional organizers, with a set of prescribed components to ensure refined leadership skills, relational work, collaborative opportunities, and democratic accountability. Faith-based community organizers, for instance, who utilize systematic one-on-one relational practices and "power-with" frames add considerable value to what congregations, local associations, or social movements might accomplish otherwise. These and other models are part of markets promoting and diffusing specific "brands" of organizing skills. See, for instance, Mark R. Warren, *Dry Bones Rattling: Community Building to Revitalize American Democracy* (Princeton, NJ: Princeton University Press, 2001); Wood, *Faith in Action*; Richard L. Wood and Brad R. Fulton, *A Shared Future: Faith-Based Organizing for Racial Equity and Ethical Democracy* (Chicago, IL: University of Chicago Press, 2015); Hahrie Han, *How Organizations Develop Activists: Civic Associations and Leadership in the 21st Century* (New York: Oxford University Press 2014); K. Sabeel Rahman and Hollie Russon Gilman,

Civic Power: Rebuilding American Democracy in an Era of Crisis (New York: Cambridge University Press, 2019).

44. Juliet B. Schor and Craig J. Thompson, eds., *Sustainable Lifestyles and the Quest for Plenitude* (New Haven, CT: Yale University Press, 2014); Gar Alperovitz, *America Beyond Capitalism: Reclaiming Our Wealth, Our Liberty, and Our Democracy*, 2nd ed. (Takoma Park, MD, and Boston, MA: Democracy Collaborative Press/ Dollars and Sense, 2011); James DeFilippis, *Unmaking Goliath: Community Control in the Face of Global Capital* (New York: Routledge, 2003); Thad Williamson, David Imbroscio, and Gar Alperovitz, *Making a Place for Community: Local Democracy in a Global Era* (New York: Routledge, 2002). On ecovillages and transition towns, see Frank Fischer, *Climate Crisis and the Democratic Prospect: Participatory Governance in Sustainable Communities* (New York: Oxford University Press, 2017).

45. Carmen Sirianni, "The Civics of a Green New Deal," *Public Administration Review*, Symposium: The Green New Deal: Pathways to a Low Carbon Economy, edited by Nives Dolsak and Aseem Prakash, July 2019; "The Civics of a Green New Deal: Toward Policy Deign for Community Empowerment and Public Participation in an Age of Climate Change" (working paper, Jonathan M. Tisch College of Civic Life, Tufts University, Medford, MA, May 2020), https://tischcollege.tufts .edu/research/civic-green-new-deal.

46. On democratic crises, see Benjamin I. Page and Martin Gilens, *Democracy in America? What Has Gone Wrong and What We Can Do About It* (Chicago, IL: University of Chicago Press, 2017); Steven Levitsky and Daniel Ziblatt, *How Democracies Die* (New York: Crown, 2018); Michael Tomasky, *If We Can Keep It: How the Republic Collapsed and How It Might Be Saved* (New York: Liveright, 2019).

Chapter 2. Urban Water and Air
in the Early Postwar Decades

1. Adam Rome, *The Bulldozer in the Countryside: Suburban Sprawl and the Rise of American Environmentalism* (New York: Cambridge University Press, 2001), qtd. on 7; Greg Hise and William Deverell, *Eden by Design: The 1930 Olmsted-Bartholomew Plan for the Los Angeles Region* (Berkeley: University of California Press, 2000); Jeffrey M. Hornstein, *A Nation of Realtors: A Cultural History of The Twentieth-Century American Middle Class* (Durham, NC: Duke University Press, 2005); Owen D. Gutfreund, *Twentieth-Century Sprawl: Highways and the Reshaping of the American Landscape* (New York: Oxford University Press, 2004); Michael R. Fein, *Paving the Way: New York Road Building and the American State, 1880–1956* (Lawrence: University Press of Kansas, 2008).

2. Paul W. Hirt, *A Conspiracy of Optimism: Management of the National Forests since World War Two* (Lincoln: University of Nebraska Press, 1994); Martin Nie, *The Governance of Western Public Lands: Mapping Its Present and Future* (Lawrence: University Press of Kansas, 2008).

3. Thomas J. Sugrue, *The Origins of the Urban Crisis: Race and Inequality in Postwar Detroit*, updated ed. (Princeton, NJ: Princeton University Press, 2014); Isabel Wilkerson, *The Warmth of Other Suns: The Epic Story of America's Great Migration* (New York: Vintage, 2010); Lizabeth Cohen, *A Consumers' Republic: The Politics of Mass Consumption in Postwar America* (New York: Vintage, 2003); Kenneth T. Jackson, *Crabgrass Frontier: The Suburbanization of the United States* (New York: Oxford University Press, 1985); Robert A. Beauregard, *When America Became Suburban* (Minneapolis: University of Minnesota Press, 2006).

4. J. Eric Oliver, *Democracy in Suburbia* (Princeton, NJ: Princeton University Press, 2001); Thad Williamson, *Sprawl, Justice, and Citizenship: The Civic Costs of the American Way of Life* (New York: Oxford University Press, 2010); Peter Dreier, John Mollenkopf, and Todd Swanstrom, *Place Matters: Metropolitics for the Twenty-First Century*, 3rd ed. (Lawrence: University Press of Kansas, 2014).

5. Mark Gottdiener, Claudia Collins, and David R. Dickens, *Las Vegas: The Social Production of an All-American City* (Malden, MA: Wiley-Blackwell, 1999); William Deverell and Greg Hise, eds., *Land of Sunshine: An Environmental History of Metropolitan Los Angeles* (Pittsburgh, PA: University of Pittsburgh Press, 2005); Philip Vander Meer, *Desert Visions and the Making of Phoenix, 1860–2009* (Albuquerque: University of New Mexico Press, 2010); Donald J. Pisani, *Water, Land, and Law in the West: The Limits of Public Policy* (Lawrence: University Press of Kansas, 1996).

6. Paul S. Sutter, *Driven Wild: How the Fight against Automobiles Launched the Modern Wilderness Movement* (Seattle: University of Washington Press, 2002); David Louter, *Windshield Wilderness: Cars, Roads, and Nature in Washington's National Parks* (Seattle: University of Washington Press, 2006); Samuel P. Hays, with Barbara D. Hays, *Beauty, Health, and Permanence: Environmental Politics in the United States, 1955–1985* (New York: Cambridge University Press, 1987).

7. Martin V. Melosi, *The Sanitary City: Environmental Services in Urban America from Colonial Times to the Present* (Baltimore, MD: Johns Hopkins University Press, 2000); *Precious Commodity: Providing Water for America's Cities* (Pittsburgh, PA: University of Pittsburgh Press, 2011); William McGucken, *Biodegradable: Detergents and the Environment* (College Station: Texas A&M University Press, 1991).

8. Jonathan H. Adler, "Fables of the Cuyahoga: Reconstructing a History of Environmental Protection," *Fordham Environmental Law Journal* 14 (2002): 89–146; David Stradling and Richard Stradling, *Where the River Burned: Carl Stokes and the Struggle to Save Cleveland* (Ithaca, NY: Cornell University Press, 2015); William McGucken, *Lake Erie Rehabilitated: Controlling Cultural Eutrophication 1960s–1990s* (Akron, OH: University of Akron Press, 2011).

9. Christopher C. Sellers, *Crabgrass Crucible: Suburban Nature and the Rise of Environmentalism in Twentieth-Century America* (Chapel Hill: University of North Carolina Press, 2012), qtd. on 122, 109, and 119; Rome, *Bulldozer in the Countryside*, 87–118; Robert D. Lifset, *Power on the Hudson: Storm King Mountain*

and the Emergence of Modern American Environmentalism (Pittsburgh, PA: University of Pittsburgh Press, 2014), 38.

10. Such alignment is stressed in the general analyses of multitiered associations in Theda Skocpol, *Diminished Democracy: From Membership to Management in American Civic Life* (Norman: University of Oklahoma Press, 2003); Theda Skocpol, Marshall Ganz, and Ariane Liazos, "A Nation of Organizers: The Institutional Origins of Civic Voluntarism in the United States," *American Political Science Review* 94 (2000): 527–546.

11. Karl Boyd Brooks, *Before Earth Day: The Origins of American Environmental Law, 1945–1970* (Lawrence: University Press of Kansas, 2009).

12. Thomas R. Huffman, *Protectors of the Land and Water: Environmentalism in Wisconsin, 1961–1968* (Chapel Hill: University of North Carolina Press, 1994).

13. Senator Willis A. Robertson, qtd. in Brooks, *Before Earth Day*, 26. See also Thomas B. Allen, *Guardian of the Wild: The Story of the National Wildlife Federation, 1936–1986* (Bloomington: Indiana University Press, 1987), 32–33.

14. Kenneth C. Davis and Walter Gelhorn, "Present at The Creation: Regulatory Reform Before 1946," *Administrative Law Review* 38 (1986): 511–533; Arthur Earle Bonfield, "The Federal APA and State Administrative Law," *Virginia Law Review* 12 (1986): 297–336; Adam M. Sowards, *The Environmental Justice: William O. Douglas and American Conservation* (Corvallis: Oregon State University Press, 2009). On the "massive, submerged, and surprisingly vibrant" administrative law that exists at the local level (including land use and environment), or the "administrative city-state," see Nestor M. Davidson, "Localist Administrative Law," *Yale Law Journal* 126 (2017): 564–634, qtd. on 569 and 570. For APA's place in broader developments to secure democratic legitimacy through reason giving, see also Jerry L. Mashaw, *Reasoned Administration and Democratic Legitimacy: How Administrative Law Supports Democratic Government* (New York: Cambridge University Press, 2018); Joanna L. Grisinger, *The Unwieldy American State: Administrative Politics Since the New Deal* (New York: Cambridge University Press, 2012), who sees little change in administrative practice due to APA. As Michael Schudson argues, however, APA "offered a charter for public access to government information" (58), helped generate a culture of "right to know," and was the specific law revised to accommodate the Freedom of Information Act in 1966. See Schudson, *The Rise of the Right to Know: Politics and the Culture of Transparency, 1945–1975* (Cambridge, MA: Harvard University Press, 2015).

15. Paul Charles Milazzo, *Unlikely Environmentalists: Congress and the Clean Water Act, 1945–1972* (Lawrence: University Press of Kansas, 2006); Richard J. Lazarus, *The Making of Environmental Law* (Chicago, IL: University of Chicago Press, 2004), 37–38; Jason Scott Smith, *Building New Deal Liberalism: The Political Economy of Public Works, 1933–1956* (New York: Cambridge University Press, 2006); Rufus E. Miles, *The Department of Health, Education, and Welfare* (New

York: Praeger, 1974); Fitzhugh Mullan, *Plagues and Politics: The Story of the United States Public Health Service* (New York: Basic Books, 1989). On Progressive-Era attempts to establish the legal basis for federal water pollution control, as well as to advance local and state approaches, see Kimberly K. Smith, *The Conservation Constitution: The Conservation Movement and Constitutional Change, 1870–1930* (Lawrence: University Press of Kansas, 2019), esp. ch. 8–9.

16. John F. Kennedy, "Special Message to the Congress on Natural Resources," February 23, 1961; Milazzo, *Unlikely Environmentalists*, 38–60; Sellers, *Crabgrass Crucible*, 105–136; Smith, *The Conservation Constitution*, 220–221, on the limited regulatory mandate of PHS, formally created in 1912.

17. Richard N. L. Andrews, *Managing the Environment, Managing Ourselves: A History of American Environmental Policy*, 2nd ed. (New Haven, CT: Yale University Press, 2006), 222. On the concept of political opportunity structure, see David S. Meyer and Debra C. Minkoff, "Conceptualizing Political Opportunity," *Social Forces* 82 (2004): 1457–1492, which includes interpretive components that help account for the ability to recognize and act upon opportunities.

18. Public Health Service (PHS), US Department of Health, Education, and Welfare, *Proceedings: The National Conference on Water Pollution; Washington D.C.; December 12–14, 1960* (Washington, DC: US Government Printing Office, 1960), 601. Although many women were often identified in the proceedings only by their husband's and married names, I have attempted to provide women's given names if available from other sources to avoid gendered language.

19. PHS, *Proceedings*, v–vi, 99–102, and 337–340. See also Joseph Lampel and Alan D. Meyer, "Field-Configuring Events as Structuring Mechanisms: How Conferences, Ceremonies, and Trade Shows Constitute New Technologies, Industries, and Markets," *Journal of Management Studies* 45 (2008): 1025–1035.

20. Katie Osbirn, PHS, *Proceedings*, qtd. on 99; Alvin B. Toffler, "Danger in Your Drinking Water," *Good Housekeeping*, no. 150, January 1960, 42–43 and 128–130; Louise M. Young, *In the Public Interest: The League of Women Voters, 1920–1970* (Westport, CT: Greenwood Press 1989), 175.

For one of the most compelling narrative templates for this kind of community work among women in the Progressive Era, lightly tinged with civic romance to ensure wide reading in club (and later league) circles, see Helen M. Winslow, *The President of Quex: A Woman's Club Story* (Boston, MA: Lothrop, Lee & Shepard, 1906); and with further civic and administrative emphasis, see Anna E. Nicholes, "How Women Can Help in the Administration of a City," in *Woman and the Larger Citizenship: City Housekeeping*, vol. 9 of *The Woman Citizen's Library*, ed. Shailer Mathews (Chicago, IL: The Civics Society, 1913), 2143–2208; Mary Ritter Beard, *Woman's Work in Municipalities* (New York: Appleton, 1915). On the history of municipal housekeeping, see Karen J. Blair, *The Clubwoman as Feminist: True Womanhood Redefined, 1868–1914* (New York: Holmes & Meier, 1980).

For important theorizations of pragmatic and democratic institutionalism, as well as styles of civic and institutional organizing among women's clubs, see Mary Parker Follett, *The New State: Group Organization the Solution of Popular Governance* (State College: Pennsylvania State Press, 1998/1918); Louise W. Knight, *Citizen: Jane Addams and the Struggle for Democracy* (Chicago, IL: University of Chicago Press, 2005); Joan K. Smith, *Ella Flagg Young: Portrait of a Leader* (DeKalb: Northern Illinois University Press, 1979). Young was the first female superintendent of a large urban school system (Chicago) and Addams the cofounder of Hull House. The work of both Addams and Young (his PhD student) had a profound influence on John Dewey while working out his democratic pragmatism at the University of Chicago.

21. Jane Freeman, qtd. in Terrianne K. Schulte, "Grassroots at the Water's Edge: The League of Women Voters and the Struggle to Save Lake Erie, 1956–1970" (PhD diss., State University of New York at Buffalo, 2006), 101–02. Freeman—a lawyer and activist in the Minnesota Democratic Farmer-Labor Party—was born Jane C. Shields and was married to Orville Freeman, governor of Minnesota (1955–1961) and later secretary of agriculture (1961–1969).

22. Patricia H. Thornton, William Ocasio, and Michael Lounsbury, *The Institutional Logics Perspective: A New Approach to Culture, Structure, and Process* (New York: Oxford University Press, 2012); Neil Fligstein and Doug McAdam, *A Theory of Fields* (New York: Oxford University Press, 2012).

23. League of Women Voters Education Fund (LWVEF), *The Big Water Fight: Trials and Triumphs in Citizen Action on Problems of Supply, Pollution, Floods, and Planning Across the U.S.A.* (Brattleboro, VT: Stephen Greene Press, 1966); Rome, *Bulldozer in the Countryside*, 87–118.

24. White House Conference on Natural Beauty, *Beauty for America: Proceedings of the White House Conference on Natural Beauty* (Washington, DC: US Government Printing Office, 1965). As a partner in a Clinton White House project on reinventing citizenship in the mid-1990s, Elizabeth Kraft, director of water resources at the League of Women Voters Educational Fund, first provided me insight into the league's civic styles. As she once noted with a wry smile, "We league ladies are always very polite."

25. Donald E. Carr, *Death of the Sweet Waters* (New York: Norton, 1966), qtd. on 12; Young, *In the Public Interest*, 176.

26. LWVEF, *Big Water Fight*, 126–206.

27. League of Women Voters (LWV), Lake Erie Basin Committee, *Lake Erie: Requiem or Reprieve?* (Cleveland, OH: League of Women Voters, 1966); McGucken, *Lake Erie Rehabilitated*, 55; Mark Neuzil, *The Environment and the Press: From Adventure Writing to Advocacy* (Evanston, IL: Northwestern University Press, 2008); Schulte, "Grassroots at the Water's Edge;" Stradling and Stradling, *Where the River Burned*; Dave Dempsey, *On the Brink: The Great Lakes in the 21st Century* (East Lansing: Michigan State University Press, 2004).

28. Wendy Read Wertz, *Lynton Keith Caldwell: An Environmental Visionary and the National Environmental Policy Act* (Bloomington: Indiana University Press, 2014); Scott H. Dewey, "Working for the Environment: Organized Labor and the Origins of Environmentalism in the United States, 1948–1970," *Environmental History* 3 (1998): 45–63; Andrew Hurley, *Environmental Inequalities: Class, Race, and Industrial Pollution in Gary, Indiana, 1945–1980* (Chapel Hill: University of North Carolina Press, 1995).

29. Author interview with Rebecca Hanmer, February 2, 2006; Christine Mueller, *Protect Your Groundwater: Educating for Action* (Washington, DC: League of Women Voters Education Fund, 1994); Adam Rome, *The Genius of Earth Day: How a 1970 Teach-In Unexpectedly Made the First Green Generation* (New York: Hill and Wang, 2013), 73; Robert Gottlieb, *Forcing the Spring: The Transformation of the American Environmental Movement* (Washington, DC: Island Press, 1993), 38–39.

30. LWVEF, *Big Water Fight*, 40–43 and 223–225; league flyer, reprinted in PHS, *Proceedings*, v–vi and 338. On cost sharing formulas, see Milazzo, *Unlikely Environmentalists*, 31–33.

31. Qtd. in John Joseph Gargan, "The Politics of Water Pollution in New York State: The Development and Adoption of the 1965 Pure Waters Program" (PhD diss., University of Syracuse, 1968), 421; Terence Kehoe, "'You Alone Have the Answer': Lake Erie and Federal Water Pollution Control Policy, 1960–1972," *Journal of Policy History* 8 (1996): 440–469; *Cleaning Up the Great Lakes: From Cooperation to Confrontation* (DeKalb: Northern Illinois University Press, 1997), 83.

32. Barry G. Rabe, *Fragmentation and Integration in State Environmental Management* (Washington, DC: Conservation Foundation, 1986); Huffman, *Protectors of the Land and Water*; Victoria S. Haskell and Elizabeth H. Price, *State Environmental Management: Case Studies of Nine States* (New York: Praeger, 1973).

33. David Zwick and Marcy Benstock, *Water Wasteland* (New York: Bantam, 1971), 431–437. The range of waters covered was extended in 1961 to all navigable waters.

34. Federal Water Pollution Control Administration (FWPCA), *Proceedings of the Conference in the Matter of Pollution of Lake Michigan and Its Tributary Basin, Chicago, January-March 1968* (Washington, DC: FWPCA, US Department of the Interior, 1968); Kehoe, *Cleaning Up the Great Lakes*, 51.

35. Zwick and Benstock, *Water Wasteland*, 431–437; Joel A. Mintz, *Enforcement at the EPA: High Stakes and Hard Choices*, rev. ed. (Austin: University of Texas Press, 2012), 22.

36. Caroline W. Lee, "Is There a Place for Private Conversation in Public Dialogue? Comparing Stakeholder Assessments of Informal Communication in Collaborative Regional Planning," *American Journal of Sociology* 113 (2007): 41–96; Francesca Polletta, "Just Talk: Public Deliberation after 9/11," *Journal of Public Deliberation* 4 (2008), art. 2.

37. Martin V. Melosi, "Lyndon Johnson and Environmental Policy," in *The Johnson Years*, vol. 2: *Vietnam, the Environment, and Science*, ed. Robert A. Devine (Lawrence: University Press of Kansas, 1987), 113–149; Henry B. Sirgo, "Water Policy Decision-Making and Implementation in the Johnson Administration," *Journal of Political Science* 12 (1985).

38. Milazzo, *Unlikely Environmentalists*.

39. Subcommittee on Air and Water Pollution of the Senate Committee on Public Works of the 88th Cong., 1st Sess., *Troubled Waters: 1964 Water Pollution Report of the U.S. Senate Committee on Public Works*, video documentary, Washington, 1964, https://www.youtube.com/watch?v=KXNMGYuznzU. On cultural narratives, see Francesca Polletta, *It Was Like a Fever: Storytelling in Protest and Politics* (Chicago, IL: University of Chicago Press, 2006). On ritual pollution, see Mary Douglas, *Purity and Danger: An Analysis of Concepts of Pollution and Taboo* (New York: Routledge, 1966).

40. Jürgen Habermas, *The Theory of Communicative Action*, vol. 2: *Lifeworld and System: A Critique of Functionalist Reason*, translated by Thomas McCarthy (Boston, MA: Beacon, 1985). On the Sierra Club's Wilderness River Trail, see Mark Harvey, *A Symbol of Wilderness: Echo Park and the American Conservation Movement* (Seattle: University of Washington Press, 1994).

41. Beatrice Hort Holmes, *History of Federal Water Resources Programs and Policies, 1961–1970*, misc. pub. no. 1379 (Washington, DC: US Department of Agriculture Economics, Statistics, and Cooperative Service, 1979), qtd. on 86 and 102; Edmund S. Muskie, "Citizens' Crusade for Clean Water," *Congressional Record*, July 7, 1969, 18424 (Lewiston, ME: Bates College Archives).

42. See especially Milazzo, *Unlikely Environmentalists*; Zwick and Benstock, *Water Wasteland*.

43. Albert E. Cowdry, "Pioneering Environmental Law: The Army Corps of Engineers and the Refuse Act," *Pacific Historical Review* 46 (1975): 331–349; Robert L. Potter, "Discharging Old Wine into New Wineskins: The Metamorphosis of the Rivers and Harbors Act of 1899," *University of Pittsburgh Law Review* 33 (1971/1972): 485–531.

44. Lifset, *Power on the Hudson*, 135 and 247; Holmes, *History of Federal Water Resources Programs and Policies*, 31–32.

45. Conservation Foundation, *Water Quality Training Institute Handbook* (Washington, DC: Conservation Foundation, 1974), qtd. on 1.

46. George A. Gonzalez, *The Politics of Air Pollution: Urban Growth, Ecological Modernization, and Symbolic Inclusion* (Albany: State University of New York Press, 2005); Devra Davis, *When Smoke Ran like Water: Tales of Environmental Deception and the Battle against Pollution* (New York: Basic Books, 2002); Scott H. Dewey, *Don't Breathe the Air: Air Pollution and U.S. Environmental Politics, 1945–1970* (College Station: Texas A&M University Press, 2000); Charles O. Jones,

Clean Air: The Policies and Politics of Pollution Control (Pittsburgh, PA: University of Pittsburgh Press, 1978); Chip Jacobs and William J. Kelly, *Smogtown: The Lung-Burning History of Pollution in Los Angeles* (Woodstock, NY: Overlook Press, 2008).

47. US Department of Health, Education, and Welfare (HEW), *National Conference on Air Pollution: Proceedings, November 18–20, 1958* (Washington, DC: US Department of Health, Education, and Welfare, 1959); HEW, *Proceedings* (Washington, DC, 1963); HEW, *Proceedings* (Washington, DC, 1966), 32–39, 435–438, and 439–441; Esther Peterson and Winifred Conkling, *Restless: The Memoirs of Labor and Consumer Activist Esther Peterson* (Caring Publications, 1997).

48. Helen Ingram, "The Political Rationality of Innovation: The Clean Air Act Amendments of 1970," in *Approaches to Controlling Air Pollution*, ed. Ann F. Friedlaender (Cambridge, MA: MIT Press, 1978), 12–56; David Vogel, "A Case Study of Clean Air Act Legislation, 1967–1981," in *The Impact of the Modern Corporation*, ed. Betty Bock (New York: Columbia University Press, 1984), 309–386; Milazzo, *Unlikely Environmentalists*, 153–160.

49. James Longhurst, *Citizen Environmentalists* (Medford, MA: Tufts University Press, 2010). See also Sherie R. Mershon and Joel Tarr, "Strategies for Clean Air: The Pittsburgh and Alleghany Smoke Control Movements, 1940–1960," in *Devastation and Renewal: An Environmental History of Pittsburgh and Its Region*, ed. Joel Tarr (Pittsburgh, PA: University of Pittsburgh Press, 2003), 145–173; Samuel P. Hays, "Beyond Celebration: Pittsburgh and Its Region in the Environmental Era—Notes by a Participant Observer," in Tarr, *Devastation and Renewal*, 193–215; Robert Martin and Lloyd Symington, "A Guide to the Air Quality Act of 1967," *Law and Contemporary Problems* 33 (1968): 239–274.

50. Hurley, *Environmental Inequalities*.

51. Longhurst, *Citizen Environmentalists*.

52. On this general concept, see Henri Lefebvre, *Writings on Cities*, ed. and trans. Eleonore Kofman and Elizabeth Lebas (Malden, MA: Wiley-Blackwell, 1996), pt. 2; Don Mitchell, *The Right to the City: Social Justice and the Fight for Public Space* (New York: Guilford Press, 2003); David Harvey, *Rebel Cities: From the Right to the City to the Urban Revolution* (London: Verso, 2012).

53. R. Shep Melnick, *Regulation and the Courts: The Case of the Clean Air Act* (Washington, DC: Brookings Press, 1983), 24–52.

54. Longhurst, *Citizen Environmentalists*, qtd. on 124. See also Thornton, Ocasio, and Lounsbury, *The Institutional Logics Perspective*; Paul Lichterman and Nina Eliasoph, "Civic Styles," *American Journal of Sociology* 120 (2014): 798–863; Huston & Williams LLC, *Clean Air Handbook*, 4th ed. (Lanham, MD: Bernan Press, 2014).

55. Lynton K. Caldwell, "Environment: A New Focus for Public Policy," *Public Administration Review* 23 (1963), 132–139; HEW, *A Strategy for a Livable Environ-*

ment: A Report to the Secretary of Health, Education, and Welfare by the Task Force on Environmental Health and Related Problems, June 1967 (Washington, DC: US Government Printing Office, 1967); Wertz, *Lynton Keith Caldwell*; Robert Kaufman, *Henry M. Jackson: A Life in Politics* (Seattle: University of Washington Press, 2000); Priscilla Coit Murphy, *What a Book Can Do: The Publication and Reception of "Silent Spring"* (Amherst: University of Massachusetts Press, 2007); Russell E. Train, *Politics, Pollution, and Pandas: An Environmental Memoir* (Washington, DC: Island Press, 2003); J. Brooks Flippen, *Nixon and the Environment* (Albuquerque: University of New Mexico Press, 2000); J. Brooks Flippen, *Conservative Conservationist: Russell E. Train and the Emergence of American Environmentalism* (Baton Rouge: Louisiana State University Press, 2006). Schudson, *The Rise of the Right to Know*, 180–227, provides a wonderfully complex account of the crafting of the bill through various stages and among differently situated congressional actors, as well as within the emerging "right to know" culture. However, he tends to underestimate how the activity of civic associations such as LWV and IWLA, as well as federal-enforcement conferences and public hearings across many locales, shaped the views of leading congressional sponsors.

56. A. Dan Tarlock, "The Story of *Calvert Cliffs:* A Court Construes the National Environmental Policy Act to Create a Powerful Cause for Action," in *Environmental Law Stories*, ed. Richard Lazarus and Oliver Houck (St. Paul, MN: Foundation Press, 2005), 77–107; Matthew J. Lindstrom and Zachary A. Smith, *The National Environmental Policy Act: Judicial Misconstruction, Legislative Indifference, and Executive Neglect* (College Station: Texas A&M University Press, 2001); Richard A. Liroff, *National Policy for the Environment: N.E.P.A. and Its Aftermath* (Bloomington: Indiana University Press, 1976); Hannah Cortner, "A Case Analysis of Policy Implementation: The National Environmental Policy Act of 1969," *Natural Resources Journal* 16 (1976): 323–338; Thomas Dietz and Paul C. Stern, eds., *New Tools for Environmental Protection: Education, Information, and Voluntary Measures* (Washington, DC: National Academy Press, 2002).

57. Lazarus, *Making of Environmental Law*, 85–87. On the views of environmental groups, see Michael McCloskey, *In the Thick of It: My Life in the Sierra Club* (Washington, DC: Island Press, 2005), 104; Wertz, *Lynton Keith Caldwell*, 168–169. See also Serge Taylor, *Making Bureaucracies Think: The Environmental Impact Statement Strategy of Administrative Reform* (Stanford, CA: Stanford University Press, 1984); Jane Mansbridge, James Bohman, Simone Chambers, Thomas Christiano, Archon Fung, John Parkinson, Dennis F. Thompson, and Mark E. Warren, "A Systemic Approach to Deliberative Democracy," in *Deliberative Systems: Deliberative Democracy at the Large Scale*, ed. John Parkinson and Jane Mansbridge (New York: Cambridge University Press, 2012), 1–26.

58. Forster O. Ndubisi, *Ecological Planning: A Historical and Comparative Synthesis* (Baltimore, MD: Johns Hopkins University Press, 2002); Robert B Keiter,

Keeping Faith with Nature: Ecosystems, Democracy, and America's Public Lands (New Haven, CT: Yale University Press, 2003); A. Clay Schoenfeld, "The Press and NEPA: The Case of the Missing Agenda," *Journalism Quarterly* 56 (1979): 577–585.

59. Council on Environmental Quality (CEQ), *Effective Use of Programmatic NEPA Reviews: Memorandum for Federal Departments and Agencies* (Washington: Executive Office of the President, December 18, 2014); Leonard Ortolano, "US Urban Environmental Planning," in *The Profession of City Planning: Changes, Images, and Challenges: 1950–2000*, ed. Lloyd Rodwin and Bishwapriya Sanyal (New Brunswick, NJ: Rutgers University Press, 2000), 144–160; Leonard Ortolano, *Environmental Regulation and Impact Assessment* (New York: Wiley, 1997); Catherine J. LaCroix, "SEPAs, Climate Change, and Corporate Responsibility: The Contribution of Local Government," *Case Western Reserve Law Review* 58 (2008): 1289–1321; Tom Daniels, *The Environmental Planning Handbook for Sustainable Communities and Regions*, 2nd ed. (Chicago, IL: APA Planners Press, 2014); Davidson, "Localist Administrative Law."

60. Lynton Keith Caldwell, *The National Environmental Policy Act: An Agenda for the Future* (Bloomington: Indiana University Press, 1999); Michael R. Greenberg, *The Environmental Impact Statement after Two Generations: Managing Environmental Power* (New York: Routledge, 2012); E. Ray Clark and Larry W. Canter, eds., *Environmental Policy and NEPA: Past, Present, and Future* (Boca Raton, FL: CRC Press, 1997).

61. Rome, *Genius of Earth Day*. See also Brian Balogh, *Chain Reaction: Expert Debate and Public Participation in American Commercial Nuclear Power, 1945–1975* (New York: Cambridge University Press, 1991); Thomas R. Wellock, *Critical Masses: Opposition to Nuclear Power in California, 1958–1978* (Madison: University of Wisconsin Press, 1998); John Wills, *Conservation Fallout: Nuclear Protest at Diablo Canyon* (Reno: University of Nevada Press, 2006).

62. Rome, *Genius of Earth Day*, 209–258; Robert Cox and Phaedra C. Pezzullo, *Environmental Communication and the Public Sphere*, 5th ed. (Los Angeles, CA: SAGE, 2018); Anders Hansen and Robert Cox, eds., *The Routledge Handbook of Environment and Communication* (New York: Routledge, 2015).

63. National Environmental Education Advisory Council, *Report Assessing Environmental Education in the United States and Implementation of the Environmental Education Act of 1990*, report prepared for Congress, (Washington, DC: US EPA, 1996); NAAEE, *Guidelines for Excellence: Community Engagement* (Washington, DC, 2017); Carmen Sirianni and Stephanie Sofer, "Environmental Organizations," in *The State of Nonprofit America*, ed. Lester M. Salamon, 2nd ed (Washington, DC: Brookings Press, 2012), 294–328; Robert B. Stevenson, Michael Brody, Justin Dillon, and Arjen E. J. Wals, eds., *International Handbook of Research on Environmental Education* (New York: Routledge, 2013). On identities in social movements, see David S. Meyer, Nancy Whittier, and Belinda Robnett,

eds., *Social Movements: Identity, Culture, and the State* (New York: Oxford University Press, 2002); Aidan McGarry and James Jasper, eds., *The Identity Dilemma: Social Movements and Collective Identity* (Philadelphia, PA: Temple University Press, 2015).

64. Fligstein and McAdam, *A Theory of Fields*, 92. See also Elizabeth A. Armstrong, "From Struggle to Settlement: The Crystallization of a Field of Lesbian/Gay Organizations in San Francisco, 1969–1973," in *Social Movements and Organization Theory*, ed. Gerald F. Davis, Doug McAdam, W. Richard Scott, and Mayer N. Zald (New York: Cambridge University Press, 2005), 161–187. Armstrong also highlights the rapid decline of the New Left at the end of the 1960s and very beginning of the 1970s as helping to account for field settlement, which likely played a parallel role for the environmental field as well. On countercultural environmental organizations, see Andrew G. Kirk, *Counterculture Green: The Whole Earth Catalog and American Environmentalism* (Lawrence: University Press of Kansas, 2007); Frank Zelko, *Make It a Green Peace! The Rise of Countercultural Environmentalism* (New York: Oxford University Press, 2013); Barbara Epstein, *Political Protest and Cultural Revolution: Nonviolent Direct Action in the 1970s and 1980s* (Berkeley: University of California Press, 1991).

65. Andrews, *Managing the Environment*, 227–254; Lazarus, *Making of Environmental Law*, 67–97; Daniel A. Mazmanian and Michael E. Kraft, "The Three Epochs of the Environmental Movement," in *Toward Sustainable Communities: Transition and Transformations in Environmental Policy*, ed. Daniel A. Mazmanian and Michael E. Kraft, 2nd ed. (Cambridge, MA: MIT Press, 2009), 3–32; Daniel J. Fiorino, *The New Environmental Regulation* (Cambridge, MA: MIT Press, 2006); Denise Scheberle, *Federalism and Environmental Policy: Trust and the Politics of Implementation*, rev. ed. (Washington, DC: Georgetown University Press, 2004).

66. Judith A. Layzer, *Open for Business: Conservatives' Opposition to Environmental Regulation* (Cambridge, MA: MIT Press, 2012), 31–81; John P. Dwyer, "The Pathology of Symbolic Legislation," *Ecology Law Quarterly* 17 (1990): 233–316; John W. Meyer, W. Richard Scott, Brian Rowan, and Terrence E. Deal, *Organizational Environments: Ritual and Rationality* (Thousand Oaks, CA: SAGE, 1985); Andrew J. Hoffman and Marc J. Ventresca, eds., *Organizations, Policy, and the Natural Environment: Institutional and Strategic Perspectives* (Stanford, CA: Stanford Business Books, 2002), intro.

67. Andrew J. Hoffman, *From Heresy to Dogma: An Institutional History of Corporate Environmentalism*, exp. ed. (Stanford, CA: Stanford University Press, 2002); Chris Laszlo and Nadya Zhexembayeva, *Embedded Sustainability: The Next Big Competitive Advantage* (Stanford, CA: Stanford University Press, 2011); Rebecca Henderson, Ranjay Gulati, and Michael Tushman, eds., *Leading Sustainable Change: An Organizational Perspective* (New York: Oxford University Press, 2015).

68. Andrews, *Managing the Environment*, 228–229; Richard A. Harris and Sid-

ney M. Milkis, *The Politics of Regulatory Change: A Tale of Two Agencies* (New York: Oxford University Press, 1989), 227–232; Alfred A. Marcus, "EPA's Organizational Structure," *Law and Contemporary Problems* 54 (1991): 5–40; Walter A. Rosenbaum, "Improving Environmental Regulation at the EPA: The Challenge of Balancing Politics, Policy, and Science," in *Environmental Policy: New Directions for the Twenty-First Century*, ed. Norman J. Vig and Michael E. Kraft (Washington, DC: CQ Press, 2006), 169–192; Robert McMahon, *The Environmental Protection Agency: Structuring Motivation in a Green Bureaucracy* (Brighton, UK: Sussex Academic Press, 2006).

69. William Ruckelshaus, "The Citizen and the Environmental Regulatory Process," *Indiana Law Journal* 47 (1971–1972): qtd. on 638; Patrick J. Dobel, "Managerial Leadership in Divided Times: William Ruckelshaus and the Paradoxes of Independence," *Administration and Society* 26 (1995): 488–514; Joel Mintz, *Enforcement at the EPA*, 21–40; John Quarles, *Cleaning Up America: An Insider's View of the Environmental Protection Agency* (Boston, MA: Houghton Mifflin, 1976); Train, *Politics, Pollution, and Pandas*.

70. Senator Edward Kennedy, Heller School forum and personal communication, Brandeis University, Waltham, MA, March 2005; Marc K. Landy, Marc J. Roberts, and Stephen R. Thomas, *The Environmental Protection Agency: Asking the Wrong Questions* (New York: Oxford University Press, 1990), qtd. on xii, 7, and 40–42; Marc K. Landy, "Public Policy and Citizenship," in *Public Policy for Democracy*, ed. Helen Ingram and Steven Rathgeb Smith (Washington, DC: Brookings Press, 1993), 19–44; Walter A. Rosenbaum, "The Paradoxes of Public Participation," *Administration and Society* 8 (1976): 355–83; "Slaying Beautiful Hypotheses with Ugly Facts: EPA and the Limits of Public Participation," *Journal of Voluntary Action Research* 6 (1978): 161–173; Walter A. Rosenbaum, "Public Involvement as Reform and Ritual: The Development of Federal Participation Programs," in *Citizen Participation in America*, ed. Stuart Langton (Lexington, MA: Lexington Books, 1978), 81–96; Richard J. Lazarus, "The Tragedy of Distrust in the Implementation of Federal Environmental Law," *Law and Contemporary Problems* 54 (1991): 311–374; Meg Jacobs, *Panic at the Pump: The Energy Crisis and the Transformation of American Politics in the 1970s* (New York: Hill and Wang, 2016).

71. Richard J. Lazarus, "The Neglected Question of Congressional Oversight of EPA: 'Quis Custodiet Ipsos Custodes' (Who Shall Watch the Watchers Themselves)?" *Law and Contemporary Problems* 54 (1991): 205–239; Melnick, *Regulation and the Courts*.

72. Malcolm F. Baldwin and James K. Page Jr., eds., *Law and the Environment* (New York: Conservation Foundation and Walker, 1970); Gordon Harrison and Stanford M. Jaffe, "Public Interest Law Firms: New Voices for New Constituencies," *American Bar Association Journal* 58 (1972): 459–467; Robert L. Graham, "Balancing the Scales of Justice: Financing Public Interest Law in America," *Loyola*

University Chicago Law Journal 8, no. 3: 1976; Senator George McGovern, "Introduction," in Joseph L. Sax, *Defending the Environment: A Strategy for Citizen Action* (New York: Knopf, 1971), qtd. on xii, italics added. See also Richard J. Lazarus, *The Making of Environmental Law*, 47–49; Joel F. Handler, Betsy Ginsberg, and Arthur Snow, "The Public Interest Law Industry," in *Public Interest Law: An Economic and Institutional Analysis*, ed. Burton Allen Weisbrod, with Joel F. Handler and Neil K. Komesar (Berkeley: University of California Press, 1978), 42–79; Loiuse G. Trubek, "Public Interest Law: Facing the Problems of Maturity," *University of Arkansas at Little Rock Law Review* 33 (2011): 417–433.

73. Jeffrey M. Berry, Kent E. Portney, and Ken Thomson, *The Rebirth of Urban Democracy* (Washington, DC: Brookings Press, 1993), 42–43; Gottlieb, *Forcing the Spring*, 143–148; Christopher J. Bosso, *Environment, Inc.: From Grassroots to Beltway* (Lawrence: University Press of Kansas, 2005), 80–81.

74. Marc K. Landy and Mary Hague, "The Coalition for Waste: Private Interests and Superfund," in *Environmental Politics: Public Costs, Private Rewards*, ed. Michael S. Greve and Fred L. Smith Jr. (New York: Praeger, 1992), 67–87, qtd. on 74; Barry G. Rabe, "Legislative Incapacity: Congressional Policymaking and the Case of Superfund," *Journal of Health, Politics, Policy, and Law* 15 (1990): 571–590; Allan Mazur, *A Hazardous Inquiry: The Rashomon Effect at Love Canal* (Cambridge, MA: Harvard University Press, 1998).

75. Fligstein and McAdam, *A Theory of Fields*, qtd. on 92; Robert Allen of the Kendall Foundation, qtd. in Gottlieb, *Forcing the Spring*, 120; Layzer, *Open for Business*; David Vogel, *Fluctuating Fortunes: The Political Power of Business in America* (New York: Basic Books, 1989); *Kindred Strangers: The Uneasy Relationship Between Politics and Business in America* (Princeton, NJ: Princeton University Press, 1996).

Chapter 3. Urban Land Conflicts and Professional Shifts

1. Raymond Mohl, "Stop the Road: Freeway Revolts in American Cities," *Journal of Urban History* 30 (2004): 674–706; Mark H. Rose and Raymond A. Mohl, *Interstate: Highway Politics and Policy Since 1939*, 3rd ed. (Knoxville: University of Tennessee Press, 2012); Tom Lewis, *Divided Highways: Building the Interstate Highways, Transforming American Life*, rev. ed. (Ithaca, NY: Cornell University Press, 2013); Adam Rome, *The Bulldozer in the Countryside: Suburban Sprawl and the Rise of American Environmentalism* (New York: Cambridge University Press, 2001).

2. William K. Reilly, *The Use of Land: A Citizens' Policy Guide to Urban Growth* (New York: Thomas Y. Crowell, 1973), qtd. on 10; Fred P. Bosselman and David Callies, *The Quiet Revolution in Land Use Control* (Washington, DC: White House Council on Environmental Quality, 1971); Fred P. Bosselman, David Callies, and

John Banta, *The Taking Issue: An Analysis of the Constitutional Limits of Land Use Control* (Washington, DC: White House Council on Environmental Quality, 1974); Robin W. Winks, *Laurance S. Rockefeller: Catalyst for Conservation* (Washington, DC: Island Press, 1997), 154–158; Alice O'Connor, "Community Action, Urban Reform, and the Fight against Poverty: The Ford Foundation's Gray Areas Program," *Journal of Urban History* 22 (1997): 586–625; Roger Biles, *The Fate of Cities: Urban America and the Federal Government, 1945–2000* (Lawrence: University Press of Kansas, 2011), 134.

3. For an earlier analysis, see Carmen Sirianni and Jennifer Girouard, "The Civics of Urban Planning," in *The Oxford Handbook of Urban Planning*, ed. Rachel Weber and Randall Crane (New York: Oxford University Press, 2012), 669–690.

4. For some classic analyses of these dynamics, see J. David Greenstone and Paul E. Peterson, *Race and Authority in Urban Politics: Community Participation and the War on Poverty* (Chicago, IL: University of Chicago Press, 1973); Peter Marris and Martin Rein, *Dilemmas of Social Reform: Poverty and Community Action in the United States*, 2nd ed. (Chicago, IL: University of Chicago Press, 1982).

5. Lawrence Brown and Bernard J. Frieden, "Rulemaking by Improvisation: Guidelines and Goals in the Model Cities Program," *Policy Sciences* 7 (1976): 455–488, qtd. on 470; Bernard J. Frieden and Marshall Kaplan, *The Politics of Neglect: Urban Aid from Model Cities to Revenue Sharing* (Cambridge, MA: MIT Press, 1975); Charles Haar, *Between the Idea and the Reality: A Study in the Origin, Fate, and Legacy of the Model Cities Program* (Boston, MA: Little, Brown, 1975). For recent studies of community action and its legacies, see Noel A. Cazenave, *Impossible Democracy: The Unlikely Success of the War on Poverty Community Action Programs* (Albany: State University of New York Press, 2007); Annelise Orleck and Lisa Hazirjian, eds., *The War on Poverty: A New Grassroots History, 1964–1980* (Athens: University of Georgia Press, 2011); Nancy Naples, *Grassroots Warriors: Activist Mothering, Community Work, and the War on Poverty* (New York: Routledge, 1998). On the emulative and isomorphic tendencies of Model Cities, see Carl Abbott, *Portland: Planning, Politics, and Growth in the Twentieth Century* (Lincoln: University of Nebraska Press, 1983).

6. Rose and Mohl, *Interstate*, 113–158; Lewis, *Divided Highways*, 179–210; Mandi Isaacs Jackson, *Model City Blues: Urban Space and Organized Resistance in New Haven* (Philadelphia, PA: Temple University Press, 2008); Jeffrey Craig Sanders, *Seattle and the Roots of Urban Sustainability: Inventing Ecotopia* (Pittsburgh, PA: University of Pittsburgh Press, 2010); Allan K. Sloan, *Citizen Participation in Transportation Planning: The Boston Experience* (Cambridge, MA: Ballinger, 1974).

7. Rose and Mohl, *Interstate*, 113–158; Lewis, *Divided Highways*, 179–210.

8. Desoto Jordan, Sherry R. Arnstein, Justin Gray, Ellen I. Metcalf, Wayne R. Torrey, and Florence W. Mills, *Effective Citizen Participation in Transportation Planning: Final Report*, 2 vols. (Washington, DC: US Department of Transporta-

tion, 1976); William M. Rohe and Lauren B. Gates, *Planning with Neighborhoods* (Chapel Hill: University of North Carolina Press, 1985).

9. National Commission on Neighborhoods, "People Building Neighborhoods: Final Report to the President and the Congress of the United States," Washington, 1979, 273–323; John H. Mollenkopf, *The Contested City* (Princeton, NJ: Princeton University Press, 1983); Ocean Howell, *Making the Mission: Planning and Ethnicity in San Francisco* (Chicago, IL: University of Chicago Press, 2015); Sudhir Venkatesh, "Chicago's Pragmatic Planners: American Sociology and the Myth of Community," *Social Science History* 25 (2001): 275–317; William M. Rohe, "From Global to Local: One Hundred Years of Neighborhood Planning," *Journal of the American Planning Association* 75 (2009): 209–230; Pierre Clavel, *The Progressive City: Planning and Participation, 1969–1984* (New Brunswick, NJ: Rutgers University Press, 1986); Carmine Scavo, "The Use of Participative Mechanisms in Large U.S. Cities," *Journal of Urban Affairs* 15 (1993): 93–109; John Clayton Thomas, *Between Citizen and City: Neighborhood Organizations and Urban Politics in Cincinnati* (Lawrence: University Press of Kansas, 1986).

10. Jeffrey M. Berry, Kent E. Portney, and Ken Thomson, *The Rebirth of Urban Democracy* (Washington, DC: Brookings Press, 1993); Ken Thomson, *From Neighborhood to Nation: The Democratic Foundations of Civil Society* (Medford, MA: Tufts University Press, 2001); Kent E. Portney and Jeffrey M. Berry, "Participation and the Pursuit of Sustainability in U.S. Cities," *Urban Affairs Review* 46 (2010): 119–139.

11. For a theoretical analysis and classification, see Joel A. C. Baum, "Organizational Ecology," in *Handbook of Organization Studies*, ed. Stewart R. Clegg, Cynthia Hardy, and Walter R. Nord (Thousand Oaks, CA: SAGE, 1996), 77–114. On Seattle, see Carmen Sirianni, "Neighborhood Planning as Collaborative Democratic Design: The Case of Seattle," *Journal of the American Planning Association* 73 (2007): 373–387.

12. Ronald F. Ferguson and Sara E. Stoutland, "Reconceiving the Community Development Field," in *Urban Problems and Community Development*, ed. Ronald E. Ferguson and William T. Dickens (Washington, DC: Brookings Press, 1999), 33–75; David J. Erickson, *The Housing Policy Revolution: Networks and Neighborhoods* (Washington, DC: Urban Institute Press, 2009); Alex F. Schwartz, *Housing Policy in the United States*, 3rd ed. (New York: Routledge, 2014); Avis C. Vidal, "Housing and Community Development," in *The State of Nonprofit America*, ed. Lester M. Salamon, 2nd ed. (Washington, DC: Brookings Press, 2012), 266–293; Michael Frisch and Lisa J. Servon, "CDCs and the Changing Context of Urban Community Development: A Review of the Field and the Environment," *Journal of the Community Development Society* 37 (2006): 88–108. For recent city initiatives, see LISC Boston, *Nine Steps Towards Green: Introducing Sustainability to Affordable Housing on a Limited Budget* (Boston, MA: LISC Green Development

Center, 2010); City of Chicago, *Green Healthy Neighborhoods* (Chicago, IL: Department of Planning and Development, 2014).

13. Vidal, "Housing and Community Development"; Julia Ann Parzen and Michal Hall Kieschnick, *Credit Where It's Due: Development Banking for Communities* (Philadelphia, PA: Temple University Press, 1992).

14. Margaret Weir, "Power, Money, and Politics in Community Development," in *Urban Problems and Community Development*, 139–192; Ross Gittell and Avis Vidal, *Community Organizing: Building Social Capital as a Development Strategy* (Thousand Oaks, CA: SAGE, 1998); Randy Stoecker, "Understanding the Development-Organizing Dialectic," *Journal of Urban Affairs* 25 (2003): 493–512; Nicole P. Marwell, *Bargaining for Brooklyn: Community Organizations in the Entrepreneurial City* (Chicago, IL: University of Chicago Press, 2007); Michael McQuarrie, "No Contest: Participation Technologies and the Transformation of Urban Authority," in *Democratizing Inequalities: Dilemmas of the New Public Participation*, ed. Caroline W. Lee, Michael McQuarrie, and Edward T. Walker, (New York: New York University Press, 2015), 83–101; Isabelle Anguelovski, *Neighborhood as Refuge: Community Reconstruction, Place Remaking, and Environmental Justice in the City* (Cambridge, MA: MIT Press, 2014); William A. Shutkin, *The Land That Could Be: Environmentalism and Democracy in the Twenty-First Century* (Cambridge, MA: MIT Press, 2000); Jason Corburn, *Toward the Healthy City: People, Places, and the Politics of Urban Planning* (Cambridge, MA: MIT Press, 2009).

15. William Scott Swearingen Jr., *Environmental City: People, Place, Politics, and the Meaning of Modern Austin* (Austin: University of Texas Press, 2010), 35–70; Josh Protas, "The Straw That Broke the Camel's Back: Preservation of an Urban Mountain Landscape," *Journal of the Southwest* 43 (2001): 379–421; Richard A. Walker, *The Country in the City: The Greening of the San Francisco Bay Area* (Seattle: University of Washington Press, 2007); Kay Franklin and Norma Schaeffer, *Duel for the Dunes: Land Use Conflict on the Shores of Lake Michigan* (Urbana: University of Illinois Press, 1983); J. Ronald Engel, *Sacred Sands: The Struggle for Community in the Indiana Dunes* (Middletown, CT: Wesleyan University Press, 1986); Rutherford H. Platt, *Reclaiming American Cities: The Struggle for People, Place, and Nature since 1900* (Amherst: University of Massachusetts Press, 2014); Daniel Press, *Saving Open Space: The Politics of Local Preservation in California* (Berkeley: University of California Press, 2002), 32–58; Richard Brewer, *Conservancy: The Land Trust Movement in America* (Lebanon, NH: Dartmouth University Press, 2003); Rome, *The Bulldozer in the Countryside*.

16. Joseph James Shomon, *Open Land for Urban America: Acquisition, Safekeeping, and Use* (Baltimore, MD: Johns Hopkins University Press / National Audubon Society, 1971); Rutherford H. Platt, *Open Land in Urban Illinois: Roles of the Citizen Advocate* (DeKalb: Northern Illinois University Press, 1971); Bernice Ben-

edict Popelka, *Saving Peacock Prairie: The Grassroots Campaign to Protect a Wild Urban Prairie* (Thiensville, WI: Caritas Communications, 2011).

17. Frank J. Popper, *Politics of Land Use Reform* (Madison: University of Wisconsin Press, 1981); Bosselman and Callies, *Quiet Revolution in Land Use Control*.

18. Noreen Lyday, *The Law of the Land: Debating National Land Use Legislation, 1970–1975* (Washington, DC: Urban Institute, 1976); Rome, *Bulldozer in the Countryside*.

19. Margaret Weir, "Planning, Environmentalism, and Urban Poverty: The Political Failure of National Land Use Planning Legislation, 1970–1975," in *The American Planning Tradition: Culture and Policy*, ed. Robert Fishman (Washington, DC: Woodrow Wilson Center Press, 2000), 193–215; Natural Resources Defense Council (NRDC), *Land Use Controls in the United States: A Handbook on the Legal Rights of Citizens* (New York: Dial Press / James Wade, 1977); Michael J. Rich, *Federal Policymaking and the Poor: National Goals, Local Choices, and Distributional Outcomes* (Princeton, NJ: Princeton University Press, 1993); Alan A. Altschuler, *Community Control: The Black Demand for Participation in Large American Cities* (New York: Pegasus, 1970).

20. J. William Futrell, "'Love for the Land and Justice for Its People': Sierra Club National and Southern Leader, 1968–1982," interview conducted by Ann Lage, in *Sierra Club Leaders II, 1960s–1970s*, Regional Oral History Office, Bancroft Library, University of California, Berkeley; Sim Van der Ryn and Peter Calthorpe, *Sustainable Communities: A New Design Synthesis for Cities, Suburbs and Towns* (San Francisco: Sierra Club Books, 1986); William H. Whyte, *The Social Life of Small Urban Spaces* (New York: Project for Public Spaces, 1980/2001); Mark Roseland, *Toward Sustainable Communities: Solutions for Citizens and Their Governments*, 4th ed. (Gabriola Island, BC: New Society Publishers, 2012), qtd. on 39 and 24.

21. Frank J. Popper, "Understanding American Land Use Regulation since 1970: A Revisionist Interpretation," *Journal of the American Planning Association* 54 (1988): 291–301, qtd. on 293; Robert G. Healy and John S. Rosenberg, *Land Use and the States*, 2nd ed. (Baltimore, MD: RFF Press, 1979); David L. Callies, "The Quiet Revolution Revisited: A Quarter Century of Progress," *The Urban Lawyer* 26 (1994): 197–213; John M. DeGrove, *Land, Growth and Politics* (Washington, DC: Planners Press, 1984); *Planning Policy and Politics* (Cambridge, MA: Lincoln Institute of Land Policy, 2005).

22. Nestor M. Davidson, "Localist Administrative Law," *Yale Law Journal* 126 (2017): 564–634; Stephen R. Miller, "Legal Neighborhoods," *Harvard Environmental Law Review* 37 (2013): 105–166; John Nolon, "In Praise of Parochialism: The Advent of Local Environmental Law," *Harvard Environmental Law Review* 26 (2002): 365–416; *Protecting the Local Environment through Land Use Law: Standing Ground* (Washington, DC: Environmental Law Institute, 2014); Leonard Orto-

lano, "U.S. Urban Environmental Planning," in *The Profession of City Planning: Changes, Images, and Challenges: 1950–2000*, ed. Lloyd Rodwin and Bishwapriya Sanyal (New Brunswick, NJ: Rutgers University Press, 2000), 144–160; Robert C. Ellickson, Vicki L. Been, Roderick M. Hills, and Christopher Serkin, *Land Use Controls: Cases and Materials*, 4th ed. (Frederick, MD: Wolters Kluwer Law & Business, 2013); John Nolon and Patricia Salkin, *Land Use in a Nutshell* (St. Paul, MN: West Academic Publishing, 2006). For explicit attention to sustainable development and climate change, see John Nolon and Patricia Salkin, *Climate Change and Sustainable Development Law in a Nutshell* (St. Paul, MN: West Academic Publishing, 2010); John Nolon and Patricia E. Salkin, *Land Use and Sustainable Development Law: Cases and Materials*, 8th ed. (St. Paul, MN: West Academic Publishing, 2012).

23. Royston Greenwood, Roy Suddaby, and C. R. Hinings, "Theorizing Change: The Role of Professional Associations in the Transformation of Institutionalized Fields," *Academy of Management Journal* 45 (2002): 58–80.

24. Albert W. Dzur, *Democratic Professionalism: Citizen Participation and the Reconstruction of Professional Ethics, Identity, and Practice* (University Park: Pennsylvania State University Press, 2008); William M. Sullivan, *Work and Integrity: The Crisis and Promise of Professionalism in America* (San Francisco: Jossey-Bass, 1995).

25. Urban Design Associates, *The Urban Design Handbook: Techniques and Working Methods*, 2nd ed. (New York: Norton, 2013), qtd. on 10; Urban Design Associates, *UDA @ 50*, (Pittsburgh, PA: UDA, 2015), qtd. on 2, https://issuu.com/urbandesignassociates/docs/p1931viewbook_issuu; Bill Lennertz and Aarin Lutzenhiser, *The Charrette Handbook: The Essential Guide to Design-Based Public Involvement*, 2nd ed. (Chicago, IL: APA Planners Press, 2014), 15–24. For a broader range of methods, see Tina Nabatchi and Matt Leighninger, *Public Participation for 21st Century Democracy* (Hoboken, NJ: Jossey-Bass, 2015), 155–194; Mary R. English, Jean H. Peretz, and Melissa J. Manderschied, "Building Communities while Building Plans: A Review of Techniques for Participatory Planning Processes," *Public Administration Quarterly* 28 (2004): 182–221; Lawrence E. Susskind, Sarah McKearnen, and Jennifer Thomas-Larmer, eds., *The Consensus Building Handbook: A Comprehensive Guide to Reaching Agreement* (Thousand Oaks, CA: SAGE, 1999).

26. Peter Batchelor and David Lewis, eds., *Urban Design in Action: The History, Theory and Development of the American Institute of Architects' Regional/Urban Design Assistance Teams Program* (Raleigh: American Institute of Architects and the Student Publication of the School of Design, North Carolina State University, 1986), qtd. on 70. See also American Institute of Architects (AIA), *Local Leaders: Healthier Communities through Design* (Washington, DC: AIA, 2012).

27. Author interview with Joel Mills, senior director of the Center for Community Design, American Institute of Architects, May 7, 2018.

28. Batchelor and Lewis, *Urban Design in Action*, qtd. on 22, 12, 97, and 13.

29. Batchelor and Lewis, *Urban Design in Action*, qtd. on 18 and 132–133. See also American Institute of Architects, *R/UDAT: Planning Your Community's Future: A Guide to the Regional/Urban Design Assistance Team Program* (Washington, DC: American Institute of Architects, 2004); *Citizen Architect Handbook*, 2nd ed. (Washington, DC: American Institute of Architects, Center for Civic Leadership, 2018); Linda C. Reeder, ed., *The Architect's Handbook of Professional Practice*, 15th ed. (Hoboken, NJ: Wiley, 2013); *Last Place in the Downtown Plan: R/UDAT Report on Portland, OR* (Washington, DC: American Institute of Architects, 1983); *Downtown Austin* (Washington, DC: American Institute of Architects, 1991); President's Council on Sustainable Development, *Sustainable America: A New Consensus for Prosperity, Opportunity, and a Healthy Environment for the Future* (Washington, DC: President's Council on Sustainable Development, 1996), 97, https://clinton whitehouse2.archives.gov/PCSD/Publications/TF_Reports/amer-top.html.

30. AIA, *Local Leaders*.

31. Interview with Erin Simmons, director of the Center for Community Design, American Institute of Architects, November 13, 2016; AIA Communities by Design, *The Rockaways R/UDAT: Bay to Beach* (AIA, 2013), 93–111, https://www .brikbase.org/sites/default/files/dat_aiab099137_therockaways_2013_reduced. pdf. See also Eric W. Sanderson, William D. Solecki, John R. Waldman, and Adam S. Parris, eds., *Prospects for Resilience: Insights from New York City's Jamaica Bay* (Washington, DC: Island Press, 2016). The challenge of governance is compounded by the twenty-five or so federal, state, and local agencies that have jurisdictional responsibilities in the Jamaica Bay watershed, making collaboration essential. The Science and Resilience Institute at Jamaica Bay, composed of a wide array of academic and other institutions, was established in 2013 to facilitate research and engage community and government stakeholders.

32. Philip R. Berke, "The Evolution of Green Community Planning, Scholarship, and Practice: An Introduction to the Special Issue," *Journal of the American Planning Association* 74 (2008): 393–407; Ian L. McHarg, *Design with Nature* (Garden City, NY: Natural History Press, 1969); Forster O. Ndubisi, *Ecological Planning: A Historical and Comparative Synthesis* (Baltimore, MD: Johns Hopkins University Press, 2002); Anne Whiston Spirn, *The Granite Garden: Urban Nature and Human Design* (New York: Basic Books, 1984); Douglas Farr, *Sustainable Urbanism: Urban Design with Nature* (Hoboken, NJ: Wiley, 2007); Frederick R. Steiner, *An Ecological Approach to Landscape Planning*, 2nd ed. (Washington, DC: Island Press, 2008); George F. Thompson and Frederick R. Steiner, eds., *Ecological Design and Planning* (New York: Wiley, 1997); Bart R. Johnson and Kristina Hill, eds., *Ecology and Design: Frameworks for Learning* (Washington, DC: Island Press, 2001); William J. Cohen, *Ecohumanism and the Ecological Culture: The Educational Legacy of Lewis Mumford and Ian McHarg* (Philadelphia, PA: Temple University

Press, 2019). See also Robert Fishman, *Urban Utopias in the Twentieth Century: Ebenezer Howard, Frank Lloyd Wright, and Le Corbusier* (New York: Basic Books, 1977).

33. Jane Jacobs, *The Death and Life of Great American Cities* (New York: Random House, 1961); Lewis Mumford, *The City in History: Its Origins, Its Transformations, and Its Prospects* (New York: Harcourt, Brace & World, 1961); Martin Needleman and Carolyn E. Needleman, *Guerrillas in the Bureaucracy: Community Planning Experiment in the United States* (New York: Wiley, 1974). On participatory democracy in 1960s movement organizations as strategic, expressive, and civic republican, see Francesca Polletta, *Freedom Is an Endless Meeting: Democracy in American Social Movements* (Chicago, IL: University of Chicago Press, 2002); James Miller, *Democracy Is in the Streets: From Port Huron to the Siege of Chicago* (New York: Simon & Schuster, 1988).

34. Herbert J. Gans, "City Planning in America: A Sociological Analysis," in *People and Plans: Essays on Urban Problems and Solutions*, ed. Herbert J. Gans, (New York: Basic Books, 1968), qtd. on ix; *The Urban Villagers: Group and Class in the Life of Italian Americans*, upd. and ex. ed. (New York: Free Press, 1982); Paul Davidoff, "Advocacy and Pluralism in Planning," *Journal of the American Institute of Planners* 31 (1965): 596–615; David E. Booher, *Citizen Participation in Planning: Selected Interdisciplinary Bibliography* (Monticello, IL: Council of Planning Librarians, 1975); Norman Krumholz and Pierre Clavel, *Reinventing Cities: Equity Planners Tell Their Stories* (Philadelphia, PA: Temple University Press, 1994); June Manning Thomas, "Social Justice as Responsible Practice: Influence of Race, Ethnicity, and the Civil Rights Era," in *Planning Ideas That Matter: Livability, Territoriality, Governance, and Reflective Practice*, ed. Bishwapriya Sanyal, Lawrence J. Vale, and Christina D. Rosan, (Cambridge, MA: MIT Press, 2012), 359–385.

35. David R. Godschalk, ed., *Planning in America: Learning from Turbulence* (Washington, DC: American Institute of Planners, 1974); Philip R. Berke, David R. Godschalk, and Edward J. Kaiser, with Daniel A. Rodriquez, *Urban Land Use Planning*, 5th ed. (Urbana: University of Illinois Press, 2006); Richard Klosterman, "Planning Theory Education: A Thirty-Year Review," *Journal of Planning Education and Research* 31 (2011): 319–331; John Randolph, *Environmental Land Use Planning and Management*, 2nd ed. (Washington, DC: Island Press, 2011); Betsy Otto, Kathleen McCormick, and Michael Leccese, *Ecological Riverfront Design: Restoring Rivers, Connecting Communities* (Chicago, IL: APA Planning Advisory Service, 2004); International City/County Management Association and National League of Cities, *Leading Your Community: A Guide for Local Elected Leaders* (Washington, DC: ICMA and NLC, 2008), https://icma.org/sites/default/files/-E-43546_Leading_Your_Community_1.pdf.

36. Author interview with John Forester, May 29, 2018. See John Forester, *Planning in the Face of Power* (Berkeley: University of California Press, 1989); *The Delib-*

erative Practitioner: Encouraging Participatory Planning Processes (Cambridge, MA: MIT Press, 1999); *Dealing with Differences: Dramas of Mediating Public Disputes* (New York: Oxford University Press; 2009); John Forester, "On the Evolution of a Critical Pragmatism," in *Encounters in Planning Thought: 16 Autobiographical Essays from Key Thinkers in Spatial Planning,* ed. Beatrix Haselsberger, (New York: Routledge, 2017), 297–314; Judith E. Innes, "Planning Theory's Emerging Paradigm: Communicative Action and Interactive Practice," *Journal of Planning Education and Research* 14 (1995): 183–189; Judith E. Innes and David E. Booher, *Planning with Complexity: An Introduction to Collaborative Rationality for Public Policy* (New York: Routledge, 2010); Patsy Healey, "Communicative Planning," in *Planning Ideas That Matter,* 333–357; Patsy Healey, *Collaborative Planning: Shaping Places in Fragmented Societies,* 2nd ed. (New York: Palgrave Macmillan, 2006); Barbara Eckstein and James A. Throgmorton, eds., *Story and Sustainability: Planning, Practice, and Possibility for American Cities* (Cambridge, MA: MIT Press, 2003).

37. Author interview with Philip Berke, director of the Institute of Sustainable Communities at Texas A&M University, June 15, 2018. See David R. Godschalk and David Rouse, *Sustaining Places: Best Practices for Comprehensive Plans* (Chicago, IL: APA Planners Press, 2015), qtd. on 7; David R. Godschalk and William R. Anderson, *Sustaining Places: The Role of the Comprehensive Plan* (Chicago, IL: APA Planning Advisory Service, 2012); Philip R. Berke, "Commentary: Twenty Years After Campbell's Vision: Have We Achieved More Sustainable Cities?" *Journal of the American Planning Association* 82 (2016): 380–383; T. J. Kent Jr., *The Urban General Plan* (Chicago, IL: American Planning Association, 1990).

38. Author interview with Ryan Scherzinger, coordinator of the Community Planning Assistance Teams, American Planning Association, May 23, 2018. See Michael Bayer, Nancy Frank, and Jason Valerius, *Becoming an Urban Planner: A Guide to Careers in Planning and Urban Design* (Hoboken, NJ: Wiley, 2010); American Planning Association (APA), with Frederick R. Steiner and Kent Butler, *Planning and Urban Design Standards* (Hoboken, NJ: Wiley, 2006); Christopher J. Duerksen, C. Gregory Dale, and Donald L. Elliott, *The Citizen's Guide to Planning,* 4th ed. (New York: Routledge, 2009), which is part of an APA citizens planning series as well as a network of citizen planning academies and institutes.

39. Daniel T. O'Brien, *The Urban Commons: How Data and Technology Can Rebuild Our Communities* (Cambridge, MA: Harvard University Press, 2018). On civic innovation and participatory planning as indispensable drivers of urban data innovation in the face of power asymmetries embedded in other innovation logics, see Jennifer Clark, *Uneven Innovation: The Work of Smart Cities* (New York: Columbia University Press, 2020); Renee E. Sieber, "Public Participation Geographic Information Systems: A Literature Review and Framework," *Annals of the Association of American Geographers* 96 (2006): 491–507; "Spatial Data Access by

the Grassroots," *Cartography and Geographic Information Science* 34 (2007): 47–62; William J. Craig and Sarah A. Elwood, "How and Why Community Groups Use Maps and Geographic Information," *Cartography and Geographic Information Systems* 25 (1998): 95–104; Sarah A. Elwood, "GIS and Collaborative Urban Governance: Understanding their Implications for Community Action and Power," *Urban Geography* 22 (2002): 737–759; Richard K. Brail and Richard E. Klosterman, eds., *Planning Support Systems: Integrating Geographic Information Systems, Models, and Visualization Tools* (Redlands, CA: ESRI Press, 2001); William J. Craig, Trevor M. Harris, and Daniel Weiner, eds., *Community Participation and Geographic Information Systems* (New York: Taylor and Francis, 2002); Nader Afzalan and Brian Muller, "Online Participatory Technologies: Opportunities and Challenges for Enriching Participatory Planning," *Journal of the American Planning Association* 84 (2018): 162–177. For global case studies, see Chiara Certomà, Mark Dyer, Lorena Pocatilu, and Francesco Rizzi, eds., *Citizen Empowerment and Innovation in the Data-Rich City* (New York: Springer, 2017). See also Lily M. Hoffman, *The Politics of Knowledge: Activist Movements in Medicine and Planning* (Albany: State University of New York Press, 1989); Tom Angotti, *New York for Sale: Community Planning Confronts Global Real Estate* (Cambridge, MA: MIT Press, 2008); Murray Bookchin, *The Rise of Urbanization and the Decline of Citizenship* (San Francisco: Sierra Club Books, 1987); Debbie Bookchin and Blair Taylor, eds., *The Next Revolution: Popular Assemblies and the Promise of Direct Democracy* (New York: Verso, 2015).

40. For various formulations and debates, see Peter Calthorpe, *The Next American Metropolis: Ecology, Community, and the American Dream* (New York: Princeton Architectural Press, 1993); Eric Mumford, *The CIAM Discourse on Urbanism, 1928–1960* (Cambridge, MA: MIT Press, 2000); *Defining Urban Design: CIAM Architects and the Formation of a Discipline, 1937–1969* (New Haven, CT: Yale University Press, 2009); Charles Waldheim, ed., *The Landscape Urbanism Reader* (New York: Princeton Architectural Press, 2006); Andrés Duany and Emily Talen, eds., *Landscape Urbanism and Its Discontents: Dissimulating the Sustainable City* (Gabriola Island, BC: New Society Publishers, 2013); Robert Fishman, "New Urbanism," in *Planning Ideas That Matter*, 65–89, who discusses East and West Coast variants—the latter more rooted in environmental concerns and passive solar design.

41. Emily Talen, *New Urbanism and American Planning: The Conflict of Cultures* (New York: Routledge, 2005). For her attempt to think through how to reconstruct neighborhoods as genuinely localized and self-governing yet diverse and inclusive, see Emily Talen, *Neighborhood* (New York: Oxford University Press, 2019).

42. Michael Leccese and Kathleen McCormick, eds., and Congress for the New Urbanism (CNU), *Charter of the New Urbanism* (New York: McGraw-Hill, 1999).

43. Andrés Duany, qtd. in *Charter of the New Urbanism*, 12; author interview

with Holly Madill, director of the National Charrette Institute, June 13, 2018, author interview with David Brain, former NCI board member, May 23, 2018, who has brought acute attention to issues of market and professional power into the initially "naïve communitarian" vision of charrette practice; Lennertz and Lutzenhiser, *The Charrette Handbook*; "CNU 26.Savannah," the 26th Annual Congress for the New Urbanism, Savannah, GA, May 16–19, 2017. See also Smart Growth America, "Opening Plenary: Getting to Just Growth and Shared Prosperity: Lessons from Communities across the Nation," 17th Annual New Partners for Smart Growth Conference, San Francisco, February 1, 2018. NCI offers regular charrette trainings, webinars, tool kits for specific topics (comprehensive and regional planning, health care planning, storm water management), and several certification programs, which are accepted as continuing education units by APA's American Institute of Certified Planners (AICP), the American Society of Landscape Architects (ASLA), AIA, and CNU. For analyses that supports some of the critiques of culture and class biases in new urbanism, see Erualdo Romero Gonzalez and Raul P. Lejano, "New Urbanism and the Barrio," *Environment and Planning A* 41 (2009): 2946–2963; Emily Talen, "New Urbanism, Social Equity, and the Challenge of Post-Katrina Rebuilding in Mississippi," *Journal of Planning Education and Research* 27 (2008): 277–293; Emily Talen and Sungduck Lee, *Design for Social Diversity*, 2nd ed. (New York: Routledge, 2018).

44. Author interview with Lynn Richards, executive director of the Congress for the New Urbanism, June 28, 2018; Congress for the New Urbanism (CNU), *CNU Strategic Plan 2016–2018* (Washington, DC: CNU, 2015), https://www.cnu.org/sites/default/files/CNU%20Strategic%20Plan%202016-18.pdf; CNU, *Combatting the Suburbanization of Poverty: The Future of Just, Sustainable Growth in the Puget Sound Region* (Washington, DC: CNU, 2017), https://www.cnu.org/sites/default/files/CombatingSuburbanizationPoverty.pdf.

45. Richards interview.

46. On HOPE VI and the debates it has sparked, see Arthur Naparstek, *Hope VI: Community Building Makes a Difference* (Washington, DC: HUD, 2000); Henry G. Cisneros and Lora Engdahl, eds., *From Despair to Hope: Hope VI and the New Promise of Public Housing in America's Cities* (Washington, DC: Brookings Press, 2009); Lawrence J. Vale, *Purging the Poorest: Public Housing and the Design Politics of Twice-Cleared Communities* (Chicago, IL: University of Chicago Press, 2013); Robert J. Chaskin and Mark L. Joseph, *Integrating the Inner City: The Promise and Perils of Mixed-Income Public Housing Transformation* (Chicago, IL: University of Chicago Press, 2017).

47. US Department of Housing and Urban Development (HUD), *Office of Sustainable Housing and Communities: Helping Communities Realize a More Prosperous Future* (Washington, DC: HUD, 2012) https://www.hud.gov/sites/documents/2012OSHCACCOMPRPT.PDF; HUD, USDOT, and EPA, *Partnership*

for Sustainable Communities: Five Years of Learning from Communities and Coordinating Federal Investments (Washington, DC: HUD, USDOT, and EPA, 2014), https://www.epa.gov/sites/production/files/2014-08/documents/partnership-ac complishments-report-2014-reduced-size.pdf; Rolf Pendall, Sandra Rosenbloom, Diane Levy, Elizabeth Oo, Gerrit Knaap, Jason Sartori, and Arnab Chakraborty, *Can Federal Efforts Advance Federal and Local De-Siloing? Lessons from the HUD-EPA-DOT Partnership for Sustainable Communities* (Washington, DC: Urban Institute, 2013), prepared for Living Cities; Athena Jade Ullah, "A Policy Story of Continuity and Change: Reflections on the Obama Administration's Metropolitan Agenda" (MA thesis in City Planning, MIT, Cambridge, MA, 2011); Karen Chapple, *Planning Sustainable Cities and Regions: Towards More Equitable Development* (New York: Routledge, 2015); "Regional Policy in the Age of Obama," in *Urban Policy in the Time of Obama*, ed. James DeFilippis, (Minneapolis: University of Minnesota Press, 2016), 259–271, qtd. on 266; Juan Sebastian Arias, Sara Draper-Zivetz, and Amy Martin, "The Impacts of the Sustainable Communities Initiative Regional Planning Grants on Planning and Equity in Three Metropolitan Regions," *Cityscape: A Journal of Policy Development and Research* 19 (2017): 93–114; Rachel S. Madsen, "Affordable Housing's Place in Social Mobility, Equity, and Sustainability: How Local Dynamics Affect Implementation of Federal Program Objectives" (PhD diss., Brandeis University, Waltham, MA, 2018).

48. Smart Growth America (SGA), "Better Choices for Communities: SGA Annual Report 2007," Washington, DC, 2007; Martin J. Rosen and Carl Wilmsen, *Trust for Public Land Founding Member and President, 1972–1997: Oral History Transcript: The Ethics and Practice of Land Conservation* (Berkeley, CA: Regional Oral History Office, Bancroft Library, 2000); John W. Frece, "Twenty Lessons from Maryland's Smart Growth Initiative," *Vermont Journal of Environmental Law* 6 (2004–2005): 106–132; *Sprawl and Politics: The Inside Story of Smart Growth in Maryland* (Albany: State University of New York Press, 2009); Gerrit-Jan Knaap and John W. Frece, "Smart Growth in Maryland: Looking Forward and Looking Back," *Idaho Law Review* 43 (2007): 445–473; Gregory K. Ingram, Armando Carbonell, Yu-Hung Hong, and Anthony Flint, eds., *Smart Growth Policies: An Evaluation of Programs and Outcomes* (Cambridge, MA: Lincoln Institute of Land Policy, 2009); Angela C. Halfacre, *A Delicate Balance: Constructing a Conservation Culture in the South Carolina Low Country* (Columbia: University of South Carolina Press, 2012); DeGrove, *Planning Policy and Politics*.

49. International City/County Management Association (ICMA), with Geoffrey Anderson, *Why Smart Growth: A Primer* (Washington, DC: ICMA, 1998), https://www.epa.gov/sites/production/files/2014-04/documents/why-smart -growth.pdf; President's Council, *Sustainable America*, 83–107; Daniel Sitarz, ed., *Sustainable America: America's Environment, Economy and Society in the 21st Century* (Carbondale, IL: EarthPress, 1998). On the Reinventing Citizenship Project,

see Carmen Sirianni and Lewis A. Friedland, *Civic Innovation in America* (Berkeley: University of California Press, 2001), ch. 7.

50. Barbara McCann, *Completing Our Streets: The Transition to Safe and Inclusive Transportation Networks*, 2nd ed. (Washington, DC: Island Press, 2013), 22–25; Smart Growth America, "National Complete Streets Coalition: SGA Annual Report 2011," Washington, DC, 2011; Donald Appleyard, *Livable Streets* (Berkeley: University of California Press, 1981); Richard K. Unterman, *Accommodating the Pedestrian: Adapting Towns and Neighborhoods for Walking and Biking* (New York: Van Nostrand Reinhold, 1984); David Crites, Sue Knaup, Barbara McCann, Stefanie Seskin, Gayle Stallings, and Kristen Steele, *Alliance for Biking & Walking Guide to Complete Streets Campaigns*, 3rd ed. (CreateSpace Independent Publishing Platforms, 2010); Barbara McCann and Suzanne Rynne, eds., *Complete Streets: Best Policy and Implementation Practices* (Chicago, IL: APA Planning Advisory Service, 2010).

51. Author interview with Emiko Atherton, executive director of the National Complete Streets Coalition, June 7, 2018. See also McCann, *Completing Our Streets*.

52. National Association of City Transportation Officials (NACTO), *Urban Street Design Guide*, 2nd ed. (Washington, DC: Island Press, 2013); NACTO, *Urban Bikeway Design Guide*, 2nd ed. (Washington, DC: Island Press, 2014); NACTO, *Transit Street Design Guide* (Washington, DC: Island Press, 2016); NACTO, *Urban Street Stormwater Guide* (Washington, DC: Island Press, 2017); "Public Engagement that Counts: Transportation Education and Civic Empowerment," webinar, February 6, 2018, https://nacto.org/wp-content/uploads/2018/01/Street-Ambassadors-NACTO-Presentation.pdf; NACTO, "*Strategies for Engaging Community: Developing Better Relationships through Bike Share* (Washington, DC: NACTO, 2018), https://nacto.org/wp-content/uploads/2018/09/NACTO_BBSP_2018_Strategies-for-Engaging-Community.pdf; NACTO, *2018 Annual Report* (Washington, DC: NACTO, 2018); US Department of Transportation (USDOT), "Memorandum: Bicycle and Pedestrian Facility Design Flexibility," Federal Highway Administration, Washington, DC, 2013, https://www.fhwa.dot.gov/environment/bicycle_pedestrian/guidance/design_flexibility.cfm.

53. American Association of State Highway Transportation Officials, *AASHTO 2014-2019 Strategic Plan Update: Draft V2* (Washington, DC: AASHTO, 2014), qtd. on 10, https://www.transportation.org/wp-content/uploads/2019/12/AASHTO-Strategic-Plan-Final-Draft-BOD-approved-112414.pdf; AASHTO, *A Policy on Geometric Design of Highways and Streets* ("Green Book"), 7th ed. (Washington, DC: AASHTO, 2018). On leading and lagging states, see Atherton interview; Frece, *Sprawl and Politics*.

54. F. Kaid Benfield, Matthew Raimi, and Donald D. T. Chen, *Once There Were Greenfields: How Urban Sprawl Is Undermining America's Environment,*

Economy, and Social Fabric (New York: NRDC, 1999); Ford Foundation, "The Just City: A Ford Forum on Metropolitan Opportunity," video, Ford Live Events, July 14, 2011, https://www.fordfoundation.org/the-latest/ford-live-events /the-just-city-a-ford-forum-on-metropolitan-opportunity/.

55. Jana Lynott, Jessica Haase, Amanda Taylor, Hannah Twaddell, Jared Ulmer, Barbara McCann, and Edward R. Stollof, *Planning Complete Streets for an Aging America* (Washington, DC: AARP, 2009); ICMA, *The Maturing of America: Communities Moving Forward for an Aging Population* (Washington, DC: ICMA, 2011), https://icma.org/sites/default/files/302655_The%20Maturing%20of%20America %20Report%202011.pdf; N4A, *National Survey of Area Agencies on Aging: Serving America's Older Adults* (Washington, DC: N4A, 2017). https://www.n4a.org /Files/2017%20AAA%20Survey%20Report/AAANationalSurvey_web.pdf.

56. AARP, "Livable Communities Archives," 2004–2017, https://www.aarp .org/livable-communities/archives/; Nancy LeaMond, *Where We Live: Communities for All Ages*, ed. Melissa Stanton (Washington, DC: AARP, 2017); Thibauld Moulaert and Suzanne Garon, eds., *Age-Friendly Cities and Communities in International Comparison: Political Lessons, Scientific Avenues, and Democratic Issues* (New York: Springer, 2016); Christine L. Day, *AARP: America's Largest Interest Group and Its Impact* (Santa Barbara, CA: Praeger, 2017). On the core dynamics of participatory policy feedback in this field, see Andrea Louise Campbell, *How Policies Make Citizens: Senior Political Activism and the American Welfare State* (Princeton, NJ: Princeton University Press, 2003). On the key role of the Americans with Disabilities Act in funding, see Bruce D. Epperson, *Bicycles in American Highway Planning: The Critical Years of Decision-Making, 1969–1991* (Jefferson, NC: McFarland, 2014), 153–159.

57. Author interview with Danielle Arigoni, director of AARP's Livable Communities program, June 5, 2018. For associational dynamics during the Clinton health reform effort, see Theda Skocpol, *Boomerang: Health Care Reform and the Turn against Government* (New York: Norton, 1997).

58. Arigoni interview; US EPA, *Growing Smarter, Living Healthier: A Guide to Smart Growth and Active Aging* (Washington, DC: USEPA, 2009).

59. David Gottfried, *Greed to Green: The Transformation of an Industry and a Life* (Berkeley, CA: WorldBuild Publishing, 2004); Gottfried, *Greening My Life: A Green Building Pioneer Takes on His Most Challenging Project* (Regenerative Publishing, 2010).

60. American Society for Testing and Materials, *ASTM 1898–1998: A Century of Progress* (Washington, DC: ASTM, 1998), qtd. on 48 and 33; Nils Brunsson, Bengt Jacobsson, and Associates, *A World of Standards* (New York: Oxford University Press, 2000). See also Carl Tobias, "Of Public Funds and Public Participation: Resolving the Issue of Agency Authority to Reimburse Public Participants in Administrative Proceedings," *Columbia Law Review* 82 (1982): 906–985; Amory B.

Lovins, *Soft Energy Paths: Towards a Durable Peace* (New York: HarperCollins, 1979).

61. On social learning within industry during these years, see Andrew J. Hoffman, *From Heresy to Dogma: An Institutional History of Corporate Environmentalism*, ex. ed. (Stanford, CA: Stanford University Press, 2002); Rachel L. Shwom, "Nonprofit-Business Partnering Dynamics in the Energy Efficiency Field," *Nonprofit and Voluntary Sector Quarterly* 44 (2014): 564–586; Christine Mondor, David Deal, and Stephen Hockley, "Building Up to Organizational Sustainability: How the Greening of Places Transforms Organizations," in *Constructing Green: The Social Structures of Sustainability*, ed. Rebecca L. Henn and Andrew J. Hoffman, (Cambridge, MA: MIT Press, 2013), 197–217; Frank Boons and Jennifer A. Howard-Grenville, eds., *The Social Embeddedness of Industrial Ecology* (Northampton, MA: Edward Elgar, 2009); Ryan Dupont, Kumar Ganesan, and Louis Theodore, *Pollution Prevention: Sustainability, Industrial Ecology, and Green Engineering*, 2nd ed. (Boca Raton, FL: CRC Press, 2016).

62. US Green Building Council, *2014 Annual Report* (Washington, DC: US Green Building Council, 2015), qtd. on 3, https://urbangreencouncil.org/sites/default/files/2014_annual_report.pdf.

63. USGBC, *2014 Annual Report*, qtd. on 3. On the broader organizational features and logics of the construction field in which green building has emerged, see Andrew J. Hoffman and Rebecca Henn, "Overcoming the Social and Psychological Barriers to Green Building," *Organization & Environment* 2 (2008): 390–419; Thomas D. Beamish and Nicole Woolsey Biggart, "The Role of Social Heuristics in Project-Centered Production Networks: Insights from the Commercial Construction Industry," *Engineering Project Organizational Journal* 2 (March–June 2012): 57–70; Nicole Woolsey Biggart, "Forward: Integrating the Social into the Built Environment," in *Constructing Green*, ix–xiv.

64. USGBC, *2014 Annual Report*, qtd. on 6. See also Beth M. Duckles, "The Green Building Industry in California: From Ideals to Buildings" (PhD diss., University of Arizona, Tucson, 2009).

65. Michele A. Meyer, Jennifer E. Cross, Zinta S. Byrne, Bill Franzen, and Stuart Reeve, "Green School Building Success: Innovation through a Flat Team Approach," in *Constructing Green*, 219–238. See also Nicholas J. Rajkovich, Alison G. Kwok, and Larissa Larsen, "LEED, Collaborative Rationality, and Green Building Public Policy," in *Constructing Green*, 57–76.

66. Poudre School District and the Brendle Group, Inc., *Sustainability Management System* (Fort Collins, CO: Poudre School District, 2006); Poudre School District, *2013 Annual Sustainability Report* (Fort Collins, CO: Poudre School District, 2013); Poudre School District, *Sustainability Management Plan*, 2017 (Fort Collins, CO: Poudre School District, 2017), https://www.psdschools.org/sites/default/files/PSD/facility_services/Sustainability/SustainabilityManagement

Plan2017Final.pdf; Chelsea Schelly, Jennifer E. Cross, William S. Franzen, Pete Hall, and Stu Reeve, "Reducing Energy Consumption and Creating a Conservation Culture in Organizations: A Case Study of One Public School District," *Environment and Behavior* 43 (2011): 316–343; "How to Go Green: Creating a Conservation Culture in a Public High School Through Education Modeling and Communication," *Journal of Environmental Education* 43 (2012): 143–161.

67. Jane Mansbridge, James Bohman, Simone Chambers, Thomas Christiano, Archon Fung, John Parkinson, Dennis F. Thompson, and Mark E. Warren, "A Systemic Approach to Deliberative Democracy," in *Deliberative Systems: Deliberative Democracy at the Large Scale*, ed. John Parkinson and Jane Mansbridge (New York: Cambridge University Press, 2012), 1–26.

68. USGBC, *LEED v.4 for Neighborhood Development* (Washington, DC: USGBC, 2014), https://www.usgbc.org/resources/leed-v4-neighborhood-development-checklist. For European comparisons, see Harrison Fraker, *The Hidden Potential of Sustainable Neighborhoods: Lessons from Low-Carbon Communities* (Washington, DC: Island Press, 2013).

69. Author interview with Lucia Athens, chief sustainability officer of Austin, Texas, and former head of green building for ten years in the city of Seattle, June 6, 2018; Aaron Welch, Kaid Benfield, and Matt Raimi, *A Citizen's Guide to LEED for Neighborhood Development: How to Tell if Development Is Smart and Green* (Washington, DC: CNU, USGBC, and NRDC, n.d.), qtd. on 18, https://www.nrdc.org/sites/default/files/citizens_guide_LEED-ND.pdf; Lucia Athens, *Building an Emerald City: A Guide to Creating Green Building Policies and Programs*, 2nd ed. (Washington, DC: Island Press, 2009); Seattle 2030 District, *Our City, Our District, Our Impact: 2015 Annual Report* (Seattle, WA: Seattle 2030 District, n.d.), http://www.2030districts.org/sites/default/files/atoms/files/Seattle_2030_District_Annual_Report_2016.pdf.

70. Welch, Benfield, and Raimi, *Citizen's Guide to LEED for Neighborhood Development*, qtd. on 13 and 17; USGBC, *A Local Government Guide to LEED for Neighborhood Development* (Washington, DC: USGBC, 2012), https://www.usgbc.org/resources/local-government-guide-leed-neighborhood-development. For a quantitative test of the positive relationship between civic capacity (measured by the proxy of presence and density of nonprofit organizations, especially environmental ones) and green building trajectories among cities, see Christof Brandtner, "Cities in Action: City Climate Action, Civil Society, and the Organization of Cities" (PhD diss., Stanford University, Stanford, CA, 2019), ch. 5.

71. USGBC, "LEED for Cities and Communities Webinar: Stories of Success," March 20, 2019; USGBC, "LEED v4.1 for Cities and Communities Webinar," January 10, 2020; STAR Communities, *STAR (Sustainability Tools for Assessing and Rating) Communities Index: Version 1.2* (STAR Communities, 2015), 77–79, and qtd. on 8; USGBC, *2013–2015 Strategic Action Plan* (Washington, DC: USGBC,

2012), https://www.usgbc.org/resources/usgbc-strategic-plan-2013-2015. STAR is now part of USGBC's LEED for Cities and Communities program.

72. Jerry Yudelson, *Reinventing Green Building: Why Certification Systems Aren't Working and What We Can Do About It* (Gabriola, BC: New Society Publishers, 2016). See also Beth Simone Noveck, *Smart Citizens, Smarter State: The Technologies of Expertise and the Future of Governing* (Cambridge, MA: Harvard University Press, 2015).

73. Jeroen van der Heijden, *Innovations in Urban Climate Governance: Voluntary Programs for Low-Carbon Buildings and Cities* (New York: Cambridge University Press, 2017), qtd. on 193 and 197. See Rachel Weber, *From Boom to Bubble: How Finance Built the New Chicago* (Chicago, IL: University of Chicago Press, 2015), on financialization dynamics. On the rolling rule regime, see Charles Sabel, Archon Fung, and Bradley Karkkainen, *Beyond Backyard Environmentalism* (Boston, MA: Beacon Press, 2000). See also Kriston Capps, "How New York Can Deliver on the First Phase of Its 'Green New Deal,'" CITYLAB, May 2, 2019; Urban Green Council, "Annual Report 2017."

Chapter 4. Biking, Walking, and Farming in Cities

1. Bruce D. Epperson, *Bicycles in American Highway Planning: The Critical Years of Decision-Making, 1969–1991* (Jefferson, NC: McFarland, 2014); James Longhurst, *Bike Battles: A History of Sharing the American Road* (Seattle: University of Washington Press, 2015); Paul Barrett and Mark H. Rose, "Street Smarts: The Politics of Transportation Statistics in the American City, 1900–1990," *Journal of Urban History* 25 (1999): 405–433; Michael R. Fein, *Paving the Way: New York Road Building and the American State, 1880–1956* (Lawrence: University Press of Kansas, 2008). See also E. F. Schumacher, *Small Is Beautiful: Economics as If People Mattered* (London: Blond & Briggs, 1973); Jane Jacobs, *The Death and Life of Great American Cities* (New York: Random House, 1961); Mark Furness, *One Less Car: Bicycling and the Politics of Automobility* (Philadelphia, PA: Temple University Press, 2010).

2. Jeff Mapes, *Pedaling Revolution: How Cyclists Are Changing American Cities* (Corvallis: Oregon State University Press, 2009), 119–140; Epperson, *Bicycles in American Highway Planning*, 86–96; Carlton Reid, *BIKE BOOM: The Unexpected Resurgence of Cycling* (Washington, DC: Island Press, 2017), 67–76.

3. Chris Carlsson, Jim Swanson, and Hugh D'Andrade, *Critical Mass: Essays, Flyers, Images (Archives 1992–1998)*, https://www.scorcher.org/cmhistory/; Chris Carlsson, *Critical Mass: Bicycling's Defiant Celebration* (Oakland, CA: AK Press, 2002); Susan Blickstein and Susan Hanson, "Critical Mass: Forging a Politics of Sustainable Mobility in the Information Age," *Transportation* 28 (2001): 347–362; J. Harry Wray, *Pedal Power: The Quiet Rise of the Bicycle in American Public Life* (Boulder, CO: Paradigm Publishers, 2008), 131–160; John S. Ahlquist and Marga-

ret Levi, *In the Interest of Others: Organizations and Social Activism* (Princeton, NJ: Princeton University Press, 2013). On the "right to the city," see Henri Lefebvre, *Writings on Cities*, ed. and trans. Eleonore Kofman and Elizabeth Lebas (Malden, MA: Wiley-Blackwell, 1996); David Harvey, "The Right to the City," *New Left Review* 53 (2008): 23–40; Margaret Kohn, *The Death and Life of the Urban Commonwealth* (New York: Oxford University Press, 2016).

4. Jason Henderson, *Street Fight: The Struggle over Urban Mobility in San Francisco* (Amherst: University of Massachusetts Press, 2013), 112–138; Longhurst, *Bike Battles*; Elinor Ostrom, *Governing the Commons: The Evolution of Institutions for Collective Action* (New York: Cambridge University Press, 1990).

5. Henderson, *Street Fight*; Barrett and Rose, "Street Smarts."

6. San Francisco Bicycle Coalition, *Strategic Plan 2012–2017* (San Francisco: SFBC, 2012), https://sfbike.org/wp-content/uploads/2014/03/Strategic-Plan_2012 -2017-v2013.pdf; San Francisco Bicycle Coalition, annual reports, 2012–2016, http://www.sfbike.org/wp-content/uploads/2017/08/2017.08.11AnnualReport .pdf.

7. Author interview with Brian Wiedenmeier, executive director of the San Francisco Bicycle Coalition, June 15, 2018; National Association of City Transportation Officials, *Cities Taking the Lead: NACTO 2018 Annual Report*, 2018, 14, https://nacto.org/wp-content/uploads/2018/12/2018-NACTO-Annual-Report .pdf.

8. Wiedenmeier interview, June 15, 2018.

9. Wiedenmeier interview, June 15, 2018; Rachel Swan, "San Francisco Supervisor Pushes to Untangle Freeway Hairball," SFGate, August 4, 2017; Teresa Gowan, *Hobos, Hustlers, and Backsliders: Homeless in San Francisco* (Minneapolis: University of Minnesota Press, 2010); Tamika Butler, "I Am Not Your Nigger: Can Vision Zero Succeed in a Racist Society?" (dinner address, Vision Zero Cities Conference, New York, NY, May 12, 2017); Ninth Annual Complete Streets Dinner, Washington, DC, January 15, 2019.

10. *Aftermass: Bicycling in a Post-Critical Mass Portland*, written and directed by Joel Biel, (Portland, OR: Microcosm Publishing, 2013), DVD; Bicycle Transportation Alliance, *A Blueprint for World-Class Bicycling: Three-Year Status Update and Annual Report* (Portland, 2015); City of Portland, *Portland Bicycle Plan for 2030* (Portland: Bureau of Transportation, 2010), https://www.portlandoregon.gov /transportation/44597; Mapes, *Pedaling Revolution*, 141–168.

11. Bicycle Transportation Alliance and Oregon Walks, *Vision Zero: A Unifying Vision for Street Safety for Oregon* (2015).

12. Author interview with Jillian Detweiler, executive director of The Street Trust, July 2, 2018; The Street Trust, "The Street Trust Racial Equity Policy Statement," 2017, https://www.thestreettrust.org/full-racial-equity-policy-statement; The Street Trust, "2017 Annual Report," 2017, https://www.thestreettrust.org

/financials. See also Melody L. Hoffmann, *Bike Lanes Are White Lanes: Bicycle Advocacy and Urban Planning* (Lincoln: University of Nebraska Press, 2016); Karen J. Gibson, "Bleeding Albina: A History of Community Disinvestment, 1940–2000," *Transforming Anthropology* 15 (2007): 3–25.

13. Transportation Alternatives, annual reports, 2012–2016, https://www.transalt.org/annual-report; Mapes, *Pedaling Revolution*, 169–194; Ginia Bellafante, "New York Was Supposedly Getting Better for Cyclists. What Happened?" *New York Times*, July 12, 2019.

14. Inbar Kishoni, "Public Engagement That Counts," NACTO webinar, February 6, 2018, https://nacto.org/wp-content/uploads/2018/01/Street-Ambassadors-NACTO-Presentation.pdf. See also Janette Sadik-Khan and Seth Solomonow, *Streetfight: Handbook for an Urban Revolution* (New York: Viking, 2016); Samuel I. Schwartz and William Rosen, *Street Smart: The Rise of Cities and the Fall of Cars* (New York: PublicAffairs, 2015).

15. John Forester, "Toy Bike Syndrome," *Bike World* 2 (1973): 24–27; Bruce D. Epperson, "The Great Schism: Federal Bicycle Safety Regulation and the Unraveling of American Bicycle Planning," *Transportation Law Journal* 37 (2010): 73–118. This John Forester is not the urban planning theorist of the same name cited in chapter 3.

16. Author interview with Andy Clarke, former executive director of the League of American Bicyclists, June 14, 2018; League of American Bicyclists (LAB), *Our 2015–2018 Strategic Framework: A Commitment to Leadership: Creating a Bicycle-Friendly America for Everyone* (2015), qtd. on 2, https://bikeleague.org/sites/default/files/League_Strategic_Plan_2015_2018.pdf; Adonia Lugo, *Integrating Equity in Bike Advocacy: An Interim Report on the Internal Equity Assessment at the League of American Bicyclists* (LAB, 2014), https://bikeleague.org/sites/default/files/League_internal_equity_web.pdf; Mapes, *Pedaling Revolution*, 27–60; Aaron Golub, Melody L. Hoffmann, Adonia E. Lugo, and Gerardo F. Sandoval, eds., *Bicycle Justice and Urban Transformation: Biking for All?* (New York: Routledge, 2016).

17. Author interview with Andy Clarke, June 14, 2018; LAB, annual reports and financials, 2004–2015, https://www.bikeleague.org/content/financials.

18. Mapes, *Pedaling Revolution*, 38.

19. Author interview with Leah Shahum, former executive director of the San Francisco Bicycle Coalition, June 27, 2018; PeopleForBikes, annual reports, 2005–2015, https://peopleforbikes.org/annual-reports-audited-financial-statements/.

20. Surface Transportation Policy Project (STPP), *Acting in the National Interest: The Transportation Agenda*, 1991, https://transact.org/wp-content/uploads/2014/04/STPP-Acting-in-the-National-Interest-1991.pdf; STPP, *"Ten Years of Progress: Building Better Communities through Transportation*, 2001, https://transact.org/wp-content/uploads/2014/04/Ten_Years_Of_Progress.pdf; Donald H. Camph, *Trans-*

portation, The ISTEA, and American Cities (STPP Monograph Series, 1996), https://transact.org/wp-content/uploads/2014/04/Transportation_ISTEA_and_American_Cities.pdf; Daniel P. Moynihan, "New Roads and Urban Chaos," *Reporter*, April 14, 1960, 13–20; Richard F. Weingroff, "Creating a Landmark: The Intermodal Surface Transportation Efficiency Act of 1991," *Public Roads* 65 (2001): 7–48; Philip M. Parker, ed., *ISTEA: Webster's Timeline History, 1991–2004* (San Diego, CA: Icon Group, 2009); Richard Brewer, *Conservancy: The Land Trust Movement in America* (Lebanon, NH: Dartmouth University Press, 2003), 253–268.

21. US General Accounting Office (GAO), *Transportation Enhancements: Status of the $2.4 Billion Authorized for Nonmotorized Transportation: Report to Congressional Requesters* (Washington, DC: GAO, 1996), https://www.gao.gov/assets/230/223102.pdf; Rails to Trails Conservancy, *Transportation Enhancement Financial Summary* (Washington, DC: RTC, 1996); Joe Distefano and Matthew Raimi, *Five Years of Progress: 110 Communities Where ISTEA Is Making a Difference* (Washington, DC: STPP, 1996).

22. Angie L. Cradock, Philip J. Troped, Billy Fields, Steven J. Melly, Shannon V. Simms, Franz Gimmler and Marianne Fowler, "Factors Associated with Federal Transportation Funding for Local Pedestrian and Bicycle Programming and Facilities," *Journal of Public Health Policy* 30 (2009): S38-S72; Progressive Management, *Twenty-First Century Complete Guide to SAFETEA-LU: Safe, Accountable, Flexible, Efficient Transportation Equity Act: A Legacy for Users* (Brooklyn, NY: Progressive Management, 2007), CD ROM.

23. Sherry R. Arnstein, "Eight Rungs on the Ladder of Citizen Participation," *Journal of the American Institute of Planners* 25 (1969): 216–224; Desoto Jordan, Sherry R. Arnstein, Justin Gray, Ellen I. Metcalf, Wayne R. Torrey, and Florence W. Mills, *Effective Citizen Participation in Transportation Planning: Final Report*, 2 vols. (Washington, DC: US Department of Transportation, 1976); Thomas A. Horan, Hank Dittmar, and Daniel R. Jordan, "ISTEA and the New Era in Transportation Policy: Sustainable Communities from a Federal Initiative," in *Toward Sustainable Communities: Transition and Transformations in Environmental Policy*, ed. Michael E. Kraft and Daniel A. Mazmanian (Cambridge, MA: MIT Press, 1999), 217–245; Hank Dittmar, *Interest-Based Convening: Toward Participatory Decision Making in Transportation Investment* (STPP, 2000); Longhurst, *Bike Battles*, 222; Weingroff, "Creating a Landmark." See also Carissa Shively Slotterback, "Building a Foundation for Public Engagement in Planning: 50 Years of Impact, Interpretation, and Inspiration from Arnstein's Ladder," *Journal of the American Planning Association* 85 (2019):183–187; John Gaber, "Building 'A Ladder of Citizen Participation': Sherry Arnstein, Citizen Participation, and Model Cities," *Journal of the American Planning Association* 85 (2019).

24. On the Interagency Council on Citizen Participation, see Sirianni and Friedland, *Civic Innovation in America*, 89–90.

25. Horan, Dittmar, and Jordan, "ISTEA and the New Era in Transportation Policy"; Dittmar, *Interest-Based Convening*; Cynthia A. Weatherby Gilliland, *An Assessment of Public Involvement Strategies* (College Station: Texas Transportation Institute, Texas A&M University, 2000); Bradford D. Hunt and Jon B. DeVries, *Planning Chicago* (Chicago, IL: APA Planners Press, 2013), 264. On emergent but limited partnership structures during the first decade, see Todd Goldman and Elizabeth Deakin, "Regionalism through Partnership? Metropolitan Planning since ISTEA," *Berkeley Planning Journal* 14 (2000): 46–75. MPOs were originally created as part of the Federal-Aid Highway Act of 1962.

26. Author discussions with William Potapchuk, Washington, DC, January 19–20, 2009; Harriet Parcells, *Citizen's Guide to ISTEA Transit and Rail Funding and Public Participation Requirements* (Campaign for New Transportation Priorities, 1993); Kristina Younger, "Public Involvement," in *ISTEA Planners Workbook*, ed. Albert C. Eisenberg and Nancy S. Willis (Washington, DC: STPP, 1994), 4–11; Federal Highway Administration, *Public Involvement Techniques for Transportation Decision Making: Update* (Washington, DC: FHA, 2015), https://www.fhwa.dot.gov/planning/public_involvement/publications/techniques/chapter00.cfm. See Michael Lipsky, *Street-Level Bureaucracy: Dilemmas of the Individual in Public Service* (New York: Russell Sage, 1980).

27. Margaret Weir, Jane Rongerude, and Christopher K. Ansell, "Collaboration is Not Enough: Virtuous Cycles of Reform in Transportation Policy," *Urban Affairs Review* 44 (2009): 455–489, qtd. on 460.

28. On the larger fields, see Brian K. Obach, *Organic Struggle: The Movement for Sustainable Agriculture in the United States* (Cambridge, MA: MIT Press, 2015); Warren James Belasco, *Appetite for Change: How the Counterculture Took on the Food Industry*, 2nd ed. (Ithaca, NY: Cornell University Press, 2007); Sally K. Fairfax, Louise Nelson Dyble, Greig Tor Guthey, Lauren Gwin, Monica Moore, and Jennifer Sokolove, *California Cuisine and Just Food* (Cambridge, MA: MIT Press, 2012); Jennifer Meta Robinson and James Robert Farmer, *Selling Local: Why Local Food Movements Matter* (Bloomington: Indiana University Press, 2017); Julie Guthman, *Agrarian Dreams: The Paradox of Organic Farming in California,* second edition (Berkeley: University of California Press, 2014); Thomas A. Lyson, *Civic Agriculture: Reconnecting Farm, Food, and Community* (Medford, MA: Tufts University Press, 2004).

29. American Community Gardening Association (ACGA), annual report, 2015, https://b1b85574-bf08-4d46-8c44-326622c7ebf1.filesusr.com/ugd/f96093_df3afa69b77c4669ba440bf35753b89a.pdf; ACGA, *American Community Garden Survey* (College Park, GA: ACGA, 1998); Laura J. Lawson, *City Bountiful: A Century of Community Gardening in America* (Berkeley: University of California Press, 2005); David J. Hess, *Localist Movements in a Global Economy: Sustainability, Justice, and Urban Development in the United States* (Cambridge, MA: MIT Press, 2009), 135–160.

30. Jim Diers, *Neighbor Power: Building Community the Seattle Way* (Seattle: University of Washington Press, 2004); Jeffrey Craig Sanders, *Seattle and the Roots of Urban Sustainability: Inventing Ecotopia* (Pittsburgh, PA: University of Pittsburgh Press, 2010); Matthew Klingle, *Emerald City: An Environmental History of Seattle* (New Haven, CT: Yale University Press, 2007); Barrett A. Lee, R. S. Oropesa, Barbara J. Metch, and Avery Guest, "Testing the Decline of Community Thesis: Neighborhood Organizations in Seattle, 1929–1979," *American Journal of Sociology* 89 (1984): 1161–1188; Margaret Gordon, Hubert Locke, Laurie McCutchen, and William Stafford, "Seattle: Grassroots Politics Shaping the Environment," in *Big City Politics in Transition*, ed. H.V. Savitch and John Clayton Thomas (Newbury Park, CA: SAGE, 1991), 216–234. For some flavor of the cultural background, see the 1974 utopian novel set in the region by Ernest Callenbach, *Ecotopia*, 40th Ann. Epistle ed. (Indore, IN: Banyan Tree Books, 2014).

31. Carmen Sirianni, "Neighborhood Planning as Collaborative Democratic Design: The Case of Seattle," *Journal of the American Planning Association* 73 (2007): 373–387.

32. Jeffrey Hou, Julie M. Johnson, and Laura J. Lawson, *Greening Cities, Growing Communities* (Seattle: University of Washington Press, 2009); Marcia Ruth Ostrom and Raymond A. Jussaume Jr., "Assessing the Significance of Direct Farmer-Consumer Linkages as a Change Strategy in Washington State: Civic or Opportunistic?" in *Remaking the North American Food System: Strategies for Sustainability*, ed. C. Clare Hinrichs and Thomas A. Lyson (Lincoln: University of Nebraska Press, 2007), 235–259; Megan Horst, "Fostering Food System Transformation: An Examination of Planning in the Central Puget Sound Region" (PhD diss., University of Washington, Seattle, 2015).

33. City of Philadelphia, Office of the City Controller, *Philadelphia: A New Urban Direction*, 1st and 2nd ed. (Philadelphia, PA: St. Joseph's University Press, [1999] 2005); Roger D. Simon, *Philadelphia: A Brief History* (Philadelphia, PA: Temple University Press, 2017); Domenic Vitiello, "Planning the Food-Secure System: Philadelphia's Agriculture, Retrospect and Prospect," in *Nature's Entrepot: Philadelphia's Urban Sphere and Its Environmental Thresholds*, ed. Brian C. Black and Michael J. Chiarappa (Pittsburgh, PA: University of Pittsburgh Press, 2012), 250–266. See also Gregory L. Heller, *Ed Bacon: Planning, Politics, and the Building of Modern Philadelphia* (Philadelphia: University of Pennsylvania Press, 2013); Lisa Levenstein, *A Movement Without Marches: African American Women and the Politics of Poverty in Postwar Philadelphia* (Chapel Hill: University of North Carolina Press, 2009); Matthew J. Countryman, *Up South: Civil Rights and Black Power in Philadelphia* (Philadelphia: University of Pennsylvania Press, 2006); Guian A. McKee, *The Problem of Jobs: Liberalism, Race, and Deindustrialization in Philadelphia* (Chicago, IL: University of Chicago Press, 2008); Carolyn Adams, David Bartelt, David Elesh, Ira Goldstein, Nancy Kleniewski, and William Yancey, *Phil-*

adelphia: Neighborhoods, Division, and Conflict in a Postindustrial City (Philadelphia, PA: Temple University Press, 1991); Monica M. White, *Freedom Farmers: Agricultural Resistance and the Black Freedom Movement* (Chapel Hill: University of North Carolina Press, 2018).

34. J. Blaine Bonham Jr., Gerri Spilka, and Darl Rastorfer, *Old Cities/Green Cities: Communities Transform Unmanaged Land* (Chicago, IL: APA Planning Advisory Service, 2002), 5, 71–104; Trust for Public Land, annual reports and audited financial statements, 2010–2015, https://www.tpl.org/financials; Louise Bush-Brown, *"Garden Blocks for Urban America": The Story of the Neighborhood Association of Philadelphia and Its Successful Struggle Against Urban Blight* (New York: Charles Scribner's & Sons, 1969); and especially Christina D. Rosan and Hamil Pearsall, *Growing a Sustainable City? The Question of Urban Agriculture* (Toronto: University of Toronto Press, 2017).

35. Pennsylvania Horticultural Society (PHS), annual reports, 2015, 2017, https://phsonline.org/about/annual-report/.

36. Stephen J. McGovern, "Philadelphia's Neighborhood Transformation Initiative: A Case Study of Mayoral Leadership, Bold Planning, and Conflict," *Housing Policy Debate* 17 (2006): 529–570.

37. Michael Nutter, *Greenworks Philadelphia Vision* (Philadelphia, PA: Office of Sustainability, 2009), https://www.phila.gov/media/20160419140515/2009-green works-vision.pdf; Michael Nutter, *Greenworks Philadelphia: 2015 Progress Report* (Philadelphia, PA: Office of Sustainability, 2015), https://www.phila.gov/media /20160419140539/2015-greenworks-progress-report.pdf; Philadelphia Water Department, *Green City, Clean Waters: The City of Philadelphia's Program for Combined Sewer Overflow Control* (Philadelphia, PA: PWD, 2009), https://www.phila .gov/media/20160421133948/green-city-clean-waters.pdf; Philadelphia Land Bank, *Strategic Plan and Performance Report* (Philadelphia, PA: PLB, 2019), https:// secureservercdn.net/104.238.71.140/k05.f3c.myftpupload.com/wp-content/up loads/2019/07/2019_StrategicPlan_DRAFTREPORT_PublicRelease_060519 _PRINT-6.5.19-REDUCED.pdf; Campaign to Take Back Vacant Land, *Put Abandoned Lands in Our Hands* (Philadelphia, PA: WCRP, 2011), files.wcrpphila .com/PutAbandonedLandinOurHandsSpring2011.pdf; Frank Alexander, *Land Banks and Land Banking*, 2nd ed. (Flint, MI: Center for Community Progress, 2015); Lynn Mandarano, "Clean Waters, Clean City: Sustainable Storm Water Management in Philadelphia," in *Sustainability in America's Cities: Creating the Green Metropolis*, ed. Matthew Slavin, 2nd ed. (Washington, DC: Island Press, 2011), 157–179.

38. Rosan and Pearsall, *Growing a Sustainable City?*

39. On some of the unresolved tensions, see Robert Gottlieb and Anupama Joshi, *Food Justice* (Cambridge, MA: MIT Press, 2010), xiv, 5–6. For broad studies of food justice, see Alison Hope Alkon and Julian Agyeman, eds., *Cultivating*

Food Justice: Race, Class, and Sustainability (Cambridge, MA: MIT Press, 2011); Alison Hope Alkon and Julie Guthman, eds., *The New Food Activism: Opposition, Cooperation, and Collective Action* (Berkeley: University of California Press, 2017).

40. Nevin Cohen and Jennifer Obadia, "Greening the Food Supply in New York," in *Sustainability in America's Cities*, 205–229; Robert Fox Elder, "Protecting New York City's Community Gardens," *New York University Environmental Law Journal* 13 (2005): 769–803; Christopher Smith and Hilda Kurtz, "Community Gardens and Politics of Scale in New York City," *Geographical Review* 93 (2003): 193–212.

41. Efrat Eizenberg, *From the Ground Up: Community Gardens in New York City and the Politics of Spatial Transformation* (New York: Routledge, 2013), 25–32, 53–54; Cohen and Obadia, "Greening the Food Supply in New York," 97.

42. Kristin Reynolds and Nevin Cohen, *Beyond the Kale: Urban Agriculture and Social Justice Activism in New York City* (Athens: University of Georgia Press, 2016); Efrat Eizenberg, "The Changing Meaning of Community Space: Two Models of NGO Management of Community Gardens in New York City," *International Journal of Urban and Regional Research* 36 (2012): 106–120.

43. Lindsay K. Campbell, *City of Forests, City of Farms: Sustainability Planning for New York City's Nature* (Ithaca, NY: Cornell University Press, 2017). See also Dana R. Fisher, Lindsay K. Campbell, and Erika S. Svendsen, "The Organizational Structure of Urban Environmental Stewardship," *Environmental Politics* 21 (2012): 26–48; ICLEI USA, with the Mayor's Office of Long-Term Planning and Sustainability, City of New York, *The Process Behind PlaNYC: How the City of New York Developed Its Long-Term Comprehensive Sustainability Plan* (New York: ICLEI USA, 2010), http://s-media.nyc.gov/agencies/planyc2030/pdf/iclei_planyc_case _study_201004.pdf.

44. Neelam Sharma, qtd. in Garrett Broad, *More Than Just Food: Food Justice and Community Change* (Berkeley: University of California Press, 2016), 62, 129–164. For more on the role of the Black Panthers, see Joshua Bloom and Waldo E. Martin Jr., *Black against Empire: The History and Politics of the Black Panther Party* (Berkeley: University of California Press, 2016), 179–198.

45. Broad, *More Than Just Food*. See also Juliet Musso, Christopher Weare, Nail Oztas, and William E. Loges, "Neighborhood Governance Reform and Networks of Community Power in Los Angeles," *American Review of Public Administration* 36 (2006); Juliet Musso, and Christopher Weare, "Citizen and City: Institutional Reform and Self-Governance in Los Angeles," in *The Politics of Self-Governance*, ed. Eva Sørensen and P. Triantafilou (Burlington, VT: Ashgate, 2009), 95–116; Juliet Musso, Christopher Weare, T. Bryer, and Terry L. Cooper, "Towards 'Strong Democracy' in Global Cities? Social Capital Building, Theory-Driven Reform, and the Los Angeles Neighborhood Council Experience," *Public Administration Review* 71 (2011): 102–111.

46. Johns Hopkins Center for a Livable Future, "Food Policy Councils in

North America" (Baltimore, MD: Johns Hopkins University, Bloomberg School of Public Health, 2015); Johns Hopkins Center for a Livable Future, "Food Policy Council Directory," Food Policy Networks, 2015, http://www.foodpolicynet works.org/directory/online/; Raychel Santo, K. Bassarab, and Anne Palmer, *State of the Research: An Annotated Bibliography on Existing, Emerging, and Needed Research on Food Policy Groups* (Baltimore, MD: Johns Hopkins Center for a Livable Future, 2017); Rebecca Schiff, "The Role of Food Policy Councils in Developing Sustainable Food Systems," *Journal of Hunger and Environmental Nutrition* 3 (2008): 206–228; Samina Raja, Branden Born, and Jessica Kozlowski Russell, *A Planners Guide to Community and Regional Food Planning: Transforming Food Environments, Facilitating Healthy Eating* (Chicago, IL: APA Planners Press, 2008); Samina Raja, Femke Hoekstra, Cecilia Delgado, Rene van Veenhuizen, "Community Involvement in Urban Planning and Policy Development to Strengthen City and Regional Food Systems," *Urban Agriculture Magazine* 31 (2016): 4–9; Samina Raja, Kevin Morgan, and Enjoli Hall, "Planning for Equitable Urban and Regional Food Systems," *Built Environment* 43 (2017): 309–314; Kimberly Hodgson, Marcia Caton Campbell, and Martin Bailkey, *Urban Agriculture: Growing Healthy, Sustainable Communities* (Chicago, IL: APA Press, 2011); April Philips, *Designing Urban Agriculture: A Complete Guide to the Planning, Design, Construction, Maintenance and Management of Edible Landscapes* (Hoboken, NJ: Wiley, 2013); Megan Horst, Nathan McClintock, and Lesli Hoey, "The Intersection of Planning, Urban Agriculture, and Food Justice," *Journal of the American Planning Association* 83 (2017): 277–295.

47. Althea Harper, Alison Alkon, Annie Shattuck, Eric Holt-Gimenez, and Frances Lambrick, *Food Policy Councils: Lessons Learned* (Oakland, CA: Food First, Institute for Food and Development Policy, 2009), https://foodfirst.org/publication/food-policy-councils-lessons-learned/; Rebecca Schiff, "Food Policy Councils: An Examination of Organizational Structure, Process, and Contribution to Alternative Food Movements" (PhD diss., Institute of Sustainability and Technology Policy, Murdoch University, AUS, 2007). See also Eva Sørensen and Jacob Torfing, "The Democratic Anchorage of Governance Networks," *Scandinavian Political Studies* 28 (2005): 195–218.

48. Nathan McClintock, *Transforming the Oakland Food System: A Plan for Action* (Oakland, CA: Oakland Food Policy Council, 2010), https://www.academia.edu/2080757/Transforming_the_Oakland_Food_System_A_Plan_for_Action; Camille Tuason Mata, *Marginalizing Access to the Sustainable Food System: An Examination of Oakland's Minority Districts* (Lanham, MD: University Press of America, 2013).

49. Mark Winne, *Stand Together or Starve Alone: Unity and Chaos in the U.S. Food Movement* (Santa Barbara, CA: Praeger, 2017), 136–137; Harper et al., *Food Policy Councils.*

50. City of Seattle, *Food Action Plan* (Seattle, WA: Office of Sustainability and Environment, 2012), http://www.seattle.gov/environment/sustainable-communi ties/food-access/food-action-plan.

51. Gillian Ferguson, "Los Angeles Food Policy Council Origin Podcast," 2017, podcast, MP3 audio, 48 minutes, https://soundcloud.com/gillian-ferguson-1; Harper et al., *Food Policy Councils*, 36–41; Gottlieb and Joshi, *Food Justice*, 204– 205.

52. Harper et al., *Food Policy Councils*, 36–41; Schiff, "Food Policy Councils"; Molly McCullagh and Raychel Santo, eds., *"Food Policy for All: Inclusion of Diverse Community Residents on Food Policy Councils* (Medford, MA: Tufts University and the Johns Hopkins Center for a Livable Future, 2014), https://foodsecurecanada .org/sites/foodsecurecanada.org/files/food-policy-all-4-8.pdf.

53. Marion Nestle, *Food Politics: How the Food Industry Influences Nutrition and Health*, rev. and exp. ed. (Berkeley: University of California Press, 2013); Parke Wilde, *Food Policy in the United States: An Introduction* (New York: Routledge, 2013); Robert Paarlberg, *Food Politics: What Everyone Needs to Know*, 2nd ed. (New York: Oxford University Press, 2013); Daniel Imhoff, *Food Fight: The Citizen's Guide to the Next Food and Farm Bill* (Healdsburg, CA: Watershed Media, 2012).

54. US Department of Agriculture (USDA), "Community Food Projects (CFP) Competitive Grants Program," webinars, 2014–2016; Winne, *Stand Together or Starve Alone*, 99; Kami Pothukuchi, Kai Siedenburg, and Jeanette Abi-Nader, *Building Community Food Security: Lessons Learned from Community Food Security Projects, 1999–2003* (Los Angeles, CA: Community Food Security Coalition, 2007), https://www.issuelab.org/resource/building-community-food-security-lessons -learned-from-community-food-projects-1999-2003.html; Iris Zippora Ahronow- itz, "Rooting the Community, Growing the Future: Two Massachusetts Urban Agriculture Organizations and Their Social Impacts" (senior thesis, Committee on Degrees in Social Studies, Harvard College, Cambridge, MA, 2004); Gottlieb and Joshi, *Food Justice*, 197–201; Audrey N. Maretzki and Elizabeth Tuckermanty, "Community Food Projects and Food System Sustainability," in *Remaking the North American Food System*, 332–344.

55. Office of Community Services, *Healthy Food Financing Grantees* (Wash- ington, DC: Office for the Administration of Children and Families, 2011–2016).

56. Matthew Benson, Matthew Russell, and Deborah Kane, *USDA Farm to School Program FY 2013-FY2015: Summary of Grant Awards* (Washington, DC: USDA, Food and Nutrition Service, 2015), 7, 25, https://fns-prod.azureedge.net /sites/default/files/f2s/F2S_Grant_Summary_Report.pdf; USDA, *The Farm to School Program: 2012–2015: Four Years in Review* (Washington, DC: USDA, 2016), https://fns-prod.azureedge.net/sites/default/files/f2s/Farm-to-School-at-USDA -4-Years-in-Review.pdf. Established by the Healthy Hunger-Free Kids Act of 2010, USDA's Farm to School program has provided grants (up to $5 million annually);

tool kits; technical assistance; curricular and other resources (in partnership with Cooperative Extension) to state and local agencies, Indian tribal organizations, nonprofits, and agricultural producers and associations to enhance the food quality and nutritional education of national school breakfast and lunch programs, school gardens, child and adult food programs, and traditional tribal foods. While the statute does not require dedicated state coordinators, as did ISTEA for biking and walking, farm-to-school coordinators have nonetheless emerged in an increasing number of states. In addition, farm-to-school teams linking school faculty and staff to parents, farmers, distributors, and food service companies typically plan and administer grants. During the fiscal years 2013 to 2015, forty-nine states, plus the District of Columbia and the Virgin Islands, received at least one award and some twelve thousand three hundred schools with 6.9 million students had been reached by the grant programs. The Know Your Farmer, Know Your Food initiative links these various programs to SNAP (Supplemental Nutrition Assistance Program), SNAP-Ed, WIC, DOD's FRESH program, and other food assistance programs. National and regional staff have facilitated network building through the School Nutrition Association's annual national and regional conferences as well as through a variety of other state and national associations, much along the lines that the EPA has fostered democratic networks through its various community-based and watershed-based initiatives.

57. Winne, *Stand Together or Starve Alone*, 71–76, 147–50; Alan R. Hunt, *Civic Engagement in Food System Governance: A Comparative Perspective of American and British Local Food Movements* (New York: Routledge, 2015), 142–168; Laura J. Miller, *Building Nature's Market: The Business and Politics of Natural Foods* (Chicago, IL: University of Chicago Press, 2017); Charlotte Biltekoff, *Eating Right in America: The Cultural Politics of Food and Health* (Durham, NC: Duke University Press, 2013); Margot S. Finn, *Discriminating Taste: How Class Anxiety Created the American Food Revolution* (New Brunswick, NJ: Rutgers University Press, 2017); Philip Howard, "Consolidation in the North American Organic Food Processing Sector, 1997–2007," *International Journal of Agriculture and Food* 16 (2009): 13–30.

58. Kathleen Ann Merrigan, "Negotiating Identity within the Sustainable Agriculture Advocacy Coalition" (PhD diss., Massachusetts Institute of Technology, Cambridge, 2000); Mrill Ingram and Helen Ingram, "Creating Credible Edibles: The Organic Agricultural Movement and the Emergence of U.S. Federal Organic Standards," in *Routing the Opposition: Social Movements, Public Policy, and Democracy*, ed. David S. Meyer, Valerie Jenness, and Helen Ingram (Minneapolis: University of Minnesota Press, 2005), 121–148; Michael Haedicke, *Organizing Organic: Conflict and Compromise in an Emerging Market* (Stanford, CA: Stanford University Press, 2016); Obach, *Organic Struggle;* Winne, *Stand Together or Starve Alone;* Robert Gottlieb, *Environmentalism Unbound: Exploring New Pathways for Change* (Cambridge, MA: MIT Press, 2001), 238–239; Gottlieb and Joshi, *Food*

Justice, 83–84. For a broad analysis of narratives in networks, including a case study of organic (but not urban) agriculture, see Raul Lejano, Mrill Ingram, and Helen Ingram, *The Power of Narrative in Environmental Networks* (Cambridge, MA: MIT Press, 2013).

59. Obach, *Organic Struggle*. For a sociological analysis of the democratic collective as an organizational form, see Joyce Rothschild-Whitt, "The Collectivist Organization: An Alternative to Rational Bureaucratic Models," *American Sociological Review* 44 (1979): 509–527. For further refinements in transportation, see Federal Highway Administration, *Public Involvement Techniques for Transportation Decision Making* (Washington, DC: FHA, 2015), https://www.fhwa.dot.gov/plan ning/public_involvement/publications/techniques/.

60. American Community Gardening Association (ACGA), *Annual Report* (College Park, GA: ACGA, 2015); ACGA, conference proceedings, 36th Annual National Conference Program, Denver, 2015; C. Clare Hinrichs and Elizabeth Barham, "Challenges and Opportunities in Remaking the Food System," in *Remaking the North American Food System*, 345–356; Farmers Market Coalition (FMC), 2014 and 2015 annual member meetings; National Sustainable Agriculture Coalition (NSAC), *Annual Reports* (Washington: NSAC, 2010–2011, 2013–2015), https://sustainableagriculture.net/publications/archived-publications/; NSAC, *Farmers' Guide to the Conservation Stewardship Program: Rewarding Farmers for How They Grow What They Grow* (Washington, DC: NSAC, 2009), http://sustainableagri culture.net/wp-content/uploads/2011/09/NSAC-Farmers-Guide-to-CSP-2011. pdf; Janet Poppendieck, *Free for All: Fixing School Food in America* (Berkeley: University of California Press, 2011); Gottlieb and Joshi, *Food Justice*.

61. Community Food Security Coalition (CFSC), publications, 2001–2015, http://foodsecurity.org/pubs/; CFSC FAQ, qtd. in Maretzki and Tuckermanty, "Community Food Projects and Food System Sustainability," 333–334; Linda Ashman, Jaime de la Vega, Marc Dohan, Andy Fisher, Rosa Hippler, and Bill Romain, *Seeds of Change: Strategies for Food Security for the Inner City* (Oakland, CA: Community Food Security Coalition, 1993), https://www.issuelab.org/resource/seeds -of-change-strategies-for-food-security-for-the-inner-city.html.

62. Will Allen, with Charles Wilson, *The Good Food Revolution: Growing Healthy Food, People, and Communities* (New York: Avery, 2012); Alfonso Morales, "Growing Food *and* Justice: Dismantling Racism through Sustainable Food Systems," in *Cultivating Food Justice*, 149–167; Gottlieb, *Environmentalism Unbound*, 227–232, 365n1; Gottlieb and Joshi, *Food Justice*, 83–85; Winne, *Stand Together or Starve Alone*, 98–110.

63. Broad, *More Than Just Food*, 101–128, qtd. on 105.

64. On city-based youth development and civic engagement institutions, see Carmen Sirianni and Diana A. Schor, "City Government as Enabler of Youth Civic Engagement: Policy Designs and Implications," in *Policies for Youth Civic*

Engagement, ed. James Youniss and Peter Levine (Nashville, TN: Vanderbilt University Press, 2009), 121–163; Milbrey McLaughlin, W. Richard Scott, Sarah Deschenes, Kathryn Hopkins, and Anne Newman, *Between Movement and Establishment: Organizations Advocating for Youth* (Stanford, CA: Stanford University Press, 2009).

65. Winne, *Stand Together or Starve Alone*, qtd. on 44.

Chapter 5. Urban Rivers and Watersheds

1. John Wesley Powell, "Institutions for Arid Lands," *Century Magazine*, June 1890, 111–116; Robert W. Adler, "Addressing Barriers to Watershed Protection," *Environmental Law* 25 (1995): 973–1106; Paul A. Sabatier, Chris Weible, and Jared Ficker, "Eras of Water Management in the United States: Implications for Collaborative Watershed Approaches," in *Swimming Upstream: Collaborative Approaches to Watershed Management*, ed. Paul A. Sabatier, Will Focht, Mark Lubell, Zev Trachtenberg, Arnold Vedlitz, and Marty Matlock (Cambridge: MIT Press, 2005), 23–52; Robert Jerome Glennon, "The Disconnect Between Water Law and Hydrology," in *Arizona Water Policy: Management Innovations in an Urbanizing, Arid Region*, ed. Bonnie G. Colby and Katharine L. Jacobs (New York: Routledge, 2007), 106–120. See also Donald Worster, *A River Running West: The Life of John Wesley Powell* (New York: Oxford University Press, 2001); Robin Craig, Robert Adler, and Noah Hall, *Water Law* (St. Paul, MN: Foundation Press, 2017); R. Neil Sampson, *For Love of the Land: A History of the National Association of Conservation Districts* (League City, TX: NACD, 1985); *With One Voice: The National Association of Conservation Districts* (Tucson, AZ: Wheatmark, 2008).

2. Michael Jungman, "Areawide Planning under the Federal Water Pollution Control Act Amendments of 1972: Intergovernmental and Land Use Implications," *Texas Law Review* 54 (1976): 1047–1080, qtd. on 1047; W. Chris Wicker, "Enforcement of Section 208 of the Federal Water Pollution Control Act Amendments of 1972 to Control Nonpoint Source Pollution," *Land and Water Law Review* 14 (1979): 418–446.

3. National Commission on Water Quality, *Assessment of Public Participation in the Implementation of the Federal Water Pollution Control Act Amendments of 1972*, draft final report (Washington, DC: National Commission on Water Quality, 1975); Walter A. Rosenbaum, "Slaying Beautiful Hypotheses with Ugly Facts: EPA and the Limits of Public Participation," *Journal of Voluntary Action Research* 6 (1978): 161–173; Adler, "Addressing Barriers to Watershed Protection," 1038–1041; Wicker, "Enforcement of Section 208."

4. Conservation Foundation, *Water Quality Training Institute Handbook* (Washington, DC: Conservation Foundation, 1974). On attention- and resource-rationing dilemmas, see Patricia H. Thornton, William Ocasio, and Michael Lounsbury, *The Institutional Logics Perspective: A New Approach to Culture,*

Structure, and Process (New York: Oxford University Press, 2012), 89–91; Michael Lipsky, *Street-Level Bureaucracy: Dilemmas of the Individual in Public Service* (New York: Russell Sage, 1980).

5. Daniel A. Mazmanian and Jeanne Nienaber, *Can Organizations Change? Environmental Protection, Citizen Participation, and the Corps of Engineers* (Washington, DC: Brookings Press, 1979). On the competitive dynamics among women's organizations of various types as well as other environmental and advocacy organizations, see Debra Minkoff, *Organizing for Equality: The Evolution of Women's and Racial-Ethnic Organizations in America, 1955–1985* (New Brunswick, NJ: Rutgers University Press, 1995); Kristin A. Goss, *The Paradox of Gender Equality: How American Women's Groups Gained and Lost Their Public Voice* (Ann Arbor: University of Michigan Press, 2013).

6. David R. Godschalk and Bruce Stiftel, "Public Participation in Statewide Water Quality Planning in North Carolina: An Evaluation" (Chapel Hill, NC: Center for Urban and Regional Studies, 1980); David R. Godschalk and Bruce Stiftel, "Making Waves: Public Participation in State Water Planning," *Journal of Applied Behavioral Science* 17 (1981): 597–614; Jungman, "Areawide Planning," 1059.

7. Godschalk and Stiftel, "Making Waves"; Adler, "Addressing Barriers to Watershed Protection," 1043–1047; Domenico Parisi, Michael Taquino, Steven Michael Grice, and Duane A. Gill, "Civic Responsibility and the Environment: Linking Local Conditions to Community Environmental Activeness," *Society & Natural Resources* 17 (2004): 97–112.

8. Karen McLeod and Heather Leslie, eds., *Ecosystem-Based Management for the Oceans* (Washington, DC: Island Press, 2009); Lance Gunderson, Garry Peterson, and C. S. Holling, "Practicing Adaptive Management in Complex Social-Ecological Systems," in *Complexity Theory for a Sustainable Future*, ed. Jon Norberg and Graeme Cumming (New York: Columbia University Press, 2008), 223–240.

9. Mary Doyle and Fernando Miralles-Wilhelm, "The Culture of Collaboration in the Chesapeake Bay Program," in *Large-Scale Ecosystem Restoration: Five Case Studies from the United States*, ed. Mary Doyle and Cynthia A. Drew (Washington, DC: Island Press, 2008), 175–203; Tom Horton, *Turning the Tide: Saving the Chesapeake Bay*, rev. ed. (Washington, DC: Island Press, 2003); John R. Wennersten, *The Chesapeake: An Environmental Biography* (Baltimore: Maryland Historical Society, 2001); Donald F. Boesch and Erica B. Goldman, "Chesapeake Bay, USA," in *Ecosystem-Based Management for the Oceans*, 268–293.

10. Chesapeake Bay Program, *Chesapeake 2000: A Watershed Partnership* (Annapolis, MD: EPA, 1999).

11. Susan L. Moffitt, *Making Policy Public: Participatory Bureaucracy in American Democracy* (New York: Cambridge University Press, 2014).

12. City of Philadelphia, *Green City, Clean Waters: The City of Philadelphia's*

Program for Combined Sewer Overflow, Amended (Philadelphia, PA: Philadelphia Water Department, 2011), https://paesaggisensibili.files.wordpress.com/2014/05/city-of-philadelphia_s-program-for-combined-sewer-overflow-control.pdf; Lynn Mandarano, "Clean Waters, Clean City: Sustainable Storm Water Management in Philadelphia," in *Sustainability in America's Cities: Creating the Green Metropolis,* ed. Matthew Slavin, 2nd ed. (Washington, DC: Island Press, 2011), 157–179; Lynn Mandarano and Kurt Paulsen, "Governance Capacity in Collaborative Watershed Partnerships: Evidence from the Philadelphia Region," *Journal of Environmental Planning and Management* 54 (2011): 1293–1313; informal discussion with Fay Strongin Vogel, a public outreach coordinator for clean waters in Philadelphia, November 22, 2018.

13. Kerry Hodges, ed., *Chesapeake Bay Communities: Making the Connection* (Washington, DC: EPA for the Chesapeake Bay Program, 1996); Jennifer Greenfeld and Brian LeCouteur, *Chesapeake Bay Community Action Guide* (Washington, DC: Metropolitan Washington Council of Governments, 1994); Chesapeake Bay Commission, *The Cost of a Clean Bay: Assessing Funding Needs throughout the Watershed* (Annapolis, MD: CBC, 2003), http://www.chesbay.us/Publications/C2Kfunding.pdf; Boesch and Goldman, "Chesapeake Bay"; Howard R. Ernst, *Chesapeake Bay Blues: Science, Politics, and the Struggle to Save the Bay* (Lanham, MD: Rowman & Littlefield, 2003); *Fight for the Bay: Why a Dark Green Environmental Awakening Is Needed to Save the Chesapeake Bay* (Lanham, MD: Rowman & Littlefield, 2010); Judith A. Layzer, *Natural Experiments: Ecosystem-Based Management and the Environment* (Cambridge, MA: MIT Press, 2008); Doyle and Miralles-Wilhelm, "The Culture of Collaboration in the Chesapeake Bay Program," 195–199.

14. US Environmental Protection Agency, *Community-Based Watershed Management: Lessons from the National Estuary Program* (Washington, DC: USEPA, 2005), 35–38, https://www.epa.gov/nep/fact-sheet-about-community-based-watershed-management-handbook. See Neil Fligstein and Doug McAdam, *A Theory of Fields* (New York: Oxford University Press, 2012).

15. Thomas Webler and Seth Tuler, "Integrating Technical Analysis with Deliberation in Regional Watershed Management Planning: Applying the National Research Council Approach," *Policy Studies Journal* 27 (1999): 530–543; Michael J. Kennish, ed., *Estuary Restoration and Maintenance: The National Estuary Program* (Boca Raton, FL: CRC Press, 2000).

16. Eva Sørensen and Jacob Torfing, "The Democratic Anchorage of Governance Networks," *Scandinavian Political Studies* 28 (2005): 195–218.

17. Author's field observations and interviews, Seattle and Bainbridge, WA, February and March 2008; Puget Sound Partnership, Action Agendas, 2012/2013, 2014/2015, 2016, 2018–2022, https://www.psp.wa.gov/action_agenda_center.php.

18. National Research Council, Committee on Assessing and Valuing the Ser-

vices of Aquatic and Related Terrestrial Ecosystems, *Valuing Ecosystem Services: Toward Better Environmental Decision-Making* (Washington, DC: National Academies Press, 2005); Robert I. McDonald, *Conservation for Cities: How to Plan and Build Natural Infrastructure* (Washington, DC: Island Press, 2015); Linwood H. Pendleton, *The Economic and Market Value of Coasts and Estuaries: What's at Stake?* (Arlington, VA: Restore America's Estuaries, 2008); Daniel Holland, James Sanchirico, Robert Johnston, and Deepak Jogleka, *Economic Analysis for Ecosystem-Based Management: Applications to Marine and Coastal Environments* (Washington, DC: RFF Press, 2010). On ecosystem services, see Dan L. Perlman and Jeffrey Milder, *Practical Ecology for Planners, Developers, and Citizens* (Washington, DC: Island Press, 2005).

19. Ronald L. Ohrel Jr. and Kathleen M. Register, *Voluntary Estuary Monitoring: A Methods Manual* (Washington, DC: Ocean Conservancy, 2006).

20. Mark Lubell, "Do Watershed Partnerships Enhance Beliefs Conducive to Collective Action?" in *Swimming Upstream*, 201–232. See also Mark Schneider, John Scholz, Mark Lubell, Denisa Mindruta, and Matthew Edwardsen, "Building Consensual Institutions: Networks and the National Estuary Program," *American Journal of Political Science* 47 (2003): 143–158; Lynn Mandarano, "Evaluating Collaborative Environmental Planning Outputs and Outcomes: Restoring and Protecting Habitat and the New York-New Jersey Harbor Estuary Program," *Journal of Planning Education and Research* 27 (2008): 456–468.

21. Kim Herman Goslant, "Citizen Participation and Administrative Discretion in the Cleanup of Narragansett Bay," *Harvard Environmental Law Review* 12 (1988): 522–556.

22. Author's field notes, Eighth National Coastal and Estuarine Summit, jointly sponsored by Restore America's Estuaries and the Coastal Society, New Orleans, LA, December 10–15, 2016; Restore America's Estuaries, *A National Strategy to Restore Coastal and Estuarine Habitat* (Arlington, VA: RAE, 2002), https://estuaries.org/wp-content/uploads/2020/02/A-National-Strategy-to-Restore-Coastal-and-Estuarine-Habitat_2002.pdf; Restore America's Estuaries, *Annual Reports, Financials* (Arlington, VA: RAE, 2001–2017), https://estuaries.org/annual-reports-financials/; dollar figures are from the 2005 annual report (5) and the NOAA National Marine Fisheries Service Restoration Center website at https://coast.noaa.gov/digitalcoast/contributing-partners/noaa-national-marine-fisheries-service-restoration-center.html.

23. Restore America's Estuaries, *Living Shorelines: From Barriers to Opportunities* (Arlington, VA: RAE, 2015), https://estuaries.org/?s=Living+Shorelines%3A+From+Barriers+to+Opportunities+; Robert I. McDonald and Daniel Shemie, *Urban Water Blueprint: Mapping Conservation Solutions to the Global Water Challenge* (Washington, DC: The Nature Conservancy, in partnership with C40 Cities and the International Water Association, 2014), https://www.h2info.us/resource

/urban-water-blueprint-mapping-conservation-solutions-global-water-challenge; Brian Needelman, Stephen Crooks, Janet E. Hawkes, et al., *Restore—Adapt—Mitigate: Responding to Climate Change through Coastal Habitat Restoration* (Arlington, VA: RAE, 2012), https://estuaries.org/wp-content/uploads/2018/08/RAE_Restore-Adapt-Mitigate_Climate-Chg-Report.pdf.

24. For the emergence of watershed framing as ecologically integrative and civically generative, see Goslant, "Citizen Participation and Administrative Discretion"; Bob Doppelt, Mary Scurlock, Chris Frissell, and James Karr, *Entering the Watershed: A New Approach to Save America's River Ecosystems* (Washington, DC: Island Press, 1993); Luna B. Leopold, *A View of the River* (Cambridge, MA: Harvard University Press, 1994). For an account of how the new river management paradigm emerged from the work of Donald Tennant within the US Fish and Wildlife Service from 1956 to 1975, see Sandra Postel and Brian Richter, *Rivers for Life: Managing Water for People and Nature* (Washington, DC: Island Press, 2003). This includes the development of a "policy toolbox."

25. River Network and the Rivers, Trails, and Conservation Assistance Program, National Park Service, *1998–1999 River and Watershed Conservation Directory* (Portland, OR: To the Point Publications, 1998); Freeman House, *Totem Salmon: Life Lessons from Another Species* (Boston, MA: Beacon Press, 1999); Robert Doherty, *Disputed Waters: Native Americans and the Great Lakes Fishery* (Lexington: University Press of Kentucky, 2014); Katherine L. Reedy-Maschner, *Aleut Identities: Tradition and Modernity in an Indigenous Fishery* (Montréal: McGill-Queen's University Press, 2010).

26. US Environmental Protection Agency (EPA), *National Directory of Volunteer Environmental Monitoring Programs* (Washington, DC: Office of Water, 1994); John Cronin and Robert F. Kennedy Jr., *The RIVERKEEPERS: Two Activists Fight to Reclaim Our Environment as a Basic Human Right* (New York: Scribner, 1997).

27. Author's field notes, participation in strategic visioning exercises, and discussions with staff and board, River Rally, Cleveland, OH, June 21–24, 2019, and Pittsburgh, PA, May 30–June 2, 2014; River Network, "River Voices," quarterly newsletter, https://www.rivernetwork.org/river-voices-newsletter/.

28. Peter Lavigne, *The Watershed Innovators Workshop: Swift River Inn, Cummington, Massachusetts Proceedings* (Portland, OR: River Network, 1995); "Watershed Councils East and West: Advocacy, Consensus and Environmental Progress," *UCLA Journal of Environmental Law and Policy* 22 (2004): 301–319. On structural design, cultural norms, and deliberative practice, see also Edward P. Weber, *Bringing Society Back In: Grassroots Ecosystem Management, Accountability, and Sustainable Communities* (Cambridge, MA: MIT Press, 2003).

29. Ken Slattery, Joy Huber, and Phil Shelton, *Four Corners Watershed Innovators Report: Washington Background Report* (Portland, OR: River Network, 1997); Fran Vitulli, Sari Sommarstrom, et al., *Four Corners Watershed Innovators Report:*

California Background Report (Portland, OR: River Network, 1998); Derek Busby and Don Elder, *Four Corners Watershed Innovators Report: Florida Background Report* (Portland, OR: River Network, 1997); Mark Smith, Ed Himlan, Bob Zimmerman, Curt Laffin, and Ian Cooke, *Four Corners Watershed Innovators Report: Massachusetts Background Report* (Portland, OR: River Network, 1998); Stephen Born and Kenneth D. Genskow, *Exploring the Watershed Approach: Critical Dimensions of State-Local Partnerships* (Portland, OR: River Network, 1999); *The Watershed Approach: An Empirical Assessment of Innovation in Environmental Management* (Washington, DC: National Academy of Public Administration, 2000). See also Mark T. Imperial and Timothy Hennessey, *Environmental Governance in Watersheds: The Importance of Collaboration to Institutional Performance* (Washington, DC: National Academy of Public Administration, 2000).

30. US EPA, *Toward a Place-Driven Approach: The Edgewater Consensus on an EPA Strategy for Ecosystem Protection* (Washington, DC: EPA, 1994).

31. DeWitt John, *Civic Environmentalism: Alternatives to Regulation in States and Communities* (Washington, DC: CQ Press, 1994); National Academy of Public Administration (NAPA), *Setting Priorities, Getting Results: A New Direction for the Environmental Protection Agency: A NAPA Report to Congress* (Washington, DC: NAPA, 1995); NAPA, *Resolving the Paradoxes of Environmental Protection: An Agenda for Congress, EPA, and the States* (Washington, DC: NAPA, 1997); DeWitt John and Marian Mlay, "Community-Based Environmental Protection: Encouraging Civic Environmentalism," in *Better Environmental Decisions: Strategies for Governments, Businesses, and Communities*, ed. Ken Sexton, Alfred A. Marcus, K. William Easter, and Timothy D. Burkhardt (Washington, DC: Island Press, 1998), 353–376. See John W. Gardner, *On Leadership* (New York: Free Press, 1990).

32. Suzanne Easton, "Watershed Assistance Grants: Building Capacity of Community-Based Watershed Partnerships: An Evaluation" (Portland, OR: River Network, 2001).

33. EPA Region 8, *Natural News*, ecosystem program newsletter, fall 2000 to fall 2007; Urban Waters National Training Workshop, Sheraton Hotel, Arlington, VA, July 26–28, 2016.

34. Tom Schueler and Anne Kitchell, *Methods to Develop Restoration Plans for Small Urban Watersheds* (Ellicott City, MD: Center for Watershed Protection, 2005).

35. Carmen Sirianni, "Bringing the State Back In through Collaborative Governance: Emergent Mission and Practice at the U.S. Environmental Protection Agency," in *Varieties of Civic Innovation: Deliberative, Collaborative, Network, and Narrative Approaches*, ed. Jennifer Girouard and Carmen Sirianni (Nashville, TN: Vanderbilt University Press, 2014), 215, table 2, for an extensive list of events and types of participants. See also Joseph Lampel and Alan D. Meyer, "Field-Configuring Events as Structuring Mechanisms: How Conferences, Ceremonies, and

Trade Shows Constitute New Technologies, Industries, and Markets," *Journal of Management Studies* 45 (2008): 1025–1035; Miller McPherson, Lynn Smith-Lovin, and James M. Cook, "Birds of a Feather: Homophily in Social Networks," *Annual Review of Sociology* 27 (2001): 415–444.

36. Anne Taufen Wessels, "Ways of Knowing the Los Angeles River Watershed: Getting from Engaged Participation to Inclusive Deliberation," in *Varieties of Civic Innovation*, 23–44. See also Bruce Evan Goldstein, Anne Taufen Wessels, Raul P. Lejano, and William Butler, "Narrating Resilience: Transforming Urban Systems through Collaborative Storytelling," *Urban Studies* 52 (2015): 1285–1303; Anne Taufen Wessels and Raul P. Lejano, "Urban Waterways and Waterfront Spaces: Social Construction of a Common Good," *Journal of the Southwest* 59 (2017): 106–132. See also Robert Gottlieb, *Reinventing Los Angeles: Nature and Community in the Global City* (Cambridge, MA: MIT Press, 2007).

37. American Rivers, *Annual Reports and Financial Statements* (Washington, DC: American Rivers, 2011–2016), https://www.americanrivers.org/about-us/; American Rivers, "*Strategic Plan 2014–2018* (Washington, DC: American Rivers, 2013). See also Noah Garrison, Robert C. Wilkinson, and Richard Horner, *A Clear Blue Future: How Greening California Cities Can Address Water Resources and Climate Challenges in the 21st Century* (New York: NRDC, 2009); Christopher J. Bosso, *Environment, Inc.: From Grassroots to Beltway* (Lawrence: University Press of Kansas, 2005), 65; Samuel P. Hays, with Barbara D. Hays, *Beauty, Health, and Permanence: Environmental Politics in the United States, 1955–1985* (New York: Cambridge University Press, 1987), 141.

38. Lisa Hollingsworth-Segedy and Peter Raabe, "Creative Engagement for Controversial Projects" (presentation at the River Rally, Cleveland, OH, June 22, 2019); American Rivers, *Annual Report 2011*, qtd. on 6; American Rivers, "*Annual Report 2016*, qtd. on 2–7; American Rivers, *Annual Report 2012*, qtd. on 5.

39. Clean Water Action/Clean Water Fund, *2016 Annual Report* (Washington, DC: Clean Water Action, 2016), qtd. on 17, https://www.cleanwateraction.org/sites/default/files/docs/publications/2016%20Annual%20Report%20CWA%20and%20CWF.pdf; Clean Water Action/Clean Water Fund, "*The Chilling Effect of Oil and Gas Money on Democracy: Environmental Policy and Oversight Influenced by Polluter Interests* (Washington, DC: Clean Water Fund, 2016), https://www.cleanwaterfund.org/sites/default/files/docs/publications/Money_in_Politics_05%2003%2016a_web%20-%20FINAL.pdf; David Zwick and Marcy Benstock, *Water Wasteland* (New York: Bantam, 1971); Bosso, *Environment, Inc.*, 64; Benjamin J. Pauli, *Flint Fights Back: Environmental Justice and Democracy in the Flint Water Crisis* (Cambridge, MA: MIT Press, 2019).

40. Glennon, "The Disconnect Between Water Law and Hydrology"; Helen Ingram, John M. Whitely, and Richard Perry, "The Importance of Equity and the Limits of Efficiency in Water Resources," in *Water, Place, and Equity*, ed. John M.

Whiteley, Helen Ingram, and Richard Warren Perry (Cambridge, MA: MIT Press, 2008), 1–32; Allison Lassiter, ed., *Sustainable Water: Challenges and Solutions from California* (Berkeley: University of California Press, 2015).

41. US EPA, *Managing Wet Weather with Green Infrastructure: Action Strategy and Municipal Handbooks* (Washington, DC: EPA, 2008); EPA, *Protecting Water Resources with Smart Growth* (Washington, DC: EPA, 2015), https://www.epa.gov /smartgrowth/protecting-water-resources-smart-growth; McDonald, *Conservation for Cities*; McDonald and Shemie, *Urban Water Blueprint.* See also Timothy Beatley, *Planning for Coastal Resilience: Best Practices for Calamitous Times* (Washington, DC: Island Press, 2009); *Blue Urbanism: Exploring Connections between Cities and Oceans* (Washington, DC: Island Press, 2014).

42. NACTO, *Urban Street Stormwater Guide* (Washington, DC: Island Press, 2017); Sirianni, *Investing in Democracy*, 105–106.

43. Andrew Karvonen, *Politics of Urban Runoff: Nature, Technology, and the Sustainable City* (Cambridge, MA: MIT Press, 2011), 123–158, qtd. on 136 and 139; Carmen Sirianni, "Neighborhood Planning as Collaborative Democratic Design: The Case of Seattle," *Journal of the American Planning Association* 73 (2007): 373–87; Slattery, Huber, and Shelton, *Four Corners Watershed Innovators Report*, 11–12; Harry Wiland, Dale Bell and Joseph D'Agnese, *Edens Lost and Found: How Ordinary Citizens Are Restoring Our Great American Cities.* Book and Seattle DVD (White River Junction, VT: Chelsea Green, 2006).

44. NACTO, *Urban Street Stormwater Guide.*

45. David Soll, *Empire of Water: An Environmental and Political History of the New York City Water Supply* (Ithaca, NY: Cornell University Press, 2013), 11–96; National Research Council, *Watershed Management for Potable Water Supply: Assessing the New York City Strategy* (Washington, DC: National Academy Press, 2000); Diane Galusha, *Liquid Assets: A History of New York City's Water System* (Fleischmanns, NY: Purple Mountain Press, 1999).

46. Keith Porter, "Fixing Our Drinking Water: From Field and Forest to Faucet," *Pace Environmental Law Review* 23 (2006): 389–422; Justin Freiberg, Xiaoting Hu, Jason Nerenberg, Fauna Samuel, and Erin Derrington, "New York City Watershed Management: Past, Present, and Future," in *Natural and Engineered Solutions for Drinking Water Supplies: Lessons from the Northeastern United States and Directions for Global Watershed Management*, ed. Emily Alcott, Mark S. Ashton, and Bradford S. Gentry (Boca Raton, FL: CRC Press, 2013), 117–171; Soll, *Empire of Water.*

47. Marilyn Gelber, in Nancy Burnett, with Virginia Scheer, "Behind the Scenes: The Inside Story of the Watershed Agreement," audio transcripts, set 2, Catskill Watershed Corporation, Margaretville, NY, 1996–2001, 52–69; Albert Appleton, "Regional Landscape Preservation and the New York City Watershed Protection Program: Some Reflections," in *The Race for Space: The Politics and*

Economics of State Open Space Programs, ed. Keith S. Goldfeld (Princeton, NJ: Princeton University, Policy Research Institute for the Region, 2006), 39–72. On "small talk," see Caroline W. Lee, "Is There a Place for Private Conversation in Public Dialogue? Comparing Stakeholder Assessments of Informal Communication in Collaborative Regional Planning," *American Journal of Sociology* 113 (2007): 41–96.

48. Keith S. Porter, in *Behind the Scenes*, 89–103; Soll, *Empire of Water*, 148–176; Freiberg, "New York City Watershed Management."

49. Robert D. Lifset, *Power on the Hudson: Storm King Mountain and the Emergence of Modern American Environmentalism* (Pittsburg, PA: University of Pittsburgh Press, 2014).

50. New York State Department of State, *New York City Watershed Memorandum of Agreement* (New York: NYSDS, 1997), https://www.dos.ny.gov/watershed/pdf/agreement/NYCMOA-VI.pdf; Robert F. Kennedy Jr., in *Behind the Scenes*, 73–86; Robert F. Kennedy Jr., "A Culture of Mismanagement: Environmental Protection and Enforcement at the New York City Department of Environmental Protection," *Pace Environmental Law Review* 15 (1997): 233–292; Cronin and Kennedy, *The RIVERKEEPERS*.

51. Kennedy, in *Behind the Scenes*, qtd. on 80; see also *Behind the Scenes*, set 1; Catskill Watershed Corporation (CWC), *2016 Annual Report* (Margaretville, NY: CWC, 2016): https://cwconline.org/wp-content/uploads/2017/04/CWC-Annual-Report-2016-with-coverspdf.pdf], qtd. on 1; Soll, *Empire of Water*, qtd. on 151.

52. Gelber in *Behind the Scenes*, set 2, 51–53; Watershed Agricultural Council (WAC), *Strategic Plans* (Arkville, NY: WAC, 2004, 2010, and 2016), https://www.nycwatershed.org/; WAC, meeting agendas and minutes, 2016–2017, https://www.nycwatershed.org/about-us/policies-agendas-minutes/. See also Land Trust Alliance (LTA), *Annual Reports* (Washington, DC: LTA, 2008–2016), https://www.landtrustalliance.org/about/annual-report; *National Land Trust Census Report: Our Common Ground and Collective Impact* (Washington, DC: LTA, 2015), http://s3.amazonaws.com/landtrustalliance.org/2015NationalLandTrustCensusReport.pdf. See also David Stradling, *Making Mountains: New York City and the Catskills* (Seattle: University of Washington Press, 2007); Sally K. Fairfax, Lauren Gwin, Mary Ann King, Leigh Raymond, and Laura A. Watt, *Buying Nature: The Limits of Land Acquisition as a Conservation Strategy, 1780–2004* (Cambridge, MA: MIT Press, 2005); Jason Corburn, *Street Science* (Cambridge, MA: MIT Press, 2005).

53. Maarten De Kadt, *The Bronx River (NY): An Environmental and Social History* (Charleston, SC: History Press, 2011); Stephen Paul DeVillo, *The Bronx River in History and Folklore* (Charleston, SC: Arcadia Publishing, 2015).

54. Soll, *Empire of Water*, 177–205; Jennifer Dodge, "The Deliberative Potential of Civil Society Organizations: Framing Hydraulic Fracturing in New York," *Policy Studies* 36 (2015): 249–266.

55. Kennedy in *Behind the Scenes*, set 2, 80; Freiberg, "New York City Water-shed Management," qtd. on 162.

56. Weber, *Bringing Society Back In*; Robert B. Keiter, *Keeping Faith with Nature: Ecosystems, Democracy, and America's Public Lands* (New Haven, CT: Yale University Press, 2003); Martin Nie, *The Governance of Western Public Lands: Mapping Its Present and Future* (Lawrence: University Press of Kansas, 2008).

Chapter 6. Governance Pathways to Urban Sustainability

1. Carl Abbott, *Portland: Planning, Politics, and Growth in the Twentieth Century* (Lincoln: University of Nebraska Press, 1983); Robert D. Johnston, *The Radical Middle Class: Populist Democracy and the Question of Capitalism in Progressive Era Portland, Oregon* (Princeton, NJ: Princeton University Press, 2003); Steven Reed Johnson, "The Transformation of Civic Institutions and Practices in Portland, Oregon, 1960–1999" (PhD diss., Portland State University, Portland, OR, 2002); Thomas Goebel, *A Government by the People: Direct Democracy in America, 1890–1940* (Chapel Hill: University of North Carolina Press, 2002).

2. Jeffrey M. Berry, Kent E. Portney, and Ken Thomson, *The Rebirth of Urban Democracy* (Washington, DC: Brookings Press, 1993); Carl Abbott, *Greater Portland: Urban Life and Landscape in the Pacific Northwest* (Philadelphia: University of Pennsylvania Press, 2001); Archon Fung, *Empowered Participation: Reinventing Urban Democracy* (Princeton, NJ: Princeton University Press, 2004). San Francisco's planning director, Allan Jacobs, who had incorporated some of the lessons of that city's freeway and other revolts into planning practices, was invited by Neil Goldschmidt, Portland's mayor (1973–1979), to attend an April 1973 weekend workshop with core staff and citizen activists, though the institutional model chosen by Portland was different.

3. City of Portland, *The River Plan: River Concept* (Portland, OR: Bureau of Planning, 2006); City of Portland, *Downtown Portland Waterfront Activation Strategy* (Portland: Bureau of Planning, 2014), https://www.pdx.edu/usp/sites/www.pdx.edu.usp/files/Downtown%20Portland%20Waterfront%20Activation%20Strategy-Part%201.pdf; William G. Robbins, *Landscapes of Conflict: The Oregon Story, 1900–2000* (Seattle: University of Washington Press, 2004); Matthew Witt, "Dialectics of Control: The Origins and Evolution of Conflict in Portland's Neighborhood Association Program," in *The Portland Edge: Challenges and Successes in Growing Communities*, ed. Connie P. Ozawa (Washington, DC: Island Press, 2004), 84–101; Steven Reed Johnson, "The Myth and Reality of Portland's Engaged Citizenry and Process-Oriented Governance," in *The Portland Edge*, 102–117; Michael Houck, "Bankside Citizens," in *Rivertown: Rethinking Urban Rivers*, ed. Paul Stanton Kibel (Cambridge, MA: MIT Press, 2007), 179–196; Abbott, *Greater Portland*, 57.

4. Sy Adler, *Oregon Plans: The Making of an Unquiet Land Use Revolution* (Corvallis: Oregon State University Press, 2012), for an especially fine-grained account of the complex processes aligning local civic engagement of various types with planning, advocacy, legislation, stakeholder strategies, conflict resolution, and monitoring of the Growth Management Act; Christopher Leo, "Regional Growth Management Regime: The Case of Portland, Oregon," *Journal of Urban Affairs* 20 (1998): 363–394; Carl Abbott, "Planning a Sustainable City: The Promise and Performance of Portland's Urban Growth Boundary," in *Urban Sprawl: Causes, Consequences, and Policy Responses*, ed. Gregory D. Squires (Lanham, MD: Rowman & Littlefield, 2002), 363–394; John M. DeGrove, *Planning Policy and Politics* (Cambridge, MA: Lincoln Institute of Land Policy, 2005), 9–41; David Oates, *City Limits: Walking Portland's Boundary* (Corvallis: Oregon State University Press, 2006).

5. Johnson, "Myth and Reality," qtd. on 113.

6. Metro (OR), *The Nature of 2040: The Region's 50-Year Plan for Managing Growth* (Portland: Portland State University, Metro Collection, 1995), https://pdx scholar.library.pdx.edu/cgi/viewcontent.cgi?article=1033&context=oscdl_metro; Judith Layzer, "Making Tradeoffs: Urban Sprawl and the Evolving System of Growth Management in Portland, Oregon," in *The Environmental Case: Translating Values into Policy*, ed. Judith A. Layzer (Washington, DC: CQ Press, 2011), 488–514; Matthew Slavin and Kent Snyder, "Strategic Climate Action Planning in Portland," in *Sustainability in America's Cities: Creating the Green Metropolis*, ed. Matthew Slavin, 2nd ed. (Washington, DC: Island Press, 2011), 21–44; Abbott, *Greater Portland*. On institutional responses to the oil crises in the 1970s, see Meg Jacobs, *Panic at the Pump: The Energy Crisis and the Transformation of American Politics in the 1970s* (New York: Hill and Wang, 2016).

7. Ethan Seltzer, "It's Not an Experiment: Regional Planning at Metro, 1990 to the Present," in *The Portland Edge*, 35–60, qtd. on 57; John Fregonese and C. J. Gabbe, "Engaging the Public and Communicating Successfully in Regional Planning," in *Regional Planning in America: Practice and Prospect*, ed. Ethan Seltzer and Armando Carbonell (Cambridge, MA: Lincoln Institute of Land Policy, 2011), 222–242; Jill Sterrett, Connie Ozawa, Dennis Ryan, Ethan Seltzer, and Jan Whittington, eds., *Planning the Pacific Northwest* (New York: Taylor & Francis, 2015).

8. City of Portland and Multnomah County, climate action plan archive, 1993–2017, https://beta.portland.gov/bps/climate-action/history-and-key-documents -climate-planning-and-action-portland; Timothy Grewe, Susan Anderson, and Laurel Butman, "Portland, Oregon: A Case Study in Sustainability," *Government Finance Review* 18 (2002): 8–12, qtd. on 9; Susan Anderson and Michael Armstrong, "Sustainability in the City of Portland," Sustainable City webinar, October 29, 2015, https://www.youtube.com/watch?v=ljVgyJkZ2Zw; Dan Salzman, Susan Anderson, and Rob Bennett, *ReThinking Development: Portland's Strategic Investment in Green Building* (Portland, OR: Office of Sustainable Development, 2003);

Wendy Mendes, Kevin Balmer, Terra Kaethler, and Amanda Rhoads, "Using Land Inventories to Plan for Urban Agriculture: Experiences from Portland and Vancouver," *Journal of the American Planning Association* 74 (2008): 435–449; Slavin and Snyder, "Strategic Climate Action Planning in Portland"; Alexander Aylett, "Relational Agency and the Local Governance of Climate Change: International Trends and an American Exemplar," in *The Urban Climate Challenge: Rethinking the Role of Cities in the Global Climate Regime*, ed. Craig Johnson, Noah Toly, and Heike Schroeder (New York: Routledge, 2015), 156–177; Timothy Beatley, *Handbook of Biophilic City Planning and Design* (Washington, DC: Island Press, 2016), 93–102.

9. City of Portland, "The Portland Plan," 2012, qtd. on 4–5, https://www .portlandonline.com/portlandplan/index.cfm?c=56527; Jill Fuglister, Ron Carley, Sheila Martin, et al., *The Regional Equity Atlas: Metropolitan Portland's Geography of Opportunity* (Portland, OR: Coalition for a Livable Future, 2007); Connie P. Ozawa, "Developing Effective Participatory Processes for a Sustainable City," in *Elgar Companion to Sustainable Cities: Strategies, Methods, and Outlook*, ed. Daniel A. Mazmanian and Hilda Blanco (Northampton, MA: Edward Elgar, 2014), 210–227; Vivek Shandas and W. Barry Messer, "Fostering Green Communities Through Civic Engagement: Community-Based Environmental Stewardship in the Portland Area," *Journal of the American Planning Association* 74 (2008): 408–418. On the role of Portland State University and its implementation of "Let Knowledge Serve the City" as a model within the movement to enrich the civic mission of higher education, see Carmen Sirianni, "The New Student Politics: Sustainable Action for Democracy," *Journal of Public Affairs* 7 (2004): 101–123; Anne Colby, Thomas Ehrlich, Elizabeth Beaumont, and Jason Stephens, *Educating Citizens: Preparing America's Undergraduates for Lives of Moral and Civic Responsibility* (San Francisco, CA: Jossey-Bass, 2003).

10. J. Allen Whitt, *Urban Elites and Mass Transportation: The Dialectics of Power* (Princeton, NJ: Princeton University Press, 1982), 40–80.

11. Chester Hartman, with Sarah Carnochan, *City for Sale: The Transformation of San Francisco,* revised and updated edition (Berkeley: University of California Press, 2002).

12. Frederick M. Wirt, *Power in the City: Decision Making in San Francisco* (Berkeley: University of California Press, 1974); Stephen J. McGovern, *The Politics of Downtown Development: Dynamic Political Cultures in San Francisco and Washington, D.C.* (Lexington: University Press of Kentucky, 1998).

13. John H. Mollenkopf, *The Contested City* (Princeton, NJ: Princeton University Press, 1983); Ralph M. Kramer, *Participation of the Poor: Comparative Community Case Studies in the War on Poverty* (Englewood Cliffs, NJ: Prenitice Hall, 1969); Stephen E. Barton, "The Neighborhood Movement in San Francisco," *Berkeley Planning Journal* 2 (1985): 85–105; Chester W. Hartman, *Yerba Buena:*

Land Grab and Community Resistance in San Francisco (San Francisco, CA: Glide Publications, 1974). On the highway revolt in San Francisco, see Katherine M. Johnson, "Captain Blake versus the Highwaymen: Or, How San Francisco Won the Highway Revolt," *Journal of Planning History* 8 (2009): 56–83; William Issel, "Land Values, Human Values, and the Preservation of the City's Treasured Appearance: Environmentalism, Politics, and the San Francisco Freeway Revolt," *Pacific Historical Review* 68 (1999): 611–646; Jason Henderson, *Street Fight: The Struggle over Urban Mobility in San Francisco* (Amherst: University of Massachusetts Press, 2013).

14. Jasper Rubin, *A Negotiated Landscape: The Transformation of San Francisco's Waterfront since 1950* (Pittsburgh, PA: University of Pittsburgh Press, 2011), qtd. on 175; Allison Isenberg, *Designing San Francisco: Art, Land, and Urban Renewal in the City by the Bay* (Princeton, NJ: Princeton University Press, 2017); Bruce Brugmann and Greggar Sletteland, eds., *The Ultimate Highrise: San Francisco's Mad Rush Toward the Sky* (San Francisco, CA: Bay Guardian Books, 1971); Tomás F. Summers Sandoval, *Latinos at the Golden Gate: Creating Community and Identity in San Francisco* (Chapel Hill: University of North Carolina Press, 2013); William Issel, *Church and State in the City: Catholics and Politics in Twentieth-Century San Francisco* (Philadelphia, PA: Temple University Press, 2013); Manuel Castells, *The City and the Grassroots: A Cross-Cultural Theory of Urban Social Movements* (Berkeley: University of California Press, 1983); Allan B. Jacobs, *Making City Planning Work* (Chicago, IL: American Planning Association, 1980); Patrick J. O'Hern, "Reclaiming the Urban Environment: The San Francisco Urban Design Plan," *Ecology Law Quarterly* 3 (1973): 535–595; Stephen L. Vettel, "San Francisco's Downtown Plan: Environmental and Urban Design Values in Central Business District Regulation," *Ecology Law Quarterly* 12 (1985): 511–566.

15. Sue Hestor, "San Francisco's Leading Slow Growth Advocate: Sue Hestor," interview by Arthur Bruzzone, pts. 1 and 2, SFunscriptedTV May 2011; McGovern, *Politics of Downtown Development*, 87–118; Tony Robinson, "Gentrification and Grassroots Resistance in San Francisco's Tenderloin," *Urban Affairs Quarterly* 30 (1995): 483–513; "Community Mobilization and Regime Transformation in San Francisco's Tenderloin" (PhD diss., University of California, Berkeley, CA, 1994); Randy Shaw, *The Tenderloin: Sex, Crime, and Resistance in the Heart of San Francisco* (Urban Reality Press, 2015).

16. Richard Edward DeLeon, *Left Coast City: Progressive Politics in San Francisco, 1975–1991* (Lawrence: University Press of Kansas, 1992), qtd. on 70; McGovern, *Politics of Downtown Development*, 119–185.

17. City and County of San Francisco, *Redevelopment Plan for the Mission Bay South Redevelopment Project* (San Francisco, CA: Office of Community Investment and Infrastructure, 2018), https://sfocii.org/sites/default/files/Redevelopment%20 Plan%20for%20the%20Mission%20Bay%20South%20Redevelopment%20Proj

ect_March_6_2018_0.pdf; David Prowler, "From Railyard to Neighborhood: The Rise of Mission Bay," *Urbanist*, August 1, 2005; Gerald D. Adams, "At Mission Bay, It's Try, Try Again," *Planning* 68 (2002): 18–23; Marcia Rosen and Wendy Sullivan, "From Urban Renewal and Displacement to Economic Inclusion: San Francisco Affordable Housing Policy 1978–2014," *Stanford Law & Policy Review* 25 (2014): 121–162; Nicole Foletta and Jason Henderson, *Low Car(Bon) Communities: Inspiring Car-Free and Car-Lite Urban Futures* (New York: Routledge, 2016), 40–71.

18. Save the Bay, annual reports, 2011–2016, https://www.savebay.org/about-us/publications/; Save the Bay, *2020 Strategic Plan* (San Francisco, CA: Save the Bay, 2017), https://savesfbay.org/wp-content/uploads/2018/10/Save-The-Bay_2020-Strategic-Plan.pdf; David Lewis, executive director of Save the Bay, plenary presentation, Eighth National Conference on Coastal and Estuarine Restoration, New Orleans, LA, December 12, 2016; Kay Kerr, Sylvia McLaughlin, and Esther Gulick, "Save San Francisco Bay Association, 1961–1986" (Berkeley: Regional Oral History Office, Bancroft Library, University of California, 1987); Sylvia McLaughlin, "Citizen Activist for the Environment: Saving San Francisco Bay, Promoting Shoreline Parks and Natural Values in Urban and Campus Planning," oral history interviews by Ann Lage, conducted in 2006–2007, Regional Oral History Office, Bancroft Library, University of California, Berkeley, CA, 2009; Richard A. Walker, *The Country in the City: The Greening of the San Francisco Bay Area* (Seattle: University of Washington Press, 2007), qtd. on 13; John Hart and David Sanger, *San Francisco Bay: Portrait of an Estuary* (Berkeley: University of California Press, 2003); Sally Fairfax, Louise Nelson Dyble, Greig Tor Guthey, Lauren Gwin, Monica Moore, and Jennifer Sokolove, *California Cuisine and Just Food* (Cambridge, MA: MIT Press, 2012); Karen Chapplle, *Planning Sustainable Cities and Regions: Towards More Equitable Development* (New York: Routledge, 2015); Barbara Epstein, *Political Protest and Cultural Revolution: Nonviolent Direct Action in the 1970s and 1980s* (Berkeley: University of California Press, 1991).

19. Greenbelt Alliance, annual reports, San Francisco, CA, 2011–2016, https://www.greenbelt.org/financials/; Greenbelt Alliance, *Urban Village Toolkit: Your Definitive Guide to Shaping San Jose's Neighborhoods* (San Jose, CA: Greenbelt Alliance, 2015), https://www.greenbelt.org/san-jose-urban-village-toolkit/; Save the Bay, *Greening the Bay: Financing Wetland Restoration in San Francisco Bay* (San Francisco, CA: Save the Bay, 2007), https://savesfbay.org/wp-content/uploads/2018/10/Save-The-Bay_Greening-The-Bay.pdf; San Francisco Water Power Sewer (2014–2015), "Water System Improvement Program: Regional Projects Quarterly Report," February 3, 2015, https://sfwater.org/modules/showdocument.aspx?documentid=6730; Ann Riley, *Restoring Streams in Cities: A Guide for Planners, Policymakers, and Citizens* (Washington, DC: Island Press, 1998); Ann Riley, *Restored Urban Streams: Case Studies in Science and Practice* (Washington, DC: Is-

land Press, 2015); Christopher K. Ansell, "Community Embeddedness and Collaborative Governance in the San Francisco Bay Area Environmental Movement," in *Social Movements and Networks: Relational Approaches to Collective Action*, ed. Mario Diani and Doug McAdam (New York: Oxford University Press, 2003), 123–144.

20. Hal K. Rothman, *The New Urban Park: Golden Gate National Recreation Area and Civic Environmentalism* (Lawrence: University Press of Kansas, 2004); Amy Meyer, with Randolph Delahanty, *New Guardians for the Golden Gate: How America Got a Great National Park* (Berkeley: University of California Press, 2006). For other urban parks and park planning in the city, see Beatley, *Handbook of Biophilic City Planning and Design*, 103–118.

21. Rothman, *The New Urban Park*; Doug Nadeau, interview by John Martini, Presidio Oral History Project, October 6, 1998.

22. Peter Berg, Beryl Magilavy, and Seth Zuckerman, *Green City Program for San Francisco Bay Area Cities and Towns* (San Francisco: Planet Drum Foundation, 1989); Beryl Magilavy, *Indicators Applications: Moving Indicators into Action—San Francisco's Experience 1988–1998* (San Francisco, CA: Sustainable City, 1998), http://sustainablecity.org/document/assess.htm; Henderson, *Street Fight*, 115.

23. City and County of San Francisco, *San Francisco Climate Action Strategy* (San Francisco, CA: Department of the Environment, 2013), https://sfenviron ment.org/sites/default/files/engagement_files/sfe_cc_ClimateActionStrategyUp date2013.pdf; City and County of San Francisco, *2014 Annual Urban Forest Report* (San Francisco, CA: Department of the Environment, 2014), https://sfen vironment.org/sites/default/files/fliers/files/2014_annual_report_final.pdf; City and County of San Francisco, "Resilient San Francisco: Stronger Today, Stronger Tomorrow" (San Francisco, CA: SFGSA, 2016), https://sfgsa.org/sites/default /files/Document/Resilient%20San%20Francisco.pdf. On field formation in the gay identity movement, see Elizabeth A. Armstrong, *Forging Gay Identities: Organizing Sexuality in San Francisco, 1950–1994* (Chicago, IL: University of Chicago Press, 2002), 154–175. On early healthy cities strategies on AIDS in San Francisco, see Carmen Sirianni and Lewis A. Friedland, *Civic Innovation in America* (Berkeley: University of California Press, 2001), 167.

24. Jason Corburn, *Toward the Healthy City: People, Places, and the Politics of Urban Planning* (Cambridge, MA: MIT Press, 2009); Christopher Lowen Agee, *The Streets of San Francisco: Policing and the Creation of a Cosmopolitan Liberal Politics, 1950–1972* (Chicago, IL: University of Chicago Press, 2014); Nan Alamilla Boyd, *Wide-Open Town: A History of Queer San Francisco to 1965* (Berkeley: University of California Press, 2003).

25. Els De Graauw, *Making Immigrant Rights Real: Nonprofits and the Politics of Integration in San Francisco* (Ithaca, NY: Cornell University Press, 2016), qtd. on 10; Carmen Sirianni and Diana A. Schor, "City Government as Enabler of Youth Civic Engagement: Policy Designs and Implications," in *Policies for Youth Civic En-*

gagement, ed. James Youniss and Peter Levine (Nashville, TN: Vanderbilt University Press, 2009), 121–163; Milbrey McLaughlin, W. Richard Scott, Sarah Deschenes, Kathryn Hopkins, and Anne Newman, *Between Movement and Establishment: Organizations Advocating for Youth* (Stanford, CA: Stanford University Press, 2009).

26. Rosen and Sullivan, "From Urban Renewal and Displacement to Economic Inclusion"; Michael Storper, Thomas Kemeny, Naji Makarem, and Taner Osman, *The Rise and Fall of Urban Economies: Lessons from San Francisco and Los Angeles* (Stanford, CA: Stanford Business Books, 2015), 138–192; Randy Shaw, *Generation Priced Out: Who Gets to Live in the New Urban America* (Berkeley: University of California Press, 2018); Cary McClelland, *Silicon City: San Francisco in the Long Shadow of the Valley* (New York: Norton, 2018); Amy L. Howard, *More Than Shelter: Activism and Community in San Francisco Public Housing* (Minneapolis: University of Minnesota Press, 2014).

27. Joel Rast, "Regime Building, Institution Building: Urban Renewal Policy in Chicago 1946–1962," *Journal of Urban Affairs* 31 (2009): 173–194; Joel Rast, "Creating a Unified Business Elite: The Origins of the Chicago Central Area Committee," *Journal of Urban History* 37 (2011): 583–605. On housing in Chicago, see Mary Pattillo, *Black on the Block: The Politics of Race and Class in the City* (Chicago, IL: University of Chicago Press, 2007); Sudhir Venkatesh, *American Project: The Rise and Fall of a Modern Ghetto* (Cambridge, MA: Harvard University Press, 2000); D. Bradford Hunt, *Blueprint for Disaster: The Unraveling of Chicago Public Housing* (Chicago, IL: University of Chicago Press, 2008); Arnold R. Hirsch, *Making the Second Ghetto: Race and Housing in Chicago 1940–1960* (Chicago, IL: University of Chicago Press, 1983).

28. Larry Bennett, *The Third City: Chicago and American Urbanism* (Chicago: University of Chicago Press, 2010), qtd. in 40; D. Bradford Hunt and Jon B. DeVries, *Planning Chicago* (Chicago, IL: APA Planners Press, 2013).

29. Amanda L. Seligman, *Block by Block: Neighborhoods and Public Policy on Chicago's West Side* (Chicago, IL: University of Chicago Press, 2005); Roberta M. Feldman and Susan Stall, *The Dignity of Resistance: Women Residents' Activism in Chicago Public Housing* (New York: Cambridge University Press, 2006); Sanford D. Horwitt, *Let Them Call Me Rebel: Saul Alinsky: His Life and Legacy* (New York: Vintage, 1992); Richard L. Wood and Brad R. Fulton, *A Shared Future: Faith-Based Organizing for Racial Equity and Ethical Democracy* (Chicago, IL: University of Chicago Press, 2015); David Moberg, "Back to Its Roots: The Industrial Areas Foundation and United Power for Action and Justice," in *The New Chicago: A Social and Cultural Analysis*, ed. John Koval, Larry Bennett, Michael Bennett, Fassil Demissie, Roberta Garner, and Kiljoong Kim (Philadelphia, PA: Temple University Press, 2006), 239–247; Robert Gioielli, *Environmental Activism and the Urban Crisis: Baltimore, St. Louis, Chicago* (Philadelphia, PA: Temple University Press, 2014), 104–136.

30. Robert J. Sampson, *Great American City: Chicago and the Enduring Neighborhood Effect* (Chicago, IL: University of Chicago Press, 2012); Dan Immergluck, "Building Power, Losing Power: The Rise and Fall of a Prominent Community Economic Development Coalition," *Economic Development Quarterly* 19 (2005): 211–224; Larry Bennett, "Postwar Redevelopment in Chicago: The Declining Politics of Party and the Rise of Neighborhood Politics," in *Unequal Partnerships: The Political Economy of Urban Redevelopment in Postwar America*, ed. Gregory Squires (New Brunswick, NJ: Rutgers University Press, 1989), 161–177; Robert Mier and Kari J. Moe, "Decentralized Development: From Theory to Practice," in *Harold Washington and Neighborhoods: Progressive City Government in Chicago, 1983–1987*, ed. Pierre Clavel and Wim Wievel (New Brunswick, NJ: Rutgers University Press, 1991), 64–99; Joan Pogge, "Reinvestment in Chicago Neighborhoods: A Twenty-Year Struggle," in *Redlining to Reinvestment*, ed. Gregory Squires (Philadelphia, PA: Temple University Press, 1992), 133–148.

31. Teresa Córdova, "Harold Washington and the Rise of Latino Electoral Politics in Chicago, 1982–1987," in *Chicano Politics and Society in the Late Twentieth Century*, ed. David Montejano (Austin: University of Texas Press, 1999), 31–57; Jaime Dominguez, "Machine Matters: The Politics of Immigrant Integration in the Chicago Metro Area," in *Unsettled Americans: Metropolitan Context and Civic Leadership for Immigrant Integration*, ed. John Mollenkopf and Manuel Pastor Jr. (Ithaca, NY: Cornell University Press, 2016), 76–101; William J. Grimshaw, *Bitter Fruit: Black Politics and the Chicago Machine, 1931–1991* (Chicago, IL: University of Chicago Press, 1992); Gary Rivlin, *Fire on the Prairie: Harold Washington, Chicago Politics, and the Roots of the Obama Presidency*, rev. ed. (Philadelphia, PA: Temple University Press, 2012).

32. City of Chicago, *Chicago Works Together: 1984 Chicago Development Plan* (Chicago, IL: Cornell, 1984), https://ecommons.cornell.edu/bitstream/handle/1813/40517/CWT-1984.pdf?sequence=2&isAllowed=y; City of Chicago, *Chicago Works Together II: Recommended Changes to the 1984 Chicago Development Plan* (Chicago, IL: Chicago Works Together Planning Task Force, 1987); Bennett, "Postwar Redevelopment in Chicago"; Robert Mier, *Social Justice and Local Development Policy* (Newbury Park, CA: SAGE, 1993), 118–119.

33. Pierre Clavel, *Activists in City Hall: The Progressive Response to the Reagan Era in Boston and Chicago* (Ithaca, NY: Cornell University Press, 2010); Hunt and DeVries, *Planning Chicago*; Mier and Moe, "Decentralized Development."

34. Elizabeth Hollander, "The Department of Planning under Harold Washington," in *Harold Washington and Neighborhoods*, 121–145; John Kretzmann, "The Affirmative Information Policy: Opening Up a Closed City," in *Harold Washington and Neighborhoods*, 199–220; Barbara Ferman, *Challenging the Growth Machine: Neighborhood Politics in Chicago and Pittsburgh* (Lawrence: University Press of Kansas, 1996), 89; Pierre Clavel, *Activists in City Hall*, 124.

35. John McCarron, "'Reform' Takes Costly Toll . . . Chicago on Hold: Politics of Poverty," *Chicago Tribune*, August 28, 1988; "Blue-Collar Dream Skews City Policy," *Chicago Tribune*, August 31, 1988; Michael Miner, "'Politics of Poverty': Why Did John McCarron Do That?" *Chicago Reader*, September 15, 1988; Rivlin, *Fire on the Prairie*, 131–218.

36. Keith Koeneman, *First Son: The Biography of Richard M. Daley* (Chicago, IL: University of Chicago Press, 2013); Costas Spirou and Dennis R. Judd, *Building the City of Spectacle: Mayor Richard M. Daley and the Remaking of Chicago* (Ithaca, NY: Cornell University Press, 2016); Terry Nichols Clark, ed., *The City as an Entertainment Machine* (Lanham, MD: Lexington Books, 2011); Rachel Weber, *From Boom to Bubble: How Finance Built the New Chicago* (Chicago, IL: University of Chicago Press, 2015), qtd. on 192; David Naguib Pellow, *Garbage Wars: The Struggle for Environmental Justice in Chicago* (Cambridge, MA: MIT Press, 2002); Adam S. Weinberg, David N. Pellow, and Allan Schnaiberg, *Urban Recycling and the Search for Sustainable Community Development* (Princeton, NJ: Princeton University Press, 2000); Saskia Sassen, "A Global City," in Charles Madigan, ed., *Global Chicago* (Urbana: University of Illinois Press, 2004), 15–34; Robert J. Chaskin and Mark L. Joseph, *Integrating the Inner City: The Promise and Perils of Mixed-Income Public Housing Transformation* (Chicago, IL: University of Chicago Press, 2017).

37. City of Chicago, *Chicago Brownfield Initiative: Recycling Our Past, Investing in Our Future* (Chicago, IL: Department of Environment, Department of Planning and Development, 2003), https://www.csu.edu/cerc/documents/ChicagoBrown fieldsInitiativeRecyclingOurPastInvestinginOurFuture.pdf; Eleonora Pasotti, *Political Branding in Cities: The Decline of Machine Politics in Bogotá, Naples, and Chicago* (New York: Cambridge University Press, 2010); Joel Rast, *Remaking Chicago: The Political Origins of Urban Industrial Change* (DeKalb: Northern Illinois University Press, 1999); Hunt and DeVries, *Planning Chicago*, 171–209; Timothy Stewart-Winter, *Queer Clout: Chicago and the Rise of Gay Politics* (Philadelphia: University of Pennsylvania Press, 2016); Clavel, *Activists in City Hall*, 137–142.

38. On participatory budgeting, see Hollie Russon Gilman, *Democracy Reinvented: Participatory Budgeting and Civic Innovation in America* (Washington, DC: Brookings Press, 2016); Victoria Gordon, Jeffery L. Osgood Jr., and Daniel Boden, *Participatory Budgeting in the United States: A Guide for Local Governments* (New York: Routledge, 2016).

39. Wesley G. Skogan and Susan M. Hartnett, *Community Policing, Chicago Style* (New York: Oxford University Press, 1997); Archon Fung, *Empowered Participation: Reinventing Urban Democracy* (Princeton, NJ: Princeton University Press, 2004); Wesley G. Skogan, *Police and Community in Chicago: A Tale of Three Cities* (New York: Oxford University Press, 2006). For strategic directions to grapple with the range of failures of Chicago policing in recent years, especially around

race in the wake of Laquan McDonald's fatal shooting in 2014, which proved a widely recognized "tipping point," see Police Accountability Task Force, *Recommendations for Reform: Restoring Trust Between the Chicago Police and the Communities They Serve* (Chicago, IL: PATF, April 2016), https://chicagopatf.org/wp-content/uploads/2016/04/PATF_Final_Report_4_13_16-1.pdf. Lori Lightfoot, chair of the task force, was elected mayor in April 2019. Wesley Skogan, a prominent Northwestern University scholar and evaluator of community policing in the city, served on the community-police relations working group. Among a broad range of analyses and recommendations, the report noted the years of recent neglect and disinvestment in the Community Alternative Policing Strategy (CAPS), including significant budget cuts in the late 2000s. It proposed to reverse this with several structural changes, renewed emphasis on beat work, further outreach to youth, enhancing "civilian organizing staff," and involvement of the community in police training (an early design feature), including ABCD and restorative justice skills (qtd. in text and endnote, 53, 14). For an ethnographic study that incorporates political competition and collaboration at the neighborhood level, see Robert Vargas, *Wounded City: Violent Turf Wars in a Chicago Barrio* (New York: Oxford University Press, 2016).

40. Robert J. Chaskin and Mikael Karlström, *Beyond the Neighborhood: Policy Engagement and Systems Change in the New Communities Program* (New York: Manpower Development Research Corporation, 2012), https://pdfs.semanticscholar.org/fcff/f97657baa0085521683039de185a0a3b279e.pdf?_ga=2.50296482.589096818.1583432252-1476452223.1583432252; Doug C. Gills and Wanda J. White, "Chicago's Empowerment Zone and Citizen Participation," in *Empowerment in Chicago: Grassroots Participation in Economic Development and Poverty Alleviation*, ed. Cedric Herring, Michael Bennett, Doug Gills, and Noah Temaner Jenkins (Urbana-Champaigne: University of Illinois Press, 1998), 140–170; David Greenberg, Sonya Williams, Mikael Karlström, Victoria Quiroz-Becerra, and Marcia Festen, *The Promise of Comprehensive Community Development: Ten Years of Chicago's New Communities Program* (New York: MDRC, 2014); Joseph P. Schwieterman and Dana M. Caspall, *The Politics of Place: A History of Zoning in Chicago* (Carbondale: Southern Illinois University Press, 2006); Dick Simpson, *Rogues, Rebels, and Rubber Stamps* (Boulder, CO: Perseus, 2001); Ferman, *Challenging the Growth Machine.* On the role of state government and special-purpose authorities, especially in attempting to bypass local protest, see James M. Smith, "'Re-Stating' Theories of Urban Development: The Politics of Authority Creation and Intergovernmental Triads in Postindustrial Chicago," *Journal of Urban Affairs* 32 (2010): 425–448. Smith also provides a basis for reconsidering Harold Washington's mayoralty in some of these institutional choices.

41. Author interview with Suzanne Malec-McKenna, former environment commissioner, City of Chicago, January 30, 2019.

42. City of Chicago, *City Space: An Open Space Plan for Chicago* (Chicago, IL: Chicago Park District and Forest Preserve District of Cook County, 1998), https:// www.chicago.gov/content/dam/city/depts/zlup/Sustainable_Development/Publi cations/CitySpace/CitySpace1a.pdf.

43. Active Transportation Alliance, annual reports, 2009–2015, https://active trans.org/about-us/our-organization/annual-reports-and-financial-information; Active Transportation Alliance, *Bikeways for All: Envisioning Chicago's Bike Network* (Chicago, IL: ATA, 2014), http://www.activetrans.org/sites/files/Bikeways%20 for%20All%20Full%20Report.pdf; City of Chicago *Bike 2015 Plan* (Chicago, IL: Mayor's Bicycle Advisory Council and Department of Transportation, 2006), http://www.bike2015plan.org/; City of Chicago, *Chicago Streets for Cycling Plan 2020* (Chicago, IL: Department of Transportation, 2012), https://www.chicago .gov/content/dam/city/depts/cdot/bike/general/ChicagoStreetsforCycling2020 .pdf.

44. Author's lunch discussion with Hank Topper, EPA headquarters staff in the Office of Pollution Prevention and Toxics (and director of Design for Environment), and EPA Region 5 Brownfields staff, EPA Community Involvement Conference, Boston, MA, August 5, 1998; Jessica Higgins, "Evaluating the Chicago Brownfields Initiative: The Effects of City-Initiated Brownfield Redevelopment on Surrounding Communities," *Northwestern Journal of Law and Social Policy* 3 (2008): 240–262; City of Chicago, "Chicago Brownfield Initiative"; Calumet Collaborative, archives, 2017–2018, http://www.calumetcollaborative.org/latest-news /archives/08-2019.

45. City of Chicago, *Adding Green to Urban Design: A City for Us and Future Generations* (Chicago, IL: City of Chicago, 2008), https://www.chicago.gov/dam /city/depts/zlup/Sustainable_Development/Publications/Green_Urban_Design /GUD_booklet.pdf; City of Chicago, *Chicago's Urban Forest Agenda* (Chicago, IL: City of Chicago, 2009), https://www.chicago.gov/content/dam/city/depts /doe/general/NaturalResourcesAndWaterConservation_PDFs/UrbanForest Agenda/ChicagosUrbanForestAgenda2009.pdf; City of Chicago, *Calumet Open Space Reserve Plan* (Chicago, IL: City of Chicago, 2002), https://www.chicago .gov/content/dam/city/depts/zlup/Sustainable_Development/Publications/Cal umet_Open_Space_Reserve/COSR_plan.pdf; Timothy J. Gilfoyle, *Millennium Park: Creating a Chicago Landmark* (Chicago, IL: University of Chicago Press, 2006); Costas Spirou, "Urban Beautification: The Construction of a New Identity in Chicago," in *New Chicago*, 295–302; Harold L. Platt, *Sinking Chicago: Climate Change and the Remaking of a Flood-Prone Environment* (Philadelphia, PA: Temple University Press, 2018); Eric Klinenberg, *Heat Wave: A Social Autopsy of Disaster in Chicago* (Chicago, IL: University of Chicago Press, 2002); Christopher R. Browning, Danielle Wallace, Seth L. Feinberg, and Kathleen A. Cagney, "Neighborhood Social Processes, Physical Conditions, and Disaster-Related Mortality: The Case

of the 1995 Heat Wave," *American Sociological Review* 71 (2006): 661–678; Julie L. Cidell, *Imagining Sustainability: Creative Urban Environmental Governance in Chicago and Melbourne* (New York: Routledge, 2017); Doug Kelbaugh, *The Urban Fix: Resilient Cities in the War Against Climate Change* (New York: Routledge, 2019), 179–182; Michael J. Lorr, "Greening Lifestyles, Homes, and Urban Infrastructure in Chicago, IL, and Jacksonville, FL," in *The Greening of Everyday Life: Challenging Practices, Imagining Possibilities*, ed. John M. Meyer and Jens Kersten (New York: Oxford University Press, 2016), 115–135; "Urban Sustainability and the 'Greening' of Neoliberal Chicago," in *Neoliberal Chicago*, ed. Larry Bennett, Roberta Garner, and Euan Hague (Chicago, IL: University of Illinois Press, 2017), 115–135. Comprehensive civic and institutional strategies for urban heat waves are now being developed in other cities; see City of New York, *Cool Neighborhoods NYC: A Comprehensive Approach to Keep Communities Safe in Extreme Heat* (New York: City of New York, 2017), https://www1.nyc.gov/assets/orr/pdf/Cool_Neigh borhoods_NYC_Report.pdf.

46. Steve Lerner, *Eco-Pioneers: Practical Visionaries Solving Today's Environmental Problems* (Cambridge, MA: MIT Press, 1997), 81–90; Bill Eyring, Kevin Green, and Franklin Lomax, *An Alternative to the Northwest Incinerator: Reducing Waste, Stimulating Economic Development, and Creating Jobs Instead of Pollution* (Chicago, IL: Center for Neighborhood Technology, 1994); Pellow, *Garbage Wars*, 137. On Design for Environment at the EPA, see Sirianni and Friedland, *Civic Innovation in America*, 121.

47. Author interview with Julia Parzen, facilitator of the Chicago Climate Task Force, April 7, 2015; Julia Parzen, *Lessons Learned: Creating the Chicago Climate Action Plan* (Chicago, IL: Global Philanthropy Partnership, ICLEI USA, and the City of Chicago, 2009), 9 and 24 for a comprehensive list of meetings, https://ledsgp.org/resource/lessons-learned-creating-the-chicago-climate-action-plan/?loclang=en_gb; Center for Neighborhood Technology, *Chicago's Greenhouse Gas Emissions: An Inventory, Forecast, and Mitigation Analysis for Chicago and the Metropolitan Region* (Chicago, IL: CNT, 2008), https://www.cnt.org/sites/default/files/publications/CNT_ChicagoGreenhouseGasEmissions.pdf; Center for Neighborhood Technology, *Industrial Ecodistricts: Primer* (Chicago, IL: CNT, 2017), https://www.cnt.org/sites/default/files/publications/CNT_EcoDistrictPrimer .pdf; Margaret Weir, Jane Rongerude, and Christopher K. Ansell, "Collaboration is Not Enough: Virtuous Cycles of Reform in Transportation Policy," *Urban Affairs Review* 44 (2009): 455–489.

48. William Stevens, *Miracle Under the Oaks: The Revival of Nature in America* (New York: Pocket Books, 1995); Stephen Packard and Cornelia F. Mutel, eds., *The Tallgrass Restoration Handbook: For Prairies, Savannas, and Woodlands* (Washington, DC: Island Press, 1997). See also William Cronon, *Nature's Metropolis: Chicago and the Great West* (New York: Norton, 1991).

49. City of Chicago, *City Space* (Chicago, IL: City of Chicago, 1998); City of Chicago, *Calumet Open Space Reserve Plan* (Chicago, IL: City of Chicago, 2002).

50. Suzanne Malec-McKenna interview, January 30, 2019. Malec-McKenna also served as executive director of Chicago Wilderness after she left city government. On the Forest Service's research intervention, see especially Paul Gobster and R. Bruce Hull, eds., *Restoring Nature: Perspectives from the Social Sciences and Humanities* (Washington, DC: Island Press, 2000); Reid Helford, "Prairie Politics: Constructing Science, Nature, and Community in the Chicago Wilderness" (PhD diss., Loyola University, Chicago, IL, 2003). See also Gavin Van Horn and Dave Aftandilian, eds., *City Creatures: Animal Encounters in the Chicago Wilderness* (Chicago, IL: University of Chicago Press, 2015).

51. Chicago Wilderness, annual reports, 2007–2008, 2010–2015, https://www.chicagowilderness.org/page/publicationsnew.

52. Julia Parzen interview, April 7, 2015; City of Chicago, *Chicago Climate Action Plan: Our City, Our Future* (Chicago, IL: City of Chicago, 2008), https://www.chicago.gov/content/dam/city/progs/env/CCAP/CCAP.pdf; Sadhu Aufochs Johnston, Steven S. Nicholas, and Julia Parzen, *The Guide to Greening Cities* (Washington, DC: Island Press, 2013), qtd. on 20–21. See also Julia Ann Parzen and Michal Hall Kieschnick, *Credit Where It's Due: Development Banking for Communities* (Philadelphia, PA: Temple University Press, 1992).

53. City of Chicago, *Progress Report: First Two Years, Chicago Climate Action Plan* (Chicago, IL: City of Chicago, 2010), https://uccrnna.org/wp-content/uploads/2017/06/05_Chicago_2010_Progress-Report.pdf; City of Chicago, *Sustainable Chicago 2015: Action Agenda and Updates* (Chicago, IL: City of Chicago, 2012–2015), https://www.chicago.gov/city/en/progs/env/sustainable_chicago2015.html; City of Chicago, *Green Healthy Neighborhoods* (Chicago, IL: Department of Planning and Development, 2014), https://www.chicago.gov/city/en/depts/dcd/supp_info/green-healthy-neighborhoods.html; Metropolitan Mayors Caucus, *The Greenest Region Compact: Opportunities + Impact* (Chicago, IL: Mayors Caucus, 2015), https://mayorscaucus.org/wp-content/uploads/2015/03/GRC-Opportunities-and-Impact-2015-final.pdf; Metropolitan Mayors Caucus, *Greenest Region Compact: Collaborating for Sustainable Communities: The Framework* (Chicago, IL: Mayors Caucus, 2018); Corina McKendry, *Greening Post-Industrial Cities: Growth, Equity, and Environmental Governance* (New York: Routledge, 2017).

54. Larry Bennett, "Contemporary Chicago Politics: Myth, Reality, and Neoliberalism," in *Neoliberal Chicago*, ed. Larry Bennett, Roberta Garner, and Euan Hague (Urbana: University of Illinois Press, 2017), 72–96; Hunt and DeVries, *Planning Chicago*; Chaskin and Joseph, *Integrating the Inner City*.

55. Steven A. Moore, *Alternative Routes to the Sustainable City: Austin, Curitiba, and Frankfurt* (Lanham, MD: Lexington Books, 2007); Steven A. Moore, *Pragmatic Sustainability: Dispositions for Critical Adaptation*, 2nd ed. (New York:

Routledge, 2016); Sara Hughes, *Repowering Cities: Governing Climate Change Mitigation in New York City, Los Angeles, and Toronto* (Ithaca, NY: Cornell University Press, 2019).

56. Baltimore Office of Sustainability, *Baltimore Sustainability Plan* (Baltimore, MD: Office of Sustainability, 2009), 18–23, https://www.baltimoresustainability.org/plans/sustainability-plan/2009-2/; Baltimore Office of Sustainability, Baltimore annual sustainability reports, 2010–2015, https://www.baltimoresustainability.org/about/achievements-2/; Baltimore Office of Sustainability, commission meeting minutes, 2010–2017, https://www.baltimoresustainability.org/commission-meeting-minutes/. On various forms of civic engagement over several decades in Baltimore, including faith-based community organizing and neighborhood associations, see Marion Orr, *Black Social Capital: The Politics of School Reform in Baltimore, 1986–1999* (Lawrence: University Press of Kansas, 1999); Harold McDougall, *Black Baltimore: A New Theory of Community* (Philadelphia, PA: Temple University Press, 1993); Matthew A. Crenson, *Neighborhood Politics* (Cambridge, MA: Harvard University Press, 1983); Antero Pietila, *Not in My Neighborhood: How Bigotry Shaped a Great American City* (Chicago, IL: Ivan R. Dee, 2010); Michael J. Rich and Robert P. Stoker, *Collaborative Governance for Urban Revitalization: Lessons from Empowerment Zones* (Ithaca, NY: Cornell University Press, 2014), 164–197. See also Matthew A. Crenson, *Baltimore: A Political History* (Baltimore, MD: Johns Hopkins University Press, 2017).

57. Blue Water Baltimore, annual reports, 2012–2015, https://bluewaterbaltimore.org/about/annual-report-and-financials/; Eric Zeemering, *Collaborative Strategies for Sustainable Cities: Economy, Environment and Community in Baltimore* (New York: Routledge, 2014).

58. Zeemering, *Collaborative Strategies for Sustainable Cities*, 96–116. See also William A. Shutkin, *The Land That Could Be: Environmentalism and Democracy in the Twenty-First Century* (Cambridge, MA: MIT Press, 2000).

59. Robert P. Stoker, Clarence N. Stone, and Donn Worgs, "Neighborhood Policy in Baltimore: The Postindustrial Turn," in *Urban Neighborhoods in a New Era: Revitalization Politics in the Postindustrial City*, ed. Clarence N. Stone and Robert P. Stoker (Chicago, IL: University of Chicago Press, 2015), 50–80.

60. Andrew Ross, *Bird on Fire: Lessons from the World's Least Sustainable City* (New York: Oxford University Press, 2011), qtd. on 4; Michael F. Logan, *The Lessening Stream: An Environmental History of the Santa Cruz River* (Tucson: University of Arizona Press, 2002), qtd. on 232; Michael F. Logan, *Desert Cities: The Environmental History of Phoenix and Tucson* (Pittsburgh, PA: University of Pittsburgh Press, 2006); Paul Hirt, Annie Gustafson, and Kelli Larson, "The Mirage in the Valley of the Sun," *Environmental History* 13 (2008): 482–514; James Lawrence Powell, *Dead Pool: Lake Powell, Global Warming, and the Future of Water in the West* (Berkeley: University of California Press, 2009); Bonnie G. Colby and

Katharine L. Jacobs, eds., *Arizona Water Policy: Management Innovations in an Urbanizing, Arid Region* (New York: Routledge, 2007).

61. Philip Vander Meer, *Desert Visions and the Making of Phoenix, 1860–2009* (Albuquerque: University of New Mexico Press, 2010); Patricia Gober, *Metropolitan Phoenix: Place Making and Community Building in the Desert* (Philadelphia: University of Pennsylvania Press, 2006); Andrew Needham, *Power Lines: Phoenix and the Making of the Modern Southwest* (Princeton, NJ: Princeton University Press, 2014).

62. Amy Bridges, *Morning Glories* (Princeton, NJ: Princeton University Press, 1997); Jessica Trounstine, *Political Monopolies in American Cities: The Rise and Fall of Bosses and Reformers* (Chicago, IL: University of Chicago Press, 2008); Vander Meer, *Desert Visions and the Making of Phoenix*; Elizabeth Tandy Shermer, *Sunbelt Capitalism: Phoenix and the Transformation of American Politics* (Philadelphia: University of Pennsylvania Press, 2013); Carl Abbott, "Real Estate and Race: Imagining the Second Circuit of Capital in Sunbelt Cities," in *Sunbelt Rising: The Politics of Space, Place, and Region*, ed. Michele Nickerson and Darren Dochuk (Philadelphia: University of Pennsylvania Press, 2011), 265–289; Douglas E. Kupel, *Fuel for Growth: Water and Arizona's Urban Environment* (Tucson: University of Arizona Press, 2003).

63. Portney, *Taking Sustainable Cities Seriously*, 80–81.

64. Grady Gammage Jr., *The Future of the Suburban City: Lessons from Sustaining Phoenix* (Washington, DC: Island Press, 2016), qtd. on 19. See also Jonathan Fink, "Phoenix, the Role of the University, and the Politics of Green-Tech," in *Sustainability in America's Cities*, 60–90; Robert W. Adler, *Restoring Colorado River Ecosystems: A Troubled Sense of Immensity* (Washington, DC: Island Press, 2007); John Fleck, *Water Is for Fighting Over: And Other Myths about Water in the West* (Washington, DC: Island Press, 2016).

65. Neal R. Peirce, with Curtis W. Johnson and John Stuart Hall, *Citistates: How Urban America Can Prosper in a Competitive World* (Washington, DC: Seven Locks Press, 1994), 41–82, for a reprint of the 1987 report; VanderMeer, *Desert Visions and the Making of Phoenix*; G. Wesley Johnson Jr., ed., *Phoenix in the Twentieth Century: Essays in Community History* (Norman: University of Oklahoma Press, 1993).

66. John Stuart Hall and Louis F. Wechsler, "The Phoenix Futures Forum: Creating Vision, Implanting Community," *National Civic Review* 80 (1991): 135–158, qtd. on 151; Rod Engelen, "Community Goal Setting: The Phoenix Experience," in *Practical Planning: New Theories for Effective Community Plans*, ed. Bruce McClendon (Washington, DC: APA Press, 1991); David D. Chrislip and Carl E. Larson, *Collaborative Leadership: How Citizens and Civic Leaders Can Make a Difference* (San Francisco, CA: Jossey-Bass, 1994); American Institute of Architects, *R/UDAT for Metropolitan Phoenix* (Washington, DC: AIA, 1974).

67. Marilyn Dantico and James Svara, "Professionalized Government: Institutionalizing the New Politics in Phoenix," in *Urban Neighborhoods in a New Era*, 108–130.

68. Downtown Voices Coalition (DVC), *Downtown Voices: Creating a Sustainable Downtown* (Phoenix, AZ: DVC, 2004), https://www.phoenixcommunityalliance.com/wp-content/uploads/2017/10/2004-Downtown-Voices_-Creating-a-Sustainable-Downtown.pdf; Serena Unrein and Diana Brown, *Bikes, Trains, and Less Driving: Transportation Trends in Arizona* (Phoenix: Arizona PIRG Education Fund, 2014); Ross, *Bird on Fire*.

69. City of Phoenix, *planPHX: 2015 General Plan* (Phoenix, AZ: City of Phoenix, 2015), https://www.phoenix.gov/pddsite/Documents/PZ/pdd_pz_pdf_00451.pdf; Vander Meer, *Desert Visions and the Making of Phoenix*, 336; Ross, *Bird on Fire*, 104–105; Paul Hirt, Rachel Snyder, Cyrus Hester, and Kelli Larson, "Water Consumption and Sustainability in Arizona: A Tale of Two Desert Cities," *Journal of the Southwest* 59 (2017): 264–301; Patricia Gober, D. A. Sampson, R. Quay, D. D. White, and W. T. Chow, "Urban Adaptation to Mega-Drought: Anticipatory Water Modeling, Policy, and Planning for the Urban Southwest," *Sustainable Cities and Society* 27 (2016): 497–504; Otto Santa Ana and Celeste González de Bustamante, eds., *Arizona Firestorm: Global Immigration Realities, National Media, and Provincial Politics* (Lanham, MD: Rowman & Littlefield, 2012); Alex P. Oberle and Daniel D. Arreola, "Resurgent Mexican Phoenix," *Geographical Review* 98 (2008): 171–196; David R. Diaz, *Barrio Urbanism: Chicanos, Planning, and American Cities* (New York: Routledge, 2005).

Chapter 7. Framing and Enabling the Sustainable Cities Field

1. Meg Holden, *Pragmatic Justifications for the Sustainable City: Acting in the Common Place* (New York: Routledge, 2017), qtd. on 22. See also Kent E. Portney, *Taking Sustainable Cities Seriously: Economic Development, the Environment, and Quality of Life in American Cities*, 2nd ed. (Cambridge, MA: MIT Press, 2013), 1–36, on the conceptual foundation of sustainable cities.

2. Robert D. Benford and David A. Snow, "Framing Processes and Social Movements: An Overview and Assessment," *Annual Review of Sociology* 26 (2000): 611–639; Hank Johnston and John A. Noakes, "Frames of Protest: A Road Map to a Perspective," in *Frames of Protest: Social Movements and the Framing Perspective*, ed. Hank Johnston and John A. Noakes (Lanham, MD: Rowman & Littlefield, 2005), 1–29; Robert D. Benford, "The Framing Perspective's Development, Diffusion, and Resonance," *Mobilization: An International Quarterly* 19 (2014): 29–30; Doug McAdam, "The Framing Function of Movement Tactics: Strategic Dramaturgy in the American Civil Rights Movement," in *Comparative Perspectives on Social Movements: Political Opportunities, Mobilizing Structures, and Cultural*

Framings, ed. Doug McAdam, John D. McCarthy, and Mayer N. Zald (New York: Cambridge University Press, 1996), 338–355; John L. Campbell, "Where Do We Stand? Common Mechanisms in Organizations and Social Movements," in *Social Movements and Organization Theory*, ed. Gerald F. Davis, Doug McAdam, W. Richard Scott, and Mayer N. Zald (New York: Cambridge University Press, 2005), 41–68; Jeff Goodwin, James M. Jasper, and Francesca Polletta, eds., *Passionate Politics: Emotions and Social Movements* (Chicago, IL: University of Chicago Press, 2001). See also Frank Fischer, *Reframing Public Policy: Discursive Politics and Deliberative Practices* (New York: Oxford University Press, 2003); Donald A. Schön and Martin Rein, *Frame Reflection: Toward the Resolution of Intractable Policy Controversies* (New York: Basic Books, 1995); Dennis Chong and James N. Druckman, "Framing Theory," *Annual Review of Political Science* 10 (2007): 103–126; Eleanora Pasotti, *Political Branding in Cities: The Decline of Machine Politics in Bogotá, Naples, and Chicago* (New York: Cambridge University Press, 2010); Lee G. Bolman and Terrence E. Deal, *Reframing Organizations: Artistry, Choice, and Leadership*, 6th ed. (Hoboken, NJ: Jossey-Bass, 2017). For an analysis of framing in a broad climate movement, see Beth Schaefer Caniglia, Robert J. Brulle, and Andrew Szasz, "Civil Society, Social Movements, and Climate Change," in *Climate Change and Society: Sociological Perspectives*, ed. Riley E. Dunlap and Robert J. Brulle (New York: Oxford University Press, 2015), 235–268.

3. See, for instance, Calvin Morrill and Jason Owen-Smith, "The Emergence of Environmental Conflict Resolution: Subversive Stories and the Construction of Collective Action Frames and Organizational Fields," in *Organizations, Policy, and the Natural Environment: Institutional and Strategic Perspectives*, ed. Andrew J. Hoffman and Marc J. Ventresca (Stanford, CA: Stanford Business Books, 2002), 90–118; Rosemary O'Leary and Lisa B. Bingham, eds., *The Promise and Performance of Environmental Conflict Resolution* (New York: Routledge, 2003); James E. Crowfoot and Julia M. Wondolleck, *Environmental Disputes: Community Involvement in Conflict Resolution* (Washington, DC: Island Press, 1990).

4. Sim Van der Ryn and Peter Calthorpe, *Sustainable Communities: A New Design Synthesis for Cities, Suburbs and Towns* (San Francisco, CA: Sierra Club Books, 1986); Mark Roseland, *Toward Sustainable Communities: Solutions for Citizens and Their Governments* (Gabriola Island, BC: New Society Publishers, 1992), and subsequent editions in 1998, 2005, and 2012; Iris Borowy, *Defining Sustainable Development for Our Common Future: A History of the World Commission on Environment and Development (Brundtland Commission)* (New York: Routledge, 2014).

5. See, for instance, F. Kaid Benfield, Jutka Terris, and Nancy Vorsanger, *Solving Sprawl: Models of Smart Growth in Communities across America* (New York and Washington, DC: NRDC and Island Press, 2001); Isabelle Anguelovski, *Neighborhood as Refuge: Community Reconstruction, Place Remaking, and Environmental Justice in the City* (Cambridge, MA: MIT Press, 2014). On federal policy supports

during these years, see Peter Dreier, John Mollenkopf, and Todd Swanstrom, *Place Matters: Metropolitics for the Twenty-First Century*, 3rd ed. (Lawrence: University Press of Kansas, 2014), 136–174. For an analysis of recycling as a field frame, emerging in competition with waste-to-energy incineration methods and rationales, and in the context of competition among grassroots nonprofit recyclers and for-profit waste management firms, see Michael Lounsbury, Marc Ventresca, and Paul M. Hirsch, "Social Movements, Field Frames, and Industry Emergence: A Cultural-Political Perspective on US Recycling," *Socio-Economic Review* 1 (2003): 71–104.

6. Leonard J. Duhl, *The Urban Condition: People and Policy in the Metropolis* (New York: Basic Books, 1963); Alice Sardell, *The U.S. Experiment in Social Medicine: The Community Health Center Program, 1965–1986* (Pittsburgh, PA: University of Pittsburgh Press, 1989).

7. Author's field notes, US Department of Health and Human Services, Washington, DC, December 8, 1994.

8. Carmen Sirianni and Lewis A. Friedland, *Civic Innovation in America* (Berkeley: University of California Press, 2001), 166–177; Tyler Norris, ed., "Twenty-Five Years of Healthy Communities," *National Civic Review* 102 (2013) and 103 (2014).

9. Jason Corburn, *Toward the Healthy City: People, Places, and the Politics of Urban Planning* (Cambridge, MA: MIT Press, 2009); *Healthy City Planning: From Neighborhood to National Health Equity* (New York: Routledge, 2013); Andrew L. Dannenberg, Howard Frumkin, and Richard J. Jackson, *Making Healthy Places: Designing and Building for Health, Well-Being, and Sustainability*, 2nd ed. (Washington, DC: Island Press, 2011); Howard Frumkin, Lawrence Frank, and Richard Jackson, *Urban Sprawl and Public Health: Designing, Planning, and Building for Healthy Communities* (Washington, DC: Island Press, 2004); Chinmoy Sarkar, Chris Webster, and John Gallacher, *Healthy Cities: Public Health through Urban Planning* (Northampton, MA: Edward Elgar, 2016).

10. On framing disputes, see Benford and Snow, "Framing Processes and Social Movements," 625–627. See also Mark R. Warren, *Dry Bones Rattling: Community Building to Revitalize American Democracy* (Princeton, NJ: Princeton University Press, 2001); Richard L. Wood, *Faith in Action: Religion, Race, and Democratic Organizing in America* (Chicago, IL: University of Chicago Press, 2002); Steven Rathgeb Smith and Michael Lipsky, *Nonprofits for Hire: The Welfare State in the Age of Contracting* (Cambridge, MA: Harvard University Press, 1994); Steven Rathgeb Smith, "Social Services," in *The State of Nonprofit America*, ed. Lester M. Salamon, 2nd ed. (Washington, DC: Brookings Press, 2012), 192–228.

11. John P. Kretzmann and John L. McKnight, *Building Communities from the Inside Out: A Path Toward Finding and Mobilizing a Community's Assets* (Evanston, IL: ACTA Publications, 1993); John P. Kretzmann and John L. McKnight, *Mobilizing a Community's Assets: Video Training Program*, produced by Civic Network Television (Chicago, IL: ACTA Publications, 1996). These two tool kits were em-

ployed widely, even when ABCD training practitioners could not possibly keep up with the rapidly burgeoning demand for their services.

12. Dorceta Taylor, "The Rise of the Environmental Justice Paradigm: Injustice Framing and the Social Construction of Environmental Discourses," *American Behavioral Scientist* 43 (2000): 508–580; *Toxic Communities: Environmental Racism, Industrial Pollution, and Residential Mobility* (New York: NYU Press, 2014); David Naguib Pellow, *Garbage Wars: The Struggle for Environmental Justice in Chicago* (Cambridge, MA: MIT Press, 2002); Stella M. Capek, "The Environmental Justice Frame: A Conceptual Discussion and Application," *Social Problems* 40 (1993): 5–24.

13. Environmental Protection Agency, *Plan EJ 2014* (Washington, DC: EPA, 2011), 78-90, https://nepis.epa.gov/Exe/ZyPDF.cgi/P100DFCQ.PDF?Dockey=P100 DFCQ.PDF; Julian Agyeman, *Introducing Just Sustainabilities: Policy, Planning, and Practice* (London: Zed Books, 2013); Julian Agyeman, Robert D. Bullard, and Bob Evans, eds., *Just Sustainabilities: Development in an Unequal World* (Cambridge, MA: MIT Press, 2003); Michael Méndez, *Climate Change from the Streets: How Conflict and Collaboration Strengthen the Environmental Justice Movement* (New Haven, CT: Yale University Press, 2020); David Konisky, ed., *Failed Promises: Evaluating the Federal Government's Response to Environmental Justice* (Cambridge, MA: MIT Press, 2015); Paul Mohai, David Pellow, and J. Timmons Roberts, "Environmental Justice," *Annual Review of Environment and Resources* 34 (2009): 405–430; Christopher H. Foreman Jr., *The Promise and Peril of Environmental Justice* (Washington, DC: Brookings Press, 1999); Holly D. Gordon and Keith I. Harley, "Environmental Justice and the Legal System," in *Power, Justice, and the Environment: A Critical Appraisal of the Environmental Justice Movement*, ed. David Naguid Pellow and Robert J. Brulle (Cambridge, MA: MIT Press, 2005), 153–170; Charles Lee, "Collaborative Models to Achieve Environmental Justice and Healthy Communities," in *Power, Justice, and the Environment*, 219–249; Lisa Schweitzer and Max Stephenson, "Environmental Justice: Right Answers, Wrong Questions: Environmental Justice as Urban Research," *Urban Studies* 44 (2007): 319–337; Michael B. Gerrard and Sheila R. Foster, *The Law of Environmental Justice: Theories and Procedures to Address Disproportionate Risks*, 2nd ed. (Chicago, IL: American Bar Association, 2009); J. Timmons Roberts and Melissa M. Toffolon-Weiss, *Chronicles from the Environmental Justice Frontline* (New York: Cambridge University Press, 2001); Scott Frickel and James R. Elliott, *Sites Unseen: Uncovering Hidden Hazards in American Cities* (New York: Russell Sage, 2018); Luke W. Cole and Sheila R. Foster, *From the Ground Up: Environmental Racism and the Rise of the Environmental Justice Movement* (New York: NYU Press, 2001). Benjamin J. Pauli, *Flint Fights Back: Environmental Justice and Democracy in the Flint Water Crisis* (Cambridge, MA: MIT Press, 2019), discusses contested partnership language and some of the conundrums of maintaining civic action and building capacity for a radical model of democracy after the initial victories.

14. On territoriality and division-of-labor motivations for urban coproduction in Boston's 311 reporting system, see Daniel T. O'Brien, *The Urban Commons: How Data and Technology Can Rebuild Our Communities* (Cambridge, MA: Harvard University Press, 2018). A parallel argument to mine here, though with different analytic purposes, is made by Thomas K. Ogorzalek, *The Cities on the Hill: How Urban Institutions Transformed National Politics* (New York: Oxford University Press, 2018). For Ogorzalek, governance logics of urban leaders representing a large, dense, and heterogeneous city upward at the federal policy level must build upon emergent and pragmatic "organic city interests" as well as "institutions of horizontal integration," even though many conflicting interests play out within any given city. How, and how much, these logics become intertwined with integrative sustainable city framing and policy logics, especially with policy design that might explicitly encourage civic engagement and partnerships, remains an intriguing question.

15. US Environmental Protection Agency, *EPA's Framework for Community-Based Environmental Protection* (Washington, DC: Office of Policy and Office of Reinvention, 1999); US EPA, *Community-Based Environmental Protection: A Resource Book for Protecting Ecosystems and Communities* (Washington, DC: EPA, 1997), https://19january2017snapshot.epa.gov/sites/production/files/2015-04/documents/communitybasedenvironmentalprotection.pdf; US EPA, *Evaluation of Community-Based Environmental Protection Projects: Accomplishments and Lessons Learned* (Washington, DC: Office of Policy Economics and Innovation, 2003), https://www.epa.gov/sites/production/files/2015-09/documents/eval-cbep.pdf.

16. On Seattle's comprehensive neighborhood and sustainability planning and indicators more generally, see Carmen Sirianni, "Neighborhood Planning as Collaborative Democratic Design: The Case of Seattle," *Journal of the American Planning Association* 73 (2007): 373–387; Meg Holden, "Revisiting the Local Impact of Community Indicator Projects: Sustainable Seattle as Prophet in Its Own Land," *Applied Research in Quality of Life* 1 (2006): 253–277; Meg Holden, "Sustainable Seattle: The Case of the Prototype Sustainability Indicators Project," in *Community Quality-of-Life Indicators: Best Cases II*, ed. M. Joseph Sirgy, Don Rahtz, and David Swain (Dordrecht, Netherlands: Springer, 2006), 177–201; Lisa Pettibone, *Governing Urban Sustainability: Comparing Cities in the USA and Germany* (New York: Routledge, 2015); Simon Bell and Stephen Morse, *Sustainability Indicators: Measuring the Immeasurable?* 2nd ed. (London: Earthscan, 2008).

17. Jane Mansbridge, James Bohman, Simone Chambers, Thomas Christiano, Archon Fung, John Parkinson, Dennis F. Thompson, and Mark E. Warren, "A Systemic Approach to Deliberative Democracy," in *Deliberative Systems: Deliberative Democracy at the Large Scale*, ed. John Parkinson and Jane Mansbridge (New York: Cambridge University Press, 2012), 1–26. See also Jerry L. Mashaw, *Reasoned Administration and Democratic Legitimacy: How Administrative Law Supports Democratic Government* (New York: Cambridge University Press, 2018).

18. Here, I also draw upon my field observations and extensive conversations at EPA annual conferences on public participation in the late 1990s (under the Clinton administration), and as the academic advisor to the EPA's Community Action for a Renewed Environment (CARE) program, in which I engaged with community grantees and EPA headquarters and regional staff in national trainings and conferences over a five-year period during the George W. Bush and Obama administrations. My perspective on institutional learning was also formed in a three-hour presentation and exchange with the EPA's Innovation Action Council, composed of all deputy administrators and deputy regional administrators (that is, the uppermost operational career staff), many of whom oversaw community-based programs and other innovations. Author's field notes, Arlington, VA, March 25, 2009, at the beginning of the Obama administration.

19. US EPA, *Environmental Justice Collaborative Model: A Framework to Ensure Local Public Problem Solving* (Washington, DC: Federal Interagency Working Group on Environmental Justice, 2002), https://www.epa.gov/sites/production /files/2015-02/documents/iwg-status-02042002.pdf. On skepticism of collaborative EJ framing, see Robert D. Bullard, "Environmental Justice in the Twenty-First Century," in *The Quest for Environmental Justice*, ed. Robert D. Bullard (San Francisco, CA: Sierra Club Books. 2005), 19–42; Robert D. Benford, "The Half-Life of the Environmental Justice Frame: Innovation, Diffusion, and Stagnation," in *Power, Justice, and the Environment*, 37–53.

20. On master frames, see David A. Snow and Robert D. Benford, "Master Frames and Cycles of Protest," in *Frontiers in Social Movement Theory*, ed. Aldon D. Morris and Carol D. Mueller (New Haven, CT: Yale University Press, 1992), 133–155; Benford and Snow, "Framing Processes and Social Movements," 618–619.

21. Portney, *Taking Sustainable Cities Seriously*; Mark Lubell, Richard Feiock, and Susan Handy, "City Adoption of Environmentally Sustainable Policies in California's Central Valley," *Journal of the American Planning Association* 75 (2009): 293–308; James H. Svara, Tanya C. Watt, and Hee Soun Jang, "How Are U.S. Cities Doing Sustainability? Who Is Getting on the Sustainability Train?" *Cityscape: A Journal of Policy Development and Research* 15 (2013): 9–44; James H. Svara, Anna Read, and Evelina Moulder, *Breaking New Ground: Promoting Environmental and Energy Programs in Local Government* (Washington, DC: IBM Center for the Business of Government, 2011); the latter two studies are based on ICMA surveys. See Paul J. DiMaggio and Walter W. Powell, "The Iron Cage Revisited: Institutional Isomorphism and Collective Rationality in Organizational Fields," *American Sociological Review* 48 (1983): 147–60. While civic norms and identities are not considered directly in DiMaggio and Powell's original formulation, one of the core arguments here is that these have become especially important in dynamic interaction with professional norms and identities in building the

sustainable cities field in the United States in a manner that informs and coheres a collective rationality that is pragmatic and democratic.

22. For important analytic perspectives, see Pamela S. Tolbert and Lynne G. Zucker, "Institutional Sources of Change in the Formal Structure of Organizations: The Diffusion of Civil Service Reform 1880–1935," *Administrative Science Quarterly* 28 (1983): 22–39; David Strang and Sarah A. Soule, "Diffusion in Organizations and Social Movements: From Hybrid Corn to Poison Pills," *Annual Review of Sociology* 24 (1998): 265–290. For international networks, see Sofie Bouteligier, *Cities, Networks, and Global Environmental Governance: Spaces of Innovation, Places of Leadership* (London: Routledge, 2013); Marco Keiner and Arley Kim, "Transnational City Networks for Sustainability," *European Planning Studies* 15 (2007): 1371–1395; Louis Albrechts and Seymour J. Mandelbaum, eds., *The Network Society: A New Context for Planning* (New York: Routledge, 2005); Christof Brandtner, "Cities in Action: City Climate Action, Civil Society, and the Organization of Cities" (PhD diss., Stanford University, Stanford, CA, 2019), ch. 3.

23. David Ribeiro, Stefen Samarripas, Kate Tanabe, Hannah Bastian, Emma Cooper, Ariel Drehobl, Shruti Vaidyanathan, Alexander Jarrah, and Mary Shoemaker, *The 2019 City Clean Energy Scorecard* (Washington, DC: American Council for an Energy Efficient Economy, 2019), https://www.aceee.org/sites/default/files /publications/researchreports/u1904.pdf. This is its fourth scorecard to date.

24. Matt Leighninger, *Civic Engagement and Recent Immigrant Communities* (Washington, DC: National League of Cities, 2010), https://www.issuelab .org/resource/civic-engagement-and-recent-immigrant-communities.html; Matt Leighninger, *Beyond Civility: From Public Engagement to Problem Solving* (Washington: NLC, 2011, https://www.nlc.org/beyond-civility-from-public-engage ment-to-problem-solving; Matt Leighninger and Bonnie C. Mann, *Planning for Stronger Local Democracy: A Field Guide for Local Officials* (Washington: NLC, 2011); Svara, Read, and Moulder, *Breaking New Ground*, 6.

25. Jeb Brugmann, *Welcome to the Urban Revolution: How Cities Are Changing the World* (New York: HarperCollins, 2009).

26. Author's field notes, ICLEI World Congress, Montreal, June 19–22, 2018; ICLEI, the International Development Research Center, and the United Nations Environment Programme, *The Local Agenda 21 Planning Guide: An Introduction to Sustainable Development Planning* (Toronto: IDRC, 1996), https://www.dem ocratsagainstunagenda21.com/uploads/4/4/6/6/4466371/iclei.local-agenda-21 .planning.guide.pdf; ICLEI-Local Governments for Sustainability, *Corporate Report 2011/12* (Bonn, Germany: ICLEI, 2011–2012), qtd. on 2; ICLEI-Local Governments for Sustainability, *Strategic Plan 2007–2012* (Cape Town, South Africa: ICLEI Council, 2006), qtd. on 12. On conflicts in California over environmental justice strategies and policy designs for public participation, community empowerment, and public health within the Global Warming Solutions Act (AB 32,

2006), see Michael Méndez, *Climate Change from the Streets: How Conflict and Collaboration Strengthen the Environmental Justice Movement* (New Haven, CT: Yale University Press, 2020).

27. ICLEI USA, *Sustainability Planning Toolkit: A Comprehensive Guide for Local Governments on How to Create a Sustainability Plan* (New York: ICLEI and the City of New York Mayor's Office of Long-Term Planning and Sustainability, 2012); ICLEI USA, with the Mayor's Office of Long-Term Planning and Sustainability, City of New York, *The Process Behind PlaNYC: How the City of New York Developed Its Long-Term Comprehensive Sustainability Plan* (New York: City of New York, 2010), http://s-media.nyc.gov/agencies/planyc2030/pdf/iclei_planyc _case_study_201004.pdf.

28. Center for Science in the Earth System and King County, Washington, in association with ICLEI USA, *Preparing for Climate Change: A Guidebook for Local, Regional, and State Governments* (Seattle, WA: ICLEI, 2007), https://icleiusa.org /wp-content/uploads/2015/08/PreparingForClimateChange_Sept2007.pdf.

29. ICLEI USA, with ecoAmerica, *Let's Talk Communities and Climate: Communication Guidance for City and Community Leaders* (Seattle, WA: ICLEI, 2016), https://icleiusa.org/wp-content/uploads/2015/06/EcoAmerica-Lets-Talk-Com munities-and-Climate.pdf; Ion Bogdan Vasi, "Organizational Environments and Compatibility: The Diffusion of the Program against Global Climate Change among Local Governments in the U.S.," *Sociological Forum* 21 (2006): 439–466; Michele M. Betsill and Harriet Bulkeley, *Cities and Climate Change* (New York: Routledge, 2003), qtd. on 81; Elaine B. Sharp, Dorothy M. Daley, and Michael S. Lynch, "Understanding Local Adoption and Implementation of Climate Change Mitigation Policy," *Urban Affairs Review* 47 (2011): 433–457; Rachel M. Krause, "Climate Policy Innovation in American Cities," in *Changing Climate Politics: U.S. Policies and Civic Actions*, ed. Yael Wolinsky-Namias (Thousand Oaks, CA: SAGE, 2015), 82–107; Michele M. Betsill, "Mitigating Climate Change in U.S. Cities: Opportunities and Obstacles," *Local Environment* 6 (2001): 393–406.

30. Author interview with Angie Fyfe, executive director of ICLEI USA, July 23, 2018.

31. Statewide Energy Efficiency Collaborative (SEEC), with ICLEI USA, *State of Local Climate Action: California 2016* (California: SEEC, 2016), https://califor niaseec.org/wp-content/uploads/2016/10/State-of-Local-Climate-Action-Califor nia-2016_Screen.pdf. My estimate of the role of ILG and Terry Amsler is derived from my examination of many of the ILG tool kits and Amsler's reputation among leading civic innovators at multiple conferences and meetings over a period of more than two decades. For broader analysis of environmental policy, public participation, and sustainability networks in California, see David Vogel, *California Greenin': How the Golden State Became an Environmental Leader* (Princeton, NJ: Princeton University Press, 2018); Judith E. Innes and Jane Rongerude, "Civic

Networks for Sustainable Regions—Innovative Practices and Emergent Theory," *Planning Theory and Practice* 14 (2013): 75–100; Myungjung Kwon, Hee Soun Jang, and Richard C. Feiock, "Climate Protection and Energy Sustainability Policy in California Cities: What Have We Learned?" *Journal of Urban Affairs* 36 (2014): 905–924; Isaac William Martin, "The Fiscal Sociology of Public Consultation," in *Democratizing Inequalities: Dilemmas of the New Public Participation*, ed. Caroline W. Lee, Michael McQuarrie, and Edward T. Walker (New York: NYU Press, 2015), 102–124.

32. Author interview with Angie Fyfe, July 23, 2018; ICLEI USA, *Toward 1.5 Degrees Celsius: Annual Report 2016* (Denver, CO: ICLEI, 2016), https://icleiusa .org/wp-content/uploads/2017/02/ICLEI-USA-2016-Annual-Report.pdf.

33. Vasi, "Organizational Environments and Compatibility."

34. Author's field notes, Seattle City Council town hall, May 7, 2013. For an evolving analysis of the complex array of factors in city participation in ICLEI and persistence in sustainability beyond peak membership, see Rachel M. Krause, Hongtao Yi, and Richard C. Feiock, "Applying Policy Termination Theory to the Abandonment of Climate Protection Initiatives by U.S. Local Governments," *Policy Studies Journal* 44 (2016): 176–195; Hongtao Yi, Rachel M. Krause, and Richard C. Feiock, "Back-peddling or Continuing Quietly? An Assessment of the Impact that Terminating Membership in ICLEI-Local Governments for Sustainability on Local Sustainability Efforts," *Environmental Politics* 26 (2017): 138–160; Christopher V. Hawkins, Rachel M. Krause, Richard C. Feiock, and Cali Curley, "Making Meaningful Commitments: Accounting for Variation in Cities' Investments of Staff and Fiscal Resources to Sustainability," *Urban Studies* 63 (2016): 1902–1924. On the rise of the Tea Party, see Theda Skocpol and Vanessa Williamson, *The Tea Party and the Remaking of Republican Conservatism*, rev. ed. (New York: Oxford University Press, 2016).

35. Author interview with Nils Moe, managing director of USDN, July 24, 2018; author's field notes, ICLEI World Congress, Montreal, June 19–22, 2018. On mayors, see Benjamin R. Barber, *If Mayors Ruled the World: Dysfunctional Nations, Rising Cities* (New Haven, CT: Yale University Press, 2013); Benjamin R. Barber, *Cool Cities: Urban Sovereignty and the Fix for Global Warming* (New Haven, CT: Yale University Press, 2017).

36. Interview with Moe; Sadhu Aufochs Johnston, Steven S. Nicholas, and Julia Parzen, *The Guide to Greening Cities* (Washington, DC: Island Press, 2013); Urban Sustainability Directors Network (USDN), Urban Sustainability Innovation report archive, 2014–2017, https://www.usdn.org/november-2017-urban-sustain ability-innovation-report.html; USDN, "Urban Sustainability Bulletin," reports, videos, 2014–2018, https://www.usdn.org/urban-sustainability-bulletin.html.

37. Author interview with Julia Parzen, April 7, 2015; USDN and Innovation Network for Communities, *Regional Networks Leadership Academy* (USDN,

2013), https://www.usdn.org/uploads/cms/documents/regional-networks-academy-main-ppt-3-1-16-13.pdf; Peter Plastrik, with Julia Parzen, *Toward a Sustainable City: The State of Innovation in Urban Sustainability* (USDN, 2013), https://www.usdn.org/uploads/cms/documents/state-of-innovation.pdf; Peter Plastrik, Madeleine Taylor, and John Cleveland, *Connecting to Change the World: Harnessing the Power of Networks for Social Impact* (Washington, DC: Island Press, 2014); USDN, with Institute for Sustainable Communities and Nutter Consulting, *Getting Smart about Smart Cities: USDN Resource Guide* (USDN, 2014), http://us.iscvt.org/wp-content/uploads/2017/01/Smart-Cities-RG.pdf. For a thoroughly pragmatic yet visionary perspective on cities as climate innovation laboratories still in their early stages of emergence, see Peter Plastrik and John Cleveland, *Life After Carbon: The Next Global Transformation of Cities* (Washington, DC: Island Press, 2018). See also Ben Green, *Smart Enough Cities: Putting Technology in Its Place to Reclaim Our Urban Future* (Cambridge, MA: MIT Press, 2019); Stephen Goldsmith and Susan Crawford, *The Responsive City: Engaging Communities Through Data-Smart Governance* (San Francisco, CA: Jossey-Bass, 2014).

38. Author interview with Garrett Fitzgerald, USDN strategic collaborations director, August 24, 2018; Garrett Fitzgerald, *Connecting People, Fostering Innovation: The Urban Sustainability Directors Network* (USDN, 2015), 7, https://sites.nationalacademies.org/cs/groups/pgasite/documents/webpage/pga_167367.pdf; USDN, *2015 Strategic Plan: External Edition* (USDN, 2015), https://www.usdn.org/uploads/cms/documents/3_-_usdn-long-term-strategic-plan-final-draft-executive-summary.pdf.

39. USDN, *Innovation Fund: 2017 Annual Report* (USDN, 2017), https://www.usdn.org/uploads/cms/documents/usdn_if_2017_annual_report_final.pdf; USDN, "Urban Sustainability Bulletin"; Regional Networks Leadership Academy, 22.

40. Environmental Grantmakers Association, "Tracking the Field," 6 vols., summary reports, 2007–2015, https://ega.org/connect/ttf. The Health and Environmental Funders Network, established in 1996, focuses specifically on building an environmental health movement.

41. Neil F. Carlson, *Looking Back: Influencing, Networking, Facilitating: A Ten-Year Retrospective of the Funders' Network for Smart Growth and Livable Communities* (Coral Gables, FL: TFN, 2009); Maureen Lawless, ed., *Looking Forward: Perspectives on Future Opportunities for Philanthropy* (Coral Gables, FL: TFN, 2009); Katherine Szczerbacki, "The Organizational and Relationship Changes in Community Foundations Engaged in Community Leadership" (PhD diss., Brandeis University, Waltham, MA, 2017); Rebecca Wolfe, "Community Foundations as Agents of Local Social Change" (PhD diss., Stanford University, Stanford, CA, 2006).

42. Baird Straughan and Tom Pollak, *The Broader Movement: Nonprofit Envi-*

ronmental and Conservation Organizations, 1989–2005 (Washington, DC: Urban Institute, 2008); Smith, "Social Services"; Bradford H. Gray and Mark Schlesinger, "Health Care," in *The State of Nonprofit America*, 89–136; Smith and Lipsky, *Nonprofits for Hire*.

43. Robert J. Brulle and J. Craig Jenkins, "Foundations and the Environmental Movement: Priorities, Strategies, and Impact," in *Foundations for Social Change: Critical Perspectives on Philanthropy and Popular Movements*, ed. Daniel Faber and Debra McCarthy (Lantham, MD: Rowman & Littlefield, 2005), 151–174; Mark Dowie, *American Foundations: An Investigative History* (Cambridge, MA: MIT Press, 2001).

Chapter 8. Democratic Resilience

1. On grassroots protest and climate justice, see Jennifer Hadden, *Networks in Contention: The Divisive Politics of Climate Change* (New York: Cambridge University Press, 2015); Michael Méndez, *Climate Change from the Streets: How Conflict and Collaboration Strengthen the Environmental Justice Movement* (New Haven, CT: Yale University Press, 2020); Benjamin J. Pauli, *Flint Fights Back: Environmental Justice and Democracy in the Flint Water Crisis* (Cambridge, MA: MIT Press, 2019). For a broad range of other strategies, see Barry G. Rabe, ed., *Greenhouse Governance: Addressing Climate Change in America* (Washington, DC: Brookings Press, 2010); Barry G. Rabe, *Can We Price Carbon?* (Cambridge, MA: MIT Press, 2018); Daniel J. Fiorino, *A Good Life on a Finite Earth: The Political Economy of Green Growth* (New York: Oxford University Press, 2018); Daniel Klein, Maria Pia Carazo, Meinhard Doelle, Jane Bulmer, and Andrew Higham, eds., *The Paris Agreement on Climate Change: Analysis and Commentary* (New York: Oxford University Press, 2017); Rebecca Henderson, Ranjay Gulati, and Michael Tushman, eds., *Leading Sustainable Change: An Organizational Perspective* (New York: Oxford University Press, 2015); Chris Laszlo, and Nadya Zhexembayeva, *Embedded Sustainability: The Next Big Competitive Advantage* (Stanford, CA: Stanford University Press, 2011); Ceres and KKS Advisors, *Systems Rule: How Board Governance Can Drive Sustainability Performance* (Boston, MA: Ceres and KKS Advisors, 2018), https://static1.squarespace.com/static/5143211de4b038607dd318c b/t/5afc5e271ae6cf3092ecd7ed/1526488627169/Systems+Rule_Final.pdf; Rutherford H. Platt, *Disasters and Democracy: The Politics of Extreme Natural Events*, 4th ed. (Washington, DC: Island Press, 1999).

2. Jane Mansbridge, James Bohman, Simone Chambers, Thomas Christiano, Archon Fung, John Parkinson, Dennis F. Thompson, and Mark E. Warren, "A Systemic Approach to Deliberative Democracy," in *Deliberative Systems: Deliberative Democracy at the Large Scale*, ed. John Parkinson and Jane Mansbridge (New York: Cambridge University Press, 2012), 1–26; Carmen Sirianni, *Investing in Democracy: Engaging Citizens in Collaborative Governance* (Washington, DC:

Brookings Press, 2009), 39–65, on core principles of collaborative governance and policy design; Neil Fligstein and Doug McAdam, *A Theory of Fields* (New York: Oxford University Press, 2012).

3. Kent E. Portney, *Taking Sustainable Cities Seriously: Economic Development, the Environment, and Quality of Life in American Cities*, 2nd ed. (Cambridge, MA: MIT Press, 2013); Mark Lubell, Richard Feiock, and Susan Handy, "City Adoption of Environmentally Sustainable Policies in California's Central Valley," *Journal of the American Planning Association* 75 (2009): 293–308.

4. Riley E. Dunlap and Aaron M. McCright, "Challenging Climate Change: The Denial Countermovement," in *Climate Change and Society: Sociological Perspectives*, ed. Riley E. Dunlap and Robert J. Brulle (New York: Oxford University Press, 2015), 300–332; Andrew Hoffman, *How Culture Shapes the Climate Change Debate* (Stanford, CA: Stanford University Press, 2015).

5. For some of these community and institutional dynamics, see Orin H. Pilkey and Keith C. Pilkey, *Sea Level Rise: A Slow Tsunami on America's Shores* (Durham, NC: Duke University Press, 2019); Orrin H. Pilkey, Linda Pilkey-Jarvis, and Keith C. Pilkey, *Retreat from a Rising Sea: Hard Choices in an Age of Climate Change* (New York: Columbia University Press, 2016); Liz Koslov, "The Case for Retreat," *Public Culture* 28 (2016): 373–401; A. R. Siders, Miyuki Hino, and Katharine J. Mach, "The Case for Strategic and Managed Climate Retreat: Why, Where, When, and How Should Communities Relocate? *Science* 365 (August 2019): 761–763; A. R. Siders, "Adaptive Capacity to Climate Change: A Synthesis of Concepts, Methods, and Findings in a Fragmented Field," *Climate Change* 10 (January 2019); Chris Chopik, "Property Value in an Era of Climate Change" (graduate thesis, OCAD University, Toronto, 2019); Harriet Bulkeley, *Cities and Climate Change* (New York: Routledge, 2013); Harriet Bulkeley, Matthew Paterson, and Johannes Stripple, eds., *Towards a Cultural Politics of Climate Change: Devices, Desires and Dissent* (New York: Cambridge University Press, 2016); Cynthia Rosenzweig, William D. Solecki, Patricia Romero-Lankao, Shagun Mehrotra, Shobhakar Dhakal, and Somayya Ali Ibrahim, eds., *Climate Change and Cities: Second Assessment Report of the Urban Climate Change Research Network* (New York: Cambridge University Press, 2018); Anne Grambsch, Ann Kosmal, Libby Larson, and Nancy Sonti, *Fourth National Climate Assessment*, chapter 11: Built Environment, Urban Systems, and Cities (USGCRP, 2018), https://nca2018 .globalchange.gov/chapter/11/; Institute of Medicine, *Healthy, Resilient, and Sustainable Communities after Disaster: Strategies, Opportunities, and Planning for Disaster* (Washington, DC: National Academies Press, 2015); Daniel A. Mazmanian, and Hilda Blanco, *Elgar Companion to Sustainable Cities: Strategies, Methods, and Outlook* (Northampton, MA: Edward Elgar, 2014). For a normatively informed planning perspective, see Susan Fainstein, "Resilience and Justice," *International Journal of Urban and Regional Research* 39 (2015): 157–167.

6. Judith Rodin, *The Resilience Dividend: Being Strong in a World Where Things Go Wrong* (New York: PublicAffairs, 2014), qtd. on 3. See also Jason Vogel et al., *Climate Adaptation: The State of Practice in U.S. Communities* (Cambridge, MA: Abt Associates, with the Kresge Foundation, 2016); 100 Resilient Cities, *Resilient Cities, Resilient Lives: Learning from the 100RC Network* (New York: Rockefeller Foundation, 2019), http://100resilientcities.org/wp-content/uploads/2019/07/100RC-Re port-Capstone-Abridged-PDF.pdf; Resilient Cities, *Cities Taking Action: How the 100RC Network is Building Urban Resilience* (New York: Rockefeller Foundation, 2017), https://www.adaptationclearinghouse.org/resources/cities-taking-action-how -the-100rc-network-is-building-urban-resilience.html; Carlos Martin and Sara McTarnaghan, *Institutionalizing Urban Resilience: A Midterm Monitoring and Evaluation Report of 100 Resilient Cities* (Washington, DC: Urban Institute, 2018), http://www.100resilientcities.org/wp-content/uploads/2019/03/100RC-2018-Ur ban-Institute-Midterm-Report.pdf. As of this writing, 100RCs has been discontinued as a project of the Rockefeller Foundation but is reorganizing as the Global Resilient Cities Network. For a broad review of literature that highlights the need to further integrate knowledge holistically across disciplines, incentivize civic participation and equity, and incorporate transformative yet conundrum-laden future scenarios, see Ebba Brink, et al., "Cascades of Green: A Review of Ecosystem Adaptation in Urban Areas," *Global Environmental Change* 36 (2016): 111–123.

7. Thomas Beamish, *Community at Risk: Biodefense and the Collective Search for Security* (Stanford, CA: Stanford Business Books, 2015).

8. Kevin Fox Gotham and Miriam Greenberg, *Crisis Cities: Disaster and Redevelopment in New York and New Orleans* (New York: Oxford University Press, 2014), qtd. on 134; Kathleen Tierney, Christine Bevc, and Erica Kuligowski, "Metaphors Matter: Disaster Myths, Media Frames, and Their Consequences in Hurricane Katrina," *Annals of the American Academy of Political and Social Science* 604 (2006): 57–81; Peter F. Burns and Matthew O. Thomas, *Reforming New Orleans: The Contentious Politics of Change in the Big Easy* (Ithaca, NY: Cornell University Press, 2015); John C. Mutter, *The Disaster Profiteers: How Natural Disasters Make the Rich Richer and the Poor Even Poorer* (New York: St. Martin's, 2015). On the importance of regional strategies, see Karen Chapple, *Planning Sustainable Cities and Regions: Towards More Equitable Development* (New York: Routledge, 2015); Chris Benner and Manuel Pastor, *Just Growth: Inclusion and Prosperity in America's Metropolitan Regions* (New York: Routledge, 2012); Chris Benner and Manuel Pastor, *Equity, Growth, and Community: What the Nation Can Learn from America's Metro Areas* (Berkeley: University of California Press, 2015); Peter Dreier, John Mollenkopf, and Todd Swanstrom, *Place Matters: Metropolitics for the Twenty-First Century*, 3rd ed. (Lawrence: University Press of Kansas, 2014); Sean Safford, *Why the Garden Club Couldn't Save Youngstown: The Transformation of the Rust Belt* (Cambridge, MA: Harvard University Press, 2009). On the potential of civic me-

dia beyond Twitter polarization, see Chris Wells, *The Civic Organization and the Digital Citizen: Communicating Engagement in a Networked Age* (New York: Oxford University Press, 2015); Ben Green, *The Smart Enough City: Putting Technology in Its Place to Reclaim Our Urban Future* (Cambridge, MA: MIT Press, 2019); Eric Gordon and Paul Mihailidis, eds., *Civic Media: Technology, Design, Practice* (Cambridge, MA: MIT Press, 2016).

9. Daniel P. Aldrich, *Building Resilience: Social Capital in Post-Disaster Recovery* (Chicago, IL: University of Chicago Press, 2012), 24–53; *Black Wave: How Networks and Governance Shaped Japan's 3/11 Disasters* (Chicago, IL: University of Chicago Press, 2019); Kathleen Tierney, *The Social Roots of Risk: Producing Disasters, Promoting Resilience* (Palo Alto, CA: Stanford Business Books, 2014); Kathleen Tierney, *Disasters: A Sociological Approach* (Medford, MA: Polity Press, 2019); Eric Klinenberg, *Heat Wave: A Social Autopsy of Disaster in Chicago* (Chicago, IL: University of Chicago Press, 2002); Eric Klinenberg, *Palaces for the People: How Social Infrastructure Can Help Fight Inequality, Polarization, and the Decline of Civic Life* (New York: Broadway Books, 2018); Amy Liu, Roland V. Anglin, Richard M. Mizelle Jr., and Allison Plyer, eds., *Resilience and Opportunity: Lessons from the U.S. Gulf Coast after Katrina and Rita* (Washington, DC: Brookings Press, 2011); Emily Chamlee-Wright, *The Cultural and Political Economy of Recovery: Social Learning in a Post-Disaster Environment* (New York: Routledge, 2010).

For more general analyses, see Robert D. Putnam, *Bowling Alone: The Collapse and Revival of American Community* (New York: Simon & Schuster, 2000); Alejandro Portes, "Social Capital: Its Origins and Applications in Modern Sociology," *Annual Review of Sociology* 24 (1998): 1–24; Ross Gittell and Avis Vidal, *Community Organizing: Building Social Capital as a Development Strategy* (Thousand Oaks, CA: SAGE, 1998); Michael Woolcock, "Social Capital and Economic Development: Toward a Theoretical Synthesis and Policy Framework," *Theory and Society* 27 (1998): 151–208; Simon Szreter, "The State of Social Capital: Bringing Back Power, Politics, and History," *Theory and Society* 31 (2002): 573–621.

10. Carmen Sirianni, "Neighborhood Planning as Collaborative Democratic Design: The Case of Seattle," *Journal of the American Planning Association* 73 (2007): 373–87; Edward P. Weber, *Bringing Society Back In: Grassroots Ecosystem Management, Accountability, and Sustainable Communities* (Cambridge, MA: MIT Press, 2003).

11. See Albert W. Dzur, *Democratic Professionalism: Citizen Participation and the Reconstruction of Professional Ethics, Identity, and Practice* (University Park: Pennsylvania State University Press, 2008); Harry C. Boyte, *Everyday Politics: Reconnecting Citizens and Public Life* (Philadelphia: University of Pennsylvania Press, 2004), 113–133; William M. Sullivan, *Work and Integrity: The Crisis and Promise of Professionalism in America* (San Francisco, CA: Jossey-Bass, 1995), who utilizes the term *civic professionalism*.

12. Kyle Dreyfuss-Wells, plenary presentation, author's field notes, River Rally, Cleveland, June 23, 2019. See ch. 5.

13. Rachel S. Madsen, Hylton J.G. Haynes, and Sarah M. McCaffrey, "Wildfire Risk Reduction in the United States: Leadership Staff Perceptions of Local Fire Department Roles and Responsibilities," *International Journal of Disaster Risk Reduction* 27 (2018): 451–458; Anna K. Schwab, Dylan Sandler, and David J. Brower, *Hazard Mitigation and Preparedness: An Introductory Text for Emergency Management and Planning Professionals,* second edition (Boca Raton, FL: CRC Press, 2016); Federal Emergency Management Agency (FEMA), *A Whole Community Approach to Emergency Management: Principles, Themes, and Pathways for Action* (Washington, DC: FEMA, 2011), https://www.fema.gov/media-library-d ata/20130726-1813-25045-0649/whole_community_dec2011__2_.pdf.

14. Carmen Sirianni and Lewis A. Friedland, *Civic Innovation in America* (Berkeley: University of California Press, 2001), 234–280; Peter Levine, *We Are the Ones We Have Been Waiting For: The Promise of Civic Renewal in America* (New York: Oxford University Press, 2013), 120–161; National Commission on Civic Renewal, *A Nation of Spectators: How Civic Disengagement Weakens America and What We Can Do About It* (College Park, MD: ERIC, 1998), https://eric.ed.gov /?id=ED424174; the executive director and deputy director of the national commission were, respectively, William Galston and Peter Levine.

15. James Jasper, "Emotions and Social Movements: Twenty Years of Theory and Research," *Annual Review of Sociology* 37 (2001): 285–303; Jeff Goodwin, James M. Jasper, and Francesca Polletta, eds., *Passionate Politics: Emotions and Social Movements* (Chicago, IL: University of Chicago Press, 2001); Marshall Ganz, "Public Narrative, Collective Action, and Power," as well as his leadership training program at the Kennedy School of Government, Harvard University; Deborah B. Gould, *Moving Politics: Emotion and ACT UP's Fight against AIDS* (Chicago, IL: University of Chicago Press, 2009); Nina Eliasoph, *Avoiding Politics: How Americans Produce Apathy in Everyday Life* (New York: Cambridge University Press, 1998); Hoffman, *How Culture Shapes the Climate Change Debate,* 1–14; Kari Marie Norgaard, "'People Want to Protect Themselves a Little Bit': Emotions, Denial, and Social Movement Non-Participation in the Case of Global Climate Change," *Sociological Inquiry* 76 (2006): 372–396; Kari Marie Norgaard, *Living in Denial: Climate Change, Emotions, and Everyday Life* (Cambridge, MA: MIT Press, 2011); Arlie Russell Hochschild, *Strangers in Their Own Land: Anger and Mourning on the American Right* (New York: New Press, 2016); Andrew McMurry, *Entertaining Futility: Despair and Hope in the Time of Climate Change* (College Station: Texas A&M Press, 2018).

16. Jasper, "Emotions and Social Movements"; Mustafa Emirbayer and Chad Alan Goldberg, "Pragmatism, Bourdieu, and Collective Emotions in Contentious Politics," *Theory and Society* 34 (2005): 469–518.

17. Author's field notes, Garrison Institute's Climate, Mind and Behavior Conference, Garrison, New York, June 9–12, 2013; River Rally, June 1, 2014, Pittsburgh, jointly sponsored by the River Network and the Waterkeeper Alliance; Global Climate Action Summit, San Francisco, September 2018, https://www .youtube.com/channel/UCor3JbUn8yqq5npEsf7Clɪg/videos. See also Rebecca Elliott, "The Sociology of Climate Change as a Sociology of Loss," *European Journal of Sociology* 59 (2018): 301–337.

18. Subcommittee on Air and Water Pollution of the Senate Committee on Public Works of the 88th Cong., *Troubled Waters: 1964 Water Pollution Report of the U.S. Senate Committee on Public Works*, documentary, written by Patricia S. Channon, 1964, https://www.youtube.com/watch?v=KXNMGYuznzU. See ch. 2.

19. See Dennis R. Judd, "EVERYTHING IS ALWAYS GOING TO HELL: Urban Scholars as End-Times Prophets," *Urban Affairs Review* 41 (2005): 119–131. On "chaos incitement" in the body politic, see Michael Bang Petersen, Mathias Osmundsen, and Kevin Arceneaux, "A 'Need for Chaos' and the Sharing of Hostile Political Rumors in Advanced Democracies" (paper presented at the American Political Science Association annual meeting, Boston, MA, August 30–September 2, 2018). On traditions of hope, see Mary Robinson, *Climate Justice: Hope, Resilience, and the Fight for a Sustainable Future* (New York: Bloomsbury, 2018); Robert Jay Lifton, *The Climate Swerve: Reflections on Mind, Hope, and Survival* (New York: New Press, 2017); Chris Doran, *Hope in the Age of Climate Change: Creation Care This Side of the Resurrection* (Eugene, OR: Cascade Books, 2017); Claire Dawson and Mick Pope, *A Climate of Hope: Church and Mission in a Warming World* (Urban Neighbours of Hope, 2014); Gleb Raygorodetsky, *The Archipelago of Hope: Wisdom and Resilience at the Edge of Climate Change* (New York: Pegasus, 2017).

Postscript: Toward a Civic Green New Deal

1. Carmen Sirianni, "The Civics of a Green New Deal," blog symposium, "The Green New Deal: Pathways to a Low Carbon Economy," *Public Administration Review*, ed. Nives Dolšak and Aseem Prakash (July 2019); Carmen Sirianni, "The Civics of a Green New Deal: Towards Policy Design for Community Empowerment and Public Participation in an Age of Climate Change" (working paper, Jonathan M. Tisch College for Civic Life, Tufts University, Medford, MA, May 2020), https://tischcollege.tufts.edu/research/civic-green-new-deal. Here I must remain agnostic on the substantive components of a Green New Deal and other proposals to tackle climate change. As of this writing in April 2020, such proposals are proliferating, mostly without coherent civic design, although some are beginning to integrate public participation.

2. On developments in the field of public participation practice, see Susan L. Moffitt, *Making Policy Public: Participatory Bureaucracy in American Democracy* (New York: Cambridge University Press, 2014); Tina Nabatchi and Matt Leigh-

ninger, *Public Participation for 21st Century Democracy* (Hoboken, NJ: Jossey-Bass, 2015); Tina Nabatchi, John Gastil, G. Michael Weiksner, and Matt Leighninger, eds., *Democracy in Motion: Evaluating the Practice and Impact of Deliberative Civic Engagement* (New York: Oxford University Press, 2012); Lawrence Susskind, Sarah McKearnan, and Jennifer Thomas-Larmer, eds., *The Consensus Building Handbook: A Comprehensive Guide to Reaching Agreement* (Thousand Oaks, CA: SAGE, 1999); John Gastil and Peter Levine, *The Deliberative Democracy Handbook: Strategies for Effective Civic Engagement for the Twenty-First Century* (San Francisco, CA: Jossey-Bass, 2005); Laurence Bherer, Mario Gauthier, and Louis Simard, eds., *The Professionalization of Public Participation* (New York: Routledge, 2017).

See also Caroline W. Lee, *Do-It-Yourself Democracy: The Rise of the Public Engagement Industry* (New York: Oxford University Press, 2015); Caroline W. Lee, Michael McQuarrie, and Edward T. Walker, "Rising Participation and Declining Democracy," in *Democratizing Inequalities: Dilemmas of the New Public Participation*, ed. Caroline W. Lee, Michael McQuarrie, and Edward T. Walker (New York: NYU Press, 2015), 3–22. In chapter 1, I briefly address the limits of movement solidarities as a binary alternative to structured and multistakeholder participation and collaboration posited by critics such as Lee, McQuarrie, and Walker. A civic GND design should certainly pay attention to trade-offs and other perverse dynamics in the overall ecology of civic engagement, but this can hardly serve as an argument for investing federal dollars in the physical infrastructure of a Green New Deal but not in its civic infrastructure. Synergies abound and skilled field actors are generally sophisticated enough to generate them.

3. Charles Heckscher and Paul S. Adler, eds., *The Firm as a Collaborative Community: The Reconstruction of Trust in the Knowledge Economy* (New York: Oxford University Press, 2006).

4. Melissa Bass, *The Politics and Civics of National Service: Lessons from the Civilian Conservation Corps, VISTA, and AmeriCorps* (Washington, DC: Brookings Press, 2013). For debates on the impacts and roles of service, as well as arguments for and against universal service, see E. J. Dionne, Kayla Meltzer Drogosz, and Robert E. Litan, eds., *United We Serve: National Service and The Future of Citizenship* (Washington, DC: Brookings Press, 2003); Peter Frumkin and JoAnn Jastrzab, *Serving Country and Community: Who Benefits from National Service?* (Cambridge, MA: Harvard University Press, 2010). On those forms of civic innovation and social entrepreneurship that are available for coproductive public work and a more robust national service strategy, see Paul C. Light, *Sustaining Innovation: Creating Nonprofit and Government Organizations That Innovate Naturally* (San Francisco, CA: Jossey-Bass, 1998); Paul C. Light, *The Search for Social Entrepreneurship* (Washington, DC: Brookings Press, 2008); Carmen Sirianni and Lewis A. Friedland, *The Civic Renewal Movement: Community Building and Democracy in the United States* (Dayton, OH: Kettering Foundation Press, 2005);

Peter Levine, *We Are the Ones We Have Been Waiting For: The Promise of Civic Renewal in America* (New York: Oxford University Press, 2013).

5. See Eric M. Patashnik, "Limiting Policy Backlash: Strategies for Taming Counter-coalitions in an Era of Polarization," *Annals of the American Academy of Political and Social Science* 685 (2019): 47–63. The broad challenges I outline are among those that theorists of collaborative and network governance call "meta-governance." See Jacob Torfing, B. Guy Peters, Jon Pierre, and Eva Sørensen, *Interactive Governance: Advancing the Paradigm* (New York: Oxford University Press, 2012).

6. Archon Fung analyzes recipes and design choices in a way that might be emulated in civic GND frameworks for specific agencies and offices so that agency staff can make informed choices on representational forms, grants, and other resources and tools, and so that civic and professional groups can appropriately apply and provide critical feedback and hence mutual learning in multiple directions. See Archon Fung, "Recipes for Public Spheres: Eight Institutional Design Choices and Their Consequences," *Journal of Political* Philosophy 11 (2003): 338–367; "Varieties of Participation in Complex Governance," in Collaborative Public Management, special issue, *Public Administration Review* 66 (2006): 66–75. For a very helpful general statement on integrating normative and empirical analysis in policy design with feed-forward effects and across a wide range of constructivist design components, see Anne Schneider and Mara Sidney, "What Is Next for Policy Design and Social Construction Theory," *Policy Studies Journal* 37 (2009): 103–119. On the surprisingly robust legacy and potential of citizen advisory committees, see Moffitt, *Making Policy Public*. As she argues, citizen advisory committees are especially relevant when there is interdependent task implementation among public agencies and increasing reliance upon third parties for coproduction. They facilitate emergent knowledge sharing and policy learning among networks of actors, and can fruitfully combine bureaucratic initiative and public accountability among the full range of implementers as well as broader publics. "In the right conditions, public participation yields not just better policy outcomes but better bureaucracy. Public participation is not necessarily bureaucracy's opposite but instead can be its complement" (226). For further background, see Stephen P. Croly and William F. Funk, "The Federal Advisory Committee Act and Good Government," *Yale Journal on Regulation* 14 (1997): 451–557.

7. Jeremy Rifkin, *The Green New Deal* (New York: St. Martin's Press, 2019), understands core challenges when he argues that "the way to ensure public engagement at every step along the way to transitioning to a green smart city or region is to embed 'deep public participation' and involvement at every stage of development, from conception to ongoing deployment" (42). He recommends federal grants to each state for $60 million to establish the centers, but one would probably want to adjust this figure according to state population.

8. Naomi Klein, *On Fire: The Burning Case for a Green New Deal* (New York: Simon & Schuster, 2019), qtd. on 51, 39. For a nuanced view of the relationships between movement and policy design across a range of fields, see David S. Meyer, Valerie Jenness, and Helen Ingram, eds., *Routing the Opposition: Social Movements, Public Policy, and Democracy* (Minneapolis: University of Minnesota Press, 2005).

Index

in New York, 191
sustainable, 149, 151, 156–157
urban, 34–35, 124, 138–160, 275–279
Watershed Agricultural Council (WAC), 193
Agyeman, Julian, 249
air pollution, 12, 63–64, 66, 147, 188. *See also* clean air
Air Quality Act (1967),64– 65
aldermanic privilege, 200, 216, 219–220, 222–223, 239, 276
Aldrich, Daniel, 283
algae blooms, 45, 55, 58
aligning and bridging, 7–8, 37, 250, 273
Alinsky, Saul, 85, 127, 217, 239, 247
Alleghany County, 64–65
Allen, Erika, 158
Allen, Will, 158
Alliance for Biking and Walking (ABW), 128–129, 134, 154, 160, 174
alliances, 80, 87, 232, 251
    Alliance for Biking and Walking (ABW), 128–129, 134, 154, 160, 174
    Alliance for Chesapeake Bay, 169
    bicycle, 129, 134
    greenbelt, 34, 88
    and Smart Growth America, 106, 109, 187
    and watersheds, 178, 196
American Association of State Highway and Transportation Officials (AASHTO), 108–109, 138
American Community Gardening Association (ACGA), 139, 157
American Council for an Energy-Efficient Economy (ACEEE), 255–256, 264, 268, 273
    City Clean Energy Scorecard, 255
American Federation of Labor-Congress of Industrial Organizations (AFL-CIO), 51, 61
American Institute of Architects (AIA), 13–14, 34, 93–97
    Center for Communities by Design, 96–97
    and civic engagement, 81, 121
    and field logics, 10, 273, 279
    and Intermodal Surface Transportation Efficiency Act, 134–135, 137
    in Phoenix, 236
    in Portland, 202
    and US Green Building Council, 112–113, 118
American Institute of Planners, 61, 101
American Municipal Association, 33, 42, 49, 51, 63, 78

American Planning Association (APA), 4, 14, 34, 81, 97–101
    and civic Green New Deal, 296, 303
    and civic organizing, 121
    and field logics, 10, 273
    and food policy councils, 149
    as intermediary, 254
    and Intermodal Surface Transportation Efficiency Act, 134, 137
    and Smart Growth America, 105
    and US Green Building Council, 116, 119
American Public Health Association, 107, 247
American Recovery and Reinvestment Act (ARRA), 238, 264
American Rivers and Clean Water Action, 36, 163, 183–185, 197
American Society for Testing and Materials (ASTM), 113–114
American Society of Landscape Architects (ASLA), 106–107, 341n43
Americans with Disabilities Act (ADA), 110, 137
AmeriCorps, 141, 232, 248, 260, 291, 300
Amsler, Terry, 260, 390n31
Anderson, Susan, 205
Andrews, Denise, 187
Andrews, Richard, 74
Angeles, Ron, 188
antihunger activism, 149, 151, 158–159
Appleton, Albert, 190
aquifers, 36, 46, 233, 235
Area Agencies on Aging (AAAs), 109–110
Arigoni, Danielle, 111
Arizona State University (ASU), 235, 238, 240, 255, 277
    Global Institute of Sustainability, 238, 255
Arnstein, Sherry, 84, 136
Asian populations, 140, 153, 202, 207
assets-based community development (ABCD), 37, 219, 242, 245, 247–248, 267
    and food justice, 143, 148, 152
Association for Biking and Walking, 12, 156, 254–255
Association of State Floodplain Managers, 14, 285
associations, 31, 34–36, 38
    American Municipal Association, 33, 42, 49, 51, 63, 78
    and asset-based community development, 247–248
    associational capacity building, 48, 294
    associational networks, 16, 177, 228
    bicycle, 11, 31, 108, 123, 131–133, 159, 250

and International Council for Local
    Environmental Initiatives, 257, 260
Oakland, California, 150, 153, 207, 257
oil spill in, 46, 61
Prop 50 in, 283
Smart Growth America in, 107
University of California, Berkeley, 125, 214,
    246, 262
urban rivers and watersheds in, 175–176,
    179, 186, 197
US Green Building Council in, 119
water pollution in, 46, 61
See also Los Angeles, California; San
    Francisco, California
California Environmental Quality Act of 1970
    (CEQA), 208–209
    environmental impact review (EIR),
        209–210
California's State Energy Efficiency
    Collaborative (SEEC), 260
Calthorpe, Peter, 90–91, 101
Campbell, Lindsay, 146
Canada, 91, 139, 205, 264
capacity building, 12, 19, 32, 141, 152, 177
    civic capacity building, 32, 39, 97, 137,
        165–166
capital, 6
    capitalism, 27, 29, 299
    global, 9, 24, 27
    and green building, 10
    social, 38, 159, 223, 283–284
    and urban agriculture, 146–147
    and urban rivers and watersheds, 191, 193
carbon emissions, 11, 119–120
    carbon pricing, 271
    reduction of, 264, 303
Carbon Neutral Cities Alliance, 264
careers, environmental, 31, 100, 291
Carlsson, Chris, 126
Carson, Rachel, 68
Carter, Jimmy, 74, 204, 233
Casciani, Cheryl, 231
Catskill-Delaware watersheds, 189–194
Catskill Watershed Corporation (CWC),
    191–194
Center for Neighborhood Technology (CNT),
    104, 134–135, 225–226, 228–229
Center for Watershed Protection, 19, 181–182
Ceres, 9, 299
chambers of commerce, 225, 298, 303
Chapple, Karen, 105
charrettes, 93–96, 103–104, 224, 275, 341n43
    National Charrette Institute (NCI), 103

Chen, Don, 109, 266
Chesapeake Bay, 167–169, 176, 185, 196–197,
    275
    and Baltimore, 230–231, 240
    Chesapeake 2000 (C2K), 169–170
    Chesapeake Bay Foundation (CBF),
        168–170, 174
    Chesapeake Bay Program, 36, 162,
        167–169, 278
Chesapeake Bay Foundation (CBF), 168–170,
    174
Chicago, Illinois
    aldermanic privilege in, 200, 216, 219–220,
        222–223, 239, 276
    bicycle advocacy in, 132, 134–135
    Chicago Association of Neighborhood
        Development Organizations (CANDO),
        217, 223
    Chicago Brownfields Initiative, 224
    Chicago Climate Action Plan, 228, 263
    Chicagoland Bicycle Federation, 132, 134,
        224
    Chicago Wilderness, 226–229
    Chicago Works Together, 218
    and democratic resilience, 276–277,
        288
    food justice in, 158
    and International Council for Local
        Environmental Initiatives (ICLEI),
        260–261
    the Loop in, 200, 216, 221
    neighborhood associations in, 84
    New Communities Program, 223, 229
    open space councils in, 88
    urban governance in, 199–201, 215–230,
        238–239
    and Urban Sustainability Directors
        Network, 263
Chicago Association of Neighborhood
    Development Organizations (CANDO),
    217, 223
Chicago Wilderness, 226–229
Chicanos Por La Causa, 237
children
    in Chicago, 222, 228
    and civic Green New Deal, 306
    and cultural politics of hope, 287–288
    and food justice, 141, 146, 150, 153
    and safe streets, 19, 107, 126–128, 160
    and water quality, 176, 184
churches, 70, 87, 252, 295
    faith-based organizing, 21, 144, 151, 217,
        295, 318n43

cities
    city agencies, 85–87, 125, 139, 149–160,
        215, 229–230
    city governments, 108, 123, 145, 149, 191,
        257
    city housekeeping frame, 12, 52, 77
    city institutions, 37, 142, 249
    city-level planning, 69, 91
    city manager-council governments, 12
    city offices, 4, 185, 255
    city officials, 8, 83, 94–95, 215, 236,
        261–262
    city practitioners, 4, 255
    city processes, 37, 268
    city tool kits, 37, 250, 268
    inner-city neighborhoods, 3, 21, 135, 142,
        230, 232
    See also Baltimore, Maryland; Chicago,
        Illinois; city councils; Los Angeles,
        California; New York City, New
        York; Philadelphia, Pennsylvania;
        Phoenix, Arizona; Portland, Oregon;
        San Francisco, California; Seattle,
        Washington; sustainable cities; urban
        environments; urban governance
Cities for Climate Protection (CCP), 261
citizen participation, 13–17, 19
    and biking and walking, 136–137
    and Chesapeake Bay, 169
    in Chicago, 227–229
    citizen advisory boards, 151, 204
    citizen advisory committees, 39, 171–172,
        292, 296, 302–304, 400n75
    citizen-driven, 258
    citizen engagement, 17, 48, 99, 117, 121,
        149, 194, 206, 208
    citizen groups, 58, 62, 68, 96, 118
    citizen science, 13, 100, 213, 227–228, 278
    citizen whistleblowers, 62
    and civic Green New Deal, 291–292, 294,
        297–298, 303–304
    and Clean Water Act, 162, 164–165, 195
    and democratic resilience, 38–39, 278, 286
    and framing anchors, 250
    and ICLEI, 262–263
    and participatory planning, 84, 102
    in Portland, 200, 202–206
    and postwar air and water, 46–49, 51,
        54–58, 61–65, 68, 76–78
    and professional organizations, 34, 82–84,
        89, 95–96, 99, 102, 121
    in San Francisco, 207, 212–213
    and Seattle water, 187–188

    and US Green Building Council, 117–118
    and water quality monitoring, 177, 183
Citizens Advisory Committee on
    Environmental Quality, 81, 169
citizen science, 13, 100, 213, 227–228, 278
city councils, 256, 275–276, 283
    in Baltimore, 230
    in Chicago, 85, 225
    and democratic policy design, 21
    and federal enforcement conference, 58–59
    and ICLEI, 261–262
    in Philadelphia, 144
    in Phoenix, 236
    in Portland, 129, 136, 202
    in Seattle, 86, 140, 151–152, 262
city housekeeping frame, 12, 52, 77
civic and conservation associations, 70, 72
civic associations, ix, 4–5, 11–12
    and bicycling, 128, 137
    and civic Green New Deal, 294–295, 303
    and democratic resilience, 278, 284
    and food justice, 145, 149
    and institutional fields, 9
    and intermediaries, 255
    and neighborhood associations, 86
    in Phoenix, 235
    and policy design, 80, 83
    and postwar environmentalism, 45, 49,
        60–61, 75–77
    and professional associations, 18–19, 107
    and urban governance, 26
    and watershed advocacy, 36, 170, 172, 197
civic Green New Deal (GND), 39, 290–292,
    305–306
    funding for, types of grants, 292–301
    strategic coordination for, 301–304
civic politics of risk and resilience, 38–39, 271,
    281–284, 290
civic professionalism, 13, 92, 177, 189, 293
civil rights movement, 16, 70, 82–84, 86, 236
    in Chicago, 218–219, 221
Clarke, Andy, 132–133
clean air, 3–4, 8, 11
    clean air policy, 64
    and land-use policy, 89, 121
    and Pittsburgh, 64–67
    and postwar advocacy, 42, 45, 56, 63–67,
        72–73, 77–78
    and sustainable cities framing, 244, 259
    See also Clean Air Act (CAA)
Clean Air Act (CAA), 63, 65, 72–73, 78, 89,
    137
    Clean Air Act of 1963, 63–64

clean water, 3–4
  and civic associations, 11, 33
  and civic Green New Deal, 296
  Clean Water Action, 36, 178, 183–184,
    197, 257
  and democratic resilience, 285
  and field logics, 8
  National Association of Clean Water
    Agencies, 178, 285
  post–Clean Water Act, 35–36, 162, 166,
    176–178, 183, 185–186, 190
  and postwar advocacy, 41–42, 45–63, 67,
    75, 77–78
  and sustainable cities frame, 244
  See also Clean Water Act (CWA)
Clean Water Act (CWA), 35–36, 61–63,
  72–73, 78, 162–164, 195–196
  amendments to, 167, 170
  and Chesapeake Bay, 168–169
  citizen suit provision in, 164–165
  civic action prior to, 33, 56, 59
  and Clean Water Action, 185
  and Edmund S. Muskie, 59
  and Environmental Protection Agency, 181
  and field dynamics, 278
  and land-use policy, 89
  and National Estuary Program, 21, 170
  and Seattle, 186
  Section 208 of, 56, 162, 164–167, 176
Clean Water Action, 36, 178, 183–184, 197,
  257
Cleveland, Ohio, 46, 55, 58, 153, 178, 285
  Cuyahoga River in, 46, 61
climate change, ix, 1, 5
  and analytic approaches, 27, 30–31
  in Chicago, 225–226, 228–229, 240
  and civic Green New Deal, 39, 290–291,
    295–298, 301, 304–306, 398n1
  climate action plans, 200–201, 205, 228,
    239, 255, 262–263, 276–277
  climate adaptation, 96, 265, 283, 285
  climate disruption, 14, 287
  climate futility, 5, 39, 286, 288
  climate mitigation, 39, 97, 259–260,
    279–280
  climate planning, 100, 122, 225–226, 250
  and contemporary activism, x
  as crisis, ix, 1, 29, 32, 38, 242, 289, 295
  and democratic policy design, 21, 23
  and democratic resilience, 38, 271, 276,
    280, 282, 285–289
  denial of, 3, 286, 288
  and ICLEI USA, 257–259, 261–262

and National Environmental Policy Act, 69
  in Portland, 200–201, 205–206, 238–239
  and professional associations, 14, 96–97,
    103, 111–112, 116
  and sustainable cities framing, 242, 250,
    254, 269
  and urban rivers and watersheds, 163, 175,
    186
Clinton, Bill, 20, 95, 106, 180, 233, 246, 248
cloud-based platforms, 100, 119, 143, 250,
  259
coal, 43, 64, 201, 239, 234
coalitions, 2, 4, 11–12
  and biking and walking advocacy, 123–125,
    127–130, 134–137, 154
  and civic Green New Deal, 298–299
  coalition building, 59
  Coalition to Restore Urban Waters, 14, 183
  and democratic resilience, 272, 275,
    279–280, 285
  and food advocacy, 144–146, 149, 155–158
  and land-use conflicts, 81–82, 85, 86, 90,
    104–109, 121
  in postwar years, 33–35, 52, 54, 57, 59, 61,
    63
  and sustainable cities frame, 244, 248–250,
    259
  and urban governance, 24–25, 199–200,
    206–209, 215–216, 226, 237, 239
  and urban rivers and watershed, 174, 183,
    185, 190–192
coastal areas, 19, 163, 167, 175, 186
  and Clean Water Act, 35
  and coastal retreat, 23, 103
  and democratic resilience, 280, 284
  and land-use conflicts, 91
  and National Estuary Program, 22
  and San Francisco, 211
cobenefits, 184, 224, 245, 250, 259
cognitive framing, 5, 60, 87, 176, 243–245,
  249–251, 267
collaboration, x, 2
  and bicycling and walking movements, 35,
    125, 128, 137
  and civic associations, 12–13
  and civic Green New Deal, 39, 290, 293,
    296–299, 304–306
  collaborative action, 35, 37, 196, 212, 297
  collaborative decision making, 137, 299
  collaborative management, 21
  collaborative planning, 137, 156, 169,
    211
  and democratic policy design, 21–22

comprehensive conservation and management
plan (CCMP), 171, 173
comprehensive planning, 105, 118–119, 150,
203
Conference of Mayors, US, 33, 38
and bicycle advocacy, 135
and land use conflicts, 90
and postwar environmentalism, 42, 49, 51,
61, 63, 78
and sustainable cities framing, 243,
256–257
and urban agriculture, 148
conflict, 2–3, 18, 25, 27, 244
and civic Green New Deal, 39, 304, 306
conflict resolution, 85, 369n4
and democratic resilience, 279, 281
and postwar air and water, 48, 73, 77
and urban agriculture, 156
and urban governance, 200, 212, 219
and urban rivers and watershed, 184, 190,
193
See also land-use conflicts
Congestion Mitigation and Air Quality
Improvement (CMAQ), 135, 137
Congrès Internationaux d'Architecture
Moderne (CIAM), 101–102
Congress, US
and bicycling, 107, 133
and civic Green New Deal, 292–294,
302–303
and Clean Water Act, 21, 73, 165, 167,
196–197
and democratic resilience, 279–280
and NAPA reports, 180
and National Land Use Policy Act, 34, 67, 69
and policy design, 17, 48–50, 80, 89
and postwar environmentalism, 41–43, 61,
63–64, 71–72, 73–75, 313n21
and San Francisco, 212–123
and urban agriculture, 155, 158
Congress for the New Urbanism (CNU), 81,
101–104, 117, 274
Conlin, Richard, 251
consensus-based multistakeholder processes,
114–115, 118
conservation
associations, 12, 33, 41, 70, 77, 88
biology, 36, 244
and civic associations, 12, 33
Conservation Foundation, 55, 63, 68, 75,
165, 265
conservationists, 17, 46, 48, 59, 64
and democratic policy design, 17

in early postwar decades, 41–43, 46–48, 59,
64, 72, 75
energy conservation, 204, 225–226
groups, 33, 46–47, 53, 58, 72
and land-use conflicts, 88–89
leagues, 88, 211
pre–World War II, 1
and urban governance, 204, 211, 225–226,
238
and urban rivers and watersheds, 164, 171,
175–176, 181, 183, 193–194
water, 116, 193, 201
Conservation Foundation, 55, 63, 68, 75,
165, 265
conservatives, 78, 89, 201, 234, 240, 266
Constitution, US, 25, 49, 70
consulting, 11, 93, 116–117, 189, 226, 255
contestation, 18, 26, 29, 238, 299, 305–306
co-ops, 138, 156, 160
coproduction
and civic Green New Deal, 291, 294–295,
297, 302, 304
and democratic policy design, 15, 18–20
and democratic resilience, 270, 273–274, 284
and food policy councils, 150
and League of Women Voters, 52
and National Estuary Program, 172
and professional associations, 101, 112
and sustainable cities framing, 247, 250
and urban governance, 26–27
Corburn, Jason, 19, 194, 247
Cornell University Extension, 191, 193
coronavirus, x, 240
Corporation for National and Community
Service (CNCS), 300–301
Council of Educational Facilities Planners
International, 10, 116
Council on Environmental Quality (CEQ), 34,
62, 68–69, 82, 244, 280
Council on Sustainable Development, 96,
106, 199
countermovements, 34, 280, 286, 306
covenants, conditions, and restrictions
(CC&Rs), 234
Coxe, Trudy, 178
Critical Mass, 123, 125–126, 129–130, 159,
214, 287
Cronon, William, 227
cross-boundary dimensions, 45, 54, 89
Croton watershed, 189–190, 194
culture
and bicycling, 123–124, 126, 129, 159–160
black cultural areas, 130

culture, *continued*
  and civic Green New Deal, 295, 306
  of conservation, 12
  cultural politics of hope, 38–39, 271,
    280–281, 286–289, 290
  cultural symbols, 8, 176
  and democratic engagement, 4, 102
  and institutional fields, 6–9
  and postwar air and water, 51, 60, 66, 72
  and Smart Growth alliances, 187, 189
  and sustainable cities framing, 243–244,
    254, 259, 268–269
  and urban agriculture, 141–142, 146, 155
  and urban governance, 201, 205, 209–210,
    228, 236, 240
  and urban rivers and watersheds, 172–173,
    176, 183, 188

Daley, Richard J., 200, 216, 218
Daley, Richard M., 138, 201, 220–225,
  228–229, 276
dams, 16, 44, 47–48, 164, 184, 189
data
  and American Planning Association,
    100–101
  and citizen water monitoring, 177
  data tools, 101, 120, 273
  and democratic policy design, 17, 19–20
  and democratic resilience, 273, 277–278
  and National Environmental Policy Act, 42
  and Pennsylvania Horticulture Society, 143
  and sustainable cities framing, 37, 255, 268
  and urban governance, 205, 219
Davis, California, 125, 159, 282
De Graauw, Els, 215
deindustrialization, 37, 142, 199, 216, 218, 276
deliberative processes, 16, 21, 23, 90
  and civic Green New Deal, 291–292, 302,
    304
  deliberative democracy, 26, 99, 172, 222,
    274–275
  deliberative design, 137
  deliberative problem-solving, 286
  systemic deliberation, 59, 69, 195, 252
  and urban agriculture, 149, 156
  and urban river and watersheds, 183, 188
democracy, ix–x
  and civic action, 2
  and civic Green New Deal, 292, 294,
    299–300, 304, 306
  deliberative, 26, 99, 172, 222, 274–275
  democratic action, ix, 8, 27, 82, 252,
    273–274, 297

democratic anchorage, 149, 172
democratic deliberation, 28, 172, 222, 274
democratic engagement, 4–5, 30, 199, 242,
  270
democratic governance, 10, 22, 123, 306
democratic institutionalism, 2, 9, 30, 274
democratic norms, x, 271, 302
democratic participation, 78, 124, 270
democratic policy design, 6, 14–17, 20–22,
  155, 166
democratic pragmatism, 2, 18, 261, 323n20
democratic professionalism, 27, 38–39, 253,
  270–271, 281, 284–286, 290
democratic resilience, 38, 270–272,
  274–275, 280–284
democratic sustainability, 9
democratization, 28, 48, 317n39
  and land-use conflicts, 83, 86–86, 91, 93
  participatory, 63, 86, 219
  in postwar years, 48, 61, 63, 77
  and professional associations, 102–103, 117
  and sustainable cities framing, 249
  systemic approaches to, 26–30
  true, 29–30
  and urban governance, 200–201, 219
  and urban rivers and watersheds, 181, 189,
    195, 198
  See also democratic legitimacy
democratic legitimacy, 5, 7
  and bicycle movement, 126, 154
  and civic Green New Deal, 39
  and democratic resilience, 272, 277, 283
  and sustainable cities framing, 250–252,
    268–269
  and urban agriculture, 140, 143, 159
  and urban governance, 212, 239
Democratic Party, United States, 74, 76
denialism, 27, 38, 280–281, 283, 286, 288
Denver, Colorado, 47, 139, 150, 257
Department of Agriculture, United States
  (USDA), 73, 151–153, 175, 193, 268
Department of Environmental Protection
  (DEP), New York City, 190, 194
Department of Health, Education, and
  Welfare, United States (HEW), 49, 55,
  57–58, 73, 180, 246
Department of the Interior, US, 44, 68, 73
Department of Transportation, US (USDOT)
  and bicycle advocacy, 133, 136
  establishment of, 84
  and professional associations, 104, 107–109,
    111
  state DOTs, 108–109, 136–138, 279

environment
  environmental countermovements, 34, 280, 286, 306
  environmental degradation, ix, 102
  environmental education, 21, 71, 169–170, 212, 228, 231, 298
  environmental equity, 248
  environmental field, 6–7, 33, 68, 120–121, 252, 272
  environmental history, 30, 55
  environmental lobbying, 33, 61
  environmental movement, 18, 78, 192, 310n16
  environmental norms, 11, 113
  environmental policy, 16–18, 22, 42, 55, 60, 67
  environmental racism, 248
  environmental regulations, 226
  environmental sustainability, 232, 240
  environmental values, 76, 135, 174, 280
  and National Environmental Policy Act, 67–69
  and US Green Building Council, 112–113
  See also environmentalism; environmental justice (EJ); environmental organizations; Environmental Protection Agency (EPA)
Environmental Action, 61, 71, 225, 253
Environmental Defense Fund (EDF), 9, 61, 76, 78, 185, 252, 265
Environmental Education and Training Partnership (EETAP), 71
Environmental Grantmakers Association (EGA), 265, 267, 304
environmental impact statements (EIS), 42, 47, 55, 68–69, 98, 136
environmentalism, 1, 3, 7
  postwar, 41–43, 46, 49, 67, 70
  and urban agriculture, 149
  and urban governance, 203, 208, 232
  and water, 174, 193, 197
environmental justice (EJ), 1, 3, 7–8, 34, 77, 248–249
  in Chicago, 225–226, 229, 240
  and civic Green New Deal, 295, 302, 304, 306
  and democratic resilience, 278, 285, 287
  and policy, 17, 19
  in Portland, 206, 239
  and professional associations, 14, 100, 114, 122
  and River Network, 178
  and San Francisco, 214, 239

  and sustainable cities framing, 248–249, 251–253, 256–257, 263, 267–268
  and transportation, 135, 137–138
  and urban agriculture, 146
environmental organizations, 9–10
  and civic Green New Deal, 293, 299
  and policy design, 80, 90
  in postwar era, 42–43, 72, 74
  and professional associations, 104, 113
  and sustainable cities framing, 266
  and urban agriculture, 151
  and watershed advocacy, 191, 197
Environmental Protection Agency (EPA)
  and AARP, 111–112
  and Chesapeake Bay, 276
  and Chicago, 225–226
  and civic Green New Deal, 294–295
  and Clean Water Act, 62–63
  development of, 42, 58, 279
  and environmental justice, 248–249
  and GASP, 65
  and institutional fields, 9, 11, 72–76, 287
  Office of Environmental Education, 20–21, 71
  Office of Sustainable Ecosystems and Communities (OSEC) in, 180, 252
  Office of Water, EPA, 20, 55, 177, 179, 185, 252
  Office of Wetlands, Oceans, and Watersheds (OWOW), EPA, 36, 163, 179, 182–183, 196
  and rivers and watersheds, 19–20, 36, 163, 165–183, 190–191, 194–198
  and Smart Growth America, 105–106
  and Smart Growth Network, 105
  and sustainable cities framing, 252, 255, 261, 268
  and US Green Building Council, 113, 116
equity
  in Chicago, 218, 226, 229
  and civic Green New Deal, 292, 304
  and food justice, 141
  gender, 129, 210
  in Phoenix, 238, 240
  and policy, 82
  in Portland, 206
  and professional associations, 96, 99–100, 102, 105–106, 108, 117
  racial, 108, 141, 200, 218, 275
  in San Francisco, 210, 214
  and sustainable cities frame, 242–243, 248–249, 263

gay community, 146, 214–215, 221
Gelber, Marilyn, 190, 193, 195
gender
    equity, 129, 210
    General Federation of Women's Clubs
        (GFWC), 12, 51, 55, 64
    and sustainable cities framing, 287
    See also League of Women Voters; women
General Federation of Women's Clubs
    (GFWC), 12, 51, 55, 64
gentrification, 23, 130, 142, 146, 225
geographic information systems (GIS), 19, 98,
    101, 205, 250, 268
Geological Survey, US, 88, 163
GHG emissions, 231, 259, 263
GI Bill, 15–16, 268, 304
Gingrich, Newt, 155, 158, 180
Giuliani, Rudolph. 145, 190
Glendenning, Parris N., 106
Global Philanthropy Partnership (GPP), 228,
    263
global scope, ix
    and Chicago climate action plan, 228
    and civic innovation, 29
    and democratic resilience, 271, 280–281
    global capital, 24, 27
    global cities network, 9, 264
    global movements, 29
    global north/south axis, 310n11
    and ICLEI USA, 38, 245, 257, 260–261
    and sustainable cities framing, 252
    and urban agriculture, 160
Global Warming Solutions Act, 260, 289n26
Goddard, Terry, 235
Golden Gate National Recreation Area
    (GGNRA), 200, 212–213
Goldschmidt, Neil, 98, 204–205, 368n2
Good Housekeeping, 52–53
Gordon, Phil, 235
Gore, Al, 261
Gotham, Kevin, 25
Gottfried, David, 112–113
Gottlieb, Robert, 157–158
governance
    and American Planning Association, 98–99
    in Chicago, 227
    and civic Green New Deal, 290, 297, 303,
        306
    collaborative governance, 27, 213, 260
    democratic governance, 10, 22, 123, 306
    and democratic resilience, 275, 277, 282
    dynamics, 94, 159, 227, 242
    metagovernance, 400n5

multilevel governance, 12, 271
participatory governance, 155, 238, 258
    in Phoenix, 236–237
    in San Francisco, 213–214, 239
    shared, 214, 282
    and sustainable cities framing, 242, 250,
        259–260
    templates, 19, 21–22
    and urban rivers and watersheds, 163, 173,
        186
    See also urban governance
grants, 19
    in Chicago, 224, 225, 228
    and civic Green New Deal, 292–299,
        300–304
    and Clean Water Act, 165, 169
    Community Development Block Grant
        program, 85–86, 90, 112, 218, 222
    and Congress for the New Urbanism,
        104–105
    and EPA OWOW, 181, 183
    federal, 39, 83, 229, 233, 269, 292,
        294–295
    and food policy, 151–154, 157
    grant programs, 20, 153, 292–293, 295
    and ISTEA, 136, 204
    and LEED-ND, 118
    and New York City water, 192
    and postwar environmentalism, 50–51, 63,
        65
    and sustainable cities frame, 248, 251,
        264–266
Gray, Freddie, 232
Great Lakes, 42, 46, 59, 62, 77
    Lake Erie, 45, 53–55, 58, 176
    Lake Michigan, 58, 60, 88
greenbelt alliances, 34, 88, 105, 117, 200, 211
Greenberg, Miriam, 25
green building, 3–4, 8, 10
    in Baltimore, 230
    in Chicago, 225–226, 240
    and civic Green New Deal, 298–299
    and community development corporations,
        87
    in Phoenix, 237
    in Portland, 205–206
    and professional associations, 92, 96–97,
        104
    in San Francisco, 211, 213
    in Seattle, 141, 188
    and sustainable cities framing, 242, 245,
        261
    See also Green Building Council (USGBC)

multistakeholder collaboration
  and analytic approaches, 27
  and bicycle advocacy, 129, 132
  and civic Green New Deal, 39, 292–293,
    302
  and democratic governance, 268, 272, 278
multistakeholder partnerships, 16, 39, 132,
  169, 178, 272, 292
multistakeholder visioning, 105, 140, 268
  and policy design, 16, 21, 51
  and professional associations, 14, 95, 99,
    105, 108, 112, 115
  and sustainable cities framing, 245,
    247–248, 250, 268
  and urban agriculture, 140, 149, 151, 153
  and urban governance, 37, 211, 220,
    225–226, 229, 236–237
  and urban rivers and watersheds, 163,
    166–167, 169–170, 173, 178–180, 183
multitiered organizations
  and policy design, 80
  in postwar era, ix, 11–12, 41–42, 46,
    51–52, 76–78
  and professional associations, 94, 110, 121
  and urban governance, 203, 215, 229, 239
  and water advocacy, 166, 172, 185
Muskie, Edmund S., 59, 61–62, 65–65, 69,
  162

Nadeau, Doug, 213
Nader, Ralph, 62, 185
Narragansett Bay, 174, 178
  Save The Bay (STB) in, 178
National Academy of Public Administration
  (NAPA), 179–180, 197, 237, 303
National Association of Area Agencies on
  Aging, 109–110
National Association of City Transportation
  Officials (NACTO), 4
  and bicycle advocacy, 128, 131, 138, 154,
    160
  and civic Green New Deal, 296
  and democratic resilience, 273, 279, 285
  and Seattle drainage system, 187–188
  and Smart Growth America, 108–109
  and sustainable cities framing, 255, 268
National Association of Clean Water Agencies
  (NACWA), 178, 285, 296
  Stormwater Management Committee, 178,
    285
National Association of Counties, 63, 135
National Association of Home Builders
  (NAHB), 43, 89

National Association of Realtors (NAR), 43,
  89, 107
National Association of State Floodplain
  Managers, 14, 285
National Audubon Society, 10, 12, 46, 64,
  77, 272
National Campaign for Sustainable
  Agriculture, 156–157
National Civic League (NCL), 138, 180, 235,
  246
  All-America Cities Award, xv, 237
National Complete Streets Coalition, 106,
  108–109, 132, 134
National Conference of Commissioners on
  Uniform State Laws, 17, 48
National Conference on Water Pollution, 50, 53
National Environmental Justice Advisory
  Council (NEJAC), 20, 248–249, 251,
  257, 304
National Environmental Policy Act (NEPA),
  17, 42, 47, 55, 60, 67–70, 279
  and bicycle advocacy, 154, 160
  environmental impact assessments, 69, 91
  and policy design, 84, 89, 91
  and professional associations, 98, 121, 136,
    137
National Estuary Program (NEP), 19, 21–22,
  36, 167, 170–174, 196
  Puget Sound NEP, 179, 259
National Farm to School Network, 157–158
National Land Use Policy Act (NLUPA), 34,
  89–92, 121, 167, 203, 279
National League of Cities (NLC), 4, 38
  and bicycle advocacy, 135, 138
  and civic Green New Deal, 296, 303
  and democratic resilience, 279
  and land-use conflicts, 81, 90
  and postwar environmentalism, 59, 61
  and professional associations, 110, 118
  and sustainable cities framing, 243,
    256–257, 260, 268
  and urban governance, 205, 229, 240
National Oceanic and Atmospheric
  Administration (NOAA), 19, 175, 185,
  259, 279, 294
National Organic Standards Board (NOSB),
  35, 152, 155–156, 160
National Parks Conservation Association
  (NPCA), 184, 228
National Park Service (NPS), 44, 88, 176,
  212–213
National Pollutant Discharge Elimination
  System (NPDES), 165, 186

and sustainable cities framing, 243, 249, 254, 258, 269
and water advocacy, 192, 194, 198
resistance
    and democratic resilience, 280–281
    and environmental racism, 249
    mass, 28, 30
    in Philadelphia, 142
    popular, 28, 39, 290
    and urban governance, 200, 207, 216–217, 220, 227, 239
resources
    associational, 13, 34
    and bicycle advocacy, 129, 132–133
    and civic Green New Deal, 305–306
    and land-use conflicts, 100, 108, 118
    natural, 50, 98, 223
    and policy design, 15–16, 19, 22
    and postwar environmentalism, 33, 50–52, 71, 74
    and sustainable cities framing, 247, 265, 269
    and urban agriculture, 143, 146
    and urban governance, 215, 222–224, 228, 236
    water, 35–36, 46, 52, 223
    and watershed advocacy, 176, 178, 185, 197
restoration
    and civic Green New Deal, 291, 293, 300–302
    and democratic resilience, 278, 284, 288
    ecosystem, 19, 266, 294
    Restore America's Estuaries (RAE), 163, 174–176, 183, 241, 255, 259
    and sustainable cities framing, 240, 245, 259
    and urban governance, 210–213, 225, 230–231
    and urban rivers and watersheds, 21–22, 31, 56, 99, 169–175, 183–185, 197
Restore America's Estuaries (RAE), 163, 174–176, 183, 241, 255, 259
revitalization
    in Baltimore, 231–232
    in Chicago, 201–203, 222
    and Model Cities program, 83
    neighborhood, 87, 139, 143, 222, 231–232, 277
    in Phoenix, 237
    and urban governance, 37
rhetoric, 56, 66, 257, 305
Richards, Lynn, 103–104
Rifkin, Jeremy, 303

rights
    and bicycle advocacy, 123–124, 127, 137
    to the city, 123, 127, 159
    to information, 1, 77
    and land-use conflicts, 83–84, 86, 90, 121
    and postwar environmentalism, 64, 70, 77
    property, 3, 89, 121, 167, 174
    rights-based policies, 16–17, 19, 137, 278, 291
    and urban agriculture, 145, 159, 167
    See also civil rights movement
risk
    and civic Green New Deal, 290, 304–305
    disputes, 282
    factors, 247, 267
    and professional associations, 13, 111, 113
    and resilience, 38–39, 271, 281–283, 290
River Network, 12, 19, 36, 163, 176–179, 181–183
    and civic Green New Deal, 294
    and sustainable cities framing, 254–256
River Rally, 20, 177–178, 182, 285, 288
rivers, 32, 35–36, 163, 196–197
    American Rivers and Clean Water Action, 36, 163, 183–185, 197
    and Chesapeake Bay, 168–170
    and civic Green New Deal, 291, 300, 306
    and EPA Office of Wetlands, Oceans, and Watersheds, 179, 181–183
    Hudson Riverkeeper, 177, 192, 197
    and New York City water, 189, 192, 194
    and postwar environmentalism, 42, 46, 50–52, 54, 57–62, 77
    river basins, 36, 52, 54–55, 168, 184
    River Rally, 20, 177–178, 182, 285, 288
    river restoration, 99, 184–185, 225, 245, 291
    Rivers and Harbors Act, 62
    and urban governance, 201–203, 231, 233, 272, 277
    and watershed associations, 176–179
    See also River Network
Rivers Council of Washington (RCW), 188
roads
    and bicycles, 123–125, 127, 132, 135
    construction of, 44
    in Phoenix, 233–234
Robertson, Willis A., 47–48
Robert Wood Johnson Foundation, 132–133, 246
Rockefeller, Nelson, 56–57, 61
Rockefeller Foundation, 82, 187, 281
Rocky Mountain Institute, 10, 112, 121

soil conservation, 54, 164, 191, 193
    Soil Conservation Service (SCS), 88, 164
solar energy, 90, 235, 340n41
solidarities, 28–30, 126, 155–156, 183, 283,
    399n2
    social solidarity, 28–29
Soll, David, 189
space, 34, 267
    bicyclists claim to, 125–127, 130, 133, 287
    in cities, 204, 216, 221
    civic spaces, 117
    public, 130, 141, 157, 183, 221, 225
    spatial inequality, 23
    spatial scarcities, 35, 126, 154, 157, 159
    See also open space movement
species protection, 6, 172, 176, 187
sportsmen's groups, 45, 47
sprawl
    and Chesapeake Bay, 168
    and land-use conflicts, 91, 102
    and Phoenix, 201, 240, 277
    suburban, 43
stakeholders
    and bicycle advocacy, 136, 159–160
    and civic Green New Deal, 296, 298
    and democratic resilience, 270, 273, 284,
        288, 291
    diverse, 69, 95, 184, 250, 270
    and ISTEA, 136
    and land-use conflicts, 85, 93, 95, 99,
        118
    multiple stakeholders, 21, 28, 37, 160, 166,
        203
    organized stakeholders, 288, 291
    and policy design, 16, 18, 21
    and sustainable cities framing, 247, 258
    and systemic approaches, 27–28
    and urban governance, 210
    and urban rivers and watersheds, 162,
        170–171, 174, 195, 197
    See also multistakeholder collaboration
standards
    and bicycle advocacy, 124, 127
    and intermediaries, 254
    and postwar environmentalism, 29, 71–73
    and professional associations, 13, 100, 108,
        112–114, 117–118, 120
    standard-setting organizations, 10, 74, 113
    and urban agriculture, 35, 152, 155, 160
    and urban governance, 229, 232, 235
Stanton, Greg, 235
state environmental policy act (SEPA), 17
state implementation plans (SIPs), 65–66

states
    and bicycle advocacy, 128, 134–136, 138,
        160
    and civic action, 12, 36, 41, 47–49
    and civic Green New Deal, 294–295, 300,
        303
    and democratic resilience, 277, 279–280
    and ICLEI USA, 260–261
    and land-use conflicts, 84, 88–89, 91
    and policy design, 16–17, 19
    and postwar environmentalism, 51, 53–58,
        61, 69, 71–73
    and professional associations, 104–106,
        108–111, 115–116
    state associations, 71, 163
    state environmental policy act (SEPA), 17
    state-funded networks, 246
    state implementation plans (SIPs), 65–66
    state policies, 260–261
    state regulation, 47, 169, 271
    statist overreach, 39, 272, 290, 294
    and urban agriculture, 150, 152
    and urban governance, 201, 203, 231–233,
        234, 238, 240
    and urban rivers and watersheds, 163–171,
        176–179, 181–183, 185, 191–194, 196
steel industry, 61–62, 65, 88, 113, 202, 221
Stein, Murray, 58
stewardship, 106, 116, 147
    and civic Green New Deal, 295, 300, 306
    and democratic resilience, 272, 276
    and urban governance, 213, 226–227
    and urban rivers and watersheds, 169–170,
        174, 176, 187, 196
Stone, Clarence, 23, 25
stormwater, 108, 163–164, 169–170,
    186–189, 264
    and democratic resilience, 276, 285
    runoff, 164, 187–188, 212
strategic action, 9, 171–172, 273, 280, 286,
    289
    fields, 6, 277, 310n11
strategic choices, 249, 272, 277, 287, 310n11
    and bicycle advocacy, 123, 125–127, 129,
        131, 159–160
    and New York City water, 189
    and postwar environmentalism, 42, 52, 76
    and professional associations, 101, 115
    and urban agriculture, 142, 148
strategic planning, 6, 31, 109, 179–180, 296,
    302
    strategic collaboration, 17, 35
    strategic coordination, 39, 291–292, 301

and sustainable cities framing, 247, 248, 255, 264

and urban agriculture, 143–144, 146, 157

and urban governance, 203, 210, 220, 224–225

and urban rivers and watersheds, 165, 172–173, 178, 181–182, 184

Transamerica Pyramid, 208, 215

transit advocacy, 129, 224

transit-oriented development, 201, 232, 275

transparency, 9, 115, 144, 210, 221, 223, 233

transportation

asymmetries, 35, 126, 154, 159

and bicycle advocacy, 124–130, 132, 134–139, 154, 279

and civic Green New Deal, 293, 296, 298

engineers, 14, 90, 107, 250, 285

equity, 26, 136, 145, 226

and land-use conflicts, 84, 90

planning, 31, 104–105, 124, 128, 136–137, 154, 279

and policy design, 19

and professional associations, 14, 104–105, 107–109, 116–117

public transit, 102, 111, 130, 202

Surface Transportation Policy Project (STPP), 105, 132, 134–135, 154, 160, 226

sustainable, 8, 109

Transportation Alternatives (Trans Alt), 130–131

and urban governance, 26, 204–205, 224, 226, 235–237

See also Bicycle Transportation Alliance (BTA); Department of Transportation, US (USDOT); Intermodal Surface Transportation Efficiency Act (ISTEA); National Association of City Transportation Officials (NACTO)

trees, 143, 147, 224, 231, 240

tribal areas, 69, 178, 296, 357n56

Troubled Waters, 60, 94, 288

Trump, Donald, 67, 198, 271

trust, 24, 38–39, 263

and bicycle advocacy, 127, 129

and civic Green New Deal, 290, 305

and democratic resilience, 272, 275, 282, 284

and professional associations, 99, 115

trust building, 21, 163, 195, 282

and urban governance, 202, 221

and water advocacy, 166, 174, 182–183, 188, 190–191, 193–195

trusteeship, 12, 158, 282, 284

Trust for Public Land (TPL), 105, 143, 145, 211, 224, 257

Udall, Stewart, 59

unions, 26, 159, 190

American Federation of Labor-Congress of Industrial Organizations (AFL-CIO), 51, 61

and bicycle advocacy, 126

and civic Green New Deal, 293, 298–299, 303

construction unions, 24, 26, 43

and postwar environmentalism, 43, 58, 61, 64

United Auto Workers (UAW), 55, 61

and urban governance, 207–209, 226, 234

United Nations (UN), 257

Brundtland Commission, 205, 245

Framework Convention on Climate Change (UNFCCC), 257

Intergovernmental Panel on Climate Change (IPCC), 205

United States, ix, 1, 5, 17–18, 26, 29, 32

Army Corps of Engineers, 44, 62, 72, 166, 168

and bicycle advocacy, 127

and civic Green New Deal, 294, 299, 303

and democratic resilience, 270–271, 280, 288–289

Department of Agriculture (USDA), 73, 151–153, 175, 193, 268

Department of Health and Human Service (HHS), 153, 246, 253

Department of the Interior, 44, 68, 73

Fish and Wildlife Service, 47, 71, 173, 175

Forest Service, US, 43, 72–73, 193

Geological Survey, 88, 163

and land-use conflicts, 81, 87–88, 90–91, 102, 104

military, 15, 207, 212

and postwar environmentalism, 61, 67, 70–73, 76, 78

and sustainable cities framing, 246, 252–253, 255, 257–258, 261, 265

United States v. Republic Steel, 62

United States v. Standard Oil Company, 62

and urban agriculture, 139

and urban governance, 29, 199–200, 209, 229, 238

and water advocacy, 45, 48, 163, 170, 175

Volpe, John, 84
Volunteer Estuary Monitoring, 173, 182
volunteering
    and civic Green New Deal, 294
    and urban agriculture, 141, 147
    and urban governance, 226–228, 231–232
    volunteer design teams, 13, 94–96
    Volunteer Stewardship Network (VSN), 227
    volunteer water-quality monitoring, 19–21,
        173, 176–177, 182, 184
Vrdolyak, Edward, 220

Walker, Edward, 27
Walker, Richard, 211
walking
    movements for, 34, 123, 127–130,
        133–135, 159–160
    and professional associations, 92, 107, 109
    and sustainable cities framing, 242,
        254–255
    and urban governance, 211, 237
    walkability, 8, 19, 109, 110, 117, 129
Warren, Mark E., 26
Washington (state)
    bicycle advocacy in, 132
    and ICLEI USA, 258
    river advocacy in, 188
    University of Washington, 141, 258
    urban agriculture in, 141
    See also Seattle, Washington
Washington, DC, 20, 57
    and rivers and watersheds, 167–168, 179,
        182, 185
    and Smart Growth Alliance, 106
    urban agriculture in, 152
    and urban governance, 203, 212
    and Urban Sustainability Directors
        Network, 264
Washington, Harold, 200–201, 218–221, 226,
    239, 276
waste, 221, 248, 287
    and postwar environmentalism, 45–56, 60,
        72
    waste incinerators, 226, 248
    wastewater treatment facilities, 49, 52, 56,
        186, 192–193
wastewater treatment facilities, 49, 52, 56, 186,
    192–193
water
    American Rivers and Clean Water Action,
        36, 163, 183–185, 197
    and Chesapeake Bay, 168–170
    and civic Green New Deal, 272, 296

    after Clean Water Act, 35–36, 162–163,
        195–198
    conservation, 116, 193, 201
    consumption, 36, 149, 235, 238
    and democratic resilience, 273, 277–278
    drinking, 46, 163, 185–186, 189
    federal water policy, 33, 47, 49, 53, 322n15
    field, 12, 190
    filtration, 163, 172, 188–192, 194–195, 277
    Flint, Michigan crisis, 185, 249
    groundwater, 46, 53, 186, 228, 233–234,
        238
    law, 44, 47, 164
    management, 231–232, 253, 257
    Office of Wetlands, Oceans, and Watersheds
        (OWOW), EPA, 36, 163, 179, 182–183,
        196
    and policy design, 20–21
    and postwar environmentalism, 41–42,
        46–57, 59–61, 63–64, 77–78
    and professional associations, 114, 116, 119
    sustainable urban, 185–195
    systems, 185, 264, 272
    and urban governance, 201, 223, 231–235,
        238, 240
    usage, 46, 54, 119
    wastewater, 49, 52, 56, 186, 192–193
    waterways, 45, 62
    See also clean water; Clean Water Act
        (CWA); National Estuary Program
        (NEP); River Network; water pollution;
        water quality; watersheds
water pollution, 164, 196, 278
    control, 164, 196, 322n16
    Federal Water Pollution Control Act
        (FWPCA), 49, 51, 56–57
    and postwar environmentalism, 46–53, 55,
        57–59, 61, 73
water quality, 36, 165–166, 169, 181, 193
    monitoring, 172, 177, 183
    and postwar environmentalism, 46, 49, 59,
        63, 70
    Water Quality Act of 1965, 59
Watershed Agricultural Council (WAC), 191,
    193–194
watersheds, 35–36, 163–185, 189–198
    Center for Watershed Protection, 19,
        181–182
    and civic Green New Deal, 291, 294, 302
    and democratic resilience, 272–273, 278,
        284
    New York City Watershed Memorandum of
        Agreement (MOA), 191–194